C999900017
KW-052-194

# INTRODUCTION
# TO THE
# TALMUD AND MIDRASH

EUR

# INTRODUCTION

# TO THE

# TALMUD AND MIDRASH

*by*

Günter Stemberger

*Translated and edited by*

Markus Bockmuehl

SECOND EDITION

T&T CLARK
EDINBURGH

T&T CLARK LTD
59 GEORGE STREET
EDINBURGH EH2 2LQ
SCOTLAND

First edition copyright © T&T Clark Ltd, 1991
Second edition copyright © T&T Clark Ltd, 1996

Authorised English Translation of *Einleitung in Talmud und Midrasch*
© C. H. Beck'sche Verlagsbuchhandlung (Oscar Beck), München 1982, 1992,
and incorporating additional material by Günter Stemberger and Markus Bockmuehl.

All rights reserved. No part of this publication may be reproduced, stored in a retrieval system, or transmitted, in any form or by any means, electronic, mechanical, photocopying, recording or otherwise, without the prior permission of T&T Clark Ltd.

First edition published 1991
Second edition published 1996

ISBN 0 567 29509 5

British Library Cataloguing-in-Publication Data
A catalogue record for this book is available from the British Library

21 FEB 2001
BIRMINGHAM LIBRARIES
R
296.12506
SU(R)

Printed and bound in Great Britain by Bell & Bain Ltd, Glasgow

# CONTENTS

## EDITOR'S PREFACE TO THE SECOND EDITION

In the seven years since the original edition of this translation was prepared, the study of rabbinic Judaism has continued to progress at a remarkable pace. It is this continuing surge in Jewish scholarship which, together with the warm reception and widespread use of this work, has now made a second edition both desirable and feasible.

Readers will note a number of significant changes. Most importantly, the present text substantially represents the eighth German edition published by Günter Stemberger in 1992. Given the extent of growth and change now embodied in the handbook originally written by H. L. Strack, it seemed most fitting that this edition should appear solely under Professor Stemberger's name – a decision which has of course been followed here. Compared to the 1991 English edition, the latest German edition included several hundred alterations, affecting both the bibliographies and the text of every chapter. Some of the most significant changes concerned the midrashim and the redaction of the Palestinian and Babylonian Talmuds.

Beyond this, however, this second English edition incorporates all of the author's further improvements until May 1995. The translation has been thoroughly revised throughout, and a number of reviewers' suggestions have been adopted. Some of these concern the format and layout, but we have also included a new appendix on computer-based resources for the study of rabbinic Judaism (below, pp. 360–66).

We offer this new edition in the hope that both students and teachers of rabbinic Judaism will find it a welcome improvement of a familiar textbook.

Markus Bockmuehl
Cambridge, July 1995

## AUTHOR'S PREFACE TO THE FIRST EDITION (1991)

Hermann L. Strack (1848–1922), professor of Old Testament at the University of Berlin, came out of the Protestant tradition of missionary activity among the Jews. Out of this interest he founded the *Institutum Judaicum* at Berlin and turned to Jewish studies. The missionary bias, however, never prevented him from defending the Jews in the anti-Semitic turmoil of his time; in his studies of Jewish literature he also endeavoured to be as objective as possible. As a result of these studies, he published his *Introduction to the Talmud* (1887), the first work of its kind ever to be written in a modern language. The book had the success which it deserved. Several revised and enlarged editions of the work were published until 1920. This last edition was reprinted several times until 1976. The highly positive reviews of the book by prominent Jewish scholars bear witness to the fact that Strack achieved his objective of impartiality. In 1931 an English translation of the book was published, sponsored by the Central Conference of American Rabbis, and reprinted ever since.

The progress of Jewish studies since the days of Strack, however, made a thorough revision of his work desirable. In order to realize his objectives for our own times, it was necessary to rewrite completely most of the book. The thorough revision of another classical work of German Jewish studies, E. Schürer's *History of the Jewish People in the Age of Jesus Christ*, by G. Vermes, F. Millar and M. Black, provided a welcome model of how to deal with an important, but in many ways now outdated work, in order to resurrect it to new life. I am happy that the English translation of this 'new Strack' is to be published by the same publishing house which undertook the 'new Schürer'.

This book is, however, not a simple translation of the German edition. Since the completion of the German manuscript in 1980, Rabbinic studies have undergone a rapid development. This made it necessary not only to bring the bibliography up to date, but also to revise the text of the book in quite a number of ways. New manuscripts have come to light, critical editions have been published, and some hitherto rather neglected writings of the rabbis have found scholarly attention. This is particularly true in the field of Midrash; here, among other developments, a new approach similar to that of redaction criticism in biblical scholarship is gaining ground (especially J. Neusner). This approach considers midrashic works not primarily as collections of material connected only by the biblical text, but as coherent works with a unified literary structure and message. This English edition of the book gave me the opportunity to bring it up to date as far as possible. My thanks are due to Dr Markus Bockmuehl who translated the work and accepted changes in and additions to the text up to the last moment. I also thank the publishers for their readiness to undertake an English edition of the book; this is particularly welcome in a time when German is no longer the main language in Judaic studies as it was in the days of H. L. Strack.

# PART ONE: GENERAL INTRODUCTION

## I

## THE HISTORICAL FRAMEWORK


***Bibliography***

***Palestine***

**Alon, G.** *The Jews*. 2 vols. Jerusalem 1980–86. **Alon, G.** *Studies*. **Avi-Yonah, M.** *Geschichte der Juden im Zeitalter des Talmud.* Berlin 1962. (Cf. *The Jews of Palestine: A Political History from the Bar Kokhba War to the Arab Conquest*, Oxford/New York 1976). **Baras, Z.** et al. (eds.). *Eretz Israel from the Destruction of the Second Temple to the Muslim Conquest* (Hebr.). 2 vols. Jerusalem 1982–84. **Baron, S. W.** *History*, vol. 2. **Levine, L.I.**, ed. *The Galilee in Late Antiquity.* New York/Jerusalem 1992. **Oppenheimer, A.** *Galilee in the Mishnaic Period* (Hebr.). Jerusalem 1991. **Oppenheimer, A. & Rappaport, U.** (eds.). *The Bar Kokhba Revolt – New Studies* (Hebr.). Jerusalem 1984. **Schäfer, P.** *Der Bar Kokhba-Aufstand.* Tübingen 1981. **Schäfer, P.** *Geschichte der Juden in der Antike.* Stuttgart 1983. **Smallwood, E. M.** *The Jews under Roman Rule: From Pompey to Diocletian.* Leiden 1976; corrected repr. 1981. **Stemberger, G.** *Das klassische Judentum: Kultur und Geschichte der rabbinischen Zeit.* Munich 1979. **Stemberger, G.** *Juden und Christen im heiligen Land: Palästina unter Konstantin und Theodosius.* Munich 1987.

***Babylonia***

**Funk, S.** *Die Juden in Babylonien.* 2 vols. Berlin 1902–08. **Gafni, I. M.** *Babylonia.* **Neusner, J.** *Babylonia.* **Oppenheimer, A.** *Babylonia Judaica in the Talmudic Period.* Wiesbaden 1983.

***Internal Organization***

**Beer, M.** *Exilarchate.* **Goodblatt, D.** *The Monarchic Principle: Studies in Jewish Self-Government in Antiquity.* Tübingen 1994. **Grossman, A.** *Reshut ha-golah be-Babel bi-tequfat ha-Geonim.* Jerusalem 1984. **Habas (Rubin), E.** *The Patriarch in the Roman-Byzantine Era: The Making of a Dynasty* (Hebr.). Diss. Tel Aviv 1991. **Levine, L. I.** 'The Jewish Patriarch (Nasi) in Third Century Palestine.' *ANRW* II 19/2 (1979) 649–88. **Mantel, H.** *Sanhedrin.*

***Origins of the Rabbinic Movement***

**Aderet, A.** *From Destruction to Restoration: The Mode of Yavneh in the Re-Establishment of the Jewish People* (Hebr.). Jerusalem 1990. **Cohen, S. J. D.** 'The Significance of Yabneh: Pharisees, Rabbis, and the End of Jewish Sectarianism.' *HUCA* 55 (1984) 27–53. **Neusner, J.** '"Pharisaic-Rabbinic" Judaism: A Clarification.' *HR* 12 (1973) 250–70. **Neusner, J.** *Development.* **Neusner, J.** 'The Formation of Rabbinic Judaism: Yavneh (Jamnia) from A.D. 70 to 100.' *ANRW* II 19/2 (1979) 3–42. **Saldarini, A. J.** 'The End of the Rabbinic Chain of Tradition.' *JBL* 93 (1974) 97–106. **Schäfer, P.** 'Die Flucht Johanan b. Zakkais aus Jerusalem und die Gründung des "Lehrhauses" in Jabne.' *ANRW* II 19/2 (1979) 43–101.


The rabbinic literature here discussed dates from the first millennium of our era. The period in question ranges approximately from the destruction of

Jerusalem and its Temple by Titus in the year 70 to the decline of the Geonic academies of Babylonia around 1040, although the latest works of rabbinic literature were compiled centuries after this date.

***1) Political History***

The following is a brief recapitulation of the basic facts about this period, since no literature can be understood without its historical context. The two most important centres of Jewish life at the time were Palestine and Babylonia; rabbinic literature developed almost exclusively in these centres.

In *Palestine* the defeat of 70 CE decisively ended the last vestige of political independence and of the Temple as the religious centre and the basis of priestly power. A reorganization of Jewish self-government developed only gradually from Yabneh, the new centre of religious learning. There, soon after 70, Yoḥanan ben Zakkai began to gather around himself Jewish scholars primarily from Pharisaic and scribal circles, but also from other important groups of contemporary Judaism. From these early beginnings there slowly developed a new Jewish leadership of Palestine, able to guide Judaism through a period without Temple and state. This leadership found its institutional expression in the patriarchate with its academy and its court; the latter became the successor to the Sanhedrin of the Second Temple period.

The Jews of Palestine apparently did not participate in the great diaspora revolt against Roman rule in 115–17 CE. But under the leadership of Bar Kokhba they then allowed themselves to be driven into the tragic second great revolt against Rome in 132–35. Reconciliation with Rome came only after the death of Hadrian in 138. Peaceful reconstruction began under the dynasties of Antoninus and Severus, culminating in the powerful patriarchate of Yehudah ha-Nasi (known simply as 'Rabbi'). After 135 the bulk of the Jewish population of Palestine was no longer in Judaea but in Galilee; following the Bar Kokhba revolt, the centre of Jewish self-government was no longer Yabneh but first Usha (until c. 170), then Beth Shearim and Sepphoris, and finally Tiberias (from the middle of the third century).

The third century brought structural consolidation for Palestinian Judaism in the form of leadership by the now hereditary patriarchate, and in the rise of the rabbinate. At the same time Palestine of course shared in the political confusion and economic decline of the Roman Empire. Two facts in particular stand out. Of far-reaching political and economic importance was the *Constitutio Antoniana* of Caracalla in 212, which bestowed Roman citizenship on (virtually) all inhabitants of the Empire, including the Jews. Palestinian Judaism was more immediately affected by the period of Palmyrene rule under Odenathus and Zenobia (260–73) over large parts of the Eastern empire, including Palestine.

Constantine's Christianization of the Roman Empire was the great turning point: the 'edict' of Milan in 313 made Christianity *religio licita*; with Constantine's sole rule from 324 this became significant for Palestine as well. The subsequent period saw a continual advance of Christianity, so that Judaism even in Palestine found itself increasingly on the defensive. A brief respite was afforded by the rule of Julian (361–63), who even permitted the rebuilding of the Temple. Then Christianity finally triumphed. The primary external documentation of this is a law of 380 CE making the Nicene creed binding on all subjects of the Empire, thereby *de facto* establishing Christianity as the state religion. Between 415 and 429 the institution of the Jewish patriarchate was abolished. The *Codex Theodosianus* of 438 and in particular the *Codex Justinianus* of 529/534 permanently settled the legal situation in the Jews' disfavour. Not surprisingly, the Jews of Palestine had high expectations of the period of Persian rule (614–28). Disappointed yet again, they endured the return of Byzantine government until they were permanently freed from Christian rule by the Arab invasion (Jerusalem fell in 638).

Since the exile of 586–538 BCE, *Babylonia* had always been home to a significant Jewish population; this group attained self-government under the exilarch shortly after 70 CE, probably in reaction to the events in Palestine. With the Bar Kokhba revolt Babylonia became important for the history of rabbinic Judaism. Many Palestinian rabbis now fled to Babylonia, and some of them remained even after the situation in Palestine had stabilized. Around 226 CE the government of Babylonia passed from the Parthians to the Sassanid Persians, who attempted to establish Zoroastrianism as the state religion. After initial difficulties for the Jews, their autonomy was fully restored c. 250 under Shapur I in return for their recognition of the state law.

A long period of stable prosperity ended abruptly in the second half of the fifth century with a number of persecutions of Jews (and Christians), culminating in 468: Jewish self-government was abolished, the Exilarch executed, synagogues were closed and many rabbis were killed. Although the situation normalized in the first half of the sixth century, the exilarchate was not restored. Jews in Babylonia, as in Palestine, were thus without any strong leadership.

In Babylonia the decisive turning point came with the Arab conquest around 640 CE. For the first time the two major Jewish centres were under a common political administration. The capital of the Umayyads was Damascus, so that Palestine was initially closer to the centre of power; but after 750 under the Abbasids Baghdad became the capital, and Babylonia attained dominance within Judaism. For a while the restored exilarchate and the leaders of the great rabbinic academies of Sura and Pumbeditha (both now in Baghdad) became the recognized representatives of Judaism in Babylonia, in the rest of the Diaspora, and even in Palestine.

However, the political decline of the Caliphate also brought a gradual shift in the Jewish population. Egypt, North Africa, and Spain became increasingly more important, while the exilarchate lost its influence and the Geonic schools dwindled. The Crusades (Jerusalem fell in 1099) meant the end of this epoch and of the Jewish world in which rabbinic literature originated. Despite a certain period of continued literary activity on the part of the rabbis, their time had clearly passed. Now the rabbinic writings themselves became the object of commentaries and compendia, i.e. they became primary texts.

### *2) The Beginnings of the Rabbinic Movement*

From the modern perspective the year 70 is a decisive turning point in Jewish history. But did contemporaries also regard it as such a clear watershed separating the period of the Temple and the Pharisees from the period after 70, without the Temple and with the rabbis? The introduction of the title 'Rabbi' (to be distinguished from 'Rabbi' as a form of address meaning 'my lord, my master') suggests such a consciousness of a new era. This is reflected in t.Eduy 3.4 (Z. 460): 'He who has students who in turn have students of their own is called Rabbi. If his students are forgotten, he is called Rabban; if even the students of his students are already forgotten, he is called [merely] by his name.' The use of terminology which this text represents was not only an external change of the period after 70 CE, but indicates a new self-understanding. This did not arise suddenly and straightforwardly, but in retrospect it already shows up clearly by the second half of the second century.

This transformation of rabbinic self-understanding also appears in the chain of tradition in Abot and ARN. These writings offer first a list of the 'pairs' up to Hillel and Shammai, all of whom are interconnected back to Moses by the reception and transmission of the Torah. There is a break after Hillel and Shammai: after them, only Yoḥanan ben Zakkai is described in the same language of tradition (*qibbel* – *masar*), while the appended list of patriarchs and the enumeration of the other rabbis does not employ this typical terminology. This illustrates the desire to link Yoḥanan with the 'pairs', i.e. to connect the rabbinic with the Pharisaic tradition.

As J. Neusner has variously emphasized (e.g. *Phar* 3:228, 282f.), this desire was not yet manifest in the days of Yabneh: a sense of discontinuity was then not yet in evidence. This only emerged at Usha, when it was clear that there would be no Temple and no restoration of earlier conditions in the foreseeable future: 'the real break in the history of the Pharisaic-rabbinic movement comes not at 70, with the destruction of the Temple, but at 140, with the devastation of southern Palestine and the reconstitution of the rabbinic movement and the patriarchal government in the north' (*Phar* 3:283). Only now was there an awareness that the break of 70 was irreparable. Now there emerged an explicit appeal to the period before 70, a deliberate representation of Hillel and Shammai and their schools as the fathers of the rabbinic movement, indeed a tracing back of the ancestors to the time of Simeon the Just and of Ezra, establishing a continuity with Moses.

The account of Yoḥanan ben Zakkai's flight from Jerusalem became the foundation document of rabbinic Judaism (see Schäfer). But it was a long time before this came to be seen as the decisive new beginning. Only the perspective of hindsight made it clear that the loss of political independence and of the Temple was the prerequisite for the rise of rabbinic Judaism. Of course it took even longer for the rabbinate to prevail as the new establishment, and to reduce the diversity of pre–70 Judaism to a certain uniformity. Rabbinic Judaism probably never represented the only manifestation of Jewish life; and it was only through centuries of development that it became the 'normative' Judaism which it was often assumed to have been for the entire period.

### *3) The Sources*

The sources for a description of the rabbinic period are so biased that the historical picture gained from them remains largely insecure – the very notion of a 'normative' Judaism, for example, derives from these sources. Only the rough outline of political history is sufficiently documented by non-Jewish sources. For the internal development of rabbinic Judaism, however, we are almost wholly dependent on the rabbis' own testimony, and thus on the literature of a single group within this Judaism: rabbinic self-understanding has shaped all of tradition. It is true that this picture can in part be checked and corrected by means of archaeological discoveries (only in Palestine), as well as by Patristic and other non-Jewish writings. But the fact remains that we depend on the rabbis' own testimony and that no other contemporary party of Judaism has left any literary evidence. Where the Geonim (e.g. the *Seder Tannaim we-Amoraim* or the *Letter of Sherira Gaon*) describe conditions in the rabbinic period, they do so once again out of a particular group interest; they therefore provide no suitable corrective to the rabbinic descriptions. We can only estimate with caution the actual significance of the rabbinic movement within Jewish life, especially of the Talmudic period. It is certain that the rabbis ascended slowly to a position of recognized leadership within Judaism, and that their party's literature could only gradually become the near-canonical literature of Judaism.

The *Seder Tannaim we-Amoraim* (*STA*) provides a theory of method: it discusses the derivation of valid halakhah from rabbinic literature, and addresses the relationship between the Mishnah on the one hand and the *baraitot* (i.e. other, 'outside' Tannaitic traditions: cf. p. 177 below) and halakhic midrashim on the other. *STA* adds to this methodological material a chain of tradition patterned after the example of Abot, but influenced also by the Islamic method of *isnad al-hadith.* This latter part offers the list of Patriarchs beginning with Hillel, as well as an enumeration of rabbinic teachers to the end of the Saboraic period. As was already noted by Azariah dei Rossi in *Me'or 'Ênayyim*, the list ends with the year 884 (dated both in Seleucid chronology and from the creation of the universe). The work is therefore commonly thought to have originated in 884, although because of its composite nature this is by no means certain. Some parts could come from Israel, others from Babylonia; later ones in turn may have developed in North Africa and France, where the fullest text was transmitted in the *Maḥzor Vitry*. Critical edition (base text *Maḥzor Vitry*): K. Kahan (ed.), *Seder Tannaim we-Amoraim*, Frankfurt 1935 (with a German introduction); cf. J. E. Ephrathi, *The Sevoraic Period*, 14–32; S. Abramson, 'Le-toldot nusaḥ "Seder Tannaim we-Amoraim"' in Y. D. Gilat et al. (eds.), *Iyyunim be-Sifrut Ḥazal, ba-Miqra u-be-Toldot Yisra'el* (*Festschrift* E. Z. Melamed, Ramat Gan 1982), 215–47 (Genizah fragments).

The *Letter of Sherira Gaon* (*Iggeret Rab Sherira Gaon*, hence *ISG*) was written in 987 by Sherira, the Gaon of Pumbeditha (c. 906–1006), to Rabbenu Nissim and the congregation of Kairouan, in answer to questions about the redaction of the Mishnah, Tosefta, and Talmud. Sherira combines a description of the rabbinic writings with a listing of the most important rabbis and the Geonim up to his own time. Two recensions have been transmitted, one French and one 'Spanish' (according to Schlüter, the latter is more likely an Ashkenazic revision). While B. M. Lewin gives precedence to the 'Spanish' version, the French is today preferred (cf. Epstein, *IAL*, 610–15). Critical edition: B. M. Lewin (ed.), *Iggeret Rab Sherira Gaon*, Frankfurt 1920 (repr. Jerusalem 1972); M. Schlüter, *Auf welche Weise wurde die Mishna geschrieben? Das Antwortschreiben des Rav Sherira Gaon: Mit einem Faksimile der Handschrift Berlin Qu. 685 (Or. 160) und des Erstdrucks Konstantinopel 1566*, Tübingen 1993 (with a commentary and translation of both versions). Cf. S. Assaf, *Geonim*, 149–53; M. Beer, 'The Sources of Rav Sherira Gaon's Igeret' (Hebrew), *Bar-Ilan* 4–5 (1967) 181–96; Ephrathi, *The*

*Sevoraic Period*, 1–13; M. Schlüter, 'A Study in a Manuscript of Iggeret Rav Sherira Gaon' (Hebr.), *10th WCJS* (Jerusalem 1990), C 1:147–54.

***4) The Division of Jewish History into Periods***

Due to the available sources, the conventional periodic division of the rabbinic era is entirely in accordance with the perspectives and interests of the rabbis. Of central significance for them is the relationship to tradition and teaching, and this is reflected in the delimitation of the different periods. Thus the time of the *Tannaim* (Aram. *tanna*, from Heb. *shanah*, 'to repeat, learn': the masters of teachings transmitted by continual oral repetition, which were later regarded as authoritative) extends from Hillel and Shammai at the beginning of our era (according to Maimonides's student Joseph Ibn Aqnin: from Simeon the Just, c. 300 BCE; according to Abraham Ibn Daud's *Sefer ha-Qabbalah* (c. 1160/61): from 70, more particularly Yoḥanan ben Zakkai) to Rabbi and his sons, i.e. to the early third century (cf. Bacher, *ET* 1:193f., 2:241). They are followed by the *Amoraim* (*amar*, 'to say, comment': the commentators of Tannaitic teachings) up to c. 500. The time of the *Saboraim* (*sabar*, 'to think': the editors of the Babylonian Talmud) found its continuation in the period of the *Geonim* (*ga'ôn*, 'eminent': the title of the heads of the Babylonian academies), until the eleventh century.

This division into periods is very old. Already the Talmudic Gemara and the Midrashim distinguish between the Tannaim and the subsequent teachers. Only the teachers of the Mishnaic period are properly called Tanna (for another meaning cf. p. 12); their sayings are introduced by corresponding verbal forms (*tenu*, *teni*, etc.). Similarly, the specific use of *'amar* is already Talmudic, while the terms *sabora* and *ga'ôn* come from the Geonic period. Thus the conventional periodic division occurs already in *STA* and *ISG*. Abraham Ibn Daud then fully developed it; he is also responsible for the continuing practice of subdividing the Tannaitic period into five, the Amoraic into seven generations.

# II

## THE RABBINIC SCHOOL SYSTEM


***Bibliography***

**Bacher, W**. 'Das alt-jüdische Schulwesen.' *Jahrbuch für jüdische Geschichte und Literatur* 6 (1903) 48–81. **Dimitrovsky, H. Z.**, ed. *Exploring the Talmud.* Vol. 1: *Education.* New York 1976. **Ebner, E.** *Elementary Education in Ancient Israel during the Tannaitic Period.* New York 1956. **Florsheim, J**. 'The Establishment and Early Development of the Babylonian Academies, Sura and Pumbeditha' (Hebr.). *Zion* 39 (1974) 183–97. **Gafni, I**. *Babylonia*, 177–236 (with additional literature). **Gerhardsson, B**. *Memory and Manuscript.* **Goodblatt, D. M**. *Instruction.* **Goodblatt, D. M**. 'New Developments in the Study of the Babylonian Yeshivot' (Hebr.). *Zion* 46 (1981) 14–38. **Lightstone, J. N**. 'The institutionalization of the rabbinic Academy in late Sassanid Babylonia and the redaction of the Babylonian Talmud.' *StudRel/SciRel* 22 (1993) 167–86. **Mirsky, S. K**. 'Types of Lectures in the Babylonian Academies.' In J. L. Blau et al. (eds.), *Essays on Jewish Life and Thought: Presented in Honor of S. W. Baron*, 375–402. New York 1959. **Sorek, Y**. *Nehardea – Mother City and Academy in the Time of the Mishna and Talmud* (Hebr.). Tel Aviv 1972.

***Regarding Ordination***

**Bacher, W**. 'Zur Geschichte der Ordination.' *MGWJ* 38 (1894) 122–27. **Epstein, A**. 'Ordination et Autorisation' *REJ* 46 (1903) 197–211. [On the ordination of Rab by Rabbi]. **Goldstein, N**. 'Conditional Ordination and Temporary Ordination' (Hebr.). *Bar-Ilan* 18–19 (1981) 136–43. **Lohse, E**. *Die Ordination im Spätjudentum und Urchristentum.* Göttingen 1951.

***Regarding Discipleship***

**Kirschner, R**. 'Imitatio Rabbini.' *JSJ* 17 (1986) 70–79. **Neusner, J**. *Talmudic Judaism in Sasanian Babylonia*, 46–135. Leiden 1976.


The *Sitz im Leben* of rabbinic literature, in addition to the synagogal sermon and to a lesser extent jurisprudence, is the school system in the broadest sense. This scholastic activity is reflected in the rabbinic texts, and significantly facilitates their interpretation. At the same time, the rabbinic school system made the greatest contribution to the spread of the rabbinic ideal, until it more or less dominated all of Judaism. At this point, therefore, we must briefly outline the development of the school system. Two of its essential aspects – hermeneutics and oral tradition – will be treated in the following chapters.

### *1) Elementary Instruction*

The Bible already places a father under the obligation of religious instruction for his sons (Deut 11.19). Sifre Deut 46 (F. 104) clarifies this by saying that the father must speak with his son in the holy language and must teach him

Torah. The instruction of girls was on the whole rejected (cf. the controversy in Sot 3.4). Most fathers were not in a position either to meet this obligation personally or to hire private tutors; and hence came about the early establishment of boys' schools. Rabbinic tradition attributes this to Simeon ben Shetaḥ under Salome Alexandra (76–67) p.Ket 8.11, 32c. Yehoshua ben Gamala, high priest in the years before the great revolt against Rome, then supposedly extended the school system to all cities, so that boys from the age of six or seven generally could attend school (BB 21a). However, in the contemporary political situation Yehoshua's initiative could hardly have met with much success: after the revolt the reconstruction of the school system must have begun afresh, as also after the Bar Kokhba revolt and the difficult years which followed until the death of Hadrian. After the middle of the second century, schools for boys will have become the general norm. Even in Tannaitic times, therefore, a scholar could be forbidden to live in a place which lacked a teacher of children, among other things (Sanh 17b).

The elementary school (*bêt sefer*, 'house of the book') was normally located in the synagogue or in an adjacent room. Children primarily learned to read the biblical text. They began with the alphabet on a slate (ARN A6, Sch. 29), then were given short pieces of the Torah on scrolls (p.Meg 3.1, 74a), and finally moved to complete Torah scrolls. The first book to be read was Lev (LevR 7.3, M. 156). In the course of his schooling, a child was in theory to study the entire Bible together with the Targum. The preferred teaching method, here as elsewhere in the Jewish school system, was reading aloud (Erub 53b–54a) and continual repetition (Ḥag 9b).

General attendance at school ended at the age of twelve or thirteen (GenR 63.9, Theodor/Albeck 692; Ket 50a; the ages cited in Abot 5.21 are a secondary addition to the text). Boys wishing to pursue further studies would go to a teacher of Mishnah in the academy (*bêt midrash* or *bêt talmud*), where they learned the rudiments of Jewish tradition and of Halakhah. A more general education beyond the level of elementary school was afforded by sermons and lectures in the synagogue and academy on the Sabbath.

### *2) Rabbinic Education in Palestine*

In Palestine, both primary and secondary schools were called *bêt ha-midrash*. The term *yeshibah* or Aramaic *metibta*, later commonly used for rabbinic schools, was not employed in this sense at least in the Tannaitic period. Instead, it was understood literally as a 'session', and occasionally to denote the subject matter conveyed at such a session; the term was also used figuratively of a lawcourt. Inasmuch as the courts were open to the public and the proceedings served at the same time as practical instruction for students, this may have suggested a transition to the meaning of 'college, academy'.

Almost nothing is known about precursors of the rabbinic school system in the Temple period, whether established by the Pharisees or the scribes. The description of the *bêt ha-midrash* on the Temple Mount in t.Sanh 7.1 (Z. 425) probably contains some anachronisms. What is, moreover, in view here is not a school in the proper sense, but the Sanhedrin's determination of the halakhah in front of the public; this of course would involve a measure of instruction. It is often claimed on the basis of p.Shab 16.8, 15d that Yoḥanan ben Zakkai directed an academy before 70 in the Galilean village of Arab, but this is not explicitly asserted in that text (cf. Neusner, *Development*, 133f.). The passage is, moreover, relatively late and anecdotal, and thus only of limited historical use. Lastly, the 'houses' of Hillel and Shammai similarly cannot be understood in the sense of organized schools (*contra* Gerhardsson 85: 'two different school foundations and not merely two tendencies'). Another legendary assertion is that Hillel had eighty students (BB 134a).

For the period after 70 CE a *baraita* in Sanh 32b is particularly informative:

> Righteousness, Righteousness, this you shall follow' (Deut 16.20). Follow the scholar to the *yeshibah*, R. Eliezer to Lydda, R. Yoḥanan ben Zakkai to Beror Ḥayil, R. Yehoshua to Peqiin, Rabban Gamaliel to Yabneh, R. Aqiba to Bene Beraq, R. Mattyah to Rome, R. Ḥananyah ben Teradion to Sikhnin, R. Yose to Sepphoris, R. Yehudah ben Bathyra to Nisibis, R. (Ḥanina, the nephew of R.) Yehoshua to the diaspora [i.e. Babylonia], Rabbi to Beth Shearim, the Sages into the Chamber of Hewn Stone.

This text derives from a shorter version cited earlier in Sanh 32b, which considers right judgement to be assured only with R. Eliezer in Lydda and with Rabban Yoḥanan ben Zakkai in Beror Ḥayil, thus probably polemicizing against Gamaliel's succession of Yoḥanan at Yabneh. This text was later transformed into a list of teaching centres which can probably be dated to the time just before 200, when Rabbi was still working at Bet Shearim and not yet at Sepphoris (unless the intention is to avoid naming Sepphoris a second time, after it had already been mentioned for R. Yose in the previous generation).

Our knowledge about the operation of the schools is sketchy, especially for the Tannaitic era. In the early period, the existence of fully organized schools can probably be assumed only for the respective seat of the patriarch, where the school was firmly linked with the court of law (not with a Sanhedrin in the original sense: see Levine, *The Rabbinic Class*, 76–83). The schools of the other scholars were more likely small groups of disciples which formed around the residence of a well-known teacher, and which would disband after his departure or death. Only from the third century on were there definite academies outside the patriarchal capital; the texts repeatedly summarize these as 'the Rabbis of Caesarea' or 'the Rabbis from the South' (probably Lydda/Lod). The most important schools of Galilee in Amoraic times were Sepphoris (even after the patriarch's move to Tiberias) and Tiberias, where reputedly even R. Meir had taught (p.Ḥag 2.1, 77b), and where R. Yoḥanan bar Nappaḥa (d. 279 according to Sherira) brought the school into high repute. Founded before the patriarch's relocation to Tiberias, this school also survived the end of the patriarchate and remained significant well into Islamic times, until Jerusalem once again became the main centre of teaching.

### *3) The Rabbinic Academies of Babylonia*

The history of these schools is transmitted only in Geonic sources from the ninth and tenth centuries (Tanḥuma, STA and especially ISG). Nineteenth and twentieth century scholarship followed Sherira's information almost without exception, essentially supplementing it only with Talmudic material. On this account, the great Babylonian academies date back to the third century: Rab, a younger contemporary of Rabbi, founded the academy of Sura on the Euphrates and was its first director. His contemporary Mar Samuel supposedly directed the academy of Nehardea; Nehardea was destroyed by Odenathus in 259, but its school was later revived. Finally, Yehudah bar Yeḥezqel is said to have founded the school of Pumbeditha after 259 to replace Nehardea.

However, one cannot simply regard the Geonic accounts as faithfully summarizing the archival records of the academies. In reality, the texts promote specific political biases: SG wanted to prevent the recovery of the school of Sura by his repeated insistence that only Pumbeditha had an uninterrupted tradition. When the Geonic statements are checked against the BT, supposedly the work of these academies, no indication can in fact be found of great Babylonian academies in Amoraic times, as D. Goodblatt has shown. The BT's term for a school is not *yeshibah* or *metibta*, but *bêt rab*, 'the Master's house', usually adding the name of the rabbi teaching there. Together with other Talmudic data this suggests that Babylonian rabbis taught small groups of students at their residence or sometimes in their own school houses; these groups would disband no later than the Master's death. The more successful teachers will occasionally have succeeded in gathering larger groups of students; in this case they may have needed to hire auxiliary teachers and thus to organize more extensive school operations. But the fact remains that the Geonim anachronistically projected their own circumstances into an earlier period. In Talmudic times, the 'academies' of Sura, Nehardea and Pumbeditha were probably no more than the particular abundance in these centres of eminent teachers with their groups of disciples; only a later tradition combined these into large individual academies. In their later form, such academies arose only in early Islamic times and probably followed Islamic examples.

There were probably no major differences in *teaching methods* between Palestine and Babylonia. Even on this level of education, memorization took absolute precedence; it was accomplished by means of continual vocal recitation of the teaching material in a set manner of cantillation (Meg 32a). The first order was to learn, even if what was learnt was not understood: the meaning of a text could always be considered later (AZ 19a, Shab 63a). Wherever the number of students was sufficient, there was also a drilling coach, the *Tanna*, who had to know by heart as much of the traditional material as possible, and who passed on this teaching by his continually repeated recitation. Indispensable as a walking library, the Tanna was on the other hand despised by many rabbis because of his purely mechanical knowledge: 'The magician mutters and does not know what he is saying. The Tanna teaches and does not know what he is saying' (Sot 22a). Despite this criticism the office of the Tanna remained alive until Geonic times: it was too closely connected with the ritual of learning to be easily abolished.

Already in Talmudic times, but more particularly in the Geonic period, Babylonian rabbinic education in groups of disciples (and later in academies) was supplemented by the institutions of *Pirqa* and *Kallah*.

The etymology of the word *kallah* (cf. also Hebr. 'bride') is not clear, even if a favourite reference is to the Torah as 'bride'; Gafni, comparing the statutes of the Christian school of Nisibis, has recently proposed the derivation from Greek *kella*, (study) 'cell' (*Tarbiz* 51 (1981–82) 572–73). The institution, described in detail by Nathan ha-Babli, was a kind of educational congress of students and graduates of rabbinic schools, lasting several days. In Geonic times these were scheduled for the month of Elul in summer and Adar in winter (the 'Kallah months'). These gatherings, first attested for the beginning of the fourth century, may well have contributed significantly to the consolidation of the rabbinic academies. They were usually quite well attended: at least ten men had to be present as a quorum to open the proceedings (BB 12b). The subject of a *kallah* would be a tractate of the rabbinic tradition (later of the Talmud), the text of which would be orally tested before the discussion of its particular problems commenced. Certainly the *kallah* meetings were of special significance for the final form of the BT (see Goodblatt, *Instruction*, 155ff.; Gafni, *Babylonia*, 213ff.).

The *Pirqa* ('section, chapter'), also attested from the fourth century onward, was an individual lecture on a partly halakhic and partly haggadic topic, delivered before a larger audience including simple lay people. In

Geonic times the *Pirqa* was regularly held on the Sabbath in the synagogues of the rabbinic academies; the lecture was given by the head of the school or by the exilarch. Thus the *Pirqa* greatly contributed to the spread of the rabbinic mentality among the common people (cf. Goodblatt, *Instruction*, 171f.; Gafni, *Babylonia*, 204ff.).

### *4) Disciples*

In addition to the academic side of rabbinic education, another aspect of at least equal importance was the practice of *discipleship* under a scholar, i.e. the 'service' of a pupil (*talmid ḥakham*) under a rabbi. Such discipleship lasts for years and is often connected with a closely-knit common life and a shared household. This training is the only way to full-fledged membership in rabbinic society; without it one remains despite all knowledge uneducated, an *'am ha'areṣ* (Sot 21b–22a). The disciple learns from his master the proper conduct and emulates him in all aspects of daily life: in dress, manner of speech, etc. This leads to a pronounced traditionalism and class consciousness and often to a hereditary rabbinic status, even at the risk of occasional criticism (e.g. Ned 81a).

The aim of education is to enable the student to make free and independent decisions in matters of religious law. In Palestine this was tied to the *semikhah*, i.e. ordination, which also bestowed one's right to use the title of 'Rabbi'. It is possible, but not certain, that in Babylonia 'Rab' was used as a title in the absence of a formal ordination.

The rabbinic *semikhah* (from Hebr. 'leaning against', hence 'laying on of hands' as a gesture of transferring an office) entitled the recipient to the authentic transmission of tradition. It assured the unbroken chain of tradition from Moses down to one's own time (Abot). Soon the laying on of hands at the *semikhah* was abandoned; instead, the naming of the ordinand was followed by the formula, 'May he teach? He may. May he judge? He may. May he permit (i.e. cancel vows)? He may' (Sanh 5a). In this fully developed form, ordination authorized independent instruction and decision in matters of halakhah, the execution of judgement, the admission of firstfruits to secular use, the cancellation of vows, participation in calendrical intercalation, and the imposition of bans.

It is likely that originally every rabbi could terminate his student's discipleship by ordination. However, ordination included admission into the Sanhedrin, which even in later times could only accommodate limited numbers. For this reason the patriarch increasingly reserved for himself the right to ordain; sometimes he might consult the other members of the Sanhedrin, but often he would not. R. Abba says in p.Sanh 1.3, 19a: 'At first everyone ordained his own students. Later they abandoned direct ordination and said, "A court ordaining without the patriarch's knowledge has not ordained lawfully; but when the patriarch ordains without knowledge of the court, his ordination is valid". Then they determined that the Sanhedrin ordains only with the patriarch's knowledge, and the patriarch only with the knowledge of the Sanhedrin.' Thus, due to the numerical restraints on ordination, Palestine had a group of men with full rabbinical training who nonetheless could not fully 'practise' since they were not ordained.

The custom of ordination ceased around the middle of the fourth century, and certainly no later than the end of the patriarchate prior to 429. By then, it would have been replaced by other forms of declaring the disciples of scholars independent, as indeed such forms must always have existed in Babylonia (e.g. acceptance into the exilarch's official staff).

# III

## RABBINICAL HERMENEUTICS

***Bibliography***

**Bacher, W.** *ET.* **Bonsirven, J.** *Exégèse rabbinique et exégèse paulinienne.* Paris 1939. **Daube, D.** 'Alex. Methods.' **Daube, D.** 'Rabb. Methods.' **Daube, D.** 'Texts and Interpretation in Roman and Jewish Law.' *Jewish Journal of Sociology* 3 (1961) 3–28. [Repr. in Fischel, *Essays*, 240–65]. **Dobschütz, L.** *Die einfache Bibelexegese der Tannaim mit besonderer Berücksichtigung ihres Verhältnisses zur einfachen Bibelexegese der Amoraim.* Breslau 1893. **Finkelstein, L.** *Sifra,* 1:120–91. **Gertner, M.** 'Terms of Scriptural Interpretation: A Study in Hebrew Semantics.' *BSOAS* 25 (1962) 1–27. **Goldberg, A.** 'Rede und Offenbarung in der Schriftauslegung Rabbi Aqibas.' *FJB* 8 (1980) 61–79. **Guttmann, A.** 'Foundations of Rabbinic Judaism.' *HUCA* 23/1 (1950–51) 453–73. **Heinemann, I.** *The Methods of the Aggada* (Hebr.). Jerusalem 1949, 3rd edn. 1970. **Heinemann, I.** 'Altjüdische Allegoristik.' *Jahrbuch Breslauer Seminar* 18 (1935). **Jacobs, L.** *Studies in Talmudic Logic and Methodology.* London 1961. [On this see E. Wiesenberg, 'Observations on Method in Talmudic Studies', *JSS* 11 (1966) 16–36.] **Lieberman, S.** *Hell.* **Lieberman, S. J.** 'A Mesopotamian Background for the So-Called Aggadic 'Measures' of Biblical Hermeneutics?' *HUCA* 58 (1987) 157–225. [Especially on *notarikon* and *gematria.*] **Loewe, R.** 'The "Plain" Meaning of Scripture in Early Jewish Exegesis.' *Papers of the Institute of Jewish Studies* [London] 1 (1964) 140–85. **Maass, F.** 'Von den Ursprüngen der rabbinischen Schriftauslegung.' *ZTK* 52 (1955) 129–61. **Ménard, J.–E.**, ed. *Exégèse biblique et Judaïsme.* Strasbourg 1973. **Mielziner, M.** *Introduction to the Talmud,* 117–264. Cincinnati/Chicago 1894. **Ostrowski, M.** *Ha-Middot she-ha-Torah nidreshet bahen.* Jerusalem 1924. **Patte, D.** *Early Jewish Hermeneutic in Palestine.* Missoula 1975. **Salomonsen, B.** 'Om rabbinsk hermeneutik.' *Dansk teologisk Tidsskrift* 36 (1973) 161–73. **Towner, W. S.** 'Hermeneutical Systems of Hillel and the Tannaim: A Fresh Look.' *HUCA* 53 (1982) 101–35. **Vermes, G.** *Studies,* 59–91. **Weingreen, J.** *From Bible to Mishna: The Continuity of Tradition,* 1–76. Manchester 1976. **Zeitlin, S.** 'Hillel and the Hermeneutic Rules.' *JQR* N.S. 54 (1963–64) 161–73.

Further literature is given in the individual sections below.

Rabbinic literature arose mostly out of the attempt to adapt the Torah as the Jewish rule of life to changing conditions. This updating of the Torah occurs in the 'oral Torah' whose development is particularly connected with biblical exegesis, be it by direct deduction of new regulations and ideas from the text or by secondary justification of a statement of tradition through a particular biblical reference. The rabbis' treatment of Scripture may often seem arbitrary, but it is in fact controlled by certain rules (*middot*). Over time, rabbinic tradition summarized these in groups: the 7 rules of Hillel, 13 of Ishmael, and 32 of R. Eliezer (ben Yose ha-Gelili).

Of course there was a definite methodology of interpretation even prior to the formal crystallization of these rules. The early biblical scholars are called *soferim.* This term derives from Hebrew *sefer*, 'book', but it is also related to the sense of 'to count', since one of the scribes' most important tasks was to count the words in every book of the Bible, as well as the frequency of the individual words and even letters (cf. Qid 30a). They also compiled lists of terms which occur only once or twice in the Bible. These lists facilitated the explanation of texts by parallels and generally by the biblical context: it was a fundamental hermeneutical principle to interpret the Torah from the Torah (according to p.Meg 1.13, 72b Noah already employed this). The co-existence of different textual recensions of Scripture in the Dead Sea Scrolls might seem to make an early date of this approach unlikely. Nevertheless, these same texts also document the concern for the precise and detailed definition of the text, a concern which is equally evident from the earliest beginnings of the rabbinic tradition.

The simple explanation of words derives from general usage as well as comparison with foreign languages. This tends to be introduced by the expression *ein... ela*: i.e. a terms means 'nothing but' this or that. On the other hand this expression is also frequently used where the explanation in no way follows from the meaning of the word, but rather constitutes a theological interpretation or even an allegorical recasting of the literal sense. (This is not necessarily a later development.) Explanations of this kind were perhaps collated in textual glosses on the Bible or even in separate collections. See W. Reiss, 'Wortsubstitution als Mittel der Deutung: Bemerkungen zur Formel *ein... ela*' *FJB* 6 (1978) 27–69.

For the application of the rules of interpretation it is important to distinguish between halakhah and haggadah. The halakhah tends to be fixed even prior to its biblical justification: biblical interpretation is then more or less constrained to the task of grounding and supporting the existing halakhah in Scripture. To this extent halakhic exegesis is more closely tied to tradition than the haggadic. On the other hand, the halakhah has to adapt to changing conditions. In each changed situation the desire is to attain uniformity of halakhah as far as possible; this leads to a continual process of adaptation. The Haggadah, however, which has no direct influence on practice, remains largely unaffected by this continual adaptation, even if here too there are various changes reflecting temporary polemical interests and the defence against certain ideas. Thus, although it is not in principle as strictly defined, haggadah tends to be more stable than halakhah.

### *1) The Seven Rules of Hillel*

#### *Bibliography*

**Schwarz, A.** *Die hermeneutische Analogie in der talmudischen Litteratur.* Karlsruhe 1897.
**Schwarz, A.** *Der hermeneutische Syllogismus in der talmudischen Litteratur.* Karlsruhe 1901.
**Schwarz, A.** *Die hermeneutische Induktion in der talmudischen Litteratur.* Vienna 1909.
**Schwarz, A.** *Die hermeneutische Antinomie in der talmudischen Literatur.* Vienna 1913.
**Schwarz, A.** *Die hermeneutische Quantitätsrelation in der talmudischen Literatur.* Vienna 1916.

**Bergman, J.** 'Gezerah shawah mahi?' *Sinai* 71 (1972) 132–39. [On the difference from the *heqqesh*.] **Chernick, M. L.** *Hermeneutical Studies in Talmudic and Midrashic Literature* (Hebr.). Tel Aviv 1984. [On *Kelal u-ferat u-kelal* and *ribbuy u-mi'ut*.] **Chernick, M. L.** 'Internal Restraints on Gezerah Shawah's Application.' *JQR* N.S. 80 (1989–90) 253–82. **Weiss, M.** 'The *Gezera Shava* and the *Kal Va-Chomer* in the Explicit Discussions of *Bet Shammai* and *Bet Hillel*' (Hebr.). *Sidra* 6 (1990) 41–61.

The seven *middot* of Hillel were not invented by Hillel but constitute a collation of the main types of argument in use at that time. The introduction of the rules into Pharisaic exegesis is usually connected with the episode of p.Pes 6.1, 33a: Hillel gives a positive answer to the question whether the Passover sacrifice may be prepared on a Sabbath which coincides with the 14th of Nisan. His reason is an argument from the lesser to the greater (the daily sacrifice suspends the Sabbath, although Scripture does not command it under penalty of extirpation; all the more clearly does the Passover sacrifice suspend the Sabbath, since it is commanded under penalty of death), with an argument from analogy (just as the Passover sacrifice, daily sacrifice must take place at its appointed time, *be mô'adô*: Num 9.2; 28.2; hence the Passover sacrifice must also be like the daily sacrifice in suspending the Sabbath) and with a topical analogy (both are offerings of the people at large). All of Hillel's logical deductions fail to persuade his audience, the clan of Bathyra, until he appeals to his teachers Shemayah and Abtalion, thereby staking his claim on tradition.

In the version of t.Pes 4.13 (L. 165f.), the same account (shorter in Pes 66a) mentions neither the people of Bathyra nor Shemayah and Abtalion as Hillel's teachers. The polemical statement that only the appeal to tradition won the argument is also absent in T (cf. Neusner, *Phar* 1:231–35, 246–51). Incidentally, the context in T suggests that Hillel's appeal to his teachers concerns the halakhah but not the rules of interpretation (Lieberman, *Hell.*, 54). Hence the proximity of Hillel's rules to the customary hermeneutical principles of Hellenistic rhetoric, which were also adopted in Roman legal interpretation (cf. Daube, *Rabb. Methods*), cannot be explained by reference to the tradition that Hillel's teachers Shemayah and Abtalion were proselytes who had studied and taught in Alexandria (*contra* Daube, *Rabb. Methods*, 241). The direct adoption of the rules from the Hellenistic world cannot be established, even if the correlation and terminology of the rules may go back to Hellenistic influence.

In t.Sanh 7.11 (Z. 427) the seven rules are introduced, 'Hillel the Elder expounded seven words before the elders of Patira.' However, this does not refer to the account in t.Pes, where the people of Patira/Bathyra are not mentioned. The story does not describe the historical reason for the introduction of the rules; neither was it invented as an illustration. Nor indeed does the list derive from it: for out of the seven rules the story mentions only the argument from the lesser to the greater and the argument from analogy (not at all explicit in T), and it adds the topical analogy (*heqqesh*) which is not contained in the list. A historical connection of Hillel with the seven rules cannot be ascertained.

Apart from t.Sanh the text of Hillel's rules is also transmitted in the introduction to Sifra (W. 3a) and in ARN A 37 (Sch. 110). In Sifra it is joined to an exposition of Ishmael's thirteen rules; rules 3 and 4 are merged (*ubinyan ab ushnê ketubim*). Rules 3 and 4 properly belong together but were separated in order to obtain the total of seven (contrast Finkelstein *ad loc.*, who takes *ushnê ketubim* to mean Ishmael's thirteenth rule). In ARN, the list appears together with other lists of seven; Neusner's contention (*Phar* 1.275) that ARN has copied it from T cannot be verified. In T, too, the list seems to be a secondary appendix to the chapter, probably occasioned by the preceding statement about 'seven'. It is a text which was generally familiar in the schools and which was applied as needed in various writings.

1. *Qal wa-ḥomer* (or more precisely *qol*, 'lightness': e.g. at the beginning of Cod. Assemani 66 of Sifra; the conventional pronunciation avoids confusion with *qôl*, 'voice'). Argument *a minori ad maius*, from the lighter (less significant) to the weightier (more significant) and vice versa. According to Ishmael this rule is already applied ten times in the Pentateuch, e.g. in Gen 44.8 (GenR 92.7, Theodor/Albeck 1145). A non-biblical example is Ket 111b: 'A *qal wa-ḥomer* of the grain of wheat: this is buried naked and emerges clothed. How much more must we expect this of the righteous who are buried in their clothes.' However, this rule may not be used to justify a greater punishment: 'It is sufficient that the deduction from a law should be equal to that from which it derives' (m.BQ 2.5).

2. *Gezerah shawah*: lit., 'equal ordinance' or 'statute'. According to Lieberman, *Hell.* 58f., this expression of uncertain etymology was formed in analogy to the Hellenistic rhetorical term *synkrisis pros ison* (first attested in Hermogenes, 2nd cent.). It is an argument from analogy. Strictly speaking this is only to be used if two given Torah statements make use of identical (and possibly unique) expressions. Moreover, these expressions which form the basis for the analogy should not be required for the understanding of the statement; in this way it can be assumed that Scripture itself already used them with a view to the intended analogy (Shab 64a). What is more, *gezerah shawah* may only be used with great restraint and should be supported by tradition: 'You shall not apply *gezerah shawah* lightly' (Ker 5a); 'No one argues from analogy on his own authority' (p.Pes 6.1, 33a). Only under these

conditions (which in later times were less strictly observed) will a particular Pentateuchal legal stipulation be valid also for another passage. Thus e.g. Lev 27.7 states that in regard to the fulfilment of a vow a certain valuation shall be placed upon 'a man of sixty years and upward'. Arakhin 4.4 applies the 'and upward' also to other age groups for which it is not explicitly given (Lev 27.3, 5). In all cases one must proceed from the completed year of life, even if this makes the regulation sometimes easier and at other times more difficult: the word 'year' must always be interpreted to mean the same (*shanah, shanah, li-gezerah shawah*). Closely related to the *gezerah shawah* is the so-called *heqqesh*, i.e. the less strictly controlled *topical analogy* (e.g. Hillel in p.Pes 6.1, 33a).

3. *Binyan ab mi-katub eḥad*, lit.: 'founding of a family' (*ab* short for *bêt ab*) 'from a single Scripture text'. 'By means of this exegetical norm, a specific stipulation found in only one of a group of topically related biblical passages is applied to them all. Thus the main passage bestows on all the others a common character which combines them into a family' (Bacher, *ET* 1:9). R. Eleazar ben Pedat says in p.Sanh 1.1, 18a, 'Wherever it says, "And God", God and his lawcourt are intended. And it is a *binyan ab*: wherever it says *wayyomer*, "And he said", a disaster is predicated.' SifreDeut §148 (F. 202) derives from Deut 17.6: wherever the expression *yimmaṣe'* 'he is found' is used in a particular context, two or three witnesses are always required.

4. *Binyan ab mi-shnê ketubim* is the expression for the same kind of derivation based on two biblical passages. Thus, for example, the regulations that a slave must be released when his owner puts out his eye or tooth (Exod 21.26, 27) are generalized: for any irreplaceable loss a slave must be compensated by being freed (Mek Neziqin 9, L. 3.72f.).

5. *Kelal u-ferat u-ferat u-kelal*: 'The general and the particular, the particular and the general', i.e. the qualification of the general by the particular, and the particular by the general. The thirteen *middot* of Ishmael divide this rule into eight (Nos. 4–11). For parallels in Roman legal exegesis see Daube, *Rabb. Methods*, 252–54. The introduction to Sifra (F. 5f.) explains the rule as follows:

> What is the argument from the general to the particular? It says first, 'Of domestic animals' (one may make an offering: Lev 1.2). This general statement includes only what is subsequently contained in the detailed statement. What is the argument from the particular to the general? 'If someone gives another an ass, an ox or a sheep to keep for him', that is the detailed statement, followed by the generalization: 'or any domestic animal' (Exod 22.10). The argument from the particular to the general means that the general expression adds something to the particular examples.

6. *Ke-yoṣe bô be-maqom aḥer*, 'something similar to this in another passage'. Daube, *Rabb. Methods*, 260, derives this peculiar phrase (lit. 'as it goes forth with this...') from the Hellenistic technical term *symbainein* 'to correspond to, to result from a deduction'. This rule is similar to the argument by analogy, but it is less strictly limited. An example is the beginning of Mek (L. 1.1–3), which refutes the assumption that 'whatever is mentioned first in Scripture has precedence' by adducing for each case a corresponding Bible verse in which the order is different. In Exod 3.6 it says, 'the God of Abraham, the God of Isaac and the God of Jacob' but Lev 26.42 states, 'I remember my covenant with Jacob, my covenant with Isaac and my covenant with Abraham'.

7. *Dabar ha-lamed me–'inyanô*: the 'argument from the context' of a Biblical statement. Because of its inherent plausibility this rule is universally recognized. Aqiba's statement in SifreNum §131 (H.169), that 'every Scripture passage which is close to another must be interpreted with respect to it' appears to say the same; however, this principle frequently leads not to a natural exegesis of context but to often farfetched expositions based on the accidental proximity of two terms. An example from Hillel's rule: a *baraita* in Sanh 86a explicitly appeals to the context in its interpretation of Exod 20.15: 'You shall not steal.' According to the opinion of the rabbis this concerns kidnapping, since the other laws also relate to persons. 'You shall not steal' in Lev 19.11, on the other hand, applies in context to the theft of money.

### *2) The Thirteen Middot of R. Ishmael*

#### *Bibliography*

**Finkelstein, L.** *Sifra*, 1:147–91. **Freimann, A.**, in S. Krauss (ed.), *Festschrift Adolf Schwarz*, 109–19. Berlin/Vienna 1917. [Lists 54 Hebrew commentaries to the 13 *middot*.] **Porton, G. G.** *Ishmael*, 4.160–211.

R. Ishmael, the great teacher of the generation before Bar Kokhba, is regarded as the antagonist of Rabbi Aqiba especially in the area of Biblical interpretation. Over against the forced interpretation of individual words, he advances the principle, 'The Torah speaks in human language' (SifreNum §112, H. 121). Thus he rejects, for example, the interpretation of the infinitive absolute *hikkaret* before the finite verb *tikkaret*: 'These are stylistic repetitions which the Torah uses in its own way' (p.Yeb 8.1, 8d); a further explanation of such dual expressions is therefore unnecessary.

Like Hillel, Ishmael has ascribed to him a series of hermeneutical rules, the 13 *middot* (the number is traditional – a normal count would distinguish 16; Aaron Ibn Ḥayyim in his commentary on Sifra of 1609–11 arrives at 17).

The text is found at the beginning of Sifra (F. 3f.). These rules are held in very high regard in Judaism: they are a part of the daily morning prayer (thus already in the earliest complete Siddur, that of Rab Amram Gaon). Numerous Jewish teachers since the Middle Ages have declared them to be transmitted from Sinai (for a compilation see G. Fischer, *Jeschurun* 7 (1860–61) 485–87). MHG Exod 21.1 (M. 458) introduces the text of the *middot*: 'R. Ishmael says, These are the thirteen *middot* by which the Torah is interpreted, which were handed down to Moses at Sinai.' D. Hoffmann included the text in his edition of MRS (Frankfurt 1905, p. 117); but the Genizah discoveries have not corroborated this, and thus the section does not appear in the edition Epstein/Melamed, p. 158. The text of the *middot* is also in MHG Lev 1.2 (p. 17), where it is expressly quoted from Sifra.

The 13 *middot* are essentially just an expanded version of Hillel's seven *middot*: I.1=H.1; I.2=H.2; I.3=H.3 and 4; I.4–11 are formed by a partition of H.5; I.12=H.7: Ḥul 63a cites this *middah* as one of the '13 *middot* according to which the Torah is interpreted' but without mentioning Ishmael. H.6 is left out.

I. 13 is new: 'Two verses of Scripture contradict each other until the third verse comes and decides between them.' An example is Mek Pisḥa 4 (L. 1.32): Aqiba points out that according to Deut 16.2 the Passover sacrifice is to be of flocks (sheep or goats) and herds (cattle), whereas in Exod 12.5 it is of sheep or goats. 'How can these two passages be maintained? Say: this is a rule in the (interpretation of) Torah – two passages contradict each other. They remain in their place until the third verse comes and decides between them.' Exod 12.21 mentions only flocks; thus it is clear that only flocks and not herds are suitable for the Passover sacrifice. Cf. D. Henschke, 'Studies in the Method of "shnê ketubim ha-makhḥishim zeh et ze"' (Hebr.), *11th WCJS* (Jerusalem 1994) C 1:39–46.

The historicity of the attribution of the 13 *Middot* to Ishmael is just as uncertain as that of the seven rules to Hillel. G. G. Porton (*Ishmael*, 2.65) shows on stylistic grounds that the list in Sifra must be composite. Hence, he sees no reason 'that it should be assigned to one man, other than the editor of this passage, or to one school'. An analysis of the exegetical traditions of Ishmael in Tannaitic collections shows that Ishmael 'never uses the majority of his exegetical methods. He most commonly employs the *a fortiori* argument and the *gezerah shawah*, the same principles which were common in the non-Jewish world of his time' (ibid., 6). If we keep to the principles of which he actually made use in these texts, he knew at most five of his rules. Moreover the clear boundaries between the methods of Ishmael and Aqiba cannot be maintained: 'frequently 'Aqiba employs techniques usually associated with Ishmael and Ishmael uses methods usually assigned to 'Aqiba' (*Ishmael*, 4.208). Thus at the time of Ishmael there were not yet two exegetical schools clearly distinguishable by their method; where the rabbinic texts already distinguish between the methods of Ishmael and Aqiba, this is usually in the Palestinian Gemara (*Ishmael*, 4.209). 'It appears that the standard picture of Ishmael's exegetical practice is, at earliest, an Amoraic construction' (*Ishmael*, 2.7).

The Karaite Yehudah Hadassi opposed these *middot* in his description of Karaite faith, *Eshkol ha-kofer* (begun in 1148; edition Eupatoria 1836, expanded repr. London 1971, 124b). He pointed to the similarity with the 12 Greek rules, *ergasiai kai epicheirémata*. This is probably a citation of a medieval scholion to Hermogenes's *Peri heureseôs*. Direct parallels to the *ergasiai* are present only in the first two rules of Ishmael and of Hillel; but certain similarities are present with some of the 32 rules of Eliezer, which Hadassi also cites (cf. Lieberman, *Hell.*, 56).

### *3) The Thirty-Two Middot*

***Bibliography***

**Enelow, H. G.**, ed. *The Mishnah of Rabbi Eliezer or the Midrash of Thirty-Two Hermeneutic Rules*. New York 1933; repr. 1970. [Text with English Introduction.] **Aptowitzer, V**. 'Das Alter der Baraita der 32 Normen. . . .' In *Festschrift A. Schwarz*, 121–32. Berlin/Vienna 1917. **Albeck**, *Derashot*, 434–36. **Bardowicz, L.** *Die Abfassungszeit der Baraita der 32 Normen für die Auslegung der Heiligen Schrift*. Berlin 1913. **Epstein, J. N**. 'On the Mishna of R. Eliezer Son of R. Jose the Galilean' (Hebr.). *Tarbiz* 4 (1932–33) 343–53. **Epstein, J. N**. 'Mishnat R. Eliezer.' *HUCA* 23/2 (1950–51) Hebr. section 1–15. [Repr. in *Studies* 2:221–47.] **Moreshet, M**. 'The Language of "Mishnat R. Eliezer"' (Hebr.). *Bar-Ilan* 11 (1973) 183–223. **Zucker, M**. 'Le-pitron ba'ayat l"b middot u-mishnat Rabbi Eliezer.' *PAAJR* 23 (1954) Hebr. section 1–39.

The 32 *Middot* are named after Eliezer ben Yose ha-Gelili (generation after Bar Kokhba). Until the nineteenth century the text, first cited by the grammarian Abulwalid Ibn Ganaḥ (11th cent.), was known only from the *Sefer Keritut* by Samson of Chinon (1260–1330; ed. J. M. Sofer, Jerusalem 1965), and in the Karaite tradition through Yehudah Hadassi. The version in MHG (M. 22f.) numbers 33 *middot* (by dividing No. 29); Enelow's text refers to 33 *middot*, but lists only 32. The source of MHG has turned out to be the *Mishnat R. Eliezer*, also called *Midrash Agur* or Midrash of the 32 *Middot*.

The dating of the midrash is disputed. Because the work quotes no teachers later than the third century, Enelow considers it to be a 'product of the Tannaic tradition' (59), 'composed not later than the closing part of the fourth century' (60). A date after Saadya, on the other hand, was already suggested by Bardowicz. This is also the assumption of M. Zucker: he sees the 32 Middot as a selection from the 49 rules of Samuel ben Ḥofni, who in turn draws especially on Saadya. Somewhat earlier are the dates suggested by Epstein (the time of Heraclius) and Albeck (8th cent.). For linguistic reasons Moreshet arrives at a date between 600 and 800. The late date applies in any case only to the final form of this work, whose traditions may date in part from Talmudic times. However, the 32 rules are not yet mentioned in the Talmud. Ḥul 89a says, 'Where you hear the words of Eliezer ben Yose ha-Gelili in the haggadah, open your ear like a funnel' (thus R. Yoḥanan). Eliezer's fame as a haggadist may have contributed to the connection of the rules with his name. In some editions of the Talmud they are printed after the tractate Berakhot. Rashi, Abraham ben David and Zakuto read in the title of the *Baraita* not '32 rules by which *the haggadah* is interpreted' but 'the Torah'. S. Krauss concludes from this that these *middot* are valid also for halakhic interpretation (*Festschrift A. Schwarz*, 572). That applies to several of these rules, but others are unequivocally haggadic.

1. *Ribbui*, 'increase, inclusion' where the Bible uses the words *af* and *gam* ('also' or the accusative particle *et*. Thus, GenR 1.14 (Theodor/Albeck 12) interprets Gen 1.1 'God created heaven and earth' (Hebr. twice has the accusative particle *et*) as follows: 'heaven: that includes sun, moon, stars and constellations; and earth: that includes trees, grass, and the Garden of Eden.' Halakhic application: according to Arak 1.4 the execution of a pregnant adulteress condemned to death is not to be postponed until her delivery. Arak 7a accounts for this on the basis of Deut 22.22: *u-metu gam shnêhem*, 'and both of them (the adulterers) shall die', i.e. the man and the woman with the embryo. See M. Chernick, *Hermeneutical Studies in Talmudic and Midrashic Literature* (Hebr.), Tel Aviv 1984; idem, 'Hitpaḥut, ṣurah u-mibneh ba-drashot shel ribbuyim u-mi'utim' *PAAJR* 49 (1982), Hebr. section, 105–22; Y. Elman, 'Towards a History of Ribbuy in the Babylonian Talmud' (Hebr.), *11th WCJS* (Jerusalem 1994) C 1:87–94.

2. *Mi'ut*, 'restriction, exclusion, reduction' indicated by the words *akh*, *raq* ('only' and *min* ('from, out of'). Gen 7.23, 'Only (*akh*) Noah remained' According to GenR 32.11 (Theodor/Albeck 298) this is to be understood as follows: '*akh* signifies a restriction: he too vomited blood because of the cold', i.e. he did not survive unharmed. A halakhic application: 'and you shall only (*akh*) rejoice' (Deut 16.15). According to Sukk 48a this includes the evening of the last holiday of Sukkot, but not the first, which is excluded by *akh*.

3. *Ribbui aḥar ribbui*, 'inclusion after inclusion' through a combination of two of the particles cited for No. 1. MidrSam 20.5 (B. 54a) interprets 1 Sam 17.36 'also the lion (*gam et ha-'ari*), also the bear (*gam ha-dob*) did your servant slay' in the name of R. Nathan: he killed four lions (one each in

addition for *gam*, *et* and the article. The halakhah differs; here 'inclusion after inclusion means a reduction' (Sifra Ṣaw 11, W. 34d). Hence, where Lev 7.12 twice requires 'with oil' for the thank offering, only half a Log of oil is to be used instead of the whole Log for other food offerings (cf. Men 89a, where this opinion is attributed to Aqiba). SifreNum §124 (H. 155f) applies the same principle, as a rule of R. Ishmael, to the burning of the red heifer (Num 19.5, twice 'burn'): only the barely necessary quantity of wood is used. R. Yehudah on the other hand regards the double *ribbui* as an intensification: one must not skimp.

4. *Mi'ut aḥar mi'ut*, combination of two restrictive or exclusive particles. 'An exclusion after an exclusion signifies an inclusion.' R. Meir applies this principle halakhically in Mak 9b: even a blind man who has unintentionally killed someone must flee to the city of sanctuary, since the two exclusions ('without seeing it' Num 35.23; 'without intention' Deut 19.4) signify an inclusion. However, this argument is not universally accepted. Another example is the haggadic application to 1 Kgs 8.9: 'in the ark was *nothing*, *only* the two stone tablets.' The twofold restriction *ein. . . raq* leads to the assumption that the ark also contained a scroll of Torah (BB 14a) and/or the fragments of the first tablets (BB 14b).

5. *Qal wa-ḥomer meforash.* An explicit argument from the lesser to the greater, and vice versa. Cf. Hillel No. 1.

6. *Qal wa-ḥomer satum.* An implicit argument from the lesser to the greater, and vice versa.

7. *Gezerah shawah* and 8. *Binyan ab*: cf. Hillel Nos. 2, 3.

9. *Derekh qeṣarah.* An abbreviated or elliptical expression. Deut 21.11, 'And if you see among the prisoners a woman who is beautiful of appearance' (*eshet yefat to'ar*). SifreDeut §211 (F. 245) already deduces from the construct state *eshet* instead of *ishah*: 'even if she is a married woman (*eshet ish*)', one may marry her. The late Midrash *Leqaḥ Tob* clarifies ad loc.: 'Wherever *eshet* is read, it must be complemented, e.g. *eshet kesilut* ('Lady Folly', Prov 9.13). And why does it say (only) *eshet* here? In order to teach: even if she is a married woman (*eshet ish*).'

10. *Repetition* is used for interpretation. Yehudah b. Ilai says in GenR 89.9 (Theodor/Albeck 1098), 'There were actually supposed to be 14 years of famine' (Gen 41.3, 6: seven lean cows, seven lean ears of grain); Neḥemyah answers, 'Actually, 28 years were appointed: Pharaoh saw 14 (in his dream), and told Joseph about them', thereby repeating the number. And because Joseph again repeats Pharaoh's words, the Rabbis think there ought to have been 42 years.

M.Sanh 1.6 uses the repetition of 'the congregation' in Num 35.24f. to prove that a small court must have 23 members: 'congregation' = 10, as deduced from Num 14.27, where 'the congregation' is understood as the twelve spies without

Joshua and Caleb. To the twice ten are added three additional members required for other reasons.

A *baraita* in Ḥul 115b reads the threefold 'You shall not boil a kid in its mother's milk' (Exod 23.19; 34.26; Deut 14.21) as pertaining to the prohibition of eating, cooking, and usufruct. But according to Aqiba the thrice-used 'kid' means that the biblical prohibition of cooking in milk does not apply to fowl, game, and unclean animals.

In Mek Wa-yassa 5 (L. 2.119), Zeriqah deduces from the threefold repetition of 'today' in Exod 16.25 (of the manna: 'Eat it today, for today is a Sabbath to the Lord; today you will not find it in the field' that it is necessary to keep three meals on the Sabbath (cf. Shab 117b).

Yoshiyyah uses the threefold occurrence of the word *elohim* in Exod 22.7f. as proof that three judges must decide in financial (civil) court cases: Mek Neziqin 15 (L. 3.119); cf. Sanh 3b.

11. *Related material which is separated* (by *sôf pasuq* or another disjunctive accent). In 2 Chr 30.18f. the verse division does in fact interfere with the sense, but in other cases it is simply ignored in order to find biblical support for a particular idea. M.Mak 3.10 connects *be-mispar* in Deut 25.2 with *arba'im*, the first word of the following verse, 'by the number forty', in order thereby to document the limitation of corporal punishment to 39 lashes – *be-mispar arba'im*, 'a number which is next to 40'.

In Mek Pisḥa 16 (L. 1.139), Yose combines 'and nothing leavened shall be eaten' (Exod 13.3) with 'today' in the following verse, in order to establish that Israel only ate unleavened bread in Egypt on this one day.

Sifra Qedoshim 2 (W. 87d) deduces from Lev 19.10 the rule that a landowner may not favour one poor man over another by helping him glean: contrary to both the context and the *atnaḥ* accent, this combines 'you shall not gather' with the subsequent 'for the needy' (cf. Git 12a). In Sifra Qedoshim 9 (W. 91a), Simeon ben Eleazar divides Lev 19.32, 'you shall honour the face of the old. And you shall fear your God' contrary to the *atnaḥ* in order to establish that the old must not bother their neighbour: 'old man, you shall fear your God'.

Related to this ungrammatical sentence division in support of a particular interpretation is the occasional ambivalence about where a word belongs. In Mek Amaleq 1 (L. 2.142), Issi ben Yehudah says that five words in the Torah have no 'excess weight' which might tip the scales in favour of a connection with the preceding or the following material (cf. also Yoma 52 a-b). A halakhic example is Sot 7.4: according to Deut 25.9, if a widow's brother-in-law refuses levirate marriage, the woman shall 'take off his shoe, spit into his face and say: *thus* may it be done to the man who does not build up his brother's house.' R. Yehudah applies the 'thus' to 'say' as well as to 'may it be done' she shall speak *thus* (i.e. with these words, in Hebrew), '*Thus* may it be done. . . .' For parallels in the Hellenistic norms of *synthesis* and *diairesis* see Daube, *Alex. Methods*, 34–44.

12. Something is adduced for comparison and thereby is itself seen in a new light (cf. Hillel No. 7). Sanh 74a treats the principle that under the threat of death one may commit any sin except idolatry, incest, and murder. Rabbi comments with regard to incest and murder: 'This is as if someone assaults and kills his neighbour' (Deut 22.26). 'What do we learn from the comparison with the murderer? That which teaches also receives instruction. Just as for the betrothed virgin (Deut 22.25), so also in the case of a murderer one may save him (the victim) with his (the aggressor's) life. And compare the betrothed virgin (i.e. her rape) with the murderer: just as one must sooner let oneself be killed than to commit murder, so also one must sooner let oneself be killed (so the reading in Yoma 82a) than to rape a betrothed virgin.'

13. If a general principle is followed by an action (*ma'aseh*), then the latter is the particular instance of the former (cf. Hillel No. 5). An example is offered by the list of the 32 rules in MHG Gen (M. 30):

> 'God said, Let there be light' (Gen 1.14). Then it goes on to say, 'Lights shall appear in the firmament' (Gen 1.14). Whoever hears this might think it to be a separate event. But it is only a detail of the first; for it is taught, These are the same lights which were created on the first day; but God only suspended them on the fourth day. This corresponds to Gen 1.27, 'And God created man in his image.' This is the general principle, and in the end he makes his actions particular: 'And God the Lord formed man from the earth' (Gen 2.7). 'Then the Lord God caused unconsciousness to fall on the man so that he slept, and he took one of his ribs' (Gen 2.21). Whoever hears this might think it to be a different matter, but it is only a detail of the first.

14. The more significant is compared with the lesser in order to achieve better understanding, e.g. in Deut 32.2 the Torah and the rain. This rule is not used for the halakhah.

15. = Ishmael 13.

16. An expression which is unique to its passage. SifreNum §110 (H. 113):

> 'At your entering into the land' (Num 15.18). . . R. Ishmael says, The Bible expresses this 'entering' differently from every other 'entering' in the Torah. Elsewhere it says, 'And when you will enter into the land' and 'when the Lord your God lets you enter (the land)'. But here it says, 'at your entering', in order to teach you that the Israelites were obliged to bring the raised dough offering as soon as they entered (deduced from Num 15.20).

17. A circumstance not clearly expressed in the main passage is mentioned elsewhere. This is especially used to supplement a Pentateuchal reference with a non-Pentateuchal one. MHG Gen (M. 32) adduces Gen 2.8 as an example: the description of paradise is to be supplemented with Ezek 28.13; and Num 3, which gives no account of priestly orders, with 1 Chr 24.19.

18. One particular instance is mentioned in a category of events, although the whole category is intended; e.g. 'nocturnal incident' (Deut 23.11), because the said incidents occur most frequently by night. – SifreDeut §194f. (F. 234f.) on Deut 20.5f.: whoever has built a new house but has not yet dedicated it, may withdraw from armed service. Only building is mentioned here, but it applies as well to inheriting, buying, and receiving as a gift. The same is true for the vineyard: only planting is mentioned, but inheriting, buying, and receiving as a gift are also intended.

19. A statement is made in relation to one object, but it is also valid for another. In Mek Neziqin 6 (L. 3.53), R. Nathan comments on Exod 21.18, 'If someone strikes the other with a stone or with his fist': 'He compares the stone with the fist and the fist with the stone. Just as the stone must be suitable for killing, so also the fist; and just as the fist can be identified, so it must be for the stone. If the stone is mixed in with other stones (which others may have thrown), the assailant is free.'

20. Something is inappropriately said about an object but must properly be applied to another. SifreNum §118 (H. 138f.) on Num 18.15:

> 'You shall redeem the firstborn of man, and the firstborn of unclean animals you shall redeem.' I might understand all unclean animals to be included. But Exod 13.13 says, 'Every firstborn of a donkey you shall redeem with a lamb', i.e. of a donkey and not of other unclean animals. Or must one interpret: the first litter of a donkey must be redeemed with a sheep; that of all other unclean animals, with garments and implements? Exod 34.20 repeats, 'The donkey's firstborn you shall redeem with a sheep'. The repetition of 'with a sheep' teaches that one redeems only with a sheep and not with garments or implements. Why then does Num 18.15 say, 'You shall redeem'? If it does not mean that (the firstborn of) unclean animals are redeemed, then apply it to the possibility that one may dedicate unclean animals to repair the Temple, in order afterwards to redeem them again.

21. Something is compared with two things and only the good properties of both are applied. E.g. Ps 92.13: 'The righteous flourishes as the palm tree.' One might say: like the palm tree he offers no shade; but the parallel line supplies: 'He grows as a cedar in Lebanon.' The cedar of course bears no edible fruits; this in turn cannot be applied to the righteous.

M.Arak 9.7 interprets Lev 25.31: houses in villages enjoy the privileges both of houses in unwalled cities and of fields. 'They are immediately redeemed, and they are redeemed every twelve months like houses in cities, and they return to their owners in the year of Jubilee, and money is subtracted (for the time of their use) as for fields', if they are to be bought back.

22. A sentence which must be supplemented from its parallel. In Mek Kaspah 2 (L. 3.161), R. Nathan interprets the sentence Exod 23.1, 'Do not join your hand with a wicked man by being a false witness'. 'Do not join your hand – do not let the wicked man testify, and do not let the robber testify'.

23. A sentence serves to supplement its parallel. Only in the haggadah. Sifre Deut §40 (F. 80) on Deut 11.12 'a land for which the Lord your God cares'. But surely God cares for all lands! Cf. Job 38.26: 'in order to send rain on a land without people, on the desert where no one lives'. What does this mean: 'a land for which the Lord your God cares'? Because of this care God cares also for other lands. It is the same for Ps 121.4: 'the keeper of Israel neither sleeps nor slumbers'. The term 'Israel's keeper' indicates: for the sake of this keeping he keeps everything else beside them.

24. Something is contained in a general statement and is then isolated in order to say something about itself. In Josh 2.1, Joshua tells two spies, 'Go, spy out the land and Jericho.' Jericho is already included in the land, but it is singled out in order to show that it was equal to the whole land of Israel (MHG Gen M. 35 is an example of this rule).

25. Something is contained in a general statement and is then isolated in order to say something about the latter (minor modification of Ishmael's No. 8). The prohibition of lighting a fire on the Sabbath (Exod 35.3) is already contained in Exod 35.2: whoever works on the Sabbath shall be put to death. But it has been emphasized for comparison and to tell you: just as one incurs guilt by kindling of fire, which is a principal labour, so one incurs guilt by any other principal labour (Shab 70a).

26. *Mashal.* 'Parable', allegorical interpretation. Ishmael interpreted three Pentateuchal references allegorically for the halakhah: Exod 22.2, Num 21.19; Deut 22.17 (SifreDeut §237, F. 269f.). Mek Neziqin 13 (L. 3.102) on Exod 22.2: 'But on this the sun has risen', i.e. after the theft; if the victim then kills the thief, 'then there is blood guiltiness'. R. Ishmael applies 'on this' ('*alaw*) not to the crime but to the thief, and he asks, 'Does the sun rise only on him, rather than on the whole world? The sun means peace for the world; so here also. If it is known that he (the burglar) lives in peace with him (the victim) and the latter nevertheless kills him, he is guilty.'

27. *Equivalence.* A number of equivalent significance. Thus the 40 days of Num 13.25 are equivalent to the 40 years of Num 14.34.

28. *Paronomasia*, play on cognate roots: e.g. Num 21.9 *neḥash neḥoshet*, 'brazen serpent'; Jer 23.2 *ha-ro'im ha-ra'im*, 'the evil shepherds'.

29. *Gematria*. Bacher, *ET* 1:127: *grammateia*, from *grammateus* 'notarius' (stenographer), or directly from *gramma*, with a facilitating transposition of consonants. For the derivation from *geômetria* see Lieberman, *Hell.*, 69 (Hellenistic parallels) and S. Sambursky, 'On the Origin and Significance of the Term Gematria' *JJS* 29 (1978) 35–38 (rev. from *Tarbiz* 45 (1975–76) 268–71). Cf. also the comprehensive investigation of R. Weißkopf, *Gematria: Buchstabenberechnung, Tora und Schöpfung im rabbinischen Judentum*, Diss. Tübingen 1978. Gematria denotes a calculation of the numerical value of letters. In LamR 1.1 (B. 21a), Ben Azzai sees in *êkhah*, the first word of Lam, the suggestion that the Israelites were not led into exile before they denied the One (*alef*) God, the ten (*yod*) commandments, the law of circumcision given after twenty (*kaph*) generations, and the five (*he*) books of the Torah. The number 318 of Abraham's servants in Gen 14.14 is in PRK 8 (M. 139) taken to signify Eliezer; the *Epistle of Barnabas* sees in this number a pointer to the cross (T=300) and Jesus (IH=18). Yoma 20a points out the numerical value of *ha-satan*=364: on 364 days of the year Satan has power over the Israelites, but not on the Day of Atonement. Shab 70a finds in Exod 35.1 *elleh ha-debarim* the 39 prohibited Sabbath labours about which Moses received instruction at Sinai: plural *debarim*=2; the article adds something (i.e. 2+1), and *elleh* has the numerical value of 36. R. Mattan deduces the 30–day duration of Nazirite vows from Num 6.5: *qadosh yihyeh*, 'he shall be holy'; *yhyh* has a numerical value of 30 (Naz 5a = Taan 17a; Sanh 22b).

One variation of *gematria* which is sometimes seen as a separate rule is the *Atbash*, the use of a secret alphabet in which the first letter of the Hebrew alphabet corresponds to the last, the second to the last but one, etc., so that *alef* is replaced by *taw*, *beth* by *shin*, etc. Using this rule, the Targum to Jer 25.26 translates 'And finally the King of Shishak must drink' by 'the king of *Babel*. . .'.

30. *Notarikon* (from *notarius*, stenographer). Division of a word into two or more; alternatively, each letter of a word is to be understood as the initial letter of another word. Shab 105a finds in the letters of the word *nimreṣet* in 1 Kgs 2.8 a suggestion of the curses used by Shimi: *no'ef*, adulterer; Moabite; *roṣeaḥ*, murderer; *ṣorer*, tormentor; *to'ebah*, abomination. In the same fashion GenR 90.4 (Theodor/Albeck 1103) interprets the name Zaphenath-Paneah given to Joseph by Pharaoh (Gen 41.45). Partition of a word: Men 66b = Shab 105a interprets 'Carmel' as *kar*

*male*', 'full of cushions' (so full are the ears of grain there). PRE 36 (L. 84a) divides the name Reuben into *re'u ben* 'Behold, a son'.

*Notarikon* can also designate an abbreviated expression in which a positive sentence includes the corresponding negative one, e.g. Mek Baḥodesh 8 (L. 2.259) on Exod 20.12: 'If you do not honour your parents, your days will be shortened. For the words of the Torah are (to be understood as) a *notarikon.*'

31. *An Antecedent that is placed subsequently.* Lev 1.15: 'And the priest shall wring off the head of the pigeon and offer it up in smoke on the altar; and its blood shall be drained out on the side of the altar.' Zeb 65a comments on this: would it occur to you to think that he only drains it after he has offered it up in smoke? Rather, the sentence intends to say: 'just as the offering up in smoke takes place on the height of the altar, so also the draining'.

'And it (the Manna) turned to worms and smelled' (Exod 16.20). According to Mek Wa-yassa (L. 2.116), this is an inverted word of Scripture (*miqra mesuras*): smell properly precedes the worms. Occasionally, the Rabbis explicitly re-arrange the biblical text so that it matches their understanding. Thus Num 9.6, 'They came before Moses and Aaron' to receive a legal response. This seems to presuppose that that Moses was asked first and then Aaron, when no answer was received from Moses. However, that seems absurd: 'If Moses did not know it, how would Aaron? Instead, invert the word of Scripture (they came before Aaron and Moses) and interpret it thus' (R. Yoshiyyah in SifreNum §68, H. 63). This method of interpretation has its parallels in the Hellenistic exegesis of Homer, in which *anastrophé* corresponds to the Rabbinic *seres* (cf. Daube, *Alex. Methods*, 27–34 and Lieberman, *Hell.*, 65–67).

32. Some biblical passages pertain to an earlier time than a preceding text, and vice versa. Num 7 (votive offerings) should precede Num 1. This phenomenon is also known as '*erub parashiyot* ('mixing of Bible passages'): thus BQ 107a, where R. Ḥiyya bar Joseph detects such a mixing in Exod 22: the words 'this is it' in v. 8 are in the paragraph about safe-keeping, but they belong in that about loans (v. 24). Generally on the sequence of biblical statements, the 'school of Ishmael' declares, 'In the Torah there is no before and after' (SifreNum §64, H. 61; Pes 6b).

## IV

## ORAL AND WRITTEN TRADITION

***Bibliography***

**Albeck, Ch.** *Einführung*, 163–70. **Achtemeier, P. J.** 'Omne verbum sonat: The New Testament and the Oral Environment of Late Western Antiquity.' *JBL* 109 (1990) 3–27. **Alexander, P. S.** 'Orality in Pharisaic-Rabbinic Judaism at the Turn of the Eras.' In H. Wansbrough (ed.), *Jesus and the Oral Gospel Tradition*, 159–84. Sheffield 1991. **Baumgarten, J. M.** 'The Unwritten Law in the Pre-Rabbinic Period.' *JSJ* 3 (1972) 7–29. **Baumgarten, J. M.** 'Form Criticism and the Oral Law.' *JSJ* 5 (1974) 34–40. **Brown, R.** 'Midrashim as Oral Traditions.' *HUCA* 47 (1976) 181–89. **Ephrati, J. E.** 'But a Man Should Quote his Teacher Verbatim' (Hebr.). *Bar Ilan* 9 (1972) 221–38. **Epstein, J. N.** *ITM*, 692–706. **Finkelstein, L.** 'The Transmission of the Early Rabbinic Tradition.' *HUCA* 16 (1941) 115–35. [Repr. in idem, *Sifra*, 5:224*–44*.] **Foley, J. M.** *Oral Formulaic Theory and Research: An Introduction and Annotated Bibliography*. New York 1985. **Gerhardsson, B.** *Memory and Manuscript*. **Güttgemanns, E.** *Offene Fragen zur Formgeschichte des Evangeliums*, esp. 136–53. 2nd edn. Munich 1971. **Heinemann, I.** 'Die Lehre vom ungeschriebenen Gesetz im jüdischen Schrifttum.' *HUCA* 4 (1927) 149–71. **Heinemann, J.** *Aggadah*, 17–47. **Jaffee, M. S.** 'How much "Orality" in Oral Torah? New Perspectives on the Composition and Transmission of Early Rabbinic Tradition.' *Shofar* 10 (1992) 53–72. **Jaffee, M. S.** 'Writing and Rabbinic Oral Tradition: On Mishnaic Narrative, Lists and Mnemonics.' *Journal of Jewish Thought and Philosophy* 4 (1994) 123–46. **Kirkpatrick, P. G.** *The Old Testament and Folklore Study*. Sheffield 1988. **Lieberman, S.** 'The Publication of the Mishnah.' In *Hell.*, 83–99. **Lord, A. B.** *The Singer of Tales*. Cambridge, MA 1960. **Neusner, J.** *Phar* 3:143–79. **Neusner, J.** 'The Written Tradition in the Pre-Rabbinic Period.' *JSJ* 4 (1973) 56–65. **Neusner, J.** *Oral Tradition in Judaism: The Case of the Mishnah*. New York 1987. [Revision of material from *Pur*, vol. 21; *Phar*, vol. 3.] **Safrai, S.** *The Literature*, 1:35–119. **Schäfer, P.** 'Das "Dogma" von der mündlichen Torah im rabbinischen Judentum.' In idem, *Studien*, 153–97. **Towner, W. S.** 'Form Criticism of Rabbinic Literature.' *JJS* 24 (1973) 101–18. **Vansina, J.** *Oral Tradition: A Study in Historical Methodology*. Chicago 1965.

### *1) The Concept of Oral Torah; a Ban on Writing?*

The idea of 'oral Torah' is a basic concept of rabbinic Judaism: God's revelation at Sinai includes not only the 'written Torah' recorded in the Bible, but also an equivalent complex of traditions. Only by means of the latter can the Bible become fully applicable and the divine rule of life appropriate to each particular situation (thus e.g. the doctrine of the two *Torot* in an anecdote about Hillel and Shammai: ARN B 29, Sch. 61f.; Shab 31a). It is undeniable that such a tradition alongside Scripture must already have existed in the biblical period, and even more so at a later time. Here we are concerned only with the practical significance of the term 'oral Torah' (which also, and above all, includes the rabbinic literature). Does this term entail a statement about the manner of transmission – viz., not in written form but by oral tradition? Or is it merely intended as a distinction over against the Bible, or a suggestion that one Torah was given at Sinai in written and the other in oral form?

This question was already disputed in the Middle Ages. Rashi on Shab 13b, for instance, writes with respect to the Scroll of Fasting, 'All the rest of the Mishnah and *baraita* was not written, for it was forbidden to write it down.' Similarly on Erub 62b: 'At that time there was no written halakhah, not a single letter, except the Scroll of Fasting.' However, Saadya, Maimonides, and others held the view that the rabbis wrote down their teachings and that Rabbi, too, published his Mishnah in writing. This contrast between the French (Rashi) and the Spanish (Maimonides) tradition appears also in ISG: the French recension repeatedly claims that nothing was written down in Talmudic times, while the Spanish version stresses that Rabbi put his Mishnah in writing (references in Lewin, *ISG* xlviii f.).

In the nineteenth century there were keen defenders of both theories. It was not only conservatives who asserted an oral mode of transmission for the halakhah (or indeed for the haggadah) during the Talmudic or at least the Tannaitic period. (Orality was regarded *inter alia* as a guarantee that the halakhah could be adapted to changing circumstances.) There were frequent assertions that the writing of the halakhah or even the haggadah was completely forbidden. Aside from this there was a widespread assumption that rabbinic material must *de facto* be assumed to have undergone a long period of oral transmission before being written down. Thus for Beit-Arié (*Codicology*, 10 n.2) the gap of several centuries between the Qumran texts and the oldest rabbinic manuscripts is due not to a complete loss but to 'the dominant oral transmission of Jewish literature' (but why then are there no *biblical* MSS from this period either?).

***2) Rabbinic Evidence for the Ban on Writing?***

The classic proof text is Tem 14b (partial parallel Git 60b): R. Dimi (A4; see p. 57 below for this notation of dates) had no messenger; otherwise he would have written a letter to Rab Joseph about a halakhic question (the drink-offering). But was he even permitted to do so?

> R. Abba the son of R. Ḥiyya bar Abba says, R. Yoḥanan (A2) said, Those who write *halakhot* are as one who burns the Torah; and he that learns from them receives no reward. R. Yehudah bar Naḥmani (A2), the interpreter of Resh Laqish, expounded: a Scripture verse says, 'Write down these words' and then it says, 'according to (*al pi*, lit. 'by the mouth') these words' (Exod 34.27), in order to teach you: whatever is (transmitted) in oral form, you may not recite from a written document (*le-omram mi-ketab*); and whatever is (transmitted) in writing you may not recite orally (i.e. by heart, from memory). A teaching from the school of R. Ishmael: 'Write these words' – these you may write, but not *halakhot*. One says: perhaps it is different with a new subject matter. Thus R. Yoḥanan and Resh Laqish used to examine

> the book of haggadah on the Sabbath and thus to interpret the Bible: 'It is time for the Lord to act; they have broken your law' (Ps 119.126). They said, it is better that one letter in the Torah is suspended than that the (whole) Torah should be forgotten in Israel.

The text is composite:

a) The sentence of Yehudah bar Naḥmani must be extracted from the bracketing statements of Yoḥanan; it then sounds less absolute. It must not be understood as a rejection of any writing of oral Torah, but it condemns instead the use of oral Targums in the synagogal reading: Yehudah bar Naḥmani was after all a meturgeman! (Cf. Epstein, *ITM*, 697.) R. Ḥaggai (A4) relates how R. Samuel bar R. Isaac (A3) saw a Bible teacher in the synagogue 'who recited the Targum from a book. He said to him, You are forbidden to do that. Things which were spoken orally are (to be transmitted) orally, written ones in written form' (p.Meg 4.1, 74d). This text can relate equally to the synagogue school proceedings as to the service; the 'book' is either a written Targum or else the Hebrew Bible, on which the teacher bases his translation – but this too is forbidden, 'lest they say the translation is written in the Torah' (Meg 32a).

b) R. Yoḥanan rejects the *writing of halakhot*, but probably only for official instruction ('whoever learns from them'). At any rate such views are not attested before the third century; and, as the polemical note suggests, they were not universally accepted.

c) Occasionally the *writing of the haggadah* is also condemned; thus R. Yehoshua ben Levi: 'Whoever writes down a haggadah has no share (in the world to come)' (p.Shab 16.1, 15c). But others value books of haggadah (p.Ber 5.1, 9a), so that on this point too there is no unanimous agreement.

The only explicit testimony of a non-Jew from this period is Augustine, *Contra adversarium legis et Prophetarum* 2.1.2 (*CCSL* 94.87f.): 'Nescit autem habere praeter scripturas legitimas et propheticas Iudaeos quasdam traditiones suas, quas non scriptas habent, sed memoriter tenent et alter in alterum loquendo transfundit, quas deuterosin vocant.' ['He does not know, however, that in addition to the legal and prophetic scriptures the Jews have certain of their traditions, which they keep not in written form but committed to memory, and orally pass on to others. These traditions they call *deuterosis* (Gk. 'repetition', i.e. *Mishnah*).'] But Augustine is too distant from the Rabbinic world to be considered a reliable witness (with regard to this text, Epstein, *ITM*, 698, supposes Augustine's ignorance).

Josephus's statement about the Pharisees in *Ant* 13.297 cannot be straightforwardly used to date the prohibition of writing halakhah as early as the first century. According to this text, the Pharisees transmit certain precepts not written in the laws of Moses (*haper ouk anagegraptai en tois Moyseôs nomois*), while the Sadducees exclusively keep to the written precepts (*nomima ta gegrammena*). Some understand this to refer to a Pharisaic distinction between written and oral Torah (Baumgarten, *Unwritten Law*, 12–14, Schäfer, 'Dogma', 190), while e.g. Neusner (*Phar* 3:163–65; cf. Epstein, *ITM*, 697) sees here only the contrast between things written in the Bible and those not written in the Bible. In any case the text says nothing about a *prohibition* of writing.

***3) Rabbinic Evidence for the Writing Down of Oral Torah***

There are also numerous rabbinic attestations of written texts of both haggadic and halakhic character. This shows that the doctrine of the oral Torah in rabbinic times did not result in a prohibition of writing; it should instead be seen primarily as a 'dogma' without any necessary practical relevance (thus Schäfer).

***a) Books of Haggadah***

The possession of books of haggadah by third-century teachers is repeatedly attested for Palestine (p.Shab 16.1, 15c; p.Ber 5.1, 9a; p.Kil 9.4, 32b; p.Maas 3.10, 51a; Tem 14b; Ber 23a-b; Sanh 57b); patristic references in this regard are only of limited value, since they do not necessarily apply to rabbinic circles – Palestinian Judaism was of course still quite diverse even at that time. In Babylonia, such books are mentioned in relation to teachers of the fourth century (Ber 23b; Ḥul 60b; BM 116a; BB 52a; Shebu 46b; Shab 89a is not explicit).

***b) Writings mentioned by name***

*Megillat Ta'anit*, Taan 2.8; Erub 62b etc.: the 'Scroll of Fasting'. This list from the time of the Second Temple (Maccabaean and Roman periods) describes 36 days on which fasting is not permitted because of the joyous events which occurred on these days. The Aramaic text dates from the first and second centuries; the corresponding Hebrew commentary (the 'scholion') is post-Talmudic, and in its longer version it is an Ashkenazic revision of the 12th or 13th century (Noam). *Megillat Ta'anit* is to be distinguished from the Hebrew Scroll of Fasting (also called *Megillat Ta'anit Batra*), a probably Geonic list of days on which one must fast (text e.g. in Abraham Ibn Daud, *Sefer ha-Qabbalah*, ed. Cohen, Hebr. section, 57; cf. M. Margolioth, 'Mo'adim we–ṣumot be-Ereṣ Yisra'el u-be-Babel bi-tequfat ha-Ge'onim', *Areshet* 1 (1943–44) 204–16; S. Z. Leiman, 'The Scroll of Fasts: The Ninth of Tebeth' *JQR* N.S. 74 (1983–84) 174–95.

***Bibliography***

***Text***

**Lichtenstein, H.** 'Die Fastenrolle: Eine Untersuchung zur jüdisch-hellenistischen Geschichte.' *HUCA* 8–9 (1931–32) 257–351. **Lurie, B.–Z.** *Megillath Ta'anith: With Introductions and Notes* (Hebr.). Jerusalem 1964.

***Studies***

**Hampel, I.** *Megillat Ta'anit* (Hebr.). Diss. Tel Aviv 1976. **Mantel, H.** 'The Megilat Ta'anit and the Sects' (Hebr.). In *Studies in the History of the Jewish People and the Land of Israel in Memory of Z. Avneri*, 51–70. Haifa 1970. **Farmer, W. R.** *Maccabees, Zealots, and Josephus*, 151–58. New York 1956. **Noam, V.** 'The Scholion to the Megillat Ta'anit – Towards an Understanding of its Stemma' (Hebr.). *Tarbiz* 62 (1992–93) 55–99. **Tabory, J.** 'When was the Scroll of Fasts Abrogated?' (Hebr.). *Tarbiz* 55 (1985–86) 261–65. **Zeitlin, S.** *Megillat Taanit as a Source for Jewish Chronology and History in the Hellenistic and Roman Periods*. Philadelphia 1922. [=*JQR* N.S. 9 (1918–19) 71–102; 10 (1919–20) 49–80, 237–90.] **Zeitlin, S.** 'Nennt Megillat Taanit antisadduzäische Gedenktage?' *MGWJ* 81 (1937) 351–55.

Additional bibliography in J.A. Fitzmyer & D.J. Harrington, *A Manual of Palestinian Aramaic Texts* (Rome 1978), 248–50.

*Megillat Yuḥasin*, a scroll of genealogies. This is a generic term, not the title of a particular document. The scroll cited by Ben Azzai in Yeb 49b, according to which a certain person is a *mamzer*, must be distinguished from the scroll which R. Levi adduces in p.Taan 4.2, 68a, according to which Hillel is descended from David (cf. GenR 98.10, Theodor/Albeck, 1259). J. Z. Lauterbach, 'The three books found in the Temple at Jerusalem' *JQR* N.S. 8 (1917–18) 385–423, suggests that even the books found in the Temple according to SifreDeut §356 (F. 423) and p.Taan 4.2, 68a were books of this kind; but the context tends to imply Pentateuch scrolls which departed from the standard text.

*Sefer Yuḥasin*, Book of Genealogies. In Pes 62b R. Yoḥanan refuses to teach R. Simlai the book of genealogies; then it says in the name of Rab: 'Ever since *Sefer Yuḥasin* was concealed, the strength of the sages has flagged and their eyesight become dull' (in a parallel, which however does not mention *Sefer Yuḥasin*, p.Pes 5.3, 32a names R. Jonathan instead of Yoḥanan; this is also supported by the variant reading 'Nathan' in Pes 62b. Cf. Bacher, *PAm* 1:60). Mar Zutra then adds that the haggadic expositions even just on the portion of text between the two occurrences of *aṣel* in 1 Chr 8.38 and 9.44 would have sufficed to load 400 camels; this probably also reflects the rich exegetical tradition especially on the books of Chronicles. In any case the *Sefer Yuḥasin* appears to have been a commentary on the genealogies of the book of Chronicles (cf. Amram Gaon ad loc., *Oṣar ha-Gaonim*, ed. B. M. Lewin, 3.2 (Jerusalem 1980), 80).

*Megillat Ḥasidim*, 'scroll of the devout'. Thus p.Ber 10.8, 14d; also MHG Deut 11.22 (F. 231) and most of the textual tradition of SifreDeut §48, where however Finkelstein 112 adopts the reading of MidrTann Deut 11.22 (H. 42): *megillat ḥarisim*, i.e. roughly 'scroll of the sun worshippers'; Finkelstein *ad loc.* with D. Hoffmann (MidrTann 7f.) relates this to the Essenes (cf. Josephus *BJ* 2.128). According to the editor of MHG, however, the reading of MidrTann must be seen as a scribal error. Yalqut §873 on Deut 11.22 reads *megillat setarim*, 'book of the secrets' or 'a scroll kept secret'.

To this context belong the passages that speak of *written Targums*. Cf. Zunz, *GV*, 65. Thus e.g. t.Shab 13.2 (L. 57) mentions a Targum on Job (cf. also Lieberman, *TK* 3.203f.); at Qumran, too, such a Targum was found in cave 11 (ed. J. P. M. Van der Ploeg and A. S. Van der Woude, Leiden 1971). Of course the prohibition applied not to the writing down of the Targum but only to its public recitation.

***c) Evidence for the Writing of Halakhot***

In the Scroll of Fasting we read for the 4th of Tammuz (Lichtenstein, 331): 'The book of decrees (*sefer gezarata*) was rescinded'. The medieval Hebrew scholion relates this text to Sadducean ordinances; similarly many modern commentators (e.g. Lichtenstein, 295–97): a Sadducean penal code, rescinded in 76 BCE when Salome Alexandra took office or in 66 CE at the onset of the Jewish War. Against this see J. Le Moyne, *Les Sadducéens*, Paris 1972, 219–23, who thinks (with S. Zeitlin, F. Baer and others) of pagan, possibly Seleucid laws.

Yoḥanan ben Nuri (a contemporary of Aqiba) receives from an old man a *megillat sammanin*, a list of the spices for incense which was an heirloom of the family of Abtina: Yoma 38a, p.Sheq 5.2, 49a.

In the house of Ḥiyya, Rab found a *megillat setarim* in which there were halakhic sentences of Issi ben Yehudah: Shab 6b; 96b; BM 92a. Rashi on Shab 6b explains the 'secret scroll' (NB no connection with Qumran's so-called 'book of mysteries', 1Q27) by reference to the supposed ban on writing: a new, unknown teaching of an individual rabbi was written down lest it be forgotten, but the writing was kept hidden.

According to Ḥul 95b, Samuel of Nehardea sends to Yoḥanan thirteen camel loads of doubts pertaining to the laws about *Terefah* (R. Ḥananel in the *Tosafot* reads 'twelve pieces of parchment'). Letters of halakhic content are mentioned (Epstein, *ITM*, 699f.).

According to Strack, 13, the discussion in BM 80a between Abbaye and Raba about BM 6.5 (the bulk of straw is as heavy as the load *ke-masui* or makes the load heavy *le-masui*) shows that they had no written Mishnah before them. But the text gives no information about this. Cf. Epstein, *ITM*, 380f.: *ke-masui*, supported by Abbaye, is the proper Mishnah text, while Raba's 'reading' is a correction to support his interpretation.

Frequently the Talmud recounts that someone who does not know something in the school house, 'went out, examined, and found' (*nafaq, daq we-ashkaḥ*): Ber 19a; Pes 19a; Hag 19a; Yeb 36a; 105a; Ket 81b and often. This turn of phrase cannot actually prove the existence of written notes, but such an understanding does seem likely.

The oldest extant written halakhic text is the extensive mosaic inscription on the floor of the synagogue of Rehob in the Beth Shean valley. On the basis primarily of PT it gives details about the halakhah of the Sabbath year and of tithing, as it is to be observed in the towns of Israel and the surrounding area. This inscription, discovered in 1974, dates from the first half of the seventh century: Y. Sussmann, 'A Halakhic Inscription from the Beth-Shean Valley' (Hebr.), *Tarbiz* 43 (1973–74) 88–158; S. Lieberman, 'The Halakhhic Inscription from the Beth-Shean Valley' (Hebr.), *Tarbiz* 45 (1975–76) 54–63 (=*Studies*, 402–11); Z. Safrai, 'Marginal Notes on the Rehob Inscription' (Hebr.), *Zion* 42 (1977) 1–23 (according to him, the inscription is to be dated no earlier than the second half of the seventh century; recent archaeological studies support a date in the sixth to seventh centuries: F. Vitto, *IEJ* 30 (1980) 217).

The oldest Genizah fragments of M, PT and midrashim, which are palimpsests on Christian texts, are probably not much later. For an analysis of these palimpsests see M. Sokoloff & J. Yahalom, 'Christian Palimpsests from the Cairo Geniza' *Revue d'Histoire des Textes* 8 (1978) 109–32.

#### *4) Schools and Oral Tradition*

Rabbinical polemics against writing down the Oral Torah are, as we have seen, attested only since the third century. Their dogmatic-homiletical rationale is even later (from the fourth century, i.e. in the Byzantine Christian environment: p.Peah 2.6, 17a; p.Ḥag 1.8, 76d; PesR 5, F. 14b, etc.): the oral Torah distinguishes Israel from the nations, who at least cannot translate this oral Torah and then claim to be (the true) Israel. This accords well with the fact that in Arabic thought, too, the preference for oral tradition appears only in later times, and never becomes universal (Widengren). An argument against the thesis of the orality of tradition is the (admittedly not very frequent) mention of written notes of the oral Torah, which, however, would appear to be restricted to private use. Hence the nature of the transmission of rabbinic texts cannot be unequivocally determined.

The fact is that written texts, either of the Mishnah or of a midrash, are never mentioned in the context of the schools. This picture of instruction on an exclusively oral basis agrees well with the constant emphasis on memorization as well as on the Tanna's function as a tutor (cf. p. 12 and p. 139). The Tanna is first mentioned in the generation of Aqiba. According to Neusner (*Phar* 3:171f.), there arose at that time the demand for a reproduction not only of previous teachings but of their precise wording. However, the proof texts Eduy 8.7 and Yad 4.3 are not necessarily an indication of 'exact words supposedly orally formulated by a master (Moses), then orally transmitted, and now set down in writing' (*Phar* 3:169) – as Baumgarten ('Form Criticism', 34f.) has rightly criticized.

If the rabbinic texts, or a part of them, originated as oral tradition and were (at least officially) transmitted orally, this ought to be demonstrable in the text on the basis of stylistic criteria. Old Testament exegesis has long investigated the stylistic devices of oral composition, using especially the results of research into Nordic epic poetry and sagas. The epic poetry of Homer, too, by contrast with living 'oral literature' in the Balkans, has been the subject of detailed research (Lord). More recently, efforts have concentrated on the living oral literatures of Africa. Several characteristics of orally generated and orally transmitted texts have been identified, but they are not suitable to establish with complete certainty that a particular written text had its origin in oral form. On this matter we can only obtain a measure of probability.

Even allowing for these limitations, however, the results of such studies are not directly applicable to rabbinic texts. The laws of oral composition are not universal, but differ according to the sociological context (the position of the literary creator or tradent in relation to his audience) and literary genre. The traditions examined to date are primarily epic or at least narrative in character, and thus perhaps most likely comparable with haggadic traditions. Rabbinic tradition is, however, dominated by legal discussions. What is more, both the midrashic and in large part the halakhic tradition are commentary, and are therefore supported by a base text. In rabbinic Judaism the close interweaving of orality and written culture must always be taken into account.

Certain linguistic and stylistic characteristics can suggest at most the likelihood that a written rabbinic text was orally generated and/or transmitted. Oral *composition* is more difficult to demonstrate, but may be indicated particularly by the use of constantly recurring linguistic and narrative patterns, which only need to be adapted to the particular circumstances. That such texts were intended for oral *transmission* can be seen from their use of mnemonic aids, including not only proper mnemonic catchwords (*simanim*, inserted late), but also certain syntactical patterns, standard phrases and a certain linguistic rhythm as well as generally stereotypical literary forms. It is also worth noting here the formation of series, numerical sayings, etc., as well as the correlation of smaller units by means of shared keywords, thematic connections or even common stylistic properties. These rules are of course more strictly applied in the halakhah, which, despite rigid narrative structures and standard phrases, is essentially concerned with the substance; and this could be noted simply in point form.

Ethnological research shows that every new recitation is at the same time a 're-creation' of the text, which especially in the early stages of transmission can, within certain limits, change considerably. This applies particularly to haggadic texts. It depends on the text's individual genre and its function in the context whether this development leads to a constant embellishment, concretization, addition of new persons, names and details, or rather to a polishing and shortening (thus W. S. Towner with respect to the rabbinic numerical sayings). It is impossible to generalize about whether a shorter form is early or late.

Greater precision is certainly to be expected in the transmission of halakhic traditions. However, this does not mean that we may expect here the *ipsissima verba* of the individual rabbis. It is true that the ideal of Eduy 1.3 applies: *adam ḥayyab lomar bilshon rabbo,* 'One must use the language (manner of expression) of one's teacher.' This sentence, however, appears here as a gloss explaining the occurrence of an unusual unit of measurement in a saying of Hillel. Since ISG introduces the statement (unlike M-statements) not with *tenan* but with *amrinan*, Ephrati at any rate suspects a reader's gloss which does not belong to the text of M. The statement is also secondary in Ber 47a (it is still missing in Rashi's text); only in Bek 5a it would seem to be original, and from there to have been transferred to the other references. This statement, therefore, cannot be used to prove the word-for-word transmission of halakhic sentences in Tannaitic times. Even if such transmission may in many circles have been regarded as the goal, it nevertheless did not represent the general norm or was at any rate not attained (D. Halivni, *Sources*, 1.7ff.). This is evident especially from the language of the Mishnah, which is so strictly regulated and uniform that it is impossible to recognize the distinctive linguistic style of the individual master (cf. e.g. Neusner, *Pur* 21:13, 299). In part this may be because the rabbinic teachers were subjecting their halakhic lecture, or an abstract intended for memorization, to the current linguistic canons (cf. legal idiom today). By and large, however, it will be due to the linguistic levelling effect of redaction.

The assumption of centuries of verbally or even factually accurate tradition by oral transmission is a postulate which cannot be proven. Although it may not be true for every single case, one will have to assume in general that traditions which first appear in late texts must for that reason be late, even if they are attributed to early masters (thus with Neusner, whose thesis J. Heinemann, *Aggadah* 44–47 criticizes). This hypothesis is modified by the fact that written tradition is necessarily selective; but only rarely can proof be offered of the antiquity of a tradition with only late attestation.

Here we must also inquire about the *extent of orally transmitted units*. Reference is often made to generalizations about the fantastic memory of oriental people. Many rabbis certainly knew the Bible by heart, just as many Islamic legal scholars even today have the text of the Koran committed to memory. R. Ḥisda rebukes R. Ḥananel because, contrary to regulation, he writes down biblical books from memory rather than from a written copy (Meg 18b: he was reputedly able to write the entire Bible by heart!). The story is told of R. Meir that he once wrote down a Hebrew scroll of Esther in Asia (t.Meg 2.5, L. 349; GenR 36.8, Theodor/Albeck 343; p.Meg 4.1, 74d: according to this version he proceeds to copy the scroll written from memory, in order that the second scroll might then be liturgically useable). We may also recall the extent of the material which a Tanna had to know from memory: e.g. according to Qid 49b, 'Halakhah, Sifra, Sifre, Tosefta'.

However, the numerous warnings against forgetting the teaching (e.g. Yoma 38b; Men 99b; Abot 3.8) indicate that even in rabbinic times much was in fact forgotten. It is possible to forget even a law as fundamental as the Sabbath (Shab 68a), and we read that in the days of mourning for Moses a vast number of halakhot, arguments, etc. were simply forgotten (Tem 15b–16a). It sounds like consolation in the face of human weakness if R. Yoḥanan says that even Moses studied the Torah and forgot it again, until it was given to him as a gift (Ned 38a). For this reason, too, the extent of orally transmitted complexes should not be exaggerated. In general it will have been relatively small units which were then compiled, perhaps already within the oral tradition, into more extensive groups of texts, without ever exceeding a certain limited length. The frequent differences between parallel textual traditions may indicate that the grouping of individual traditions took place only in written form. (Nevertheless, one must always bear in mind the possibility of an intentional re-arrangement of the written *Vorlage*.) The large, ordered textual units will most often have come about at the stage of written composition.

The *inscripturation* of an initially oral tradition introduces into the history of tradition a break that cannot be overemphasized. M. Dibelius's observation on the gospels applies also to rabbinic texts, viz., that writing signifies 'not an organic development of the process by means of collecting, trimming, and binding together, but the beginning of a new and purely literary development' (*From Tradition to Gospel*, trans. B. L. Woolf (London 1934), 11; cf. Güttgemanns, 91ff.). Textual processing at the written stage differs from that at the oral stage, especially by being more conscious and deliberate. Now glosses are inserted (cf. Neusner, *The Written Tradition*; however, no cogent proof can be based on this) which often disrupt the original structure. Typically visual (reading) errors take the place of aural ones, etc. Nevertheless, in the case of parallel versions it is frequently uncertain whether one text is based on the other in written form, whether an author quotes a written text from memory, or whether he merely relies on the same, even more variable oral tradition. One common redaction critical device to distinguish a copy from an original is an analysis of the respective author's bias. This, however, is problematic for rabbinic texts, since the question of a consistent bias in large blocks of text or entire documents remains largely unexplored.

Still more complicated is the simultaneous occurrence of written and oral tradition of the same material, which was the case for the Mishnah and probably for other texts as well. Private written notes (of what length?) stand side by side with the official oral tradition, which is transmitted by the Tannaim. Lieberman (*Hell.*, 97) in this context speaks of an 'oral publication', in regard to which written notes have no authority. He sees an illustration of the scholastic practice of such oral publication in Erub 54b, where the *rabbanan* teach how the teaching was transmitted (literally: how the 'order of teaching' *seder mishnah*, took place): Moses learns from the mouth of God; then Moses teaches Aaron his passage, and similarly he teaches the sons of Aaron, the elders and the whole people their passage. Then Aaron, his sons and the elders in turn repeat the passage so that all have heard it four times. Thus, if the text about the transmission of traditions through Moses roughly reflects the rabbinic school system (and not just a Babylonian ideal), we would need to assume that the redactor of the Mishnah trained several Tannaim, who then took turns reciting the material until they had memorized it. This system of 'publication', however, does not result in a text which is settled once and for all; the master can still always correct and change the text which the Tanna recites before him (Lieberman, *Hell.*, 93 and Epstein, *ITM*, 676).

If this description is on the whole correct, it will have certain consequences for *textual criticism*: the latter in this case cannot count on a fixed original which an edition ought to reconstruct. The co-existence of oral and written tradition, priority being due to the oral text, implies a certain mobility of the text. Where this co-existence of oral and written tradition applies, it cannot be the task of textual criticism to reconstruct an original text. Instead, it must investigate mistakes which clearly originated in the later scribal and printing tradition, in order thus to attain to the oldest possible form of a text; this should normally be represented by an individual manuscript. The apparatus of variants then is added in the first instance as an attestation of the early history of the text and of its interpretation. One consequence of this method is the practice, now common for editions of rabbinic texts, of using as a base text an individual manuscript (thus e.g. the Tosefta editions of Rengstorf and Lieberman as against the only complete edition, viz., that of Zuckermandel) or the textual form of an early or representative printed edition (thus the Romm-Wilna edition of the BT). However, this should not lead to a reduction of text critical work to a mere selection of the optimal base text and a collection of variants. Of course this editorial practice implies that the interpreter of rabbinic texts must always also work with the critical apparatus, to a much greater extent than in the case of other ancient texts (cf. K. H. Rengstorf, 'Grundsätzliche und methodische Überlegungen zur Bearbeitung von rabbinischen, insbesondere tannaitischen Texten', *Theokratia* 1 (1970) 76–87).

*Why* in any case did the rabbis cultivate *oral tradition*, since they lived in surroundings characterized by a literary culture, and would as a matter of course have learned to write as children? The high cost of writing materials at the time is certainly a factor, but it does not explain the principle of preference for oral tradition, especially that of the halakhah. Oral transmission, after all, was not regarded as a makeshift measure! The reason, rather, is twofold: one, the doctrine of the oral Torah, which according to the rabbinic perspective could be appropriately transmitted only in oral form; and secondly, in the understanding of teaching as *mishnah*, the meaning of which already included the element of continual (oral) 'repetition'. Parallels also occur elsewhere in the history of religion (Parsiism, Buddhism, Islam).

According to Baumgarten ('The Unwritten Law', 29), the emphasis on oral transmission is 'a natural consequence of the canonization of the Torah', i.e. it serves the delimitation of Holy Scripture against all later holy tradition. According to Neusner, however, the anachronistic method of oral tradition was introduced at Yabneh as a means of rabbinic group propaganda, in order to substantiate the claim to be passing on the oral Torah of Moses in the rabbinic teaching; oral tradition would thus have been 'part of the Torah-myth most pertinent to their political needs'. Nevertheless, Neusner himself qualifies this by saying that outside the rabbinic movement such a claim would as yet hardly have been known, much less acknowledged, so that it would have been restricted to the inner circle of the rabbis themselves (*Phar* 3:174f.). A political rationale of the oral method just for internal use is of course easily open to criticism: see Schäfer, 'Dogma', 193–95, who prefers a technical to a dogmatic rationale: 'It is not the mnemonic method which is new at Yabneh, but the comprehensive attempt at a structuring and formulaic mastery of the (received) traditions' (195). In fact the two rationales are not mutually exclusive; and as Neusner has rightly observed, without the 'dogma' of the oral Torah it would hardly be conceivable that the mastery of the traditional material finds expression not primarily in written form but in a text to be recited orally.

It is not possible to determine the date of the transition from purely private written rabbinic texts to the public use of written copies; the answer would be significant for textual criticism, but is not as important in our context. The institution of the Tanna certainly survived even in Geonic times, despite the existence of written texts. Probably it was only the decline of the Babylonian academies and the spread of rabbinic Judaism across North Africa and Spain which meant the final demise of the oral tradition.

It is at any rate important that even early Amoraic scholastic discussion of the Mishnah sometimes already assumes a written text. Thus for instance in discussing the vocalization of individual words: should one read *nas'u* or *nis'u* (Ket 2b), *natnah* or *nitnah* (Ned 35a; cf. Epstein, *ITM*, 703)? Albeck (*Einführung*, 174) finds evidence of different *readings* in the discussion between Rab and Samuel in Erub 53a about whether *me'abberin* or *me'abberin* should be read in Erub 5.1, *'ayin* or *'alef* (no difference in meaning, but a differing derivation of the word). However, this does not necessarily prove a written text, but might instead reflect a pronunciation which no longer distinguishes between *'ayin* and *'alef*. A better indication of a written *Vorlage* is the assumption of a loss of text through *homoioteleuton* in Zeb 11.8 (the text creates great difficulties for the Amoraim in Zeb 97a), as Albeck supposes with reference to the parallel Sifra *Ṣaw* 7.5, W. 32d–33a (*Einführung*, 179f.). Such observations at any rate prove the existence of written texts (of what length?) as background to the rabbinic discussion. The implications of this, however, will then apply *a fortiori* to the other rabbinic texts which were not so centrally regarded as 'oral Torah'.

In conclusion, some remarks on the technical aspects of writing down rabbinic texts. The aforementioned passages speak of scrolls as well as of *pinqasim* with notes on the oral Torah. *Pinqas* = *pinax*, 'tablet', is the wax-covered note pad. M.Kel 24.7 is often taken to mean that it could consist of papyrus. However, one should read not *epiforin*, 'papyrus', but *epifodin* =

*hypopodion*, 'footstool', since a folded *pinqas* could be used in this fashion. Cf. W. Bunte *ad loc.* and esp. M. Haran. A *pinqas* can be composed of several smaller panels, so that it is also suitable for longer writings: thus p.MSh 4.9, 55b speaks of a *pinqas* of 12 leaves; in the parallel LamR 1.14 (B. 52) it is 24 leaves. The *pinqas*, then, can be the equivalent of a codex, although it differs from the latter in its harmonica-like design. Originating in the West, the codex as the predecessor of the book (initally made of wood and later of papyrus or parchment) later came to prevail in the East as well, as can be seen from the late fourth-century Coptic papyrus codices of Nag Hammadi. Rabbinic literature, however, does not mention the codex, which was probably not used for rabbinic texts until relatively late. Just as Roman legal texts were transferred in the late third century from scrolls to codices for greater ease of use, so here the easier access to voluminous texts may have been the primary motive for the change. Perhaps the distinction over against Torah scrolls also played a part, as Lieberman thinks: 'The employment of the note-book was the most suitable way of indicating that they were writing the Oral Law for private, or unofficial use, and not for publication' (*Hell.*, 204f.; according to him it was the same consideration, rather than practical reasons, which also contributed to the Christian preference of the codex). Nevertheless, the scroll also continued to be used (e.g. a Genizah fragment of ARN: see M. Bregman, *Tarbiz* 52 (1982–83) 201ff., who treats this question quite fully in his notes). In keeping with the private character of these notes, they were probably always produced individually rather than in scriptoria in which the text to be copied was dictated to several scribes (for the Bible this was in fact forbidden). As M. Beit-Arié stresses, even in the Middle Ages no information 'about any kind of institutional copying and production of books' can be found (*Codicology* 11). This also explains why copies of rabbinic texts were still an absolute rarity even at the end of the Geonic period.

***Bibliography***

**L. Blau**, *Studien zum althebräischen Buchwesen*. Budapest 1902. **M. Haran**, 'The Codex, the Pinax and the Wooden Slats' (Hebr.). *Tarbiz* 57 (1987–88) 151–63. **M. Haran**, 'More Concerning the Codex and the Pinax' (Hebr.). *Tarbiz* 58 (1988–89) 523–24. **S. Krauss**, *Talmudische Archäologie*, 3.144–58. Leipzig 1912. **S. Lieberman**, *Hell.*, 203–8. **C. H. Roberts & T. C. Skeat**, *The Birth of the Codex*. London 1983.

# V

# HANDLING RABBINIC TEXTS: THE PROBLEM OF METHOD

***Bibliography***

**Bloch, R.** 'Methodological Note for the Study of Rabbinic Literature.' In W. S. Green (ed.), *Approaches*, 1:51–75. **Bokser, B. M.** 'Talmudic Form Criticism.' *JJS* 31 (1980) 46–60. **Goldberg, A.** 'Entwurf einer formanalytischen Methode für die Exegese der rabbinischen Traditionsliteratur.' *FJB* 5 (1977) 1–41. **Goldberg, A.** 'Distributive und kompositive Formen: Vorschläge für die descriptive Terminologie der Formanalyse rabbinischer Texte.' *FJB* 12 (1984) 147–53. [Esp. on Midrash.] **Goldberg, A.** 'Form-Analysis of Midrashic Literature as a Method of Description.' *JJS* 36 (1985) 159–74. **Green, W. S.** 'Reading the Writing of Rabbinism: Toward an Interpretation of Rabbinic Literature.' *JAAR* 51 (1983) 191–206. **Mayer, R.** 'Zum sachgemäßen Verstehen talmudischer Texte.' In O. Betz et al. (eds.), *Abraham unser Vater: Juden und Christen im Gespräch über die Bibel: Festschrift für Otto Michel zum 60. Geburtstag*, 346–55. Leiden 1963. **Müller, K.** 'Zur Datierung rabbinischer Aussagen.' In H. Merklein (ed.), *Neues Testament und Ethik: Für Rudolf Schnackenburg*, 551–87. Freiburg 1989. **Neusner, J.** 'Types and Forms in Ancient Jewish Literature: Some Comparisons.' *HR* 11 (1972) 354–90. [More fully *Phar* 3:5–100.] **Neusner, J.** 'The Use of the Mishnah for the History of Judaism Prior to the Time of the Mishnah: A Methodological Note.' *JSJ* 11 (1980) 177–85. **Saldarini, A. J.** '"Form Criticism" of Rabbinic Literature.' *JBL* 96 (1977) 257–74. **Schäfer, P.** 'Research into Rabbinic Literature: An Attempt to Define the Status Quaestionis.' *JJS* 37 (1986) 139–52. [Cf. C. Milikowsky, *JJS* 39 (1988) 201–11; and Schäfer's reply in *JJS* 40 (1989) 89–94.] **Smith, M.** 'On the Problem of Method in the Study of Rabbinic Literature.' *JBL* 92 (1973) 112f. **Towner, W. S.** 'Form Criticism of Rabbinic Literature.' *JJS* 24 (1973) 101–18.

The problem of the oral transmission of rabbinic texts leads naturally to the methodological problems of textual criticism and text critical editions of rabbinic literature. Here we are dealing with general questions of method, many of which have only been clearly recognized in the last few years. So far, advances especially in the methods of biblical exegesis have been applied to the treatment of rabbinic texts only in very small measure. It is particularly the widespread theory that the rabbinic tradition was handed down orally through the centuries with absolute faithfulness which has led to an utterly uncritical use of rabbinic material. This is true both for the historian who often accepts the rabbinic texts without examination as factual reports, merely eliminating, for example, numerical exaggerations and obviously legendary traits; and for the scholar dealing in rabbinic theology, who often does not pay (sufficient) attention to the different periods of origin of the various writings, nor to the specific intention of a literary genre, and thus arrives at a rather undifferentiated image of 'the' rabbinic theology. Because of its simplicity and homogeneity, this image is readily adopted in the comparative history of religion and especially in New Testament exegesis (see K. Müller, *Das Judentum in der religionsgeschichtlichen Arbeit am Neuen Testament*

(Frankfurt 1983), 69ff.). Symptomatic of this situation is not just the use of (H. L. Strack &) P. Billerbeck's *Kommentar zum Neuen Testament aus Talmud und Midrasch* as a quarry of useful quotations. Despite its deliberately historical orientation, even E. E. Urbach's book *The Sages: Their Concepts and Their Beliefs* (Cambridge, MA 1987), in many respects an eminent standard work on rabbinic theology, does not escape the danger of an almost entirely unhistorical description.

The methodology developed for biblical studies cannot of course be adopted for rabbinic texts without scrutiny. Nevertheless, it offers important insights, as indeed it has been the source of all the relevant stimuli that have galvanized the study of rabbinic texts in recent decades. Until now, there have only been scattered attempts at a methodology specifically suited for rabbinic texts. Here of course we can only offer a few brief pointers.

***1) Literary History***

A basic requirement is that rabbinic texts should be integrated into a literary history which will then be consistently adhered to. A literary *history, however,* is highly problematic for rabbinic texts. *How does one date rabbinic writings*? One must always remember the hypothethical nature of such dates, since too many of the relevant criteria are subjective. In the first place, one can only speak of the final version of a work; layers of individual traditions may of course be much older than the document as a whole, although this needs to be established in each case. Already the Geonic introductions – e.g. ISG – attempt to answer this question, as do nineteenth-century introductions like those by Z. Frankel or L. Zunz. The question is usually answered by identifying the final redactor of a given document: accordingly, Rabbi is the redactor of the Mishnah, R. Ḥiyya of the Tosefta; the PT is attributed to Yoḥanan, BT to Rab Ashi and Rabina, and so on. This introduces a notion of authorship which, with very few exceptions, is not adequate for rabbinic literature: rabbinic writings tend to be composite works, incorporating earlier texts which are normally edited before being re-used. There is a widespread assumption that rabbinic texts are mere compilations with no intrinsic bias; but this must be demonstrated in each case.

Many, including Zunz, have attempted to date texts on the basis not just of internal criteria, but also of external attestation: when is a text first cited? This would suggest a *terminus ante quem*. But how does one recognize a quotation as such? In Geonic times the names of rabbinic writings vary considerably, and even in the Middle Ages they are not standardized. Moreover the same name can designate different writings. The quotation itself may also come from a similar writing or from the common teaching of the rabbinic schools. Then too it is not always possible to determine the relative priority. The problematic nature of the criterion of citation can be seen, for example, in the assessment of the halakhic midrashim: if PT and BT do not cite them (as e.g. Ch. Albeck thinks), this does not of itself mean that they are unknown to the Talmuds and therefore later. More objective is the identification of a *terminus post quem* according to the latest rabbis named in a document (but one needs to be aware of problems of identification in specific cases, of pseudonymity, later additions, etc.), or even according to historical events which are mentioned or presupposed (but here too it is often a matter of interpretation: e.g. not every reference to Ishmael or the Arabs necessarily points to the Islamic period).

On the linguistic front, it is true that there have been significant advances in the recognition of distinct developmental stages of Hebrew. But the ritualized and formalized language of the rabbis often makes precise statements impossible. What is more, the textual tradition often smoothed out the linguistic peculiarities of a particular period or region. Inasmuch as rabbinic texts are a literature of citation, one must of course expect different linguistic layers within one and the same document. Finally, the possibility of a deliberately archaic style must also be considered (the Zohar being the classic example; but e.g. B. Z. Wacholder also claims this for Mek).

In spite of these difficulties, at least a preliminary chronological outline of rabbinic literary history can be achieved. However, this would also have to find appropriate recognition in the interpretation of rabbinic texts. Unfortunately it is still not considered self-evident that the Mishnah or the Tosefta, for example, must be interpreted on their own and not by means of the Talmuds; the Talmuds already belong to the history of interpretation and are no more and no less useful in determining the original meaning of the Mishnah than patristic texts are for the interpretation of the New Testament. Similarly self-evident, but not always observed, is the fact that Tannaitic texts must take absolute precedence over later texts in the reconstruction of historical facts or ideas of the Tannaitic period, even where a later source cites a statement in the name of a Tanna or as a *baraita*. The same reservation applies to the utilization of Geonic statements for the Amoraic period or of Babylonian sources for conditions in Palestine.

The dating of individual texts or of particular ideas is normally accomplished on the basis of rabbinic names (see pp. 57ff. below). Above all, however, one should attempt to categorize such texts or ideas in relation to a comprehensive history of tradition, especially also by adducing references from non-rabbinic literature, which can often be dated with greater certainty. Parallels in the pseudepigrapha, at Qumran, in the New Testament, in the

Church Fathers or in Arabic literature can be just as important as non-literary attestations (like the frescoes of the synagogue at Dura Europos, which are the earliest datable evidence for a good many haggadic traditions). Here too, however, caution is required: one cannot automatically assume the continuity of an idea between two chronologically distant literary references (e.g. the parallels between PesR 131b–132a and 4 Ezra 9.38–10.57), or even assert a direct literary connection.

### *2) Cultural and Religious History*

The traditional interpretation of rabbinic texts almost exclusively regards them as literature. Contemporary history and empirical study are largely ignored; and the texts thereby become peculiarly timeless. But the study of Palestine in particular, and to a much smaller extent also that of Babylonia in the rabbinic period, has been greatly advanced in recent decades; and archaeological discoveries in Palestine have contributed to a better understanding of the texts. The interpretation of texts must consider questions of the history of settlement, population structure and economic conditions as well as the excavation of synagogues, Christian churches and pagan cultic sites and objects. These findings shed light on such matters as the laws of the tractate Abodah Zarah. On the other hand, the synagogal discoveries must be confronted with the rabbinic statements about the permissibility of artistic images. As a result, the picture which rabbinic literature gives us of the contemporary conditions proves to be completely biased: instead of a monolithic rabbinic Judaism there comes to light a much more complex social reality of Judaism in the rabbinic period (see e.g. E. M. Meyers & J. F. Strange, *Archaeology, the Rabbis, and Early Christianity*, Nashville 1981).

Beginning with this insight, we must also inquire about possible traces of an after effect in rabbinic literature of the pseudepigraphical writings, of Qumran, Philo and Josephus. These internal Jewish connections still remain largely unaccounted for.

As far as the general history of culture is concerned, research has primarily dealt with the relations between rabbinic Judaism and Hellenistic culture. During the nineteenth century this was confined in the first instance to the demonstration of individual Greek-Hellenistic motifs in rabbinic texts. S. Krauss then collected the 'Greek and Latin Loan Words in the Talmud and Midrash' – a pioneering study which is now badly in need of revision; a great deal of preliminary work for this has been done by S. Lieberman and D. Sperber. In a number of books, A. A. Hallewy has investigated Hellenistic influence on the haggadah, while H. A. Fischel has researched the influence on the rabbis of Hellenistic popular philosophy and of certain literary conventions. Less fruitful to date has been the treatment of the relationship of Babylonian Judaism with Parthian-Persian culture and religion.

The connections between rabbis and Church Fathers and the mutual influence of rabbinic Judaism and Islam have frequently been examined (on the former see J. R. Baskin, 'Rabbinic-Patristic Exegetical Contacts in Late Antiquity: A Bibliographical Reappraisal', in W. S. Green (ed.), *Approaches*, 5:53–80). However, in many cases the question of dependences and borrowings has yet to receive methodologically flawless treatment: citations of rabbinic opinions in the Church Fathers have often been assumed in cases that actually represent parallel developments from the same presuppositions. Here, too, one must always examine who is citing whom, or indeed whether a citation is present at all. Moreover, the many-layered nature of Palestinian Judaism in the rabbinic period has not been sufficiently considered, and the possibility of Christian traces on the rabbinic side has been either rejected *a priori* or too easily assumed.

### *3) Form, Tradition and Redaction History*

The methods designated by these names have dominated Biblical scholarship for decades. The term *Formgeschichte* first appears in M. Dibelius, *Die Formgeschichte des Evangeliums*, Tübingen 1919 (E.T. *From Tradition to Gospel*, trans. B. L. Woolf, London 1934). The method itself is about twenty years older: H. Gunkel, harking back to initiatives in Lessing and Herder, introduced it into Old Testament studies as *Gattungsgeschichte* (genre criticism). The method is based on the recognition of clearly defined literary forms in the literature both of the present and especially of antiquity. The primary interest lies in small units of tradition of possibly oral origin, which only grew together during an extended history of tradition, being joined into a larger literary work by means of a secondary 'framework'. Today the term 'genre' (*Gattung*) is often preferred instead of 'form', which really means only the linguistic appearance of a concrete text, but which has gained almost universal acceptance, particularly in rabbinic scholarship. One should distinguish between form or genre criticism, which identifies the individual literary forms with their governing principles and conditions of origin (the *Sitz im Leben*), and form history proper, which is concerned with the origin and transformation of forms in the course of history (cf. K. Koch, *The Growth of the Biblical Tradition: The Form-Critical Method*, trans. S. M. Cupitt, London 1969).

In rabbinic scholarship there have long been individual attempts to apply the form historical method. Examples include P. Fiebig in a series of (methodologically less than satisfactory) studies beginning in 1904, and F. Maass, who in 1937 attempted a form history of the Mishnah using the example of the tractate *Abot* (which is particularly suited to such studies, although untypical of the Mishnah). For form *history* proper, Maass relied entirely on the attributions of sayings to the individual rabbis, which of course is very problematic; but otherwise his study is very well executed. A systematic application of this method, however, has only been achieved since about 1970, for halakhic texts especially by J. Neusner and his students, for midrashic material especially by A. Goldberg and his students, and for liturgical texts by J. Heinemann. We are still a long way from a comprehensive rabbinic form history – thus far, only a few genres been studied in a larger body of texts. All the same, it is already possible to compile a rough, preliminary framework of the most important rabbinic forms – though this is barely more than a list, and should be seen as a programme of study rather than a result of research. In this connection, one discovers here a considerable discontinuity with the forms of the Bible and of intertestamental literature.

Some would demand a classification of forms regardless of the content of a text (cf. Neusner, *Pur* 3:192ff). In actual fact, however, the substance determines the form. If form criticism is not to become mere style criticism (the latter is necessary, but should not be pursued in the name of form criticism), one cannot exclude substantive criteria from the identification of forms.

Using the example of the rabbinic traditions about the Pharisees, J. Neusner has compiled a catalogue of forms (*Types*, 354–58), which with extensions and modifications has served for the following framework. The fundamental distinction is between halakhic, haggadic, and exegetical material; the latter shares in both halakhah and haggadah.

**Halakhah**

1. *Sayings*

In this area, scholarship has yet to progress beyond the most basic syntactical forms.

a) *Simple statement:* 'X says' + direct speech.

b) *Controversy*: this can be a simple juxtaposition of two statements with their respective author, either as a dispute (*X omer. . .*; *Y omer. . .*) or a debate (*X amar lahem/lo. . .*; *Y amar lahem/lo*: i.e. with a historical context, even if limited to a minimum; statement and audience appear in the perfect tense). In the lemma form, the description of the problem precedes the contrary decisions (problem – 'X says' – 'Y says'). In the chiastic form, a halakhic decision is followed by the author's name (decision – 'thus says X; but Y says: [another halakhic decision]').

c) *Attestation* ('X *he'îd*, testifies that...' (or 'regarding'): esp. in the tractate 'Eduyot).

d) *Forms* (*prosbul*, divorce, ordination, etc.).

e) *Letter* (X dictates a letter, which is then reproduced). Leaving aside the content itself, only a few examples reveal a distinct letter form; these cases then follow well-known Aramaic letters such as those from Wadi Murabba'at.

f) Chains and Lists.

2. *Narrative*

a) *Taqqanah*: 'It used to be thus; but X *tiqqen*, ordained that. . . .'

b) *Precedent*, usually simple statements with little dialogue, often introduced by *ma'aseh*, 'actual case'.

c) *Sayings and narratives in the first person.*

d) *Narratives introduced by a biblical text and its exegesis.*

3. *The Talmudic Sugya*

This self-contained logical unit of rabbinic discussion is a composite form comprising not only different literary forms, but also haggadic alongside halakhic material. See further p. 203 below.

***Bibliography***

**Goldberg, A.** 'Form und Funktion des Ma'ase in der Mischna.' *FJB* 2 (1974) 1–38. **Gulak, A.** *Das Urkundenwesen im Talmud: Im Licht der griechisch-ägyptischen Papyri und des griechischen und römischen Rechts.* Jerusalem 1935. **Jaffee, M. S.** 'The Taqqana in Tannaitic Literature: Jurisprudence and the Construction of Rabbinic Memory.' *JJS* 41 (1990) 204–25. **Maass, F.** *Formgeschichte der Mischna mit besonderer Berücksichtigung des Traktats Abot.* Berlin 1937. **Neusner, J.** 'Form and Meaning in Mishnah.' *JAAR* 45 (1977) 27–54. **Neusner, J.** 'Form-Analysis and Source Criticism: The Case of Mishnah Kelim 1:1–4.' In R. H. Fisher (ed.), *A Tribute to A. Vööbus*, 133–52. Chicago 1977. **Pardee, D.** *Handbook of Ancient Hebrew Letters: With a Chapter on Tannaitic Letter Fragments by S. D. Sperling.* Chico 1982. **Segal, E. L.** 'The Terminology of Case-Citation in the Babylonian Talmud: A Study in the Limitation of Form Criticism.' *JSJ* 9 (1978) 205–11.

## Haggadah

The primary distinction between poetry and prose is largely incidental in rabbinic literature, since *poetic forms* occur only occasionally. Of major significance is only the genre of lament for the dead (see E. Feldman, 'The Rabbinic Lament', *JQR* N.S. 63 (1972–73) 51–75).

1. *Narrative*: The most important forms here are the *historical anecdote*, the short *biographical note* without direct speech, the *biographical*

*narrative* (with the sub-genres of call narrative, school narrative, death narrative, etc.), the *miracle narrative*, the *narrative with a moral*, the *narrative in the first person*, as well as those in which a *bat qol* intervenes, *fairy tale*, *fable* and *legend*.

2. *Description* of 'scientific' content (geographical, ethnological, medical, astronomical, etc.).

3. *Speech: sayings in the first person, without narrative context*, *apophthegms* with narrative context, *declamations of woe*, *parables* (various sub-genres, e.g. parables about a king), *proverbs*, *wisdom sayings*, *numerical sayings*, *chain sayings* (*Sorites*), *series* and *lists*, *prayer* and *sermon*.

***Bibliography***

**Avery-Peck, A. J.** 'Classifying Early Rabbinic Pronouncement Stories.' *SBLSP* 22 (1983) 223–44. **Avery-Peck, A. J.** 'Rhetorical Analysis of Early Rabbinic Pronouncement Stories.' *Hebrew Annual Review* 13 (1991) 1–23. **Ben-Amos. D.** *Narrative Forms in the Haggadah: Structural Analysis.* Diss. Indiana University 1966. **Ben-Amos, D.** 'A Structural and Formal Study of Talmudic-Midrashic Legends' (Hebr.). In *4th WCJS* (Jerusalem 1968) 2:357–59. **Dschulnigg, P.** *Rabbinische Gleichnisse und das Neue Testament.* Berne 1988. **Fraenkel, J.** 'The Structures of Talmudic Legends' (Hebr.). In *Studies in Aggadah and Jewish Folklore*, Hebr. section, 45–97. Folklore Research Center Studies 7. Jerusalem 1983. **Goldberg, A.** 'Das schriftauslegende Gleichnis im Midrasch.' *FJB* 9 (1982) 1–87. **Heinemann, J.** *Prayer in the Talmud: Forms and Patterns.* Berlin/New York 1977. **Johnston, R. M.** *Parabolic Interpretations Attributed to Tannaim.* Diss. Hartford, CT: Hartford Seminary Foundation, 1977. **Porton, G. G.** 'The Pronouncement Story in Tannaitic Literature: A Review of Bultmann's Theory.' *Semeia* 20 (1981) 81–99. **Saldarini, A. J.** 'Last Words and Deathbed Scenes in Rabbinic Literature.' *JQR* N.S. 68 (1977–78) 27–45. **Sharvit, S.** 'The Introductory Formulae of Proverbs in Talmudic Literature' (Hebr.). *Hebrew Linguistics* 28–30 (1990) 197–206. **Singer, A. M.** *Animals in Rabbinic Teaching: The Fable.* Diss. New York: Jewish Theological Seminary, 1979. **Stern, D.** *Parables in Midrash: Narrative and Exegesis in Rabbinic Literature.* Cambridge, MA 1991. **Thoma, C.** 'Prolegomena zu einer Übersetzung und Kommentierung der rabbinischen Gleichnisse.' *Theologische Zeitschrift* 28 (1982) 514–31. **Thoma, C. & Lauer, S.**, (eds.), *Die Gleichnisse der Rabbinen.* Vol. 1: *Pesiqtà de Rav Kahana*; vol. 2: *Bereschit Rabba 1–63.* Berne 1986–91. **Thorion-Vardi, T.** *Das Kontrastgleichnis in der rabbinischen Literatur.* Frankfurt 1986. **Towner, W. S.** *Enumeration.* Ziegler, I. *Die Königsgleichnisse des Midrasch beleuchtet durch die römische Kaiserzeit.* Breslau 1903.

## Exegesis

Here one must again distinguish between halakhah and haggadah. In both groups one finds mere *references* to Scripture, uses of biblical texts as *proofs*, as well as the proper *interpretation of texts*; the intensity of the latter can range from a mere *gloss* via simple *exegesis of words* to a full *midrash*, which in turn can be either a purely text-based expositional midrash or a homiletical midrash (see further pp. 237ff. below).

*Homilies* are a composite form in which introduction and conclusion in particular follow definite laws of form (*proem* and *peroratio*; but also *petiḥah* as a complete short sermon); the main body itself may again contain different genres (parable, *ma'aseh*, etc.). See further pp. 243ff. below.

Beyond this descriptive genre criticism, our work must proceed to *Gattungsgeschichte* (history of genre). However, even this exists only in rudimentary attempts, and is in fact only feasible in very limited ways. Neusner, for example, speaks in regard to the Mishnah deliberately only of form analysis, not of form *history*, since this work attained its formal appearance within a relatively short period of time ('the naive conception that we may "date" a unit by the formal traits exhibited therein. This has not been proved, and I think it cannot be proved' *JQR* N.S. 70 (1979–80) 142 n.16; but cf. also the reservation of R. S. Sarason, ibid. 150f.).

What results can form critical work on rabbinic texts produce? Clearly a mere classification of the material is not enough and must not remain an end in itself. Two results above all should be mentioned: first, the delimitation of the given form and of the creativity of its user permits one to decide what is important for a given text. This leads to a more appropriate interpretation, and prevents an overemphasis on traits which belong to the formal pattern and which therefore may not immediately be interpreted as a historical reminiscence, for instance in the case of narratives. Secondly, knowledge of rabbinic forms frequently enables one to separate the base text from later accretions. Nevertheless, the expected form *historical* information about the chronological context of a given genre can be attained only rarely and in rough outline. Occasional judgements about the age of a given tradition can be achieved only in conjunction with other criteria.

*Tradition history* is on the one hand a *topical history* (*Motivgeschichte*), establishing the continuity and change of certain themes during the rabbinic period. On the other hand, it can be studied above all in relation to the numerous rabbinic parallel traditions (the same unit of tradition in different settings): the *synoptic reading* of these parallel texts is a basic task of rabbinic research, even if suitable aids for this are still largely unavailable. We still do not even have a synopsis of Mishnah and Tosefta, let alone a synopsis of the entire rabbinic text material, which M. Smith among others has called for (though the volume of material probably makes this impractical). Parallel texts in particular indicate which textual units were only composed in the course of transmission, whether this transmission should be thought of as primarily written or oral, which interests have shaped it, etc. J. Neusner's polemical injunction against 'synoptic studies' in rabbinic research (e.g. 'Studying Synoptic Texts Synoptically: The Case of Leviticus Rabbah' *PAAJR* 53 (1986) 111–45) is intended to affirm the literary independence of the individual rabbinic writings and to oppose the use of texts without respect for their context and function within the context. In other words, he stresses concerns of redaction history, but without addressing synoptic studies in the sense here advocated.

*Redaction history* deals with the personality of the final redactor of a work, his scribal or theological distinctiveness as displayed in the way he selects and collates traditional material, inserts it into a certain framework, handles it and thus interprets it (cf. J. Rohde, *Die redaktionsgeschichtliche Methode*, Hamburg 1966).

Redaction history thus endeavours to see the redactor as an author and not merely as the collector of traditions. However, in rabbinic literature this turns out to be much more difficult than, say, in the gospels. This is because only a few late rabbinic writings such as SER go back to real authorial personalities whose intentions can be isolated from the tradition without major difficulties. Thus it is precisely a work on SER which has realized the intentions of redaction history for a rabbinic text (viz., M. Kadushin, *The Theology of Seder Eliahu: A Study in Organic Thinking*, New York 1932: thus the view of P. Kuhn, *Gottes Trauer und Klage in der rabbinischen Überlieferung*, Leiden 1978, 25). It is also worth mentioning various studies by Jacob Neusner, who particularly highlights redactional intentions (e.g. in Sifra vis-à–vis M).

Rabbinic literature is not just traditional literature, but for the most part *citation literature* (A. Goldberg). The citation form applies already to the earliest stages of this literature and its most primitive units. In contrast with pseudepigraphical literature, for example, the rabbis attached great importance to naming the author of each quoted saying (on the problem of these attributions see the next chapter). This, however, reflects not an increased self-confidence of a saying's respective author, but rather the tradent's knowledge that he is bound to a given tradition. At the same time, the named quotation is determined by the view that a statement is worth only as much as its author. In Amoraic times this engenders an endeavour to trace the authors of anonymous statements from the Tannaitic period, in order thereby to establish these statements as the opinion of an individual: anonymous sayings carry higher authority (whether as an old undisputed opinion or as the opinion of the final redactor of a document). The ordering principle in the collection of quotations is therefore not the name of the originator (even if individual cases of such small collections existed): at issue is not the author but the subject matter. Incidentally, it is characteristic of rabbinic thought that while Yoḥanan ben Zakkai as the supposed progenitor of rabbinic tradition is often cited, he himself never cites his authorities. And in the final phase of Talmudic tradition, be it in the late strata of the BT or in late midrashim, the material again becomes equally anonymous; already the Saboraim and even more the later rabbis feel that their names can no longer be mentioned as equivalent to those of the earlier rabbis, that the quality of their own contribution to the rabbinic work of tradition is fundamentally different from that of their predecessors.

At the stage of the final redaction of a rabbinic text, the personality of the redactor can primarily be perceived in the selection, order and treatment of the citations. A merely additive redaction is hardly ever to be assumed. By and large, even the exegetical midrash proper does not merely collate a catena citations according to the order of the biblical text. Usually, the redactor assembles the citations to correspond to his own objective, and argues with them as though they were his own words. Furthermore it should be remembered that frequently the existing citations are already reworked, 'traditional forms' which in abbreviation enable a much wider range of material to be transmitted (Goldberg, *Entwurf*, 7). They are already encountered as such by the redactor, who uses them for his own purpose: the respective change of purpose of a citation must be ascertained by means of a diachronic analysis of function (Goldberg, *Entwurf*, 20). The redactor's intention can be discerned from this, as well as from the anonymous text material, where this must be ascribed to the redactor.

Particularly in the case of extensive texts, one should also first clarify in how far a uniform redaction may be assumed at all, and to which units of text such a redaction may be applied. This is also true especially for the two Talmuds. But even in the case of more limited text complexes one has yet to explain to what extent there is a uniform arrangement or merely the combination of larger blocks of previously edited material. Not even for the Mishnah can the intention of the final redactor be taken for granted (if indeed strictly speaking we may assume such a redactor): even the fundamental question of whether the Mishnah was intended as a teaching manual, a collection of material or an authoritative lawbook remains unresolved. One would have to approach a resolution of this question by applying redaction critical methods; in the same way, basic problems of the redaction of the Tosefta and other writings could be answered. Another unsolved question is that of the political intentions of the redactors (e.g. in relation to a possible pro-Hillelite redaction of the entire Mishnah). Here there are major tasks for the redaction history of rabbinic texts, even if one must remain aware of the difficulty of separating tradition and redaction particularly for this material. A comprehensive, comparative treatment of Mishnah and Tosefta could provide the necessary tools for this task.

# VI

# THE RABBIS

***Bibliography***

**Beer, M.** *The Babylonian Amoraim: Aspects of Economic Life* (Hebr.). 2nd edn. Ramat Gan 1982. **Cohen, S. J. D.** 'Epigraphical Rabbis.' *JQR* N.S. 72 (1981–82) 1–17. **Fraenkel, J.** 'Paronomasia in Aggadic Narratives.' *SH* 27 (1978) 27–51. [The influence of word-plays on the shaping of narratives about the Rabbis.] **Gafni, I.** 'On the Talmudic Chronology in Iggeret Rav Sherira Gaon' (Hebr.). *Zion* 52 (1987) 1–24. [= idem, *Babylonia*, 239–65.] **Green, W. S.** 'What's in a Name? – The Problematic of Rabbinic "Biography".' In idem, *Approaches*, 1:77–96. **Green, W. S.** 'Context and Meaning in Rabbinic "Biography".' In idem, *Approaches*, 2:97–111. **Levine, L. I.** *The Rabbinic Class of Roman Palestine in Late Antiquity.* Jerusalem 1989. **Neusner, J.** 'The Present State of Rabbinic Biography.' In G. Nahon & C. Touati (eds.), *Hommage à Georges Vajda: Études d'histoire et de pensée juives*, 85–91. Leuven 1980. **Safrai, S.** 'Tales of the Sages in the Palestinian Tradition and the Babylonian Talmud.' *SH* 22 (1971) 209–32. **Sperber, D.** 'Studies in Talmudic Chronology – I' (Hebr.). In *Michtam le-David: Rabbi David Ochs Memorial Volume (1905–1975)*, 77–85. Ramat-Gan 1978. **Urbach, E. E.** *The Sages: Their Concepts and Beliefs*, 564–678. Cambridge, MA 1987.

## *1) Our Sources*

Our information about the individual rabbis stems from rabbinic literature and the Geonic texts, above all STA and ISG. These also provide a number of absolute dates according to Seleucid chronology, especially the years in which various rabbis died (e.g. R. Yoḥanan bar Nappaḥa). But it should be noted that these figures often do not agree between the Spanish and the French recensions of ISG. Moreover, these references, often directly cited in modern works, can only rarely be verified and are thus only of relative value. The systematic investigation of these figures was pioneered by D. Sperber (on the death dates of 38 Babylonian Amoraim) and I. Gafni, who found the chronological frame of ISG to be generally reliable. More accurate analyses, however, remain to be implemented – if indeed they are possible, given the nature of the sources.

The rabbinic texts themselves never transmit dates. It is only rarely possible to correlate rabbinic references about events in the life of a particular rabbi with dates known from secular history (exceptions include the destruction of Jerusalem, the Bar Kokhba revolt, the revolt under Gallus); even then they are only of limited use. The fact of Aqiba's execution during or just after the Bar Kokhba revolt is well attested in rabbinic sources, albeit embellished by legends. But the texts offer no more precise date. Even for this reason alone the statement that Rabbi was born in the year of Aqiba's death is chronologically useless; to deduce from it the year 135 as the year of

Rabbi's birth is quite inappropriate. What is more, the sentence 'X was born when Y died' is a theologoumenon, as is clear from Qid 72b:

> Mar said: when R. Aqiba died, Rabbi was born; when Rabbi died, Rab Yehudah was born; when Rab Yehudah died, Raba was born; when Raba died, Ashi was born. This teaches you: no righteous man goes out of the world before a righteous man like him has been created. For it says, ' The sun rises and the sun sets' [Eccl 1.5]. Before Eli's sun set, Samuel's sun rose at Ramah.

(Yoma 38b contains this principle with the example of Eli and Samuel in the name of Ḥiyya b. Abba, who cites Yoḥanan).

The *chronology of the Rabbis*, therefore, like that of the rabbinic literature, is relative – i.e. to be determined by a rabbi's relationship to another as his teacher, conversation partner, student, or tradent (always assuming that the nomenclature is clear and the name is correctly preserved). In this way *generations* of rabbis can be co-ordinated. This relational grid has led to the classic division of the rabbinic period into five generations of Tannaim and seven of Amoraim. Instead of absolute biographical dates, one therefore classifies a rabbi as a Tannaite of the second generation (T2) or an Amora of the fifth (A5; a prefixed 'P' or 'B' indicates Palestinian or Babylonian origin). This also provides an approximate reference to absolute chronology. A question mark remains for rarely mentioned rabbis. Occasionally it is unclear if in fact two rabbis of the same name are in view, since otherwise the passages in question remain irreconcilable (e.g. for Mar Uqba). Errors of later tradents or copiers are also to be expected; indeed even the outright invention of rabbis' names (as in the Zohar) cannot be entirely excluded (assumed e.g. by B. Z. Wacholder, *HUCA* 39 (1968) 132–34 for Mek).

### *2) Rabbis' Names as an Aid for Dating*

The date of a rabbinic writing applies to the complete work. While the individual parts and traditions may be much older, this must first be demonstrated. The names of rabbis mentioned in such passages are often used as points of reference for dating purposes. Yet as active participants in the narrative, rabbis can of course only provide the *terminus a quo*; where they are identified as the originator or tradent of a saying, this could serve to date the statement or at least its substance, if the tradition is reliable. The study of extensive text units (e.g. by J. Neusner) has shown that at least in Tannaitic collections these attributions are largely reliable. Even if the accuracy of the tradent's name cannot be positively proven, the historical period connected with that name generally can. It is often possible to verify this where a rabbi of the subsequent generation(s) provides a quotation, comment or gloss of an idea, or obviously takes it for granted. (This method of *attestation* is associated with J. Neusner, *Phar* 3:180ff.; cf. idem, 'The History of Earlier Rabbinic Judaism, *HR* 16 (1977) 216–36. D. Kraemer would allow even for the possibility of verifying named attributions in BT: 'On the Reliability of Attributions in the Babylonian Talmud', *HUCA* 60 (1989) 175–90.). Others, however, are much more sceptical in this regard and baldly assert that 'attributions are simply not historically reliable data' (W. S. Towner, *Enumeration*, 34; cf. W. S. Green, 'Name', 83f.; D. Halivni, 'Doubtful Attributions in the Talmud' *PAAJR* 46f. (1979–80) Hebr. section, 67–83); S. Stern, 'Attribution and Authorship in the Babylonian Talmud', *JJS* 45 (1994) 28–51. Dating according to rabbis' names certainly involves numerous problems. Apart from the problem of pseudepigraphy (this is the more acute the later a narrative or dictum first appears: very different reasons may account for putting certain words into a rabbi's mouth after the event), such factors of uncertainty are to be seen most of all in the *transmission of names*:

a) Often the rabbinic text itself already indicates that the precise name of the tradent is uncertain (esp. his patronym or designation of origin: the BT presents the variant with the formula *we-amri le*) or that the same statement is attributed to various rabbis (*we-itay-ma'*): cf. Bacher, *TT*, 524–40.

b) Often *several rabbis have the same name*, especially where the father's name is omitted. Whether Yehudah is Yehudah b. Ilai (T3) or Yehudah bar Yeḥezqel (BA3) can usually be settled by means of the context; but is the context original, or was the text incorrectly composed because the redactors already misidentified the speaker? If no real discussion is offered, but opinions are merely set in contrast (see below, e)), the context does not help either. A decision is also impossible if no other rabbi is named in the context and no rabbinic parallel provides clarification. Circular reasoning is often unavoidable, but must nevertheless be acknowledged as such. Thus the halakhic midrashim are usually dated to the Tannaitic period *inter alia* because they cite (almost) only Tannaites. Based on this date, one then opts in doubtful cases for the identification of a rabbi with a Tannaite.

c) The *textual transmission* in manuscripts and printed editions is particularly unstable in the case of names, as the critical apparatus of textual editions clearly shows. Thus Nathan and Jonathan are constantly confused, as are Jonathan and Yoḥanan. Similarly, Eleazar and Eliezer are interchanged, Aḥa and Aḥai, Yoshiyyah and Hoshayah. The frequent use of abbreviations can lead to different readings: thus Simeon is confused with Ishmael; R. Yoḥanan or R. Yoshiyyah (both *R"Y*) with Rabbi (Yehudah ha-Nasi), who may also intrude into the text where, after 'Rabbi' written out in full, the scribe forgot to add the name. Simeon ben Shetaḥ becomes Simeon ben Azzai (where the *shin* of the abbreviated patronym was misread as *'ayin*).

d) Where *rabbinic parallel traditions* attribute the same dictum or the same incident to different rabbis and this cannot be explained through errors of transmission (as described under c)), there is of course the possibility that two or more rabbis did indeed say or experience the same thing. However, often one must expect migrating logia or narratives, as is clear also from parallels in non-rabbinic literature. There are erroneous attributions as well as pseudepigraphical quotations of famous (especially Tannaitic) masters or, for example, the attribution of later discussions to the 'houses of Hillel and Shammai'.

e) Where a text has two *rabbis of different periods* discussing with each other, this is not necessarily to be blamed on the redactor as an anachronism (nor the text consequently to be dated late). Fictitious discussions do exist, but equally and above all one finds simply topical arrangements of various rabbis' sayings, with no implied claim that a historical dialogue occurred.

f) *The dating of anonymous sayings* raises additional problems. Occasionally the context allows such cases to be identified as the presupposition or else the concluding decision of a datable discussion; parallels can sometimes help to identify the speaker (especially where the rabbinic texts themselves already indicate the intentional suppression of certain names, like that of Meir in the school of Rabbi: cf. A. Goldberg, *Tarbiz* 38 (1968–69) 231–54). Still other sayings can be linked to datable ideas, be it by the reliable attribution of similar ideas to a certain rabbi or by means of non-rabbinic sources. Nevertheless, a relatively large proportion remains undatable. An anonymous statement is not automatically old, not in the Mishnah and much less in the Talmud (the anonymous share increases over time). See J. Neusner, *From Mishnah to Scripture: The Problem of the Unattributed Saying*, Chico 1984.

g) It must be stressed that we can probably expect to be dealing with the *ipsissima verba* of certain rabbis only in exceptional cases (cf. Neusner, *Development*, 5f.). Rabbinic tradition is concerned not with the precise wording of a teaching but with its content, which either attains its own traditional form – shortened, formalized and mnemonically shaped – or else is reproduced in a completely free rendition. (This is the case particularly in haggadah, but it does not preclude the use of fixed linguistic clichés in the language of sermon, school or liturgy.)

### *3) Problems of Rabbinic Biography*

For a long time, Jewish historiography of the Talmudic period was mostly a stringing together of scholars' 'biographies' (typically e.g. I. H. Weiss, *Dor*).

However, this biographical work did not make significant progress, so that L. Finkelstein (*Akiba*, New York 1936, repr. 1975, ix) observes: 'The lack of suitable life-sketches of the rabbinic sages is especially deplorable because only biography can serve as an introduction to the spirit of the Talmud'. The kind of biography he means is illustrated in his own portrayal of Aqiba, viz., an ordered and embroidering narration of the individual rabbinic traditions about Aqiba; the result is hagiography or a historical novel, but not a biography. The latter can in fact hardly be written, since the concern of rabbinic literature is by no means biographical. Not only the dates of birth and death of the individual rabbis are lacking, but in most cases even their personal circumstances are not at all or only incidentally disclosed. Even shorter periods of at least the most important rabbis' lives cannot be coherently reconstructed: the rabbinic texts provide almost only unconnected individual narratives, which are in any case not specifically biographical in orientation.

The traditions about the rabbis consist primarily of halakhic, exegetical, or other statements without any narrative context, simply introduced by 'R. X said, expounded, etc.' and set alongside the sayings of other masters.

> We know about early rabbinic figures what the various authorities behind the documents want us to know, and we know it in the way they want us to know it. Consequently, the historical context. . . for any saying attributed to a given master or story about him is the document in which the passage appears, *not* the period in which he is alleged to have lived (Green, *Name*, 80).

As far as the narrative material is concerned, we find no birth or childhood story, only occasional descriptions of how a master converted to the Torah and began his study, incidents characterizing the political situation of the Jews in a particular period, travelogues, death scenes, but above all a mass of very diverse kinds of school narratives (relationship with disciples, scenes of controversy, incidents in the synagogue) and narratives which can serve as precedent for practical halakhah. What is more, the rabbinic sources are highly selective not only in the type of narrative, but also regarding the persons about whom more detailed accounts are given. It is above all characters of the Tannaitic period about whom we seem to be more fully informed: Hillel, Gamaliel II, Yoḥanan ben Zakkai, Eliezer ben Hyrcanus, Aqiba, Meir and Rabbi, as well as some (especially early) Amoraim such as Rab, Samuel, Yoḥanan and Resh Laqish.

How reliable are the narrative traditions? At present, methodologically faultless studies are available only for a few Tannaites (mostly works of J. Neusner and his students). They consistently show that narrative traditions are almost always later than the halakhic materials attributed to the particular master. Narratives about early Tannaites hardly ever appear in the Mishnah or Tosefta, and only rarely in the halakhic midrashim and in *baraitot*; instead, they are primarily located in the Amoraic layer of tradition or even only in the late midrashim. The primarily halakhic nature of the Tannaitic texts cannot by itself account for this fact. Instead, it would appear that the interest in preserving narratives is a later development. One cannot of course exclude the possibility that authentic biographical reminiscences were preserved through other channels (especially the much-touted oral tradition), so that it is only the fixed written form which is late. But because the frequency of narrative material increases with the temporal distance from a particular rabbi, one must seriously expect later inventions and embellishments. A large part of the rabbinic narratives is useless for serious biography (*contra* the optimism of S. Safrai, who does emphasize the lack of biographical interest in the rabbinic writings but nevertheless remains confident that even in the case of divergent parallel traditions about individual rabbis 'the common feature of all such Aggadot is their genuine historical core. . . it is possible to determine what constitutes the historical element in the narrative' *SH*, 210).

The 'biographical' narratives about the rabbis are not accurately transmitted eyewitness reports; most of them are relatively late texts intended for edification, exhortation or political ends (such as support of the patriarchate or other institutions). They are usually legendary, stereotyped narratives, which do not manifest the marked formal structure of the speech material. This formal distinction might suggest that they were transmitted through other channels; but it probably indicates instead that the transmission of narrative materials is not as regulated or as important, which in turn of course implies a reduced reliability. The primary interest in individuals in these texts is only superficial; in reality their intention is above all to inculcate certain attitudes of life, the rabbinic way of life and its ideal of study. This probably also explains a considerable number of the differences between the Babylonian and the Palestinian version of many narratives (Safrai), which reflect the different situations of their narrators. Internally, then, the texts pursue pedagogical purposes; externally they are rabbinic group propaganda.

Many narratives about rabbinic scholars demonstrate remarkable parallels with biographies of Hellenistic philosophers, as especially H. A. Fischel has shown (cf. the critique in Green, *Name*, 86). This is true especially for certain Tannaites, especially Hillel, whose accounts are very strongly reminiscent of Hellenistic clichés (*chria*), but also, for example, for the figure of Beruryah, which can be connected with narratives about learned daughters and spouses of Greek philosophers. At the same time, Beruryah's depiction as the daughter of Ḥananyah ben Teradion and Meir's wife first appears in BT and thus cannot be historically verified (D. Goodblatt; S. Safrai, 229, rightly stresses that BT generally likes to create relations of kinship between eminent rabbis). It would be worth investigating the extent to which such a *topos* of the Hellenistic scholars' biography still survived in Sassanid Babylonia. The example of Beruryah at any rate illustrates a further characteristic of the formation of biographical narrative, viz. the tendency to identify various figures after the fact and to forge close relations between the individual rabbis: thereby one can reduce the number of the unknown and make the lives of known figures more vivid and concrete (this is a general trait of haggadah: cf. I. Heinemann, *Darkhê ha-Aggadah*, 27ff.).

Finally, the potential cross-links between biographical narratives in rabbinical texts and Christian hagiography merit closer examination, since the latter also integrated the heritage of the Hellenistic scholars' biography into the biblical tradition. What we need above all, however, is a comprehensive inventory and literary-critical assessment of all the biographical material in the rabbinic texts, in order to progress beyond the (admittedly necessary) studies of individual rabbis to a typology of biographical narrative that would reveal its clichés and development potential. At present, biographical statements about individual rabbis are possible only with serious reservations. A biography in the usual sense will always remain unattainable. Nevertheless, 'biographical' studies can contribute essentially to a closer knowledge of rabbinic history and its intellectual currents; they are therefore an ongoing task.

### *4) The Most Important Rabbis*

#### *Bibliography*

**Albeck, Ch.** *Einführung*, 391–414. **Albeck, Ch.** *Mabo*, 144–451. **Bacher, W.** *Tann*; *PAm*; *BAm*; *TT*. **Duensing, H.** *Verzeichnis der Personennamen und der geographischen Namen in der Mischna*. Stuttgart 1960. **Frankel, Z.** *Darkhê*; *Mabo*. **Halevy, I.** *Dorot*. **Hallewy, A. A.** *Ha-Aggadah ha-historit-biografit le-or meqorot yewaniim we-latiniim*. Tel Aviv 1975. **Hallewy, A. A.** *Aggadot ha-Amoraim*. Tel Aviv 1977. **Halperin, R.** *Atlas Eytz Chayim: Tannaim wa-Amoraim*. 2 Parts. Tel Aviv 1980. **Hyman, A.** *Sefer Toldot Tannaim we-Amoraim*. 3 vols. London 1910; repr. Jerusalem 1964. **Jawitz, W.** *Sefer Toldot Yisrael*. Vols. 6–9. Tel Aviv 1935. **Konovitz, I.** 'Tannaitic Symposia: Complete Collected Sayings'. In idem, *Halakah and Aggadah, in the Talmudic and Midrashic Literature* (Hebr.). 4 vols. Jerusalem 1967–69. **Margalioth, M.**, ed. *Encyclopedia of Talmudic and Geonic Literature, being a Biographical Dictionary of the Tanaim, Amoraim and Geonim* (Hebr.). 2 vols. Tel Aviv 1960. **Naftal, A. M.** *Ha-Talmud we-Yoṣraw*. 5 vols. Tel Aviv 1969–79. **Rabinowitz, Z. W.** *Sha'arê Torat Babel*, 315–547. Jerusalem 1961. **Weiss, I. H.** *Dor*.

In addition to these works, which are for the most part uncritical collections of material, see the various encyclopaedias, especially *EJ*, under the name of the respective Rabbi. The listings below offer primarily a classification according to the rabbinic sequence of generations; bibliographical references deliberately do not discriminate between 'historical' and literary studies.

***a) The Earliest Period and the Five 'Pairs'***

*'The Men of the Great Synagogue'* (or 'Synod': *anshê knesset ha-gedolah*) in Abot 1.1–2 connect the time of the prophets with the Pharisaic movement, whose first named representative is Simeon the Just. These men, therefore, bridge a period of about two centuries. Later rabbinic literature attributes to them the writing of Ezekiel, the twelve minor prophets, Daniel and Esther (BB 15a), as well as exegetical and liturgical activities. A historical reconstruction of their organization (such as the assumption of 120 members, based on the 120 elders who arrange the 18 benedictions in Meg 17b) and activity is baseless. They are instead a fiction derived from the great national assembly of Neh 8–10, as was already shown by A. Kuenen.

A. Kuenen, *Abhandlungen zur biblischen Wissenschaft*, Freiburg 1894, 125–60; I. J. Schiffer, 'The Men of the Great Assembly', in W. S. Green, *Persons*, 237–76 (bibliography), Schürer/Vermes 2:358f. H. D. Mantel, 'The Period of the Great Synagogue' (Hebr.), in A. Oppenheimer et al. (eds.), *Jerusalem in the Second Temple Period* (Memorial Volume A. Schalit: Jerusalem 1980), 22–46, relocates the Great Synagogue to the Hellenistic period; Simeon the Just therefore becomes Simeon II, c. 200 BCE. A historically uncritical reconstruction is that of L. Finkelstein, 'The Men of the Great Synagogue (circa 400–170 B. C. E.)', in W. D. Davies & L. Finkelstein (eds.), *The Cambridge History of Judaism*, vol. 2 (Cambridge 1989), 229–44.

According to Josephus, *Ant* 12.43, *Simeon the Just* (m.Abot 1.2) was high priest under Ptolemy I, i.e. c. 300; in view of Sir 50.1–21, however, this epithet would better suit the high priest Simeon II (c. 200; cf. *Ant* 12.224). Did Josephus confuse the two? G. F. Moore doubts the very existence of Simeon I. The chronology of Abot also would speak more in favour of Simeon II. Rabbinic tradition casts Simeon archetypically as the good high priest and has no historical conceptions about him: it lets him meet Alexander the Great (LevR 13.5, M. 293) as well as making him the father of the Onias who under the Maccabees built the temple in Egypt (Men 109b). G. F. Moore, 'Simeon the Righteous', in G. A. Kohut (ed.), *Jewish Studies in Memory of I. Abrahams* (New York 1927); J. Neusner, *Phar* 1:27–59; Schürer/Vermes 2:359f.

*Antigonos of Sokho*, in Abot 1.3 Simeon's student, had two students according to ARN A5 and B10 (Sch. 26), Ṣadoq and Boetos, from whom the Sadducees and Boetoseans are supposed to derive (a historically worthless anecdote). E. J. Bickerman, 'The Maxim of Antigonus of Socho', *HTR* 44 (1951) 153–65; Neusner, *Phar* 1:60f.; Schürer/Vermes 2:360.

Five 'pairs' (*zugôt*) follow in the chain of tradition of Abot 1; this is probably a schematization of the tradition in analogy to Hillel and Shammai.

The rabbinic portrayal of them as respectively *Nasi* and *Ab Bêt-Din*, chairman and deputy (in the Sanhedrin?), is an anachronism. But cf. H. Mantel, *Sanhedrin* 7–18; E. E. Urbach, *EJ* 16:1232–34.

*Yose ben Yo'ezer* of Ṣereda and *Yose ben Yoḥanan* are in Sot 9.9 called the last 'grapes' (cf. G. G. Porton, 'The Grape-Cluster in Jewish Literature and Art of Late Antiquity', *JJS* 27 (1976) 159–76); Ḥag 2.7 names Yose ben Yo'ezer as a devout man among the priesthood. On their controversy about the *Semikhah* in Ḥag 2.2. see E. E. Hallewy, 'The First Mishnaic Controversy' (Hebr.), *Tarbiz* 28 (1958–59) 154–57; S. Zeitlin, 'The Semikah Controversy between the Zugoth' *JQR* N.S. 7 (1916–17) 499–517. J. Goldin, 'The First Pair (Yose Ben Yoezer and Yose ben Yohanan) or The Home of a Pharisee', *AJSR* 5 (1980) 41–61; J. Neusner, *Phar* 1:61–81. J. Genot-Bismuth attempts to identify Yose ben Yo'ezer with Qumran's Teacher of Righteousness (*Le scénario de Damas: Jérusalem hellénisée et les origines de l'essénisme*, Paris 1992; cf. G. D. Sixdenier, *JSJ* 23 (1992) 260–67).

*Yehoshua ben Peraḥyah* and *Mattai* (variant reading Nittai) of Arbel (Irbid near Tiberias). In Sanh 107b and Sot 47a, Yehoshua is named as the teacher of Jesus – apparently a gloss from the early Middle Ages (J. Maier, *Jesus*, 117–29); he also appears thus on the Babylonian magic bowls (Neusner, *Bab* 5:235–41; J. Naveh & S. Shaked reproduce a previously unpublished text in *Amulets and Magic Bowls* (Jerusalem 1985), 162). Apart from Abot 1.6f., Mattai appears only in Ḥag 2.2. J. Neusner, *Phar* 1:82–86.

*Yehudah ben Tabbai* and *Simeon ben Shetaḥ*. Only the second is of significance in rabbinic literature. He is reputed to have successfully supported the Pharisaic party under Alexander Jannaeus (103–76) and Salome Alexandra (76–67), as whose brother he appears. J. Efron, *Studies on the Hasmonean Period* (Leiden 1987), 143–218; M. Hengel, *Rabbinische Legende und frühpharisäische Geschichte: Schimeon b. Schetach und die achtzig Hexen von Askalon*, Heidelberg 1984; J. Neusner, *Phar* 1:86–141.

*Shemayah* and *Abtalion* are often identified with Samaias and Pollion mentioned in Josephus (*Ant* 14.172–75; 15.3, 370); but others prefer to see the latter Hillel and Shammai (thus A. Schalit, *König Herodes* (Berlin 1969), 768–71). In favour of this view is the similarity of the names, but against it stands Josephus's claim that Pollion was the teacher of Samaias. And unlike Josephus, rabbinic tradition does not connect the two with Herod. H. Feldman, 'The Identity of Pollio, the Pharisee, in Josephus', *JQR* N.S. 49 (1958–59) 53–62; J. Neusner, *Phar* 1:142–59; Schürer/Vermes 2:362f.

*Hillel* 'the Elder' is reputed to come from Babylonia; according to certain (late) traditions he was descended from the house of David. He lived at the time of Herod. The widespread opinion that he was the teacher of Jesus is unfounded. Tradition attributes to him seven hermeneutical rules and the introduction of the *prosbul*. The traditions about his life are entirely characterized by clichés; they contrast the gentle Hillel with the harsh Shammai and have much in common with the *topoi* of the Hellenistic scholar's biography. I. Gafni, *Babylonia*, 70–76; N. N. Glatzer, *Hillel: Repräsentant des klassischen Judentums*, Frankfurt 1966; L. Finkelstein, 'Shub al ha-mu"m ben Hillel u-benê Batirah', in *Harry Austryn Wolfson: Jubilee Volume on the Occasion of his 75th Birthday* (Jerusalem 1965), Hebr. volume, 203–24 (repr. in idem, *Sifra*, 5:123–44); H. A. Fischel, 'Studies in Cynicism and the Ancient Near East: The Transformation of a Chria', in J. Neusner (ed.), *Religions in Antiquity: Memorial Volume Erwin Ramsdell Goodenough* (Leiden 1968), 372–411; J. Neusner, *Bab* 1:36–38; *Phar* 1:212–340; 3:255–72; J. Neusner & A. J. Avery-Peck, 'The Quest for the Historical Hillel: Theory and Practice', in J. Neusner, *Formative Judaism* (Chico 1982), 45–63; M. Stern in Safrai/Stern 2:615–18; Schürer/Vermes 2:363–67; E. E. Urbach, *The Sages* (Cambridge, MA 1987), 576–92.

*Shammai* is sometimes also called 'the Elder'. Jerome (*Comm. on Isaiah* 3.8, *CCSL* 73.116): 'Sammai igitur et Hellel non multo priusquam Dominus nasceretur, orti sunt in Iudaea, quorum prior *dissipator* interpretatur, sequens *profanus*; eo quod per traditiones et *deuteroseis* suas legis praecepta dissipaverit atque maculaverit.' ['Sammai and Hellel arose in Judaea not long before the Lord's birth; the former's name means "scatterer", and the latter's "unclean", since by their traditions and *deuteroseis* (lit. "repetitions", *Mishnayot*) they scattered and defiled the precepts of the Law.'] Jerome may have misunderstood the saying of Hillel quoted in t.Ber 6.24 (L. 40): *pizar*, 'to scatter', viz. to spread the Torah; *profanus*, because Hillel is derived from *ḥol*. Since the Hillelite trend prevailed, the traditions of Shammai are almost exclusively transmitted as a contrast to those of Hillel. Neusner, *Phar* 1:185–211, 303–40.

***b) First Generation of Tannaites***

Immediately prior to the quotation just given (*CCSL* 73.116), Jerome on Isaiah presents gives a brief, historically inaccurate list of early teachers of the law: 'Sammai et Hellel, ex quibus orti sunt scribae et pharisaei; quorum suscepit scholam Akibas, quem magistrum Aquilae proselyti autumat et post eum Meir, cui successit (!) Joannan filius Zachai, et post eum Eliezier et per ordinem Telphon [Tarphon] et rursum Joseph Galilaeus et usque ad captivitatem Hierusalem Iosue.' ['Sammai and Hellel, from whom came the Scribes and Pharisees; their school was taken up by Akibas, whom his successor Meir calls the teacher of Aquila the proselyte. Meir in turn was succeeded (!) by Joannan son of Zachai, and after him Eliezier, and in turn

Telphon (Tarphon) and then Joseph the Galilaean, and Joshua until the capture of Jerusalem.']

*School of Shammai and School of Hillel*: two scholastic tendencies in first-century Pharisaism and in the period of Yabneh, in which the halakhic controversies of the two schools are already largely recorded in fixed literary forms (though one should also allow for later pseudepigraphical imitations). The c. 300 pertinent pericopes virtually never include names. The account of the 80 students of Hillel, of whom Jonathan ben Uzziel was the greatest and Yoḥanan ben Zakkai the least, is a historically unusable legend. In the controversies, about two-thirds of which deal either directly or indirectly with the food laws, the school of Shammai usually decides more severely (exceptions in Eduy 4–5); that of Hillel, more leniently. It is not possible to identify generally applicable principles that the schools would have followed. Nevertheless, in the school of Shammai one can discern a halakhically more conservative tendency, based probably on a more literal reading of Scripture; here an event is assessed strictly in terms of the action, while the Hillelites take into account the intention. A sociological explanation – the Shammaites as representatives of the land-owning middle class, the Hillelites as the lower class – cannot be substantiated. At Yabneh, the Hillelite faction tended to prevail; this in turn also influenced the formation of the tradition. – I. Ben-Shalom, *The School of Shammai and the Zealots' Struggle against Rome* (Hebr.), Jerusalem 1993; Y. D. Gilat, 'Intent and Act in Tannaitic Teaching' (Hebr.), *Bar-Ilan* 4–5 (1967) 104–16; idem, 'The Teachings of R. Eliezer ben Hyrcanos' (Hebr.), Tel Aviv 1968, 20–31. A. Guttmann, 'Hillelites and Shammaites – A Clarification', *HUCA* 28 (1957) 115–26; I. Konovitz, *Beth Shammai – Beth Hillel: Collected Sayings* (Hebr.), Jerusalem 1965; J. Neusner, *Phar* 2; S. Safrai, *EJ* 4:737–41; idem, 'The Decision According to the School of Hillel in Yavneh' (Hebr.), *7th WCJS* (Jerusalem 1981) 3:21–44; idem, *The Literature*, 1:185–200; Schürer/Vermes 2:365f.; M. Weiss, 'The authenticity of the explicit discussions in Bet Shammai-Bet Hillel disputes' (Hebr.), *Sidra* 4 (1988) 53–66; idem, 'Traces of Pre-Bet Shammai – Bet Hillel Explicit Halakhic Decisions' (Hebr.), *Sidra* 8 (1992) 39–51.

*Aqabyah ben Mahalalel* (Abot 3.1; Eduy 5.6f., etc.) cannot be precisely located in history. Suggested dates range from the first century BCE to the time of Gamaliel II at Yabneh. S. B. Hoenig, 'New Light on the Epoch of Akabiah ben Mahalalel' in M. Ben-Horin et al. (eds.), *Studies and Essays in Honour of A. A. Neuman*, (Leiden 1962) 291–98; H. Mantel, *Sanhedrin* 106–18; A. Neher, 'Aqabia ben Mahalalel: Un héros méconnu de l'époque Talmudique' *REJ* 133 (1974) 225–33; J. Neusner, *Phar* 1:144f., 416; A.

Saldarini, 'The Adoption of a Dissident: Akabya ben Mahalalel in Rabbinic Tradition' *JJS* 33 (1982) 547–56.

*Rabban Gamaliel I*, 'the elder', teacher of the apostle Paul (Acts 22.3), described in Acts 5.34–39 as a member of the Sanhedrin who advocates the release of the accused apostles. He is supposed to have been the son of a certain Simeon who in turn was Hillel's son. The existence of this Simeon is highly doubtful (he appears only in Shab 15a); but even the assumption that Gamaliel was Hillel's son, or at least belonged to his school, cannot be demonstrated. J. Neusner, *Phar* 1:341–76; Schürer/Vermes 2:367f.

*Ḥananyah* (or Ḥanina), the prefect of the priesthood (*s$^{e}$gan ha-kohanim*), was active probably towards the end of the Temple and also after 70. J. Neusner, *Phar* 1:400–413.

*Neḥunya ben ha-Qanah* (or *ha-Qaneh*: the meaning of the name is uncertain). In Shebu 26a he appears as the teacher of Ishmael, who reputedly learned from him a special preference for the rule of the general and the particular (cf. p. 19 above). He is important in the hekhalot literature. In the Kabbalah he is regarded as the author of the *Sefer ha-Bahir*. L. Finkelstein, 'Mi-torato shel R. Neḥunya ben ha-Qanah', in *Sefer Yovel le-Rabbi Ḥanokh Albeck* (*Festschrift* Ch. Albeck, Jerusalem 1963), 352–77; idem, ''Od mi-torato shel R. Neḥunya ben Ha-Qanah, (be-Torat Kohanim)', in *Hagut 'Ibrit be-Ameriqah*, vol. 1 (Tel Aviv 1972), 257–60; idem, 'Additional Teachings of R. Neḥunya Ben Ha-Qana' (Hebr.), *Tarbiz* 50 (1980–81) 88–93 (all three studies repr. in idem, *Sifra* 5:145–80); L. H. Schiffmann, 'The Recall of Rabbi Neḥuniah Ben Ha-Qanah from Ecstasy in the Hekhalot Rabbati', *AJSR* 1 (1976) 269–81; M. Schlüter, 'Die Erzählung von der Rückholung des R. Neḥunya ben Haqana aus der Merkava-Schau in ihrem redaktionellen Rahmen', *FJB* 10 (1982) 65–109.

*Rabban Simeon ben Gamaliel I*, was active during the Jewish War; Josephus, *Vita* 38 (191) describes him as 'a man full of insight and understanding, who by his genius could restore even a bad situation'. J. Neusner, *Phar* 1:413f.

*Naḥum the Mede*. He himself or his family came from Babylonia. He was still alive at the fall of the Temple. J. Neusner, *Phar* 1:413f.

*R. Ṣadoq* (vocalized *Ṣadduq* in MS Parma Ter 10.9; cf. *Saddouk* in LXX Ezek, Esra, Neh; similarly *Saddoukaioi*) lived in Jerusalem before the destruction of the Temple, and subsequently belonged to the group around Gamaliel II. All 'biographical' traditions about him are late; the conjecture of one Ṣadoq II as a grandson of this figure is based on the inconsistent nature of the material, but cannot be demonstrated. J. N. Lightstone, 'Ṣadoq the Yavnean', in W. S. Green (ed.), *Persons*, 49–147.

*Rabban Yoḥanan ben Zakkai* fled Jerusalem during the revolt against Rome and was later interned by the Romans at Yabneh, where he founded an 'academy' which was to become the basis of rabbinic Judaism. Rabbinic tradition developed this into a foundation legend. Whether Yoḥanan belonged to the school of Hillel is just as unverifiable as his membership of the Pharisees before 70. Even in the early tradition, Yoḥanan is considered a mystic. According to Abot 2.8f. his five most important students were Eliezer ben Hyrcanus, Yehoshua ben Ḥananyah, Yose the Priest, Simeon ben Nathanael and Eleazar ben Arakh. – G. Alon, *Studies*, 269–343; M. Cohen, 'Quelques observations au sujet de la personnalité et du rôle historique de Raban Yoḥanan ben Zakkay', *RHR* 187 (1975) 27–55; J. Goldin, 'Mashehu 'al Bêt Midrasho shel Rabban Yoḥanan ben Zakkai', *Harry Austryn Wolfson: Jubilee Volume on the Occasion of his 75th Birthday* (Jerusalem 1965), Hebr. vol., 69–92; A. Kaminka, 'Rabbi Jochanan Ben Zaccai and His Disciples' (Hebr.), *Zion* 9 (1943–44) 70–83; J. Neusner, *Life*; idem, *Development*; idem, *Eliezer*, 2.437–58; S. Safrai, 'Beḥinot ḥadashot le-ba'ayat ma'amado u-ma'asaw shel Yoḥanan ben Zakkai le-aḥar ha-ḥorban', *In Memory of Gedaliahu Alon: Essays in Jewish History and Philology* (Jerusalem 1970), 203–26; A. J. Saldarini, 'Johanan ben Zakkai's Escape from Jerusalem: Origin and Development of a Rabbinic Story', *JSJ* 6 (1975) 189–204; P. Schäfer, 'Die Flucht Joḥanan b. Zakkais aus Jerusalem und die Gründung des 'Lehrhauses' in Jabne', *ANRW* II 19/2, 43–101.

*R. Eliezer ben Jacob the Elder* (certainly to be distinguished from Aqiba's student of the same name, even if in a given case it is not always clear which of the two is intended). He transmits traditions about the Temple in particular; in Yoma 16a he is even regarded as the author of Middot. Bacher, *Tann* 1:62–67; L. Finkelstein, *The Pharisees*, 3rd edn. Philadelphia 1962, 731–34.

*R. Ḥanina ben Dosa* was a charismatic, miracle worker and faith-healer in the first century. He is connected with Yoḥanan ben Zakkai and Gamaliel II, but was probably neither a Pharisee nor a rabbi. – B. M. Bokser, 'Ḥanina Ben Dosa and the Lizard: The Treatment of Charismatic Figures in Rabbinic Literature', *8th WCJS* (Jerusalem 1982) C:1–6; idem, 'Wonder-working and the Rabbinic Tradition: The Case of Ḥanina ben Dosa', *JSJ* 16 (1985) 42–92; J. Neusner, *Phar* 1:394–96; idem, *Life*, 47–53; S. Safrai, 'The Pious (Hassidim) and the Men of Deeds' (Hebr.), *Zion* 50 (1985) 42–92; G. B. Sarfatti, 'Pious Men, Men of Deeds, and the Early Prophets' (Hebr.), *Tarbiz* 26 (1956–57) 126–53, especially 130–42; G. Vermes, 'Ḥanina ben Dosa: A Controversial Galilean Saint from the First Century of the Christian Era', *JJS* 23 (1972) 28–50; 24 (1973) 51–64 (=*Studies*, 178–214).

*Ḥananyah ben Ḥizkiyyah ben Garon* (or Gorion). Shab 13b attributes to him *Megillat Ta'anit* as well as special efforts to resolve contradictions in the Bible and to have the book of Ezekiel recognized as canonical. See J. Neusner, *Phar* 1:416. The rabbinic traditions about him are closely connected with those about the biblical king Hezekiah: see G. Stemberger, 'Il contributo delle baraitot babilonesi alla conoscenza storica della Palestina prima del 70 D.C.', in P. Sacchi (ed.), *Il Giudaismo palestinese: dal 1 secolo a.C. al 1 secolo D.C.* (Bologna 1993) 213–29.

*Naḥum of Gimzo* (in Southwestern Judaea). Aqiba reputedly learned from him the rules of inclusion and exclusion (*ribbui* and *mi'ut*): Sheb 26a. Bacher, *Tann* 1:57–59.

### *c) Second Generation of Tannaites (c. 90–130)*

#### *1. Older Group*

*Rabban Gamaliel II*, son of Simeon ben Gamaliel I, often called Gamaliel of Yabneh to distinguish him from his grandfather of the same name; Yoḥanan ben Zakkai's successor. He was the leader of rabbinic Judaism during the time between 80 or 90 and c. 110. Nevertheless, his position was not undisputed, as can be seen from his temporary deposition while Eleazar ben Azaryah, who was of priestly descent, took over the leadership. Rabbinic tradition also knows about a sea voyage to Rome, which Gamaliel undertook together with Eleazar ben Azaryah, Aqiba and Yehoshua ben Ḥananyah. This voyage is occasionally associated with the persecution of the Jews under Domitian, but this is problematic. – A. Y. Bittmann, *Rabban Gamaliel of Yavneh: His Teachings and Role in the Development of Talmudic Law* (Hebr.), Diss. New York: Yeshiva University, 1974; R. Goldenberg, 'The Deposition of Rabban Gamaliel II: An Examination of the Sources', *JJS* 23 (1972) 167–90 (=W. S. Green (ed.), *Persons*, 9–47); D. Goodblatt, 'The Origins of Roman Recognition of the Palestinian Patriarchate' (Hebr.), *Studies in the History of the Jewish People and the Land of Israel* 4 (Haifa 1978) 89–102 (assumes an appointment of Gamaliel by the Romans, which was only subsequently followed by efforts to secure recognition by the people); S. Kanter, *Rabban Gamaliel II: The Legal Traditions*, Chico 1980; B.–Z. Rosenfeld, 'The Standing and Activities of Rabban Gamaliel Prior to his Move to Yavneh' (Hebr.), *Zion* 55 (1990) 151–69 (appointed as patriarch c. 85).

*R. Papias* still transmits halakhot from the time of the Temple. He is sometimes confused in the MSS with the later R. Pappos (b. Yehudah). Bacher, *Tann* 1:317–19.

*R. Eliezer ben Hyrcanus* (m.Abot 2.8), in M simply R. Eliezer (more than 320x). He taught at Lydda and was often in dispute with Yehoshua ben Ḥananyah and Aqiba. His halakhic interests link him with the Pharisees, but it is not possible to assign him to the house of Hillel or of Shammai (for the latter see e.g. S. Safrai, *The Literature*, 1:186, 198–200). The Sanhedrin at Yabneh pronounced the ban on him, an incident which rabbinic tradition then strongly embellished. The assumption that Eliezer favoured Christianity is groundless, even if his arrest by the Roman authorities may have been based on such a suspicion: thus, for example, S. Lieberman, 'Roman Legal Institutions in Early Rabbinics and in the Acta Martyrum', *JQR* N.S. 35 (1944) 1–57, especially 20–24 (=*Texts and Studies*, 76–80; cf. J. Maier, *Jesus*, 144–60). M. Aberbach, 'Did Rabban Gamaliel II Impose the Ban on Rabbi Eliezer ben Hyrcanus?', *JQR* N.S. 54 (1963–64) 201–7; R. D. Aus, 'Luke 15.11–32 and R. Eliezer ben Hyrcanus's Rise to Fame', *JBL* 104 (1985) 443–69; Epstein, *ITL*, 65–70; Y. D. Gilat, *R. Eliezer ben Hyrcanus: A Scholar Outcast*, Ramat Gan 1984; Z. Kagan, 'Divergent Tendencies and their Literary Moulding in the Aggadah', *SH* 22 (1971) 151–70; I. Konovitz, *Rabbi Eliezer – Rabbi Joshua: Collected Sayings* (Hebr.), Jerusalem 1965; J. Neusner, *Eliezer* (and cf. Abr. Goldberg, *JSJ* 6 (1975), 108–14); idem, *In Search of Talmudic Biography*, Chico 1984.

*Yehoshua ben Ḥananyah*, in M simply R. Yehoshua (more than 140x). He worked in Peqiin and was often engaged in controversy with Eliezer ben Hyrcanus. On his Greek education see S. Lieberman, *Greek*, 16–19; his contribution to M: Epstein, *ITL*, 59–65. W. S. Green, 'Redactional Techniques in the Legal Traditions of Joshua ben Ḥananiah', in J. Neusner (ed.), *Christianity, Judaism and other Greco-Roman Cults: Studies for Morton Smith at Sixty* (Leiden 1975), 4.1–17; idem, *The Traditions of Joshua ben Ḥananiah*, part 1: *The Early Legal Traditions*, Leiden 1981; I. Konovitz, *Rabbi Eliezer – Rabbi Joshua: Collected Sayings* (Hebr.), Jerusalem 1965; R. Loewe, 'Rabbi Joshua ben Ḥananiah: Ll.D. or D. Litt.?' *JJS* 1974 (special issue: *Studies in Jewish Legal History in Honour of David Daube*, ed. B. S. Jackson), 137–54; J. Podro, *The Last Pharisee: The Life and Times of R. Joshua ben Hananiah*, London 1959 (attempt at a conventional biography).

*Yose the Priest*, *Simeon ben Nathanael* and *Eleazar ben Arakh* were, like Eliezer ben Hyrcanus and Yehoshua, students of Yoḥanan ben Zakkai, Abot 2.8. Neusner, *Life*, 106–17.

*Yose the Priest*, Abot 2.12, in p.Ḥag 2.1 as Joseph the Priest. Bacher, *Tann* 1:67–69.

*R. Eleazar ben Arakh* appears as the favourite student of Yoḥanan ben Zakkai, especially in mystical texts. Bacher, *Tann* 1:69–72; A. Goshen-Gottstein, 'Rabbi Eleazar ben Arakh: Symbol and Reality' (Hebr.), in A.

Oppenheimer et al. (eds.), *Yehudim ve-Yahadut bi-yemê ha-bayit ha-shenî: Meḥkarim li-khebodo shel Shmuel Safrai* (*Festschrift* S. Safrai; Jerusalem 1993), 173–97; J. Neusner, *Development*, 247–52 and index.

*R. Eleazar ben Azaryah* worked at Yabneh as an aristocratic, wealthy priest. He briefly replaced Gamaliel II as leader of the rabbinic movement at Yabneh, even though he is a marginal figure in its tradition: T. Zahavy, *The Traditions of Eleazar Ben Azariah*, Missoula 1977.

*R. Eleazar ben Ṣadoq*, son of the Ṣadoq mentioned above. He had a grandson of the same name. Bacher, *Tann* 1:50.

*Samuel the Small* reputedly formulated the *Birkat ha-Minim* in the Prayer of Eighteen Benedictions (Ber 28b) before Gamaliel II. However, this was not primarily or even exclusively formulated against Christians, as might appear to be the case from the church fathers Justin, Epiphanius and Jerome that the Jews in their daily prayer pronounce curses against the Christians. Even the version found in the Cairo Genizah, which explicitly speaks of *noṣrim* instead of *minim*, is no evidence of the original text. Sem 8 preserves the lament of Gamaliel II and Eleazar ben Azaryah at Samuel's death. N. Cohen, 'Mah ḥiddesh Shmuel ha-Qatan be-Birkat ha-Minim?', *Sinai* 48 (1983–84) 57–70; M. Hirshman, 'Shmuel ha-Qatan' (Hebr.), in A. Oppenheimer et al. (eds.), *Yehudim ve-Yahadut bi-yemê ha-bayit ha-shenî: Meḥkarim li-khebodo shel Shmuel Safrai* (*Festschrift* S. Safrai; Jerusalem 1993), 165–72; P. Schäfer, 'Die sogenannte Synode von Jabne', *Judaica* 31 (1975) 54–64 (=*Studien*, 45–55).

*Simeon ha-Paqoli* ('the flax dealer') ordered the Prayer of Eighteen Benedictions at the time of Gamaliel II (Ber 28b). N. Cohen, 'The Nature of Shim'on Hapekuli's Act' (Hebr.), *Tarbiz* 52 (1983–84) 547–55.

*R. Eleazar of Modiim* was active at the time of the Bar Kokhba revolt and is supposed to have been killed by Bar Kokhba. Bacher, *Tann* 1:187–211; P. Schäfer, *Der Bar-Kokhba-Aufstand* (Tübingen 1981), 44f., 173f. Some wish to identify him with the priest Eleazar on the Bar Kokhba coins: see S. Applebaum, *PEQ* 116 (1984) 41; L. Mildenberg, *The Coinage of the Bar Kokhba War* (Aarau 1984), 29f.

*R. Levitas of Yabneh*, Abot 4.4; according to Bacher, *Tann* 1:444, he was probably active before the Hadrianic period. He is also repeatedly named in PRE.

### *2. Younger Group of the Second Generation*

The most famous teachers of this group are Ishmael and Aqiba.

*R. Ishmael ben Elisha*, usually just R. Ishmael, came perhaps from a priestly family (cf. t.Ḥal 1.10, L. 277). He was a student of Neḥunya ben ha-

Qanah and lived mostly at Kefar Aziz on the border with Edom. To him is attributed the principle, 'The Torah speaks in human language' (as against the hermeneutical exploitation of the Bible's stylistic peculiarities assumed of Aqiba: SifreNum §112, H. 121). See pp. 20ff. above for the interpretative rules attributed to him. I. Konovitz, *Tannaitic Symposia*, 3:261–367; G. G. Porton, *Ishmael*; idem, 'The Artificial Dispute: Ishmael and 'Aqiva' in J. Neusner (ed.), *Christianity, Judaism and other Greco-Roman Cults: Studies for Morton Smith at Sixty* (Leiden 1975), 4:18–29.

*R. Aqiba ben Joseph*, usually just R. Aqiba. He was an eminent teacher of the period of Yabneh; after the Bar Kokhba revolt, his students made his traditions the foundation of M. His name is connected with mystical traditions (Ḥag 14b) as well as with a particular method of biblical interpretation: he is said to have been able to read mountains of halakhot in every jot and tittle of the written law (Men 29b). Historically, this would appear to be just as untrue as in the case of R. Ishmael. Various 'biographical' accounts, too (e.g. that he only turned to study at the age of 40, or even the accounts of his imprisonment and execution), are relatively useless for a description of the historical Aqiba. That he considered Bar Kokhba to be the 'star of Jacob', i.e. a Messianic figure, would fit his other views; but his numerous journeys can hardly be seen in terms of a publicity campaign for Bar Kokhba. Jerome, in addition to his reference to Aqiba on Isa 8.11 (see p. 65 above), also mentions him in *Epist.* 121.10 (*CSEL* 56:48) '[Judaei] solent respondere et dicere: Barachibas et Symeon et Helles [Hillel], magistri nostri, tradiderunt nobis, ut duo milia ambulemus in sabbato.' ['The Jews usually reply by saying, Barachibas and Symeon and Helles (Hillel) our teachers have passed on to us that we may walk two miles on the Sabbath.'] – G. S. Aleksandrow, 'The Role of 'Aqiba in the Bar Kokhba Rebellion', in Neusner, *Eliezer* 2.422–36 (=*REJ* 132 (1973) 65–77); S. Applebaum, 'The Burial Place of R. 'Aqiva', *7th WCJS* (Jerusalem 1981) 3:37–47; J. Elbaum, 'Models of Storytelling and Speech in Stories About the Sages' (Hebr.), *7th WCJS* (Jerusalem 1981) 3:71–77 [on Aqiba in ARN]; L. Finkelstein, *Akiba: Scholar, Saint and Martyr*, New York 1936=1970; A. Goldberg, 'Das Martyrium des R. 'Aqiva: Zur Komposition einer Märtyrererzählung (bBer 61b)', *FJB* 12 (1984) 1–82; A. Guttmann, 'Akiba,"Rescuer of the Torah"', *HUCA* 17 (1942–43) 395–421; D. Ḥoshen, 'Suffering and Divinity in R. Akiva's Philosophy' (Hebr.), *Da'at* 27 (1991) 5–33; I. Konovitz, *Rabbi Aqiba: Collected Sayings* (Hebr.), 2nd edn. Jerusalem 1965; P. Lenhardt & P. von der Osten-Sacken, *Rabbi Aqiva: Texte und Interpretationen zum rabbinischen Judentum und Neuen Testament*, Berlin 1987; C. Primus, *Aqiva's Contribution to the Law of Zera'im*, Leiden 1977; S. Safrai, *Rabbi*

*Akiba ben Josef: His Life and Teaching* (Hebr.), Jerusalem 1970; P. Schäfer, 'R. Aqiva und Bar Kokhba', in idem, *Studien*, 65–121 (cf. W. S. Green (ed.), *Approaches*, 2:113–30).

*R. Tarfon* (Jerome on Isaiah 8.11: Telphon). Of priestly stock, he came from Lydda and was the teacher of Yehudah bar Ilai. His halakhic sayings, deriving mostly from discussions with Aqiba, are concerned on the one hand with the preference of objective fact before subjective intention, and on the other hand with the interests of priests, in whose favour he always decided. Rabbi Tarfon is probably not identical with the Trypho named by Justin Martyr: see M. Freimann, 'Die Wortführer des Judentums in den ältesten Kontroversen zwiscen Juden und Christen', *MGWJ* 55 (1911) 555–85, 565ff.; L. W. Barnard, *Justin Martyr: His Life and Thought* (London 1967), 24f. J. D. Gereboff, *Rabbi Tarfon: The Tradition, the Man and Early Judaism*, Missoula 1979; J. Neusner, 'A Life of Rabbi Tarfon, ca. 50–120 CE', *Judaica* 17 (1961) 141–67.

*R. Ilai* was a student of Eliezer ben Hyrcanus and the father of Yehudah (b. Ilai). He often passes on the tradition of Eliezer.

*Aqilas*, 'the proselyte'. According to Epiphanius, he came from Sinope in Pontus. He was a student of R. Eliezer and of R. Yehoshua ben Ḥananyah and translated the Bible into Greek. Scholarly opinion is divided as to whether in doing so he came under the influence of the exegetical method attributed to Aqiba (thus Barthélemy; contrast Grabbe). D. Barthélemy, *Les Devanciers d'Aquila*, Leiden 1963. L. L. Grabbe, 'Aquila's Translation and Rabbinic Exegesis', *JJS* 33 (1982) 527–36; A. Silverstone, *Aquila and Onkelos*, Manchester 1931.

*R. Yoḥanan ben Torta* in p.Taan 4.7, 68d criticizes Aqiba's support of Bar Kokhba. Bacher, *Tann* 2:557f.

*Pappos ben Yehudah*, or simply Pappos (without the title of Rabbi), was a haggadist. He is said to have been in prison with Aqiba (Ber 61b).

*R. Yoḥanan ben Nuri*, a close adherent of Gamaliel II, disputes with Aqiba and is generally depicted as the latter's adversary. Bacher, *Tann* 1:366–68; L. A. Rosenthal, 'Die Malkhijot R. Jochanan b. Nuri's', in S. Eppenstein et al. (eds.), *Festschrift zum siebzigsten Geburtstage David Hoffmann's* (Berlin 1914), 234–40.

*R. Yose ha-Gelili*, the Galilean, disputes particularly with Aqiba, Tarfon and Eleazar ben Azaryah; his sayings concern sacrifice and temple service. J. N. Lightstone, *Yose the Galilean: I. Traditions in Mishnah – Tosefta*, Leiden 1979; idem, 'Yosé the Galilean in Mishnah – Tosefta and the history of Early Rabbinic Judaism', *JJS* 31 (1980) 37–45; J. Fraenkel, *SH* 27 (1978) 28–35; D. J. Stevens, *Rabbi Yose the Galilean: A Representative Selection of his Legal Traditions*, Diss. Durham, NC: Duke University, 1978.

*R. Eleazar Ḥisma* (LevR 23.4 gives an explanation of the name), sometimes also called Eleazar ben Ḥisma, is supposed to have been a student of Yehoshua ben Ḥananyah and active in the academy of Gamaliel II. The halakhot transmitted in his name are concerned above all with agricultural and purity laws. D. Levine, 'Eleazar Ḥisma', in W. S. Green (ed.), *Persons*, 140–205.

*R. Yoḥanan ben Beroqa*, student of Yehoshua ben Ḥananyah, Abot 4.4. Bacher, *Tann* 1:448f.

*R. Yose, son of the Damascene woman* (ben Dormasqit), student of Eliezer ben Hyrcanus, advocated the literal sense in biblical interpretation (SifreDeut §1, F. 6–8). Bacher, *Tann* 1:389–94.

*R. Ḥananyah ben Teradion.* According to (late) rabbinic tradition, he was Meir's father-in-law through his daughter Beruryah, and one of the martyrs in the Hadrianic persecution. Bacher, *Tann* 1:394–97; H. W. Basser, 'Hanina's Torah: A Case of Verse Production or of Historical Fact?', in J. Neusner (ed.), *Approaches to Ancient Judaism*, New Series vol. 1 (Atlanta 1990), 67–82 (=idem, *In the Margins of the Mishnah* (Atlanta 1990), 49–63); on the alleged family relationships see D. Goodblatt, 'The Beruriah Traditions', *JJS* 26 (1975) 68–85 (=W.S. Green (ed.), *Persons*, 207–35); E. E. Urbach, 'Ascesis and Suffering in Talmudic and Midrashic Sources' (Hebr.), in S. W. Baron et al. (eds.), *Yitzhak F. Baer Jubilee Volume on the Occasion of His Seventieth Birthday* (Jerusalem 1960), 48–68, especially 61–64.

*R. Eleazar ben Parta* (cf. *peruta* in Palestinian Syriac, 'money-changer'; others think of Greek *prôtos*). Bacher, *Tann* 1:400–403. He should be distinguished from his grandson of the same name.

*R. Yehudah ben Baba*, with the epithet Ḥasid. He reputedly ordained seven students of Aqiba soon after the latter's death, and was killed by Roman soldiers while attempting to escape (Sanh 13b–14a). G. A. Wewers, 'Rabbi Jehuda-ben-Baba: Skizze zum Problem der Individualüberlieferung in der frühen rabbinischen Literatur', *Kairos* 19 (1977) 81–115.

*R. Yose ben Qismah*, Abot 6.9. Bacher, *Tann* 1:397–400; J. Gutmann, 'Milḥemet ha-Yehudim bimê Tiryanos', *Sefer Assaf* (Jerusalem 1953), 149–84 (especially 171f.).

*Simeon ben Azzai*, usually just Ben Azzai (an abbreviation of Azaryah). In Ḥag 14b he belongs with Ben Zoma, Elisha ben Abuyah and Aqiba to the four who entered 'Paradise' i.e. who engaged in esoteric speculation; only Aqiba survived this unharmed. G. Scholem, *Jewish Gnosticism, Merkabah Mysticism, and Talmudic Tradition* (New York 1960), 14–19; H. A. Fischel, *Rabbinic Literature*, 1–34, 90–98, 99–128, 161–65.

*Simeon ben Zoma*, usually just Ben Zoma. H. A. Fischel, *Rabbinic Literature*, 51–89, 138–61.

*Elisha ben Abuya*, repeatedly called *Aḥer* ('the other'), in order to avoid naming him after his apostasy. He was the teacher of R. Meir. A. Büchler, 'Die Erlösung Elisa' b. Abujahs aus dem Höllenfeuer', *MGWJ* 76 (1932) 412–56; G. Stroumsa, 'Aḥer: A Gnostic', in B. Layton (ed.), *The Rediscovery of Gnosticism*, vol. 2 (Leiden 1981), 808–18; H. Yalon, 'Acher im Talmudisch-Hebräischen', *MGWJ* 79 (1935) 238–40; cf. also idem in *Leshonenu* 29 (1965) 213–17.

*R. Ḥananyah* (or Ḥanina) *ben Gamaliel II*. Bacher, *Tann* 1:436–40.

*R. Eleazar ben Yehudah* of Bartota (Birtota? thus Cod. Kaufmann on Abot 3.7) sometimes appears without mention of his father Eleazar Ish Bartota.

*R. Simeon of Timna* (*ha-Timni*: thus e.g. Yeb 4.13 Cod. Kaufmann; others prefer the vocalization *ha-Temani*, 'from Teman', i.e. probably Edom, cf. Job 2.11). He was a student of Aqiba and Yehoshua (t.Ber 4.18, L. 23).

*The older students of Aqiba* are also included in this generation:

*Ḥananyah ben Ḥakhinai* lived in Yabneh and Benê Beraq; in late sources he is considered one of the 'ten martyrs'. Bacher, *Tann* 1:434–36.

*R. Simeon of Shiqmonah*. Bacher, *Tann* 1:445f.

*R. Ḥidqa*. Bacher, *Tann* 1:446f.

*Mattyah ben Ḥeresh* (for Ḥeresh as proper name, see 1 Chr 9.15; others read Ḥarash) was active in Rome just before the Bar Kokhba revolt. L. A. Segal, 'R. Matiah ben Ḥeresh of Rome on Religious Duties and Redemption: Reaction to Sectarian Teaching', *PAAJR* 58 (1992) 221–41; A. Toaff, 'Matia Ben Cheresh e la sua academia rabbinica di Roma', *Annuario di Studi Ebraici* 2 (1964–65) 69–80.

*R. Yehudah ben Bathyra* (others: Betera) worked in Palestine with Eliezer ben Hyrcanus, later in Nisibis, where Yoḥanan the Sandal-Maker and Eleazar ben Shammua learned Torah under him. According to Neusner, *Bab* 1:43–49, 121–24, two rabbis of this name must be assumed: one c. 20/30–90, the other c. 100–160, both in Nisibis.

*Ḥananyah*, the nephew (brother's son) of Yehoshua ben Ḥananyah, lived in Bablonia at Nehar Peqod, where he fled after the Bar Kokhba revolt. There he independently attempted to intercalate the calendar, which was a privilege reserved for Palestine. A. Burstein, *Sinai* 38 (1956) 32–37; 40 (1957) 387f.; J. Neusner, *Bab* 1:113–21.

***d) Third Generation of Tannaites (c. 130–160)***

***1. Ishmael's most Eminent Students***

*R. Yoshiyyah*, who perhaps came from Ḥuṣal and settled in Babylonia after the Bar Kokhba revolt (Neusner, *Bab* 1:128–31), and *R. Jonathan*, probably also a Babylonian (Neusner, *Bab* 1:132). They are frequently mentioned in Mek and Sifre; but Jonathan appears only once in M (m.Abot 6.9) and Yoshiyyah never, perhaps because Meir and Rabbi followed the views of Aqiba rather than Ishmael. Bacher, *Tann* 2:351–64.

*Abba Ḥanin* (Ḥanan) also appears to have belonged to this circle; he is often mentioned as a tradent of sayings of Eliezer ben Hyrcanus, and was perhaps also a Babylonian (Neusner, *Bab* 1:130).

***2. The Later Students of Aqiba***

Of these, the first four are mentioned most frequently (on Aqiba's students, cf. Abr. Goldberg, 'All Base Themselves upon the Teachings of Rabbi 'Aqiva' (Hebr.), *Tarbiz* 38 (1968–69) 231–54.

*R. Meir* was a student first of Ishmael and then of Aqiba; Elisha ben Abuyah also taught him. He lived for a time in Tiberias or in the adjacent Ḥammat Tiberias. According to a late tradition, he was the son-in-law of Ḥananyah ben Teradion through his wife Beruryah. He was important as both a halakhist and a haggadist (Sanh 38b: one-third of his lecturing was halakhah, one-third haggadah, one-third parables). In addition, he played a significant part in the redaction of M, in which he is mentioned about 330 times. N. G. Cohen, 'Rabbi Meir, A Descendant of Anatolian Proselytes: New Light on his Name and the Historical Kernel of the Nero Legend in Giṭṭin 56a', *JJS* 23 (1972) 51–59; R. Goldenberg, *The Sabbath-Law of Rabbi Meir*, Missoula 1978; S. Lieberman, *Hell.*, 24–26; Bacher, *Tann* 2:1–69; I. Konovitz, *Rabbi Meir: Collected Sayings* (Hebr.), Jerusalem 1967; A. Shinan, '"Aḥiw" shel Rabbi Meir', *JSHL* 2 (1983) 7–20 (on GenR 92.6); J. P. Siegel, *The Severus Scroll and 1QIsa*$^{a}$ (Missoula 1975), 43–48.

*R. Simeon ben Yoḥai* (=abbreviation of Yoḥanan), in M always (more than 300x) simply R. Simeon. He was long considered to be the author of the Zohar; but in reality this principal work of the Kabbalah was written in the second half of the thirteenth century by Moshe ben Shem Tob de Leon in Spain. MRS has also been attributed to his circle. Bacher, *Tann* 2:70–149; M. Beer, 'Shim'on bar Yoḥai and Jerusalem' (Hebr.), in A. Oppenheimer et al. (eds.), *Jerusalem in the Second Temple Period* (Memorial Volume A. Schalit) (Jerusalem 1980), 361–75; I. Konovitz, *Rabbi Simeon bar Yohai: Collected Sayings* (Hebr.), Jerusalem 1966; L. Levine, 'R. Simeon b. Yoḥai and the Purification of Tiberias: History and Tradition', *HUCA* 49 (1978) 143–85; O. Meir, 'Sippur Rabbi Shim'on ben Yoḥai ba-Me'arah', *'Alê Siaḥ* 26 (1989) 145–60.

*R. Yose ben Ḥalafta*, in M always simply R. Yose (c. 330x). He taught at Sepphoris and was an important halakhist. Tradition also regards him as the main tradent of the accepted Jewish chronology, as it is fixed in the Seder Olam Rabbah. He is frequently considered the author of Kelim. Bacher, *Tann* 2:150–90; R. Gershenzon & E. Slomovic, 'A Second-Century Jewish-Gnostic Debate: Rabbi Jose ben Halafta and the Matrona', *JSJ* 16 (1985) 1–41; T. Ilan, 'Matrona and Rabbi Jose: An Alternative Interpretation', *JSJ* 25 (1994) 18–51; I. Konovitz, *Rabbi Jose ben Halafta: Collected Sayings* (Hebr.), Jerusalem 1966; K. H. Rengstorf, *Die Mischna: Jebamot* (Giessen 1929, repr. 1958), 32*–37*.

*R. Yehudah bar Ilai* (an abbreviation from Eleazar or Elyoënai: 1 Chr 3.23, etc. (thus G. Dalman, *Grammatik des jüdisch-palästinischen Aramäisch* (2nd edn. Leipzig 1905, repr. Darmstadt 1960), 179). In M he is always simply R. Yehudah (more than 600x) and appears as the main representative of his generation (Sanh 20a 'the generation of Yehudah b. Ilai'). Sanh 86a attributes to him the basis, or the anonymous sayings, of Sifra. Bacher, *Tann* 2:191–228, 237–74; I. Ben-Shalom, 'Rabbi Judah b. Ilai's Attitude towards Rome' (Hebr.), *Zion* 49 (1984) 9–24 (cf. D. Rokéaḥ, *Zion* 52 (1987) 107–10 and once more Ben-Shalom, *ibid.*, 111–13); I. Konovitz, *Rabbi Judah bar Ilai: Collected Sayings* (Hebr.), Jerusalem 1965.

*R. Neḥemyah* frequently appears in controversy with Yehudah bar Ilai. According to Sanh 86a he is the author of the anonymous part of T. Bacher, *Tann* 2:225–74; I. Konovitz, *Tannaitic Symposia,* 4:23–55.

*R. Eleazar ben Shammua*, in M and in the *baraita* always simply R. Eleazar. Born in Alexandria, he visited his teacher Aqiba in prison and later went to Nisibis with Yoḥanan ha-Sandelar in order to study under Yehudah ben Bathyra. Bacher, *Tann* 2:275–82; I. Konovitz, *Tannaitic Symposia*, 1:178–216; Neusner, *Bab* 1:126f.

*R. Eliezer ben Jacob* (the younger one so named, second half of second century) took part in the assembly at Usha after the Bar Kokhba revolt. S. Horovitz (*Siphre*, xviii) is inclined to consider Sifre Zutta as the product of his school. Konovitz, *Tannaitic Symposia*, 1:48–86.

*R. Yoḥanan ha-Sandelar*, 'the sandal-maker'. Others derive his epithet from his native city of Alexandria. Bacher, *Tann* 2:365f.; Neusner, *Bab* 1:126–28.

### *3. Other Teachers of the Same Generation*

*Eliezer* (sometimes Eleazar) *ben R. Yose ha-Gelili* was an acclaimed haggadist (Ḥul 89a). The 32 *Middot* of R. Eliezer are attributed to him (cf. pp. 22ff. above).

*R. Yehoshua ben Qarḥa* (or Qorḥa: 'baldhead') was an eminent haggadist. Bacher, *Tann* 2:308–21.

*R. Eleazar ben Ṣadoq II* was the grandson of Eliezer ben Ṣadoq I, discussed earlier.

*R. Yose ben Yasyan* was a contemporary of Rabban Simeon ben Gamaliel II., also known simply as Ben Yasyan. Bacher, *MGWJ* 45 (1901) 300f. and 46 (1902) 83f. identifies him with Yose beR. Issi in Mek Baḥodesh 3 (L. 2:211); however, all textual witnesses except the Yalqut on that passage read 'beR. Yehudah'.

*Rabban Simeon ben Gamaliel II* was the father of Yehudah ha-Nasi. After Hadrian's death he took over the rabbinic centre which Aqiba's disciples had newly founded at Usha instead of Yabneh. Hor 13b relates the attempt of R. Meir and R. Nathan to depose him. See A. Büchler, 'La conspiration de R. Nathan et R. Méïr contre le Patriarche Simon ben Gamaliel', *REJ* 28 (1894) 60–74; D. Goodblatt, 'The Story of the Plot against R. Simeon B. Gamaliel II' (Hebr.), *Zion* 49 (1984) 349–74 [he considers the story to be essentially a Babylonian fabrication]; Alon, *The Jews in their Land*, 2:667–73; Bacher, *Tann* 2:322–34; Konovitz, *Tannaitic Symposia*, 4:159–228; Neusner, *Bab* 1:73–80. Cf. A. I. Baumgarten, 'The Akiban Opposition', *HUCA* 50 (1979) 179–97, on early developments at Usha.

*R. Ishmael, Son of Yoḥanan ben Beroqa*, belonged to the circle of Rabban Simeon ben Gamaliel II. Bacher, *Tann* 2:369f.; Konovitz, *Tannaitic Symposia*, 3:267–75.

*Abba Saul.* His date is determined by his controversy with Yehudah b. Ilai. Bacher, *Tann* 2:366–69; I. Konovitz, *Tannaitic Symposia*, 1:14–28; I. Lewy, *Über einige Fragmente aus der Mischna des Abba Saul*, Berlin 1876 (cf. also Epstein, *ITL*, 160–63).

*R. Ḥananyah ben Aqabyah* (or Aqiba), probably the son of Aqiba ben Mahalalel; esteemed by Rab for his cleverness (Shab 83b). Bacher, *Tann* 2:370.

*Issi* (abbrev. of Joseph) *ben Yehudah*, a Babylonian, is probably identical with Eleazar ben Shammua's student Issi the Babylonian; also with others, according to Pes 113b. Bacher, *Tann* 2:373–76; M. Hakohen, 'Toldot ha-Tanna Issi ben Yehudah', *Sinai* 33 (1953) 355–64; 34 (1954) 231–40, 325–34, 407–23; Neusner, *Bab* 1:138f., 188–90.

*R. Nehorai*, a contemporary of Yose ben Ḥalafta, probably resided at Sepphoris. Bacher, *Tann* 2:377–83.

*Reuben ben Istrobeli* (according to H. Graetz and S. Krauss: *Strobilos*; according to Bacher, *Aristobulos*). Me'ilah 17a–b tells of his intervention at Rome during the time of the Hadrianic persecution. Bacher, *Tann* 2:383f.; S. Klein, 'Eine Tannaim-Familie in Rom', *Jeschurun* 3 (1916) 442–45.

*Abba Yose ben Dostai* (Dositheos). Bacher, *Tann* 2:388f.

***e) Fourth Generation of Tannaites***

***1. Rabbi's Contemporaries***

*R. Dostai ben Yannay* transmits the sayings of Meir, Yose and Eleazar. He was in Babylonia as the patriarch's emissary. Bacher, *Tann* 2:385–87; Neusner, *Bab* 1:136f.

*R. Simeon ben Yehuda*, from Kefar Ikos (also written K. Akum or K. Akko). Bacher, *Tann* 2:392.

*Aḥai ben Yoshiyyah* taught at Ḥuṣal; after some time in Palestine he returned to Babylonia, where he was Rab's teacher. Bacher, *Tann* 2:393f.; Neusner, *Bab* 1:129–32, 136.

*R. Jacob*, according to Qid 39b the son of Elisha ben Abuya's daughter. During the conspiracy of R. Meir and R. Nathan, he supported Simeon ben Gamaliel. He has the occasional epithet 'ben Korshai'. Bacher, *Tann* 2:395–97.

*Symmachos* (ben Joseph) was a student of R. Meir. Some would identify him with the author of the Greek version of the Bible. Bacher, *Tann* 2.397; D. Barthélemy, 'Qui est Symmaque?', *CBQ* 36 (1974) 451–65 (=idem, *Études d'Histoire du Texte de l'Ancien Testament* (Fribourg/Göttingen 1978), 307–21); J. R. Busto Saiz, *La traducción de Símaco en el libro de los Salmos* (Madrid 1978) 311–23.

*R. Isaac* is often mentioned in Mek and SifreNum. He intervened with R. Nathan against R. Ḥananyah's intercalation in Babylonia. Bacher, *Tann* 2:397–99; Neusner, *Bab* 1:117–21.

*R. Yose ben Kipper* (Neusner: Kefar), a student of Eleazar ben Shammua, appears repeatedly in T. He travelled between Palestine and Babylonia. Bacher, *Tann* 1:386; Neusner, *Bab* 1:116–18.

*R. Dosa* was a tradent of Yehudah bar Ilai. He is not identical with Dosa ben Arḥinos. Bacher, *Tann* 2:389f.

*R. Dostai ben Yehuda* was a tradent of Simeon ben Yoḥai. Bacher, *Tann* 2:390–92.

*R. Eleazar ben Simeon* (ben Yoḥai) is described as a Roman government servant. Bacher, *Tann* 2:400–407; Konovitz, *Tannaitic Symposia*, 1:216–52; S. Krauss, 'R. Eleazar ben R. Simeon als römischer Befehlshaber', *MGWJ* 38 (1894) 151–56; Y. Gutman, 'R. Elazar b. R. Shimon in the Roman Government Service of Palestine' (Hebr.), *Zion* 18 (1953) 1–5; O. Meir, 'On the Hebrew Expression *ḥomeṣ ben yayin*' (Hebr.), *Dappim* 4 (1988) 9–18.

*R. Pinḥas ben Yair* was an ascetic and the son-in-law of R. Simeon ben Yoḥai, apparently resident in Lydda. Midrash Tadshê is occasionally attributed to him. Bacher, *Tann* 2:495–99; O. Meir, 'The She-Ass of R. Pinhas ben Yair', in *Studies in Aggadah and Jewish Folklore*, Folklore

Research Center Studies 7 (Jerusalem 1983), Hebr. section 117–37; on his chain saying in Sot 9.15 see P. Schäfer, *Die Vorstellung vom heiligen Geist in der rabbinischen Literatur* (Munich 1972), 118–21.

*R. Ishmael ben Yose* (ben Ḥalafta). He is supposed to have travelled to Rome with Simeon ben Yoḥai and to have seen the Temple treasure which had been looted by Titus. Bacher, *Tann* 2:412–15.

*R. Menaḥem ben Yose* (ben Ḥalafta), or simply R. Menaḥem. Bacher, *Tann* 2:415f.

*Eurydemos ben Yose* (ben Ḥalafta). Bacher, *Tann* 2:416f.

*R. Yose ben Yehudah* (ben Ilai) often appears in controversy with Rabbi. Bacher, *Tann* 2:417–21; Konovitz, *Tannaitic Symposia*, 3:147–78.

*R. Yehudah ben Laqish* transmits in the name of Simeon ben Gamaliel II, in halakhic controversy with Yose ben Yehudah (ben Ilai). Bacher, *Tann* 2:292f.

*R. Eleazar ben Yehudah.* Bacher, *Tann* 2:417 n.4 considers him to be identical with the teacher of the same name from Bartota.

*R. Simeon ben Eleazar* (ben Shammua), a student of Meir, often disputes with Rabbi, particularly in T. He also engages in controversy with Samaritans. Bacher, *Tann* 2:422–36; Konovitz, *Tannaitic Symposia* 4:117–56; J. Fraenkel, *SH* 27 (1978) 42–50.

*R. Yose ben Meshullam* appears in controversy with Simeon ben Eleazar. Together with Simeon ben Menasyah he apparently led the 'holy congregation' which had formed in Jerusalem by the end of the second century despite the banning of Jews from the city: S. Safrai, 'The Holy Assembly of Jerusalem' (Hebr.), *Zion* 22 (1957) 183–94; idem, 'The Holy Congregation in Jerusalem', *SH* 23 (1972) 62–78; Bacher, *Tann* 2:489.

*R. Nathan* carries the epithet *ha-Babli*, because he had come to Palestine from Babylonia at the time of Simeon ben Gamaliel II. At the latter's court, he exercised important functions together with R. Meir; according to Hor 13b this was due to his father's eminent position in Babylonia (exilarch?). Later he appears in frequent controversy with Rabbi. Occasionally he is regarded as the author of the recension of Abot on which ARN is based. Bacher, *Tann* 2:437–52; M. Beer, *Exilarchate*, 29f.; Konovitz, *Tannaitic Symposia*, 4:58–89; Neusner, *Bab* 1:73–79.

*R. Eleazar* (also attested: Eliezer) *ha-Qappar*. The name is perhaps to be derived from Qefira, a town in the Golan near Dabbura, where an inscription has been discovered: *Eliezer ha-Qappar. Zeh bêt midrashô shel Rabbi.* Or he may be connected with Syriac *qufra*, 'the asphalt dealer', alternatively his name may derive from *kapparis*, 'caper blossom', in which case it designates a producer of drugs or spices from this plant. He is usually regarded as the father of Bar Qappara, who may be the subject of the cited inscription. Others wish to identify the two outright, but this is rather improbable. Bacher, *Tann* 2:500–502; D. Urman, 'Jewish Inscriptions from Dabbura in the Golan', *IEJ* 22 (1972) 16–23; idem, 'Eliezer HaKappar and Bar Kappara – Father and Son?' (Hebr.), *Beer-Sheva* 2 (1985) 7–25.

*R. Simeon ben Yose ben Laqonyah* was Eleazar ben Simeon's brother-in-law, the uncle and educator of Jonathan ben Eleazar (ben Simeon). Bacher, *Tann* 2:488f.

Together with Yose ben Meshullam, *R. Simeon ben Menasyah* led the 'holy congregation' in Jerusalem, which was concerned to divide all its time equally between the study of Torah, prayer and work. Bacher, *Tann* 2:489–94; S. Safrai, *Zion* 22 (1957) 183ff. and *SH* 23 (1972) 62ff.

*R. Mana* (like Mani an abbreviation of Menaḥem) is not to be confused with the two Palestinian Amoraim Mani or Mana.

*R. Yehudah ha-Nasi*, the 'Prince' or 'patriarch', is often simply known as 'Rabbi', sometimes *Rabbenu* or *Rabbenu ha-qadosh*, 'holy' because of his strictly moral way of life. Son of Rabban Simeon ben Gamaliel II; according to tradition he was born on the day of Aqiba's death. He studied under Yehudah ben Ilai, later under Simeon ben Yoḥai and Eleazar ben Shammua as well as Nathan (although subsequently he often contradicts the latter's views). He later resided in Beth Shearim, then in Sepphoris. He brought the institution of the patriarchate to full recognition; his good relations with the Roman authorities are reflected in the legends about 'Antoninus and Rabbi'. Inasmuch as this expresses historical reminiscences, 'Antoninus' is most likely Caracalla, who visited Palestine in the years 199 and 215. Yehudah ha-Nasi, who must be regarded as the actual redactor of M, died in the year 217 (thus A. Guttmann). – Ch. Albeck, *Einleitung*, 145–70; M. Aberbach, 'Hezekiah King of Judah and Rabbi Judah the Patriarch – Messianic Aspects' (Hebr.), *Tarbiz* 53 (1983–84) 353–71. G. Alon, *The Jews in their Land*, 2.705–25; A. I. Baumgarten, 'The Politics of Reconciliation: The Education of R. Judah the Prince', in E. P. Sanders et al. (eds.), *Jewish and Christian Self-Definition*, vol. 2 (London 1981), 213–25, 382–91; idem, 'Rabbi Judah and his Opponents', *JSJ* 12 (1981) 135–72; J. N. Epstein, *ITL*, 180–211; Bacher, *Tann* 2:454–86; A. Guttmann, 'The Patriarch Judah I – His Birth and His Death: A Glimpse into the Chronology of the Talmudic Period', *HUCA* 25 (1954) 239–61; I. Konovitz, *Rabbi Judah ha-Nasi (Rabbi): Collected Sayings* (Hebr.), Jerusalem 1965; S. Krauss, *Antoninus und Rabbi*, Vienna 1910; O. Meir, 'The Story of Rabbi's Death: A Study of Modes of Traditions' Redaction' (Hebr.), *JSHL* 12 (1990) 147–77; G. Stemberger, 'Die Beurteilung Roms in der rabbinischen Literatur', *ANRW* II 19/2 338–96, especially 367–75; J. S. Zuri, *Toldot ha-Mishpat ha-Ṣibburi ha-'Ibri*, vol. 1.2: *Tequfat R. Yehudah ha-Nasi*, Paris 1931.

***f) Fifth Generation of Tannaites***

These are Rabbi's younger contemporaries, and in part his students. They constitute the transition to the period of the Amoraim, in which Rabbi's Mishnah was soon recognized as the authoritative compilation of traditional law.

*Gamaliel III*, the son of Rabbi, who appointed him as his successor in the patriarchate (Ket 103b). A tomb in Beth Shearim bearing the name R. Gamaliel, next to another one with the name R. Simeon, might belong to him and his brother (catacomb 14). Bacher, *Tann* 2:554; A. Wasserstein, 'Rabban Gamaliel and Proclus the Philosopher (Mishna Aboda Zara 3,4)' (Hebr.), *Zion* 45 (1980) 257–67.

*R. Ḥiyya* (probably abbreviated from Aḥiyya) the Elder (Ruba or Rabba). Ḥiyya bar Abba was born in Babylonia, perhaps of the Patriarch's family (he claims Davidic descent). Later he came to Palestine, where he lived at Tiberias and was active in the silk trade. He was a student and friend of Rabbi; uncle and teacher of Rab. Rabbinic tradition repeatedly mentions his collection of Mishnayot. Sherira regards him as the redactor of T; others assign him a leading part in the compilation of Sifra. Ḥul 141a: every *baraita* which has not been edited by R. Ḥiyya or R. Oshayyah is flawed (unreliable). Bacher, *Tann* 2:520–30; A. Engle, *Rabbi Hiyya the Great – Halachist and Travelling Salesman* (Niv Hamidrashia 1972), Engl. section, 63–72; P. Minzberg, *Toldot R. Ḥiyya u-banaw*, Jerusalem 1953; Neusner, *Bab* 1:101–10; E. S. Rosenthal, 'Rab Ben Aḥi, R. Ḥiyya gam Ben Aḥoto (Perat eḥad le-toldot ha-nusaḥ shel ha-Babli)', in S. Lieberman (ed.), *Henoch Yalon: Jubilee Volume* (Hebr.), (Jerusalem 1963), 281–337.

*Bar Qappara* (thus usually in the Talmud), properly R. Eleazar ben Eleazar ha-Qappar (see p. 80 above), also R. Eleazar ha-Qappar beRabbi. He was the teacher of Hoshayah and of Yehoshua ben Levi. His academy in 'the South' was probably at Lydda (but see D. Urman), where in S. Lieberman's opinion he edited Sifre Zutta (*Siphre Zutta* (New York 1968), 104ff.). Rabbinic tradition attributes a Mishnaic collection to him as well. Bacher, *Tann* 2:503–20; D. Urman, 'Regarding the Location of the Batei-Midrash of Bar Kappara and R. Hoshaya Rabbah', (Hebr.), *8th WCJS* (Jerusalem 1982), Hebr. section, 2:9–16.

*R. Simeon ben Ḥalafta*, Ḥiyya's friend, lived in 'En Te'enah near Sepphoris. A haggadist and teller of parables, he was repeatedly exalted in legends. Bacher, *Tann* 2:530–36.

*Levi bar Sisi* (Sosius?), in BT usually just Levi (e.g. Yoma 24a), a student of Rabbi, not to be confused with the Amoraic haggadist R. Levi. Bacher, *Tann* 2:536–39; B. Ratner, 'Die Mischna des Levi ben Sisi', in

*Zikkaron le-Abraham Eliyahu* (*Festschrift* A. Harkavy, St. Petersburg 1908), Hebr. section, 117–22.

*R. Banna'ah,* or Bannayah/Benayah. His main tradent was Yoḥanan bar Nappaḥa. Bacher, *Tann* 2:539–43.

*R. Yose ben Saul,* a student and tradent of Rabbi. Bacher, *PAm* 3:598f.

*Rab Huna* served as exilarch at the time of Rabbi (p.Ket 12.3, 35a). His corpse was brought to Palestine (p.Kil 9, 32b). Beer, *Exilarchate*, 66f., 96f.; Neusner, *Bab* 1:100–108.

For the Babylonian Tannaim see Neusner, *Bab* 1:113–63. Bacher, *Tann* 2:547–61 discusses Tannaim whose date is uncertain.

***g) First Generation of Amoraim***

***1. Palestine***

*R. Ḥama bar Bisa* was the father of one R. Hoshayah (H. Rabbah?). Bacher, *PAm* 1:89f.

*R. Efes* (=Pas), from Southern Judaea, was instituted by Rabbi as as head of the academy at Sepphoris (thus Ket 103b; but cf. p.Taan 4.2, 68a). Bacher, *PAm* 1:2, 91, 341.

*R. Ḥanina* (sometimes Ḥanina bar Ḥama) came to Palestine after studying in Babylonia. He was a student of Rabbi and an eminent teacher at Sepphoris (acc. to Ket 103b he became the successor of R. Efes). Bacher, *PAm* 1:1–34; S. S. Miller, 'R. Ḥanina bar Ḥama at Sepphoris', in L. I. Levine, (ed.), *The Galilee in Late Antiquity* (New York/Jerusalem 1992), 175–200.

*R. Yannai* lived in Sepphoris. He is also called Sabba, 'the Elder', to distinguish him from his grandson of the same name (R. Yannai Ze'ira). He was a student of Ḥiyya, and Yoḥanan's teacher. Bacher, *PAm* 1:35–47; A. Oppenheimer, 'Those of the School of Rabbi Yannai' (Hebr.), *Studies in the History of the Jewish People and the Land of Israel* 4 (Haifa 1978) 137–45.

*Yehudah and Ḥizkiyyah,* the sons of Ḥiyya, came from Babylonia to Palestine with their father. Yehudah was Yannay's son-in-law; Ḥizkiyyah is occasionally regarded as the redactor of MRS. Bacher, *PAm* 1:48–57.

*R. Jonathan ben Eleazar,* usually just R. Jonathan. Originally from Babylonia, he lived at Sepphoris and was close to R. Ḥanina. He was the student of Simeon ben Yose ben Laqonya, and teacher of Samuel bar Naḥman. Bacher, *PAm* 1:58–88.

*Bar Pedayah* (full name: Yehudah bar Pedayah). A nephew of Bar Qappara, he became the teacher of Yehoshua ben Levi. Bacher, *PAm* 1:124f.

*R. Hoshayah* (usually Oshayah in PT). He was the son of Ḥama ben Bisa; to distinguish him from the third-generation Amora, he is also called Hoshayah Rabba ('the Great, the Elder'). He was a student of Bar Qappara and of R. Ḥiyya, and Yoḥanan's teacher. He lived in Sepphoris and later headed a school in Caesarea. Like Ḥiyya and Bar Qappara, he collected Mishnayot. Bacher, *PAm* 1:89–108; D. Barthélemy, 'Est-ce Hoshaya Rabba qui censura le "commentaire allégorique?"', *Colloques Nationaux du CNRS, 'Philon d'Alexandrie' (Lyon 1966)* (Paris 1967), 45–78 (=idem, *Études d'histoire du texte de l'AT* (Fribourg/Göttingen 1978), 140–73); L. I. Levine, *Caesarea*, 76, 87–89, 103f.

*Yehudah II*, son of Gamaliel III, in PT R. Yudan Nesia or R. Yehudah Nesia. As patriarch and Rabbi's grandson, he maintained friendly relations with Hoshayah as well as with Yoḥanan bar Nappaḥa. The patriarchate declined under his leadership, in part because of the sale of judgeships: cf. G. Alon, *Studies*, 374ff.

*R. Yose ben Zimra*. His daughter was married to one of Rabbi's sons. Eleazar ben Pedat transmitted his haggadic sayings. Bacher, *PAm* 1:109–18; Alon, *Studies*, 405f.

*R. Simeon ben Yehoṣadaq*. His sayings were transmitted by Yoḥanan. Bacher, *PAm* 1:119–23.

*R. Yehoshua ben Levi* lived in Lydda. He was one of the most eminent Amoraim of Palestine in the first half of the third century, especially because of his work in the haggadah. A student of Bar Qappara, Yehudah bar Pedayah and Pinḥas ben Yair, he was the teacher of Simeon ben Pazzi and of Tanḥum ben Ḥanilai. Bacher, *PAm* 1:124–94; Y. Frankel, 'The Image of Rabbi Joshua ben Levi in the Stories of the Babylonian Talmud' (Hebr.), *6th WCJS* (Jerusalem 1977) 3:403–17; D. J. Halperin, *The Faces of the Chariot* (Tübingen 1988), 253ff., 307ff.; I. Levy, *La légende de Pythagore de Grèce en Palestine*, (Paris 1927), 154ff.; S. Lieberman, *Shkiîn* (2nd edn. Jerusalem 1970), 34–42 (a story about Yehoshua ben Levi in Petrus Venerabilis, for which the Alphabet of Ben Sira is a likely source); A. Marmorstein, *Jeschurun* 13 (1926) 375–83.

*R. Zabdai ben Levi* belonged to Hoshayah's circle; he conversed with Yehoshua ben Levi, whom he survived, and with Rab. Bacher, *PAm* 3:640–42.

*R. Ḥiyya ben Gamda* lived in Palestine and Babylonia. He transmits in the name of Simai and Yose ben Saul, the last Tannaim.

***2. Babylonia***

*Rab Shêla* was already a respected teacher in Nehardea when Rab returned from Palestine. J. Fraenkel, 'The Story of R. Sheila' (Hebr.), *Tarbiz* 40 (1970–71) 33–40; Neusner, *Bab* 2:32–34, 109–12.

*Abba bar Abba* (usually named 'the father of Samuel' after his famous son) also lived in Palestine, where he maintained a friendship with Levi bar Sisi. Bacher, *BAm* 34; Neusner, *Bab* 2 (Index).

*Ze'iri* or *Zera* the Elder, a Babylonian belonging to Yoḥanan's circle. He was the student of R. Ḥanina (bar Ḥama) and often transmits in his name. It is frequently difficult to distinguish between several Amoraim of this name. Halevi, *Dorot* 2:242–46; Neusner, *Bab* 2:145, 147.

*Qarna*, 'the judge of the diaspora', worked especially on the doctrine of damages (*Neziqin*). Bacher, *BAm* 34f.; Neusner, *Bab* 2 (Index).

*Mar Uqba(n) I* probably served as exilarch around 210–40. He is reported to have presided over the court at Kafri. Neusner, *Bab* 2:98–107; Beer, *Exilarchate*, 65–73 and Index.

*Abba Arikha*, 'the Tall' (probably because of his unusual physical height): properly Abba, he is usually just called *Rab*. He was Ḥiyya's nephew and followed him to Palestine in order to study under Rabbi. According to Geonic tradition (ISG, Lewin, 78–81) he was the founder and head of the rabbinic school at Sura on the Euphrates from the year 219, when he returned from Palestine, until his death in 247. However, historically we cannot speak of an academy but only of a group of disciples around Rab (see Goodblatt, *Instruction*). 'The halakhah in prohibitions is according to the view of Rab, both in more lenient and in more rigorous interpretations' (Nid 24b; cf. Bek 24a). In some places we read of him, 'He counts as a Tanna and may dispute (against the view adopted in M)' (Erub 50b; BB 42a; Sanh 83b). – M. Beer, 'The Political Background of Rav's Activities in Babylonia' (Hebr.), *Zion* 50 (1985) 155–72; I. Konovitz, *Rab – Samuel*, Jerusalem 1974; Neusner, *Bab* 1:105–12, 173f.; 2 passim, especially 2:111–19, 126–34, 180–87, 232–36; J. S. Zuri, *Rab: Biografia Talmudit*, Jerusalem 1925.

*Rabba bar Ḥana*, the son of R. Ḥiyya's brother. Like his cousin Rab he was a student of Rabbi, from whom he received the authority to decide in matters of religious law (Sanh 5a). In printed editions he is often called Rabba bar bar Ḥana (e.g. Ḥul 8b).

*Assi* (Issi, Assa) was highly esteemed by Rab and Samuel (Sanh 29b). Neusner, *Bab* 2 (Index).

*Mar Samuel* (died in 254, according to ISG, Lewin, 82), also called Samuel Yarḥina'ah, 'the astronomer' and 'Ariokh the Great' (BM 85b), son of Abba bar Abba. According to ISG 79f. he was the head of a rabbinic school at Nehardea (cf. Goodblatt, *Instruction*). He is the author of the oft-quoted sentence *dina de-malkhuta dina*: 'The legal decision of (even a non-Jewish) government is valid law' (BQ 113a; cf. S. Shilo, *Dina de-malkhuta Dina*, Jerusalem 1974. He should be distinguished from Mar Samuel Mar(i). M. Beer, *Exilarchate* (Index) and *Exilarchs*, 70–73; B. M. Bokser, *Samuel's Commentary on the Mishnah* 1 (Leiden 1975); idem, *Post-Mishnaic Judaism in Transition: Samuel on Berakhot and the Beginnings of Gemara*, Chico

1980 (cf. E. Segal, *Tarbiz* 51 (1981–82) 315–18); J. Horovitz, 'Mar Samuel und Schabur I.: Zur Erklärung der letzten Zeilen des Talmudtraktats Baba mezia', *MGWJ* 80 (1936) 215–31 (generally on the Talmudic tradition about Shabur: G. A. Wewers, 'Israel zwischen den Mächten: Die rabbinischen Traditionen über König Schabhor', *Kairos* 22 (1980) 77–100); I. Konovitz, *Ma'arekhot ha-Amoraim III: Rab – Samuel*, Jerusalem 1974; Neusner, *Bab* 2 passim, especially 2:64–72, 111–19, 134–44, 232–36; F. Rosner, 'Mar Samuel the Physician', in idem, *Medicine in the Bible and the Talmud* (New York 1973), 156–70.

### *h) Second Generation of Amoraim*

#### *1. Palestine*

*R. Yoḥanan bar Nappaḥa* ('the blacksmith'), usually just R. Yoḥanan. His chief teachers were Yannay, Hoshayah and Ḥanina ben Ḥama; among his peers Simeon b. Laqish is the most eminent. Another of his contemporaries was Rab Yehudah bar Yeḥezqel (Pes 118a). Yoḥanan first taught at his birthplace Sepphoris and later at Tiberias. ISG 83f. records that by the time of his death in 279 he had been head of an academy (*malakh*) for 80 years. Maimonides attributes to him the redaction of the PT. Bacher, *PAm* 1:205–339; Z. M. Dor, *Teachings*; R. R. Kimelman, *R. Yohanan of Tiberias: Aspects of the Social and Religious History of Third Century Palestine*, Diss. New Haven, CT: Yale University, 1977; idem, 'Problems in Late Rabbinic "Biography": The Case of the Amora Yohanan', in P. J. Achtemeier (ed.), *SBL Seminar Papers* 2 (1979) 35–42; idem, 'Rabbi Yoḥanan and Origen on the Song of Songs: A Third Century Jewish-Christian Disputation' *HTR* 73 (1980) 567–95; idem, 'The Conflict between R. Yohanan and Resh Laqish on the Supremacy of the Patriarchate' *7th WCJS* (Jerusalem 1981) 3:1–20; I. Konovitz, *Ma'arekhot ha-Amoraim*, vol. 1: *Rabbi Yoḥanan – Resh Laqish*, Jerusalem 1973; J. S. Zuri, *R. Jochanan, der erste Amoräer Galiläas*, Berlin 1918.

*R. Simeon ben Laqish*, usually called Resh Laqish. He was married to Yoḥanan's sister and like him lived in Tiberias, but died earlier. Bacher, *PAm* 1:340–418; M. Z. Brettler & M. Poliakoff, 'Rabbi Simeon ben Lakish at the Gladiator's Banquet: Rabbinic Observations on the Roman Arena', *HTR* 83 (1990) 93–98; I. Konovitz, *Ma'arekhot ha-Amoraim* 1: *Rabbi Yoḥanan – Resh Laqish*, Jerusalem 1973; I. Unna, *R. Simon ben Lakish, als Lehrer der Halakha und Agada*, Frankfurt 1921; A. Wasserstein, 'A Good Man Fallen Among Robbers' (Hebr.), *Tarbiz* 49 (1979–80) 197f.

*R. Isaac ben Eleazar*, usually Isaac ben Ḥaqola. He was a contemporary of R. Yehoshua ben Levi and of R. Yoḥanan (Yoma 78a). According to MQ 25b he delivered a eulogy at Yoḥanan's funeral.

*R. Alexander* (or Alexandrai) transmitted sayings of Yehoshua ben Levi, and thus cannot be included in the first Amoraic generation. Bacher, *PAm* 1:195–204.

*Rab Kahana* (in PT invariably without the title). A student of Rab, he came from Babylonia to Palestine, where he belonged to the circle of Yoḥanan and Simeon ben Laqish. The sermon collection usually known as PRK is in fact of a later date. No fewer than six Babylonian Amoraim were called R. Kahana; three of them also came to Palestine. Bacher, *PAm* 3:607–9; Neusner, *Bab* 2 (Index); D. Sperber, 'On the Unfortunate Adventures of Rav Kahana', in S. Shaked (ed.), *Irano-Judaica* (Jerusalem 1982), 83–100.

*R. Ḥiyya bar Joseph* also migrated from Babylonia to Palestine, where he became Yoḥanan's student; he is repeatedly mentioned in discussion with the latter. Bacher, *PAm* 3:560.

*R. Yose ben Ḥanina* (not to be confused with the Tanna of the same name) was an older student of Yoḥanan; controversies between these two are also extant. His most important student was Abbahu. Bacher, *PAm* 1:419–26; J. S. Zuri, *Rabbi Yose bar Ḥanina me-Qisrin*, Jerusalem 1926.

*R. Ḥama bar Ḥanina*, son of Ḥanina bar Ḥama at Sepphoris. Bacher, *PAm* 1:447–76.

*R. Me'asha*, Yehoshua ben Levi's grandson. Bacher, *PAm* 3:614–16.

*R. Simlai* (Samlai), son of Abba, came from Nehardea and then lived at Lydda (Rab already calls him an inhabitant of Lydda), and later in Galilee with Yannay at Sepphoris. His sayings were transmitted by R. Tanḥum bar Ḥiyya. Bacher, *PAm* 2:552–66; Neusner, *Bab* 2:144; B. Rosenfeld, 'The Activity of Rabbi Simlai: A Chapter in the Relations between Eretz Israel and the Diaspora in the Third Century' (Hebr.), *Zion* 48 (1983) 227–39 (Simlai as the patriarch's emissary); for his controversies with Minim see A. F. Segal, *Two Powers in Heaven* (Leiden 1977), Index.

*R. Jonathan of Beth Gubrin* (Eleutheropolis), transmits a saying of Yehoshua ben Levi. Bacher, *PAm* 3:592–94.

*Mani I*, also known as Mani bar Tanḥum, was Yoḥanan's contemporary. Bacher, *PAm* 3:444, 612, 751.

*Reuben* was an eminent haggadist, a contemporary of Mani I, and transmitted sayings of Ḥanina bar Ḥama. His tradents were Bebai and Pinḥas. Bacher, *PAm* 3:79–86.

*R. Abba* (or Ba) *Bar Zabdai* (or Zabda) spent a short time also in Babylonia. He survived Rab Huna of Sura and still belonged to the circle of Ammi and Assi in Tiberias. Bacher, *PAm* 3:533–55.

*R. Tanḥum ben Ḥanilai*, in PT usually corrupted to Ilai, was a tradent of Yehoshua ben Levi. He belongs in part already to the third generation. Bacher, *PAm* 3:627–36.

***2. Babylonia***

Y. Florsheim, 'The Relationships amongst Second Generation Babylonian Amoraim' (Hebr.), *Zion* 51 (1986) 281–93.

*Rab Huna* (died in 297 according to ISG) was Sura's most eminent teacher after Rab. Various texts suggest an exilarch Huna II, though the latter's existence is uncertain; he is perhaps to be identified with Rab Huna. Bacher, *BAm* 52–60; Beer, *Exilarchate*, 77f., 92–97, 108f.; I. Konovitz, *Ma'arekhot ha-Amoraim*, vol. 3: *Rab Huna – Rab Hisda*, Jerusalem 1977; Neusner, *Bab* 3:48–53 and Index.

*Rab Yehudah bar Yeḥezqel* (died in 299 according to ISG), usually just Rab Yehudah. A student of Rab, he was a distinguished teacher at Pumbeditha, and after Rab Huna's death the most important teacher of Babylonia. In Qid 72a he is counted among those who kept the study of Torah from being forgotten. The meaning of his epithet 'Shinena' (Qid 33b) is uncertain: Hai Gaon reads 'with great teeth'; Bacher relates it to iron endurance, others to keen intellect. He was concerned particularly with Neziqin. Nid 24b mentions his tall stature. Bacher, *BAm* 47–52; Neusner, *Bab* 2 (Index).

*Efa and Abimi*, 'the keen intellects' (*Ḥarifin*), of Pumbeditha. L. Bank, 'Les gens subtils de Poumbedita', *REJ* 39 (1899) 191–98.

*Mar Uqba(n) II* served as exilarch like his grandfather Mar Uqba I. On his mother's side he was also a grandson of Rab. He transmitted sayings of Samuel. Neusner, *Bab* 2:98–107; 3:48–50, 54–58.

*Giddel* was a younger student of Rab and often transmitted in his name. Bacher, *PAm* 3:564f.

*Rab Qattina and Geniba*, both at Sura, were also Rab's students. Because of his opposition to the Persian authorities, Geniba was handed over to execution by the exilarch: Neusner, *Bab* 3:75–81.

*Rab Adda (Ada) bar Ahaba*, at Sura, was reputedly born on the day of Rabbi's death (Qid 72a–b). He was a student of Rab and became famous on account of his long life and piety, being regarded as a miracle worker. He is considered to be the author of the *baraita* deRab Adda on intercalation, which was still cited in the fourteenth century. Bacher, *BAm* 74f.; Neusner, *Bab* 2 and 3 (Index).

*Rabbah bar Abuha*, Rab Naḥman's father-in-law, was related to the exilarch's family. Neusner, *Bab* 3:58–61 and Index.

*Rab Mattena* was a student of Samuel and then probably of Rab Yehudah. Bacher, *BAm* 83–85; Neusner, *Bab* 3 (Index).

*Rab Yirmeyah bar Abba*, in PT Rab Yirmeyah bar Wa or simply R.Y., was an older student of Rab and lived in Palestine for a time. Bacher, *BAm* 7, 51 and *PAm* 3:582f.; Neusner, *Bab* 2 and 3 (Index).

***i) Third Generation of Amoraim***

***1. Palestine***

*R. Samuel bar Naḥman* (in BT and sometimes in PT: bar Naḥmani) was a student of Jonathan ben Eleazar and a highly respected haggadist working in Tiberias. He was born in Palestine, but went to Babylonia on two occasions: once for a longer period in his youth, and later on an official mission to enact the intercalation in Babylonia. His main student and tradent was Ḥelbo. Bacher, *PAm* 1:477–551.

*R. Isaac II*, in BT often with the epithet Nappaḥa 'the blacksmith', was a student of Yoḥanan and worked partly in Tiberias, partly (probably later) in Caesarea. He also spent some time in Babylonia, where he conversed especially with Naḥman b. Jacob. He was one of the most prolific haggadists (often in controversy with Levi), but also a respected halakhist. Bacher, *BAm* 79f., 86 and *PAm* 2:205–95; Levine, *Caesarea* (Index); Neusner, *Bab* 3 (Index).

*R. Levi* was the student of Yoḥanan and an eminent haggadist. Bacher, *PAm* 2:296–436.

*R. Eleazar ben Pedat*, usually without the patronym (not to be confused with the Tannaite Eleazar ben Shammua); in PT (except in Ber) he appears as Leazar. He enjoyed instruction from Samuel and Rab in his native Babylonia, and from Yoḥanan in Palestine. From the latter he received the leadership of the school at Tiberias, but died in the same year, 279 (ISG). His main tradents were Abbahu and Benjamin ben Yefet. Bacher, *PAm* 2:1–87; Epstein, *ITM* 292–307.

*R. Abbahu*, one of Yoḥanan's later students as well as a student of Yose ben Ḥanina, was head of the school of Caesarea. He was conversant in Greek language and culture and had controversies with Minim (Christians?). S. Lieberman dates his death to the year 309 (in *Salo Wittmayer Baron: Jubilee Volume on the Occasion of his Eightieth Birthday* (Jerusalem 1975), 3:239–41 (Hebr.); repr. in *Studies*, 374–76); Bacher, *PAm* 2:88–142; S. T. Lachs, 'Rabbi Abbahu and the Minim', *JQR* N.S. 60 (1969–70) 197–212; L. I. Levine, 'Rabbi Abbahu of Caesarea' (Hebr.), *6th WCJS* (Jerusalem 1975) 2:47–50; idem, 'R. Abbahu of Caesarea', in J. Neusner (ed.), *Christianity, Judaism and other Greco-Roman Cults: Studies for Morton Smith at Sixty* (Leiden 1975), 4:56–75; idem, *Caesarea* (Index); J. Maier, *Jesus*, 80ff.

*R. Ammi* (ben Nathan), in PT also Immi, a student of Yoḥanan and Hoshayah. He was a highly respected teacher in Tiberias and is frequently mentioned together with Assi and Ḥiyya II, both contemporaries of the Emperor Diocletian. On Ammi and Assi see Bacher, *PAm* 2:143–73; Neusner, *Bab* 3 (Index).

*R. Assi* (thus BT; PT usually Yose, but also Assa, Assi or Issi: the name seems to be a diminutive of Joseph) immigrated from Babylonia, where he had been Samuel's student. In Palestine he became Yoḥanan's student. Neusner, *Bab* 3 (Index).

*R. Yehudah III* the Patriarch, in PT R. Yehudah Nesia or R. Yudan Nesia, was the son of the insignificant Gamaliel IV, and a student of Yoḥanan. He charged Ammi and Assi with the establishment of schools for children. During his time the emperor Diocletian visited Palestine. L. I. Levine, 'The Jewish Patriarch (Nasi) in Third Century Palestine', *ANRW* II 19/2 (Berlin 1979), 649–88.

*R. Ḥiyya II bar Abba*, probably the brother of Simeon b. Abba, immigrated to Palestine from Babylonia in his youth and there became a student chiefly of Yoḥanan. Bacher, *BAm* 86f. and *PAm* 2:174–201.

*R. Simeon* (in Palestine with the Hellenized name Simon), in Babylonia called Simeon ben Pazzi, was a student and tradent of Yehoshua ben Levi. He lived in the South and is often in discussion with Ḥanina ben Papa, the teacher of Tanḥum ben Ḥiyya and of Ḥilqiyah, who frequently transmits in his name. Bacher, *PAm* 2:437–74.

*R. Zera I*, a Babylonian and a student of Rab Yehudah bar Yeḥezqel, against whose will he moved to Palestine. There he was in close contact with Ammi, Assi, and Abbahu. Zera's students include Yirmeyah, Abba b. Zebina and Ḥaggai. He should not be confused with the later Palestinian Zera, who was a student of Yirmeyah. He was no friend of the haggadah: 'The haggadah can be turned this way and that, and we learn nothing (practical) from it' (p.Maas 3, 51a). Bacher, *PAm* 3:1–34; L. Bank, 'Rabbi Zeira et Rab Zeira' *REJ* 38 (1899) 47–63 (he distinguishes three men of this name: two Babylonians, viz., the student of Rab Yehudah and a contemporary of Abbaye and of Rabba, and the Palestinian); Abr. Goldberg, 'Rabbi Ze'ira and Babylonian Custom in Palestine' (Hebr.), *Tarbiz* 36 (1966–67) 319–41.

*R. Abba II*, a Babylonian and a student of Rab Huna and of Rab Yehuda, repeatedly travelled to Palestine and eventually settled there: first in Caesarea (in contact with Abbahu), then in Tiberias (in contact with Ammi and Assi). Bacher, *PAm* 3:517–25.

*R. Samuel bar R. Isaac*, a student of Ḥiyya II bar Abba, Hoshayah II's father-in-law, spent some time in Babylonia in the circle of Rab Huna. His most significant student and tradent was Yirmeyah. Bacher, *PAm* 3:34–54.

Next to Zera I, *R. Hela* (or Ela) was the most important scholar in early fourth-century Tiberias. Zera I called him 'builder of the teaching of the law', i.e. a great scholar (p.Yoma 3, 40c; p.Git 7, 48d). He was a teacher of Abin I, of Yonah and Yose. Bacher, *PAm* 3:600–702.

*R. Zeriqa* (in PT also Zeriqan) was a student of Eleazar ben Pedat and of Ammi, and conversed with Yirmeyah and Yehudah bar Simon. Bacher, *PAm* 3:754f.

*Hoshayah* (II) and *Ḥananyah* were non-ordained brothers from Babylonia who were known as *ḥabrehon de-rabbanan*, 'companions of the scholars'. They were students of Yoḥanan at Tiberias, where they made a living as shoemakers. Both were glorified in later legend. Hoshayah became a son-in-law of Samuel bar Isaac. Bacher, *PAm* 3:550–52, 565.

*R. Yoshiyyah*, a student of Yoḥanan and of Rab Kahana. To distinguish him from the second-generation Amora of the same name at Ḥuṣal, he is repeatedly called the 'contemporary of Eleazar (ben Pedat)'. Bacher, *PAm* 3:599–603.

*R. Abba bar Memel*, in PT R. Ba, a respected halakhist. He conversed with Zera I, Samuel b. Isaac and Yirmeyah; Yose bar Abin transmits in his name. Bacher, *PAm* 3:530–32.

*R. Jacob bar Idi*, a student of Yoḥanan. Bacher, *PAm* 3:571f.

*R. Isaac bar Naḥman*, a student of Yehoshua ben Levi. Bacher, *PAm* 1:131; 3:440.

*R. Bebai* (cf. Ezra 2.11), a student of Abbahu, to be distinguished from the roughly contemporary Babylonian Amora. Bacher, *PAm* 3:667–69.

*R. Abba bar Kahana*, a student of Yoḥanan and an eminent haggadist. His main tradent was Berekhyah. Bacher, *PAm* 2:475–512; A. Marmorstein, *Jeschurun* 13 (1926) 369–75.

*R. Ḥanina b. Pappai* (thus BT, an Aramaization of Pappos; in PT mostly Ḥinena, in the midrashim mostly Ḥanina b. Pappa). A student of Samuel b. Naḥman, he often debated with Simon ben Pazzi. He worked in Caesarea alongside Abbahu, and temporarily in Babylonia. He is repeatedly glorified in legends. Bacher, *PAm* 2:513–32.

*R. Benjamin ben Levi* was mainly a haggadist. His tradents were Yudan and Huna. Bacher, *PAm* 3:661–66.

*R. Aḥa b. Ḥanina* engaged in controversies with Ḥanina b. Pappai and transmitted statements e.g. of Yoḥanan and Yehoshua ben Levi. He also spent some time in Babylonia. Bacher, *PAm* 3:504–506.

*Tanḥum b. Ḥiyya* of Kefar Akko lived in Tiberias. He was a student of Simon ben Pazzi and conversed with Assi and Ḥanina b. Pappai. Bacher, *PAm* 3:636–39.

*R. Abba of Akko* was known for his modesty. Bacher, *PAm* 3:526.

***2. Babylonia***

*Rab Huna b. Ḥiyya* was the successor of R. Yehudah b. Yeḥezqel at Pumbeditha. Beer, *Exilarchate*, 101–3; Neusner, *Bab* 4:95–97.

*Rab Ḥisda*, d. 309, a student and friend of Rab Huna, was the most important teacher at Sura after the death of Rab Yehudah. He was chiefly a haggadist, and famous for his astute discussions (Erub 67a: *pilpulê deRab Ḥisda*). Bacher, *BAm* 61–71; J. Florsheim, *R. Chisda's place in Seder Moed of the Babylonian and Palestinian Talmuds* (Hebr.), Diss. Jerusalem 1970; idem, 'Rav Ḥisda as Exegetor of Tannaitic Sources' (Hebr.), *Tarbiz* 41 (1971f.) 24–48; idem, 'Le-Toldot Ḥayyâw shel Rab Ḥisda', *Sinai* 71 (1972) 121–31; I. Konovitz, *Ma'arekhot ha-Amoraim*, vol. 3: *Rab Huna – Rab Hisda*, Jerusalem 1977; Neusner, *Bab* 3 passim (Index).

For 13 years after Ḥisda's death, *Rabbah bar Rab Huna* was the most important teacher at Sura; he died in 322. Neusner, *Bab* 3 (Index), 4:107–9 and Index; Bacher, *BAm* 62f.

*Rab Sheshet* was first in Nehardea as a student of Samuel. He then moved to Maḥoza and later taught at Shilhi. He had a large volume of the traditional teaching committed to memory (Erub 67a; Shebu 41b). Bacher, *BAm* 76–79; Neusner, *Bab* 3 and 4 (Index).

*Rami (R. Ammi) bar Abba*, alongside Eleazar ben Pedat and Ḥiyya II (Beṣa 25b). Several of his haggadic sentences appear in Ned 32a, b; Meg 15b.

*Rab Naḥman bar Jacob* (d. 320), usually just Rab Naḥman, was a student of Samuel, under whom his father served as a court clerk (BM 16b). Naḥman was the son-in-law of Rabba b. Abuha in Maḥoza, and the guest of the Palestinian Isaac II. Discussion in his house often dealt with the Masorah. Bacher, *BAm* 79–83; Neusner, *Bab* 3:61–75 and passim; 4 (Index).

*Rabbah* (PT Abba) *bar bar Ḥana* (his father was called Abba bar Ḥana, hence the doubled *bar*) spent some time in Palestine, and was later at Pumbeditha and Sura. R. became known especially for his fantastical travel accounts (BB 73a–74a). Bacher, *BAm* 87–93; Neusner, *Bab* 3 (Index).

*Ulla bar Ishmael* (in BT Ulla without patronym, in both BT and PT without title) emigrated from Palestine to Babylonia, but repeatedly returned to visit his native country. Bacher, *BAm* 93–97; Neusner, *Bab* 3 (Index).

*Rabba(h) bar Naḥmani*, or simply Rabbah, d. 330, succeeded Rab Huna bar Ḥiyya as the most important teacher and (according to tradition) director of the academy at Pumbeditha. He was probably never in Palestine. Because of his sharp dialectical style he was called 'uprooter of mountains' (*oqer harim*). Bacher, *BAm* 97–101; M. Beer, 'The Removal of Rabba bar Nachmani from the Office of Head of the Academy' (Hebr.), *Tarbiz* 33 (1963–

64) 349–57; Neusner, *Bab* 4 (Index); D. Sperber, 'Ha–'im 'alah Rabbah le-Ereṣ Yisra'el?', *Sinai* 71 (1972) 140–45.

*Rab Raḥba* of Pumbeditha was a tradent of his teacher Yehudah bar Yeḥezqel. Pes 13b, 52b.

*Rab Joseph* (bar Ḥiyya), d. 333, was given the honorary epithet 'Sinai' because of his extensive knowledge of the traditional law. After Rabbah's death he is supposed to have directed the school at Pumbeditha. The redaction of a (partial) Aramaic translation of the Bible is attributed to him. He is also known as a merkabah mystic. Bacher, *BAm* 101–7.

### *j) Fourth Generation of Amoraim*

#### *1. Palestine*

*R. Yirmeyah*, originally from Babylonia, was a student of Zera I and after the latter's death became the recognized authority of the school of Tiberias. He transmitted sayings of Ḥiyya II bar Abba and taught Ḥizqiyyah, Yonah, Yose, and Zera II. Bacher, *PAm* 3:95–106.

*R. Ḥaggai*, also a student of Zera, was a respected member of the academy at Tiberias. He was Jonathan's father and tradent of Isaac II. Bacher, *PAm* 3:670–73. His cousin Jacob of Kefar Niburaya is often alleged to have connections with Jewish Christians: Bacher, *PAm* 3:709–11; O. Irsai, 'Ya'akov of Kefar Niburaia: A Sage turned Apostate' (Hebr.), *Jerusalem Studies in Jewish Thought* 2 (1982–83) 153–68.

*R. Ḥelbo*, a student of Samuel bar Naḥman, was close to Ammi and spent some time in Babylonia with Rab Huna. His student was Berekhyah. Bacher, *PAm* 3:54–63.

*R. Aḥa* of Lydda was later in Tiberias, studied under Yose b. Ḥanina and Tanḥum b. Ḥiyya and was the teacher of Huna b. Abin. He was respected in the areas of halakhah and especially of haggadah. Bacher, *PAm* 3:106–60.

*R. Abin* I (in PT also Abun and Bun), or abbreviated Rabin (thus usually in BT), came from Babylonia, where later he also lived for a long time. He was a friend of Abaye (d. 338). His teachers were Assi and Hela; his tradents, Yudan, Huna, Pinḥas (b. Ḥama) and Berekhyah. In many cases it is impossible to distinguish him from his son of the same name, who was born on the day of his death. Bacher, *PAm* 3:397–432. D. Urman, 'Jewish Inscriptions of the Mishna and Talmud Period from Kaẓrin in the Golan' (Hebr.), *Tarbiz* 53 (1983–84) 513–45, wants to apply to this rabbi the epitaph *Rabbi Abun, Mishkabo be-Shalom* (pp. 542–44); but this is doubtful.

*R. Samuel b. Ammi.* Primarily haggadic sayings are preserved of him. Bacher, *PAm* 3:681–85.

*R. Ḥanina b. Aḥa* was probably the son of Aḥa b. Ḥanina. Bacher, *PAm* 3:679f.

*R. Ḥanin* (Ḥanan) of Sepphoris transmitted for Samuel b. Naḥman; his tradent was Pinḥas. Bacher, *PAm* 3:674–76.

*R. Yudan* often transmits earlier authorities. He was the student of Abba II (R. Ba) and teacher of Mana II. Bacher, *PAm* 3:237–72.

*R. Huna* (also called Ḥuna, Ḥunya or Neḥunya), whose full name is R. Huna b. Abin, was a student and tradent of Yirmeyah and Aḥa. Alongside Yose, he was one of the authorities of the school of Tiberias. He lived for a while in Babylonia and frequently debates with Yudan about haggadic matters. His main student was Tanḥuma bar Abba. Bacher, *PAm* 3:272–302.

*R. Yehudah bar Simon* was also known as the son of Simon ben Pazzi. In PT he also appears in the short form Yehudah ben Pazzi, and frequently just R. Yehudah. He came from Lydda and was a student of his father Simon b. P. and of Zera. He was involved in controversies, particularly with Aibo. Bacher, *PAm* 3:160–220.

*R. Aibo* debates with Yehudah bar Simon. Bacher, *PAm* 3:63–79.

*R. Yehoshua ben Neḥemyah* was exclusively a haggadist and appears almost solely in midrashic literature. Bacher, *PAm* 3:303–9.

*R. Ḥanina b. Abbahu* was the son of the academic head of Caesarea. He appears once in short as Ḥanina of Caesarea. Bacher, *PAm* 3:676–79.

*R. Ahaba* (or Aḥawa) ben Zera was the son of Zera I in Caesarea, where Mani II heard his lectures. He was primarily a haggadist. Bacher, *PAm* 3:656–59.

*R. Dimi* or Abudimi (the 'voyager to Babylonia' *naḥota*, who presented Palestinian teachings and traditions at Pumbeditha, especially in the presence of Abaye). Bacher, *PAm* 3:691–93.

*Hillel II*, Patriarch (c. 330–65), was the son of the Patriarch Yehudah III. He appears only twice in connection with halakhot (p.Ber 1, 5a; p.Ter 1, 41a). He is credited with the introduction of a fixed calendar in the year 358, although this tradition is first attested in 1122 by Abraham bar Hiyya with reference to Hai Gaon. He is probably the Patriarch mentioned in the synagogue inscription of Ḥammat Tiberias. During his lifetime Julian attempted to rebuild the Temple. E. Mahler, *Handbuch der jüdischen Chronologie* (Frankfurt 1916; repr. Hildesheim 1967), 455–79; M. Schwabe, 'A New Document relating to the History of the Jews in the 4th Century C.E.: Libanius ep. 1251 (F)' (Hebr.), *Tarbiz* 1.3 (1930) 107–21. Libanius's other letters to a Patriarch (cf. M. Schwabe, *Tarbiz* 1.2 (1930) 85–110) probably concern Hillel's son, Gamaliel V.

### *2. Babylonia*

*Abaye* lived c. 280–339 and was the son of Kailil, who was a brother of

Rabba(h) bar Naḥmani. He was a student of this Rabba(h), and especially of Joseph, whom according to ISG he succeeded as head of the academy at Pumbeditha for five years. Bacher, *BAm* 107–13; D. Hanschke, 'Abbaye and Rava – Two Approaches to the Mishna of the Tannaim' (Hebr.), *Tarbiz* 49 (1979–80) 187–93; R. Kalmin, 'Friends and Colleagues, or Barely Acquainted? Relations Between Fourth-Generation Masters in the Babylonian Talmud', *HUCA* 61 (1990) 125–58; Y. L. Maimon, 'Le-toldot Abaye', in *Sefer Yovel le-Rabbi Ḥanokh Albeck* (Jerusalem 1963), 306–23; Neusner, *Bab* 4 (Index).

*Raba*, d. 352, whose full name was Raba bar Joseph bar Ḥama, studied under Rab Naḥman (bar Jacob) and Rab Joseph. He taught at Maḥoza on the Tigris. Talmudic dialectics reached its high point under Abaye and Raba; the BT devotes a great deal of space to their debates. Except in a few cases, the halakhah decided for Raba and against Abaye (Erub 15a; Sanh 27a). Ch. Albeck, 'Raba ha-shenî', in *Festschrift Dr. Jakob Freimann zum 70. Geburtstag* (Berlin 1937), Hebr. section, 1–71 (he distinguishes this Raba from another who belonged to the late Amoraim, towards the end of Rabina and R. Ashi's lifetime); Dor, *Teachings*, 11–78; Neusner, *Bab* 4 (Index); M. Weiss, 'Amar Raba matnitin qashiteh – mai irya: A Study of Talmudic Terminology' (Hebr.), *Tarbiz* 51 (1981–82) 543–65 (like Albeck he assumes a second Raba in the fourth or fifth generation).

*R. Adda II bar Ahaba*, a contemporary and student of Abaye and Raba: BB 22a; Taan 8a.

*Rab Naḥman bar Isaac*, d. 356, studied together with Raba under Naḥman bar Jacob. After Raba's death he became head of the academy at Pumbeditha (thus ISG). Since Rab N. bar Isaac is also known for short as Rab Naḥman, it is sometimes difficult to distinguish him from his teacher N. bar Jacob. Bacher, *BAm* 133–37; Neusner, *Bab* 4 (Index).

*R. Rami bar Ḥama*, Ḥisda's son-in-law and student, d. around 350. Neusner, *Bab* 4 (Index).

*R. Idi bar Abin I*, student of Ḥisda, lived around 350 in Naresh and later in Shekhanṣib.

*R. Joseph bar Ḥama* in Maḥoza was R. Sheshet's student.

*Rabbah bar Mari* was a Babylonian who spent some time in Palestine. Bacher, *BAm* 124–27; Neusner, *Bab* 4:381–83 and Index.

*R. Aḥa bar Jacob* in Pafunya (probably Epiphaneia, in the district of Pumbeditha). Bacher, *BAm* 137–39.

### *k) Fifth Generation of Amoraim*

#### *1. Palestine*

*R. Yonah* was a student of Yirmeyah and Hela. Yonah and Yose II were the heads of the academy at Tiberias around 350, at the time of Ursicinus (who after 351 was a general of Gallus, the Caesar of the Orient under Constantius). Bacher, *PAm* 3:220–31; Epstein, *ITM* 395–99.

*R. Yose II bar Zabda*, also a student of Hela. Bacher, *PAm* 3:231–37.

*R. Yehudah IV* the Patriarch (c. 385–400) was the son of Gamaliel V and grandson of Hillel II. With his son Gamaliel VI, the patriarchate ceased in Palestine.

*R. Pinḥas* (full name: Pinḥas bar Ḥama), a student of Yirmeyah, belonged to the circle of Yose and was a contemporary of the patriarch Yehudah IV. Bacher, *PAm* 3:310–44.

*R. Ḥizqiyyah*, a student of Yirmeyah, presided over the academy in Caesarea. Bacher, *PAm* 3:690f.

*R. Berekhyah* (in the midrashim often B. ha-Kohen) was a student of Ḥelbo and is very frequently cited as a tradent. Bacher, *PAm* 3:344–96.

*R. Yose bar Abin* (Abun), also known as Yose beR. Bun, was the last eminent halakhist in Palestine, and the teacher of Abin II. N. Aminoah, 'An Inquiry into the Talmudic Tradition of R. Jose Bé R. Bun' (Hebr.), *8th WCJS* (Jerusalem 1982) C:13–18; Bacher, *PAm* 3:449, 724–29.

*R. Abin II* was born the day his father Abin I died. In the third and fourth orders of PT he frequently appears alongside Mani II; he is also often found in the Tanḥuma midrashim. Bacher, *PAm* 3:397f., 404, 407.

*R. Mani II* or Mana (abbreviation of Menaḥem), son of Yonah, studied under Yose II, Ḥizqiyyah and Yudan. He lived and taught mostly at Sepphoris. His most important student was the haggadist Azaryah; his main tradent, Naḥman. He repeatedly appears in PT. Bacher, *PAm* 3:397, 433–57.

*R. Ḥananyah* II (also Ḥanina) of Sepphoris often appears in connection with Mani, in whose favour he declined the honour of head of the academy. Bacher, *PAm* 3:673f., 446f.

*R. Tanḥum(a) bar Abba* (more precisely: Berabbi Abba), a student of Huna, systematically collected the haggadah. His midrashic compilations have frequently been regarded as the basis for PRK, PesR, and the Tanḥuma-Yelamdenu midrashim. He was the last of the more eminent Palestinian haggadists. Bacher, *PAm* 3:465–511.

*R. Naḥman* was a student and tradent of Mani II (to be distinguished from the older Naḥman, the son of Samuel b. N., and from the Babylonian Rab N. bar Jacob). Bacher, *PAm* 3:739–43.

*R. Azaryah*, a student of Mani II, transmits sayings of Yehudah bar Simon. Bacher, *PAm* 3:458–65.

*Ulla II* appears several times in PT (not in BT). He was a younger contemporary of Raba, and later emigrated from Palestine to Babylonia. In 1986, excavations near Tiberias uncovered a basalt block on which one R.

Ulla and his brother are named as benefactors of the synagogue: see Z. Ilan, *Excavations and Surveys in Israel* 6 (1987–88) 110.

*Zera II*, a student of Yirmeyah, belonged to the circle of Mani. Bacher, *PAm* 3:17, 99, 106, 225, 449.

### *2. Babylonia*

*Rab Papa bar Ḥanan* (d. 375), a student of Abaye and Raba, founded a school at Naresh near Sura. He often cites popular proverbs. Bacher, *BAm* 141–43; Dor, *Teachings*, 79–115; idem, 'The Palestinian Tradition and the Halakhic Teaching of Rabbi Pappa' (Hebr.), *4th WCJS* (Jerusalem 1967) 1:157–62; Neusner, *Bab* 4 (Index). M. Schiff, *The Contribution of Rav Pappa to the Redaction of 'Talmud' (according to the Tractates of Seder Moed)* (Hebr.), Diss. Tel Aviv 1979.

*Rab Huna, son of Rab Yehoshua*, like Papa a student of Raba, was learned and wealthy. Bacher, *BAm* 141; Neusner, *Bab* 4 (Index).

*Rab Bebai bar Abaye*. There are numerous legends about his dealings with the angel of death and with demons.

*Rab Ḥama in Nehardea*, Sanh 17b. According to ISG, he led the academy at Pumbeditha for 21 years after the death of Rab Naḥman bar Isaac; d. 377. Neusner, *Bab* 5 (Index).

*R. Papi* was a student of Raba and teacher of Ashi. He lived at Maḥoza and had good relations with the exilarch.

*Dimi of Nehardea* was academic head at Pumbeditha from 385 to 388 (according to ISG).

*Rafram I* ben Papa, in Pumbeditha, was a student of Rab Ḥisda and Dimi's successor.

*Rab Zebid*, also called Z. of Nehardea, led the school of Pumbeditha from 377 to 385 (according to ISG). Neusner, *Bab* 5 (Index).

### *l) Sixth Generation of Amoraim in Babylonia*

*Amemar*, a teacher of Ashi, re-established and for a long time directed the school at Nehardea (according to ISG). Bacher, *BAm* 146; Neusner, *Bab* 5 (Index).

*Rab Kahana* in Pum Nahara (near Nehardea) was a student of Papa and of Huna b. Yehoshua, and the teacher of Ashi. Neusner, *Bab* 5.

*Rabina I*, d. c. 420, was a student of Raba, friend of Rab Naḥman b. Isaac, and the colleague of Rab Aḥa b. Raba and later of Rab Ashi. A. Cohen, 'The Identification of Ravina, Rav Ashi's Colleague' (Hebr.), *11th WCJS* (Jerusalem 1994) C 1:95–102 (if Rabina was much younger than Ashi and lived to a very old age, the assumption of a second Rabina would be superfluous); Neusner, *Bab* 5 (Index).

*Huna bar Nathan*, a student of Papa whom Ashi mentions repeatedly. Sherira reports that he was an exilarch. A seal which possibly belonged to this Huna is described in S. Shaked, 'Epigraphica Judaeo-Iranica', in S. Morag et al. (eds.), *Studies in Judaism and Islam* (*Festschrift* S. D. Goitein, Jerusalem 1981), 65–68 (65–82). M. Beer, *Exilarchs*, 62–70.

*Rab Ashi* (d. 427) is also known under the honorary title Rabbana Ashi (Ket 22a); he is reported to have led the academy at Sura for 52 years, and during the months of Kallah to have taught through the entire Talmud, much of it twice. This ensured for him a prominent place in the various theories about the origin of the BT: see Neusner (ed.), *Formation* (Index); idem, *Bab* 5 (Index); J. Jacobowitz, *Aspects of the Economic and Social History of the Jews in Babylonia with Special Emphasis on the Teachings and Decisions of R. Ashi and the Sixth Generation of Amoraim*, Diss. New York University 1978; J. S. Zuri, *Rab Ashi* (Hebr.), Warsaw 1924.

*Rab Kahana*, d. 414, taught at Pumbeditha. Neusner, *Bab* 5.

*Rab Aḥa bar Raba*, son of Raba bar Joseph, d. 419, taught at Pumbeditha and often debated with Rabina I. Neusner, *Bab* 5.

*Mar Zutra*, a friend of Ashi, d. 417. Beer, *Exilarchs*, 49–55; cf. Neusner, *Bab* 5:48–51 and Index.

***m) Seventh Generation of Amoraim in Babylonia***

ISG mentions the following heads of the academy at Sura:

*R. Yemar*, Ashi's successor, 427–32 is often identified with the exilarch Meremar. Beer, *Exilarchs*, 55–61; Neusner, *Bab* 5 (Index: Maremar, Yemar).

*R. Idi bar Abin II*, student of Papa, 432–52.

*Rab Naḥman bar Rab Huna*, 452–55. S. Albeck, *Sinai – Sefer Yobel* (1958) 70f.

*Mar bar Rab Ashi* (=Tabyomi), 455–68. Neusner, *Bab* 5 (Index).

*Rabba Tosfa'a*, 468–70. The name T. refers to his native town of Tospitis, or else should be understood as 'supplementer'. Neusner, *Bab* 5 (Index).

*Rabina (Rab Abina) II bar Huna*, 470–99, nephew of Rabina I (but see above on Rabina I).

According to ISG the heads of the academy at Pumbeditha were the following:

*Rab Gebiha* of Be Qatil, 419–33.

*Rab Rafram II*, 433–43. Neusner, *Bab* 5 (Index).

*Rab Riḥumai* (Niḥumai), 443–49. Neusner, *Bab* 5:137f., 143–45.

*Rab Sama son of Raba*, 449–76.

*Rab Yose*. Along with Rabina II, ISG describes him as *sôf hôra'ah*, the end of authoritative teaching and of the Amoraim. Hence he is commonly dated at the time of the redaction of BT. Cf. Neusner (ed.), *Formation* (Index); idem, *Bab* 5:143–45.

For the Geonic and medieval traditions about the late masters including the Saboraim, see Neusner, *Bab* 5:135–46 (note his synoptic table of the different sources, p. 144f.).

***n) The Saboraim***

For the Saboraic input into the BT see pp. 204ff. below. ISG 98f. names the following Saboraim, some of whom belong to the later fifth, the others to the first half of the sixth century.

***1. The Older Group of Saboraim***

*Sama bar Yehuda*, d. 504.

*Rab Aḥai bar Rab Huna*, d. 506, sometimes additionally designated as 'from Be Ḥatim' Neusner, *Bab* 5:143–45.

*Rab Riḥumai* (variant: Niḥumai), d. 506. Ephrathi, *The Sevoraic Period*, 123.

*Rab Samuel bar R. Abbahu* of Pumbeditha, d. 506. Ḥul 59b. Ephrathi, *The Sevoraic Period*, 122f.

*Rabina of Amuṣya* (or Amusa), d. 507.

*Rab Aḥa*, son of (Rabba bar) Abbuha, d. 510.

*Rab Taḥna* (variant: Taḥina) and *Mar Zutra*, sons of Rab Ḥinena, d. 515 (Mar Zutra must not be identified with the exilarch of the same name who at this time reportedly attempted to establish a Jewish state in Babylonia: cf. Neusner, *Bab* 5:95–105).

*Rabba Joseph* (variant: Yose), head of the school at Pumbeditha, d. 520.

***2. The Younger Group of Saboraim***

*Rab Aina* at Sura is probably not to be identified with Rab Giza. Ephrathi, *The Sevoraic Period*, 33f., 36–44.

*Rab Simona* at Pumbeditha. Ephrathi, *The Sevoraic Period*, 36–45.

*Rabbai* of Rob in Pumbeditha. Some already count him as a Gaon (cf. ISG 47: *we–'amrin de-ga'on hawah*). In this case the time of the Saboraim would already conclude with Rab Simona around 540; but this is untenable. Ephrathi, *The Sevoraic Period*, 33f., 37–42.

On the *Geonim* cf. Assaf, *Geonim*. The beginning of the Geonim of course depends on the end of the Saboraim, if one takes these terms as designating strict periods and does not assume a time of Saboraim and

Geonim as parallel heads of academies. The properly Geonic period, at any rate, begins only in Islamic times. This is despite the fact that Simona and Rabbai are sometimes regarded as the first Geonim, while *Mar bar Rab Ḥanan* of Isqiya usually figures as the first Gaon at Sura (after 589) and *Rab Mar ben Mar Rab Huna* as the first at Pumbeditha (after 609). The end of the Geonic period must be assumed with *Samuel ha-Kohen ben Ḥofni* at Sura, d. 1034, and *Rab Hai* at Pumbeditha, d. 1038. For the even later use of the title Gaon, especially in relation to the heads of academies in Palestine and Egypt, see S. Poznanski, *Babylonische Geonim in nachgeonäischer Zeit*, Berlin 1914; idem, 'Die Anfänge des palästinischen Geonats', in S. Krauss (ed.), *Festschrift Adolf Schwarz* (Berlin/Vienna 1917), 471–88; L. Ginzberg, *Geonica*, 2 vols., New York 1909 (repr. 1968); S. Assaf, *Geonim*; idem, *EJ* 7:315–24 (revised by the editor).

# VII

# THE LANGUAGES OF RABBINIC LITERATURE

Rabbinic literature has been transmitted in different linguistic stages of Hebrew and Aramaic. In addition to Mishnaic Hebrew, there is the Hebrew of Amoraic and Geonic times. Aramaic, which occurs only occasionally in Tannaitic texts, is used above all in Amoraic literature. It is regionally divided into the Galilean and the Babylonian dialect. An important aspect of rabbinic language lies in the foreign influences. These have already been quite carefully explored for Greek and Latin foreign and loan words; but they can also be detected for the oriental languages (Akkadian, Persian, Arabic). In this context we can only briefly outline the issues; our main emphasis is to give the linguistic aids for dealing with rabbinic texts. Somewhat more detailed treatments are given by B. M. Bokser in J. Neusner (ed.), *The Study*, 2:63–70; D. Goodblatt, ibid., 136–44.

## *1) Mishnaic Hebrew (MH$^1$)*

***Bibliography***

**Albeck**, *Einführung*, 189–390. **Bar-Asher, M.** 'The Different Traditions of Mishnaic Hebrew' (Hebr.), *Tarbiz* 53 (1983–84) 187–220. **Bar-Asher, M.** 'La langue de la Mishna d'après la tradition des communautés juives d'Italie.' *REJ* 145 (1986) 267–78. **Bar-Asher, M.** 'Quelques phénomènes grammaticaux en hébreu mishnique.' *REJ* 149 (1990) 351–67. [On the participle; useful bibliography.] **Bar-Asher, M.** 'L'Hébreu mishnique: Esquisse d'une description.' *Académie des Inscriptions et Belles-Lettres: Comptes rendus des séances de l'année 1990*, 1 (1990) 199–237. **Bar-Asher, M.** 'Introduction to Mishnaic Hebrew' (Hebr.), in M. Bar-Asher (ed.), *Rabbi Mordechai Breuer Festschrift*, 2:657–88. Jerusalem 1992. **Bar-Asher, M.** 'The Conjugations of Tannaitic Hebrew (A Morphological Study)' (Hebr.). In *Language Studies* 5–6 (= *Festschrift* I.Yeivin, Jerusalem 1992) 123–51. **Bar-Asher, M.** 'Ha-nisteret be–'abar be-po'alê l"y – l"' bi-leshon ha-Tannaim.' In *Talmudic Studies*, 2:39–84. **Bendavid, A.** *Biblical Hebrew and Mishnaic Hebrew* (Hebr.). 2 vols. Tel Aviv 1967 (2nd edn. Vol. 1), 1971 (Vol. 2). **Epstein**, *ITM*, 1207–69. **Haneman, G.** *A Morphology of Mishnaic Hebrew* (Hebr.). Tel Aviv 1980. **Kaddari, M. Z.** 'On the Verb Hyh in the Language of the Mishnah' (Hebr.). *Bar-Ilan* 16–17 (1979) 112–25. **Kutscher, E. Y.** 'The Present State of Research into Mishnaic Hebrew (Especially Lexicography) and its Tasks' (Hebr.). *Archive* 1:3–28. **Kutscher, E. Y.** 'Some Problems of the Lexicography of Mishnaic Hebrew and its Comparisons with Biblical Hebrew' (Hebr.). *Archive* 1:29–82. [Both of these articles include a detailed English summary; repr. with other important studies in idem, *Hebrew and Aramaic Studies*, vol. 1, Jerusalem 1977.] **Kutscher, E. Y.** *EJ* 16: 1590–1607. **Kutscher, E. Y.** *A History of the Hebrew Language*, 115–47. Leiden 1982. **Mishor, M.** 'On the Style of Mishnaic-Talmudic Literature: The Imperfect with Indicative Meaning' (Hebr.). *Tarbiz* 55 (1985–86) 345–58. **Moreshet, M.** 'The Hif'il in Mishnaic Hebrew as Equivalent to the Qal' (Hebr.). *Bar-Ilan* 13 (1976) 249–81. **Moreshet, M.** 'The Present Participle with Enclitic Nominative Pronoun in Mishnaic Hebrew' (Hebr.). *Bar-Ilan* 16–17 (1979) 126–48. **Moreshet, M.** *Lexicon of Verbs Renewed by the Tannaim* (Hebr.). Ramat Gan 1980. **Moreshet, M.** 'Polel/Hitpolel in Mishnaic Hebrew and Aramaic Dialects' (Hebr.). *Bar-Ilan* 18–19 (1981) 248–69. **Sarfatti, G. B.** 'The Use of the Syntagm *nimtsa 'ose* in Mishnaic Hebrew to Express Before-Future and After-Past Time' (Hebr.). *Language Studies* 2–3 (Jerusalem 1987) 225–43. **Sharvit, S.** 'The Crystallization of Mishnaic Hebrew Research.' *Bar-Ilan* 18–19 (1981) 221–32. **Sharvit, S.** 'The Tense System of Mishnaic Hebrew' (Hebr.). In G.B. Sarfatti et al. (eds.), *Studies in Hebrew and Semitic Languages Dedicated to the Memory of Professor E. Y. Kutscher*, 110–25. Ramat-Gan 1980. **Sharvit, S.** 'Verbs Containing Infinitive as their only Complement in Mishnaic Hebrew' (Hebr.). *Language Studies* 2–3 (Jerusalem 1987) 279–96. **Van Bekkum, W. J.** 'The Origins of the Infinitive in Rabbinical Hebrew.' *JSS* 28 (1983) 247–72. **Weinberg, W.** 'Observations about the Pronunciation of Hebrew in Rabbinic Sources.' *HUCA* 56 (1985) 117–43. **Yalon, H.** *Introduction to the Vocalization of the Mishnah* (Hebr.). Jerusalem 1964. **Yalon, H.** *Studies in the Hebrew Language* (Hebr.). Jerusalem 1971.

***Grammar***

**Pérez-Fernández, M.** *La Lengua de los Sabios*, vol. 1: *Morfosintaxis*. Estella (Navarra) 1992. **Segal, M. H.** *A Grammar of Mishnaic Hebrew*. Oxford 1927; repr. London 1978. [Very dated.]

Except for a few Aramaic sentences (sayings of Hillel and other early masters: Abot 1.13; 2.6; 4.5; 5.22f.; Eduy 8.4; quotations from the fasting scroll: Taan 2.8; from the Targum: Meg 4.9; and from documents: marriage contracts Ket 4.7–12; Yeb 15.3; divorce certificate Git 9.3; lease contracts BM 9.3; BB 10.2), the Mishnah is written in what is called Mishnaic Hebrew. With some nuances, this stage of the language is also found in the Tosefta and the halakhic midrashim as well as in the baraitot of the PT. The rabbis already distinguished this form of the language stage from Biblical Hebrew (BH): 'The language of the Torah stands by itself and the language of the sages stands by itself' (R. Yoḥanan in AZ 58b).

Following A. Geiger, MH used to be seen as an artificial language of the Tannaites. M. H. Segal then showed it to be a further development of BH (*JQR* 20 (1908) 647–737). The Bar Kokhba letters have now demonstrated that this language was actually spoken in Judaea. It was only after the second revolt and the shift of the centre of Rabbinism to Aramaic-speaking Galilee that MH could not prevail in the long run; by the end of the Tannaitic period, it had become a dead language of scholars (thus especially Kutscher). MH differs from BH both in terms of vocabulary and grammar:

***a) Vocabulary***

This is largely taken over from BH. However, many words now assume a different meaning (e.g. *ṣedaqah*: BH 'righteousness'; MH 'charity') or become rabbinic technical terms. Occasionally there are changes in gender or plural formation; in orthography, *plene* spelling prevails. Numerous Akkadian, Persian, Greek and Latin loan words supplement the vocabulary; but the main influence is from Aramaic.

### *b) Grammar*

The genitival construct state of nouns is largely replaced by *shel*. A proleptic possessive suffix is also frequent (e.g. *ribbono shel 'olam*, 'Lord of the world'). The rules of the article are not yet fully understood. *Shel* plus possessive suffix now also frequently replaces the suffix on the noun itself; indeed the pronominal system becomes generally more flexible (e.g. *'eṣem* plus suffix as reflexive pronoun; *et* plus proleptic suffix: e.g. *oto ha-yom*, 'on the same day', etc.). The *verbal system* is simplified by the loss of a separate form for the 2nd pers. fem. plural (in the perfect tense, by the conventional assimilation of final *mem* and *nun*), and by a certain standardization of the weak verbs.

The Pual disappears almost entirely, while the Hithpael is replaced by the Nithpael. Of decisive significance, however, is the alteration of the tense structure (under Aramaic and perhaps also Greek influence). Only now does the morphology itself permit a clear distinction between present, future and past: the perfect tense is assigned to the past, the imperfect to the future, and the participle replaces the present tense. A continuing action in the past is now expressed by *hayah* plus participle: *hayah omer*, 'he used to say'. Of course these changes have also altered the syntax of MH; the greater frequency of relative clauses is particularly worth noting.

It appears that linguistic differences between the Palestinian and Babylonian rabbis already exist at the stage of $MH^1$. They are primarily phonological (e.g. the almost complete disappearance of laryngeal sounds in Babylonian pronunciation) or orthographical in character, but remain at any rate relatively minor.

## *2) Amoraic Hebrew ($MH^2$)*

#### *Bibliography*

**Abramson, S.** 'On the Hebrew in the Babylonian Talmud' (Hebr.). *Archive* 2:9–15. **Abramson, S.** 'Some Aspects of Talmudic Hebrew' (Hebr.). *Language Studies* 2–3 (Jerusalem 1987) 23–50. **Breuer, Y.** 'On the Hebrew Dialect of the Amoraim in the Babylonian Talmud' (Hebr.). *Language Studies* 2–3 (Jerusalem 1987) 127–53. **Breuer, Y.** ''Al gilgulê leshon Ḥazal ba-Talmud ha-Babli.' In *Talmudic Studies* 2:91–125. **Breuer, Y.** *The Babylonian Talmudic Hebrew* (Hebr.). Diss. Jerusalem 1993. **Kutscher, E. Y.** [See §1 above]. **Moreshet, M.** 'The Language of the Baraytot in the T. B. is not $MH^1$' (Hebr.). In E. Y. Kutscher et al. (eds.), *Henoch Yalon Memorial Volume*, 275–314. Jerusalem 1974. **Moreshet, M.** 'New and Revived Verbs in the Baraytot of the Babylonian Talmud (In Comparison with $MH^2$ in the Babylonian and Palestinian Talmudim' (Hebr.). *Archive* 1:113–62. **Moreshet, M.** 'Further Studies of the Language of the Hebrew Baraytot in the Babylonian and Palestinian Talmudim' (Hebr.). *Archive* 2:31–73. **Sokoloff, M.** 'The Hebrew of Berēšit Rabba according to Ms. Vat. Ebr. 30' (Hebr.). *Leshonenu* 33 (1968–69) 25–42, 135–49, 270–79.

In the Amoraic period, Hebrew continues to be spoken for some time in certain parts of Judaea; but but it has otherwise become a dead language. As such, it changes in two ways in relation to MH$^1$: a) through the influence of the living Aramaic vernacular, whosc different dialects in Galilee and Baylonia also differently influenced MH$^2$. In Palestine there is an additional influx of forms not previously attested, as well as of words from the Hebrew still spoken in Judaea. And there is b) a growing orientation toward BH in vocabulary and forms.

As for the *baraitot*, Moreshet has shown that they are by and large MH$^1$ in the Palestinian tradition, but that in BT they reflect a language already strongly influenced by MH$^2$. Hence the language of the Babylonian baraitot must be regarded as an intermediate stage between MH$^1$ and (Babylonian) MH$^2$; indeed at times it becomes entirely MH$^2$ (fictitious baraitot).

### *3) Galilean Aramaic*

***Bibliography***

**Kutscher, E. Y.** *Studies in Galilean Aramaic.* Ramat Gan 1976. [Revised translation of *Tarbiz* 21 (1950) 192–205; 22 (1951) 53–63, 185–92; 23 (1952) 36–60.] **Kutscher, E. Y.** *Hebrew and Aramaic Studies.* Vols. 1 (Hebr.), 2 (English/German). Jerusalem 1977. **Kutscher, E. Y.** *EJ* 3:270–75. **Sokoloff, M.** 'Notes on the Vocabulary of Galilean Aramaic' (Hebr.). In G. B. Sarfatti et al. (eds.), *Studies in Hebrew and Semitic Languages Dedicated to the Memory of Professor E. Y. Kutscher*, 166–73. Ramat-Gan 1980. **Svedlund, G.** *The Aramaic Portions of the Pesiqta de Rab Kahana.* Uppsala 1974.

***Grammars***

**Dalman, G.** *Grammatik des jüdisch-palästinischen Aramäisch.* 2nd edn. Leipzig 1905; repr. Darmstadt 1960. **Levias, C.** *A Grammar of Galilean Aramaic* (Hebr.). English Introduction by M. Sokoloff. New York 1986. [Cf. Cincinnati 1900; still relevant on matters of syntax.] **Odeberg, H.** *The Aramaic Portions of Bereshit Rabba: With Grammar of Galilean Aramaic.* Lund 1939. [NB syntax.] **Stevenson, W. B.** *Grammar of Palestinian Jewish Aramaic.* Edited, with an Appendix on the Numerals by J. A. Emerton. Oxford 1962.

***Lexicon:*** see M. Sokoloff in §6 below.

'Galilean' Aramaic (whose scope probably extended beyond Galilee to include all of Palestine) is particularly poorly preserved in the manuscripts and printed editions. This is because European copyists approached their texts (PT, midrashim) from the more familiar perspective of BT. On the other hand, they were also influenced by the language of the Targumim, which, although of Palestinian provenance, were revised in Babylonia and therefore constitute a mixed form. The reconstruction of the original Galilean Aramaic in recent decades (especially by Kutscher) was only made possible by the discovery of numerous Aramaic inscriptions from Talmudic Palestine and the subsequent sifting of the most linguistically reliable manuscripts.

### *4) Babylonian Aramaic*

***Bibliography***

**Epstein, J. N.** 'Babylonisch-Aramäische Studien.' In J. Fischer et al. (eds.), *Festskrift i Anledning af D. Simonsens 70–aarige FØdelsedag*, 290–310. Copenhagen 1923. **Friedman, S.** 'Three Studies in Babylonian Aramaic Grammar' (Hebr.). *Tarbiz* 43 (1973–74) 58–69. **Kara, Y.** *Babylonian Aramaic in the Yemenite Manuscripts of the Talmud: Orthography, Phonology and Morphology of the Verb* (Hebr.). Jerusalem 1983. **Kaufman, S. A.** *The Akkadian Influences on Aramaic*. Chicago 1974. **Kutscher, E. Y.** *Hebrew and Aramaic Studies*. 2 vols. Jerusalem 1977. **Kutscher, E. Y.** *EJ* 3:277–82. **Morag, S.** *Babylonian Aramaic: The Yemenite Tradition. Historical Aspects and Transmission; Phonology; The Verbal System* (Hebr.). Jerusalem 1988.

***Grammars***

**Epstein, J. N.** *A Grammar of Babylonian Aramaic* (Hebr.). Jerusalem 1960. [On this see E. Y. Kutscher, *Leshonenu* 26 (1961–62) 149–83; repr. in idem, *Hebrew and Aramaic Studies*, 1:227–52.] **Levias, C.** *A Grammar of the Aramaic Idiom Contained in the Babylonian Talmud*. Cincinnati 1900; repr. Westmead 1971. **Marcus, D.** *A Manual of Babylonian Jewish Aramaic*. Washington, DC 1981. **Margolis, M.** *Lehrbuch der aramäischen Sprache des babylonischen Talmuds*. Munich 1910. **Schlesinger, M.** *Satzlehre der aramäischen Sprache des babylonischen Talmuds*. Leipzig 1928.

Together with Mandaean and Syriac, Babylonian Aramaic belongs to the Eastern branch of Aramaic. Research into this dialect has been hampered particularly by the lack of inscriptions as a corrective to the MSS, whose linguistic transmission has suffered especially from biblicisms and standardization. Even the magical bowls of Nippur, although linguistically related, can be used only with caution. The linguistic classification of the 'extraordinary tractates' of the BT also continues to be disputed: are they witnesses of an earlier stage of linguistic development (thus Kutscher), or rather late and close to the Geonic language (Epstein)? The Genizah fragments, especially the (vocalized) Geonic texts, can assist in furthering the reconstruction of the linguistic development; they permit above all a more accurate distinction between the Amoraic and Geonic language. Unfortunately there is as yet no reliable grammar, even though that of Epstein is very valuable (Kutscher, *Leshonenu* 26 (1961–62) 170: 'the only scholarly grammar of Babylonian Aramaic which we have today').

### *5) Foreign and Loan Words*

***Bibliography***

**Lieberman, S.** *Greek*; *Hell.*; *Texts and Studies*. [And almost all his other works.] **Krauss, S.**

*Griechische und lateinische Lehnwörter im Talmud, Midrasch und Targum.* 2 vols. Berlin 1898–99; repr. Hildesheim 1987 (with valuable notes by I. Löw). **Rosenthal, E. S.** 'For the Talmudic Dictionary – Talmudica Iranica.' In S. Shaked (ed.), *Irano Judaica*, Hebr. section, 38–134. Jerusalem 1982. **Sperber, D.** 'Greek and Latin Words in Rabbinic Literature: Prolegomena to a New Dictionary of Classical Words in Rabbinic Literature.' *Bar-Ilan* 14–15 (1977) 9–60; 16–17 (1979) 9–30. **Sperber, D.** *Essays on Greek and Latin in the Mishna, Talmud and Midrashic Literature.* Jerusalem 1982. **Sperber, D.** *A Dictionary of Greek and Latin Legal Terms in Rabbinic Literature.* Jerusalem 1984. [Cf. R. Katzoff, *JSJ* 20 (1989) 195–206.] **Sperber, D.** *Nautica Talmudica.* Ramat-Gan 1986.

With the Hellenization of the Eastern Mediterranean area, the Hebrew and Aramaic languages also came under the influence of Greek; over the centuries, numerous words entered their vocabulary. These borrowings pertain to almost every aspect of life, the law and industry as well as agriculture and the home. Where these loan words are used alongside proper Hebrew and Aramaic ones, they often designate luxury or imported goods. The Latin influence, which begins with the Roman rule over Palestine, is relatively minor and primarily limited to the military and administrative spheres.

The problems of these loan words are characterized not only by the mutations common to any adoption into a foreign language, but above all by the history of the transmission of rabbinic texts. With the Islamic conquest, rabbinic Judaism moved out of the Graeco-Latin cultural sphere; many loan words soon became unintelligible and were bastardized or replaced by similar sounding Hebrew or Aramaic words. The copyist's ignorance further compounded this effect, so that it has often become extremely difficult to recognize loan words. For this reason many entries in S. Krauss are flawed. Major progress in this regard has been made especially in the works of S. Lieberman, who emphasized *inter alia* the need to rely not only on the classical dictionaries but also on the vocabulary of the provincial Greek current in Palestine. D. Sperber has done significant preparatory work for the urgently needed revision of S. Krauss's dictionary: in addition to his two specialized lexicons see especially the article in *Bar-Ilan*, which contains a selected list of new examples along with a Greek and Latin index. As regards the adoption of Persian terminology, there are indeed a few studies from the nineteenth and early twentieth century, whose results were subsequently incorporated in the Talmudic lexicons; however, much in this area remains highly uncertain or entirely unexplored, as has been pointed out by E. S. Rosenthal in particular.

## *6) Lexicons*

***Bibliography***

**Jastrow, M.** *A Dictionary of the Targumim, the Talmud Babli and Yerushalmi, and the Midrashic Literature.* 2 vols. London 1886–1903; repr. New York 1950. **Kohut, A.** *Aruch Completum.* 8 vols. Vienna 1878–92. **Kohut, A.** *Additamenta ad Aruch Completum.* Ed. S. Krauss. Vienna 1937. **Levy, J.** *Neuhebräisches und chaldäisches Wörterbuch über die Talmudim und Midraschim.* 4 vols. Leipzig 1876–89. *Nachträge und Berichtigungen*, Berlin 1929. [Repr. Hildesheim 1964.] **Sokoloff, M.** *A Dictionary of Jewish Palestinian Aramaic of the Byzantine Period.* Ramat Gan 1990. [Cf. K. Beyer, *Abr-Nahrein* 30 (1992) 195–201; R. Macuch, *BSOAS* 55 (1992) 205–30; J. Blau, *Leschonenu* 57 (1992–93) 59–65; M. A. Fridman, *ibid.*, 67–94.]

In addition, there are specialized dictionaries: **Löw, I.** *Die Flora der Juden.* 4 vols. Vienna/Leipzig 1926–34; repr. Hildesheim 1967. **Löw, I.** *Fauna und Mineralien der Juden.* Hildesheim 1969.

A new lexicon of rabbinic literature is being compiled at Bar-Ilan University (see the two volumes of *Archive*); the first volume by M. Sokoloff on Palestinian Aramaic has now been published. All the other listed lexicons are outdated, etymologically unreliable, and incomplete. Advances in comparative semitics necessitate numerous corrections, as do the textual discoveries from the Cairo Genizah, the results of the study of Hebrew and Aramaic linguistic development, and today's much more accurate differentiation between Palestinian and Babylonian Aramaic.

# PART TWO: TALMUDIC LITERATURE

## I

## THE MISHNAH

***General Bibliography***

**Albeck, Ch**. *Einführung*. **Albeck, Ch**. *Untersuchungen über die Redaktion der Mischna*. Berlin 1923. **Brüll, J**. *Einleitung in die Mishnah* (Hebr.). 2 vols. Frankfurt am Main 1876–85; repr. Jerusalem 1970. **De Vries, B**. 'The Early Form of Certain Halakhot' (Hebr.). *Tarbiz* 24 (1954–55) 392–405; 25 (1955–56) 369–84. **Eilberg-Schwartz, H**. *The Human Will in Judaism: The Mishnah's Philosophy of Intention*. Decatur, GA 1986. **Ephrati, J. M**. 'On the Literary Sources of the Mishnah' (Hebr.). *Bar-Ilan* 11 (1973) 49–68. **Epstein, J. N**. *ITM*; *ITL*. **Feldblum, M. S**. '"Mishnah Yeterah": Siddur ha-Mishnah ba-Aspeqlaryah shel ḥomer ha-stami ba-Talmud.' In L. Landman (ed.), *Rabbi Joseph H. Lookstein Memorial Volume* (New York 1980), 7–15. **Frankel, Z**. *Darkhe*. **Ginzberg, L**. 'Zur Entstehungsgeschichte der Mishnah.' In S. Eppenstein et al. (eds.), *Festschrift zum siebzigsten Geburtstage David Hoffmann's*, 311–45. Berlin 1914. **Goldberg, A**. 'The Mishna – A Study Book of Halakha.' In S. Safrai, *The Literature*, 1:211–51. **Goldberg, A**. 'Form und Funktion des Ma'ase in der Mischna.' *FJB* 2 (1974) 1–38. **Gruber, M. I**. 'The Mishnah as Oral Torah: A Reconsideration.' *JSJ* 15 (1984) 112–22. **Guttmann, A**. 'The Problem of the Anonymous Mishna.' *HUCA* 16 (1941) 137–55. **Halivni, D. W**. 'The Reception Accorded to Rabbi Judah's Mishnah.' In E. P. Sanders et al. (eds.), *Jewish and Christian Self-Definition*, 2:204–12, 379–82. London 1981. **Halivni, D. W**. 'Mishnas which were changed from their Original Forms' (Hebr.). *Sidra* 5 (1989) 63–88. **Hoffmann, D. Z**. *The first Mishna and the Controversies of the Tannaim*. Translated by P. Forchheimer. New York 1977. [*Die erste Mischna und die Controversen der Tannaim*. Berlin 1882.] **Krochmal, N**. *The Writings* (Hebr.), 194–237. Ed. S. Rawidowicz. 2nd edn. London 1961. **Lieberman, S**. 'The Publication of the Mishnah.' In idem, *Hell.*, 83–99. **Maass, F**. *Formgeschichte der Mischna mit besonderer Berücksichtigung des Traktates Abot*. Berlin 1937. **Melammed, E. Z**. *Introduction*. **Melammed, E. Z**. 'Interpolations in the Mishnah and their Identification' (Hebr.). *Tarbiz* 31 (1961–62) 326–56. **Melammed, E. Z**. 'The Parallelism in the Mishnah' (Hebr.). *6th WCJS* (Jerusalem 1977) Hebrew section, 275–91. **Melammed, E. Z**. 'Ma'asim Collections of Tannaim' (Hebr.). *7th WCJS* (Jerusalem 1981): *Studies in the Talmud, Halacha and Midrash*, 93–107. Jerusalem 1981. **Neusner, J.**, ed. *The Modern Study*. [Introduction revised in idem, *The Study of Ancient Judaism*, vol. 1 (New York 1981), 3–26.] **Neusner, J**. *Introduction*, 97–128. **Neusner, J**. *Judaism*, 27–135. **Neusner, J**. *Form-Analysis and Exegesis: A Fresh Approach to the Interpretation of Mishnah with Special Reference to Mishnah-Tractate Makhshirin*. Minneapolis 1980. **Neusner, J**. *Judaism: The Evidence of the Mishnah*, Chicago 1981. [Cf. J. J. Petuchowski, *Religious Studies Review* 9 (1983) 108–13.] **Neusner, J**. *The Memorized Torah: The Mnemonic System of the Mishnah*. Chico 1985. [Revised from idem, *Phar* and *Pur*.] **Neusner, J**. *The Mishnah before 70*. Atlanta 1987. [Revised from idem, *Pur*.] **Neusner, J**. *The Philosophical Mishnah*. 4 vols. Atlanta 1989. **Neusner, J**. 'Redaction, Formulation and Form: The Case of Mishnah; With Comments by R. S. Sarason.' *JQR* N.S. 70 (1979–80) 131–52. **Neusner, J**. *The Mishnah: Introduction and Reader*. Philadelphia 1992. **Rosenthal, L. A**. *Über den Zusammenhang, die Quellen und die Entstehung der Mischna*. Berlin 1918. **Segal, B.-Z**. *Ha-Geografia ba-Mishnah*. Jerusalem 1979. **Urbach, E. E**. *EJ* 12:93–109. **Weiss, A**. *Al ha-Mishnah*. Ramat Gan 1969. **Weiss, M**. 'Mishnah Tractates which Open with Numbered Lists' (Hebr.). *Sidra* 1 (1985) 33–44. **Yalon, H**. *Introduction to the Vocalization of the Mishna* (Hebr.). Jerusalem 1964. **Zlotnick, D**. *The Iron Pillar – Mishnah: Redaction, Form, and Intent*. Jerusalem 1988.

### 1) Explanation of Terms

***Bibliography***

**Abramson, S.** '"Mishnah" we-"Talmud" (Gemara) be-fî Qadmonim.' In S. Werses et al. (eds.), *Sefer Dov Sadan* (*Festschrift* D. Sadan), 23–43. Tel Aviv 1977. **Albeck**, *Einführung*, 1–3. **Bacher**, *ET* 1:122f., 193–95. **Finkelstein, L.** 'Midrash, Halakhot, and Aggadot' (Hebr.). In S. W. Baron et al. (eds.), *Yitzhak F. Baer Jubilee Volume on the Occasion of His Seventieth Birthday*, 28–47. Jerusalem 1960. [Repr. in idem, *Sifra* 5:100–119.]

The Hebrew verb *shanah* 'to repeat' in its technical sense means to learn (e.g. Abot 2.4; 3.3) or teach (e.g. Erub 54b) oral tradition by repeated recitation, in contrast to *qara'*, to study the Holy Scriptures. The Aramaic equivalent is *teni* or *tena'*, the derivative noun is *mishnah* or *matnita'*.

*Mishnah* therefore means study (m.Abot 3.7) as well as oral instruction (t.Ber 2.12, L. 8). In this sense the Mishnah comprises the three branches of tradition: midrash as the interpretation of the text of Scripture; the halakhot as the statutes formulated independently of Scripture; and finally the haggadot, i.e. all non-halakhic material. Thus a baraita in Qid 49a answers the question, 'What is Mishnah?' R. Meir says, 'Halakhot.' R. Yehudah says, 'Midrash' (cf. further Finkelstein).

More specifically, Mishnah designates the entire religious law formulated until c. 200, but also the teaching of a teacher (Tannaite) active in this period as well as an individual proposition (=*halakhah*) or collections of such propositions (e.g. p.Hor 3, 48c *mishnayot gedolot*, the great mishnaic collections such as the Mishnah of Ḥiyya [read thus instead of 'Ḥuna' in printed editions], of Hoshayah and of Bar Qappara). The Mishnah *par excellence* is the collection attributed to R. Yehudah ha-Nasi, with which we are here concerned.

In his *Arukh*, Nathan ben Yeḥiel gives a different derivation of the word: 'Why is it called Mishnah? Because it is the "second" in relation to the Torah'. A similar derivation is reflected in the patristic custom of translating Mishnah as *deuterosis* (thus also Justinian's *Novella* 146).

Rabbi's Mishnah is cited as *mishnatenu* or *matnitin* (rarely *matnita'*) in BT, and as *matnitin* or *matnita* in PT. Other mishnaic collections are called *matnita* or *baraita* in BT, *mishnayot* in PT. In both BT and PT, Mishnah sentences are introduced by *tenan* or *tenayna*, 'we have learned'.

### 2) Structure and Contents

In its extant form, M (like T and the Talmuds) consists of six main divisions or orders (*sedarim*, occasionally *arakhim*). This explains the traditional designation of the Talmud as *Shas* (an abbreviation of *shishah sedarim*, 'six orders'). Each *seder* has a number (7–12) of tractates, *massekhet* (properly 'fabric'; for the change in meaning, cf. Latin *textus*) or Aramaic *massekhta*; attested plural forms are *massekhot*, *massekhtot* and *massekhiot*. The tractates are subdivided into chapters (*pereq*), and these in turn into sentences (*mishnah* or PT *halakhah*).

### *a) Survey of Contents*

(The name of each tractate is followed by the number of its chapters in parentheses.)

#### *§1 First Order: Zera'im, 'Seeds'*

(11 Tractates, of laws pertaining especially to agriculture)

1. *Berakhot* (9), 'benedictions'. Regulations on the *Shema'* prayer, morning, noon and evening prayer, on the 18 benedictions (*shemoneh 'esreh*) and on the supplementary prayer. Various benedictions for the consumption of fruit and other occasions. Common prayer after meals. The use of the divine name in greeting.

2. *Peah* (8), the 'corner' of the field, the harvest of which must according to Lev 19.9f.; 23.22; Deut 24.19ff. be left for the poor; generally, the law of the poor. Of which plants must *Peah* be given? What constitutes the corner of a field? How is the *Peah* given? Gleanings, the forgotten things, the tithe of the poor, the travelling poor. Who can claim the dues of the poor?

3. *Demai* (7), 'doubtful', i.e. fruits regarding which it is doubtful whether the tithe for the priests and (in the respective years) the second tithe should be given of them. When does the second tithe apply? Who can be trusted to keep these regulations? Behaviour in cases of common property or of mixing *Demai* with things not tithed.

4. *Kilaim* (9), 'different kinds'. According to Lev 19.19; Deut 22.9–11, these are illicit mixtures of things (plants, animals, textiles) of the same class but different in kind. Which kinds of plants and which kinds of animals constitute *Kilaim*? Mixing two kinds of seed; sowing different seeds in a field or vineyard. Bastards.

5. *Shebi'it* (10), the 'seventh year' in which according to Exod 23.11 and Lev 25.1–7 fields must lie fallow, and according to Deut 15 debts must be cancelled and indebted slaves must be freed. Which agricultural labours may be done in a Sabbath year? How may Sabbath year produce be used? Cancellation of debt and *Prosbul* (a declaration in court, *pros boulèn*, that a debt may be recalled at any time).

6. *Terumoth* (11) 'levies' or 'heave offerings' (priestly heave offering Num 18.8ff. and Deut 18.4: a levy out of the tithe due to the Levites, which

according to Num 18.25f. they must give to the priests). How is this levy set aside; how is it measured? What happens where it is mixed with other fruits? How are forgotten or stolen levies treated? Defilement of heave offerings, etc.

7. *Ma'aserot* or *Ma'aser Rishon* (5), 'tithe' or 'first tithe', to which according to Num 18.21ff. the Levites are entitled. Of which fruits must this tithe be given, and which are free of tithe?

8. *Ma'aser Sheni* (5), 'the second tithe' (Deut 14.22ff.; cf. 26.12ff.; and according to rabbinic interpretation also Lev 27.30–33) which, or the monetary equivalent of which, was to be consumed in Jerusalem. Regulations about the sale of the second tithe, its defilement, the use of the money obtained from it. Vineyards in the fourth year; the disposal (*bi'ur*) of the tithe. Abolition of the conventional confession (Deut 26.13–15) and other changes ordered by the High Priest Yoḥanan (=John Hyrcanus).

9. *Ḥallah* (4), 'dough offering' (Num 15.8ff.). Of what and in what measure must Ḥallah be given? How does the Ḥallah resemble a heave offering? How do various countries differ regarding the Ḥallah?

10. *'Orlah* (3), 'foreskin' of trees: cf. Lev 19.23, where trees are considered uncircumcised for the first three years, and hence their fruit is forbidden. When does this law apply to trees and vines? Mixing of *'Orlah*, *Kilaim*, heave offerings, etc. The application of these laws in Israel, Syria and elsewhere.

11. *Bikkurim* (3), 'firstfruits', cf. Deut 26.1ff.; Exod 23.19. Who offers them, of what, and from what time? In what do firstfruits, heave offerings and the second tithe coincide and in what do they differ? How are firstfruits brought to Jerusalem? Many Mishnah and Talmud texts add a fourth chapter on the bisexual (*androgynos*), which recurs with variants in T.

### *§2. Second Order: Mo'ed, 'Festival Days'*

(12 Tractates)

1. *Shabbat* (24): Exod 20.10; 23.12; Deut 5.14, etc. The few Pentateuchal Sabbath regulations are here developed in great detail, and derived in part from the connection in Exod 35 of the commandment of the Sabbath rest with the regulations for the construction of the sanctuary. Public, private, neutral and free domains are distinguished with regard to transport from one place to another. Which occupations are permitted on the Sabbath? Thirty-nine major kinds of forbidden tasks.

2. *'Erubin* (10), 'mixtures' by which certain Sabbath laws can be bypassed: a deposit of food at the end of a Sabbath day's walk (2,000 cubits) constitutes a 'residence' from which a further Sabbath day's walk is permitted. By a fictitious mixing of courtyards one may carry things from one

private domain to another, after a dish prepared from joint contributions has been deposited in one of the dwellings.

3. *Pesaḥim* (10), 'Passover (pesaḥ) lambs, Passover offerings'. Exod 12.23; 15.34; 34.18; Lev 23.5–8; Num 28.16ff.; Deut 16.1ff. Disposal of leaven; preparation of unleavened bread; the bitter herbs; labours permitted on the day of preparation; the slaughter of the Passover lamb and its preparation; who may eat of it? The Passover celebration in the second month (Num 9.10ff.); order of the Passover meal.

4. *Sheqalim* (8), 'sheqels', viz., the half-shekel tax used for the services in the Second Temple. (Exod 30.12ff.; Neh 10.33). Who is obliged to pay it? Exchange of money for the prescribed old coins. What may be acquired with it? Offering boxes in the Temple, the ark of the covenant, the cleaning of the temple curtain, the costliness of the curtain in front of the sanctuary.

5. *Yoma* (8), 'the day', i.e. the Day of Atonement, (*Yom ha–*) *Kippurim* Lev 16. The preparation of the high priest; casting lots for the two male goats; three confessions of sins by the high priest, and his three entrances into the Holy of Holies. Prohibitions for the Day of Atonement. The means of atonement (sin offering, guilt offering, death, Day of Atonement, repentance).

6. *Sukkah* (5), 'booth'; or plural *Sukkot*, the Feast of Booths, Lev 23.33–36; Num 29.12ff.; Deut 16.13ff. The construction and composition of the booth; eating and sleeping in it; the festive bouquet (*lulab*, *etrog*); the drawing of water. The 24 priestly divisions, their work in sacrifices, their portion in the offered pieces and the loaves of showbread.

7. *Beṣah* (5) 'egg' (from the first word) or *Yom Tob* 'holy day'. What must be observed on holy days. Differences from the Sabbath. Different opinions on this matter between the schools of Hillel and Shammai. The purchase of provisions on holy days, transport of food, prohibition of lighting a fire, etc.

8. *Rosh ha-Shanah* (4), 'New Year's Festival', Lev 23.24f.; Num 29.1ff. Four kinds of New Year (Nisan, Elul, Tishri, Shebat). Attestation and hallowing of the new moon. Blowing of the Shofar. The order of benedictions on the New Year's Festival: ten *malkhiyyot* (Scripture verses mentioning the Kingdom of God), ten *zikhronot* (Scripture verses about remembering God), ten *shofarot* (verses mentioning the shofar).

9. *Ta'anit* (4), or plural *Ta'aniyot*, 'fasting'. When does one begin to pray for rain, when to fast for it? Seven day fasts and the respective prayers. On which days does one refrain from fasting? What are other occasions for fasting? Ḥoni the Circle Drawer. Why is the fast broken when it begins to rain? The 17th of Tammuz, the 9th of Ab and the 15th of Ab.

10. *Megillah* (4), 'scroll', especially the scroll of Esther which is read in the synagogue on Purim (cf. Esth 9.28). When and how is the Esther scroll

read? The sale of holy things; the liturgical readings from the Torah and the Prophets; which texts may not be read in public, and which may not be translated?

11. *Mo'ed Qatan* (3), 'lesser holy days' (*qatan* 'small' distinguishes the tractate Moed from the order of the same name), sometimes also known as *mashqin* ('one waters'), from the first word. Regulations for the days between the first and seventh day of Passover and between the first and eighth day of Sukkot, on which certain labours are permitted.

12. *Ḥagigah* (3), 'celebration of a festival'. The three festivals of pilgrimage (Passover, Feast of Weeks, Feast of Booths: Deut 16.16). Who must appear in the Temple, and how much must he spend on the sacrifices? Subjects about which not everyone is instructed. Differences of opinion about *Semikhah*. Ritual hand washing. Seven stages of purity and purity regulations.

***§3. Third Order: Nashim, 'Women'***
(7 Tractates)

1. *Yebamot* (16), 'sisters-in-law', also vocalized as *Yabmut* 'affinity by marriage', and sometimes called *Nashim*, 'women'. Deals especially with levirate marriage (Deut 25.5–10; cf. Ruth 4 and Matt 22.24) and the *ḥaliṣah* which cancels this obligation. Who is required to perform it, and under which circumstances? Whom is a (high) priest not permitted to marry? The admission of Ammonites, etc., into the congregation. The position of proselytes. A minor's refusal to remain with her husband. Attestation of a husband's death.

2. *Ketubboth* (13), 'marriage contracts', cf. Exod 22.16. A *ketubbah* is both the marriage contract and the amount it assigns to the woman in case of divorce or her husband's death. Marriage of virgins; penalty payable for raping a girl. Mutual duties of husband and wife. Women's property and right of inheritance; widows' rights.

3. *Nedarim* (11) 'vows' and their cancellation (Num 30). What counts as a vow? Qorban; qualified vows; escapes. Four *a priori* invalid vows. White lies. The interpretation of vows. Which vows may a scholar remit? Who may cancel his wife's or daughter's vows, and which vows?

4. *Nazir* (9), 'Nazirite', or *Nezirut*, 'Nazirite vow', Num 6. Which formulations require the Nazirite observance, and how long does it last? The time of cutting the hair. Remission of Nazirite vows. Prohibitions for the Nazirite. Defilement of the Nazirite; the sacrifices he is required to offer. Nazirite vows of women and slaves.

5. *Sotah* (9), 'the suspected adulteress', Num 5.11–31. Application of the jealousy ordeal before the great court. Differences of rights and

punishments between Israelites and priests. When is the water of jealousy not given to drink? Formulas which may only be pronounced in Hebrew. Explanation of Deut 20.2–9 (the priest's address before battle); slaughter of a calf where a murderer remains unknown (Deut 21.1–9). Appendix: the signs of the Messiah's coming.

6. *Gittin* (9), 'divorce certificates' (Deut 24.1). Transmission, certification and retraction of divorce certificates. Form, signature. Re-acceptance of the dismissed wife. Divorce in cases of illness, conditional divorce. The validity of oral instructions regarding a divorce certificate. Reasons for divorce.

7. *Qiddushin* (4), 'betrothal, engagement': distinct from the ensuing stage of taking home the bride, the wedding itself (*nissuin*). How does a man acquire a wife (by money, a document, sexual intercourse)? Acquisition of other possessions. Which commandments are only required of men; which are valid only in Israel? Betrothal by proxy, conditional betrothal. Marriages of equal standing. Moral precepts.

### *§4. Fourth Order: Neziqin, 'Damages'*

(10 Tractates)

1. *Baba Qamma* (10), 'first gate' (of the originally undivided tractate Neziqin with 30 chapters). Damages in the narrower sense, including theft, robbery, and bodily harm. Damage caused by the goring ox, the uncovered pit, by grazing and fire. Assessment of damage, compensation. Doubtful purchase. Scraps belonging to the manufacturer or craftsman.

2. *Baba Meṣia* (10), 'middle gate'. Found objects claimed by two people. Who has no claim to found objects? Safekeeping of objects. Purchase, time-limit for reconsideration, illegal profit, duty of compensation, interest and speculation. Hiring of workers and animals. Renting and leasing; deposits; wage demands. Claims arising from the collapse of a building.

3. *Baba Bathra* (10) 'last gate'. Division of common property. Restrictions on the use of landed property. Positive prescription (*ḥazaqah*). Sale of real estate and movable property. The seller's warranty obligation. Law of inheritance. Division of assets. Wedding presents. Issuing of documents. Surety.

4. *Sanhedrin* (10) from Greek *synhedrion*, 'lawcourt'. A court of three men; a small Sanhedrin of 23, a great Sanhedrin of 71 members. Selection of arbitrators. Testimony. Who can be neither judge nor witness? The difference between civil and criminal litigation. Types of the death penalty. The disobedient son (Deut 21.18ff.). The burglar. The second offender.

Execution without judgement. Who has no share in the world to come? The rebellious teacher (*zaqen mamre*) and the false prophet.

5. *Makkot* (4), 'stripes'. On the penalty of beating (Deut 25.1–3). Beating of false witnesses. Involuntary manslaughter and the cities of asylum (Deut 19.1ff.; Num 35.9ff.). When does the penalty of beating apply? The number of stripes, manner of application. The penalty of lashing exempts one from extirpation. The reward of the commandments.

6. *Shebuot* (8), 'oaths' (cf. Lev 5.4ff.). The main types of oaths. Thoughtless and vain oaths. The testimonial oath; oath imposed by a judge. When does one refrain from swearing? Oaths relating to wages, in business and other matters. Four kinds of custodians (with or without pay, borrower, tenant).

7. *'Eduyot* (8), 'testimonies' of later teachers about the statements of earlier masters; also called *beḥirta*, selection. According to Ber 28a they were taught on the day when Eleazar ben Azaryah was installed in place of Gamaliel II. All in all there are 100 statements; also 40 cases in which the Shammaites interpret more leniently and the Hillelites more severely. Most of the statements recur elsewhere in M (following the thematic order).

8. *'Abodah Zarah* (5), 'idolatry'. Feasts of the idolaters. Regulations against unduly close contact with them. Idols. Wine of idolaters. How to purify utensils purchased from idolaters.

9. *Abot* (5), (sayings of the) 'Fathers', also *Pirqe Abot*, 'sections, chapters of the Fathers'. It is also possible to understand Abot as the 'fundamental principles' of the Mishnah: thus M. B. Lerner in Safrai, *The Literature*, 264. Chain of tradition from Moses to the end of the Tannaitic period. Maxims of these teachers. Anonymous number sayings and moral observations. Chapter 6, the praise of the Torah (*qinyan torah*, the 'acquisition of the Torah'), was only added later and does not belong to M.

10. *Horayot* (3), 'instructions, decisions'. Erroneous judgements in religious law. The sin offering, Lev 4.13f. Differences between the court, the high priest, and others in case of erroneous judgements. Other distinctions between the high priest and ordinary priests, etc.

### *§5. Fifth Order: Qodashim, 'Holy Things'*
(11 Tractates)

1. *Zebaḥim* (14), 'sacrificial victims' (cf. Lev 1ff.). Necessary intention. What makes a sacrificial victim unsuitable and under which conditions it remains suitable after all. Sprinkling of blood. Offering of birds. Precedence of offerings before other things. Purification of vessels. The priests' portion in the offerings. Burning of oxen and male goats. History of the sacrificial sites.

2. *Menaḥoth* (13), 'meal offerings', cf. Lev 2; 5.11ff.; 6.7ff.; 7.9f.; Num 6.13ff., etc. The necessary intention. Which infractions leave a meal offering suitable or render it unfit. Preparation of the meal offering. Loaves of the thank offering, the consecration and the Nazirite's offering. Measures for the meal offering. Drink offering. Sacrificial vows.

3. *Ḥullin* (12), 'profane things'. The slaughter of animals not intended for sacrifice, and other regulations about the consumption of animal foods. Who is permitted to perform ritual slaughter: by what means and how is this done? Clean and unclean animals. Meat may not be boiled in milk. Portions of slaughtered animals due to the priests. Firstfruits of sheep-shearing. The law of the bird's nest (Deut 22.6f.).

4. *Bekhorot* (9), the 'first-born', cf. Exod 13.2, 12f.; Lev 27.26f.; Num 8.16ff.; 18.15ff.; Deut 15.19ff. The first-born of donkeys, of unclean animals; inspection of the first-born. First-born animals unfit as offerings. Blemishes rendering a person unfit to serve as a priest. Hereditary rights of the first-born. Priestly rights in regard to the redemption money. Tithing cattle (Lev 27.32).

5. *Arakhin* (9), 'assessments', i.e. sums which must be paid for a vow, according to age and gender (Lev 27.2ff.). Who may assess? Minimum and maximum amounts. Consideration of the wealth of the person vowing. Obligation of the descendants. Confiscation in case of failure to pay the equivalent. Redeeming an inherited, purchased or sold field; walled cities (Lev 25).

6. *Temurah* (7) 'exchange' of sacrificial animals (Lev 27.10, 33). What may be exchanged. Difference between individual and communal offerings. Exchange for a sin offering. What may not be put on the altar? Which of the consecrated things must be burnt or buried?

7. *Keritot* (6), 'extirpations'. The punishment of 'extirpation' mentioned in the Torah (Exod 12.15, etc.) is interpreted as death of natural causes between the ages of 20 and 50, and without descendants. Extirpation applies to 36 intentional sins. Guilt offering in case of doubt. The power of the Day of Atonement.

8. *Me'ilah* (6), 'embezzlement' of consecrated things (Num 5.6–8; Lev 5.15f.). For which offering and from which time is embezzlement committed; where is it impossible? Use of consecrated things.

9. *Tamid* (6, now 7 due to the later subdivision of chapter 6), short for *'olat tamid*, the 'daily burnt offering', cf. Exod 29.38ff.; Num 28.3ff. The priests' night-watch in the sanctuary. Clearing up the altar. The various priestly tasks. The offering of the sacrificial lamb. Morning prayer. The

smoke offering. The high priest's sacrificial service. The priestly blessing and the Levites' songs.

10. *Middot* (5), temple 'measures' and furnishings. Night-watch in the temple. Temple gates; the fireplace. The Temple mount, walls and outer courts. The holocaust altar. The Temple. The outer court and its chambers. Thc Chamber of Hewn Stone.

11. *Qinnim* (3) 'bird's nests'. The offering of pigeons brought by poor women after childbirth (Lev 12.8) and paupers for certain offences (Lev 5.1ff.), which is also possible as a voluntary burnt offering (Lev 1.14ff.). Complications arising from the confusion of birds belonging to different people or to different types of offerings.

### *§6. Sixth Order: Toharot, 'Purities'*

(12 Tractates)

1. *Kelim* (30), 'utensils'. Which kinds of impurity can apply to utensils. Biblical points of reference: Lev 6.20f.; 11.32ff.; Num 19.14ff.; 31.20ff. Major kinds of impurity, degrees of impurity and of holiness. Earthen vessels; ovens and stoves; vessels with lids; utensils of metal, leather, etc. Beds, tables, riding equipment, etc. Distinction of the vessel's exterior, interior, stand, rims, handles, etc., with respect to possible pollution.

2. *Ohalot* (18), 'tents', or *Ahilot*, 'tent coverings'. On impurity spread by a corpse. This occurs not only by touching, but already if something is in the same 'tent' (Num 19.14). Which openings prevent or promote the spread of impurity? Discovery of corpses. Graveyards. Houses of Gentiles.

3. *Nega'im* (14), 'plagues', i.e. leprosy (Lev 13–14). Types of leprosy, inspection by the priest. Doubtful cases. The bright spots of leprosy. Leprous boils and burns. Skin diseases. Leprosy of clothes and houses. Purification of a leper.

4. *Parah* (12), the '(red) heifer' (Num 19). Age and properties of the red heifer. Slaughter and preparation of the ashes. Preparation and storage of the sprinkling water. How it may become unfit or impure. Effectual and ineffectual sprinkling.

5. *Toharot* (10), 'purities', euphemism for 'impurities'. Defilements lasting only until sunset. Animals not ritually slaughtered (*nebelah*). Degrees of defilement by touching unclean things. Doubtful impurity. Defilement through liquids. Defilement of oil and wine during pressing and treading.

6. *Miqva'ot* (10), 'immersion pools' for purification (origin in Lev 15.12; Num 31.23 for vessels; Lev 14.8 for lepers; 15.5ff. for those defiled by sexual emissions). Dimensions and nature of the bath. How is it to be applied and what renders it ineffectual?

7. *Niddah* (10), '(menstrual) uncleanness'; cf. Lev 15.19ff. (menstrual flow) and Lev 12 (woman in childbed). The menstruating woman; the woman in childbed. Samaritan, Sadducean and non-Israelite women. Various ages, female puberty, etc.

8. *Makhshirin* (6) 'what predisposes (to defilement)', also called *Mashqin*, 'liquids'. After being moistened by one of seven liquids, dry foodstuffs can become unclean by contact with something unclean (cf. Lev 11.34, 37f.).

9. *Zabim* (5), 'those with an unclean emission' (cf. Lev 15). On counting the seven clean days before the *zab* can be considered clean again. Questions on inspecting the emission; defilement by a *zab*. Comparison with different kinds of uncleanness. Enumeration of the things which render heave offerings unfit (*pasul*).

10. *Tebul Yom* (4) 'one who has taken a ritual bath on the same day' and who is still unclean until sunset (Lev 15.5; 22.6f.). He may touch profane things; but he renders heave offerings, Ḥallah and consecrated things unfit (*pasul*), although not unclean. How does contact with a part affect the whole?

11. *Yadayim* (4), 'hands', i.e. ritual impurity and purification of the hands; cf. Matt 15.2, 20; 23.25; Mark 7.2ff.; Luke 11.38f. Cleansing of hands by pouring water over them. How do hands become unclean? Writings which defile the hands, i.e. which belong to the biblical canon: debate about the Song of Songs and Qohelet. The Aramaic in Ezra and Daniel. Differences between Pharisees and Sadducees.

12. *Uqṣin* (3), 'stalks'. How stalks, peels and kernels transmit impurity to the fruit, and *vice versa*.

### *b) Is this Structure Original?*

(Cf. Epstein, *ITM*, 980–1006; Albeck, *Einführung*, 184–88.)
The division of the Mishnah into *six orders* is cited in Ket 103b in the name of R. Ḥiyya (T5): *shita sidre* (cf. BM 85b). Palestinian texts also use *erekh* instead of *seder*: e.g. PRK 1.7 (M. 11), *shesh erkhê ha-mishnah*. The Talmud repeatedly mentions the names of the individual orders. As for the sequence of the six orders, the extant arrangement already appears in an interpretation of Resh Laqish (A2) on Isa 33.6; he relates each term of the verse in turn to the orders of the Mishnah: 'stability' = Zeraim; 'your times' = Moed; 'abundance' = Nashim; 'salvation' = Neziqin; 'wisdom' = Qodashim; 'knowledge' = Toharot (Shab 31a). The connection of the orders with the individual terms is only partly plausible. This suggests that the sequence of the orders is a given, rather than derived from the Bible verse. Nevertheless, the text cannot prove that this sequence was already fixed by the third century. In MidrPsa 19.14 (B. 86a), R. Tanḥuma (A5) interprets Ps 19.8–10

of the six orders of the Mishnah, citing in this order Nashim, Zeraim, Toharot, Moed, Qodashim and Neziqin. The adduced references from the Psalm do not correspond to the order of the biblical text. In order to match the biblical order, Toharot was probably later moved into fifth place with the corresponding verse of the Psalm. This suggests that the author had the cited sequence of Mishnah orders before him (NB here, too, the link between Scripture verses and orders is highly tenuous). But this in turn means that in Talmudic times there was not yet a required sequence of the individual orders, even if the sequence familiar to us became more and more accepted (it is also compatible with BM 114b, where Neziqin is the fourth and Toharot the sixth order).

The *names of the tractates* are already largely attested in the Talmuds: thus e.g. Ber in BQ 30a, Yoma in Yoma 14b, RH in Taan 2a; Ket, Ned, Naz and Sot in Sot 2a; BQ and BM in AZ 7a; Sanh (incl. Mak) in p.Mak 1, 31b; Mak and Shebu in Shebu 2b; Eduy in Ber 28a, Abot in BQ 30a; Tam in Yoma 14b, Mid in Yoma 16a, Kel in Kel 30.4; Ahilot and Nega'im in p.MQ 2.5, 81b; Uqṣin in Hor 13b. The names usually derive from the content, and sometimes from the first word (thus Beṣah is more frequent than Yom Tob; Sheḥitat Qodashim is older than Zebaḥim; Mashqin older than MQ).

The *number of tractates* is now 63. However, originally the three 'gates' (*babot*) at the beginning of the fourth order constituted only one tractate, also called Neziqin: 'All of Neziqin is *one* tractate' (BQ 102a; cf. BM 10a, b). Like Kelim, this contained 30 chapters (LevR 19.2, M. 417). This original state of affairs is reflected in MSS Kaufmann and Parma; other MSS also number the chapters of the three 'gates' sequentially. It is only because of its size that this tractate was already in Talmudic times divided into three (similarly Kelim in T). The division was purely mechanical, into three 'gates' of 10 chapters each; thematically, BM 10 should be part of BB. Makkot originally constituted a single tractate with Sanh, viz., Sanhedrin containing 14 chapters as attested by MSS Kaufmann and Parma. This is also assumed in p.Mak 1.14, 31b: 'We learn here something which we do not learn in the entire (tractate) Sanhedrin. . . .' Here too the separation from Sanh was not carried out thematically: Mak 1 should still belong to Sanh. In the introduction to his Mishnah commentary, even Maimonides still reluctantly attests that in the MSS Mak and Sanh are connected and counted as a single tractate. Thus we arrive at 60 as the original number of tractates; this is also confirmed by R. Isaac Nappaḥa's (A3) interpretation of the 'sixty queens' of Cant 6.8 as the 'sixty tractates of halakhot' (CantR 6.14).

The *sequence of tractates* within the orders has not been uniformly transmitted: MSS and printed editions of M disagree just as much as the arrangement of the tractates in the transmission of T and the two Talmuds. The sequence here presented coincides with that of Maimonides in the introduction to his Mishnah commentary. The exception is the arrangement of Naz – Sot – Git: Maimonides here opts for the order Naz – Git – Sot, which because of the explicit testimony of Naz 2a and Sot 2a (was Maimonides unaware of these references?) has not prevailed. Otherwise there is little unequivocal Talmudic information on the sequence (Taan 2a: RH – Taan; Shebu 2b: Mak – Shebu). A consistent original sequence of tractates cannot be assumed. Within the orders, the guiding principle of the MSS appears to have been the number of chapters of the individual tractates, as was already supposed by A. Geiger (*Wissenschaftliche Zeitschrift für jüdische Theologie* 2 (1836) 489–92). This is at any rate the case for all orders except Zeraim, if the three 'gates' in the order of Neziqin are treated as a single tractate Neziqin, and Sanh and Mak taken together as the tractate Sanh with 14 chapters. In the order Qodashim, one should note that Tamid originally had not seven but six chapters. Where the sequence of individual MSS differs, this is consistently due to a switch of tractates with the same number of chapters. If the first edition of M includes Abot (five chapters) after Horayot (three chapters), this will be because of the unique status of Abot within the order (and M as a whole), and because it may once in fact have formed the conclusion of M. Nevertheless, it is worth noting that even this edition places Abot ahead of Horayot in its summarizing list of the fourth order.

The arrangement of the order Zeraim, however, altogether diverges from this principle, even if a group of longer tractates precedes the smaller ones. In the usual sequence, the numbers of chapters are 9 – 8 – 7 – 9 – 10 – 11 – 5 – 5 – 4 – 3 – 3. MS Vienna of T transposes this in the first part: Ter (11), Shebi (10), Kil (9); a Genizah MS also attests the sequence Shebi – Kil. But even if this were the original sequence, the arrangement of the first three tractates would still remain unexplained. Nor are we particularly helped by Abr. Goldberg's suggestion that this may be the secondary attachment of a partial order (in Safrai, *The Literature*, 234). Demai, the 'doubtfully tithed', which now is in third place, should on purely topical grounds follow Maas and Ter (NB MS Erfurt of T does in fact have Demai after Ter). The second place of Peah, too, can hardly be justified thematically. As for Ber, its position at the beginning of M may be due to its content (in the Munich Codex of the BT, Ber appears at the end of the order Moed). It is at any rate no longer possible to give a satisfactory clarification of the present arrangement of Zeraim. Some have surmised that the sequence Kil – Shebi – Ter, for example, should be explained on the basis of the underlying biblical texts (Lev 19; Lev 25; Num 18). However, it is impossible to substantiate the general assumption that the oldest arrangement of tractates is determined by the place of the relevant laws in the Pentateuch – even if the sequence of not a few regulations within the individual tractates can be explained by the proximity of pertinent statements in the Pentateuch. Certain tractates were doubtless placed next to each other because of topical connections (thus Maas and MSh). But even Maimonides' attempt to give a topical explanation of his supposedly original arrangement of tractates (in the introduction to his Mishnah commentary: configuration of like with like, precedence of the indispensable, succession in the Torah) remains unconvincing.

If within their orders the *massekhtot* are indeed primarily arranged according to the number of chapters, then the *chapter divisions* themselves must be older than this arrangement. And indeed we find as early as LevR 19.2 (M. 417) that Neziqin and Kelim are divided into 30 chapters each. In the Talmuds, certain chapters of M are in fact cited by the titles, formed by the first words, which are still in use today: e.g. p.Git 8.5, 49c 'he who divorces his wife' (m.Git 9); Yeb 96b 'four brothers' (m.Yeb 3); Nid 48a 'a child delivered by Caesarean section' (m.Nid 5). This of course does not preclude the possibility that some chapters were only later detached (m.Tam 6 and 7 count as one chapter in the MSS and the early commentaries) or added (Abot 6; Bik 4 from the T tradition). Moreover, occasional chapter divisions are topically incorrect, e.g. in Shab, where 9.1–4 thematically belongs with 8.7 (both are statements for which a cited Scripture passage serves not as a proof but as an allusion). Such inappropriate divisions can sometimes be older than the Talmuds and may go back to the reciters of M in the schools, the Tannaim.

The *sequence of chapters* within a tractate is not always unambiguously transmitted: e.g. in Erub, MS Oxford has the sequence 6, 5, 7, 4, while MS Munich places 5 before 3. The Geonim divide Pes into two: a) Chap. 1–4 and 10; b) Chap. 5–9. For this reason MS Munich directly attaches Chap. 10 to Chap. 4. In Tam, MS Florence has 4 before 3. In Ber, Rashi read 4 after 2. Printed editions of BT have Meg 3 in fourth place. In Git, Rabbenu Asher and many French texts switch 6 and 7. In MS Hamburg 19, BB 5 comes after 6, and 7 after 8. In the BT, Sanh 10 is in eleventh, Men 10 in sixth place.

The subdivision of chapters into *halakhot* or *mishnayot* is in any case old, and is already presupposed in the Talmuds.

The inconsistent arrangement of the tractates within their orders shows that this subdivision of M does not follow a normative original structure of the text, but was subject to the changing interests in the scholarly activity of the Rabbis and their successors. It was only the MS tradition and above all the effort of Maimonides which standardized the arrangement of the blocks of tradition within M, but without ever producing complete uniformity.

***c) A Structuring Principle of the Mishnah***

Despite a certain inconsistency in its textual tradition, the outline of M is fixed enough to raise the question of its structuring principle, even if we cannot accept Maimonides's explanation regarding the logical succession of the tractates. *The assignment of the individual tractates to their respective Sedarim* is almost without exception thematically justified. Ber, Naz, Eduy and Abot remain problematic.

1. *Ber* deals above all with the daily prayers; as such it does not really fit the order Zeraim, which is concerned with the laws of agriculture and agricultural products. It may have been assigned to this order because it also includes detailed discussions of table graces with their benedictions for the various foods. The theme of prayer commends a place for the tractate at the very beginning of the order and hence of the Mishnah as a whole, thus establishing its religious character from the outset.

2. The classification of *Naz* already raises questions in Sot 2a and Naz 2a. Its connection with Sot is explained in moral terms: one who considers the suspected adulteress accursed will forswear the seductive consumption of wine. In reality Naz belongs together with Ned: the special problem of women's vows (subject to cancellation by husband or father: Ned 10–11) warranted the inclusion of Ned in the order Nashim; Naz therefore took its place as a special case of vows, even though only 4.1–5 and 9.1 deal with Nazirite vows of women.

3. *Eduy*, 'Testimonies', will have entered the order Neziqin along with Shebu, 'Oaths'; due to its arrangement according to teachers (unique to M) and without thematic unity, the latter tractate could not be otherwise classified. Albeck, *Mishnah* 4:277 considers that Eduy was incorporated in Neziqin because the sayings it contains were attested before the Sanhedrin at Yabneh.

4. *Abot* is the only purely haggadic tractate in the Mishnah, and thus together with Eduy the second abnormal tractate. According to Albeck (*Mishnah* 4:348f.) it was included because the 'Fathers' were the members of the Sanhedrin. However, this explanation is quite doubtful. R. Yehudah says in BQ 30a, 'Whoever wants to be devout shall keep the laws of the "damages". Raba said, The instructions of the "Fathers".' If Raba here specifies Yehudah's statement, this would attest for his period the inclusion of Abot in Neziqin; but it would not explain it. A logical explanation may not be possible. More conceivable is the historical explanation of A. Guttmann: he considers that Abot was only inserted into M at a late date (c. 300) and hence was placed at the end of the work, which at that time was usually formed by the order Neziqin.

*Within the individual tractates*, a thematic arrangement predominates; but it is frequently interrupted by associations of substance, form, or the tradent's identity. Thus, for example, in Sotah the main theme is the suspected adulteress. Just as she is subject to a retaliation 'measure for measure', so also others – both for good and for evil (1.7–9). Yehoshua's statement about immoral women is followed by another in his name, regarding those who by their behaviour destroy the world (3.4). In the Sotah's meal offering there is a distinction between the daughter of a priest and the wife of a priest who is the daughter of an ordinary Israelite. This leads in turn to a discussion of the general differences between priests and daughters of priests, as well as between men and women. Formally, these statements are connected by the introduction *mah bên*, 'what is (the distinction) between. . .?' (3.7–8). A saying of R. Aqiba with R. Yehoshua's commentary in 5.1 is followed in 2–5 by two other sayings of R. Aqiba on the same day (*bo ba-yom darash R. Aqiba*), supplemented respectively by R. Yehoshua and others. The connection here is provided by the names of Aqiba and Yehoshua, and probably also by the cue of 'defilement'. Such associative insertions are most extensive in 7–9: the adjuration of the Sotah may be pronounced in any language; what else may be recited in any language, and what only in Hebrew? This leads to liturgical questions and to the subject of the calf whose neck is broken when a murderer is not found. The latter custom ceased with the increase in homicides; what else has changed in the course of time? From here, connections are drawn to the signs of the end.

In other places, the textual arrangement of M has apparently been influenced by the halakhic midrash and depends on the context of the biblical passage: e.g. MSh 5.10–14 explains Deut 26.13–15. Immediately following certain regulations about men with a mutilated penis (Deut 23.2f.), Yeb 8 speaks about the non-acceptance into the congregation of Ammonites and Moabites as well as the acceptance of Egyptians and Edomites (Deut 23.4ff.). The explanation of Deut 20.2–9 in Sot 8 is followed by that of Deut 21.1–9 in Sot 9. Despite its inappropriateness to the subject matter, BM 2.10 mentions the donkey collapsing under its burden (Exod 23.5) because the context deals with animals gone astray (Exod 23.4). Mak 2 has regulations about involuntary manslaughter Deut 19.4ff. and the cities of asylum Deut 19.2ff; these do not belong in the tractate, but are included because Mak 1 discusses cases in which false witnesses are to receive lashes (Deut 19.19). Shebu is largely composed of an explanation of Lev 5 (Chap. 1–4) and Exod 22.5–14 (Chap. 6–8).

Thus the composition of materials in M, which to the modern reader seems unsystematic, is due to various structuring principles in use at the time.

Complete coherence and uniformity are by definition not to be expected in the system of the rabbis. With all due caution, however, the differences in the arrangement of the material in the Mishnah may indeed be used to analyse its sources and history of tradition.

### *3) Origin*

#### *a) According to Tradition*

Almost all descriptions of the genesis of M are based on *Gaon Sherira*'s letter of 987, in which he answers the questions of the congregation of Kairouan: How was the Mishnah written down? Did the men of the Great Synagogue begin to write and did the sages write a section in each generation until Rabbi came and brought M to a conclusion? They are aware that the extensive anonymous material in M corresponds to the teaching of R. Meir, and that the most frequently mentioned scholars – Meir, Yehudah, Yose and Simeon – are students of Aqiba, with whom the halakhah agrees. But if the earlier sages transmitted a wealth of material to the later ones, why was nothing written down until the end of the time of Rabbi? Furthermore, the congregation at Kairouan desires an explanation of the arrangement of tractates in M, information about T, etc. (ISG, 4–6).

Sherira's answer combines scattered Talmudic information into a historical outline of the Talmudic period. Prior to Rabbi there was no homogeneous formulation of the laws, much less an ordered M. Concerned that the teaching might be lost, Rabbi took up the redaction of M. He did not proceed at his own discretion, but examined the tradition all the way back to the men of the Great Synagogue, in order to adopt verified sentences verbatim (Sanh 5.2 is cited as proof: Ben Zakkai's appearance without the title Rabban is taken to mean that this tradition dates from a time before his ordination). Some tractates like Uqṣin (taught at the time of Simeon b. Gamaliel, according to Hor 13b) and Eduyot (recited on the day of Eleazar ben Azaryah's installation, according to Ber 28) pre-dated Rabbi; he merely supplemented them with teachings from the time of his father. Sherira considers that the anonymous teaching in M is indeed that of Meir, based on Aqiba who in turn receives from his teachers. A written version of M was not previously necessary, since all agreed and taught the same; differences of opinion only arose because of the numerous students of Hillel and Shammai.

This depiction of a uniform transmission of M from ancient times until its edition by Rabbi is based on the notion in ISG that the oral Torah derives directly from Moses (others state this explicitly). Sherira avails himself of this uniform image of the development of tradition in his fight against the Karaites and their devaluation of the rabbinic tradition. Saadya also stresses the great age of the oral Torah in his *Sefer ha-Galuy* (S. Schechter, *Saadyana*

(Cambridge 1903), 5); but according to him it was already the men of the Great Synagogue who began to write down the Mishnah. Finally, STA (*Maḥzor Vitry* (Jerusalem 1963), 484) claims on the basis of Ḥag 14a: 'From the days of Moses until Hillel there were 600 orders of the Mishnah, as the Holy One had given them to Moses on Sinai; but in Hillel's time respect for the Torah became weak, and so Hillel and Shammai only established six orders' (cf. also Responsum 20 in *Shaare Teshubah: Responsa of the Geonim*, New York 1946; and Bereshit Rabbati, ed. Albeck, 48).

Modern scholarly introductions have generally not advanced beyond these rudimentary beginnings (cf. J. Neusner (ed.), *The Modern Study*). Almost without exception, a long prehistory of M is assumed. Some take it back to the revelation to Moses on Sinai (D. Hoffmann); but in general its origin is seen in the exilic study of Scripture or in the men of the Great Synagogue (e.g. Z. Frankel), in which case Ezra also warrants the direct connection with biblical times. Another popular idea is the haggadah of the 600 orders of M before Hillel, or at least the creation of the six orders by Hillel himself or in his time (e.g. N. Krochmal). Ch. Albeck and others, following Sherira, do not assume a fixed order of M prior to Rabbi, but they nevertheless maintain that the origins of the mishnaic halakhah are centuries older than M itself. Only J. N. Epstein largely dispenses with a reconstruction of the pre-mishnaic period and generally relies on a literary-critical examination of M itself.

The following, then, are the points of reference of a traditional common opinion: Rabbi Yehudah ha-Nasi edited M; his main source was the Mishnah of R. Meir, who in turn is based on the Mishnah of his teacher Aqiba. Yet even Aqiba was not the Mishnah's first redactor, but resorted to a 'first Mishnah' whose roots go back to biblical times.

This description appears to find support in rabbinic evidence. Frequently quoted is a statement of R. Yoḥanan, 'Anonymous statements of M (*stam matnitin*): R. Meir; those of T: R. Neḥemyah; those of Sifra: R. Yehudah; those in Sifre: R. Simeon. And all follow R. Aqiba' (*we-kulhu 'aliba deR. Aqiba*: Sanh 86a). Quite apart from the problem of the reliability of this tradition, the text does not explicitly speak of ordered or even written M collections of Aqiba or Meir, but can also be understood of the halakhah underlying M. The same is true of Sanh 3.4, where Aqiba's M is contrasted with the first M (similarly Naz 6.1 and t.MSh 2.12, L. 253; Ket 5.3 and Git 5.6: the first M vs. later decisions; t.MSh 2.1, L. 249, and Sifre Zutta *Naso* 5.10, H. 232 designate certain teachings as M of R. Aqiba): 'Mishnah' here can also mean a single halakhah. This does not necessarily imply a redactional activity of Aqiba. Two other texts, however, do seem to affirm such activity: 'When R. Aqiba ordered halakhot for his students' (*mesader*: t.Zab 1.5, R. 337), he had them produce counter-arguments. S. Lieberman (*Hell.*, 91) understands this as an examination of the *hypomnēmata*, the students' written notes; he interprets this statement (like p.Sheq 5.1, 48c: 'R. Aqiba, who established (*hitqin*) midrash, halakhot and haggadot') as referring to Aqiba's redactional activity.

Despite the difficulty of evaluating these rabbinic statements, they cannot simply be neglected. This is also clear from non-Jewish sources, viz., two unfortunately imprecise or corrupt references in Epiphanius: 'Among the Jews the traditions of the elders are called *deuteroseis*. These are four: one is in the name of Moses [*mishneh torah*, i.e. Deut? but N.B. the context implies a non-biblical work], the second is according to the so-called R. Aqiba, the third according to Adda or Judah, the fourth according to the sons of the Hasmonaeans' (instructions of John Hyrcanus? or a mutilation of Hoshayah? *Haer*. 33.9, *GCS* 25.1:459f.). The parallel text (*Haer*. 15.2, p. 209f.) reads, 'For there were four *deuteroseis* among them: one is named after the prophet Moses, the second after their teacher Akiba or Barakiba, another after Adda or Annas who is also called Judah, another after the sons of the Hasmonaeans.'

### *b) Biblical Interpretation as the Origin of the Mishnah?*

***Bibliography***

**Aicher, G.** *Das Alte Testament in der Mischna.* Freiburg 1906. **Avery-Peck, A. J.** 'Scripture and Mishnah: The Case of the Mishnaic Division of Agriculture.' *JJS* 38 (1987) 56–71. **Halivni, D. W.** *Midrash, Mishnah, and Gemara: The Jewish Predilection for Justified Law.* Cambridge, MA 1986. **Lauterbach, J. Z.** 'Midrash and Mishnah: A Study in the Early History of the Halakah.' *JQR* N.S. 5 (1914–15) 503–27; 6 (1915–16) 23–95, 303–23. [Repr. in idem, *Rabbinic Essays*, 163–256. New York 1973 (=Cincinnati 1951).] **Melamed, E. Z.** 'Halakhic Midrashim in the Mishna and Tosephta' (Hebr.). *Bar-Ilan* 2 (1964) 84–99. **Neusner, J.** *Method and Meaning in Ancient Judaism*, 2:101–213. Chico 1981. **Neusner, J.** *Judaism: The Evidence of the Mishnah* (Chicago 1981), 167–229. **Neusner, J.** 'Accommodating Mishnah to Scripture in Judaism: The Uneasy Union and Its Offspring.' In idem, *Formative Judaism*, 2:153–68. Chico 1982. **Rosenblatt, R. S.** *The Interpretation of the Bible in the Mishnah.* Baltimore 1935. **Safrai, S.** *The Literature*, 1:146ff. **Sarason, R. S.** 'Mishnah and Scripture: Preliminary Observations on the Law of Tithing in Seder Zera'im.' In W. S. Green (ed.), *Approaches to Ancient Judaism*, 2:81–96. Chico 1980. **Urbach, E. E.** 'The Derasha as a Basis of the Halakha and the Problem of the Soferim' (Hebr.). *Tarbiz* 27 (1957–58) 166–82. **Weingreen, J.** *From Bible to Mishnah: The Continuity of Tradition.* Manchester 1976. **Zeitlin, S.** 'Midrash: A Historical Study.' In idem, *Studies in the Early History of Judaism. History of Early Talmudic Law*, 4:41–56. New York 1978.

The rabbinic view of the Sinaitic origin of the oral Torah naturally lets M begin at Sinai, too. Alongside this theory of a coexistence of oral and written Torah from the beginning, the other traditional opinion is that oral Torah derives from the written, and is the latter's consistent exegesis. Sherira already claimed (ISG 39) that the early teachers at the time of the Second Temple proceeded according to the midrashic method of Sifra and Sifre, i.e. that they derived the halakhah from the Bible or taught in connection with it, even where the halakhah is independent of the Bible. Sherira's statement, which probably also reflects anti-Karaite polemics, has been adopted by N. Krochmal, Z. Frankel, J. Brüll, D. Hoffmann, etc. (implicitly in apologetic defence against the Christian thesis of *Spätjudentum*, 'Late Judaism': J. Neusner, *Method*, 158). J. Z. Lauterbach (*Rabb. Essays*, 163ff.) expanded it: he considered the Maccabean period as the time when the mishnaic method of teaching halakhah without reference to Scripture arose alongside the midrashic method. To explain this rise of the mishnaic method, Lauterbach points out that in a period without teaching authority numerous biblically unfounded halakhot had become so accepted that they could no longer be displaced; at the same time, the Pharisees could use the doctrine of the oral Torah connected with these underived halakhot to support their own teaching authority. Against this chronological explanation, Halivni (pp. 18ff.) argues that it was only the pressure of external circumstances after 70 which temporarily caused the mishnaic method to displace the midrashic approach: the Mishnah is 'a composite work, excerpted from earlier sources, from Midrash' (p. 53).

On the other hand there are those who believe that the halakhah was not originally derived from Scripture, nor taught within the framework of exegesis: and that therefore the mishnaic method precedes the midrashic one. This view finds support in the fact that the halakhot of the earliest masters are always transmitted without biblical argumentation. Also worth mentioning is the account of Hillel's decision regarding the preparation of the Passover sacrifice on the Sabbath (p.Pes 6.1, 33a: cf. p. 17 above), assuming that it has at least a usable historical core. This opinion is held by Halevy (*Dorot*, 1c:292ff.; 1e:467ff.), G. Aicher and S. Zeitlin. According to Zeitlin the midrashic form was only adopted in order to bestow a higher authority on the halakhot from the time of the Second Temple. From Qid 49a ('What is M?' R. Meir says, 'halakhot'; R. Yehudah says, 'midrash'; cf. Sanh 86a: the anonymous M agrees with Meir, the anonymous Sifra with R. Yehudah), Zeitlin deduces that during the collection of the halakhah in a single corpus, Meir favoured a thematic arrangement and Yehudah an arrangement according to the Pentateuch.

Others take a mediating position and hold to a co-existence of both methods (thus e.g. S. Safrai, *The Literature*, 1:154). J. N. Epstein (*ITL* 503ff.) and Ch. Albeck (*Einführung*, 56–93) follow Sherira in assuming the temporal precedence of the midrashic teaching method; but they emphasize that although the halakhah is frequently supported by the Bible, it does not derive from there. E. E. Urbach assumes that in the earliest period the established authorities (the Sanhedrin and its scholars as well as the courts) appointed the halakhah in the form of *taqqanot* and *gezerot*, while the non-authoritative *soferim* based themselves on biblical interpretation. Thus, he believes that biblical interpretation only slowly developed into an equivalent source of halakhah. After 70, scholars were becoming *soferim* (m.Sot 9.15: but in the context the *soferim* should rather be seen as school teachers, so that the passage affirms a decline of scholarship before the end of the world!); finally the day was won by Aqiba's school, which wanted to derive every halakhah from Scripture.

In the present state of our knowledge, such historical reconstructions are hardly possible. The simple evidence of the M text itself shows that there are essentially three groups of halakhot: 1) those derived from Scripture; 2) halakhot independent of Scripture; 3) halakhot which arose independently of Scripture but were later connected with it. This corresponds with an anonymous statement in Ḥag 1.8:

> (The laws about) the cancellation of vows are suspended on air and unsupported. (The halakhot about) the Sabbath, festivals and the profaning of consecrated things are like mountains suspended on a hair. Here there is little Scripture and many halakhot. Civil law, temple service, purities and impurities, and incest (laws) have something to support them. They are the essence of the Torah (*gufê torah*).

Ephrati (*Bar-Ilan* 11) stresses the poor attestation of the reading 'on a hair' (*be-sa'arah*) as opposed to the other reading 'in the storm' (*samekh* in place of *sin*). He regards the statement as polemical against the Yabnean attempt to teach the halakhah systematically: while some principles are unbiblical or only weakly supported in Scripture, the others constitute biblical teaching (*gufê torah*) and require no systematic reorganization. However, even if Ephrati's analysis is historically correct, the mere absence of a negative reply to the statement already shows it to have been positively adopted; it is thus to be understood simply as a factual declaration of the relationship of the halakhah to Scripture.

Only a precise analysis of every single M tractate, indeed of every single complex of laws, can lead to a more accurate definition of the relationship of M to the Bible. M has comparatively few biblical quotations, and even these are in part later additions. Arguments from Scripture ('as it is written') are, moreover, relatively rare. In general, the Mishnah creates the impression of a deliberate effort to be independent of the Bible. A closer observation of individual tractates, however, shows that each one has a different relation to

Scripture. Some tractates appear as a mere paraphrase, commentary and expansion of the biblical text: thus, for example, almost all of the fifth order of M, except for Tam and Mid which are intended not as scriptural interpretation but as a representation of actual circumstances at the time of the Temple; similarly those tractates of Seder Toharot which discuss the sources of uncleanness. At thc same time J. Neusner rightly stresses, 'Sameness, five hundred years later, is the greatest difference' (*Method*, 170): at issue is not merely the reproduction and treatment of certain biblical passages, but also the respective selection and perspective of reproduction (in which Qodashim entirely ignores the priesthood). 'Mishnah constitutes a statement on the meaning of Scripture, not merely a statement of the meaning of Scripture' (ibid., 168). Other M passages indeed are also expanding commentaries on Scripture, but they could never be developed from the biblical text alone (e.g. the tractate Qinnim). Finally there are numerous passages of M which are completely independent of the Bible, or even contradict it. This is true for long stretches of the sixth order, which deal with places and objects of uncleanness and with ways of their elimination. A considerable number of fundamental hermeneutical principles are here presupposed (e.g. that purity regulations also apply outside the cult).

A historical conclusion about early preliminary stages of M cannot be gained from such insights. Even in tractates which are obviously based on the Bible, M itself does not claim very early origins: the earliest cited authorities are from the beginning of our era. Other tractates (like Makhshirin) which are quite independent from Scripture commence after 70; but even tractates with biblical foundations arrive at their interpretation only on the basis of presuppositions that are alien to Scripture. The identification of M units which are constructed not systematically or by association but in accordance with the Biblical text may therefore in individual cases serve to isolate sources within M, but it cannot verify an extended prehistory connecting M directly with the Bible.

***c) Preliminary Stages of Our Mishnah***

The attempt to illustrate a long prehistory of M by way of an early stage of halakhic presentation, based on Scripture and deriving from exegesis, can be considered a failure. Nevertheless, the question of preliminary stages of our M remains. Sherira already assumes that in his redaction of M, Rabbi had certain tractates before him, viz., Eduyot and Uqṣin. Various Amoraim also claim such sources for Rabbi, not merely in Yoḥanan's general statement that the anonymous M comes from R. Meir and all follow R. Aqiba (Sanh 86a), but also in the attribution of individual tractates (their basic core, their anonymous portions, or only individual halakhot?) to certain Tannaites before Rabbi.

J. N. Epstein (*ITL*, 25–58; similarly concise E. E. Urbach, *EJ* 12: 93–102) works out a number of M collections which are supposed to have their origin in the period of the Temple or shortly after its destruction. He includes the basic core of Sheq (author Abba Yose ben Ḥanin: p.Sheq 6.2, 49d), Tam (Simeon of Miṣpah: thus Yoḥanan, p.Yoma 2.3, 39d; contrast Jacob bar Aḥa: not all is from him, but only the 'sayings which were required by the Rabbanan', *millin ṣerikhin le-rabbanan*, i.e. with which they agreed), Mid (Eliezer ben Jacob: Yoma 16a; p.Yoma 2.3, 39d with the same restriction as for Tam) and Yoma, where he believes Tam has already been used as in Mid. Likewise Epstein takes into account parts of Taan, Suk, Ḥag, Qid and individual sections in almost all tractates. He allows for later revision and complementation in all of these tractates, even Sheq, Tam and Mid (names of later rabbis), but he relies on the all but complete originality of the M texts he has identified.

Epstein's argumentation has many predecessors (e.g. D. Hoffmann and L. Ginzberg). Some of his primary criteria are substantive (matters concerning the Temple (service) or which still presuppose a king) and others linguistic in nature (e.g. on Tam or Bik 3.1–8, a frequently cited text which describes Agrippa's offering of firstfruits in the Temple: archaic language, idiosyncratic expressions – do these few remarks suffice to isolate sources or even to establish such an early date?). Above all, however, Epstein's criteria consist of Amoraic attestations that this or that Tannaite is responsible for a given tractate. Such Talmudic data, however, do not constitute proof but can at best suggest a possible solution that must be substantiated by other means. Thus when e.g. Eliezer b. Jacob in Mid 2.5 and 5.4 says, '*I* have forgotten what its use was', Epstein (*ITL*, 31) takes this to denote explicitly that the entire preceding description comes from him; his name has been inserted in order to explain the first person singular. But this is hardly conclusive. Similarly, Urbach's reference to Demai 2.2–3; Ḥag 2.7; 3.6f. as conditions of admittance to a society, for which there are parallels at Qumran, demonstrates not 'the antiquity of the formulation and phraseology of these halakhot' (*EJ* 12:96), but at best the antiquity of their content.

In order to arrive at convincing results, the internal criteria for a separation of sources – language, contradictions within M, dependence of one halakhah on another, and perhaps form critical considerations – would need to be applied on a much greater scale. What is at issue here is not the dating of the content of two halakhot, but their literary treatment (for criticism cf. J. Neusner, *Method*, 166f., n.8). By means of a form critical analysis, Neusner (*Eliezer*, 2:52) arrives at a negative conclusion regarding a fixed formulation of M before 70: 'We do not have any significant evidence that a corpus of Mishnah – whether in writing or orally formulated and orally transmitted in exactly the language of the original formulation – lay before Eliezer.'

Ch. Albeck (*Einführung*, 94–129) feels compelled to accept the Amoraic attributions of Tam and Mid (127), but he weakens them by saying that several anonymous teachings in these tractates appear in our M in the style prescribed by R. Simon of Miṣpa in Tam and R. Eliezer b. Jacob in Mid (128). In his view the tractate first subjected to redaction is Eduyoth, which according to t.Eduy 1.1 (Z. 454) dates back to the scholars at Yabneh: fearing that the Torah might be forgotten, they formally ordered the halakhah, beginning with Hillel and Shammai (122ff.). Unlike the rest of M, the arrangement of the material is according to names of tradents and formal criteria, much of it recurring in topically appropriate contexts in the other tractates. Albeck considers this to be due merely to the chronological priority of Eduy, although he concedes that we have the tractate not in its original form but with many later alterations and additions (for a more discriminating analysis of the tractate see Epstein, *ITL*, 422–44, who rejects Albeck's opinion (428); cf. also Neusner, *Phar* 2:326ff.). Albeck's theory is indeed untenable; yet the peculiarity of Eduy remains a fact, whether one explains it by the tractate's greater age or by its provenance from a school different from the rest of M. However, a verifiable evaluation of these observations for the redaction criticism of M has yet to be achieved.

As for R. Aqiba, whom according to Sanh 86a all follow, his importance for the development of the M tradition is undoubted. The Amoraim already pointed out the fact that in his presentation of halakhah Meir never quotes in the name of Aqiba (this is in fact true for M). R. Yoḥanan explains this by saying, 'Everyone knows that Meir is a student of R. Aqiba' (p.Ber 1, 4b). Many anonymous statements of M can indeed be identified as Aqiba's teaching (time and again in BT). A tradition in ARN A 18 (Sch. 67) compares Aqiba to a worker who collects in his basket everything he finds, wheat, barley, etc., and then sifts it at home. 'Thus did R. Aqiba, and he made the whole Torah into rings and rings', i.e. he ordered it systematically, in the shape of 'rings'. We should also recall the text of Epiphanius cited earlier. Similarly EcclR 6.2; 12.7 and CantR 8.1 merit attention: they each cite the M of R. Aqiba as one example of *mishnayot gedolot* (on the problem of these texts see Epstein, *ITL*, 71). Another relevant fact is the significant volume of quotations of Aqiba in M as well as his share in its anonymous material.

Our question here, however, is not the extent of Aqiba's contribution to the *material* of M, but whether Aqiba created an ordered, edited M collection which is still identifiable by *literary criteria*. The relatively homogeneous style of our M not only makes unlikely the discovery in M of Aqiba's *ipsissima verba*, but all the more renders impossible the verification of a literary preliminary stage of M. If, for example, Epstein (*ITL,* 71) calls Aqiba the father of our M, this may be true for the material, but it cannot be established for the literary form of M (cf. Ch. Primus, *Aqiva's Contribution of the Law of Zera'im* (Leiden 1977), 7: 'In Aqiva's traditions on agriculture I see no evidence to suggest the existence of an Aqivan proto-mishnah'; cf. ibid., 194). If Aqiba did create a proto-Mishnah, this must have been completely absorbed in the work of his students.

A similar case is the *Mishnah of Meir*, who is mentioned time and again in M, and who undoubtedly stands behind many anonymous halakhot. His M was reputedly the direct basis of Rabbi's M, even if according to Hor 13b–14a one does not mention the names of those who once wanted to undermine the dignity of the dynasty (i.e. Meir and Nathan). Some have attempted to trace entire chapters of today's M directly back to Meir (thus Git 8, Eduy 4 and Ber 8: Epstein, *ITL,* 99f.). However, it is possible at most to establish the agreement of the teaching in these chapters with Meir or his generation, but not the assumption that Meir himself so formulated the statements and collated them into closed chapters. Although frequently mentioned as the teacher of certain halakhot in M, Meir in fact is entirely without a profile of his own. It is true of him as of the other students of Aqiba (Yehudah ben Ilai, Eleazar ben Shammua, Simeon ben Yoḥai and Yose ben Ḥalafta, but also Abba Saul, whose M some have attempted to reconstruct) that we can at best identify the traditional material attributed to them, but not discover their literary traces (if indeed they were ever engaged in literary activity!): 'The men of the generation(s) following Meir were so successful at leaving their mark on these traditions that any reconstruction of the earlier shape of things must remain hypothetical at best' (R. Goldenberg, *The Sabbath-Law of Rabbi Meir* (Missoula 1978), 246).

Further, one cannot safely infer from Hor 13b (Meir and Nathan wanted to embarrass Simeon ben Gamaliel by challenging him to recite Uqṣin; he did not know this tractate but learned it just in time, after Jacob b. Qodshi alerted him by his continual vocal recitation of it) that the tractate was already in a fixed shape at that time; even less does the text establish that the tractate entered our M in that shape (as is assumed by ISG and many others). Neither is anything proved on the basis of Kel 30.4, where Yose b. Ḥalafta says, 'Happy are you, Kelim: for you began with impurity but ended with purity'. W. Bunte (ad loc. in the Giessen M) supposes Yose to be the redactor of the tractate, or to have had the tractate already before him in completed form; on p. 7, however, he does allow for the possibility of a final redaction by Rabbi. The statement could apply just as well to an earlier form of the tractate or to an unspecified unit of teaching in Kelim; or it might indeed merely refer to the practice of seeking a positive ending even for negative subjects.

At least with the presently available methods, then, the prehistory of M is not feasible as a reconstruction of its literary sources. 'Mishnah's formulation and its organization are the result of the work of a single "generation" of tradents-redactors: tradents who formulate units of thought, and redactors who organize aggregations of said units of thought. Mishnah is not the product of tradents succeeded by redactors.' This verdict of Neusner (*JQR* N.S. 70 (1979–80) 142) may be a little too pessimistic with regard to the elucidation of preliminary stages of M (cf. the strictures of R. S. Sarason, ibid., 150), but it does correspond to what can at present be demonstrated. Even where textual units in M are arranged according to a principle different from the rest of M (e.g. by purely formal criteria in Meg 1.4–11; Men 3.4–4.4, etc.), we may indeed suppose relatively fixed prior formulations, but their unchanged transmission is not guaranteed.

By contrast, at least the major stages in the growth of the *material* in the Mishnah can be traced with relative certainty, as especially Neusner has shown: possible origins before 70 – Yabneh – Usha – final redaction. Even though the attribution of given sayings to individual masters will frequently be in doubt, nevertheless they can quite safely be assigned to specific *generations* of scholars; in the same way the extensive anonymous material is largely subject to historical classification. Beyond this, particularly in regard to whether the final redactor of M used fixed oral or written sources, progress may perhaps be hoped for with a future refinement of methods, but it cannot at present be achieved.

***d) The Redaction of the Mishnah***

Rabbinic tradition unanimously regards R. Yehudah ha-Nasi, simply called 'Rabbi', as the author of M (cf. Epstein, *ITL*, 200). 'Rabbi and Rabbi Nathan are the end of the Mishnah; Rab and Rabina the end of the (authoritative) teaching' (*hora'ah*: BM 86a). This much-quoted sentence does not of course directly attribute the composition of M to Rabbi, but merely uses his and R. Nathan's name to mark the end of the mishnaic period. However, the unself-conscious attribution of mishnaic decisions to Rabbi clearly suggests that M is his work (e.g. Ket 95a: 'Here Rabbi decided anonymously according to R. Meir, there according to R. Yehudah'; R. Yoḥanan in p.Qid 3.14, 64c; R. Simeon ben Laqish in p.Shab 14.1, 14b, etc.).

Nevertheless, M in its present shape cannot possibly come from Rabbi himself. On the contrary, numerous additions were made in the course of time. Among these are above all passages in which Rabbi himself is named and his opinion is contrasted with that of others (Naz 1.4; Mak 1.8, etc.: cf. *ITL*, 194–99), and also passages mentioning teachers who lived after Rabbi: this is the case especially in Abot (2.2 Rabbi's son Gamaliel; 6.2 Yehoshua ben Levi; all of 6 is a later addition) and at the end of certain tractates (e.g. Sot 9.15 (which also mentions the death of Rabbi); AZ 2.6, where 'Rabbi and his court' probably refers to Yehudah Nesia; and Uqṣin 3.12 Yehoshua ben Levi). In general, these must be seen as later augmentations of M from T, halakhic midrashim and baraitot, and partly also from the Amoraic discussion of M; in other cases the transmitting Tanna has simply substituted 'Rabbi' for the speaker's 'I' (but this is a source of errors: not only Yehudah ha-Nasi is Rabbi, but every Tanna calls his own teacher 'Rabbi'). Hence these passages do not present a decisive objection against the assumption of Rabbi as the redactor of M, as long as we suppose that for a time the text retained a certain flexibility (cf. Epstein, *ITM*, 946ff.). What is more, the term 'redactor' must be broadly understood, and Rabbi must be seen as the main figure under whose authority M essentially took its shape. We must continue to stress that the role of Rabbi in the formation of M cannot be strictly proven: the fact is merely that there are no decisive arguments against the tradition which links the redaction of M with his name.

The attribution of a document to a certain author can usually also be verified by comparing the document with the author's other opinions transmitted elsewhere. For M such a comparison is already greatly complicated by the fact that the very mention of Rabbi is very often due to errors of transmission (mistaken omission of the name after the title 'Rabbi'; incorrect reading of abbreviations such as R.Y., and thereby the displacement of Yoḥanan or Jonathan by Rabbi, etc.). We have as yet no comprehensive examination of the traditions attributed to Rabbi. Above all, this question is closely related to the problem of the intention of M, which will be discussed below.

As the Amoraim stress time and again, the anonymous teaching of M (i.e. the part which can be seen as the redactor's opinion) in many cases does not correspond to the opinion of Rabbi as attested elsewhere (cf. *ITL*, 200ff.). Repeatedly we read, 'M is not like Rabbi' (p.Beṣah 2.3, 61b on Beṣah 2.3; RH 19b on RH 1.3; Arak 31a on Arak 9.3, etc.). Men 72a refers to a contradiction within M and attributes one opinion to Rabbi, the other to R. Eleazar ben R. Simeon. There are also contradictions between anonymous teachers and statements attributed to Rabbi in T (cf. e.g. t.Ber 3.18, L. 16, with Ber 4.5; t.Shab 10.19, L. 45, with Shab 11.6, etc.). In explanation of such contradictions one can cite the statement attributed to Rabbi, 'I consider their words as better compared with my words' (Kil 2.11; the reading *Rabbi omer* is to be preferred in place of the *R. Meir omer* in the conventional editions; cf. *ITM*, 1203). In Erub 38b it says about such passages, 'Rabbi taught this, but he does not hold this view.' This takes into account later changes in Rabbi's opinion, as well as his inclusion of established opinions even where he is not of the same opinion.

These assumptions are not implausible, but they do require a further explanation: why does Rabbi transmit statements with which he does not (any longer) agree? Granted this presupposition, what is his intention for M? Has he in this case deposited his own opinions anywhere? E. Z. Melammed (*Introduction*, 120) assumes a private collection of Rabbi's household; this was edited by his students and sons, and according to Melammed (similarly Abr. Goldberg in S. Safrai, *The Literature*, 1:294f.) has been preserved primarily in T, where Rabbi is mentioned about 250 times, but also in the Talmuds and in the halakhic midrashim (cf. Epstein, *ITM*, 43ff. on the numerous traditions *debê Rabbi*). Albeck (*Einführung*, 161f.), too, supposes a private collection of the school of Rabbi, a 'Talmud' of Rabbi (p.Shab 16.1, 15c) which was recited as a supplement to M and which contained the legal decisions. Of course this assumption of a private halakhic collection is no more than a supplementary hypothesis, if, on the presupposition of Rabbi as the redactor of M, one wants to give a comprehensive explanation of statements in M, as well as other material attributed to Rabbi, which differs from the latter's opinion. Goldberg's view (in Safrai, *The Literature*, 1:217), that the successive redactors of M up to and including Rabbi always merely officially formulated the teachings of the preceding generation, is a hypothesis which unnecessarily complicates matters.

The reason for Rabbi's transmission of statements with which he disagrees, as well as for the further definition of his supposed private collection, is closely linked with the old problem of the purpose of M: is it a mere *collection of sources*, a *teaching manual*, or a *law code* of current halakhah?

Ch. Albeck is of the opinion that Rabbi's principles in the redaction of M represent the fundamentals of any purely 'academically' oriented *collection.* The redactor collected the sources and clarified the most important readings, thereby transmitting an 'eclectic' text of the 'thirteen kinds' of halakhah he had learned (cf. Ned 41a); but he did not change them and did not insert his own opinions (*Einführung*, 157). Albeck considers that in the final redaction the halakhot were not changed but fixed and arranged in exactly the formulation in which they had been transmitted; this implies for him that the redactor's intention in M was not to organize halakhic decisions 'for practical application' (*lema'aseh*) (*Einführung*, 155; cf. 156, 463f.). Albeck's decision is based on his view that 'the redactor of the Mishnah made no changes, adjustments, or cuts in the material before him, but established it in our Mishnah in the form in which he had received it' (149).

Like his teacher Albeck, Abr. Goldberg ('Purpose') deduces from the repetitions and linguistic irregularities within M, etc. that the latter cannot be a code of current law. Instead, he sees M as a teaching manual designed above all on the basis of pedagogical criteria, which offers the most material in the shortest possible form. This intention he believes to be evident above all in Rabbi's combination of the sources. The editor's aim was 'an official text of study for the academy, regardless of whether the source chosen is the accepted law or not. The editor does not commit himself to any particular point of view, other than a general acceptance of the Akivan line in the Hillelite tradition' (Goldberg in Safrai, *The Literature*, 1:227).

J. N. Epstein (*ITL,* 224–26), finally, holds to the most widespread opinion of M as a *legal canon* in which the anonymous decisions respectively represent the current halakhah, even if in a given case the legal decision of M may not be immediately apparent. With a view to this law code, Rabbi changed, augmented or deleted, scrutinized and revised existing halakhot, combined various sources, but also preferred majority opinion to his own.

Beginning no later than the third generation, the Amoraim did indeed regard M as a legal code and as an internally altogether consistent system. This often led to rather forced interpretations, occasional corrections of the text, and the frequent assumption of elliptical speech in M (*ḥasore meḥasra*, 'something is missing', as an interpretative principle: cf. Epstein, *ITM,* 595–672). Much as in biblical interpretation, the assumption was that M contained no unnecessary repetitions. This Amoraic interpretation is of importance with respect to the historical impact of M, but it says nothing about the original intention of M. The latter is rather to be ascertained from internal criteria; these, however, are not unambiguous, as is sufficiently demonstrated by the widely differing assessments of such eminent experts as Epstein and Albeck.

The view of M *as a collection of sources* appears to find support in the repetitions of halakhot, internal contradictions, anonymous decisions diverging from Rabbi's views as cited elsewhere (in T and the baraitot), as well as in some linguistic observations. Repetitions and particularly contradictions are difficult to account for in a code of current law. On the other hand M must not be judged by modern criteria. Repetitions often occur because tractates or even chapters are intended as far as possible to form closed and self-contained units, or because M sometimes quotes extended units of text even if not everything pertains to the respective context (especially for the halakhot compiled according to formal criteria, or in the collation in Beṣah of the alleviations of the school of Shammai over against that of Hillel). Similarly, the inclusion of laws which are no longer valid (e.g.

Toharot) points less to a code than to a collection of traditions or a teaching manual, although it may have been done with a view to the future, when the observation of these halakhot might again become possible.

However, a verbatim adoption of unchanged sources does not suffice to explain all the literary peculiarities of M: nor is it a necessary explanation. Moreover, the question arises whether a mere collection of sources, without any revision or definite intention, would really have met a need for the rabbinate of the day (especially since this collection is by no means complete).

As for the contradictions in M, Men 72a for instance resorts to an identification of the authors: Men 10.9 declares the sheaf of the first fruits valid if it was reaped in the daytime; but Meg 2.6 considers the whole night suitable for reaping the barley sheaf. According to Men 72a, the one decision is from R. Eleazar and the other from Rabbi. M would thus not always decide a discussion, nor would the anonymous opinion necessarily agree with that of Rabbi; but instead the redactor would transmit a discussion undecided, and insert his own opinion elsewhere. The resolution of contradictions in M is particularly problematic, and it is too easily influenced by preconceived opinions about Rabbi's intentions.

The theory of *M as a teaching manual* is a mediating position. The formal requirements for such a manual are less strict than for a law code. Didactic motivations could be paramount; and this would explain both the manner of the redaction of sources (but how is this recognized?) and above all repetitions. Of course M would in no way meet modern requirements for a teaching manual: too much is taken for granted. As a teaching manual, M certainly could not have been intended for the self-taught; instead, it might have served as a guide for teaching, a summary of doctrine in a broader presentation and description, always accompanied by explanations and tied to particular presuppositions of knowledge which are not shared today. What is more, we do not know enough about the rabbinic school system and its pedagogical methods to attain certainty in this matter.

The view of *M as a law code* has indeed become traditional, but it is (from today's perspective) beset with the greatest difficulties. The main counter-arguments include the aforesaid aspects which cause Albeck to opt for a collection of sources. In a law code, moreover, the rebuttals featured in the discussion leading up to the decision would only confuse the reader. What also speaks against this view is the frequent difficulty (not just for the modern reader) of deciding what in fact is the valid halakhah. Apart from its historical impact, this theory (along with that of M as a collection) has in its *favour* above all the fact that M presents statements as halakhah which contradict what is elsewhere offered as Rabbi's opinion. Together with the much more frequent agreement of the anonymous final decision in a discussion with theses elsewhere attributed to Rabbi, this suggests that Rabbi attempted to arrive at a universally accceptable summary of the halakhah, even if he himself does not agree with every detail of it. It is, moreover, not necessary to regard M as entirely the personal work of Rabbi. Indeed, it is more plausible to regard M as the instruction offered in his school, i.e. as the work not of an individual but of a group headed by Rabbi. This might also have contributed to the fact that M really shows no personal stylistic peculiarities.

Given today's knowledge, it is no longer possible unequivocally to determine whether M was originally conceived as a collection, a teaching manual or a law code. Indeed this alternative probably arises only for modern readers; what is more, it fails to account sufficiently for the utopianism of M, its idealized order of the perfect harmony of heaven and earth, and the underlying philosophy. In principle, the ancient tradition is of course regarded as law which must be transmitted in teaching – and thus the three concepts almost coincide. And a certain development cannot be excluded. The summary of the halakhah in Rabbi's school, with its endeavour to include a great variety of rabbinical opinions, will at the same time have been a political move intended to unite Judaism under the direction of the patriarchate: although primarily the basis of teaching in schools, it was also the foundation for the judgements in Rabbi's court. Rabbi's exceptional authority then led to the work being regarded as a code of binding law for all of rabbinic Judaism, like the Bible the cornerstone and basis of new developments by interpretation (cf. Epstein, *ITM*: the attitude to M changes from about the third Amoraic generation; where necessary, it now came to be interpreted very unnaturally or subjected to textual correction, but it was no longer contradicted with baraitot).

How should the *redaction and publication of M* be imagined? The redactional work essentially consisted of sorting, compiling, selecting and supplementing received traditions to produce an organic whole of stylistic unity. This was accomplished not by clerical work but in the school, as a team effort under Rabbi's leadership, and in questions of practically applicable law probably also in cooperation with the patriarch's court. Publication should not be pictured as an official written edition, the original of which might for purposes of reference and control have been deposited at the patriarch's court. There were only unofficial copies containing individual sections; this accounts for the flexibility in the transmission of the work as a whole and of its organization. Should there really have been an official publication, this is best seen in the form suggested by S. Lieberman (cf. p.

41f. above): viz., a number of Tannaim painstakingly committed the text to memory and were then able to recite the desired portions. This implied a certain textual fluidity, inasmuch as these 'living editions' could supplement the text with short explanations offered in the schools, were permitted to add influential decisions even of Rabbi's grandsons, corrected mistakes that had arisen in the course of transmission (NB not necessarily restoring the original version), and so on. But at the same time this mode of transmission also involved a certain rigidity of the text, an autonomy of the tradition which the original editor could no longer freely dispose of. Changes of opinion could not easily be incorporated into the text; attempts to do so may in fact have contributed to the diversification of the textual tradition, especially after M had also found acceptance in other scholastic centres.

The 'canonization' of M after the middle of the third century did not necessarily effect a freezing of the textual tradition, but in turn caused textual changes (harmonization with the practised halakhah), explicative and supplementary additions. Commentary on M in the Amoraic period also had a retroactive effect on the text. New possibilities of textual alteration then arose from the mainly written transmission of M. Only this stage of textual development is accessible to textual criticism; the latter cannot trace an autograph of M, since such a document probably never existed. The earlier textual development of M is indeed sporadically discernible through various MSS and Talmudic discussions, but it does not permit a definite judgement about M at the time of Rabbi.

In summary, we can only observe the crystallization of the tradition into an ordered whole in the circle around Rabbi; certain avenues of growth remained open for about fifty years, until M was subjected to the usual textual development of documents which have become canonical. Our sketch of the redaction and publication of M has a certain plausibility in its favour, but it is contingent on too many unknown factors to be considered certain.

### *4) The Text: Manuscripts and Editions*

***Bibliography***

**Epstein, J. N.** *ITM*. **Krupp, M.** 'Manuscripts of the Mishna.' In Safrai, *The Literature*, 1:252–62. **Schachter, M.** 'Babylonian-Palestinian Variations in the Mishna.' *JQR* N.S. 42 (1951–52) 1–35. **Schachter, M.** *The Babylonian and Jerusalem Mishnah textually compared* (Hebr.). Jerusalem 1959. **Sossman** (=Sussman), **Y.** 'Manuscripts and Text Traditions of the Mishna' (Hebr.). *7th WCJS* (Jerusalem 1981) 3:215–50. **Zeitlin, S.** 'Ha-Mishnah she-ba-Talmud Yerushalmi we-ha-Mishnah she-ba-Babli.' In B. Z. Luria (ed.), *Zer li-gevurot: The Zalman Shazar Jubilee Volume*, 539–48. Jerusalem 1973.

### *a) Manuscripts*

In the manuscript transmission of the M text one must distinguish between the Palestinian and the Babylonian text type. Both types date back to the earliest Amoraic textual tradition. However, they were never uniformly developed in their respective countries, but will have differed slightly from school to school (cf. B. M. Bokser in Neusner (ed.), *The Modern Study*, 33f., in critique of Epstein). Even in their later manifestation these types are not purely preserved but have influenced each other (e.g. Babylonian vocalization of a Palestinian text). Independent Mishnah MSS (i.e. without commentary or Gemara) belong exclusively to the Palestinian textual tradition. The Gemara of PT was transmitted without the text of M – even in MS Leiden of PT the latter was always only added from MS Parma. MSS of BT, on the other hand, always included M in its Babylonian recension. Maimonides's commentary on M, too, is based on the Palestinian text type of M, although he often alters it according to the Babylonian tradition. This mixed version was then also adopted by the first printed edition of Naples.

### *1. Genizah Fragments*

The oldest extant M texts are individual fragments from the *Cairo Genizah.* They are now dispersed among different libraries and museums (especially Cambridge, Oxford, London, Leningrad and New York). Their value varies considerably: the oldest ones date perhaps to the late seventh or eighth century, the latest are more than 800 years younger. Of particular significance are the vocalized texts: both the old Palestinian and the Tiberian and Babylonian vocalization are represented. The Genizah fragments have been published only in part.

#### *Bibliography*

**Alloni, N.**, ed. *Geniza Fragments.* [12 Fragments from M, mostly prior to the 11th cent.; comprehensive Hebrew introduction.] **Katsh, A. I.** *Ginze Mishna: One Hundred and Fifty Nine Fragments from the Cairo Geniza* (Hebr.). Jerusalem 1970. [Fragments from the particularly valuable Antonin Collection, Leningrad; incl. MS 262 containing a large part of Toharot. The edition is not satisfatory.] **Yeivin, I.** *A Collection of Mishnaic Geniza Fragments with Babylonian Vocalization: With Description of the Manuscripts and Indices* (Hebr.). Jerusalem 1974.

**Allony, N.** 'Qeta' Mishnah 'im Niqqud Ereṣ–yisraeli.' In *Sefer Yovel le-Rabbi Ḥanokh Albeck* (*Festschrift* Ch. Albeck), 30–40. Jerusalem 1963. [And cf. ibid., 114–22: A. Greenbaum, 'Biurim. . . .'] **Allony, N.** 'Qeta' Mishnah Nusaf be-Niqqud Ereṣ–yisraeli.' *Sinai* 72 (1973) 11–29. [2 leaves, 10th–11th cent., Sanh 10.6–Mak 1.1; Shebu 6.3–7.7.] **Friedmann, C. B.** 'Zur Geschichte der ältesten Mischnaüberlieferung: Babyl. Mischna-Fragmente aus der Altkairoer Geniza, veröffentlicht und kritisch untersucht.' *Jahrbuch der Jüdisch-Literarischen Gesellschaft* 17 (Frankfurt am Main 1927) 265–88. **Kahle, P. & Weinberg, T.** 'The Mishna-Text in Babylonia: Fragments from the Geniza.' *HUCA* 10 (1935) 185–222. **Kahle, P.** 'The Mishnah Text in Babylonia II.' *HUCA* 12–13 (1937–38) 275–325. **Katsh, A. I.** 'Unpublished Geniza Fragments of Pirke Aboth in the Antonin Collection in Leningrad.' *JQR* N.S. 61 (1970–71) 1–14. **Mirkin, R.**

'Two Mishna Fragments from the Cairo Genizah' (Hebr.). In E. Y. Kutscher et al. (eds.), *Henoch Yalon Memorial Volume*, 371–84. Jerusalem 1974. **Morag, S.** 'Mishnayot min ha-pereq "Ba-meh madliqin" bi-shnê kitbê-yad shel Genizat Qahir.' In J. Blau et al. (eds.), *Studia Orientalia Memoriae D. H. Baneth Dedicata*, 111–23. Jerusalem 1979. [Shab 2]. **Murtonen, A.** 'Qeta'ê Mishnah be-Niqqud Babli.' *Leshonenu* 21 (1956–57) 1–6. **Sharvit, S.** 'Tractate Bikkurim: The Printed Edition Compared with Genizah Fragments' (Hebr.). *Bar-Ilan* 6 (1968) 22–32.

Brief descriptions and lists of Genizah fragments are given in **Sacks, N.**, ed. *Mishnah Zeraim*, vol. 1 (Jerusalem 1972), 87–112; vol. 2 (Jerusalem 1975), 39–43.

For a general survey see **Sussmann, Y.** 'Talmud Fragments in the Cairo Geniza' (Hebr.). In M. A. Friedman (ed.), *Cairo Geniza Studies*, 21–31. Tel Aviv 1980.

### *2. The Most Valuable Complete Mishnah Manuscripts*

*MS Kaufmann*: Library of the Hungarian Academy of Sciences, Budapest, Collection Kaufmann A 50. The most important Mishnah MS, usually dated to the beginning of the thirteenth century. M. Beit Arié, 'K"Y Kaufmann shel ha-Mishnah [Budapest A50]: Moṣa'o u-zemano', in *Qobeṣ Ma'amrim bi-lshon Ḥazal* 2 (Jerusalem 1979–80) 84–99) proposes the early twelfth century; D. Rosenthal, *Mishna Aboda Zara* (Hebr.), Diss. Jerusalem 1980, 123–30, dates the MS to the eleventh century at the latest, since MS Parma is assumed to depend on it; M. Krupp ('Manuscripts', 253) adopts this early date. This MS has a Palestinian text type with subsequent Tiberian vocalization; the script is probably Italian. There are 286 leaves in all; the text is complete except for one leaf (m.Ker 3.7–5.2). For a description see S. Krauss, *MGWJ* 51 (1907) 54–66, 142–63, 323–33, 445–61; the vocalization is discussed in G. Birnbaun, *Leshonenu* 48–49 (1984–85) 269–80; facsimile ed. by G. Beer, The Hague 1929, reduced reprint Jerusalem 1968.

*MS Parma*, Biblioteca Palatina, De Rossi 138. This MS contains 195 leaves and reveals a Palestinian text type in Oriental square script, later partially vocalized. It is usually dated in the mid-thirteenth century. However, G. Haneman in his dissertation (Jerusalem 1972) already identified one scribe of this MS with that of MS Vatican 31 (dated to 1072/73). In any case the close relationship between the two MSS suggests a date for MS Parma in the eleventh century, which would make it the oldest extant complete manuscript of M: M. Krupp, 'The Relationship Between MS Parma De Rossi 138 of the Mishna and MS Vatican 31 of the Sifra, Seder Eliyahu Rabba, and Zutta' (Hebr.), *Tarbiz* 49 (1979–80) 194–96; I. Z. Feintuch, 'On the Parma Manuscript' (Hebr.), *Bar-Ilan* 18–19 (1981) 196–217. Feintuch already previously attempted to show that MS Parma was used as *Vorlage* in MS Leiden of PT (*Tarbiz* 45 (1975–76) 178–212). Facsimile edition Jerusalem 1970, 2 vols.

*MS Cambridge*: University Library Add. 470:1. 250 leaves, c. 1400. Jerusalem text family, Sephardic-Greek script. Published by W. H. Lowe, *The*

*Mishnah on which the Palestinian Talmud Rests*, Cambridge 1883, repr. Jerusalem 1967.

A complete text of M is also contained in the two complete Talmudic MSS: *Leiden*, University Library Collection Scaliger 3, for PT; for BT: *Munich*, State Library, Cod. Hebr. 95.

Of particular significance is the M text in the autograph of the M commentary of Maimonides (see below, p. 146). Codex Paris 328–29 is also important (facsimile with introduction by M. Bar Asher, 3 vols., Jerusalem 1973): in two volumes it contains the entire M with a Hebrew translation of the M commentary of Maimonides. Written 1398–1401 at Cesena; a linguistic analysis of the MS is offered by M. Bar-Asher, *The Tradition of Mishnaic Hebrew in the Communities of Italy* (Hebr.), Jerusalem 1980. Codex Parma 'B' De Rossi 497, Seder Toharot (facsimile with introduction by M. Bar Asher, Jerusalem 1971).

For a short description of the MSS see N. Sacks, *Mishnah Zeraim* vol. 1 (Jerusalem 1972), 65–81; 2 (Jerusalem 1975), 55.

### *b) Printed Editions*

#### *1. Early Printed Editions*

Only a few pages remain of the first printed Mishnah of 1485; hence the edition of Naples 1492, a work of J. S. Soncino, is considered the *editio princeps*. This also contains the Hebrew commentary of Maimonides, and it has probably been the main source for the M text. It is a mixed text: although closer to the Palestinian type, it also betrays Babylonian influence. Cf. Epstein, *ITM* 1275–8 and A. M. Haberman in the introduction to the reprinted edition, Jerusalem 1970. Later editions generally present the Babylonian text type, e.g. the Justiniani print, Venice 1546–47, and the edition Venice 1548–49 with the commentary by Obadiah of Bertinoro. Yom Tob Lipmann Heller produced an edition corrected on the basis of MSS with his own commentary (*Tosafot Yom Tob*): Prague 1614–17; Cracow 1643–44. This became the basis of all later printed editions, among which we should mention especially the Romm edition, 13 vols., Wilna 1908–09 (begun as early as 1887, but expanded, reprinted and completed in 1908 after an interval).

#### *2. Modern Complete Editions*

Ch. Albeck, *Shishah Sidre Mishnah*, 6 vols., Jerusalem 1952–58, repeatedly reprinted. This contains a text vocalized by H. Yalon, with introductions and brief annotations to each of the tractates. It is a conveniently practical but uncritical edition (see Abr. Goldberg, *KS* 34 (1958–59) 274–80).

Two *critical editions* are in process:

The so-called '*Giessen Mishnah*'. Publication began in 1912 under the tutelage of G. Beer and O. Holtzmann, and was later supervised by K. H. Rengstorf, L. Rost and S. Herrmann. Until 1935 it appeared in Giessen, then in Berlin, where publication resumed in 1956. Text, German translation, introduction, commentary in the form of footnotes; and a valuable text-critical appendix. Compared with the earlier issues, the quality of the volumes published in Berlin is much improved. While the earlier volumes produced a mixed text, the later volumes use Codex Kaufmann; the MSS variants are placed in the critical apparatus, in keeping with the current state of textual criticism in M. All in all, 42 tractates had appeared by 1991; only the order Zeraim is now complete.

Tractates published so far:

*Zeraim.* Ber: O. Holtzmann, 1912; Peah: W. Bauer, 1931; Demai: W. Bauer, 1931; Kil: K. Albrecht, 1914; Shebi: D. Correns, 1960; Ter: E. Güting, 1969; Maas and MSh: W. Bunte, 1962; Ḥallah, Orlah, Bik: K. Albrecht, 1913, 1916, 1922.

*Moed.* Shab, Erub: W. Nowack, 1924, 1926; Pes: G. Beer, 1912; Yoma: J. Meinhold, 1913; Suk: H. Bornhäuser, 1935; Beṣah: W. E. Gerber, 1963; RH: P. Fiebig, 1914; Taan: D. Correns, 1989; Meg: L. Tetzner, 1968; MQ: E. L. Rapp, 1931.

*Nashim.* Yeb: K. H. Rengstorf, 1929 (corr. repr. 1958); Naz: M. Boertien, 1971; Sot: H. Bietenhard, 1956; Git: D. Correns, 1991.

*Neziqin.* BQ, BM, BB, Hor: W. Windfuhr, 1913, 1923, 1925, 1914.

*Qodashim.* Arak: M. Krupp, 1971; Tam, Mid, Qin: O. Holtzmann, 1928, 1913, 1931.

*Toharot.* Kel: W. Bunte, 1972; Ohal: W. Bunte, 1988; Parah: G. Mayer, 1964; Toh: W. Bunte, 1981; Nid: B. Z. Barslai, 1980; Zab: W. Bunte, 1958; Tebul Yom, Yad, Uqṣim: G. Lisowsky, 1964, 1956, 1967.

The Institute for the Complete Israeli Talmud, Jerusalem, has begun a large M edition of which the first order has been published thus far: *The Mishnah with Variant Readings Collected from Manuscripts, Fragments of the 'Genizah' and Early Printed Editions and Collated with Quotations from the Mishnah in Early Rabbinic Literature as well as with Bertinoro's Commentary from Manuscript: Order Zeraim I*, ed. N. Sacks, Jerusalem 1972; *Order Zeraim II*, ed. N. Sacks, Jerusalem 1975. The base text is not a MS but the Romm edition, Wilna 1908–09.

### *3. Editions of Individual Tractates* (in alphabetical order)

D. Rosenthal, *Mishna Aboda Zara – A Critical Edition (with Introduction)*, Diss. Jerusalem 1980 (textual basis MS Kaufmann; detailed introductory volume in Hebrew); idem, '"Nusaḥ Ereṣ Yisra'el" we–"Nusaḥ Babel" be-Mishnat Abodah Zarah', in S. Raam (ed.), *Meḥqarim be-Sifrut ha-Talmudit (Festschrift* S. Lieberman, Jerusalem 1983), 79–92. – R. T. Herford, *The Ethics of the Talmud: Sayings of the Fathers*, London 1925, frequently reprinted (Aboth: text, translation, commentary); S. Sharvit, *Textual Variants and Language of the Treatise Abot and Prolegomena to a Critical Edition*, Diss. Ramat Gan 1976; S. Sharvit, 'The Textual Criticism of Tractate Avot', in Safrai, *The Literature*, 1:277–81; S. Sharvit, 'An Oriental Mishnah of the 12th Century' (Hebr.), *Alei Sefer* 17 (1992–93) 5–17; M. Assis, 'Mabo le-mahadurah madda'it shel Massekhet Arakhin', *Asufot* 5 (1990–91) 9–101. – M. Krupp, *Mischnatraktat 'Arakin': Computergesteuerte textkritische Ausgabe*, Hildesheim 1977. – Abr. Goldberg, *The Mishna Treatise Eruvin: Critically Edited and Provided with Introduction, Commentary and Notes* (Hebr.), Jerusalem 1986. – P. R. Weis, *Mishnah Horayoth, Its History and Exposition*, Manchester 1952 (cf. Abr. Goldberg, *KS* 32 (1956–57) 163–68). – T. Hirth, *Der Mischnatraktat 'Keritot' nach Handschriften und Erstdrucken herausgegeben, übersetzt und kommentiert*, Diss. Tübingen 1973. – J. Rabbinowitz, *Mishnah Megillah: Edited with Introduction, Translation, Commentary and Critical Notes*, London 1931 (repr. Westmead 1970). – A. S. Kaufman, *The Temple of Jerusalem: Tractate Middot. An Ancient Version composed from manuscripts* (Hebr.), Jerusalem 1991 (an eclectic edition based on 33 MSS, including Genizah fragments and early printed editions). – T. Z. Meacham, *Mishnah Tractate Niddah with Introduction: A Critical Edition with Notes on Variants, Commentary, Redaction, and Chapters in Legal History and Realia* (Hebr.), 2 vols., Diss. Jerusalem 1989. – Abr. Goldberg, *The Mishnah Treatise Ohaloth: Critically Edited and Provided with Introduction, Commentary and Notes* (Hebr.), Jerusalem 1955. – Abr. Goldberg, *Commentary to the Mishna: Shabbat; Critically Edited and Provided with Introduction, Commentary and Notes* (Hebr.), Jerusalem 1976 (cf. Z. A. Steinfeld, *KS* 55 (1979–80) 571–83). – Y. Feliks, *Mishna Tractate Shevi'it: A Study of the Mishnaic Text on its Botanical and Agricultural Background* (Hebr.), Jerusalem 1987 (critical text with commentary); E. Z. Melammed, 'Shevi'ith Tractate (according to Manuscripts and Geniza Fragments)' (Hebr.), E. Y. Kutscher et al. (eds.), *Henoch Yalon Memorial Volume* (Jerusalem 1974), 385–417. – H. Fox, *A Critical Edition of Mishnah Tractate Succah with an Introduction and Notes* (Hebr.), 2 vols., Diss. Jerusalem 1979. – A. Brody, *Der Mišna-Traktat Tamid*, Uppsala 1936.

***c) Translations***

Among the early translations it is worth mentioning *Mischna... cum Maimonidis et Bartenorae commentariis integris: Accedunt variorum auctorum notae ac versiones: Latinitate donavit ac notis illustravit* Guilielmus Surenhusius, Amsterdam 1698–1703 (in part translated by others); Johann Jacob Rabe, *Mischnah oder der Text des Talmuds. . . übersetzt und erläutert*, 6 parts, Onolzbach 1760–63.

An excellent complete translation is H. Danby, *The Mishnah: Translated from the Hebrew with Introduction and Brief Explanatory Notes*, Oxford 1933, often reprinted. J. Neusner, *The Mishnah: A New Translation*, New Haven 1988. Complete translations are also in the Soncino (English) and L. Goldschmidt (German) editions of BT. Spanish: C. del Valle, *La Misná*, Madrid 1981. An antiquated translation is *Mischnajoth. . . Hebr. Text mit Punktuation, deutscher Übersetzung und Erklärung*, Berlin 1887ff., 3rd edn. Basel 1968 (Zeraim: A. Sammter; Moed: E. Baneth; Nashim: M. Petuchowski; Neziqin: D. Hoffmann; Qodashim: J. Cohn; Toharot: D. Hoffmann). There are numerous translations of individual tractates (see also above on the textual editions and below on M commentaries).

***d) Concordance***

Ch. Y. Kasovsky, *Thesaurus Mishnae: Concordantiae verborum quae in sex Mishnae ordinibus reperiuntur*, 4 vols., Jerusalem 1957–61; H. Duensing, *Verzeichnis der Personennamen und der geographischen Namen in der Mischna*, Stuttgart 1960.

**5) The Interpretation of the Mishnah**

The Interpretation of M begins in part already in T and then above all in the two Talmuds, whose understanding of M largely determined the later interpretation of M. Independent study and interpretation of M apart from the Talmud were only resumed relatively recently.

Saadya Gaon (882–941) is reputed to have written a commentary on M, but this does not survive. The commentary of Hai Gaon (939–1038) likewise has been lost. The *Perush ha-Geonim* was erroneously attributed to him by its first editor, J. Rosenberg (Berlin 1856), but it probably derives from the circle of his students. This oldest preserved M commentary is a compendium; it is extant only for Seder Toharot. It contains linguistic explanations in particular (comparison with Arabic, Persian, Greek and Aramaic) and relies on the Talmuds, T, the Targums and LXX. J. N. Epstein, *Der Gaonäische Kommentar zur Mischnaordnung Teharoth zugeschrieben R. Hai Gaon*, 2 fascicles, Berlin 1921–24; idem, *Der Gaonäische Kommentar zur Ordnung Tohoroth: Eine kritische Einleitung. . .*, Berlin 1915 (Hebrew summary with additional units of text: 'The Supplement to the Gaonic Taharot' (Hebr.), *Tarbiz* 16 (1944–45) 71–134.

There is an Arabic commentary with short explanations of vocabulary and subject matter by R. Nathan, the head of the Palestinian Yeshibah in the eleventh century (Hebr. translation by J. Qafiḥ in the M edition *El Hamekoroth*, 13 vols. Jerusalem 1955–58). Almost nothing survives of the numerous glossaries on M: see N. Aloni, 'Two Fragments from the Geniza Dealing with Mishnaic Vocabulary' (Hebr.), in Y. Hocherman et al. (eds.), *Yaacov Gil Jubilee Volume* (Jerusalem 1979), 249–55.

Between the ages of 23 and 30, Maimonides (1138–1204; on the year of his birth see S. D. Goitein in G. Nahon & C. Touati (eds.), *Hommage à Georges Vajda* (Leuven 1980), 155) wrote a M commentary in Arabic, which was later called *kitab as-sirag* or *sefer ha-ma'or*, 'Book of the Light', since *ha-ma'or* was Maimonides's title of honour. This work contains an introduction to M and a treatise on the Tannaites. Parts of it, e.g. the introduction, the commentary on Abot and especially the *Pereq Ḥeleq* (m.Sanh 10) with the 13 principles of faith, were also transmitted separately. Already during Maimonides's lifetime, the work was partly translated into Hebrew; in 1297 a complete translation was jointly produced by several contributors in Spain. The Hebrew translation was first printed in the M edition of Naples in 1492, and rendered in Latin in the translation of M by G. Surenhusius, Amsterdam 1698–1703. Arabic text with Hebrew translation: J. Qafiḥ (ed.), *Mishnah 'im Perush Rabbenu Moshe Ben Maimon, Maqor we-Targum*, 7 vols., Jerusalem 1963–68 (3rd edn. 1976–78 in 3 vols., Hebr. only). Cf. on this J. Blau, *Leshonenu* 30 (1965–66) 54–60; 31 (1966–67) 235–39; 32 (1967–68) 399–401; 35 (1970–71) 75–78. Maimonides's own copy (others consider it the autograph) has also been preserved; it is today divided into several MSS: Oxford Bodl. 393 (Zeraim) and 404 (Neziqin, Qodashim), and Sassoon 72 (Moed) and 73 (Nashim), NB now in Jerusalem; Toharot is entirely missing, but even the rest of the MS is not complete (e.g. Shab and Erub 1–7 are missing). Facsimile with Hebrew-English introduction: S. D. Sassoon & R. Edelmann, *Maimonidis Commentarius in Mischnam*, 3 vols., Copenhagen 1954–56. On the MS: S. M. Stern, 'Autograph Manuscripts of the Commentary on the Mishnah by Mainonides' (Hebr.), *Tarbiz* 23 (1953–54) 72–83; J. Blau, 'Do We Really Possess an Autograph of Maimonides' Mishna-Commentary?' (Hebr.), *Tarbiz* 27 (1957–58) 536–43; S. M. Stern & S. D. Sassoon, 'The Autograph Manuscript of Maimonides' Commentary on the Mishna' (Hebr.), *Tarbiz* 29 (1959–60) 261–67. English Translation: F. Rosner, *Moses b. Maimon: Commentary on the Mishnah: Introduction to Seder Zeraim and Commentary on Tractate Berachoth*, New York, 1975; cf. also G. Stemberger, 'Maimonides als Mischna-Ausleger', *Kairos* 28 (1986) 196–208.

Isaac ben Melchizedek of Siponto (c. 1090–1160) wrote a commentary on Zeraim based especially on PT, but also T, Sifra, BT and the Geonim. In the Middle Ages his commentary on Toharot, too, was frequently cited, but it is not preserved. Critical edition: N. Sacks, *Perush ha-RIBMAṢ le-Rabbenu Yiṣḥaq be-R. Malkiṣedeq me-Simpont la-Mishnah Zeraim*, Jerusalem 1975. Samson b. R. Abraham of Sens (c. 1150–1230) wrote a commentary on M Zeraim (except Ber) and Toharot (except Nid), which is contained in most editions of the Talmud. A commentary on the same tractates was also produced by Asher ben Yeḥiel (Rosh), who was from Germany and died in Spain in 1327. His commentary essentially summarizes his predecessors and supplements them; it was first printed in abbreviated form in the 1717 Amsterdam edition of the Talmud, and fully at Altona in 1735 (Zeraim) and Frankfurt in 1720–22 (Toharot).

The outstanding authority is the commentary by Obadiah of Bertinoro (Italy; after 1486 in Jerusalem, where he died in 1510): first published in Venice in 1548–49, and since then in almost all editions of M. A Latin translation was prepared by G. Surenhusius. He relies on Rashi's commentary on the Talmud; in Zeraim and Toharot, where there is no Gemara, he generally follows Samson of Sens. He also normally appends the decision of the halakhah, following Maimonides.

Yom Tob Lipmann Heller (1579–1654) of Wallerstein in Bavaria, later rabbi at Prague and Cracow, supplemented Bertinoro's commentary. These 'additions', *Tosafot Yom Tob*, were first printed at Prague in 1617, and in revised and enlarged form at Cracow in 1642–44. Since then they appear in most M editions. Solomon ha-Adani (1567–c.1625) also wrote a commentary to supplement that of Bertinoro: *Melekhet Shlomo*; like Heller, he too is important for the textual criticism of M because of his knowledge of MSS. The commentary is printed in M Romm, Wilna. The latter also contains the commentaries of the Gaon Elijah of Wilna (1720–98) on Zeraim, Toharot and certain tractates of the other orders, as well as the commentary *Tif'eret Yisra'el* by R. Yisrael Lipschütz (1782–1861), which first appeared with M in six volumes at Hannover, Danzig (Gdansk), Königsberg (Kaliningrad) 1830–50. This commentary is concerned above all with practical halakhah according to the Shulḥan Arukh. It consists of two parts – a literal explanation (*peshat*) and an explanation in the style of the *pilpul* – which Lipschütz calls Jachin and Boaz after 1 Kgs 7.21.

In addition to the cited works, the M edition Romm, Wilna, contains numerous other traditional commentaries (see Albeck, *Einführung*, 415–38; A. Marx, 'The "Romm" Mishnah', *JQR* N.S. 2 (1911–12) 266–70).

All the cited commentaries are loyal to tradition. This means above all that M is interpreted in light of the Talmud. The remarks are usually kept in the form of glosses which deal with linguistic or halakhic details and almost never take into account a larger context; they are generally not interested in the material documentation of life in mishnaic times or in the historical context.

If we omit the numerous specialized studies of individual tractates (especially Abot) or sections of text, there are only two *modern commentaries* (NB Albeck's commentary in his edition of M is also traditional in nature, and limited to short glosses):

(i) After their general introductions, the individual volumes of the '*Giessen Mishnah*' are limited to a gloss-like commentary; but this does comprise the essential issues of language, substance, and (to a lesser extent) the history of religion. Nevertheless, this type of commentary prevents a more detailed treatment of literary questions such as those concerning the structure of a pericope, relationships with parallels, matters of form and tradition criticism.

(ii) This more comprehensive treatment has been provided by J. Neusner in his commentary on the order Toharot, and much more briefly on the orders Qodashim, Nashim, Moed and Neziqin: *A History of the Mishnaic Law of Holy Things*, 6 vols., Leiden 1978–80; *A History of the Mishnaic Law of Women*, 5 vols., Leiden 1980; *A History of the Mishnaic Law of Appointed Times*, 5 vols., Leiden 1981–83; *A History of the Mishnaic Law of Damages*, 5 vols., Leiden 1983–85. In the same fashion Neusner's students have treated most of Zeraim: R. Brooks, *Support for the Poor in the Mishnaic Law of Agriculture: Tractate Peah*, Chico 1983; H. S. Essner, 'The Mishnah Tractate 'Orlah: Translation and Commentary', in W. S. Green (ed.), *Approaches*, 3:105–48; P. J. Haas, *A History of the Mishnaic Law of Agriculture: Tractate Maaser Sheni*, Chico 1980; M. S. Jaffee, *Mishnah's Theology of Tithing: A Study of Tractate Maaserot*, Chico 1981; I. Mandelbaum, *A History of the Mishnaic Law of Agriculture: Kilayim*, Chico 1982; L. E. Newman, *The Sanctity of the Seventh Year: A Study of Mishnah Tractate Shebiit*, Chico 1983; A. J. Avery-Peck, *The Priestly Gift in Mishnah: A Study of Tractate Terumot*, Chico 1981; R. S. Sarason, *A History of the Mishnaic Law of Agriculture*, III/1 *Demai*, Leiden 1978; T. Zahavy, *The Mishnaic Law of Blessings and Prayers: Tractate Berakhot*, Atlanta 1987. Parts of Bikkurim and Ḥallah: M. W. Rubenstein, D. Weiner & A. Havivi in W. S. Green (ed.), *Approaches*, vol. 3. A summary is given in A. J. Avery-Peck, *Mishnah's Division of Agriculture: A History and Theology of the Seder Zeraim*, Chico 1985. These commentaries (especially *Pur*) are systematically concerned with the form criticism and the history of tradition of M and generally with the literary problems, without (at least in *Pur*) neglecting the material facts.

# II

# THE TOSEFTA


***General Bibliography***

**Albeck, Ch.** *Mabo*, 51–78. **Albeck, Ch.** 'Die Herkunft des Toseftamaterials.' *MGWJ* 69 (1925) 311–28. **Albeck, Ch.** *Meḥqarim ba-Baraita u-ba-Tosefta we-Yaḥsan la-Talmud.* Jerusalem 1944; repr. 1969. **Dünner, J. H.** *Die Theorien über Wesen und Ursprung der Tosephta kritisch dargestellt.* Amsterdam 1874. **Elitzur, Y.** 'Meeting-Points between Reality and Language in Tannaitic Hebrew and the Question of the Ancestry of the Tosefta' (Hebr.). *Language Studies* 5–6 (=*Festschrift* I.Yeivin, Jerusalem 1992) 109–21. **Elman, Y.** *Authority and Tradition: Toseftan Baraitot in Talmudic Babylonia.* New York 1994. **Elman, Y.** 'Babylonian Baraitot in the Tosefta and the "Dialectology" of Middle Hebrew.' *AJSR* 16 (1991) 1–29. **Epstein, J. N.** *ITL*, 241–62. **Frankel, Z.** *Darkhe*, 322–25; *Mabo*, 22–27. **Goldberg, Abr.** 'The Tosefta – Companion to the Mishna.' In Safrai, *The Literature*, 1:283–301. **Goldberg, Abr.** 'The Use of the Tosefta and the Baraitha of the School of Samuel by the Babylonian Amora Rava for the Interpretation of the Mishna' (Hebr.). *Tarbiz* 40 (1971–72) 144–57. **Goldberg, Abr.** 'Seder ha-Halakhot u-Tekhunot ha-Tosefta 'al-pi shnê ha-peraqim ha-rishonim shel Masekhet Baba Qamma ba-Tosefta.' In *Talmudic Studies*, 2:151–96. **Guttmann, A.** *Das redaktionelle und sachliche Verhältnis zwischen Mišna und Tosephta.* Breslau 1928. **Herr, M. D.** *EJ* 15: 1283–85. **Malter, H.** 'A Talmudic Problem and Proposed Solutions.' *JQR* N.S. 2 (1911–12) 75–95. [Argues for Zuckermandel.] **Melammed, E. Z.** *Introduction*, 148–60. **Melammed, E. Z.** 'Halakhic Midrashim in the Mishna and Tosephta' (Hebr.). *Bar-Ilan* 2 (1964) 84–99. **Milikowsky, Ch.** 'Seder 'Olam and the Tosefta' (Hebr.). *Tarbiz* 49 (1979–80) 246–63. **Neusner, J.** *Introduction*, 129–52. **Neusner, J.** *The Tosefta: Its Structures and Its Sources.* Atlanta 1986. [Revised from idem, *Pur*; cf. Y. Elman, *JQR* N.S. 78 (1987–88) 130–36.] **Neusner, J.** *The Tosefta: An Introduction.* Atlanta 1992. **Rosenblatt, S.** *The Interpretation of the Bible in the Tosefta.* Philadelphia 1974. **Schwarz, A.** 'Studien über die Tosifta.' *MGWJ* 23 (1874) 464–70, 561–68; 24 (1875) 25–31, 87–90, 126–39, 274–81, 325–30, 351–66, 460–72, 492–500. **Schwarz, A.** *Die Tosifta des Traktates Sabbath, in ihrem Verhältnis zur Mischna.* Karlsruhe 1879. **Schwarz, A.** *Tosifta juxta Mischnarum Ordinem recomposita et Commentario instructa.* Vol. 1: Wilna 1890; vol. 2: Frankfurt 1902. **Spanier, A.** *Die Toseftaperiode in der tannaitischen Literatur.* Berlin 1922. **Weis, P. R.** 'The Controversies of Rab and Samuel and the Tosefta.' *JSS* 3 (1958) 288–97. **Zeitlin, S.** 'The Tosefta.' *JQR* N.S. 47 (1957) 382–99. **Zuckermandel. M. S.** *Tosefta, Mischna und Boraitha in ihrem Verhältnis zueinander.* 2 vols. Frankfurt 1908–09; Supplement 1910. **Zuckermandel, M. S.** *Gesammelte Aufsätze.* 2 vols. Frankfurt 1911–12.

***On individual tractates***

**Mayer, G.** *Ein Zaun um die Tora: Tradition und Interpretation im rabbinischen Recht, dargestellt am Toseftatraktat Kil'ajim.* Stuttgart 1973. **Di Segni, R.** 'Indagini sul trattato di Meghillà della Toseftà.' *Annuario di Studi Ebraici (Collegio Rabbinico Italiano, Roma) 1975–76* (Rome 1977) 17–43.

***On the relationship of T to M and the Talmuds***

**Bunte, W.** 'Der Mischnatraktat Zabim in seinem Verhältnis zum gleichnamigen Traktat der Tosefta.' *ZDMG* 107 (1957) 31–66. **Cohen, B.** *Mishnah and Tosefta: A Comparative Study.* Vol. 1: *Shabbat.* New York 1935. **Friedman, S.** 'The Primacy of Tosefta in Mishnah-Tosefta Parallels – Shabbat 16.1: *kol kitbê ha-qodesh*' (Hebr.). *Tarbiz* 62 (1992–93) 313–38. **Friedman, S.** 'The Primacy of Tosefta in Mishnah-Tosefta Parallels' (Hebr.). *11th WCJS* (Jerusalem 1994) C 1:15–22.

**Goldberg, Abr.** 'The Order of the Halachot in the Mishna and the Tosefta' (Hebr.). *6th WCJS* (Jerusalem 1972) 3:81–94. **Goldberg, Abr.** 'Tosefta to the Tractate Tamid' (Hebr.). In E. Z. Melamed (ed.), *Benjamin de Vries Memorial Volume*, 18–42. Jerusalem 1968. **Goldberg, Abr.** 'The Relationship of Mishnah to Tosefta and Baraitha as Seen Differently by R. Yohanan and Resh Laqish' (Hebr.). *7th WCJS* (Jerusalem 1981) 3:109–16. **Houtman, D.** 'The Interdependence of Mishnah and Tosefta of Tractate Shevi'it.' *11th WCJS* (Jerusalem 1994) C 1:17–24. **Schmida, S.** 'Mishna and Tosefta in the first section of Eduyot' (Hebr.). In E. Z. Melamed (ed.), *Benjamin de Vries Memorial Volume*, 1–17. Jerusalem 1968. **Steinfeld, Z. A.** 'The Order of Halachot in Mishna and Tosefta Horayot' (Hebr.). *8th WCJS* (Jerusalem 1982) C:9–12. **De Vries, B.** *Meḥqarim*, 96–129 [on BM, Mak and Me'ilah], 148–60 [relation to the Talmuds]. **Weiss, M.** 'The arrangement of the Mishna in Tractate Peah and its relationship to Tosefta' (Hebr.). Diss. Tel Aviv: Bar Ilan, 1978. **Weiss, M.** 'Tosefta-like Chapters in the Mishnah' (Hebr.). *11th WCJS* (Jerusalem 1994) C 1:55–62.

### *1) Name, Structure and Contents*

The Aramaic *tosefta* (poss. *tosifta*; Hebr. *tosefet*, plur. *tosafot*) means generally 'addition, supplement', viz., an additional halakhic teaching which supplements M (in the wider sense as the officially taught halakhah). Thus, for example, Abbahu in p.Shab 8.1, 11a denies that he knows a new halakhah (*oraita ḥadata*); he claims rather to have heard a *tosefta 'atiqta*, an 'old supplement'. In the narrower sense, *tosefta* can designate a book of such supplementary teachings, especially the work preserved under this title. In a comprehensive formula in Meg 28a, the rabbinic teaching syllabus is described as *hilkheta, sifra, sifre we-tosefta* (Shebu 41b also adds *talmud*); in Qid 49b this describes the material which a Tanna must control. This undoubtedly already envisages firmly defined complexes of tradition – the halakhah with its supplements and the halakhic midrash – , but probably not the writings known to us by these names. Even if Yoma 70a explicitly quotes the *tosefta* (the quotation recurs with some variations in t.Yoma 6.19, L. 247f.), this is not necessarily our T.

T is a halakhic work which corresponds in structure to M: the same six orders (*sedarim*) also comprise the same tractates, whose names and arrangement vary slightly both within the transmission of T and in relation to M (for present purposes we will cite the names of tractates and the numbering of chapters according to Zuckermandel, even where page references are according to the editions of Lieberman or Rengstorf: e.g. t.Yoma 4.19 is t.Kippurim 3.19 in Lieberman). Our earlier remarks on M, therefore, are equally relevant here. Only the tractates Abot, Tamid, Middot and Qinnim have no equivalent in T; the tractate Kelim is divided into three 'gates' (BQ, BM, BB). T is about four times as extensive as M.

The language of T is Mishnaic Hebrew; as in M, this is interspersed with occasional Aramaic sentences and with numerous loan words, especially of Greek and Latin origin. The rabbis named in T also correspond to those of M, although not in quite the same distribution.

### *2) Origin*

#### *a) Tradition*

Sanh 86a says in the name of R. Yoḥanan, *stam tosefta R. Neḥemyah.* Should our T be in view here, then its anonymous sections are attributed to a teacher of Usha (T3), one generation after the anonymous statements of M which reputedly go back to R. Aqiba. Sherira (ISG L. 34) names R. Ḥiyya bar Abba (T5), a friend and student of Rabbi, as the actual author of T; in doing so he confirms the opinion of the inquirers at Kairouan. Rashi holds the same view (e.g. on BM 85b), as does Maimonides (in the preface to *Mishneh Torah* (Jerusalem 1957), 9; also in the introduction to his M commentary, ed. Qafiḥ, 1:33f.).

It is worth noting that various medieval scholars do not apply Sanh 86a to our T: so R. Samson of Chinon in *Sefer Keritut* IV 1.12 (ed. J. M. Sofer, 158), 'What they call T in the Talmud is not what we call T, but an addition which they supply in order to explain M.' He refers to our T as a work of R. Ḥiyya and R. Hoshayah (A1: a text cited by S. Schechter, *Saadyana* (Cambridge 1903), 141 n.1 also regards Hoshayah to be the author of T). The same opinion is held by R. Nissim (990–1062) in the introduction to his *Sefer ha-Mafteaḥ* (printed in BT Romm, preceding Ber); he bases this on Taan 21a, where Ilfa (A2) says, 'If someone asks me about a baraita of R. Ḥiyya or of R. Hoshayah and I cannot explain it from M, may I throw myself from the ship's mast and drown.' This view is later still found in Hameiri, who describes T as 'baraitot' of R. Ḥiyya or of R. Hoshayah (introduction to his commentary on Abot, 12a). Assuming the validity of this theory, the few passages where T mentions R. Ḥiyya (e.g. t.Neg 8.6, R. 180; t.Beṣa 1.7, L. 281 also mentions R. Abba=Rab!) would then have to be regarded as later additions.

In the history of modern criticism, the attribution of T to Ḥiyya and Hoshayah has been adopted by Z. Frankel in particular. In his view our T comprises Tosefta collections of R. Ḥiyya and to a lesser degree also of R. Hoshayah (*Mabo*, 22a–27b). Opponents of this position include Albeck, (*Mabo*, 55f.), who argues that T contains only a small part of the baraitot which in the Talmuds are attributed to these two rabbis. Abr. Goldberg bypasses this objection by means of the theory that a redactor officially edited only the teachings of the preceding generation; the redaction of T began a generation after that of M and culminated in the work of R. Ḥiyya, Rabbi's literary heir. The teachings of R. Ḥiyya and his contemporaries were then probably edited by R. Hoshayah; and a final, less extensive layer was reputedly published by Rab. Goldberg wants to assume 220–30 as the date of T (thus in Safrai, *The Literature*, 1:283, 294f.).

If one combines the traditional view of R. Ḥiyya as the author of T with

Sanh 86a, the frequently assumed history of the development of T appears in parallel to that of M: one would then need to suppose a T of Neḥemyah supplementing the M of Aqiba or Meir, which R. Ḥiyya then revised and completed in dependence on Rabbi's M. The purpose of T according to this traditional perspective is the augmentation of M (lest the Tannaitic material omitted from M be forgotten), or a commentary on M.

J. N. Epstein (*ITL*, 242ff.) also accepts the traditional statements connecting T with Neḥemyah and Ḥiyya; however, he sees Neḥemyah's T not as an augmentation of the M of Aqiba, but of that of Simeon ben Gamaliel II, which he believes to have been the original M at the time. In his view, R. Ḥiyya in turn collected halakhot which differed from Rabbi or originated after him; nevertheless his collection is not our T. Epstein's reconstruction not only introduces further variables, but also goes far beyond what can be shown from the sources.

***b) The Relationship between Tosefta and Mishnah***

T has almost always been regarded as supplementing M, having originated shortly after the latter. Hence T has in the history of research always been seen in relation to M, and never on its own. Such a treatment is indeed legitimate as long as T is not rashly evaluated and interpreted on the basis of M. A closer definition of the relationship of T to M, as well as to the baraitot and the Talmuds, is an essential task of T research.

A comparison reveals a multitude of different connections between T and M, similar to the basic facts of the synoptic problem in New Testament studies. Hence it seems plausible to take methodological stimuli from that research. This applies also to the compilation of an urgently needed synopsis of T and M (and the other parallels). The connections between T and M can be summarized as follows:

1. T agrees verbatim with M or varies only slightly.
2. T offers authors' names for sentences which are anonymous in M, or augments M by additional glosses and discussions.
3. T functions like a commentary on unquoted M material.
4. T offers additional substance without direct reference to material in common with M (especially more haggadic and midrashic material).
5. T contradicts M in halakhah or tradents' names.
6. The *arrangement* of material parallel to M is largely the same in T, but also frequently different. T often seems to have the more original arrangement as well as the more primitive form of the halakhah itself (S. Friedman).
7. The *style* of T is not as succinctly formulated and polished as that of M. Mnemonic traits are present, but are not as important as in M. It seems that unlike M, T was not formulated so as to be memorized (J. Neusner).

Together with observations on parallels to T in the Talmudic baraitot (are these taken from T, from a parallel tradition, or did they serve in fact as building blocks of T?), the facts here outlined have been the subject of very different and contradictory interpretations in the *history of research.* However, this abundance of explanations reflects not only the ambiguity of the facts, but also often a highly selective evaluation of these facts. The most comprehensive studies of T are by M. S. Zuckermandel, the editor of T. He worked on his theory for several decades before publishing it in its final form in 1908–12. He considers T to be the Mishnah underlying PT, but our M to be Babylonian. Thus he accounts for the fact that PT sometimes agrees with T against M; where PT agrees with M against T, he sees interpolations or textual alterations. Later he revised his theory to say that Rabbi's work contained our M and T, and hence that PT presupposes both. The Babylonian Amoraim recognized only parts of this work, viz., our M. When M became the generally recognized codex, many parallel texts in T were omitted, so that T lost its original coherence. This theory, which Zuckermandel also wanted to substantiate with his edition of T, has almost invariably been received with emphatic rejection, and is indeed untenable. Nevertheless, Zuckermandel is justified in the desire not to consider the T–M relationship exclusively from the perspective of M.

J. H. Dünner's study of T was published at the same time as the earliest version of Zuckermandel's theory. Like Zuckermandel he departed from tradition, though in another direction: in his view, T is a post-Talmudic compilation of Talmudic baraitot and authentic Tannaitic material (he assumes the latter in order to explain the differences between T and the Talmudic baraitot). Dünner is thus an important precursor of Ch. Albeck and his school. I. H. Weiss, *Dor,* 2:193ff., argues similarly: he derives T from a Palestinian compiler working in Babylonia in the fifth or perhaps the fourth century, and who is supposed among several other sources to have used the Talmuds (Weiss adduces the fact that numerous statements in T appear in the Gemara as sayings of Amoraim).

A. Spanier has attempted a new solution of the M–T relationship; his precursor is A. Schwarz in his endeavour to re-arrange T according to M. Spanier calls T a 'special edition of scholia on the Mishnah: in detaching it from the Mishnah and independently collating it, the compiler added and removed many things in order to give the new work at least to a modest extent the appearance of a unified whole' (*Toseftaperiode*, 47). Such scholia to M, he believes, were already in existence at the time of Aqiba. Rabbi partly incorporated them in his M; this explains many of the parallels between M and T which far transcend the character of scholia (ibid., 74). Of course Spanier's theory assumes a written M from the very beginning.

A. Guttmann represents a similar theory: 'The aim of the redactor of the Tosefta appears at first to have been the collection of relevant Tannaitic material not included in the Mishnah, regardless of whether it supplements, explains or contradicts the Mishnah, or merely offers variants to it' (ibid., 1). The author compiled this material into a relatively independent work, even if T only constituted a complement to M (ibid., 2). Guttmann explains the different arrangement of T over against M by suggesting that there was at first merely a 'card file' of Tannaitic statements, in which some tractates were already grouped together. When the cards were translated into the form of books or scrolls, these tractates retained the order of M while the order of others was mixed up (176f.). Like Spanier's theory, this one has found few admirers and must be regarded as an inadequate makeshift solution, which moreover unduly projects modern literary conventions into the Talmudic period (even if hypotheses similar to Spanier's theory of scholia might be adduced for the Fragment Targum).

The theories of T we have cited are all intended as global solutions. The cited connections between M and T, however, are not uniformly distributed over the work; instead, their composition and distribution varies from tractate to tractate. A global assessment of the relationship between T and M is therefore impossible, and one must begin by examining the individual tractates of T in their own right.

This independent standing of the tractates is already clear from the length of T compared with M: all in all, T is four times as long as M. Thus many tractates in T, too, are longer than in M; a few are almost equal in length (e.g. Yad), but some are shorter (e.g. Sheq).

In terms of form and structure, many tractates of T presuppose M, even if T contains lengthy interpolations of material, bypasses some passages of M without comment, or indeed features a different arrangement of the material. An example of the latter is Ter (cf. E. Güting in the Gießen M, from which the following references are also taken, 27–31), where T frequently makes use of M for a better understanding, but M hardly depends on T. Matters are similar in Shebi (D. Correns, 28f.), where T also refers to M, but may presuppose an earlier form of the M text (cf. also De Vries, *Meḥqarim*, 101, on BM, and 108 on Mak). This suggests not a direct dependence on the M text, but the dependence of both M and T on a common, already largely defined and ordered tradition; W. Bunte suggests this for Maas and MSh (16–26), where T is entirely comprehensible without M. Suk is a different case again, inasmuch as many terms of T are virtually unintelligible without M, and T in fact cannot be interpreted without M (thus H. Bornhäuser, 18–25). Conversely, K. H. Rengstorf observes on Yeb (46–52): M is here not clearly presupposed in T, but for the most part T in M. It would be easier to supplement T from M. For H. Bietenhard, yet another picture emerges from Sot (18–22), where M is more easily supplemented from T than vice versa. Finally, J. Neusner states with regard to the entire order of Toharot (*Pur* 21:15) that T is here indeed to be understood as the complement of M, and its first commentary. Seder Qodashim in turn is the main argument for those who regard T as a work independent from M.

This list of assessments could be significantly expanded. The differences derive not merely from the individual scholars' personal opinions, nor solely from the doubtless diversity of approaches to the comparison of M and T. They are due, rather, to the actual differences in the relationships between the corresponding tractates of M and T, which must probably be attributed to the differing origins of the various tractates and orders of T. An even more detailed comparison would probably no longer permit a unified assessment even of individual tractates (thus rightly Schäfer, *JJS* 37 (1986) 147–49).

### *c) The Relationship of the Tosefta to the Talmuds*

In the preceding references to the history of research we also briefly addressed the relationship of T to the Talmudic baraitot. Again the facts are ambiguous in this question of such importance for the historical classification of T:

1. The only explicit quotation of T in the Talmuds is in Yoma 70a. But the textual variants do not permit a decision about whether the text here quoted as T is indeed from our T rather than from a similar collection of the same name.
2. Numerous baraitot in the Talmuds correspond (almost) verbatim to T.
3. Other baraitot of the Talmuds agree with T in substance but differ considerably in wording.
4. In the Talmuds, Amoraim frequently discuss problems with whose solutions they ought to be familiar from T. Are they ignorant of T, do they not accept T as an authority deciding the halakhah, or were they simply unable to recall the respective text of T (after all, even the most appropriate quotations from M are not always adduced as proof, although knowledge of M must surely be assumed for the Amoraim)?

These observations allow for a variety of interpretations, which basically fall into one of two schools of thought. Their most prominent representatives in the last few decades have been J. N. Epstein and Ch. Albeck, but both conceptions go back much further.

According to Epstein, the Talmuds knew T in different ways: a primitive form of today's T led to the baraitot of the BT, while the baraitot of PT, which textually are much closer to T, are directly dependent on our T. One must not overrate the fact that the Talmuds occasionally fail to cite T even where it would benefit a given discussion: this does not imply a general ignorance of T.

For Albeck, on the other hand, the frequent textual deviation of Talmudic baraitot from T-parallels, along with the Talmud's failure to cite T in crucial passages, is proof that the redactors of the Talmuds did not yet know T; instead, they cited from other collections of baraitot which then became the sources of our T (perhaps together with the Talmuds). The final redaction of T thus should be pegged towards the end of the Amoraic period.

B. De Vries occupies a mediating position. For him, the neglect of T in Talmudic discussions is no proof of the ignorance of T, neither at the time of origin of the particular sugya, nor of course at the final redaction. The latter would perhaps not even have regarded it as its task to interfere with existing sugyot by means of T quotations. De Vries traces the baraitot from a baraita-collection already before the Amoraim in written form, which does not agree with our T (he explains this less by means of the variant readings than by variations in the arrangement of the text), which moreover is not a primitive form of T, but which employs an earlier stage of tradition in common with T. Others (e.g. P. R. Weis and A. Weiss) gloss over the problem by assuming that some Amoraim knew T while others did not.

Y. Elman has now presented an in-depth study based on the tractate Pesaḥim. His position resembles that of Albeck, but is more sophisticated: many of the Tosefta-like baraitot in BT were independently received by the redactors, 'as individual baraitot, perhaps loosely connected, and not as part of a Tosefta-like composition' (*Authority*, 278). This neither denies nor confirms the possibility of an early origin: 'If the Tosefta's language points to an early date, that is either because it was reduced to written form at an early date but then neglected, or because its constituent components existed in writing and were not altered by its redactors. . . . In any case, early or late, the Tosefta was not known as such in Amoraic Babylonia' (p. 281).

### *d) Is a Solution Possible?*

The variety of the suggested solutions shows that we are still far removed from a generally acceptable description of the development and intent of T. Perhaps even our posing of the questions is not quite appropriate to the problem. At any rate, as Y. Elman rightly stresses, Albeck's arguments do not suffice to secure his late dating of T. Textual variants of the baraitot vis-a-vis T might well be due either to free citation and revision or to alternative collections that are parallel with T. One periodically encounters the argument that the redactors frequently neglected T because of its lesser authority (cf. already Alfasi: T is not halakhah); at least in the case of BT, however, this oversimplifies the problem. What is more, even if certain circles were in fact unfamiliar with T (or parts of it), this does not imply that T did not exist at the time. In the absence of compelling evidence, the common ground between T and M is too great to permit a significant chronological distance between their respective dates of composition.

A measure of the complexity of the evidence may be indicated by the development in the views of J. Neusner. He first included a translation and commentary on T in his *History of the Mishnaic Law*, but soon concluded that this had been a mistake: instead, he considered T to be a post-Mishnaic document with nothing to say on the history of law in the Mishnah (*The Tosefta: Translated from the Hebrew*, vol. 4 (New York 1981), xv–xvi). In 1977, he designates the date of T as unknown, between 200 and 450 (vol. 6, p. xi); in 1981 he identifies the end of the fourth century (vol. 2, p. ix). By 1986, however, he had returned to his earlier view, dating 'the major work of redaction of T. – that is, the organization and arrangement of its already extant materials – between the preliminary redaction of M. and its ultimate conclusion' (*The Tosefta: Its Structures and Its Sources*, 99; cf. p. 7). In 1990 he expressed a similar, though once again more cautious view in the new introduction his reprinted Tosefta translation, vol. 6 (p. xxiii): T was compiled after the conclusion of M, but before PT, and probably dates from the third century. Only a small proportion of its contents 'can have reached formulation prior to the closure of the Mishnah' (cf. *Introduction*, 131).

As a fully edited work, T is certainly post-Mishnaic and therefore Amoraic, although quite probably from the beginning of the Amoraic period. It is at any rate hardly possible to sustain serious objections to the assumption of a final redaction in the late third or early fourth century. For reasons of language as well as of the particular proximity to PT, it is indisputable that the redaction of T took place in Palestine; this is also where the Babylonian baraitot were probably later inserted (cf. Y. Elman, *Babylonian Baraitot*, on t.Suk 2.8–3.1).

There are, of course, additional reasons to expect a subsequent growth of T, especially through the intrusion of M texts, just as T texts conversely encroached on M. Talmudic baraitot probably also continued to be inserted into T at a later stage. Such textual alterations will have been bolstered by the fact that T did not attain to the official status of M and was therefore less controlled in its literary shape. On the other hand, this same fact meant that T was less prone to be deliberately adapted to later halakhah. Instead, the textual shape of T probably suffered more from prolonged neglect.

Given these observations, the question of the relationship between T and M cannot be answered unequivocally. In how far is T indeed a 'supplement' to M; in how far is it an independent work and its name 'misleading', as others claim? An 'either–or' will hardly do. Besides this, a historical development must be considered. T might at first have been a halakhic collection parallel to M but independent from it. With the canonization of M, however, it was increasingly seen only as a function and complement of M; this in turn would have had a corresponding influence on the further textual development, but without resulting in a uniform and thorough revision of T. Or one may think of a separate genesis of the individual T tractates, which led respectively to different relationships with M. Both possibilities could also be combined.

Equally open is the closely related question of the *purpose of T*: was T originally conceived as valid halakhah (in competition with M), or as a teaching manual complementing M, as a first commentary on M? This question cannot be answered, *inter alia* because we are unable sufficiently to isolate the sources of T, and because we can say very little with certainty about its original shape. M. D. Herr's theory (*EJ* 15: 1284: 'The compiler did not add, omit, or change his material in any way, but collected the material that was at his disposal') depicts the author of T as a mere archivist of baraitot, but this is unprovable and indeed entirely unrealistic. One cannot establish that T knew none of the baraitot which we know from the Talmuds but which are not contained in T; neither can it be demonstrated that despite all textual deviations T always transmitted the original shape of the text of the Talmudic baraitot. Even the internal contradictions and repetitions in T are insufficient grounds for the assumption that the redactor of T worked merely as a collator. We are at present unable positively to identify the purpose of T. Similarly, we cannot answer many other questions on the literary development of T; despite all efforts to date, this development remains obscure.

### *3) The Text of the Tosefta*

#### *a) Manuscripts*

Only one Tosefta manuscript is very nearly complete: *MS Vienna* (National Library Vienna, Hebr. 20, Catalogue Schwarz No. 46). However, even here we are missing some leaves in the middle that were later replaced; one leaf has disappeared at Zab 1.3–3.1, and there are numerous minor lacunae. The MS contains 227 leaves and dates from the early fourteenth century. The text type resembles that of the Genizah texts and of the Sefardic family of texts on which the printed editions are based. Description: M. S. Zuckermandel, *Der Wiener Tosefta-Codex*, Magdeburg 1877.

*MS Erfurt* is older than the Vienna Codex, but contains only the first four orders (the writer broke off after three and a half chapters of Zeb, although there was more space). 222 leaves in Ashkenazic script, twelfth century (there is a pawn receipt of 1260 on the last page). In the parallels with M, MS Erfurt often departs more significantly from M than is the case in MS Vienna (though the converse is not uncommon). This comparatively greater independence from M might suggest a preference for MS Erfurt. However, further study of this issue is needed, as is the case for the common counterargument that that the text of MS Erfurt is in fact closer to the Babylonian baraitot than to the Palestinian recension. Peter Schäfer has suggested that an 'aggressive Ashkenazi revision' may lie behind MS Erfurt (thus P. Schäfer, *JJS* 40 (1989) 92, following I. Ta-Shma); but this is made doubtful *inter alia* by a possibly tenth-century fragment of t.Erub 10.25f. and (verso) 10.2f. from Faenza (M. Perani, *Henoch* 14 (1992) 303f.). – Originally catalogued as a manuscript of PT, MS Erfurt was later mistaken for M, and only in 1870 identified as T by Z. Frankel. From 1879 it was in the Royal Library of Berlin, and is now in the Oriental department of the State Library in Berlin (Preussischer Kulturbesitz, 2°1220). Description: M. S. Zuckermandel, *Die Erfurter Handschrift der Tossefta*, Berlin 1876. Linguistic analysis: H. Nathan, *The Linguistic Tradition of Codex Erfurt of the Tosefta* (Hebr.), Diss. Jerusalem 1984; N. Braverman, 'An Examination of the Nature of the Vienna and Erfurt Manuscripts of the Tosefta' (Hebr.), *Language Studies* 5–6 (=*Festschrift* I. Yeivin, Jerusalem 1992), 153–70.

The order Moed (plus Ḥullin) is also preserved in *MS London* (British Museum, Add. 27296). It is written in Sefardic script and dates from the fifteenth century; the text is very defective. It seems to represent an attempt to reconcile the text of MS Erfurt with that of MS Vienna. In the State Archives at Bologna, M. Perani discovered four leaves of a Tosefta MS (parts of RH, Yoma, Meg) closely related to MS Vienna. This MS may have been the main *Vorlage* of the first printed edition (see M. Perani & G. Stemberger, 'Nuova luce sulla tradizione manoscritta della Tosefta: I frammenti rinvenuti a Bologna', *Henoch* 17 (1995)).

Numerous fragments from the *Cairo Genizah* are at Cambridge (e.g. Erub 8 – Pes 4, fragments of Yeb and Par 1–4) and in the Jewish Theological Seminary, New York (almost all of Yeb in various fragments). See J. Bowman, 'Fragments of the Tosefta from the Cairo Genizah and their Importance for the Text of the Tosefta', *Transactions of the Glasgow University Oriental Society* 11 (1942–44; Hertford 1946) 38–47. There is a brief description of the MSS by M. Lutzki in S. Lieberman, *Tosefta Zeraim*, 8–13. This does not yet include a manuscript of the Zurich Central Library (Z Heid 38), which probably dates from the seventeenth century and comprises the first four orders; perhaps in addition to a printed text, the scribe used at least one MS (K. H. Rengstorf, *The Tosefta: Text*, vol. 1 (Stuttgart 1983), xxi n. 43). The poor manuscript transmission of T assigns particular importance to the textual witness of medieval authors, whose quotations S. Lieberman has collected: *Tosefet Rishonim*, 4 vols., Jerusalem 1937–39.

***b) Printed Editions***

T was first printed in the Talmudic compendium of Alfasi, Venice 1521–22. This edition is based on a MS which is now lost; it became the basis of almost all later editions. The printer already recognized the defectiveness of his MS, but did not want to make corrections on his own account. In the BT edition Wilna 1860–73, T is printed after the respective BT tractate (the appended variants from MS Vienna gradually decrease and are entirely absent from Seder Toharot). For the early printed editions see M. E. Abramsky, 'The Printed Tosefta (Bibliography)' (Hebr.), *KS* 29 (1953–54) 149–61.

M. S. Zuckermandel, *Tosephta*, Pasewalk 1880; Supplement with survey, index and glossary, Trier 1882. He claims to have used first MS Erfurt (up to Zeb 5.5) and then MS Vienna, all the while noting variants from the other manuscript and from the printed edition. But MS Erfurt is not accurately copied, and MS Vienna is used even less thoroughly. Lieberman considers that beginning with Zeb 5.6, Z.'s edition corresponds essentially to the Romm edition (in BT of the edition Romm, Wilna). In its time, the edition was a great achievement, even if it is not fully satisfactory. It has not yet been replaced by another complete edition, although Lieberman has augmented it with a valuable supplement: *Tashlum Tosefta*, bound together with the reprint of Zuckermandel, Jerusalem 1937, repr. Jerusalem 1970.

S. Lieberman, *The Tosefta*, New York 1955–88, comprises in five volumes the orders Zeraim, Moed, Nashim, and the three Babot of Neziqin. The three *Babot* are to be published posthumously. The basis of the edition is MS Vienna; the variants from MS Erfurt, from the first printed edition and from the Genizah are given in the apparatus (Genizah fragments are appended in facsimile). In contrast to Zuckermandel, L. thus does not offer a mixed text, even if in exceptional cases he accepts the reading of MS Erfurt or of the first printed edition into the text (this is always stated). There is a brief Hebrew commentary and an extensive list of rabbinic parallels.

K. H. Rengstorf, in collaboration with others, has so far published two volumes of text in his series *Rabbinische Texte. Erste Reihe: Die Tosefta*. These are *Toharot* (Stuttgart 1967) and *Zeraim* (Stuttgart 1983); there is also a fascicle with text, translation and explanation: Yeb (1953). Rengstorf uses MS Erfurt as his base text, but naturally has to switch to MS Vienna beginning with Zeb. This edition is an important complement to L; where either of the two editions is available, it must of course be preferred to Z.

Methodologically dependent on the Stuttgart T are the following: F. Hüttenmeister, *Der Toseftatraktat Schekalim: Text, Übersetzung, Kommentar*, Diss. Saarbrücken 1970; H. Bietenhard, *Der Toseftatraktat Soṭa: Hebräischer Text mit kritischem Apparat, Übersetzung, Kommentar*, Berne 1986.

G. Larsson, *Der Toseftatraktat Jom hak-Kippurim: Text, Übersetzung, Kommentar*, Part One: Chapters 1 & 2, Lund 1980 (cf. T. Kronholm, *Svensk Exegetisk Årsbok* 46 (1981) 130–52).

D. E. Y. Sarnor collaborated with others on an edition of t.Sot: *Tosefta Messekhet Sota*, Boston 1970 (on the basis of MS Vienna. Introduction: 'Computer-Aided Critical Editions of Rabbinic Texts').

R. Neudecker, *Frührabbinisches Ehescheidungsrecht: Der Tosefta-Traktat Giṭṭin*, Rome 1982 (translation, commentary, reproduction of MS Erfurt).

***c) Translations***

A Latin translation of 31 tractates of T was edited by Biagio Ugolini together with the Hebrew text: *Thesaurus Antiquitatum Sacrarum*, vols. 17 & 18 (Moed), 19 (Qodashim), 20 (Zeraim), Venice 1755–57.

The only complete to date is J. Neusner: *The Tosefta: Translated from the Hebrew*, 6 vols., 1977–86 (vol. 1, *Zeraim*, ed. J. Neusner & R. S. Sarason). The translations are taken from the *History of the Mishnaic Law* by Neusner and his students (see p. 148 above).

A German translation and explanation appears in K. H. Rengstorf (ed.), *Rabbinische Texte*, Stuttgart 1960–. Six volumes have appeared to date: 1:2 Demai & Shebi, trans. by W. F. Krämer & P. Freimark (1971); 1:3 Suk, Yom Tob (=Beṣah), RH, trans. by H. Bornhäuser & G. Mayer (1993); 4:3 Sanh, Mak, trans. by B. Salomonsen (1976); 6:1–3 *Seder Toharot*, trans. by W. Windfuhr, G. Lisowsky, E. Schereschewsky, G. Mayer & K. H. Rengstorf (1960–67). Individual fascicles have contained Ber, half of Peah, Yeb (1953–58).

Individual tractates: O. Holtzmann, *Der Toseftatraktat Berakhot: Text, Übersetzung und Erklärung*, Giessen 1912; M. Kern, *Der Tosefta-Traktat Yom Tob: Einleitung, Übersetzung und Erklärung*, Diss. Würzburg 1934; E. L. Rapp, 'Der Tosephtatraktat Mo'ed Ḳaṭan', *Journal of the Society of Oriental Research* 12 (1928) 100–106 (also in the Giessen M: MQ, 2–13); P. Schlesinger, *Die Tosefta des Traktat Qiddusin: Übersetzt und erklärt*, Diss.

Würzburg 1926. F. Hüttenmeister, Sheq; G. Larsson, Yoma; and R. Neudecker, Git (see under b).

***d) Concordance***

H. J. Kasowski, *Thesaurus Thosephtae: Concordantiae Verborum quae in Sex Thosephthae ordinibus reperiuntur*, 6 vols., Jerusalem 1932–61 (vols. 5 & 6 ed. by M. Kasowski).

***4) Commentaries on the Tosefta***

The Geonim attest that T was already studied in their day (e.g. ISG 42, Spanish recension). However, for a long time T was studied only in relation to M (especially Zeraim: important also Melkizedek of Siponto and Samson of Sens) or PT. Independent commentaries on T originated only in the seventeenth century. The first commentary was by R. Abraham ha-Yakini, a follower of Shabbetai Ṣevi, and is not preserved. His younger contemporary Abraham Gombiner (c. 1637–83) wrote a short commentary on t.Neziqin: published in 1732 in Amsterdam under the title *Magen Abraham*, as an appendix to the work of his son-in-law Moses Yekutiel Kaufmann, *Leḥem ha-Panim*. The most important traditional T commentary is by David Pardo (1718–90): *Sefer Ḥasde David*, vol. 1: Zeraim, Moed, Nashim, Livorno 1776; vol. 2: Neziqin, Livorno 1790; vol. 3: Qodashim, Jerusalem 1890 (1–3 repr. Jerusalem 1971); vol. 4:1–3: Toharot, Jerusalem 1970–7. Also worth mentioning is the commentary of Elijah Gaon of Wilna (1720–97) on t.Toharot (in T Romm, Wilna 1881). Elijah Gaon fostered the considerable flourishing of T studies in Lithuania. Also from Lithuania is Yeḥezqel Abramsky, the author of the last great traditional T commentary: *Ḥazon Yeḥezqel*, vol. 1: Zeraim, Wilna 1925; vol. 2:1: Moed (Shab, Erub, Pes), Jerusalem 1934; Ḥul, Jerusalem 1938; Zeb, Jerusalem 1942; vol. 2:2: Moed (RH, Yoma), London 1942; vol. 2:3: Moed (Suk, Beṣah, Ḥag) 1950; Yeb 1957, Git 1957, Ned 1958, Sot 1963, BQ 1948; BM 1952, BB 1953, Men 1954, Shebu–Mak 1960; Qodashim, 2 vols., 1982–86 (some fascicles appeared earlier); Nid–Miqw 1986 (all Jerusalem).

There is as yet no modern commentary on the entire T, but there are three partial projects of considerable significance: S. Lieberman, *TK*, comprises the orders Zeraim, Moed and Nashim. It is very detailed, and far exceeds what one would expect of a T commentary. Many parallel passages from M and the Talmuds are also expounded. There are valuable linguistic explanations, especially of Greek loan words. However, due to the formal layout from glosses up to extensive excursuses on individual passages, larger contexts are not sufficiently considered as a unit, and the conventional introductory questions are in fact left out of consideration. But even without this, *TK* is the most important commentary on T in existence today. Also of importance is Lieberman's *Tosefet Rishonim*, 4 vols., Jerusalem 1937–39, for comments on T from the early textual tradition.

The translation volumes of the Stuttgart T, edited by K. H. Rengstorf with his team (cf. 3c), also provide a commentary. Like *TK*, although less extensive, the Stuttgart commentary is in the form of individual glosses and therefore not sufficiently attentive to the literary context. While it also fails to give due consideration to the Jewish interpretative tradition, it is good on empirical questions and serves as a valuable complement to *TK* (especially in Toharot, where *TK* is lacking).

In *A History of the Mishnaic Law* (which for Zeraim is the work of his students), J. Neusner has also commented on all of T in relation to M, generally giving due attention to the major literary questions which had previously been neglected (see p. 148 above).

# III

# THE PALESTINIAN TALMUD

***General Bibliography***


**Assis, M.** *Parallel Sugyot in the Jerusalem Talmud.* Diss. Jerusalem 1976. **Assis, M.** 'On the Question of the Redaction of Yerushalmi Nezikin' (Hebr.). *Tarbiz* 56 (1986–87) 147–70. **Avery-Peck, A. J.** 'Yerushalmi's Commentary to Mishnah Terumot: From Theology to Legal Code.' In W. S. Green (ed.), *Approaches*, 4:113–36. **Benovitz, M.** 'Transferred Sugyot in the Palestinian Talmud: The Case of Nedarim 3:2 and Shevuot 3:8.' *PAAJR* 59 (1993) 11–57. **Bokser, B. M.** 'An Annotated Bibliographical Guide to the Study of the Palestinian Talmud.' *ANRW* II 19:2, 139–256. [Repr. in J. Neusner (ed.), *The Study,* 2:1–119, but also with the pagination of ANRW as used here. An important presentation of the critical *status quaestionis.*] **Epstein, J. N.** *IAL*, 271–606. **Florsheim, Y.** 'Le-Arikhat ha-Talmud ha-Yerushalmi.' *Sinai* 79 (1976) 30–43. **Frankel, Z.** *Mabo.* [A Classic.] **Gartner, S. J.** *Studies in Tractate Ta'anit – Palestinian Talmud: A Comparative Analysis of Parallel Sources in Talmudic and Midrashic Literature* (Hebr., 54pp. Engl. Summary). Diss. New York: Yeshiva University, 1976. **Ginzberg, L.** *A Commentary on the Palestinian Talmud*, vol. 1, Hebrew Introduction [=*Mabo*]. New York 1941; repr. 1971. **Goldberg, Abr.** 'The Palestinian Talmud.' In Safrai, *The Literature*, 1:303–19. **Hezser, C.** *Form, Function and Historical Significance of the Rabbinic Story in Yerushalmi Neziqin.* Tübingen 1993. **Jaffee, M. S.** 'The Mishnah in Talmudic Exegesis: Observations on Tractate Maaserot of the Talmud Yerushalmi.' In W. S. Green (ed.), *Approaches*, 4:137–57. **Jaffee, M. S.** 'Oral Torah in Theory and Practice: Aspects of Mishnah-Exegesis in the Palestinian Talmud.' *Religion* 15 (1985) 387–410. **Lieberman, S.** *On the Yerushalmi* (Hebr.). Jerusalem 1929, 2nd edn. 1969. **Lieberman, S.** *The Talmud of Caesarea* (Hebr.). *Tarbiz* Supplement 2. Jerusalem 1931. **Lieberman, S.** *Siphre Zutta (The Midrash of Lydda).* Vol. 2: *The Talmud of Caesarea.* New York 1968. **Melammed, E. Z.** *Introduction*, 499–644. **Moscovitz, L.** 'Sugyot Muḥlafot in the Talmud Yerushalmi' (Hebr.). *Tarbiz* 60 (1991–92) 19–66. **Moscovitz, L.** 'Parallel Sugiot and the Text-Tradition of the Yerushalmi' (Hebr.). *Tarbiz* 60 (1991–92) 523–49. **Moscovitz, L.** 'Lishanei Aharinei in the Talmud Yerushalmi' (Hebr.). *Sidra* 8 (1992) 63–75. **Neusner, J.** *Judaism in Society: The Evidence of the Yerushalmi.* Chicago 1983, repr. Atlanta 1991. **Neusner, J.** *The Talmud of the Land of Israel: A Preliminary Translation and Explanation.* Vol. 35: *Introduction: Taxonomy.* Chicago 1983. **Neusner, J.** *The Yerushalmi – The Talmud of the Land of Israel: An Introduction.* Northvale, NJ 1993. **Neusner, J.** *Introduction*, 153–81. **Neusner, J.** *Judaism*, 139–93, 224–48. **Rabinowitz, L. I.** *EJ* 15:772–79. **Sussman, Y.** 'We-shub li-Yrushalmi Neziqin.' In *Talmudic Studies*, 1:55–133. **Sussman, Y.** 'Pirqê Yerushalmi.' In *Talmudic Studies*, 2:220–83. **Wewers, G. A.** *Probleme der Bavot-Traktate: Ein redaktionskritischer und theologischer Beitrag zum Talmud Yerushalmi.* Tübingen 1984.


## *1) Terms and Definitions*

*Talmud* (from *lamad*, 'to learn', or *limmad*, 'to teach') means 'study' (a theoretical activity, as opposed to *ma'aseh*, 'action', practising the commandments), but also 'instruction, teaching' (thus already at Qumran: 4QpNah 2.8), especially instruction from Scripture and hence Scriptural proof. This occurs in the frequent expressions *talmud lomar*, 'There is an instruction from Scripture, where it says. . .' or in short, 'Scripture teaches';

*mai talmuda*, 'What Scriptural proof is there?'; *yesh talmud*, 'There is a Scriptural proof.' Since *limmad* therefore also means 'to derive something from Scripture', 'Talmud' can occasionally be synonymous with 'Midrash'. However, 'Talmud' can also designate the entire traditional 'teaching', particularly the teaching derived from the interpretation of M, which is contrasted with Scripture and M (e.g. Qid 30a). Sherira (ISG L.51) defines similarly, 'Talmud is the wisdom of the early teachers, who interpreted in it the grounds of the M.' Cf. Bacher, *ET* 1:199–202; 2:234f.; Albeck, *Mabo*, 3f.; Melammed, *Introduction*, 323–26.

*Gemara* (*gemar* in Babylonian Aramaic means not only 'to complete' but also 'to learn') is the 'learning of tradition' or the 'traditional teaching' itself, in contrast to *sebara*, the logical deduction of new teachings (e.g. Erub 13a; 60a). This teaching of the oral Torah is seen as the 'completion' of the written Torah, or as the completion of study itself. The phrasing of Erub 32b, 'Have you included it in the Gemara (the traditional exposition of M)?' leads to the Geonic usage, which understands Gemara as the rounding off of M by the interpretation of the Amoraim. Censorship leads to the use of 'Gemara' rather than 'Talmud' in the printed Talmud (since the edition of Basle 1578–80). There, the M-text is followed by 'Gemara' as the headline for the Amoraic interpretation; this becomes its usual designation. Cf. Bacher, *ET* 2:28–33; Albeck, *Mabo*, 4–7; Melammed, *Introduction*, 326–30.

The PT, which in its country of origin would initially have been known simply as 'Talmud', appears in early quotations under a variety of names. In the Responsa of the Geonim it is cited as *Talmud Ereṣ Yisra'el* (Saadya, Hai Gaon, etc.) and also as *Gemara de-Ereṣ Yisra'el*. The *Halakhot Gedolot* call it *Talmud de-Ma'arba*, 'Talmud of the West', apparently reflecting the frequent expression 'in the West they say' – which in the BT denotes Palestine, from a Babylonian perspective. The *Tosafot* (on Ḥul, beginning) have *Hilkhot Ereṣ Yisra'el*. The designation *Yerushalmi* is already occasionally found in the Geonim, regularly in R. Ḥananel of Kairouan, sometimes in Alfasi, and often in the medieval authors. It would certainly be wrong to apply this now almost universally adopted designation to the place of origin, since Jerusalem at that time was forbidden to the Jews. Perhaps that designation arose in Islamic times, when Jerusalem became the residence of the academy previously located at Tiberias (thus Baron, *History*, 6:331 n.25). For bibliographical information see Bokser, 149f.

### *2) Content and Structure*

PT is the M commentary of the Palestinian Amoraim. This definition, however, holds only in the broadest sense. This is because PT does not follow

M closely, but offers much additional material which is only loosely connected with M. PT not only develops the halakhah of M in ways which are often entirely unexpected, but also supplements it by diverse haggadic materials and biblical expositions; it is, moreover, significant as a source for the history of Palestine, the development of Jewish liturgy, etc. In its arrangement, PT follows M; hence it is cited according to the respective M tractate with its chapter and halakhah (although the numbering of the various editions differs), supplemented by reference to the folio and column (a – d).

***a) The Absence of Many Tractates***

PT exists not for the entire M but only for the first four orders and for Nid 1–3 of Seder Toharot. The Gemara is also missing for Abot and Eduyot, for Shab 21–24 and Mak 3. Hence PT contains the Gemara for 39 of the 63 M tractates.

What explains the absence of the Gemara for such extensive tractates of M? Was it perhaps part of the Palestinian teaching curriculum, but was for various reasons not included in the final version of PT? Or were parts of the PT lost in the course of textual transmission?

Scholars use to believe that there was originally a Gemara for all six orders. This theory would explain the loss of Qodashim and Toharot as due to unfavourable times and the long absence of recognized academies in Palestine, as well as to the inferior reputation of PT as compared with BT. Such a loss of text seems to be supported by numerous medieval Yerushalmi quotations which are not found in our PT (collected by S. Buber, *Yerushalaim ha-benuyah*, Jerusalem 1906). But these quotations are very problematic. Often they are secondary quotations adopted especially from R. Ḥananel in particular, where it is not always possible to distinguish quotation from paraphrase or to identify the end of the actual quotation. Moreover, Spanish scholars also cite the Palestinian midrash, Midrash Rabba, Tanḥuma, etc. as Yerushalmi. Thus Yehudah ben Barzillai (11th–12th cent.) in his Yeṣira commentary (S. J. Halberstam (ed.), *Commentar zum Sepher Jezira von R. Jehuda b. Barzillai* (Hebr.), Berlin 1885, 58f.) cites as Yerushalmi a haggadah from TanB Lekh 24 (which was subsequently also incorporated in GenR: cf. Theodor/Albeck 499). Rashi's Yerushalmi quotations follow a similar pattern. Kabbalistic writings are also cited as Yerushalmi, not necessarily in deliberate forgery, but because they were regarded as Palestinian midrashim. Thus e.g. a Yerushalmi quotation in the Kad-ha-Qemaḥ of Baḥya ben Asher (13th cent.) turns out to be taken from the book of Bahir (see Ginzberg, *Mabo*, 29–32). Other texts, too, are occasionally cited as Yerushalmi; e.g. the *Sefer Ma'asim* (cf. J. N. Epstein, 'Ma'asim li-benê

Ereṣ Yisrael', *Tarbiz* 1 (1929–30) 33–42 (=*Studies*, 2:326–35), especially 36–38; see Lieberman, *On the Yerushalmi*, 36–46; idem, *Studies*, 274–95; Z. M. Rabinowitz, 'Sepher ha-Ma'aṣim livnei Ereẓ Yisrael: New Fragments' (Hebr.), *Tarbiz* 41 (1971–72) 282–305; M. A. Friedmann, 'Shnê Qeta'im me-Sefer ha-Ma'asim li-Benê Ereṣ Yisra'el', *Sinai* 74 (1974) 14–36); idem, 'Marriage Laws Based on Ma'asim Livne Ereẓ Yisra'el' (Hebr.), *Tarbiz* 50 (1980–81) 209–42; idem, '"An Important Ma'ase" – A New Fragment of Ma'asim Livnei Eretz Israel' (Hebr.), *Tarbiz* 51 (1981–82) 193–205; idem, 'On the New Fragment of Ma'asim Livnei Eretz Israel' (Hebr.), *Tarbiz* 51 (1981–82) 662–64; H. Newman, *Ha-Ma'asim li-bnê Ereṣ Yisra'el u-reqa'am ha-histori*, M. A. thesis, Jerusalem 1987 (pp. 107–62 offer a new edition of the estimated original Byzantine extent of the texts). Further bibliography: Bokser, 227–29.

Equally unsuccessful is the attempt of Z. Frankel, B. Ratner, et al. to identify references to lost tractates of Qodashim in the extant text of PT (cf. Epstein, *IAL*, 332–34). In the preface to his M commentary, Maimonides affirmed that 'there are five complete orders of the Yerushalmi'; but even this cannot serve to prove anything in the absence of a single assured quotation from p.Qodashim. (Y. Sussmann, 'Pirqê', 278ff. suspects a break in the text, suggesting that Maimonides meant BT and PT together.) In 1907–08, S. Friedländer published a manuscript supposedly dating from the year 1212, which contained most of the order Qodashim. Although at first considered genuine by S. Buber and S. Schechter, this was soon recognized to be a forgery or a thematic collection from the known portions of PT (possibly based on an older work): see e.g. V. Aptowitzer, *MGWJ* 54 (1910) 564–70; A. Schischa, *EJ* 7:182f.

Despite his polemical tendency to devalue the Palestinian traditions, Pirqoi ben Baboi (late 8th cent.) therefore should be taken seriously: according to him the Palestinian Jews do not keep all the food regulations, 'because they have not a single halakhah from the Talmud concerning the Sheḥitah, nor indeed from the Seder Qodashim. The Seder Qodashim and the whole Talmudic order Toharot has fallen into oblivion among them' (Ginzberg, *Ginze Schechter*, 2:560).

The PT fragments found in the Cairo Genizah also contain nothing of the missing tractates. Hence the latter would seem never to have been contained in PT. This of course does not mean that they were not studied in Palestine – pertinent references in PT, along with quotations on these subjects by Palestinian Amoraim in BT, prove the opposite. The study of the tractates missing in PT is also evident from the fragments published by M. Margulies (*Hilkhot Ereṣ Yisra'el min ha-Genizah*, Jerusalem 1973). It remains unclear, however, why this material was not included in the redaction of PT (perhaps because the laws of the two orders were no longer practised?). The theory that external conditions urged a speedy conclusion of the work (Frankel, *Mabo*, 48b) cannot be proven.

It is likely that the tractates Shab, Mak and Nid were originally complete. Their final chapters were already lost during the Genoic period: there is no trace of them in the MSS (including the Genizah) or in confirmed medieval quotations (Sussmann, 'Pirqê'). Shab 21–24 was already missing from the *Vorlage* of the Genizah fragment, as the scribe expressly confirms (text: J. N. Epstein, *Tarbiz* 3 (1931–32) 245; repr. in *Studies*, 2:287). As for p.Nid 4–10, the Tosafot at Nid 66a refer to Yerushalmi, Pereq Dam Niddah. This led some to conclude that at least the text of chapter 7 was still known in the middle ages. *Or Zaru'a*, however, cites the same passage from 'the end of Niddah', where its subject matter seems to fit better than in chapter 7. Sussmann ('Pirqê', 249–55) assumes that the author of this statement used a MS which simply attached a number of baraitot to p.Nid 3, as is commonly done at the end of tractates; the MS therefore does not confirm knowledge of a text that was subsequently lost. Ch. Albeck (introduction to GenR, 72) suspects that GenR 18.1 (Theodor/Albeck 160) is a quotation from p.Nid 5.6; but while the subject matter would fit there, the text need not derive from a redacted version of PT. S. Lieberman reconstructed the text of p.Mak 3 on the basis of parallels in PT as well as of medieval quotations (*Hilkhot Ha-Yerushalmi* (New York 1947), 67f.). Lieberman was still unaware of a Genizah fragment containing Mak 3 (published by S. Wiedder, *Tarbiz* 17 (1945–46) 129–35), which seemed initially to corroborate his reconstruction (though it also illustrated yet again the need for caution in using medieval quotations: cf. J. N. Epstein, *Tarbiz* 17 (1945–46) 136f.). However, Sussmann has subsequently demonstrated that this fragment does not contain the original text of p.Mak 3 ('Pirqê', 263–69): the text is assembled from a number of haggadic midrash quotations and was probably compiled to replace what was, even at that time, the missing conclusion of the tractate. Further bibliography in Bokser, 165–68.

***b) Repetitions within the Palestinian Talmud***

In addition to the missing tractates, the appearance of PT is characterized especially by numerous and frequently (almost) literal repetitions of long passages. The following list has been compiled by W. Bacher (*JE* 12 (New York 1906), 6f.); the significance of these parallels for the redactional and textual history of PT will be discussed later.

Of the first Seder, 39 long sections are repeated in the second, some more than once (references here are only according to page, column and line; for the parallels, only the first line is given): Ber 3b,10–55 = Shab 3a,69; 4a,30–56 = Sheq 47a,13 = MQ 83c,40; 5a,33–62 = MQ 82b,14; 5d,14–20 = Shab 3a,55; 5d,65 – 6a,9 = MQ 83a,5; 6c,4–17 = Yoma 44d,58; 6d,60–67 = Meg 73d,15; 7b,70 – 7d,25 = Taan 67c,12; 7d,75 – 8a,59 = Taan 63c,2; 8c,60–69 = RH 59d,16; 9a,70 – 9b,47 = Taan 63c,66; 9c,20–31 = Meg 75c,8; 9c,49–54 = Meg 75b,31; 10a,32–43 = Pes 29c,16; 11c,14–21 = Pes 37c,54; 12c,16–25 = Erub 22b,29; 12c,44–62 = Suk 24a,6 = Meg 72a,15; 13d,72 – 14a,30 = Taan 64a,75; Peah 15a,67 – 15b,21 = Ḥag 76b,24; 17a,39–72 = Ḥag 76b,13; 18d,16–33 = Sheq 46a,48; 18d,66–19a,5 = Sheq 48c,75; 21a,25–29 = Sheq 48d,55; Demai 22a,31–40 = Sheq 48d,40; Kilaim 29b,27–61 = Erub 19c,15 = Suk 52a,40; 29b,62–76 = Suk 52a,73; Shebi 34c,27–49 = MQ 80b,26; 38a,50–60 = Shab 3c,55; Ter 44a,32–8 = Shab 44d,4; 45d,42–51 = Shab 3d,2 (cf. AZ 41d,13–28); 46a,41–46b,35 = Pes 28a,34; Maas 49a,22–28 = Suk 53d,43; 49b,14–32 = Shab 6b,17; 49b,39–48 = Beṣah 62b,72; MSh 53b,6–44 = Yoma 45c,2 (cf. Shebu 32b,56–34c,3); 54b,48–58 = Sheq 51b,15; 55a,23–55 = Erub 24c,33; 55d,62–67 = MQ 80b,72; Ḥal 57c,16–20 = RH 57b,60.

Sixteen sections of the first Seder are repeated in the third: Ber 6a,35 – 6b,17 = Naz 56a,12; 6b,51–56 = Qid 61c,11; 9d,3–19 = Git 47b,49; 11b,42–68 = Naz 54b,2; 14b,45–70 = Sot 20c,40; Peah 15b,41–47 = Ket 32c,10; 15c,7–16 = Qid 61a,75; Demai 25b,60 – 25c,7 = Qid 63a,75; Kil 32a,64 – 32d,7 = Ket 34d,74; Shebi 36b,25–68 = Qid 61c,56; Ter 40c,42 – 40d,6 = Yeb 13c,70; 42b,44–53 = Naz 43d,16; 44c,9–44d,44 = Ket 27b,5; MSh 55a,69 – 55b,13 = Git 47d,55; Orlah 61b,8–33 = Naz 55c,32; Bik 64a,32–44 = Yeb 9b,71.

Ten sections from the first Seder are repeated in the fourth: Ber 3a,52–69 = Sanh 30a,65 = AZ 41c,46; 6b,20–41 = Sanh 20a,43; Peah 16b,22–25 and 43–60 = Sanh 27c,38; Shebi 35b,26–40 = AZ 44b,27; 39b,14–38 = Mak 31a,33; Ter 45c,24 – 45d,11 = AZ 41a,18; 47c,66 – 47d,4 = AZ 41c,13; MSh 54d,71 – 55a,8 = Sanh 19a,63; 56c,9–18 = Sanh 18d,13; Orlah 62b,49 – 62c,10 = AZ 45a,32.

Certain sections of the second order also recur in the fourth. Of particular length are Shab 9c,62 – 9d,59 = Sanh 24c,19; 14d,10 – 15a,1 = AZ 40d,12.

### *3) The Origin According to Tradition*

Maimonides identifies R. Yoḥanan (bar Nappaḥa, d. 279 according to ISG) as the author of PT (preface to the M commentary, ed. Qafiḥ 1:46). In the introduction to *Mishneh Torah*, he specifies, 'And R. Yoḥanan wrote the PT in the land of Israel c. 300 years after the destruction of the Temple,' i.e. about 100 years before Rab Ashi wrote the BT. Approximately contemporary with *Mishneh Torah*, and apparently following Maimonides (thus Cohen 122 n. 18), a gloss in manuscripts and in the first printed edition of Abraham Ibn Daud's *Sefer ha-Qabbalah* (Cohen, Hebr. text, p. 24) adds the following comment on R. Yoḥanan, 'And he wrote the PT on five Sedarim; for of the Seder Toharot there is only the tractate Niddah. And the PT was written about 200 years after the destruction of the Temple.' This chronological reference corrects Maimonides, whose '300 years after the destruction of the Temple' of course does not match the biographical data of Yoḥanan bar Nappaḥa. Cf. also the *Sefer Keritut* of Samson of Ḥinon.

The difficulties besetting this statement of Maimonides were soon recognized: PT names numerous rabbis who lived until the late fourth century, as well as other events from that period (e.g. Ursicinus, Gallus's general around 351–54, is named repeatedly). Together with the discrepancy in Maimonides's chronological reference, one thus arrives at the assumption of another, later Yoḥanan as the author of PT. This is the opinion of Estori ha-Parḥi (1280–c.1355) in *Kaftor wa-Feraḥ*, who argues that while Yoḥanan bar Nappaḥa was a student of Rabbi, the PT was in fact written c. 280 years after M (Ch. 16; ed. A. M. Luncz, Jerusalem 1897, 280). In modern authors, too, there is no lack of attempts to harmonize Maimonides with the facts: thus Frankel (*Mabo*, 48a) considers that the name of Yoḥanan only refers to his school, the academy of Tiberias; W. Bacher (*JE* 12:17) on the other hand takes the reference to Yoḥanan as the author of PT to mean no more than that he created its basic core.

### *4) The Redaction*

#### *a) The Terminus Post Quem*

The latest rabbis mentioned in PT are fifth-generation Amoraim, especially Mana II bar Yona (in BT called Mani) who worked in Sepphoris, and the well-known halakhist Yose bar Abin (= Yose beR. Bun), both of whom were active in the latter half of the fourth century. But even R. Samuel, the son of R. Yose bar Abin, and students of R. Mana (e.g. R. Azaryah (Ezra?) and R. Naḥman) are mentioned; this brings us to the fifth century. The last Babylonian scholar cited in PT is Raba (d. c.350). The last identifiable historical event noticed in PT is the unrest under Gallus c. 351; if (with Epstein, *IAL*, 274) the reading of p.Ned 3.2, 37d (Julian) is to be preferred to the parallel p.Shebu 2.9, 34d (Diocletian), even the emperor Julian's mobilization for his Persian campaign in 363 is mentioned.

No precise date can be deduced from on these facts. Y. Sussmann

('Neziqin', 132f.) stresses the uncertain chronology of the last Amoraim: he considers R. Yose beR. Bun to be the last independent master of PT and thus argues for the 360s as the latest possible date of final redaction. Most scholars, however, would accept a later date for the last named teachers in PT, thereby inferring a date of redaction in the first half of the fifth century. Epstein (*IAL*, 274) attempts to date PT more precisely around 410–20. A somewhat later date results if one links the final redaction of PT with the end of the patriarchate before 429 (e.g. Ginzberg, *Mabo*, 83), and thus regards it as a reaction to this serious intervention in the organization of Palestinian Judaism. This once popular 'theory of catastrophe' has recently been somewhat discredited; but it still has much in its favour, as long as it is not abused in order rashly to explain away the problems of the PT redaction, or even – as was already done by Pirqoi ben Baboi – to devalue the Palestinian tradition as incomplete.

The most likely *place of final redaction* must be Tiberias, for time and again it is clear that in the PT 'here' means Tiberias and 'the rabbis from here' are contrasted with 'the rabbis of the South' (p.Ber 2.7, 5b) or 'the rabbis of Caesarea' (p.Shab 13.1, 14a). What is more, in many sections of the PT the Tiberian rabbis are not only numerically very prominent, but they also determine the latest layer of the respective pericope. This also fits the eminent position of the academy at the seat of the patriarch. However, it is impossible to generalize: various considerations show that one cannot speak of a uniform and central redaction of PT.

***b) Nature of the Redaction***

Together with the absence of numerous M tractates and chapters, the many repetitions of pericopes might suggest that PT was not in fact edited in the proper sense, but merely represents a hasty collection of material. I. Halevy (*Dorot*, 2:528f.) arrives at this view principally because of the many contradictions in PT, but also because the order of the Gemara in PT often fails to match that in M. He concludes that the 'redactor' must have simply collated the blocks of material directly and without order. This view has been opposed, especially by S. Lieberman (*The Talmud of Caesarea*, 20–25) and L. Ginzberg (*Mabo*, 69–81); cf. the summary in Melammed, *Introduction*, 564–67). G. A. Wewers, on the other hand, without reviving the theory of a mere collection of material, writes, 'The fragmentary character of the extant PT and the assumption of a concluding and comprehensive final redaction are mutually exclusive' (*Probleme*, 311). But did the redactors really intend to comment on the whole Mishnah? In any case, a redaction of PT is clearly not to be understood in the sense of a final definition of the text; in this respect one can speak of the fundamentally unfinished state of PT (*Probleme*, 3ff.). The boundaries between redaction and the formation of tradition cannot always be determined in detail; and work on the text itself continued even later, resulting in different textual recensions.

We must assume a real redaction of PT, even if this of course cannot be assessed by modern principles of order (cf. e.g. J. Neusner, *Judaism in Society*, 49: PT 'did not just grow, but rather, someone made it up'; on the other hand, not many would agree with him (p. 70) that PT is 'a single, stunningly cogent document. . . in the bulk of its units of discourse'). A particular characteristic of the redactor was to repeat sugyot wherever there was a thematic connection, even if only part of the sugya pertained in substance to the other passage (cf. Lieberman, *On the Yerushalmi*, 34). In doing so, he has occasionally reconstructed pericopes in order to adapt them to their new environment. Thus, for example, p.Ber 3.1, 6a–b changes the order as compared with the parallel p.Naz 7.1, 56a, in order to establish a connection with the preceding material (Ginzberg, *Mabo*, 76). In the course of textual transmission, these parallel traditions in turn caused numerous textual corruptions. In copying the entire PT, parallel passages were not repeated, the omission simply being noted; but if only a single tractate was copied, these passages had to be reinserted. This often resulted in an incorrect beginning or ending of the passage, or in an improper insertion in the context, thus giving the impression of complete disorder in PT. Similarly, a parallel passage sometimes ended up being transmitted only in its secondary context (or in extreme cases being lost altogether), but in the version which should have belonged in the other passage (cf. M. Assis, *Parallel Sugyot*; G. A. Wewers, *Probleme*). Elsewhere, too, the present disorder in PT is often due to copying errors (e.g. omission of tradents' names, transposition of sentences, *homoioteleuta*, etc.).

Where the *arrangement of the Gemara* differs from the order in M, this is frequently because the M underlying PT was ordered differently. The confusion has merely been increased by rearrangements at the hands of copyists or printers of PT in order to adapt the order of PT to that of M. Departures from the order of M are moreover often found in parallel pericopes; in this case they are simply due to a copyist's incorrect insertion of a passage which in the *Vorlage* was omitted because it had already been used elsewhere. Most cases can be resolved by applying one of the two proposed explanations, so that in the remaining references one should also expect errors of transmission.

*Contradictions* in PT are usually encountered within a given sugya. As is usually already clear from the names of tradents, they tend to be due to the seamless joining of pericopes from different schools. In this way differences of opinion are found side by side, even though it is explicitly stated that the respective point is not in dispute. Where there are contradictions between a sugya and its parallel version, the redactor is likely to have used versions of the same sugya from different schools (the extent to which divergent or contradictory parallels may indicate earlier redactions of PT is examined by L. Moscovitz, 'Sugyot Muḥlafot'). Other possibilities of textual changes in the course of transmission were already discussed above.

This being said, one must in any case assume a real and systematic redaction of PT which assures that even in traditions of Babylonian masters teaching in Palestine, unrecognized Babylonian school rules are not used (Lieberman, *Talmud of Caesarea*, 22 cites as an example p.Yeb 8.2, 9b, where Yirmeyah's statement presupposes but does not mention the Babylonian rule, 'What does the generalization include? *Klala le-atoye mai*?'). Particulars of the redaction, of its sources and their treatment, etc. are not yet sufficiently clarified.

***c) The Redaction of Neziqin***

Apart from the observation that certain sugyot were formulated in different schools, a substantial portion of PT shows a redaction diverging from the rest of PT, viz., the tractate Neziqin with its three 'gates'. Already I. Lewy in his commentary on p.BQ 1–6 (*Jahrbuch Breslau 1895–1914*) deduced a different redaction of this part of PT because of the contradictions between sugyot in Neziqin and their parallels in the rest of PT; S. Lieberman (*Talmud of Caesarea*) systematically examined this question and arrived at the following results:

The three Babot differ from the rest of PT not only generally in their much terser language, but also in many details of style and vocabulary as well as in the spelling of Amoraic names. One must assume that these differences were originally much more pronounced, being frequently blurred by textual assimilation to the rest of PT. Sugyot from Neziqin which have parallels in the rest of PT differ from the latter in both structure and content as well as in the names of Amoraim. Judging from their content, some sugyot in Neziqin have their original place in another tractate, but without appearing there in PT; conversely, other tractates explain mishnayot from Neziqin, of which however Neziqin makes no mention and apparently has no knowledge. Amoraim frequently referred to in Neziqin are hardly ever mentioned elsewhere in PT, while important (especially late) Amoraim in the rest of PT appear never or rarely in Neziqin. From this it must follow that Neziqin was not edited in Tiberias together with the rest of PT, but in another school.

Neziqin in fact originated in the school of Caesarea, which from the third century on was an important Talmudic centre (cf. L. I. Levine, *Caesarea*, 82–96; he agrees with Lieberman's theory). The rabbis there, who on about 140 occasions in PT are collectively referred to as *Rabbanan de-Qesarin*, apparently constituted a kind of 'rabbinic guild' (Levine 95–97). The rabbis connected with Caesarea, of whom Abbahu is the most important, are particularly frequently mentioned in Neziqin. Moreover, exemplary narratives and other illustrations of halakhot apply mostly to Caesarea, while the formula *it amrin*, 'others say', usually refers to rabbis in Tiberias. The fact that Neziqin contains numerous Greek words which elsewhere in rabbinic literature are not used or have a different meaning, also suggests a Greek-speaking environment such as Caesarea.

Almost all the Amoraim mentioned in Neziqin belong to the first three generations. Of later generations only R. Yose b. Zabdi (c. 40x) and R. Yose beR. Bun (c. 30x) are cited frequently, and that regularly to conclude a discussion; their statements are never followed by anonymous comments. These observations are complemented by halakhic differences vis-à-vis the rest of PT, and by frequently archaic terminology. All this indicates an early redaction of Neziqin, probably around 350. Ginzberg (*Mabo*, 81f.) accepts these principles – he sees the 'Talmud of Caesarea' as a manual for the judges of the Jewish congregation of Caesarea who were uneducated in the halakhah.

J. N. Epstein (*IAL*, 286) has objected that many sayings which elsewhere in PT are attributed to the rabbis of Caesarea or to Abbahu are either missing in Neziqin or cited in the name of other rabbis. What is more, p.BB 10.1, 17c speaks of 'the rabbis of Caesarea' (NB unlike the parallel p.Git 7.12, 49d), even though 'the Rabbis from here' should be expected if Caesarea had been the place of redaction. Certainly there was a 'Talmud of Caesarea'; but according to Epstein this was used in the entire PT, including Neziqin but not excluding the rest. Furthermore he believes the frequent mention of R. Yose beR. Bun makes it impossible to date the redaction of Neziqin before that of the rest of PT. According to Epstein Neziqin also was not redacted in the proper sense, but in many places only contains short summaries and allusions as mnemonic aids (*IAL*, 290; Melammed, *Introduction*, 572, follows Epstein). S. Lieberman (*Sifre Zutta*, 125–36) replied to the objections and reaffirmed his theory.

Some of Epstein's arguments against Lieberman may be refuted by the general textual corruption of PT and by the observation that even the 'Talmud of Caesarea' will not have included everything taught by the rabbis of Caesarea. However, the recently discovered MS Escorial with its linguistic particularities and loan words invalidates certain aspects of Lieberman's argument. What is more, this MS's localization of narrative illustrations does not point so clearly to Caesarea as the place of redaction (M. Assis, 'On the Question'). The distribution of rabbinic names in p.Neziqin does not sufficiently differ from the rest of PT to serve as an argument (Y. Sussmann, 'Neziqin', 121ff.). C. Hezser's analysis of the narratives in Neziqin leads her to conclude that Lieberman's three arguments for locating the stories in Caesarea (language, rabbis, local setting) are not complementary and provide no assured results: 'Caesarea may have been the place where y.Neziqin was edited, but the material under discussion does not provide clear-cut evidence that this was so' (*Form*, 405). With regard to the proposed place and early date of the redaction of Neziqin, G. A. Wewers (*Probleme*, 308f.) points out that Lieberman's appeal to the differences between Neziqin and the rest of PT actually bears only on the traditions themselves but not the redaction itself, for which these differences supply merely a *terminus post quem*. Y. Sussmann, on the other hand, dates the redaction of PT as a whole so early that a much earlier composition of Neziqin becomes impossible. The only effective result of this lively discussion is a much clearer recognition of the independence of Neziqin, which attests a separate redaction of these tractates in a different school from the rest of PT. However, neither the place nor the time of this redaction can be clearly determined; nor is it possible to corroborate L. Ginzberg's theory on the intended audience of Neziqin.

***d) Sources of the Palestinian Talmud***

At issue here are not so much written sources in the proper sense but rather the materials which were available to the redactors of PT or to the Amoraim of the Palestinian Gemara: M, baraitot, halakhic midrashim, and Babylonian traditions.

***1. The M of the PT***

In as far as PT is a commentary on M, the latter of course is its most important source. However, the precise identification of the M text underlying the discussions of PT is beset with great difficulties. The original version of PT did not contain a M text, but only quotations and allusions within the Gemara itself. It was only later MSS which broke up the continuous text according to the textual units of M in order to insert the M text chapter by chapter before the Palestinian Gemara. This was also the procedure followed by the scribe of MS Leiden: he copied the M text and the text of PT from different sources (see I. Z. Feintuch, 'The Mishna of the MS Leiden of the Palestinian Talmud' (Hebr.), *Tarbiz* 45 (1975–76), 178–212: the *Vorlage* for M is ususally MS Parma, De Rossi 138). At times, however, the copyist did not properly divide the chapters in the Gemara. In Yeb 15–16 his PT *Vorlage* was incomplete, so that he failed to recognize the demarcation between the two chapters and therefore simply placed both M chapters together before the subsequent text of the Gemara. The first printed edition, normally dependent on MS Leiden, has corrected this on the basis of another MS (Epstein, *IAL*, 605; cf. *ITM*, 932f.).

This means that the M text of our MSS and printed editions of PT is not necessarily the text discussed by the Amoraim. Instead, it is a mixed text between the Palestinian and the Babylonian recension of M (inasmuch as one can in fact distinguish between the two recensions as clearly as Epstein does).

The actual base text of PT must be inferred from the Gemara. The latter often deviates from the M text which in our editions is given at the head of the chapter, but also from the textual version of the M manuscripts themselves as well as from that presupposed by the Gemara of BT. Ber 1.1, for example, lists commandments which one must fulfill 'before midnight', but whose fulfillment the scholars have appointed before the following dawn. In the M text underlying BT, the 'eating of the Passover lamb' is not mentioned here (Ber 9a), but it is in the version discussed by PT (p.Ber 1.3, 3a: the MS transmission of M is here irregular). In Shab 2.6 we read that women die in childbirth (*be-sha'at ledatan*) because of three transgressions. However, the Palestinian Gemara assumes the reading *yldot* and discusses whether the vocalization should be *yoldot* ('women giving birth') or *yeladot* ('girls'): p.Shab 2, 5b). The reading *be-sha'at ledatan* appears to be a clarifying paraphrase of the ambivalent expression (Ginzberg, *Mabo*, 54).

Additional examples could easily be cited. In all these cases the formulation of M assumed in PT differs from that of BT. L. Ginzberg considers that in Palestine a version of Rabbi's M prevailed which had been edited by Rabbi himself, while in Babylonia the original version could no longer be displaced (*Mabo*, 51; the contrary theory, viz., that in Babylonia the version of Rabbi's old age prevailed, is now again advocated by D. Rosenthal, *Mishnah Abodah Zarah*, Diss. Jerusalem 1980). But he himself points out that not all M variants between PT and BT can be explained in this way, but that one must also allow for deliberate corrections of the M text by the Amoraim. A reconstruction of *the* M of PT, therefore, remains impossible even by way of the Gemara, because not every example of a textual divergence in PT can automatically be attributed to a uniform Palestinian recension of M; indeed even the existence of a completely uniform version of M throughout Palestine must be doubtful. (Cf. Epstein, *ITM*, 706–26, 771–803; *IAL*, 604–6; Ginzberg, *Mabo*, 51–56; Melammed, *Introduction*, 535–48; Bokser, 171f.; titles by M. Schachter and S. Zeitlin cited above, p. 139).

### 2. *Baraitot in PT*

*Baraita*, lit. the 'outside' teaching (short for Aram. *matnita baraita*), designates all Tannaitic teachings and sayings outside of M. The Hebrew term *mishnah ḥiṣonah* has only late attestation (NumR 18.21). In PT the designation 'baraita' occurs only in p.Nid 3.3, 50d; elsewhere *matnita* is normal, as for M itself. The language of the baraitot is usually a later form of Mishnaic Hebrew.

***Bibliography***

**Higger, M.** *Oṣar ha-Baraitot.* 10 vols. New York 1938–48. [Collection of the baraitot in both Talmuds.] **Abramson, S.** ''Al shnê leshonot haba'ah min ha-Mishnah.' *Sinai* 79 (1975–76) 211–28. [On the distinction between *tanya* and *tenan* in the introduction of quotations.] **Albeck, Ch.** 'Die Herkunft des Toseftamaterials.' *MGWJ* 69 (1925) 311–28. **Albeck, Ch.** *Meḥqarim ha-Baraita we-Tosefta we-Yaḥasan la-Tosefta.* **Bacher, W.** *TT.* **Epstein, J. N.** *ITM.* **Stieglitz, M.** *Die zerstreuten Baraitas der beiden Talmude zur Mischna Berachot.* Diss. Berne 1908. **De Vries, B.** 'Baraita, Beraitot.' *EJ* 4: 189–93.

The numerous baraitot in PT are only partly introduced by one of the conventional formulas (e.g. *teni R. X* or anonymously, *teno rabbanan*, etc.); often there is no indication of their origin in the baraita. A comparison with MSS shows that these quotation formulas were later frequently dropped (cf. Higger, *Oṣar*, 2:227ff.). The baraitot of PT (as also of BT) derive mostly from the Tannaim as tradents of the academies, as well as from undoubtedly written collections of Tannaitic material. Whether T must be seen as such a collection of baraitot, or whether with M it should be contrasted with the baraitot, is a question that has been debated since the Middle Ages; it is in the end irrelevant to the present context. In any case a clear decision on whether PT uses T itself as a source (thus J. N. Epstein) or merely draws T material from common sources (thus Ch. Albeck) cannot at present be reached (see pp. 155ff. above).

The great majority of baraitot in PT is anonymous. However, a number of collections are also cited (Bacher, *TT*, 203–14; Melammed, *Introduction*, 549–54); the most important are the baraita collections from the schools of R. Ḥiyya (cited c. 200x), of R. Hoshayah (c. 80x) and of Bar Qappara (c. 60x). It is unclear whether these collections are identical with the *Mishnayot Gedolot* of these three rabbis (p.Hor 3:4, 8c: NB instead of Ḥuna read Ḥiyya), but this is more likely than the assumption of additional collections of these masters. There are also important baraita collections from the schools of R. Simeon bar Yoḥai (c. 70x) and of R. Ishmael (c. 80x), of R. Samuel (c. 20x, only in the orders Zeraim and Moed) and of R. Ḥalafta b. Saul (c. 20x).

The transmission of the baraitot raises a number of problems. Sometimes baraitot are cited elsewhere as sayings of Amoraim; both could be true, but it may also indicate texts which are erroneously or even pseudepigraphically transmitted as baraitot. Baraitot also frequently diverge from their parallels in T, in the halakhic midrashim or in BT; this implies a less standardized transmission of baraitot than in M (NB and even there the standard is only relative). Baraitot often are not quoted verbatim but only in abbreviation, in allusion, expanded by a later interpretation, or adapted to a different linguistic usage (cf. Ginzberg, *Mabo*, 60f.). Above all, however, the fragmentary transmission makes problematic any reconstruction of possible (written) collections of baraitot and their use or unfamiliarity in PT (as in the other rabbinic writings); any conclusions on this basis must remain uncertain.

For additional bibliography see Bokser, 173–78.

### *3. Midrashim*

Although to a much lesser extent than BT, PT also includes midrashic material. In addition to mishnaic material, the aforementioned baraitot also contain a great deal of midrash, so that Bacher assumes several Tannaitic midrash collections as sources of PT (*TT*, 210–13): viz., midrashim on the Pentateuch (Exod through Deut) from the school of R. Ḥiyya (often on Lev and with parallels in Sifra, which for this reason is sometimes attributed to R. Ḥiyya), of R. Ishmael, of R. Simeon ben Yoḥai and of R. Ḥizkiyyah.

As for halakhic midrash, E. Z. Melammed (*Introduction*, 275–96 has collected all the material in PT. There are about 1,300 quotations from halakhic midrashim attributed to particular Tannaites or cited anonymously as baraita. Their distribution is as follows: c. 270 quotations concern Exod; 440, Lev; 190, Num; 230, Deut; and over 100, Gen and the rest of Scripture. In part these quotations recur verbatim or in altered form in the extant halakhic midrashim, and in part they have no parallel. None of the quotations is very long; many indeed are extremely short, containing less than one line and sometimes only individual explanatory words. This of course makes it extremely difficult to determine whether one is dealing with a genuine quotation, with a mere allusion, or with a reference to a particular interpretative tradition. Frequently the midrash from the school of Aqiba is explicitly contrasted with that from R. Ishmael: it is impossible to decide whether this derives from the respective source of PT or whether it is the work of the redactor of the particular passage.

PT also cites over 1,100 midrashim in the name of Amoraim. These are mostly haggadic in nature and pertain to Gen, the Prophets and Writings (but there is also an admittedly much smaller proportion of haggadic midrashim on Exod through Deut). Here too the quoted midrashim are very short. Even the longer ones comprise only a few lines. PT likes to connect several midrashim of a particular Amora; the halakhic midrashim often provide the biblical rationale for the halakhic controversies of the Tannaites. Linguistically, most of these midrashim are in Hebrew, but compared with the Tannaitic texts they are much more pervaded by Aramaic words or even whole sentences. Aramaic is of course particularly prevalent in the haggadah, since this was intended primarily for ordinary people (Melammed, *Introduction*, 312–17).

Many of the midrashim quoted in PT have parallels in the midrashic literature and in BT. However, due to the brevity of the quotations and the general condition of the extant PT and rabbinic writings, the question of the possible use of midrashic writings or collections on the whole cannot be answered, even though the existence of midrashic writings in Amoraic Palestine can probably be assumed. Thus M. B. Lerner (*The Book of Ruth in Aggadic Literature and Midrasch Ruth Rabba* (Hebr.), Diss. Jerusalem 1971) supposes that PT at a later stage of redaction used an early recension of RuthR. At times this relationship between PT and midrash may have been reciprocal, so that (for example) an early form of the midrash was known to PT, while the final version in turn was influenced by PT. It is also to be expected that midrashim which are approximately contemporary with PT used earlier versions of PT or of individual tractates. Since the same Amoraim worked both on the design of PT and in the area of midrash, the relative dependence of various writings can only be asserted with the greatest caution (cf. also L. Moscovitz, 'The Relationship between the Yerushalmi and Leviticus Rabbah: A Re-Examination' (Hebr.), *11th WCJS* (Jerusalem 1994) C 1:31–38).

#### *4. Babylonian Traditions*

Palestinian scholars were in continuous contact with Babylonian rabbis, be it through colleagues travelling between the two countries for professional reasons (the so-called *naḥote*), or through Babylonians who temporarily or permanently settled in Palestine. Strong connections with Babylonia are attested especially for Caesarea (Levine, *Caesarea*, 89–92, 96). Of course these Babylonians also brought their traditions with them, even if they tried to adapt to their new environment (cf. BM 85a on R. Zera: when he moved to Palestine he fasted 100 days in order to forget the Babylonian Gemara. See Abr. Goldberg, *Tarbiz* 36 (1966–67) 319–41). In this way, numerous sayings of Babylonian Amoraim entered the PT, usually introduced by 'there they say' or 'the Rabbis from there say' (Bacher, *TT*, 311–17; 477–505; Epstein, *IAL*, 314–22). But NB 'there' in PT need not always refer to Babylonia; it may also designate another rabbinic school in Palestine. Many of the sayings of

Babylonians quoted in PT are missing in BT or appear in a different form. In this context one should certainly not imagine extensive units of fully edited (written or oral) traditions which could properly be termed 'sources' of the PT; instead, we are dealing with traditional material which became known in Palestine through Babylonian scholars. Cf. also Bokser, 187–91. J. Schwartz, 'Tension between Palestinian Scholars and Babylonian Olim in Amoraic Palestine', *JSJ* 11 (1980) 78–94.

***e) The Reception of the Tradition***

Studies of the redaction of PT generally confine themselves to the redactional particularities of its final condition, and they regard PT as a whole. The eminent exception is S. Lieberman's examination of the three 'gates' of Neziqin, consolidated in many points by the work of G. A. Wewers, M. Assis Y. Sussmann and C. Hezser. There is widespread agreement that different Amoraic schools stand behind PT. But we have as yet no systematic investigation of the prehistory of PT or of its parts, even though it is taken for granted that the final redactors did not compile and prepare an amorphous mass of traditional material in a single operation.

Z. Frankel (*Mabo*, 45a–49a) supposed a development of PT in three stages: (i) commentary on M in the schools; (ii) collection and completion of such academic notes at the hands of various masters, in the form of tractates corresponding to the structure of M; (iii) selection, combination and preparation of these collections in Tiberias (cf. Epstein, *IAL*, 275, who also observes three layers for individual examples). This assumption is reasonable and can even be substantiated in the individual case of Neziqin. However, it provides no more than the rough outline of a development. It remains for future research to determine in detail the literary development of PT (the development of the sugya, the genesis of the individual tractates and the formative work of the various masters and schools, the relative age of the individual pieces and their amalgamation). Based on the existing studies, it remains unclear to what extent such a goal could be achieved. Such a detailed examination would need to take us beyond the overly optimistic approach that simply dates individual sayings by the masters they cite as their authors or tradents, but without resorting to the opposite extreme of accepting only the stage of final redaction (a tendency found in J. Neusner, *Judaism in Society*). Only this would enable us to use PT in a historically warranted fashion. But that is still a long way to go.

***5) The Text***

More than other rabbinic writings, PT has suffered in its textual transmission.

We have already pointed out the numerous textual corruptions due to the omission and reinsertion of parallel pericopes. Other reasons for textual corruption must be seen in the neglect of PT, once BT had attained absolute predominance in the academic syllabus of European Judaism and even managed to displace PT in Palestine. As a result of this there are only very few surviving MSS of PT, which moreover (with the exception of the Genizah fragments) are strongly influenced by the text and language of the BT. Ignorance of the proper language of PT led not only to orthographic and grammatical assimilations to BT, or in the case of Hebrew sections to the Bible, but also to a complete adulteration of numerous Greek and Latin loan words and quotations, followed by further 'corrections' in order to wrest a meaning out of the text (cf. especially the works of S. Lieberman). See p. 37 above on the inscription of Rehob as the oldest witness to the tradition of PT.

### *a) Manuscripts*

*MS Leiden*, Scaliger 3 (University Library Leiden) is the only complete MS of PT (of equal extent as the printed editions). 672 leaves in two folio volumes, completed in 1289. In a colophon the scribe, Yeḥiel b. R. Yequtiel b. R. Benjamin ha-Rofe', deplores his very defective *Vorlage*, which he has endeavoured to correct where possible. Despite his quick work (he completed the orders Nashim and Neziqin in 36 working days: Melammed, *Introduction*, 508) which led to numerous omissions due to homoioteleuton, the MS is extremely valuable for text criticism. There are many marginal glosses, mostly textual corrections; in part these are from the scribe himself. Facsimile editions with introduction by S. Lieberman, Jerusalem 1971 (poor reproduction); new edition: M. Edelmann (ed.), *Early Hebrew Manuscripts in Facsimile*, vol. 3: *The Leiden Yerushalmi Part 1: Ms. Leyden, Univ. Library Scaliger 3*, with an introduction by E. S. Rosenthal, 1979.

***Bibliography***

**Elizur, B**. 'Traces of a Lost Page from Ms. Leiden of the Yerushalmi' (Hebr.). *KS* 63 (1990–91) 661–68. **Elizur, B**. 'Le-nusaḥ Yerushalmi Horayot.' In *Talmudic Studies*, 2:1–12. **Epstein, J. N.** 'Some Variae Lectiones in the Yerushalmi I: The Leiden MS' (Hebr.). *Tarbiz* 5 (1933–34) 257–72; 6 (1934–35) 38–55. [Repr. in *Studies*, 2:291–325.] **Epstein, J. N**, 'Diqduqe Yerushalmi.' In *IAL*, 335–606 (completed only to Shab 15, supplemented by Melammed). **Liebermann, S.** *Hayerushalmi Kiphshuto, Mabo*, 15–21. Jerusalem 1934. **Liebermann, S**. 'Further Notes on the Leiden Ms. of the Jerushalmi' (Hebr.). *Tarbiz* 20 (1949) 107–17. [Repr. in *Studies*, 219–29.] **Melammed, E. Z.** 'Ms Vatican as the Source for the Marginal Glosses in the Leiden Manuscript of Talmud Yerushalmi' (Hebr.). *Tarbiz* 50 (1980–81) 107–27.

*MS Rome*, Codex Vat. Ebr. 133. 152 leaves. Sotah and Zeraim (without Bik; M missing in Sotah 9 and in all of Zeraim except Ber 2). A little older than

MS Leiden, it is very defective but supplies some gaps in MS Leiden and has some valuable readings. It uses four different MSS as *Vorlage* (Melammed, *Introduction*, 513). Facsimile: *Talmud Yerushalmi Codex Vatican (Vat. Ebr. 133)* with an introduction by S. Lieberman (= idem, *On the Yerushalmi* (Hebr.), Jerusalem 1929), Jerusalem 1971. Selected variants to Seder Zeraim from MS Rome: L. Ginzberg, *Yerushalmi Fragments from the Geniza* (New York 1909; repr. Hildesheim 1970), 347–72.

*MS Escorial* G I–3, a Spanish MS of BT from the fifteenth century; as E. S. Rosenthal discovered, its top margin contains the three Babot of PT Neziqin. This important textual witness is close to the Genizah fragments and in many places helps to complement or correct MS Leiden: E.S. Rosenthal (ed.), *Yerushalmi Neziqin: Edited from the Escorial Manuscript with an Introduction*, Introduction and Commentary by S. Lieberman (Hebr.), Jerusalem 1983. A synopsis of MS Escorial with the Krotoshin edition is presented by G. A. Wewers, *Übersetzung des Talmud Yerushalmi*, vol. IV/1–3 *Bavot* (Tübingen 1982), 526–33; on the MS see also M. Assis, 'On the Question'; Y. Sussmann, 'Neziqin', 116.

*Zeraim and Sheqalim with the commentary of S. Sirillo*: Suppl. Hébreu 1389 at the National Library in Paris contains the text from Berakhot to Kilaim. Becker has confirmed the earlier assumption that this is an autograph of Sirillo, written at Safed in 1541–42, but without awareness of the first printed edition (Venice 1523–24). The continuation of this MS is MS Moscow, Günzburg 1135, which contains Terumot through Bikkurim. More recent, but still partly from Sirillo's pen, are MSS British Museum 403–405 = Or. 2822–2824 and MS Amsterdam (collection Etz Ḥayyim, now in Jerusalem). Editions: M. Lehmann (ed.), *Berakhot*, Mainz 1875; C. J. Dinklas (ed.), *Zeraim*, 11 vols., Jerusalem 1934–67; K. Kahana (ed.), *Shebiit*, 2 vols., Jerusalem 1972–73. Cf. H.-J. Becker, 'Die "Sirillo-Handschriften" des Talmud Yerushalmi', *FJB* 16 (1988) 53–73; idem, 'Zwei neue Yerushalmi-Handschriften und die "Gemara" zu Eduyot mit dem Kommentar des Shlomo Sirillo', *FJB* 17 (1989) 57–66; idem, 'Verstreute Yerushalmi-Texte in MS Moskau 1133', *FJB* 19 (1991–92) 31–61.

The tractate Sheqalim was connected with the text of BT at an early stage. It is found e.g. in MS Munich of BT (facsimile edition H. L. Strack, repr. Jerusalem 1971) as well as in a MS with commentary by R. Meshullam (ed. A. Schreiber, *Treatise Sheqalim*, New York 1954). A critical edition of the tractate is being prepared by M. Assis; cf. idem, 'On the Textual History of the Tractate Shekalim' (Hebr.), *7th WCJS* (Jerusalem 1981): *Studies in the Talmud, Halacha and Midrash*, 141–56; Y. Sussmann, 'Masoret limmud u-masoret nusaḥ shel ha-Talmud ha-Yerushalmi Massekhet Sheqalim', in S.

Raam (ed.), *Meḥqarim be-Sifrut ha-Talmudit* (*Festschrift* S. Lieberman, Jerusalem 1983), 12–76.

*Other MSS*: Z. M. Rabinovitz, 'A Fragment of Mishna and Yerushalmi Shevi'it' (Hebr.), *Bar-Ilan* 2 (1964) 125–33 (p.Shebi 7, a 14th-cent. Yemenite MS; Bokser, 158 notes that Sussmann regards this MS as a Genizah fragment whose continuation is at Cambridge); M. Assis, 'A Fragment of Yerushalmi Sanhedrin' (Hebr.), *Tarbiz* 46 (1976–77) 29–90; 327–9; and cf. S. Lieberman, 'On the New Fragments of the Palestinian Talmud' (Hebr.), ibid. 91–6 (a 12th-cent. North African MS containing most of p.Sanh 5.1, 22c – 6.9, 23c); A. H. Freimann, 'A Fragment of Yerushalmi Baba Kama' (Hebr.), *Tarbiz* 6:1–2 (1934) 56–63; cf. J. N. Epstein, ibid. 64f., repr. in *Studies*, 2:866f. (Vat. Ebr. 530, no later than the fourteenth century; BQ 2.4, 3a – 3.4, 3c). A number of PT leaves have in recent years been reclaimed from book bindings: M. Perani, *Momenti e testimonianze di vita e cultura ebraica a Bologna* (Bologna 1990) lists two twelfth-century leaves containing Shebi 34c–d. T. Kwasman, *Untersuchung zu Einbandfragmenten und ihre Beziehung zum Palästinischen Talmud* (Heidelberg 1986), sees in fragments from the libraries of Darmstadt, Munich and Trier the remains of a MS from the thirteenth century; but due to the textual divergences he suspects this to be a textual witness of a *Sefer Yerushalmi* rather than of PT itself.

### *b) Fragments from the Genizah*

Numerous fragments are found in various libraries and have only partly been published. A comprehensive examination of the date of the various pieces is still to be accomplished; a sweeping general assignment to the tenth century is highly questionable (Y. Sussmann, *Tarbiz* 43 (1973–74) 155f. n. 497; Sussmann plans a comprehensive edition of the PT fragments from the Genizah). Apart from their age and the special rarity of MSS of PT, the particular value of the fragments lies in the fact that they all stem from the Orient and preserve the original orthography much better than the European MSS.

#### ***Bibliography***

**Ginzberg, L.** *Yerushalmi Fragments from the Genizah*, vol. 1 (no more published), New York 1909, repr. Hildesheim 1970. **Ginzberg, L.** *Ginze Schechter*, 1:387–448. **Abramson S.** 'Qeta' Genizah mi-Yerushalmi Shabbat Pereq ha-Maṣni'ah.' *Kobez Al Yad* 8 [18] (Jerusalem 1975) 3–13 (corrections and additions to this are in *Kobez Al Yad* 10 [20] (Jerusalem 1982) 323f.). **Alloni, N.** *Geniza Fragments*, 35–43. **Epstein, J. N.** 'Additional Fragments of the Yerushalmi' (Hebr.). *Tarbiz* 3 (1931–32) 15–26, 121–36, 237–48. **Katsh, A. I.** 'A Genizah Fragment of Talmud Yerushalmi in the Antonin Collection of the Saltykov-Shchedrin Library in Leningrad.' *JQR* N.S. 71 (1980–81) 181–84. [Sheq 7, 31a, b, 32a; continuation of Ginzberg p. 139]. **Loewinger, S.** 'New Fragments from the Yerushalmi Pesaḥim ch. 5–7.' In S. Lieberman (ed.), *Alexander Marx Jubilee Volume*, Hebr. section, 237–83. New York 1950. [Cf. Lieberman, ibid. 284–6.] **Rabinovitz, Z. M.**

'New Genizah Fragments of the Palestinian Talmud' (Hebr.), in E. Y. Kutscher et al. (eds.), *Henoch Yalon Memorial Volume*, 499–511. Jerusalem 1974. **Wiedder, S.** 'A Fragment of Jerushalmi from Geniza Fragments in Budapest' (Hebr.), *Tarbiz* 17 (1945–46) 129–35. [Cf. J. N. Epstein, ibid. 136f.; repr. in *Studies*, 2:868f.]

On PT MSS and Genizah fragments see **Bokser**, 153–63; **Ginzberg**, *Mabo*, 36–40; **Melammed**, *Introduction*, 508–15; **N. Sacks**, *Mishnah Zeraim I* (Jerusalem 1972), 72–76.

Due to the poor MS support of PT, quotations in medieval literature are of special importance. For the orders of Zeraim and Moed (except Erub) they have been collected by B. Ratner, *Ahawath Zion we-Jeruscholaim*, 12 vols., Wilna 1901–17, repr. Jerusalem 1967; despite many mistakes, this work is outstandingly valuable (important reviews, etc.: V. Aptowitzer, *MGWJ* 52 (1908); 54 (1910); 60 (1916); W. Bacher, *REJ* 43 (1901) – 64 (1912)). Also of importance for medieval quotations is S. Lieberman, 'Emendations in Jerushalmi' (Hebr.), *Tarbiz* 2 (1930–31) 106–14, 235–40, 380; 3 (1931–32) 337–39, as well as his other works; also H.-J. Becker, 'Die Yerushalmi-Midrashim der Ordnung Zera'im in Ya'aqov ibn Ḥavivs "'En Ya'aqov"', *FJB* 18 (1990) 71–173 (early 16th cent., Thessaloniki); idem, 'Die Yerushalmi-Zitate im Mishnakommentar des Shimshon aus Sens, Seder Zera'im', *FJB* 20 (1993) 97–173, 21 (1994) 131–70; M. Katz, 'Yerushalmi Citations in Manuscripts of the Bavli' (Hebr.), *Sidra* 7 (1991) 21–44.

### c) Printed Editions

#### Bibliography

**Habermann, A. M.** 'Ha-Talmud ha-Yerushalmi.' In the re-issue of R. Rabbinovicz, *Ma'amar 'al Hadpasat ha-Talmud*, 203–22. Jerusalem 1952. **Malachi, E. R.** ''Al ha-Defus ha-Yerushalmi.' *Sinai* 60 (1967) 169–73. See also **Bokser**, 151f.

The Palestinian Talmud was first printed by D. Bomberg, Venice 1523–24 (on the date see I. Z. Feintuch, 'On the Talmud Yerushalmi, Venice Edition' (Hebr.), *KS* 59 (1984) 268–70). His basis was MS Leiden (cf. most recently: M. Mishor, 'An Impress from the Venice Edition in the Leiden Ms. of Talmud Yerushalmi' (Hebr.), *KS* 53 (1977–78) 578). The editor claims to have used three additional MSS. These must have been lost, unless p.Hor in BT ed. 1520–23 stems from one of these three MSS; Melammed, *Introduction*, 514 further assumes that MS Rome was known to the printer in Venice. As was shown by S. Lieberman, 'Yerushalmi Horayot', in *Sefer Yovel le-Rabbi Ḥanokh Albeck* (*Festschrift* Ch. Albeck, Jerusalem 1963), 283–305, the editor used exclusively MS Leiden and often 'corrected' his *Vorlage*. In BT ed. 1520–23, p.Hor has been printed in place of the Tosafot to the Babylonian Gemara, and p.Sheq has also been reproduced according to a different MS from that used for PT.

*Other editions*: Cracow 1609 with a short commentary; Krotoshin 1866 (repr. Jerusalem 1969, the most widely used edition); Zhitomir, 5 vols. with commentaries, 1860–67; Romm Wilna, 7 vols. with commentaries, 1922, repr. Jerusalem 1973.

Attempts at a critical edition: the most significant contribution to the textual processing of PT is made in P. Schäfer & H.–J. Becker (eds.), *Synopse zum Talmud Yerushalmi*, Part I: *Ordnung Zera'im*, 3 vols. (Tübingen 1991–92); Part IV: *Ordnung Neziqin* (Tübingen 1995). This synopsis presents the texts of Venice 1523, Constantinople 1662 and Amsterdam 1710, MSS Leiden and Rome, and the Sirillo MSS. Genizah and other MSS fragments have been deliberately excluded. See further A. M. Luncz, *Talmud Hierosolymitanum ad exemplar editionis principis*, 5 vols., Jerusalem 1907–19 (Ber through Shebi; he uses MS Leiden, Vat. 133, the MS with Sirillo's commentary and certain Genizah fragments); E. A. Goldman, 'A Critical Edition of Palestinian Talmud, Tractate Rosh Hashana', *HUCA* 46 (1975) 219–68; 47 (1976) 191–268; 48 (1977) 219–41; 49 (1978) 205–26. J. Feliks, *Talmud Yerushalmi Massekhet Shebi'it*, 2 vols. (Jerusalem 1980–86), follows the text of MS Leiden with variants from MSS, Genizah and the first printed edition; he includes a commentary on botanical and agricultural matters. See further E. S. Rosenthal, *Yerushalmi Neziqin* (Jerusalem 1983); A. Steinsaltz, *Talmud Yerushalmi: Massekhet Pe'ah* (Jerusalem 1987).

***d) Translations***

The only complete modern translation is J. Neusner, *The Talmud of the Land of Israel*, 35 vols., Chicago 1982–94 (Ber: T. Zahavy; Peah: R. Brooks; Demai: R. S. Sarason; Kil: I. J. Mandelbaum Shebi and Ter: A. J. Avery-Peck; Maas: M. S. Jaffee; MSh: R. Brooks; all other volumes by J. Neusner, incl. vol. 35: *Taxonomy*). Critical annotations to the initial volumes are offered in J. Neusner (ed.), *In the Margins of the Yerushalmi: Glosses on the English Translation*, Chico 1983.

An excellent German translation has been appearing in Tübingen since 1975: Ch. Horowitz, *Der Jerusalemer Talmud in deutscher Übersetzung*, vol. 1: *Berakhot*, 1975. Subsequent volumes were published under the collective title: *Übersetzung des Talmud Yerushalmi*, ed. by M. Hengel, J. Neusner (later replaced by H.–P. Rüger), P. Schäfer. Published to date: Peah (1986), Ter (1985), Ḥag (1983), the entire order Neziqin (1980–84), all translated by G. A. Wewers; Yoma (1995), translated by F. Avemarie; Suk (1983 = Düsseldorf 1963) and Ned (1983 = Düsseldorf 1957), translated by Ch. Horowitz; Meg (1987) and Sheq (1990), translated by F.G. Hüttenmeister; MQ (1988), translated by H.-P. Tilly.

Earlier (partial) translations: Biagio Ugolini edited 20 tractates with his own Latin translation: *Thesaurus Antiquitatum Sacrarum*, vols. 17–30, Venice 1755–65 (17: Pes; 18: Sheq, Yoma, Suk, RH, Taan, Meg, Ḥag, Beṣah, MQ; 20: Maas, MSh, Ḥallah, Orlah, Bik; 25: Sanh, Mak; 30: Qid, Sot, Ket). M. Schwab, *Le Talmud de Jérusalem*, 11 vols., Paris 1871–89, repr. in 6 vols. Paris 1969 (very unreliable French translation). A. Wünsche, *Der Jerusalemer Talmud in seinen haggadischen Bestandtheilen übertragen*, Zurich 1880, repr. Hildesheim 1967.

*Individual tractates*: A. W. Greenup, *Taanith from the Palestinian Talmud*, London 1918; J. Rabbinowitz, *The Jerusalem Talmud (Talmud Yerushalmi): Bikkurim: Text, Translation, Introduction and Commentary*, London 1975.

### *e) Concordance*

M. Kosovsky, *Concordance to the Talmud Yerushalmi (Palestinian Talmud)*, Jerusalem 1979ff. (5 vols. to 1993, up to and including the letter *nun*; based on the first printed edition); *Oṣar ha-Shmot*, Jerusalem 1985.

## *6) Commentaries*

#### *Bibliography*

**Bokser**, 225–49. **Ginzberg, L.**, *Mabo*, 90–132. **Lieberman, S.** 'The Old Commentators of the Yerushalmi' (Hebr.). In idem (ed.), *Alexander Marx Jubilee Volume*, Hebr. section, 287–319. New York 1950. **Melammed, E. Z.** *Introduction*, 515–34. **Rubinstein, J.** 'Quntras ha-shalem shel Mefarshê ha-Yerushalmi.' In the appendix to the PT edition New York 1948. **Twersky, I.** *Rabad of Posquières*. 2nd edn. Philadelphia 1980.

Apart from a possible use of PT or one of its previous stages in various midrashim, we find the earliest evidence for the influence of PT in the seventh-century inscription of Rehob (see p. 37 above): p.Demai 2, 22c–d and p.Shebi 7, 36c are here used either directly from a PT version or from a halakhic treatment of PT like the Sefer ha-Maasim whose original version arose around the middle of the seventh century. The fairly rapid displacement of PT by BT (after 750, Yehudai Gaon already endeavoured to achieve this even in Palestine) means that for a long time there were no separate commentaries on PT, but PT was only adduced as parallel evidence or explanation to BT: thus especially in the tenth-century *Sefer Methiboth*, ed. B. M. Lewin (Jerusalem 1933; repr. 1973), whose author was a Babylonian active probably at Kairouan (but note that he still frequently decides the halakhah against BT); also in R. Ḥananel of Kairouan in the eleventh century (cf. A. Y. Friezler, 'Yaḥaso shel Rabbenu Ḥananel li-Yerushalmi be-Ferush le-Babli', *Nib ha-Midrashiyah* (Tel Aviv 1972–73), 126–34). Similarly R. Nissim and Alfasi in the eleventh century, as well as Maimonides (S. Lieberman, *Hilkhot ha-Yerushalmi le-ha-Rambam*, New York 1947). In the twelfth century, *Sefer Rabia* by Eliezer b. Joel ha-Levi (ed. E. Prisman, 4 vols., Jerusalem 1965) is also of importance for the historical impact of PT; similarly the Tosafists, who used PT to a greater extent than is commonly assumed (E. E. Urbach, *The Tosafists*, 543ff.).

The oldest surviving actual commentaries on PT both deal with the tractate Sheqalim, which was transmitted together with BT. They are attributed to R. Meshullam, thirteenth century, and the contemporary student of R. Samuel ben R. Shneur of Evreux; edited by A. Schreiber (Sofer), *Treatise Shekalim with two Commentaries of Early Rabbinic Authorities*, New York 1954; E. E. Urbach doubts this attribution and regards the commentaries as works of early Tosafists: *KS* 31 (1955–56) 325–28. For the order Zeraim one may also draw upon the early M commentaries which strongly rely on PT, since BT is lacking here.

Solomo Sirillo from Spain, later in Safed, completed his commentary on Zeraim and Sheq around 1530, probably still without knowledge of the first printed edition (cf. p. 182 above).

Eleazar b. R. Moshe Azikri (1533–1600, Safed) wrote commentaries on Ber (in PT Zhitomir 1860) Peah, Demai, Ter and Pes (extant only in quotations in Solomon Adani's *Melekhet Shlomo*, in M Romm), Beṣah (ed. I. Francis, *Talmud Yerushalmi Massekhet Beṣah 'im Perush... Rabbenu El'azar Azikri*, New York 1967, with a detailed introduction).

Samuel Ashkenazi (c. 1525–95) commented on the haggadot of the PT, perhaps still based on PT MSS: *Yefe Mareh*, Venice 1590 and often (M. Benayahu, 'R. Samuel Yaffe Ashkenazi and Other Commentators of Midrash Rabba: Some Biographical and Bibliographical Details' (Hebr.), *Tarbiz* 42 (1972–73) 419–60, especially 428–30).

Yehoshua Benveniste (c. 1590–1665, Turkey) wrote a comprehensive commentary on the halakhic parts of 18 tractates: Zeraim Constantinople 1662 (repr. in: *Yerushalmi Zeraim*, 1972), the rest Constantinople 1749. Benveniste is important for his use of medieval authors.

David Darshan produced a brief, mainly linguistic commentary on the Cracow PT edition of 1610.

Elijah b. Loeb Fulda (c. 1650–1720): a concise commentary on 15 tractates – Zeraim and Sheq, Amsterdam 1710; BQ, BM and BB, Frankfurt 1742. This stimulated the study of PT in Germany and Eastern Europe.

Moshe Margolies (d. 1780, Lithuania) wrote a commentary on the entire PT: *Penê Mosheh*, addenda *Mar'eh ha-Panim*. Amsterdam 1754: Nashim; Livorno 1770: Neziqin; complete in PT Zhitomir.

David Fränkel, the teacher of Moses Mendelssohn, 1704–62: *Qorban ha–'Edah*; addenda *Shirê Qorban*. He wants to supplement the commentary of Fulda (only Sheq is common to both). Dessau 1742, Berlin 1757, 1760–62. Margolies and Fränkel are the two most important traditional commentaries.

Elijah Gaon of Wilna dealt with PT in various works, above all in his commentary on the Shulḥan Arukh. He shows an interest in textual criticism; unlike his predecessors, he attempts to explain PT on its own rather than from BT. K. Kahana, *Le-Ḥeqer Be'urê ha-GeRa"' li-Yerushalmi we-la-Tosefta*, Tel Aviv 1957; S. Goren (ed.), *Sefer ha-Yerushalmi we-ha-GeRa"' me-Wilna*, Jerusalem 1991.

The traditional stance represented in these commentaries continues into the present, especially in Yehoshua Isaac Shapiro, *Noam Yerushalmi*, 4 vols., Wilna 1863–69; repr. in 2 vols. Jerusalem 1968; Abraham Krochmal, *Yerushalaim ha Benuyah*, Lemberg (L'vov) 1867, repr. Jerusalem 1971; and Joseph Engel, *Kommentar zu Zeraim: Gilyon ha-Shas*, Vienna 1924, repr. in *Talmud Yerushalmi: Zeraim*, Jerusalem 1972. Cf. also the collection of important commentaries: *Hashlamah li-Yerushalmi*, Wilna 1928, repr. Jerusalem 1971 (additional title: *Shittah mequbbeṣet 'al ha-Yerushalmi*). S. Goren, *Ha-Yerushalmi ha-meforash*, vol. 1 *Berakhot*, Jerusalem 1961, also shares a traditional orientation, even though he employs textual criticism and draws particularly on the work of Ginzberg and Lieberman.

Among *modern commentaries*, the following deserve special mention for their conscious and systematic application of critical methods:

I. Lewy, *Introduction and Commentary to Talmud Yerushalmi*, BQ 1–6, Jerusalem 1970 (=repr. of 'Interpretation des 1. [2. etc.] Abschnittes des palästinischen Talmud-Traktats Nesikin', Hebrew with German introduction, *Jahrbuch des jüdisch-theologischen Seminars Breslau*, 1895–1914). Cf. E. Urbach, 'Der Einfluß des Seminars auf das Studium des Jerusalemischen Talmuds' (Hebr.), in G. Kisch (ed.), *Das Breslauer Seminar* (Tübingen 1963), 175–85, especially 177–82.

Saul Liebermann (*sic*), *Hayerushalmi Kiphshuto*, Part 1 vol. 1: *Sabbath Erubin Pesahim*, Jerusalem 1934 (no more published); idem, *Yerushalmi Neziqin* (commentary), ed. E. S. Rosenthal, Jerusalem 1983. His other works also contribute significantly to the interpretation of PT.

Z. W. Rabinovitz, *Sha'are Torat Erets Jisrael: Notes and Comments on the Yerushalmi*, ed. E. Z. Melammed, Jerusalem 1940 (especially also on the style and composition of PT; cf. the review of G. Allon, *Tarbiz* 12 (1940–41) 88–95).

L. Ginzberg, *A Commentary on the Palestinian Talmud: A Study of the Development of the Halakah and Haggadah in Palestine and Babylonia*

(Hebr.), 4 vols., New York 1941–61. A text-critically important 'commentary' on Ber 1–5 with extensive excursuses on a wide range of problems, especially of Jewish liturgy. Aside from an extensive Hebrew introduction, vol. 1 contains a general 'Introductory Essay' in English. Vols. 1–3 repr. New York 1971. Cf. Abr. Goldberg, *KS* 38 (1962–63) 195–202.

M. Assis, 'Hagahot u-Ferushim bi-Yerushalmi Shabbat', *HUCA* 48 (1977) Hebr. section 1–11.

# IV

# THE BABYLONIAN TALMUD

*General Bibliography*

**Agus, R. E.** *The Literary Sources of the Babylonian Talmud, Moed Katan* (Hebr.). Diss. New York: Yeshiva University, 1977. **Albeck, Ch.** *Mabo*, 452–575. **Aminoah, N.** *The Redaction of the Tractate Qiddushin in the Babylonian Talmud* (Hebr.). Tel Aviv 1977. **Aminoah, N.** *The Redaction of the Tractates Betza, Rosh-Hashana and Ta'anith in the Babylonian Talmud* (Hebr.). Tel Aviv 1986. **Aminoah, N.** 'The Transition from "Early Redaction" to "Final Redaction" in the Babylonian Talmud' (Hebr.), *Tarbiz* 52 (1982–83) 134–38. **Aminoah, N.** 'L'attitude des 'Amoraïm à l'égard des sources talmudiques antérieures.' *REJ* 145 (1986). **Berkovits, E.** *EJ* 15: 755–68. **Brüll, N.** 'Die Entstehungsgeschichte des babylonischen Talmuds als Schriftwerkes.' *Jahrbuch für jüdische Geschichte und Literatur* 2 (1876) 1–123. **Burgansky, I.** *The Babylonian Talmud Tractate of Sukka: Its Sources and Methods of Compilation* (Hebr.). Diss. Tel Aviv: Bar Ilan, 1979. **Dor, Z.** 'On the Sources of Gittin in the Babylonian Talmud' (Hebr.). *Bar-Ilan* 4–5 (1967) 89–103. [Repr. in idem, *Teachings*.] **Epstein, J. N.** *IAL*, 9–270. **Goldberg, Abr.** 'The Babylonian Talmud.' In Safrai, *The Literature*, 1:323–45. **Goldberg, A.** 'Der Diskurs im babylonischen Talmud: Anregungen für eine Diskursanalyse.' *FJB* 11 (1983) 1–45. **Goodblatt, D.** 'The Babylonian Talmud.' *ANRW* II 19:2 (1979) 257–336. [Repr. in J. Neusner (ed.), *The Study*, 2:120–99, but also with the pagination of ANRW as used here.] **Jacobs, L.** *The Talmudic Argument: A Study in Talmudic Reasoning and Methodology*. Cambridge 1984. **Jacobs, L.** *Structure and Form in the Babylonian Talmud*. Cambridge 1991. **Kalmin, R.** *Sages, Stories, Authors, and Editors in Rabbinic Babylonia*. Atlanta 1994. **Kaplan, J.** *The Redaction of the Babylonian Talmud*. New York 1933; repr. Jerusalem 1973. **Kraemer, D.** *The Mind of the Talmud: An Intellectual History of the Bavli*. New York/Oxford 1990. [Cf. Y. Elman, *JQR* N.S. 84 (1993–94) 261–82.] **Lightstone, J. N.** *The Rhetoric of the Babylonian Talmud, Its Social Meaning and Context*. Waterloo, Ont. 1994. **Melammed, E. Z.** *Introduction*, 319–97. **Neusner, J.** *Introduction to the Talmud: A Teaching Book*. 2nd edn. San Francisco 1984. **Neusner, J.**, ed. *Formation*. **Neusner, J.** *Judaism: The Classical Statement: The Evidence of the Bavli*. Chicago 1986. **Neusner, J.** *The Bavli and Its Sources: The Question of Tradition in the Case of Tractate Sukkah*. Atlanta 1987. **Neusner, J.** *Language as Taxonomy: The Rules for Using Hebrew and Aramaic in the Babylonian Talmud*. Atlanta 1990. **Neusner, J.** *The Rules of Composition of the Talmud of Babylonia*. Atlanta 1991. **Neusner, J.** *The Bavli's One Voice: Types and Forms of Analytical Discourse and their Fixed Order of Appearance*. Atlanta 1991. **Neusner, J.** *Decoding the Talmud's Exegetical Program*. Atlanta 1992. **Neusner, J.** *The Bavli's Massive Miscellanies*. Atlanta 1992. **Neusner, J.** *The Bavli's Unique Voice. A Systematic Comparison of the Talmud of Babylonia and the Talmud of the Land of Israel*. 7 vols. Atlanta 1993. **Neusner, J.** *Introduction*, 182–220. **Neusner, J.** *Judaism*, 283–339. **Rabinowitz, Z. W.** *Sha'are Torath Babel*. Jerusalem 1961. **Rosenthal, D.** ''Arikhot qedumot ha-meshuqa'ot ba-Talmud ha-Babli.' In *Talmudic Studies*, 1:155–204. **Rosenthal, D.** '"The Talmudists Jumped to Raise an Objection into the Baraita" – Bavli Kettubot 77a–b' (Hebr.). *Tarbiz* 60 (1990–91) 551–76. [On glosses in BT.] **Segal, E.** *Case Citation in the Babylonian Talmud: The Evidence of the Tractate Neziqin*. Atlanta 1990. **Sussmann, J.** *Babylonian Sugiyot to the Orders Zera'im and Tohorot* (Hebr.). Diss. Jerusalem 1969. **Tenenblatt, M. A.** *The Babylonian Talmud in its Historical Development: Its Origin and Arrangement* (Hebr.). Tel Aviv 1972. **Weiss, A.** *The Babylonian Talmud as a Literary Unit, Its Place of Origin, Development and Final Redaction* (Hebr.). New York 1943. **Weiss, A.** *The Talmud in its Development* (Hebr.). New York 1954. **Weiss, A.** *SLA*.

***1) Structure and Contents***

For the terms 'Talmud' and 'Gemara' see pp. 164f. above. The Geonim, R. Nissim, Alfasi and others refer to BT simply as *talmud dilan*, 'our Talmud'. *Talmuda de-Babel* in BM 85a does not denote our BT but simply the traditional teaching in Babylonia in Amoraic times. *Talmud babli* is intended to differentiate between BT and PT; however, Talmud (or Gemara) usually suffices to indicate BT, which in Jewish understanding is the Talmud *par excellence*.

In a very approximate manner, BT can be called the Babylonian commentary on M. Yet BT comprises Gemara for only 36½ of the 63 tractates of M: there is no Gemara for Zeraim with the exception of Ber; in Moed, Sheq is missing (in MSS and printed editions it is replaced by PT), in Neziqin Eduy and Abot, in Qodashim Mid, Qin and Tam (excluding chapters 1, 2, 4); in Toharot only Nid is treated.

Were these missing tractates discussed in the Babylonian schools? This, among other things, seems to be implied in the saying of Raba (4th cent.), 'In the days of Rab Yehudah (bar Yeḥezqel) the entire course of study consisted in (Seder) Neziqin; we, however, learn the six orders. . . we even learn (the tractate) Uqṣin in thirteen sessions' (Taan 24a, b; Ber 20a has the same in the name of Papa, a student of Raba). Discussions on topics of the M tractates without Gemara are dispersed in the other tractates of BT. It is, however, uncertain whether the origin of such Babylonian sayings lies in the actual interpretation of Zeraim and Toharot (thus e.g. B. M. Bokser, *Samuel's Commentary on the Mishnah*, vol. 1 (Leiden 1975), 4 on Zeraim) or not (thus Sussmann, *Babylonian Sugiyot*, 316: Zeraim and Toharot were not studied separately in the Babylonian schools).

Why did these tractates remain without Gemara in BT? If chance or external reasons are to be excluded, one is left with the traditional answer that the laws of Zeraim except Ber as well as of Toharot except Nid had no practical relevance: the agricultural laws were largely tied to the land of Israel; the purity laws generally were no longer practicable because there was no temple cult. Yet the same would be true for Qodashim, for which there is a Babylonian Gemara: this may be because according to Men 110a the study of the sacrificial regulations or of the Torah is generally put on a par with the sacrificial service in the Temple.

In the usual printed editions, BT (including M for the tractates without Gemara, and with the 'extra-canonical' and 'minor' tractates) comprises almost 2,900 folio leaves and is thus much more extensive than PT. This is due to the more elaborate style of BT as well as to its much longer period of growth, and above all to the fact that BT has incorporated a great deal of material which no longer has anything to do with a M commentary (to a lesser extent this is, of course, also true for PT). BT has above all integrated numerous and extensive *midrashim*, which in Palestine remain restricted to a separate literary genre (if minuscule midrashic units in PT are excluded). Quite generally the haggadah in BT is much more extensive than in PT (two thirds of BT compared with one sixth of PT). Thus BT contains e.g. a 'dream book' in Ber 55a–57b (cf. p.MSh 4.9, 55b–c), a tractate on miracles and visions in BB 73a–75b, illustrative narratives on the behaviour of the rabbis in the academies in Suk 27b–28a, narratives from the time of the two great revolts against Rome in Git 55b–58a (cf. LamR). Midrashim include Meg 10b–17a on Esther (cf. EsthR) and Sot 11a–13a on Exod (cf. ExodR).

The overall character of BT is encyclopaedic. Its editors included everything that was taught in the rabbinic schools and considered worth preserving: many kinds of legends (e.g. about appearances of the dead), anecdotes about the rabbis, historical reminiscences, knowledge about medicine, biology, mathematics, astronomy, astrology, etc. Thus BT is less a thematically closed book than a national library of Babylonian Judaism whose structure emulates M.

***2) Origin: According to Tradition***

The traditional history of the origin of BT rests essentially on two Talmudic quotations: BB 157b speaks of two *mahadurot* of Rab Ashi which could mean not only 'edition' but also 'revision, version' of the teaching in view. BM 86a calls 'Rabbi and R. Nathan the end of the *mishnah*, Rab Ashi and Rabina the end of the *hora'ah*.' It is not certain how *hora'ah* should be more precisely interpreted. Most likely it is to be regarded as a particular form of the teaching and authoritative decision of the halakhah, which is limited to the time of the Amoraim. This is the understanding in STA 8, according to which the *hora'ah* lasts for 204 (alternative reading: 280) years from Rab to Rab Ashi and Rabina. The different numbers result from the uncertainty about whether the person in question is Rabina I, a contemporary of Ashi who according to STA died in 424, or Rabina II who died in 499 (STA 6). The former possibility would correspond more closely with the wording of BM 86a (the end of the *hora'ah* at a particular point in time, rather than extending over almost a century). But the second possibility was generally accepted in Geonic times: thus as early as STA 6, where the Talmud is said to have been 'closed' (*nistam*) or 'sealed' (*neḥetam*, so another reading).

The most influential version turned out to be that of ISG, which, in addition to these Talmudic references, makes particular use of school traditions from Pumbeditha:

> And Rab Ashi led his academy for almost sixty years. Therefore we read in the chapter *mi she-met* (here BB 157b) about the first *mahadura* of Rab Ashi and about the last *mahadura* of Rab Ashi. For so the Rabbanan determined: to teach in each Kallah two *metibata*, be they short or long. And so he repeated (or revised) his teaching (*talmudeh*) in 30 years. And since Rab Ashi presided for almost 60 years, he had two *mahadure*. And he died in the year 424 (Spanish recension: 427; ISG 93f.).

'And on Wednesday, the 13th of Kislev of the year 499 Rabina the son of Rab Huna died, who is the end of the *hora'ah*' (ISG 95). 'And after him Rab Assi presided, and in his days was the end of the *hora'ah* and the Talmud was closed' (*istetem talmuda*; Goodblatt, 309, also considers the possibility of translating 'the Talmud was made anonymous', inasmuch as the authors of sayings and texts are no longer named) (ISG 97). The reference to Rab Assi (Spanish recension: Yose) as *sof hora'ah* incidentally finds no support in the text of the Talmud. Finally Sherira touches only briefly on the period of the Saboraim, observing on the basis of Geonic chronicles that most of them died within a few years (ISG 97f.). He resumes his fuller treatment only for the Geonic period.

ISG nowhere explicitly refers to Rab Ashi as the editor of BT; what is more, *talmud* in his text need not always mean BT, but can also simply designate the Talmudic teaching. However, ISG appears to understand the two Talmudic references from the perspective of the Geonic period, and its institutions, as statements about the conclusion of the Talmudic teaching (whether in general or in form of the edited BT). The two *mahadurot*, therefore, represent two complete revisions of this teaching during the Kallah months of Rab Ashi's 60–year term of office (or, according to the Spanish recension, during the semesters of these academic years).

Medieval tradition is entirely dependent on ISG. It further elaborates the latter's facts and specifies them (BT is now unequivocally in view). This is the case, for instance, in Rashi's commentaries on BM 86a and BB 157b. Similarly Abraham Ibn Daud: Rab Ashi 'began to write down the Talmud' (*Sefer ha-Qabbalah*, ed. Cohen, 27); Rab Yose is the beginning of the Saboraim, and in the 24th year of his presidency (i.e. in 500) the Talmud was sealed. 'It began to be written down under Rab Ashi and it was sealed 73 years after his death' (ibid., 33).

These premises have been adopted time and again up to the present, and they still constitute the classic view. According to this, Ashi twice revised the entire Talmud; several decades later it was finally closed and written down. The only open question in this perspective is the role of the Saboraim. But even E. Berkovits (*EJ* 15:760–62), who attributes to them not only the conventional, almost exclusively stylistic revision but also longer pieces of text, regards BT as finally completed around the middle of the sixth century; in this he agrees with the great authorities Epstein and Albeck. All reconstructions also assign a major role to the time of persecution mentioned by Sherira (ISG 99) for the end of the Persian period. This is usually regarded as a motivation for Ashi's redaction of BT (according to this view he would have worked in anticipation of the coming persecution), or at least as the reason for writing down the BT after such an extended time of oral tradition.

The traditional premise is problematic for several reasons. Not only are the two BT texts an insufficient, equivocal and not *a priori* guaranteed basis, but Sherira's interpretation further presupposes in BB 157b a system of academies, and especially the institution of the Kallah months, in a manner which can be fully substantiated only for the Geonic period. Finally, the analysis of BT itself indicates that while Ashi contributed a lot of material, he certainly does not stand out among other masters of his own and the subsequent period to such an extent that he emerges as the redactor of the first version of BT. The names of Ashi and Rabina undoubtedly indicate a time frame which was decisive for the redaction of BT. More specific conclusions, however, can only result from an investigation of BT itself.

### *3) Redaction*

#### *a) No Uniform Redaction*

J. Neusner asserts an entirely homogeneous redaction of BT: 'The facts before us do not indicate a haphazard, episodic, sedimentary process of agglutination and conglomeration'; rather, he views BT as 'a well-considered and orderly composition, planned from beginning to end and following an outline that is definitive throughout' (*The Rules*, 190). Further, he speaks in terms of a 'single, cogent and rhetorically consistent discourse', a coherent whole with 'a plan and program', which is 'the creation of single-minded geniuses of applied logic and sustained analytical enquiry' (*The Bavli's One Voice*, 460f.). On this account, most of the material in BT was shaped during a period of perhaps half a century, before being grouped around sections of the Mishnah and then redacted to attain the form of the present work (ibid., 464). Neusner rightly rejects the traditional idea of a 'sedimentary' growth of BT, assuming instead a planned redaction according to uniform criteria. This global perspective, however, drowns out the many details that point to a rather more eventful history of development, which the redactors of BT did not iron out for the sake of greater homogeneity.

In contrast, J. N. Epstein underlines that BT is not a work of one piece, but uses many sources and unites layers from different eras and generations, different authors, redactors, and schools: 'Every single tractate is a book in itself.' Epstein infers this from the many differences, contradictions and duplications within BT and even within its individual tractates, as well as from linguistic and stylistic variations and the occurrence of different Amoraim within various tractates and their subsections (*IAL*, 12; followed by E. Z. Melammed, *Introduction*, 426f.). It is perhaps not just due to circumstances, therefore, that Epstein himself was unable to complete his introduction; indeed it seems logically consistent that *IAL* offers not an introduction to 'the Babylonian Talmud' but merely introductions to (nine of) its tractates.

Five tractates – Ned, Naz, Me'ilah, Ker, Tam – differ from the rest of BT in a number of linguistic and grammatical peculiarities, which were already observed by the Tosafists (Urbach, *The Tosafists*, 561). These 'extraordinary tractates' also include those parts of Tem that are characterized by the expression *lishana aḥarina*. These tractates differ in their vocabulary, in grammatical peculiarities (distinctive possessive suffixes, demonstrative and personal pronouns) as well as divergent terminology: e.g. *tibae* instead of *teiqu*, a matter remains 'undecided' (cf. L. Jacobs, *Teyku: The Unsolved Problem in the Babylonian Talmud: A Study in Literary Analysis and Form of the Talmudic Argument*, London/New York 1981); the usual *ḥasore meḥasra*, an interpretation assuming an omission in the text M, is lacking where one might expect it. These and other, originally much more pronounced linguistic differences were in part adapted to the conventional style of BT by copyists and printers (cf. Epstein, *A Grammar of Babylonian Aramaic* (Hebr.) (Jerusalem 1960), 14–16; and idem, *IAL*, 54, 72–74; Melammed, *Introduction*, 464–70).

Rashi designates the *lishana aḥarina* as *lashon yerushalmi* (e.g. Tem 6b). He is followed by I. Halevy (*Dorot*, 3:48–50), who assumes that this and the other extraordinary tractates do indeed reflect Palestinian usage. Based on Geonic testimony that Ned was not studied after Yehudai Gaon (cf. B. M. Lewin, *Otzar ha-Gaonim*, vol. 11 (Jerusalem 1942), 5–12: explicitly attested only for Ned, it could also be inferred for the other tractates on the basis of Geonic lists of tractates), he assumes that while these Massekhtot were not taught among the Geonim in the Babylonian Yeshibot, they were indeed taught and written down in Palestine. This in turn, he believes, influenced the linguistic style as well.

This view is contradicted above all by Z. W. Rabinowitz (*Scha'are Torath Babel*, 299–310): as late as the eleventh century, PT and not BT was studied in Palestine. The substantive differences between these tractates and the rest of BT are without parallel in PT; the linguistic peculiarities cannot be traced back to Palestine but are due to dialectal differences in Babylonian Aramaic. Most of BT was edited at Sura, where Rab Ashi worked; but the linguistically divergent tractates manifest the dialect of Pumbeditha and Nehardea, which is closely related to Palestinian Aramaic. They were edited in Pumbeditha (thus already I. Lewy in his commentary on p.Neziqin, p. 74); this would appear to be suggested by the similarity of the language with that of the Geonim, most of whom are from Pumbeditha (but note that even the writings of the Geonim from Sura use the same language: De Vries, *Meḥqarim*, 231).

Others attempt to account for the peculiarity of these tractates by appealing not to a different place of redaction but rather to chronological considerations. A. Weiss (*MGWJ* 73:186–89; 83:261–76; *The Babylonian Talmud as a Literary Unit*, 46–128) and similarly B. De Vries (*Meḥqarim*, 223–38) regard the extraordinary tractates as older. A. Weiss, who plays down the differences with the other tractates, thinks that all of BT was first edited at Pumbeditha and only then introduced into the other schools; there the regularly studied tractates were subject to linguistic adaptation, while the neglected five-and-a–half tractates retained their more primitive linguistic form. De Vries, who considers the five-and-a–half tractates to be older in their subject matter as well, assumes a redaction in the school of Rab Papa especially for Me'ilah (*Meḥqarim*, 237f.), but like Weiss he emphasizes the older linguistic form of these tractates as compared with the others which were regularly studied and correspondingly adapted in Geonic times.

J. N. Epstein on the other hand holds that the five-and-a–half tractates are later than the rest of BT. In his view they contain quotations from the rest of BT (De Vries dismisses these instances as later additions; however, in contrast to his usual view this would appear to presuppose the study of these tractates in Geonic times). Above all, however, their language is already so close to Geonic Aramaic that an early date is ruled out (*IAL*, 54–71, 72–83, 131–44).

At present, a clear solution remains out of reach. While an explanation of the differences in terms of different places of redaction is conceivable, no proof of this is possible in the present state of knowledge. Similarly, too little is known about the linguistic developments to justify a reasoned defence of either an early or a late dating of these tractates. We may be nearer to a solution in the special case of Temurah, which frequently juxtaposes two linguistically different versions of the same subject matter, labelling one of them as *lishana aḥarina*. Rabinowitz explained this in terms of two redactions of this tractate, one at Sura and one at Pumbeditha, which were later combined. E. S. Rosenthal's analysis of the textual transmission of

Temurah allowed him to demonstrate that there were indeed two recensions ('The Renderings of TB Tractate Temura' (Hebr.), *Tarbiz* 58 (1988–89) 317–56). The standard version is supported by the four complete MSS of the tractate. Excerpts of the other (*lishana aḥarina*) were included in MS Florence (Beṣalel Ashkenazi has additional quotations), while fragments from the Genizah (Cambridge) and from Modena also attest its independent existence. Even for other tractates, the question of textual recensions and their aftermath is likely to have a pronounced effect on future scholarship.

## *b) Sources*
### *1. Mishnah*

***Bibliography***

See the titles by M. Schachter and S. Zeitlin on p. 139 above. **Bokser, B. M.** *Samuel's Commentary on the Mishnah: Its Nature, Forms, and Content.* Part One: *Mishnayot in the Order of Zera'im.* Leiden 1975. **Bokser, B. M.** *Post-Mishnaic Judaism in Transition: Samuel on Berakhot and the Beginnings of Gemara.* Chico 1980. **Florsheim, J.** 'Rav Hisda as Exegetor of Tannaitic Sources' (Hebr.). *Tarbiz* 41 (1971–72) 24–48. **Fraenkel, J.** 'Ha Gufa Qashya: Internal Contradictions in Talmudic Literature' (Hebr.). *Tarbiz* 42 (1972–73) 266–301. **Goldberg, Abr.** 'The Use of the Tosefta and the Baraitha of the School of Samuel by the Babylonian Amora Rava for the Interpretation of the Mishna' (Hebr.). *Tarbiz* 40 (1970–71) 144–57. **Zucker, M.** 'Ha-"Ḥasore Meḥasra" ba-Talmud.' In *Minḥat Bikkurim* (*Festschrift* A. Schwarz), 47–53. Vienna 1926.

M of course is the basis for BT as well. For this reason a complete M text is already provided by the MSS, followed by the printed editions. As was stressed before, this is not a uniform base text; and, as in the case of PT, the M text presupposed in the discussion occasionally diverges from that preceding the Gemara (cf. *ITM*, 166ff.). Insofar as M presupposes a Palestinian situation, the exegesis of M in Babylonia would of course take place under conditions different from those in Palestine. With the recognition of M as a codex of current law probably as early as the third century, Babylonian exegesis saw itself compelled to reconcile M with the sometimes divergent Babylonian halakhah. This necessitated a much more liberal treatment of M than was common in Palestine.

Particularly popular in Babylonia is the reference to the M's elliptical mode of expression by the formula *ḥasore meḥasra*, calling for appropriate supplementation. Sometimes this is justified, but sometimes it occurs without an appropriate basis in the text (cf. M. Zucker; Epstein, *ITM*, 595–672). Equally distinctive of BT is the formula *ha-gufah qashiah*, 'this contains a difficulty', to point out contradictions between two parts of a M. Here too some real internal contradictions have been observed, but most are read into the text to achieve a particular interpretation (cf. J. Fraenkel). As J. Florsheim stresses with regard to Rab Ḥisda, 'The main goal of interpretation is the renewal of the halakhah. That is, the essence of interpretation is to let the source agree with the halakhah as determined according to Rab Ḥisda's system. This does not mean that Rab Ḥisda did not know the literal interpretation of the sources; but the latter was not his main goal. . . . This system is not peculiar to Rab Ḥisda, but is typical for the entire Talmud' (*Tarbiz* 41, p. 48).

### *2. Baraitot*

***Bibliography*** (In general and on the term see p. 177 above.)

**Albeck**, *Mabo*, 44–50. **Bacher**, *TT*, 222–34. **Goodblatt**, *ANRW*, 286–88. **Hauptman, J.** 'Development of the Talmudic Sugya by Amoraic and Post-Amoraic Amplification of a Tannaitic Proto-Sugya.' *HUCA* 58 (1987) 227–50. **Hauptman, J.** *Development of the Talmudic Sugya: Relationship between Tannaitic and Amoraic Sources*. Lanham, MD 1988. [One chapter is already in *PAAJR* 51 (1984) 73–104.] **Jacobs, L.** 'Are there Fictitious Baraitot in the Babylonian Talmud?' *HUCA* 42 (1971) 185–96. **Melammed, E. Z.** *Introduction*, 258–70 (=Summary of: idem, *Halachic Midrashim of the Tannaim in the Talmud Babli* (Hebr.), 2nd ed. Jerusalem 1988), 392–94, 407–12. **Weiss, A.** *SLA*, 167–71.

We cannot know with certainty whether and to what extent BT or individual masters knew T and the halakhic midrashim (cf. p. 155 above for T, p. 250 below for the midrashim). The possibility cannot be excluded that the parallels between BT and these works derive from merely similar collections. On the other hand, the differences of wording in these parallels do not necessarily imply different sources, but may have arisen in the course of textual transmission or from paraphrasing quotations. This question indeed is not of primary importance for the analysis of BT itself: 'Whether or not the Babylonian Amoraim knew the extant Tannaitic collections, they obviously had at their disposal compilations of Tannaitic sources. Some of these compilations bore the same name as the extant collections; others bore different names' (Goodblatt, 287).

No particular problems are raised by the baraitot which are common to BT and PT: in this case the Palestinian and probably Tannaitic provenance of the material (not necessarily of the formulation) is generally assured. Matters are different, however, in the case of texts introduced as baraita which are found only in BT. This is true especially where a parallel exists in PT, but not as a baraita (e.g. in a story about R. Eliezer ben Hyrcanus, BM 59b; cf. p.MQ 3:1, 81c). Equally questionable are baraitot which in the immediate context or elsewhere are cited as sayings of Amoraim, frequently introduced by the phrase *tanya' nami hakhi*. These baraitot are widely held to have been very late insertions into the text. J. Hauptman, however, attempts to show that these baraitot belong to the earliest layer of commentary on M: they were often prefixed by later Amoraic statements and then made to conform to them in the course of textual transmission. Like other theories, therefore, this thesis does not guarantee the verbatim transmission even of halakhic baraitot, while narrative ones are even more problematic. As for sayings of Tannaim from Amoraic times, even the Amoraim are not prepared to accept these as of equal authority to a genuine baraita.

The Geonim already recognized the problematic nature of some baraitot (cf. Rab Hai Gaon's Responsum on Pes 105a in B.M. Lewin, *Otzar ha-Gaonim*, vol. 3 (Jerusalem 1930), 104, which was already pointed out by I. H. Weiss, *Dor*, 3:195f.). A. Weiss (*The Talmud in its Development*, 35–63) attempted to explain the parallel attestation of sayings as baraitot and as Amoraic sayings by suggesting that by Amoraic times many baraitot were common property and hence were not explicitly quoted as such. While this may be true in isolated cases, L. Jacobs rightly emphasizes that it cannot explain all instances: at least some baraitot in BT must at any rate be considered fictitious.

### *3. Midrashim*

In addition to the midrashic material attributed to the Tannaites, BT also contains numerous midrashim from the Amoraic period. In part this material will have arisen from the interpretation of M, for example where Scripture passages are to support the halakhah of M or Amoraic decisions. These mostly short pieces probably cannot be regarded as sources of BT in the proper sense; the same is true for the many places in which haggadic interpretation of Scripture – usually in complete accord with the principles currrent since Tannaitic times – appears only briefly and rather incidentally (Melammed, *Introduction*, 296–311, 384–91). But BT also contains longer and continuous midrashim whose *Sitz im Leben* is not the exegesis of M but the interpretation of Scripture, which was fostered as a separate discipline in the schools and synagogue sermons of Palestine or Babylonia (examples on p. 192 above; cf. e.g. Suk 52a, which offer an allegorical interpretation of Joel 2.20 to signify the evil inclination; Suk 6b has a halakhic interpretation of Lev 23.42f., although this might come directly out of the interpretation of M; see A. Weiss, *SLA*, 256–59, 276–92). In these cases one must probably assume fully formulated oral or written units of tradition, which the redactors of BT received as completed texts and incorporated into the framework of Mishnah interpretation. It is true that much of the material in these midrashim derives from Palestinian tradition, even if in individual cases one must also expect the later expansion of BT using Palestinian sources (Abr. Goldberg in Safrai, *The Literature*, 1:336 with reference to MS Vat 134 and *S'ridei Bavli*). The more extensive units, however, were composed in Babylonia and are characterized by Babylonian interests (see D. Börner-Klein, *Eine babylonische Auslegung der Esther-Geschichte*, Frankfurt 1991; E. Segal, *The Babylonian Esther Midrash: A Critical Commentary*, 3 vols., Atlanta 1994; G. Stemberger, 'Midrasch in Babylonien: Am Beispiel von Sota 9b–14a', *Henoch* 10 (1988) 183–203; D. Kraemer, 'Scripture Commenary in the Babylonian Talmud: Primary or Secondary Phenomenon', *AJSR* 14 (1989) 1–15).

In this connection we should also mention the Targums, which the Amoraim had available as sources in a relatively fixed form, although not necessarily as we know them today.

### *4. Palestinian Sources from the Amoraic Period*

***Bibliography***

**Aminoah, N.** 'Qit'ê Talmud mi-Siddur Qadum be-Massekhet Rosh Ha-Shanah.' In Y.D. Gilat et al. (eds.), *'Iyunim be-Sifrut Ḥazal, ba-Miqra' u-be-Toldot Yisra'el* (*Festschrift* E.Z. Melammed, Ramat Gan 1982), 185–97. **Bacher**, *TT*, 506–23. **Dor, Z. M.**, *Teachings*. **Epstein**, *IAL*, 290–312. **Goldberg, Abr.** 'Palestinian Law in Babylonian Tradition, as Revealed in a Study of Pereq 'Arvei Pesaḥim' (Hebr.). *Tarbiz* 33 (1963–64) 337–48. **Jaffee, M. S.** 'The Babylonian Appropriation of the Talmud Yerushalmi: Redactional Studies in the Horayot Tractates.' In A. J. Avery-Peck (ed.), *New Perspectives on Ancient Judaism*, 4:3–27. Lanham, MD 1989. **Melammed**, *Introduction*, 442–51. **Schwartz, J.** 'Southern Judaea and Babylonia.' *JQR* N.S. 72 (1981–82) 188–97. **Weiss, A.** *SLA*, 264ff.

It used to be commonly assumed that BT knew and used PT as a source. Alfasi (*Sefer ha-Halakhot*, end of Erub: ed. N. Sacks (Jerusalem 1969), 1:198), probably based on Rab Paltoi Gaon (thus Ginzberg, *Mabo*, 85), declines a decision for PT against BT, since the authors of BT supposedly already checked PT and rejected it in many questions. In his comparison of Hor in BT and PT, M. S. Jaffee claims to find 'suggestive evidence' for the view that PT presents the structural presupposition of the Mishnah commentary in BT: 'the Yerushalmi, in more or less its extant form, shapes the Babylonians' conception of their own task and, moreover, supplies the dominant exegetical themes appropriated by them for amplificiation or revision' (p. 7). J. Neusner, on the other hand, while allowing that BT and PT follow a common agenda, would nevertheless insist that 'the rhetoric and literary program of the Bavli owed remarkably little to those of its predecessor' (*Judaism: The Classical Statement*, 75).

However, the relative proximity of a given BT tractate to PT does not permit a general conclusion about the form in which the redactors of BT knew PT. Detailed comparisons of PT with BT usually conclude that BT did not make use of our PT (cf. Epstein, *IAL*, 290–92), but that we must instead expect the dissemination of Palestinian material in Babylonia – unshaped traditions as well as entire sugyot, albeit not yet in their final form enountered in PT. This explains the undeniable parallels between the two Talmuds, and also their divergences and contradictions in the names of tradents, halakhah, etc., as well as the fact that many sayings of Babylonian Amoraim are contained only in PT (for a list see Bacher, *TT*, 311–17; 477–505) and that sayings of Palestinian Amoraim in BT strongly deviate from their rendering in PT.

The dissemination of Palestinian transmissions in Babylonia is mainly due to Babylonian teachers who spent some time studying in Palestine (e.g. Rab), as well as to the *naḥote* (cf. p. 179 above). BT itself repeatedly refers to such borrowing from Palestinian tradition with phrases like, 'in the West they say' (e.g. Sot 18b), 'when X came' (e.g. Shab 45b) or 'X sent' (e.g. Git 66a), to express the personal or written communication of traditions. Certain rabbis are particularly interested in such Palestinian traditions and engage in their interpretation and evaluation: especially Raba and his student Papa, who deal intensively with the teaching of Yoḥanan (cf. Z. M. Dor).

The Palestinian influence ranges from the mere adoption of halakhic decisions and customs (cf. Goldberg) to the transfer of entire sugyot, which of course were subject to appropriate revision in Bayblonia (Dor passim; Bacher, *TT*; Epstein, *IAL*; Melammed, *Introduction*). Smaller tractates, such as the dream book of Ber 55a–57b, also come from Palestinian sources (p.MSh 4.9, 55b and LamR on 1.1), even if they were suitably elaborated and expanded in Babylonia (cf. B. Stemberger, 'Der Traum in der rabbinischen Literatur', *Kairos* 18 (1976) 1–42, especially 8–14).

***c) The Redactional Development of the Tradition***

Some scholars doubt that there was ever an actual final redaction of BT, preferring to think instead in terms of local Talmuds that developed layer by layer (A. Weiss, *The Babylonian Talmud as a Literary Unit*, 256). While certain great masters doubtless exercised a formative influence, the Babylonian traditions on this view continued to grow organically until shifting interests and other factors caused it to cease (thus e.g. A. Weiss, *SLA*, 117f.). This account would agree with ISG that the Talmud was expanded from generation to generation.

But the question of the earlier stages of BT remains relevant even if, with J. Neusner (p. 194 above), one counters the idea of sedimentary growth (which he criticizes in D. W. Halivni) by highlighting the final redaction and seeing in BT 'not patchwork quilts, but woven fabric' (*The Bavli's One Voice*, 461). However formative the actual redactors' concluding intervention may have been, there must have been prior stages of BT which went beyond the sources we have already described towards a continuous exposition of the Mishnah. We may leave open the question of whether passages not concerned with Mishnah interpretation (i.e. above all midrashim or minor topical discourses) were already integrated at this stage or only by the actual redactors of BT. Be that as it may, the compilation of BT from various sources was at any rate not left to Rab Ashi in the fifth century or another final redactor. Instead, one must assume a long development of BT and diverse earlier forms in which the aforesaid sources were already available and used to varying degrees. Expressed by way of overstatement: every great master of the Amoraic period taught 'his' Talmud, be it comprehensive or specialized in particular tractates or topics. (Bokser has shown this for Samuel; cf. also D. Rosenthal, 'Pirqa de 'Abbaye (TB Rosh Ha'shana II)' (Hebr.), *Tarbiz* 46 (1976–77) 97–109, who with the exception of minor additions attributes the Gemara of RH 2 to Abaye and his school at Pumbeditha; the collection of sayings of individual masters also occasionally entered BT as a source, e.g. BQ 11a–b, where Ulla speaks seven times in the name of R. Eleazar; cf. A. Weiss, *SLA*, 221–25).

That such different sources of the Babylonian Gemara underlie BT (cf. especially Albeck, *Mabo*, 557–75; further bibliography in Goodblatt, 289–93) is clear especially from the parallel pericopes. Where these are transmitted (almost) identically in different places, they could be attributed to a redactional decision. But some of these parallel versions are very disparate, attribute the same saying to different masters, or contradictory sayings to the same master. These sugyot refer to different sources as much as passages in which a rabbi's saying is first accepted and then completely rejected, or which quote from a Gemara that does not correspond to our BT (often with the formula *we-hawenan ba*: cf. De Vries, *Meḥqarim*, 200–214). Another indication of different sources is the introduction *ikka de-amri* 'some say' or the like, followed once again by the aforementioned with only slight variations (also with *lishana aḥarina*), as well as the non-chronological arrangement of rabbis in a given section: when in the usually chronological structure of a pericope later masters are followed by earlier teachers, this may indicate a later supplementation of the section from another source (Albeck, *Mabo*, 573f.; contrast A. Weiss, *Meḥqarim*, 160–212).

The present state of scholarship does not permit a reconstruction of the various sources underlying the final redaction of BT, even if various substantial and self-contained blocks of material can be removed without a trace (thus e.g. BB 73a–75b: cf. G. Stemberger, 'Münchhausen und die Apokalyptik', *JSJ* 20 (1989) 61–83). What is more, we must assume the independent literary development of the individual tractates, which significantly differ in age (similarly J. N. Epstein; see also the studies of individual tractates by D. Aminoah and others). Various attempts have been made to identify basic building blocks of BT, in order thereby to trace its historical development. Thus, J. Kaplan distinguished between a short and a long form of BT, which he called *gemara* and *talmud*, and which in his opinion chronologically followed each other. A. Weiss similarly distinguishes *Mêmra* and *Sugya*, as well as other forms such as collections, midrashim and tractates.

The *Mêmra* is 'a short Amoraic statement which comprises a certain succinct idea without any discussion' (*SLA*, 1). It may be in Hebrew or Aramaic, anonymous or attributed to an Amora, independent or commentary on either the Bible, Mishnah or baraita. The date of such a mêmra must be determined case by case.

*Sugya* (from Aramaic *segi*, 'to go', hence 'course' (cf. *halakhah*), the course of a discussion, the decision in a controversy) designates a self-contained basic unit of Talmudic discussion which is often based on one mêmra (or several), and may discuss a M or be independent from M. The sugya as such is also indigenous to Palestine, but it was developed and shaped especially in Babylonia.

Sugyot as basic elements of BT cannot be globally evaluated. Some are short and simply constructed, others are complex and hence longer; sometimes they even make use of other sugyot or incorporate parts of them. Although they are self-contained, sugyot may nevertheless presuppose knowledge of other sugyot and their terminology. This provides points of reference for dating sugyot and discerning their growth. At the same time one ought to avoid hasty judgements such as the global early dating of the anonymous material (e.g. Albeck, *Mabo*, 577; on this cf. G. G. Porton in Neusner (ed.), *Formation*, 131); more helpful are criteria such as those worked out by S. Friedman (*6th WCJS*, 3:390). The comparatively rudimentary nature of the sugyot of the extraordinary tractates (De Vries, *Meḥqarim*, 194) is an argument for their early date.

Some sugyot are undoubtedly early, and have influenced other sugyot. Some of the later sugyot make use of these earlier ones along with other sources – midrashim, collections of sayings, etc. Like other materials, such sugyot were probably sorted according to M and collected; this led to more and more extensive volumes which in turn were combined with other collections. Ch. Albeck assumes that the later redactors merely strung together blocks of material without change. This appears to find support in the deviations, contradictions and repetitions between the various parts of BT. Nevertheless, the redaction of BT must not be assessed by modern criteria. Given the essentially integral design of BT, it is unacceptably simplistic to conceive of its redaction merely in terms of a collection of material.

***Bibliography on the Sugya***

**Albeck**, *Mabo*, 576–601. [Cf. on this G.G. Porton in Neusner (ed.), *Formation*, 127–33.] **Atlas, S.** 'Le-toldot ha-sugya.' *HUCA* 24 (1952–53) Hebrew section, 1–21. **Cohen, A.** 'On the non-chronological Location of Mar Bar Rav Ashi's Statements in Babylonian Talmud Sugyot' (Hebr.). *Sidra* 2 (1986) 49–66. **Ephrati, J. A.** 'Contributions of Succeeding Generations to a Sugya in Bava Metzia' (Hebr.). *Bar-Ilan* 6 (1968) 75–100. **Etz-Chayim, Y.** *Contradictory Passages (Sugiot Muḥlafot) in the Tractate Nezikin (Bava Kama, Bava Mezia and Bava Batra) itself and between it and the Rest of the Babylonian Talmud* (Hebr.). Diss. Tel Aviv: Bar Ilan, 1976. **Friedman, S.** 'Some Structural Patterns of Talmudic Sugiot' (Hebr.). *6th WCJS* (Jerusalem 1977) 3:389–402. **Friedman, S.** 'A Critical Study of Yevamot X with a Methodological Introduction' (Hebr.). *Texts and Studies: Analecta Judaica*, vol. 1, 275–441. Ed. H. Z. Dimitrovsky. New York 1977. **Friedman, S.** 'Form Criticism of the Sugya in the Study of the Babylonian Talmud' (Hebr.). *7th WCJS* (Jerusalem 1981) 3:251–55. **Goldberg, Abr.** 'The Sources and Development of the Sugya in the Babylonian Talmud' (Hebr.). *Tarbiz* 32 (1962–63) 143–52. **Goldberg, Abr.** 'Le-hitpaḥut ha-sugya ba-Talmud ha-Babli.' In *Sefer Yovel le-Rabbi Ḥanokh Albeck* (*Festschrift* Ch. Albeck), 101–13. Jerusalem 1963. **Hauptman, J.** *Development of the Talmudic Sugya: Relationship Between Tannaitic and Amoraic Sources.* New York 1968. **Hauptman, J.** 'Development of the Talmudic Sugya by Amoraic and Post-Amoraic Amplification of a Tannaitic Proto-Sugya.' *HUCA* 58 (1987) 227–50. **Jacobs, L.** 'The Talmudic Sugya as a Literary Unit: An Analysis of Baba Ḳamma 2a–3b.' *JJS* 24 (1973) 119–26. **Jacobs, L.** 'A Study of Four Parallel Sugyot in the Babylonian Talmud.' *JJS* 25 (1974) 398–418. **Jacobs, L.** *The Talmudic Argument: A Study in Talmudic Reasoning and Methodology.* Cambridge 1984. **Kraemer, D.** 'The Origins of the Sugya as a Literary Unit.' *9th WCJS* (Jerusalem 1986) 23–30. **De Vries, B.** *Meḥqarim*, 181–99, 239–58. **Weiss, A.** *The Talmud in its Development* (Hebr.). New York 1954. **Weiss, A.** *SLA*; *Meḥqarim.* [On Weiss see S. Kanter and D. Goodblatt in Neusner (ed.), *Formation*, 87–94 and 95–103; M. S. Feldblum, 'Prof. Abraham Weiss – his approach and contribution to Talmudic scholarship', in *The Abraham Weiss Jubilee Volume* (New York 1964), 7–80, especially 13–36.]

## *d) The Contribution of the Saboraim*

***Bibliography***

**Bard, T.R.** In J. Neusner (ed.), *Formation*, 61–74. **Cohen, A.** 'On the Phrase 'La schmia li klomar la sbira li' in the Babylonian Talmud' (Hebr.). Tarbiz 53 (1983–84) 467–72. **Ephrathi, J. E.** *The Sevoraic Period.* **Etz-Ḥaim, Y.** 'Saboraic Material as a Factor in the Development of Non-Identical Parallel Sugiot' (Hebr.). In *Michtam le-David: Rabbi David Ochs Memorial Volume (1905–1975)*, 137–52. Ramat-Gan 1978. **Francus, I.** 'Additions and Parallels in T. B. Bava Qamma VII' (Hebr.). *Bar-Ilan* 12 (1974) 43–63. **Friedman, S.** 'Glosses and Additions in T. B. Bava Qamma VIII' (Hebr.). *Tarbiz* 40 (1970–71) 418–43. **Friedman, S.** [The two articles in the previous section on sugya.] **Goodblatt, D.** *ANRW*, 294f., 314–18. **Kalmin, R.** 'The Post-Rav Ashi Amoraim: Transition or Continuity? A Study of the Role of the Final Generations of Amoraim in the Redaction of the Talmud.' *AJSR* 11 (1986) 157–87. **Kalmin, R.** *The Redaction of the Babylonian Talmud: Amoraic or Saboraic?* Cincinnati 1989. **Klein, H.** 'Gemara and Sebara.' *JQR* N.S. 38 (1947–48)

67–91. **Klein, H.** 'Gemara Quotations in Sebara.' *JQR* N.S. 43 (1952–53) 341–63. **Klein, H.** 'Some Methods of Sebara.' *JQR* N.S. 50 (1959–60) 124–46. **Lewin, B. M.** *Rabbanan Sabora'ê we-Talmudam.* Jerusalem 1937. **Melammed, E. Z.** *Introduction*, 473–78. **Segal, E. L.** *Case Citation*, 122ff. **Spiegel, J. S.** *Later (Saboraic) Additions in the Babylonian Talmud* (Hebr.). Diss. University of Tel Aviv 1975. **Spiegel, J. S.** 'Comments and Late Additions in the Babylonian Talmud' (Hebr.). In M. A. Friedman, A. Tal and G. Brin (eds.), *Studies in Talmudic Literature*, 91–112. Tel Aviv 1983. **Weiss, A.** *The Literary Activities of the Saboraim* (Hebr.). Jerusalem 1953.

The term 'Sabora' derives from *sabar*, 'to reflect, examine, deduce'. The teachers so designated are the successors of the Amoraim. However, little is known in detail about their history and even less about their work. Sherira Gaon cites as the Saboraic period the time from 500 until 589, while according to Abraham Ibn Daud it lasted for another century, until 689. For a long time, scholars accepted Sherira's information; as a result of poor textual versions of ISG (and STA), this period was further whittled down to last only until the middle of the sixth century, or just one generation: 'The Saboraim proper belong to only a single generation' (H. Graetz, *Geschichte der Juden*, vol. 5 (4th edn. Leipzig 1909), 398; cf. also I. H. Weiss, *Dor*, 4:3f.).

The work of the Saboraim was correspondingly underestimated, since scholars were convinced that Rab Ashi and Rabina constituted the end of the *hora'ah* and that the Talmud was 'sealed' around 500. In traditional depictions, therefore, the Saboraim are left only with the delicate task of final literary redaction: the insertion of explicative glosses, information as to which of the cited Amoraic statements represents the halakhah, the supplementation of scriptural proof texts or complete parallels where only a terse reference had been given, the indication of *simanim*, mnemonic aids, and the like. Even J. N. Epstein limits their activity considerably: their work is 'the external arrangement (of BT), usually without changing anything . . . except for additions and links between mêmrot and sugyot, although these often change the entire sugya and its original shape. They transferred sugyot from one place to another, supplemented one with another and sought to compare them' (*IAL*, 12).

Meanwhile, a reassessment of the Saboraim is under way. The longer time frame of Ibn Daud's *Sefer ha-Qabbalah* is beginning to be accepted (reasons given in Ephrathi, 74–81), and the sizeable contribution of the Saboraim in BT is increasingly being recognized. J. Kaplan and A. Weiss above all have shown that one cannot speak of a 'sealing' of the Talmud around 500. The Saboraim, 'by whose merit the heavens are stretched out and the earth is founded' (STA, 9) did not just cosmetically touch up BT, but added numerous sugyot to it. This is indicated already by the Geonim (ISG 71!) who frequently cite BT in a version which still lacks Saboraic additions, and also by the MS tradition of BT which often does not contain Saboraic pieces or varies considerably in such cases. Statements of medieval authors are also frequently helpful in this regard.

N. Brüll already pointed out that some tractates begin with Saboraic sugyot. A. Weiss demonstrated this for almost all tractates and for the beginnings of many chapters within the tracatates: these sugyot are either the work of Saboraim providing an introduction to the tractate or chapter, or they were created by Saboraim using Amoraic sources. Detailed studies like those of S. Friedman and I. Francus have shown Weiss's assumptions to be justified. Saboraic additions are particularly numerous in BM, but also in BQ and BB, thus showing that here too Neziqin is a homogeneous tractate (Friedman, *Glosses*); they are nowhere entirely absent.

As for the anonymous pieces of BT, D. Halivni (*Sources,* vol. 2, introduction) surmises that they are late, at any rate after Rabina and R. Ashi; he concludes that on this basis 'we must consider the Gemara as a composite work of two books, a book of the Amoraim and a book of anonymous traditions' (7f.). J. S. Spiegel, too, finds anonymity to be the common denominator of Saboraic additions (*Additions*, 250). Might this also be suggested in ISG 97: *istetem talmuda*, 'the Talmud was made anonymous', as Goodblatt, 309 proposes to translate? No general conclusions can as yet be drawn here; but these approaches should certainly be considered and examined in detail. It has at any rate become clear that the contribution of the Saboraim is immense. It may well be inappropriate, therefore, to speak merely of Saboraic additions to an existing BT, instead of viewing the Saboraim with J. Kaplan (*Redaction*, 312) as the true redactors of BT.

***e) Geonic Additions***

'Thus the claim that the Talmud was concluded at the end of the fifth century is very much up in the air. The Talmud was not continued past the middle of the eighth century because independent literary efforts were seeking expression, as is shown by the *Halakhot Pesukot* and *Gedolot*, and because Karaism detracted from the Talmudic movement' (L. Löw, *Gesammelte Schriften*, vol. 5 (Szegedin 1900; repr. Hildesheim 1979), 67).

This judgement is fundamentally correct; for even after the Saboraim had given the Talmud tractates their essentially final shape, scholars during the transition from the Saboraim to the Geonim (whose eras cannot be clearly delimited) did not shy away from inserting further explanations into the text of BT itself. However, in the middle of the eighth century BT was already regarded as a closed work (see also Y. Sussmann in *Talmudic Studies*, 1:101ff.: BT as we know it is that of the eighth-century Geonic schools). Further additions still enter the text, particularly at the hands of Yehudai

Gaon (d. c. 761), but only indirectly by way of explicative marginal glosses (Assaf, *Geonim*, 135f.). Many of these additions are marked in MSS as *perush*, are missing, or are identified by medieval authors as Geonic additions. Further additions to BT from the time of Yehudai or later are identified by D. Rosenthal, 'Lishna de-Kalla' (Hebr.), *Tarbiz* 52 (1982–83) 273–308. Of particular importance in this context is the *Sefer ha-Ittur* of Isaac ben Abba Mari of Marseille (12th cent.). On the other hand, many references attributed to Yehudai (cf. Brüll, 73ff.; Melammed, *Introduction*, 472) go back to earlier Geonim and Saboraim (Assaf, *Geonim*, 136). E. S. Rosenthal appeals to oral recitation as the reason for subsequent changes in BT into the ninth century and to account for different textual recensions ('The History of the Text and Problems of Redaction in the Study of the Babylonian Talmud', *Tarbiz* 57 (1987–88) 1–36); whether or not this explanation is correct, future scholarship will need to pay greater attention to the problem of textual recensions, rather than merely to common variants in the MSS. (See further S. Friedman, 'On the Origin of Textual Variants in the Babylonian Talmud' (Hebr.), *Sidra* 7 (1991) 67–102; A. Schremer, '"Tre lishane" – mesoret ha-nusaḥ shel Babli Mo'ed Qatan', *Asufot* 2 (1987–88) 17–28; idem, 'Between Text Transmission and Text Redaction: A Different Recension of Mo'ed-Qatan from the Genizah' (Hebr.), *Tarbiz* 61, (1991–92) 375–99; E. Wajsberg, 'The Contribution of the Forms R. Schim'on ben Laqisch and ke-eize tsad to the Taxonomy of Talmudic Manuscripts' (Hebr.) *Leshonenu* 55 (1990–91) 367–82.) Even later explanations, especially Rashi, found their way into the text by way of marginal glosses. In the Middle Ages, BT was generally edited in keeping with Rashi's explanations and emendations (cf. J. A. Ephrati, *Bar-Ilan* 6 (1976) 75–100). What is more, until quite recently there was a very generous attitude to the insertion of conjectures into the text, so that D. Goodblatt 264 considers that 'BT reached its present state only in the last century'. This, however, already brings us to the textual history of BT; its history of redaction was finally closed with the early eighth century.

#### *4) The Text*

As its history of redaction shows, BT was not edited by a specific editor or a group of editors at a precisely datable time. Hence we also cannot assume a uniform and universally accepted BT text at any time. Not only is it impossible to draw a clear boundary between redaction and text criticism, but the coexistence of two Geonic academies will also have prevented the standardization of the textual shape of BT. Thus the Geonim already point out textual variants in their Responsa. The latter of course continued to increase in the subsequent textual tradition.

It cannot therefore be the task of textual criticism to reproduce an 'original text' (*Urtext*), but it must be to reconstruct the text form(s) of the time when BT was regarded a closed work, i.e. of the eighth century. This is possible only after appropriate preliminary studies in the history of the text and after sorting the different MSS (and quotations from them) into textual families, as was already demanded by A. Marx (*JQR* N.S. 1 (1910–11) 279–85) in protest against the mixed text of the Berakhot edition of N. Pereferkovitch (St. Petersburg 1909). The medieval quotations of BT also have yet to be fully evaluated. But as for the text critical use of rabbinic parallels, e.g. in the midrashim, extreme caution is needed in order not to misunderstand different expressions of a tradition as textual variants.

An important point in text critical work is the filling of *lacunae due to censorship*. S. Lieberman (*Shkiin*, 2nd edn. Jerusalem 1970) supposes that internal Jewish censorship at a very early point deleted magical and theosophical texts which invited Karaite attack. Such internal censorship must also be assumed later on. After 1263 (disputation of Barcelona), however, Christian censorship was in the foreground. With the arrival of the printing press this became fully effective: in the 1578–80 Basle edition of BT, for example, AZ was completely eliminated! Jewish printers would frequently omit certain passages in anticipation, to avoid offending the censors: thus already Gershom of Soncino. While the blank spaces in the copies of tractates printed at Soncino are probably due to lacunae in the underlying (Spanish) MSS, the fairly frequent omissions in the tractates printed at Pesaro likely derive from Gershom himself, who had to show regard for the duke's dependence on the Pope. Passages are left blank in AZ Pesaro, in the first Sulzbach printing of the tractate Sanh and in many later editions. Beginning with the 1835 Wilna edition, Russian censorship prohibited the use of blank spaces to point out deletions.

Some of the censored passages from BT and its commentaries were collected in small booklets published which were by and large published anonymously. Apart from these there have been several collections not printed in book form, such as the one-sided sheets printed in Amsterdam in 1708 by Simeon and Isaac Shammash, to be pasted into the edition Frankfurt on Oder. Cf. A. Berliner, *Censur und Confiscation hebräischer Bücher im Kirchenstaate*, Frankfurt 1891; M. Carmilly-Weinberger, *Censorship and Freedom of Expression in Jewish History*, New York 1977; W. Popper, *The Censorship of Hebrew Books*, New York 1899, repr. 1969; I. Sonne, *Expurgation of Hebrew Books*, New York 1943, repr. in Ch. Berlin (ed.), *Hebrew Printing and Bibliography* (New York 1976), 199–241.

***a) Manuscripts***

The first mention of a complete BT manuscript dates from the tenth century: Samuel ha-Nagid writes (quoted in Yehudah of Barcelona's *Sefer ha-Ittim*) that Natronai bar Ḥakinai, who in 773 was banned from Babylonia, wrote down BT from memory for the Spanish Jews (text in B.M. Lewin, *Otzar ha-Geonim*, vol. 1 (Haifa 1928), 20). According to a letter sent in 953 from Babylonia to Spain (the Genizah text is published in *JQR* 18 (1906) 401), Gaon Paltoi (842–58) had a MS of BT with explanations produced for Spain. A. Marx (*JQR* 18 (1906) 770) therefore considers the information about Natronai to be very dubious; but S. Abramson (*Tractate 'Abodah Zarah* (New York 1957), xiii n.1) regards the two statements as reconcilable. Maimonides claims to have used a piece of an approximately 500–year-old Gemara (*Mishneh Torah*, vol. 16 (Jerusalem 1965), 201). Naḥmanides refers to the correct Talmud copies produced in the school of Ḥushiel (late 10th cent.): *Milḥamot Adonai* BQ 85b (the text is preserved in various editions of Alfasi, e.g. Romm, Wilna 1922). However, almost nothing remains of such early MSS. Not only was a greater distribution and preservation of MSS prevented by the voluminous text of BT, but time and again many MSS were destroyed in Talmud burnings ordered by the Church (first in Paris in 1242, when 24 cartloads of Hebrew MSS were burned). A comprehensive list of BT MSS is given by M. Krupp in S. Safrai, *The Literature*, 1:346–66.

*MS Munich*, Cod. Hebr. 95 of the State Library at Munich. This is the only complete MS of BT (but even here 18 leaves are missing: Pes 119a–121b; 58a–67b; Ket 84a–87a; Men 76b–77b of the usual editions). 570 leaves in Ashkenazic script, produced in Paris in 1343. Numerous marginal glosses (variants, short comments). Facsimile edition by H. L. Strack, Leiden 1912 (with 43 pp. of introduction, in which the missing pieces are reproduced from other MSS); Jerusalem 1971 in 3 vols. Description in N. Sacks, *Mishna Zeraim*, vol. 1 (Jerusalem 1972), 69f.

*MS Leningrad*-Firkovitch. 177 leaves, Oriental script, very poorly preserved. Contains Ket and Git. According to Firkovitch it is dated to 1112, but already R. Rabbinovicz (*Diqduqe Soferim*, introduction to Megillah) could no longer read this passage.

*MS Oxford*, Bodleian Library 2673, contains half of Ker and is the oldest firmly dated MS of BT: 1123. Published in S. Schechter & S. Singer, *Talmudical Fragments in the Bodleian Library*, Cambridge 1896, repr. Jerusalem 1971.

*MS Florence*, National Library III 7–9. The volume containing Bek, Tem, Ker, Tam, Me'ilah and Qin was completed in 1177 (Ber in the same volume is from a different hand). The other two volumes are presumably from the same hand or at least from the same period: BQ, BM, BB, Sanh and Shebu. All three MSS comprise about one third of the BT. Facsimile: *Babylonian Talmud: Codex Florence (National Library III 7–9)*, introduction by D. Rosenthal, 3 vols., Jerusalem 1972.

*MS Hamburg* 165 comprises the three Babot. Written in 1184 at Gerona. Facsimile by L. Goldschmidt, Berlin 1914, repr. Jerusalem 1969 (with a new facsimile). Ḥul in MS 169 should also be mentioned: *Babylonian Talmud: Tractate Hullin: Codex Hamburg 169*, Jerusalem 1972.

*Vatican.* Of the Vatican Library's Talmud MSS, many of which once belonged to the Palatina at Heidelberg, (cf. Catalogue Assemani, Rome 1756, according to which 31 codices contain 57 Talmudic tractates and several 'minor tractates'. List of the MSS: N. Allony & D. S. Loewinger, *The Institute of Hebrew Manuscripts: List of Photocopies in the Institute*, Part III: *Hebrew Manuscripts in the Vatican*, Jerusalem 1968) the following have been published to date: *Manuscripts of the Babylonian Talmud from the Collection of the Vatican Library*, Series A, 3 vols., Jerusalem 1972 [I: Vat. Ebr. 109 (Erub, Beṣah), 108 (Shab, MQ); II: Vat. Ebr. 134 (Yoma, RH, Taan, Suk, Beṣah, Meg, Ḥag, MQ); III: Vat. Ebr. 130 (Git, Ket); 110 (Sot, Ned, Naz)]; Series B, 3 vols., Jerusalem 1974 [IV: Vat. Ebr. 118 (Zeb, Men); V: Vat. Ebr. 119 (Zeb, Tem, Arak, Bek, Me'ilah, Ker); 114 (Yeb, BM); VI: Vat. Ebr. 111 (Yeb, Qid, Nid)].

*New York*, Jewish Theological Seminary No. 44830, completed in 1290 at Ubeda, Spain; contains AZ. Facsimile: *Tractate 'Abodah Zarah of the Babylonian Talmud: Ms. Jew. Theol. Sem. of America*, with introduction and notes by S. Abramson, New York 1957. S. Friedman, 'Avodah Zara, Cod. JTS – a Manuscript Copied in Two Stages' (Hebr.), *Leshonenu* 56 (1991–92) 371–74.

*Göttingen*, University Library Cod. Hebr. 3, 110 leaves, early thirteenth century; contains part of Taan as well as Ḥag, Beṣah, Meg, and MQ up to 10a.

*Karlsruhe*, Badische Hof– und Landesbibliothek, Reuchlin 2: Sanh; once owned by Reuchlin.

*London*, British Museum, Harley 5508: RH, Yoma, Ḥag, Beṣah, Meg, Suk, MQ Taan. 236 leaves, probably twelfth century. Add. 25717: Bek (in part), Arak, Ker. 102 leaves, fourteenth century.

*New York*, Columbia University. Written in 1546–48, this MS was brought from Yemen to New York by E. Deinhard; its two volumes contain Beṣah, Pes, Meg, MQ, Zeb. J. M. Price (ed.), *The Yemenite Manuscript of Megilla*, Toronto 1916; idem (ed.), *The Yemenite Manuscript of Mo'ed Katon*, n.d. n.p., repr. Jerusalem 1970; E. L. Segal, 'The Textual Traditions of Ms. Columbia University to TB Megillah' (Hebr.), *Tarbiz* 53 (1983–84) 41–69.

### *b) Genizah Fragments*

There are numerous and in some cases very extensive MS fragments of BT from the Cairo Genizah, only some of which have been published to date. Some fragments may go back to the ninth century, but there is as yet no systematic investigation of the palaeography of these texts, which might lead to a well-founded dating. Similarly, the readings of the various fragments still need to be classified in relation to the textual history of BT.

#### *Bibliography*

W. H. Lowe published a fragment of Pes (4 leaves) as early as 1879: **Lowe, W. H.** *The fragment of Talmud Babli Pesachim of the ninth or tenth century, in the University Library, Cambridge.* Cambridge 1879. [Fragment (4 leaves) of Pes.] **Alloni, N.** *Geniza Fragments.* [Includes 7 fragments of BT.] **Friedman, S.** 'A Talmud Fragment of the Gaonic Type' (Hebr.). *Tarbiz* 51 (1981–82) 37–48. [BM 21b–22b.] **Hasidah, Y.** 'Me-Ginzê Yehudah: Daf Gemara Ketab-Yad.' *Sinai* 73 (1973): 224–29. [Ber 27a–b; 14th cent.] **Katsh, A. I.** *Ginzê Talmud Babli.* Jerusalem 1975. [178 fragments to Ber through Yeb from the Saltykov-Shchedrin Library in Leningrad.] **Katsh, A. I.** *Ginzê Talmud Babli*, vol. 2. Jerusalem 1979. [90 fragments to Ket through Nid. Katsh compares 32 examples from this volume with other MSS in *Essays on the Occasion of the Seventieth Anniversary of The Dropsie University* (Philadelphia 1979), 219–35.] **Katsh, A. I.** 'Unpublished Geniza Talmudic Fragments from the Antonin Collection.' *JQR* N.S. 58 (1967–68) 297–309. **Katsh, A. I.** 'Unpublished Geniza Talmudic Fragments of Tractate Shabbath in the Antonin Collection in the U.S.S.R.' *JQR* N.S. 63 (1972–73) 39–47. **Katsh, A. I.** 'Massekhet Berakhot min ha-Genizah.' In B. Z. Luria (ed.), *Zer li-gevurot: The Zalman Shazar Jubilee Volume*, 549–96 and 16 pp. facsim. Jerusalem 1973. **Katsh, A. I.** 'Unpublished Geniza Talmudic Fragments.' *Journal of the Ancient Near Eastern Society of Columbia University* 5 (1973; *Festschrift* T. H. Gaster) 213–23. **Katsh, A. I.** 'Unpublished Geniza Talmudic Fragments of the Tractates Baba Mezia, Baba Bathra and Sanhedrin in the Antonin Collection in Leningrad Library in the USSR.' *JQR* N.S. 66 (1975–76) 129–42. **Katsh, A. I.** 'Unpublished Genizah Fragments of the Tractate Shabbat in the Dropsie University Collection.' *JQR* N.S. 69 (1978–79) 16–26. **Katsh, A. I.** 'Unpublished Genizah Fragments in the Antonin Collection of the Saltykov-Shchedrin Library in Leningrad.' *JQR* N.S. 69 (1978–79) 193–207. **Morag, S.** *Vocalised Talmudic Manuscripts in the Cambridge Genizah Collections.* Vol. 1. Cambridge 1988. **Morag, S.** 'On the Vocalization of the Babylonian Talmud in the Geonic Period' (Hebr.). *4th WCJS* (Jerusalem) 2:223–25. **Sussmann, Y.** 'Talmud Fragments in the Cairo Geniza' (Hebr.). In M. A. Friedman (ed.), *Cairo Geniza Studies*, 21–31. Tel Aviv 1980.

Detailed descriptions of the Genizah fragments are also contained in the individual volumes of the BT edition of the Institute for the Complete Israeli Talmud (see below, p. 213).

#### *On the MS Transmission of Individual Tractates*

**Friedman, S. J.** 'Le-ilan ha-yuḥasin shel nuseḥê Baba Meṣia.' In S. Raam (ed.), *Meḥqarim be-Sifrut ha-Talmudit (Festschrift* S. Lieberman), 93–147. Jerusalem 1983. **Golinkin, D. R.** *Rosh Hashana Chapter IV of the Babylonian Talmud (Part 2): A Critical Edition and Commentary* (Hebr.). Diss. New York: Jewish Theological Serminary, 1988. **Schreiner, A.** 'The Manuscript of Tractate Moed Katan' (Hebr.). *Sidra* 6 (1990) 121–50. **Segal, E.** *The Textual Traditions of Tractate Megillah in the Babylonian Talmud* (Hebr.). Diss. Jerusalem 1981. **Traube, I. M.** *Studies in Texts and Manuscripts of Tractate Kiddushin* (Hebr.). Diss. New York: Jewish Theological Seminary, 1975.

The lack of good early MSS of BT makes the collation of Talmud quotations in the Geonim and the Middle Ages with the textual variants of the MSS an urgent necessity. R. Rabbinovicz, *Diqduqe Soferim: Variae Lectiones in Mischnam et in Talmud Babylonicum*, 15 vols., Munich 1868–86; vol. 16, Przemysl 1897; repr. in 12 vols., New York 1960, was a pioneer in this area. His work comprises the orders Zeraim, Moed, Neziqin (without Abot); Qodashim (only Zeb, Men, Ḥul). Additions: M. S. Feldblum, *Diḳduḳe Sopherim: Tractate Gittin*, New York 1966; H. Malter, *The Treatise Ta'anit of the Babylonian Talmud*, New York 1930, repr. Jerusalem 1973; the BT edition begun by the Complete Israeli Talmud Institute (see below) understands itself to be a *Diqduqe Soferim ha-Shalem*. The Geonic texts have been collected by B. M. Lewin, *Otzar ha-Gaonim*, 13 vols., Haifa and Jerusalem 1928–43; H. Z. Taubes (ed.), *Oṣar ha-Geonim le-Massekhet Sanhedrin*, Jerusalem 1966. See also J. Brody, 'Sifrut ha-Geonim we-ha-Teqst ha-Talmudi', in *Talmudic Studies*, 1:237–303.

***c) Printed Editions***

R. Rabbinovicz has presented a history of the printed BT (*Ma'amar 'al hadpasat ha-Talmud*, Munich 1866 in vol. 1 of *Diqduqe Soferim*, 1877 separately; re-edited and brought up to date by A. M. Haberman, Jerusalem 1952); M. J. Heller, *Printing the Talmud: A History of the Earliest Printed Editions of the Talmud*, New York 1992.

Around 1480 the family of Alqabet published individual tractates in a Spanish recension; members of the family later continued the work in Thessaloniki. Cf. H. Z. Dimitrovsky, *S'RIDEI BAVLI: Spanish Incunabula Fragments of the Babylonian Talmud*, 2 vols., New York 1979. In Morocco (Fez), too, individual tractates were printed between 1516 and 1521; only Erub (1521) is completely preserved. From 1484 to 1519, Yehoshua Shlomo and his nephew Gershom of Soncino printed at least 25 tractates at Soncino, Barco and Pesaro (E. N. Adler, 'Talmud Printing before Bomberg', in J. Fischer et al. (eds.), *Festskrift i Anledning af D. Simonsens 70–aarige Fødelsedag* (Copenhagen 1923), 81–84; A. M. Haberman, *Ha-Madpisim Benê Soncino*, Vienna 1933; M. Marx, 'Gershom (Hieronymus) Soncino's Wanderyears in Italy, 1498–1527: Exemplar Judaicae Vitae', *HUCA* 11 (1936) 427–500).

Daniel Bomberg, a non-Jew in Venice, printed the first complete editions of BT, completing the first in 1520–23 (repr. Jerusalem 1968), the second in 1531. His first printed edition has determined the external appaearance of BT printings ever since: each tractate begins on sheet two, since the first sheet is reserved for the title page; the front and back of each leaf are counted as a and b. The page division remains the same for all editions; so also the addition of Rashi's commentary on the inside of the text, and of the Tosafot on the outside. (See A. M. Haberman, *The Printer Daniel Bomberg and the List of Books Published by his Press* (Hebr.), Safed/Tel Aviv 1978).

In subsequent years there were printed editions in various Jewish congregations, e.g. M. A. Justiniani, Venice 1546–51; Basle 1578–80, greatly mutilated by censorship (J. Prijs, *Der Basler Talmuddruck, 1578–1580*, Olten 1960); Cracow 1602–05 follows Basle, but restores most of the censorship's mutilations and takes the absent tractate AZ from Cracow 1579; Amsterdam 1644–48, by Immanuel Benveniste, adopts the text of Lublin 1617–39; Frankfurt on Main 1720–22 (begun in Amsterdam in 1714–17; these parts reprinted in Frankfurt) served as the basis for almost all subsequent editions. The most comprehensive collection of commentaries is in the edition Romm, Wilna 1880–86 (cf. A. M. Haberman, *Peraqim be-toldot ha-madpisim ha-'ibrim we-inyanê sefarim, 1476–1896*, Jerusalem 1978; list of typographical errors: D. Choen, *He-Aqob le-Mishor*, Jerusalem 1993).

In 1972 the Institute for the Complete Israeli Talmud began editing a BT which uses the edition Romm Wilna as a base text and offers critical apparatus with the variants from the Genizah, MSS and medieval quotations. The following have been published in Jerusalem to date: Ket, ed. M. Hershler, 2 vols. 1972–77; Sot, ed. A. Liss, 2 vols. 1977–79; Yeb, ed. A. Liss, 3 vols. 1983–89; Ned, ed. M. Hershler, 2 vols. 1985–91.

A. Steinsaltz has begun an edition of particular benefit to the non-specialist, which presents the vocalized BT text with Rashi's commentary and a short modern Hebrew commentary with Hebrew translation of the Aramaic parts, textual variants, parallels, etc. Published to date: Ber, all of Moed, Yeb, Ket, Qid, Sot, Ned, Naz, Git, BM and Sanh (Jerusalem 1967–94). A bilingual English edition has been appearing in New York since 1989.

Individual tractates: Taan, ed. H. Malter, Philadelphia 1928 (repr. Philadelphia 1978), *editio maior* 1930 (here without English translation; unlike the tractates cited below, Malter attempts to establish a mixed text on the basis of 24 MSS, which not surprisingly led to criticism), repr. 1967 and Jerusalem 1973; Git, ed. M. S. Feldblum, New York 1966; BQ, ed. E. Z. Melammed, Jerusalem 1952; BM, ed. M. N. Zobel and H. Z. Dimitrovsky, Tel Aviv/Jerusalem 1960; BB, ed. S. Abramson, Jerusalem 1952; AZ, ed. S. Abramson, Jerusalem 1957. S. J. Friedman, *Talmud Arukh; BT Bava Mezi'a VI: Critical Edition with Comprehensive Commentary* (Hebr.), New York 1990 (commentary; the text volume is due to appear shortly).

***d) Translations***

I. Epstein (ed.), *The Babylonian Talmud: Translated into English with Notes,*

*Glossary and Indices*, 35 vols., London 1935–52, repr. in 18 vols., London 1961, etc.; Hebrew-English bilingual edition, 36 vols. (plus *Minor Tractates* and *Indices*), London 1960–90. J. Neusner (ed.), *The Talmud of Babylonia: An American Translation* (Chico/Atlanta 1984–). Most of these volumes were translated by Neusner and had appeared by 1994; but Neusner himself has now declared them 'obsolete' in the light of his own revision: *The Talmud of Babylonia: An Academic Commentary*, Atlanta 1994ff. (published in 1994: Yoma, Suk, Beṣah, RH, MQ, Ḥag; Sot; all of Neziqin; Ḥul, Bek, Arak, Tem, Ker, Meilah, Tam; Nid. The commentary consists primarily in the visual layout of the text in its logical structure, the identification of sources and of the language of the original. Each tractate ends with a chapter on 'Structure and System'). L. Goldschmidt, *Der babylonische Talmud*, 12 vols., Berlin 1929–36 (repr. Königstein/Taunus 1980–81); index volume, ed. R. Edelmann, Copenhagen 1959; bilingual edition in 9 vols., Berlin 1897–1935. M. Cales & H. J. Weiss (eds.), *El Talmud de Babilonia*, Buenos Aires 1964–79 (text of the edition Romm Wilna and Spanish translation; Ber, Yeb, Ned, BQ, BM, BB); E. Zolli, *Il Talmud babilonese*, Bari 1958 (only Ber; repr. Rome 1968 under the title *Il trattato delle Benedizioni del Talmud babilonese*, with an introduction by S. Cavalletti; critique by A. Toaff, *La Rassegna Mensile di Israel* 34 (1968) 642–47). For earlier translations see E. Bischoff, *Kritische Geschichte der Thalmud-Übersetzungen aller Zeiten und Zungen*, Frankfurt 1899.

***e) Concordance***

C. J. & B. Kassovsky, *Thesaurus Talmudis: Concordantiae Verborum quae in Talmude Babilonico Reperiuntur*, 42 vols., Jerusalem 1954–89; also B. Kosovsky, *Thesaurus Nominum Quae in Talmude Babylonico Reperiuntur*, 5 vols., Jerusalem 1976–83.

### *5) The Authority of the Babylonian Talmud*

The BT attained its (almost) final shape in the eighth century, i.e. at a time when the Babylonian academies were flourishing and when the newly ascendant Abbassids founded Baghdad. Thus the Babylonian Jewish community was at the political centre of the contemporary world; through trade connections it was, moreover, relatively easy to reach from every direction. Rabbinic Judaism, which by now had finally consolidated itself in Baylonia and was continually extending its sway beyond the sphere of Talmudic schools to the people, was thus enabled to spread its intellectual influence far beyond the country's borders.

Around the same time, however, Babylonian rabbinic Judaism was also seriously endangered by the growing movement of the Karaites with their rejection of the oral tradition and the Talmud. This danger in turn would have provoked the rabbis to attack. In any case Yehudai Gaon endeavoured as early as c. 750 to promote the Babylonian halakhah in Palestine (see p. 186 above). Babylonian synagogue congregations, which existed in Palestine from Amoraic times, would certainly have facilitated this advance. Another factor was the proximity of Karaite halakhah to Palestinian tradition, which for this reason easily became suspect. Pirqoi ben Baboi also intervened around 800: in a letter to the congregation of Kairouan, which belonged to the Palestinian sphere of influence, he openly criticized the Palestinian halakhah (the text has been published by B. M. Lewin: 'Geniza Fragments: I. Chapters of Ben Baboi' (Hebr.), *Tarbiz* 2 (1930–31) 383–404; cf. J. N. Epstein, ibid., 411f.; S. Spiegel, 'Le-parashat ha-polmos shel Pirqoi Ben Baboi', in S. Lieberman (ed.), *Harry Austryn Wolfson Jubilee Volume on the Occasion of his Seventy-Fifth Birthday*, Hebrew section (Jerusalem 1965), 243–74). An early ninth-century tombstone (probably from Venosa) contains the earliest European reference to a text from BT (Ber 17a) or at least to some of its phrases: C. Colafemmina, 'Una nuova epigrafe ebraica altomedievale a Lavello', *Vetera Christianorum* 29 (1992) 411–21; idem, 'Epigraphica hebraica Venusina', *Vetera Christianorum* 30 (1993) 353–58 (p. 357f. offers a corrected reading, which also attests a phrase from Ber 58b). In the ninth century the *Sefer ha-Yerushalmi* in Palestine attempted to strike a compromise between Palestinian and Babylonian halakhah; but Babylonian tradition finally prevailed no later than the demise of the academy of Jerusalem in the eleventh century.

The triumph of BT in Kairouan, however, was almost more decisive. While the *Sefer ha-Metibot* (10th cent.) still retains the tradition of PT alongside that of BT, Ḥananel and Nissim already clearly relegate it to second place, and for Alfasi the precedence of BT over PT is unquestioned. Alfasi's influence on the further development of Talmudic studies in Spain finally ensured the absolute primacy of BT in that country; it was also never questioned in the Ashkenazic region. Thus the Babylonian Talmud became 'the' Talmud *par excellence*; it has determined the entire halakhah until the present, and at least until the eighteenth century constituted the absolutely primary or even exclusive teaching syllabus in all the academies of Judaism (cf. Ginzberg, *Mabo*, 88–110).

***6) Commentaries***

The exposition of BT begins within BT itself: essentially, each new layer of BT serves simulatneously as an interpretation of the previous one. In the *Geonic period*, the interpretative efforts in BT concentrate on three types of writings:

***a) Introductions to the Talmud***

These introductions contain short statements about the teachers of the Talmud, as well as rules for its interpretation, especially for deciding the halakhah (cf. Assaf, *Geonim*, 147–54). The Arabic introduction to the Talmud by Saadya Gaon is mentioned in the book lists of the Genizah, but only five sections of it are preserved in Hebrew translation in Beṣalel Ashkenazi's *Klale ha-Talmud* (late 16th cent.): published by A. Marx, in *Festschrift zum siebzigsten Geburtstage David Hoffmann's* (Berlin 1914), Hebrew section, 196f., 205, 210 (S. Abramson, 'On "Darkei ha-Talmud", Attributed to R. Saadya Gaon' (Hebr.), *KS* 52 (1976–77) 381–82, regards the quotations as excerpts from Samuel b. Ḥofni; cf. idem, *'Inyanut be-sifrut ha-Geonim* (Jerusalem 1974), 164–73). Samuel ben Ḥofni also wrote an Arabic introduction to the Talmud, parts of which have been discovered in the Genizah. In 148 chapters it treats the Talmudic teachers, the sources mentioned in BT, and the rules for determining the halakhah (E. Roth, 'A Geonic Fragment Concerning the Oral Chain of Tradition' (Hebr.), *Tarbiz* 26 (1956–57) 410–20; S. Abramson, 'R. Samuel b. Ḥofni's Introduction to the Talmud, ibid., 421–23, also on fragments published earlier; idem, *Inyanot be-sifrut ha-Geonim* (Jerusalem 1974), 173–76); idem, 'Min ha-pereq ha-ḥamishi shel 'Mabo ha-Talmud' le-Rab Shmuel ben Ḥofni', *Sinai* 88 (1981) 193–218; idem, *Rabbi Shmuel B. Chofni Liber Prooemium Talmudis: Textum Arabicum Edidit et Versione Hebraica, Introductiones Notisque Instruxit*, Jerusalem 1990 (Chapters 141–44; chapter 143 also appeared in *Sefer Abraham Eben-Shoshan* (Jerusalem 1985), 13–65); M. Assis, 'Linguistic Aspects of Chapter 143 of R. Shmuel ben Ḥofni Gaon's Introduction to the Talmud', *Leshonenu* 56 (1991–92) 27–43.

***b) Responsa***

Responsa in reply to various questions from the Jewish world also contain a great deal on the interpretation of the Talmud.

Collected in **Lewin, B. M.** *Otzar ha-Gaonim*. 13 vols. Haifa/Jerusalem 1928–43. **Taubes, H. Z.** *Oṣar ha-Geonim le-Massekhet Sanhedrin*. Jerusalem 1966. **Harkavy, A.** *Responsen der Geonim*. Berlin 1887. **Assaf, S.** *Teshubot ha-Geonim*. 2 vols. Jerusalem 1927–29.

Note also the *Halakhic Compendia*, the *Sheiltot*: see **Mirsky, S.**, ed. *Sheeltot de Rab Ahai Gaon*. 5 vols. Jerusalem 1960–77. [Cf. S. Abramson, *Inyanut be-sifrut ha-Geonim* (Jerusalem 1974), 9–23.] Brody, R. *The Textual History of the She'iltot* (Hebr.). New York/Jerusalem 1991.

For Yehudai Gaon's *Halakhot Pesuqot, see* **Sasoon, S.**, ed. *Sefer Halachot Pesuqot: Auctore R. Jehudai Gaon (Saec. VII)*. Jerusalem 1950. [Facsimile of Codex Sassoon 263 with introduction by S. Abramson, Jerusalem 1971.] **Hildesheimer, E.** 'An Analysis of the Structure of "Halachot Pesukot"' (Hebr.). In *Michtam le-David: Rabbi David Ochs Memorial Volume (1905–1975)*, 153–71. Ramat-Gan 1978. **Morel, S.** 'Meqorotaw shel Sefer Halakhot Pesuqot: Nituaḥ ṣurani.' *PAAJR* 49 (1982) Hebr. section, 41–95.

Simon Qayyara's *Halakhot Gedolot*: **Hildesheimer, E.** *Sefer Halakhot Gedolot*. 3 vols. Jerusalem 1971–88. [Edition according to the MS of the Ambrosiana Library, Milan.] **Hildesheimer, J.**, ed. *Halachoth Gedoloth nach dem Texte der Handschrift der Vaticana*. Berlin 1890. **Hoenig, S. N.** 'Halakhot Gedolot: An Early Halakhic Code.' *The Jewish Law Annual* 2 (1979) 45–55. [Facsimile of Codex Paris 1402 with Introduction by S. Abramson, Jerusalem 1971.]

### *c) Commentaries of the Geonim*

Some of these are quoted in medieval authors (Melammed, *Introduction*, 479–86), but for the most part they have been lost. Thus the commentary of Paltoi Gaon, which is known to us from a letter to Ḥasdai Ibn Shaprut of 952. Sherira's commentaries on Ber and Shab are known from medieval quotations; that on BB 1–3, from a book list of the Genizah as well as from fragments published by S. Assaf and J. Mann (J. Mann, *Texts and Studies in Jewish History and Literature*, vol. 1, New York 1930, repr. 1972 with an introduction by G. D. Cohen, has a piece of Sherira's commentary on BB (568–72), pieces of Hai Gaon on Ber (573–607); J. N. Epstein, 'On the Commentary of R. Sherira and R. Hai Gaon to Baba-Bathra' (Hebr.), *Tarbiz* 5 (1933–34), 45–49; repr. in *Studies*, 2:604–8). The commentary on Ber attributed to Saadya (published by S. A. Wertheimer, Jerusalem 1908, according to a Genizah fragment; repr. in idem, *The Geniza Fragments: 'Ginze Jerusalem'*, ed. A. J. Wertheimer, Jerusalem 1981) probably derives not from him but from a later author, who begins by citing a piece of Saadya's M commentary (thus Assaf, *Geonim*, 143). Hai Gaon has composed commentaries on many tractates of BT; these are known partly from medieval quotations, and now also in fragments from the Genizah. He is also the likely author of the Genizah texts on Git and Qid (S. Löwinger, 'Gaonic Interpretations of the Tractates Gittin and Qiddushin', *HUCA* 23/1 (1950–51), 475–98 and 10 pp. of facsimile), although these are not from a proper commentary but are designed as a Responsum (thus S. Assaf, *KS* 29 (1959–60) 64f.). E. Hurwitz, 'Fragments of the Geonim Commentary to Tractate Shabbath from Cairo Geniza, and Selections from Commentaries of Rishonim from MSS' (Hebr.), *Hadorom* 46 (1977–78) 123–227. Generally on the commentaries see S. Assaf, *Geonim*, 135–46.

### *d) Medieval Introductions to the Talmud*

Of particular significance here is the introduction of Samuel ha-Nagid, which is reproduced after Ber in many BT editions and which explains especially difficult terms. Quotations indicate that only part of the introduction survives. Maimonides's introduction to his M commentary is to some extent also an introduction to the Talmud. There is an Arabic introduction to BT by Joseph Ibn Aqnin, a student of Maimonides (H. Graetz (ed.), 'Einleitung in den Talmud von Joseph Ibn-Aknin', in *Jubelschrift zu Ehren Z. Frankel*, Breslau [Wroclaw] 1871, repr. Jerusalem 1967). We should also mention Samson of Chinon (early 14th cent.) with his *Sefer Keritut* (ed. S. Sofer, Jerusalem 1965), as well as Beṣalel Ashkenazi (16th cent., Egypt) whose *Klalê ha-Talmud* contain methodological remarks of the most eminent interpreters of the Talmud (ed. A. Marx, in *Festschrift zum siebzigsten Geburtstage David Hoffmann's* (Berlin 1914), 369–82 and Hebrew section 179–217).

***e) Compendia of Halakhah***

The tradition of these compendia was continued in the Middle Ages by Isaac ben Jacob Alfasi, who in *Sefer ha-Halakhot* (ed. N. Sacks, *Hilkhot Rab Alfas*, 2 vols., Jerusalem 1969) combines the current law of BT with a short version of BT itself. Eliezer ben Yoel ha-Levi (13th cent., Germany, acronym 'Rabyah') has collected halakhic decisions, novellas and Responsa to the Talmud in *Sefer Rabiah* (V. Aptowitzer (ed.), *Sefer Rabiah*, Berlin 1913; vol. 2 Jerusalem 1935; supplement 1936; *Introductio ad Sefer Rabiah* (Hebr.), Jerusalem 1938; revised form of this edition in four vols. by S. Y. Cohen and E. Prisman, Jerusalem 1964–5). Another Talmud compendium is by Asher ben Yeḥiel (=Rosh; from Germany, d. 1327): this is printed in most BT editions. We should also mention Maimonides' *Mishneh Torah* (20 vols., Jerusalem 1957–65) which contains the entire halakhah in topical order, and also the *Arba'ah Turim* by Jacob ben Asher (d. c. 1340). Joseph Karo (1488–1575) commented on the latter work in *Beth Joseph*; an abbreviation of this, the *Shulḥan Arukh*, was completed in 1554 at Safed. Having been supplemented by Moses Isserles (1520–72) in *Mappat ha-Shulḥan*, the *Shulḥan Arukh* was generally accepted as current law.

***f) Actual Commentaries on BT after the Geonim***

The first commentary is that of Ḥananel ben Ḥushiel of Kairouan (c. 990–1050). He probably commented on all of BT, making extensive use of PT. The work on Moed and Neziqin except BB is contained in BT Wilna (*Perushê Rabbenu Ḥananel bar Ḥushiel la-Talmud*, Jerusalem 1988– (5 vols. to 1994: Ber; RH and Suk, ed. D. Metzger; BQ; BM, ed. D. Domb; BB, ed. J. D. Cohen); S. Assaf, 'Me-pirushê Rab Ḥananel le-Sanhedrin', in *Ish ha-Torah we-ha-Ma'aseh: Le-yobel ha-shishim shel ha-rab Mosheh Ostrovsky* (*Festschrift* Ostrovsky, Jerusalem 1946), 69–84). His commentary on Nid has been edited by E. Hurwitz: 'Perush Rabbenu Ḥananel le-Massekhet Niddah me-Genizat Qahir', *Hadorom* 51 (1981) 39–109.

Nissim ben Jacob of Kairouan (d. c. 1062) wrote a commentary on Ber, Shab and Erub, printed in BT Wilna. Genizah fragments have been published in B. M. Lewin, 'Perush Rabbenu Nissim le-'Erubin', in *Festschrift Dr. Jakob Freimann* (Berlin 1937), Hebr. section 72–80; D. Metzger's appendix to his edition of Ḥananel's commentary on Erub (Jerusalem 1993), also including excerpts from *Sefer ha-Mafteaḥ* on Erub (ed. E. E. Dickman), RH and Suk (ed. D. Metzger); J. Rovner, 'Ha re'ayot le-mahadurah qedumah shel perush Rab Ḥananel ben Ḥushiel mi-Qairowan le-Babli Qamma Meṣia', *PAAJR* 60 (1994), Hebr. section, 31–84.

Commentaries on nine tractates are attributed to Gershom ben Yehudah (d. 1028 in Mainz) (in BT Wilna; N. Sacks, *Qobeṣ Rishonim le-Massekhet Mo'ed Qatan*, Jerusalem 1966, also contains among other things the commentary attributed to Gershom); these, however, are lecture notes of his students which were later greatly expanded, and edited at the beginning of the twelfth century. Particularly eminent among those who studied under Gershom's pupils are Nathan ben Yeḥiel, who composed the Arukh (ed. A. Kohut, 8 vols., Vienna 1878–92; important for textual criticism), a lexicon on the Talmud in Rome in the eleventh century; and Rashi.

Rashi (=R. Shlomo Yiṣḥaqi of Troyes, d. 1105) wrote a commentary on most of the BT tractates supplied with Gemara; this has become a classic and is printed in almost all editions of BT. However, the commentaries on Taan Ned, Naz, Hor and MQ which are printed as Rashi's are not in fact his; the tractates Pes, BB and Mak were completed by his students. Based on a Spanish MS, E. F. Kupfer published a commentary on MQ which he considered to be the genuine Rashi commentary (Jerusalem 1961). But see recently J. Florsheim, 'Rashi's Commentary on Mo'ed Katan' (Hebr.), *Tarbiz* 51 (1981–82) 421–44, according to whom the MS complements quotations from Rashi's commentary with numerous additions from other commentaries or from the compiler himself. J. Fraenkel, *Rashi's Methodology in his Exegesis of the Babylonian Talmud* (Hebr.), Jerusalem 1975; A. Aptowitzer, 'Le-toldot perushê Rashi la-Talmud', in A. Scheiber (ed.), *Jubilee Volume in Honour of Prof. Bernhard Heller on the Occasion of his Seventieth Birthday* (Budapest 1941), 3–17; M. Hershler, 'Mahadura qamma shel Rashi le-massekhet Sukkah', *Genuzot* 1 (1984) 1–66 (MS Escorial G-II 4: a commentary on Suk 1, more likely composed by one of his students, rather than an early version by Rashi himself); J. Malchi, *Rashi's Commentary to Tractate 'Berachot'; A Comparison of the Standard Version with other Versions* (Hebr.), Diss. Tel Aviv: Bar Ilan, 1983; Ḥ. Merḥavya, 'Regarding the Rashi Commentary to "Ḥelek" (Talmud Bavli, Sanhedrin, Chap. XI)' (Hebr.), *Tarbiz* 33 (1963–64) 259–86 (unlike J. N. Epstein et al., he considers this piece to be genuine but permeated with numerous glosses; thus also J. Fraenkel, *Rashi's Methodology*, 304–25); Z. A. Steinfeld (ed.), *Rashi Studies* (Hebr.), Ramat Gan 1993.

Yehudah ben Nathan, a son-in-law of Rashi, completed the latter's commentary on Mak (beginning at 19b) and commented on almost the entire BT. BT Wilna incorrectly attributes Pseudo-Rashi on Naz to him; this commentary is likely the work of Meir bar Samuel, another son-in-law of Rashi: J. N. Epstein, 'The Commentaries of R. Yehuda ben Nathan and the Commentaries of Worms' (Hebr.), *Tarbiz* 4 (1932–33) 11–34, 153–92, 295f. (repr. in *Studies*, 3:11–76). See also E. Kupfer (ed.), *Perushê ha-Talmud mi-Beth Midrasho shel Rashi: Perush Massekhet Qiddushin*, Jerusalem 1977; A. Schreiber (Sofer), *Shnê Perushim Qadmonim 'al-Massekhet Me'ilah*, Jerusalem 1965.

The Tosafists ('supplementers' of Rashi's commentary) worked especially in the twelfth and thirteenth centuries in Germany and France. They provide not a continuous commentary but the detailed explanation of individual passages. They are concerned to remove internal contradictions in BT by means of *pilpul* (lit. 'peppering': acute logic which later degenerated into mental acrobatics). Among the older Tosafists were three of Rashi's grandsons: Isaac ben Meir, Samuel ben Meir (he completed Rashi's commentary to BB, beginning at 29a) and Jacob ben Meir (Rabbenu Tam); also the latter's nephew Isaac ben Samuel of Dampierre. Isaac's student Samson of Sens produced the earliest compilation of these Tosafot, the 'Tosafot of Sens'; these became the basis of subsequent collections like that of Eliezer of Touques ('Tosafot of Touques'), which constitute the majority of the Tosafot printed in the outer margin of the BT editions.

***Bibliography***

**Urbach, E. E.** *The Tosafists.* **Urbach, E. E.** 'Die Entstehung und Redaktion unserer Tosafot.' *Jahrbuch des Jüdisch-theologischen Seminars*, Breslau 1936. **Urbach, E. E.** 'Mi-toratam shel Ḥakhamê Anglia mi-lifnê ha-gerush.' In H. J. Zimmels et al. (eds.), *Essays Presented to Chief Rabbi Israel Brodie*, Hebr. section, 1–56. London 1966. **Faur, J.** 'Tosafot ha-Rosh le-Massekhet Berakhot.' *PAAJR* 33 (1965) Hebr. section, 41–65. **Fridman, S.** *Sefer Sha'are Shalom.* Tel Aviv 1965. **Schreiber, A.** et al. (eds.). *Tosfoth Chachmei Anglia.* Jerusalem 1968–71. [Git, Sanh 1968; Pes, BM 1969; Beṣah, Meg, Qid 1970; Nid, AZ 1971.] **Wacholder, B. Z.** 'Supplements to the Printed Edition of the Tosafot Yesanim, Yevamot, Chapter I.' *HUCA* 40/41 (1969–70) Hebr. section, 1–30.

Moses ben Naḥman (d. 1270) wrote Ḥiddushim ('innovations', detailed discussions of individual passages in BT) on numerous tractates, and thereby introduced a new development in the interpretation of BT. Edition in 3 vols., Jerusalem 1928–29, repr. Jerusalem 1972; critical edition: M. Hershler (ed.), *Ḥiddushe ha-Ramban*, Jerusalem 1970ff. (vol. 1, 1970: Mak, AZ, Sanh; vol. 2, 1973: Shab, Erub, Meg; vol. 3, 1976: Shebu, Nid; vol. 4, 1987: Yeb, Sot, Ber, Taan, RH).

Menaḥem ben Solomon, usually called *Meiri*, whose Provençal name was Don Vidal Solomon (1249–1306), composed Ḥiddushim under the title *Beth ha-Beḥira*; most of these have by now been published (between 1942 and 1971, 28 vols. on 31 tractates in Jerusalem, Ḥag in Tel Aviv; also on M. Ḥallah, Abot and Miqwaot; repr. in 13 vols., Jerusalem 1965–78).

Solomon ben Abraham Adret (1235–1310, Barcelona): Ḥiddushim, 3 vols., Jerusalem 1962. Critical Edition: H. Z. Dimitrovsky et al. (eds.), *Ḥiddushê ha-Rashba*, 12 vols., Jerusalem 1981–93.

Asher ben Yeḥiel: *Tosafot ha-Ro'sh ha-Shalem*, ed. S. Wilman, 3 vols. 1987 (repr. of Brooklyn 1971–78); Ned is not included here, but appears in most editions of BT.

Yom Tob ben Abraham of Seville (=Ritba, 1250–1320) *Ḥiddushe ha-Ritba*, ed. M. Goldstein et al., 18 vols., Jerusalem 1974–93 (Ber, Shab, Erub, Pes, Yoma, Suk, Beṣah, RH, Taan, Meg, MQ, Yeb, Ket, Ned, Git, Qid, BM, Mak, Shebu, AZ, Ḥul, Nid); BM, ed. A. Halpern, London 1962; BB, ed. B. J. Menat, Jerusalem 1975; for other tractates see the edition Tel Aviv 1958 (6 vols.).

Beṣalel ben Abraham Ashkenazi (c. 1520–1591/94) collected Talmud interpretations of the Geonim and medieval authors in his *Shittah Mequbbeṣet*, 11 vols., Tel Aviv 1963; new edition by J. D. Ilan, 3 vols., Bene Beraq 1992 (Zeb, Men, Bek, Arak, Tem, Ker, Me'ilah, Tam, Qin).

Of the later commentators we shall merely name the following: Solomon Luria of Lublin, d. 1573; Samuel Edels, d. 1631 in Ostrog; Elijah Gaon of Wilna, d. 1797; Aqiba Eger, d. 1837 in Posen. Numerous commentaries are also printed in BT Wilna. Early commentaries are edited in M. Hershler (ed.), *Ginze Rishonim*, 3 vols., Jerusalem 1962–67 (Suk, RH, Yoma, Taan, Ber). Many commentaries are summarized in *Otzar Mefarshei Hatalmud*, Jerusalem 1971ff. (no verbatim reproduction, main emphasis is on authors after 1600). Ten vols. were published up to 1991 (Suk, Mak, BQ, BM). A. Freimann, 'List of the Early Commentaries on the Talmud' (Hebr.), in *Louis Ginzberg: Jubilee Volume* (New York 1945), 2:323–54; M. M. Kasher and J. Mandelbaum, *Sarei ha-Elef: A Millennium of Hebrew Authors (500–1500 C.E.)* (Hebr.), New York 1959; I. Ta-Shmah, '"Ḥiddushei ha-Rishonim" – their Order of Publication' (Hebr.), *KS* 50 (1974–75) 325–36.

There are no *modern commentaries* on BT which go beyond the discussion of individual passages. Perhaps Z. W. Rabinowitz comes closest with his *Sha'are Torath Babel: Notes and Comments on the Babylonian Talmud* (Hebr.), ed. E. Z. Melamed, Jerusalem 1961; also D. Halivni, *Sources and Traditions: A Source Critical Commentary on the Talmud* (Hebr.), vol. 1: *On Seder Nashim*, Tel Aviv 1968; vol. 2: *Seder Moed from Yoma to Hagiga*, Jerusalem 1975; vol. 3: Shab, Jerusalem 1982; vol. 4: Erub-Pes, Jerusalem 1982; BQ, Jerusalem 1993. Cf. possibly also the brief Hebrew commentary in the Steinsaltz edition, although this rarely goes beyond Rashi. In any case, scholarly engagement with halakhic or literary critical problems as well as the sheer size of BT have thus far prevented a thorough commentary. The terse analysis in J. Neusner's translation also promises to offer an important advance at least in certain respects.

### *7) The Talmud in Controversy*

***Bibliography***

**Chazan, R.** 'The Condemnation of the Talmud Reconsidered (1239–1248).' *PAAJR* 55 (1988) 11–30. **Chazan, R.** *Daggers of Faith.* Berkeley 1989. **Cohen, J.** *The Friars and the Jews.* Ithaca, NY 1982. **Delitzsch, F.** *Rohling's Talmudjude beleuchtet.* Leipzig 1881. **Eckert, W. P.** In *Kirche und Synagoge: Handbuch zur Geschichte von Christen und Juden,* 1:227–35, 278–82, 285–87. Ed. K. H. Rengstorf & S. von Kortzfleisch. Stuttgart 1968. **Grayzel, S.** *The Church and the Jews in the XIIIth Century.* New York 1966. **Grayzel, S.** 'The Talmud and the Medieval Papacy.' In W. Jacob et al. (eds.), *Essays in Honor of S. B. Freehof,* 220–45. Pittsburgh 1964. **Hellwing, I. A.** *Der konfessionelle Antisemitismus im 19. Jahrhundert in Österreich.* Vienna 1972. [On Rohling and Deckert.] **Kirn, H.–M.** *Das Bild vom Juden im Deutschland des frühen 16. Jahrhunderts.* Tübingen 1989. [On J. Pfefferkorn.] **Klibansky, E.** 'Zur Talmudkenntnis des christlichen Mittelalters.' *MGWJ* 77 (1933) 456–62. **Merchavia, Ch.** *The Church versus Talmudic and Midrashic Literature (500–1248)* (Hebr.). Jerusalem 1970. **Merchavia, Ch.** 'The Talmud in the Additiones of Paul of Burgos.' *JJS* 16 (1965) 115–34. **Millás, J. M.** 'Extractos de la Biblioteca de la Catedral de Gerona.' *Sefarad* 20 (1960) 17–49. **Orfali, M.** 'Jerónimo de Santa Fe y la polemica cristiana contro el Talmud.' *Annuario di Studi Ebraici* 10 (1980–84, Rome 1984: *Festschrift* E. Toaff) 157–78. **Pelli, M.** *The Age of Haskalah,* 48–72. Leiden 1979. [The attitude of the *Maskilim.*] **Rappaport, S.** 'Christian Friends of the Talmud.' In H. J. Zimmels et al. (eds.), *Essays Presented to Chief Rabbi Israel Brodie,* 1:335–54. London 1966. **Rembaum, J.** 'The Talmud and the Popes: Reflections on the Talmud Trials of the 1240s.' *Viator* 13 (1982) 203–23. **Rosenthal, J. M.** 'The Talmud on Trial: The Disputation of Paris in the Year 1240.' *JQR* N.S. 47 (1956–57) 58–76, 145–69. **Stern, M.** *Urkundliche Beiträge über die Stellung der Päpste zu den Juden,* 98–108, 117–22, 126–38, 156–82. Kiel 1893. [16th cent.] **Von Mutius, H. G.** *Die christlich-jüdische Zwangsdisputation zu Barcelona: Nach dem hebräischen Protokoll des Moses Nachmanides.* Frankfurt 1982.

As the work of a powerful, but not unchallenged movement in Judaism, the Talmud has always had its opponents even in Jewish circles. Already before the completion of BT, Jewish internal controversies lead to Justinian's *Novella* 146 of 553 C.E., which not only supported the advocates of Greek Scripture readings in the synagogue but also prohibited any *deuterosis*, which presumably meant any traditional interpretation which went beyond Scripture itself. Leo VI (886–912) reiterated this prohibition; although it might have been used against BT, it appears to have had no practical effect. More threatening was the *Karaites*' opposition to the Talmud. Anan ben David, who founded this trend around the middle of the eighth century, is reputed to have issued a challenge to abandon the words of the Mishnah and the Talmud; he would devise his own Talmud (thus the Gaon Natronai in *Seder Rab Amram Gaon*, ed. D. Goldschmidt (Jerusalem 1971), 111).

Nicholas Donin became an opponent of the Talmud because of Karaite tendencies or perhaps merely a radical rationalism in the wake of Maimonides. When in 1224 he was banned by the rabbis for this reason, he converted to Christianity in 1236. In 1238 he presented to Gregory IX a document with 35 arguments against the Talmud, which led in 1240 to the *Paris Disputation* about the Talmud between Nicholas and Rabbi Yeḥiel, and resulted in 1242 in the burning of the Hebrew books which had been confiscated in 1240. Innocent IV wrote in 1247 that he had permitted the Jews possession of the Talmud because without it they would be unable to live according to their religion, but that he also ordered censorship of the Talmud. A different aspect of the battle for the Talmud emerges in the *Barcelona Disputation* of 1263 between the former Jew Pablo Christiani, who wanted to derive proofs of Christianity from Talmud and Midrash, and Naḥmanides, who by contrast emphasized the halakhah as the only obligatory part of the Talmud. The somewhat later *Pugio Fidei* of Raymond Martini also attempted to use the Talmud for Christian propaganda among the Jews. In the subsequent period, however, the situation in the Christian countries was characterized by condemnations of the Talmud (e.g. after the Disputation of Tortosa, 1413–14), prohibitions of Jewish study of the Talmud (thus Eugenius IV after the Council of Basle), burnings of the Talmud (e.g. in 1553 in Rome and Venice, where the flourishing Hebrew printing presses perished) and censorship.

In the sixteenth century it was again a converted Jew, Johannes Pfefferkorn, who led the fight against the Talmud, since he saw the Jewish books as the only reason why Jews did not become Christians. When in 1509 the Emperor Maximilian appointed him to examine the Hebrew books, the humanist Johannes Reuchlin spoke decisively in favour of the Talmud; Pfefferkorn in return brought against him lengthy proceedings before the Inquisition. The Roman measures against the Reformation finally aggravated the atmosphere of religious intolerance, and thus the Talmud also appeared on the first Index of forbidden books in 1559.

Christian Hebraists of the seventeenth century recognized the value of rabbinic literature for a deeper understanding of the New Testament: John Lightfoot, *Horae Hebraicae et Talmudicae*, Cambridge 1658, initiated an approach which for the time being has culminated in [H. L. Strack &] P. Billerbeck, *Kommentar zum Neuen Testament aus Talmud und Midrasch*, 6 vols., Munich 1922–61 (M. Smith, *Tannaitic Parallels to the Gospels*, Philadelphia 1951, rightly follows strict methodological limitations); J. Buxtorf, *Lexicon chaldaicum, talmudicum et rabbinicum*, Basle 1639, also deserves mentioning.

The main work of anti-Talmudic literature is Johann Andreas

Eisenmenger, *Entdecktes Judentum*, 2 vols., Frankfurt 1700. Pretending to seek conversion to Judaism, Eisenmenger spent years studying rabbinic literature under Jewish mentors; but in reality he compiled all the references which were intended to prove Jewish errors or attacks on the Christian religion. In his work, which was to become a veritable treasure trove of later anti-Jewish arguments, he always cites the original Hebrew sources with his translation which, though at times faulty, was doubtless not intentionally false; charges that he forged references are unfounded. The Jews at Frankfurt secured a ban on distribution, but a second edition appeared in Berlin in 1711 (impressum Königsberg), and an English translation in 1732–33.

Eisenmenger's collection of quotations, presented without their context, was open to every misinterpretation and hence also served as 'proof' of ritual murder, poisoning of wells, and other 'Jewish crimes'. August Rohling (1839–1931, professor of Old Testament at Prague from 1876) made it the basis of his plagiarizing *Der Talmudjude*, Münster 1871. This sorry effort, which went through a total of 17 editions, served as ammunition for antisemitic agitation, especially that of the Christian-Social Party in Austria, in which the Viennese clergyman Joseph Deckert (1843–1901) was also prominent.

But internal Jewish attacks on the Talmud also were not infrequent during this period, which at the same time witnessed the *haskalah* – the Jewish enlightenment. Moses Mendelssohn, himself rabbinically educated, endeavoured to assign to the sources (i.e. the Bible) their due place, and primacy over the Talmud. The curriculum of the free school he initiated in Berlin (founded in 1778) gave no place to the study of the Talmud. Later Jewish thinkers of the enlightenment at times became directly polemical against the Talmud; thus e.g. Abraham Buchner, lecturer at the rabbinical college of Warsaw (*Der Talmud in seiner Nichtigkeit*, Warsaw 1848). However, most are content to avoid rabbinic literature (Talmudic studies became important only at a relatively late stage of the *Wissenschaft des Judentums*) or to point out its purely historical significance. With the foundation of rabbinic seminaries and Jewish universities, these institutions took up the historical-critical investigation of rabbinic literature, while the Eastern European Yeshibot continued to foster the traditional study of these writings. It was these orthodox circles, too, which continued to affirm the halakhic authority of BT for the present, while many Jewish circles (especially Reform Judaism) attempted to adapt the Talmudic halakhah to circumstances or shelved it outright, considering it to be entirely obsolete.

# V

# THE EXTRACANONICAL TRACTATES

At the end of the order Neziqin of BT, one usually finds printed a number of texts known as 'extracanonical' tractates (since they do not have the authority of the actual BT) or 'minor tractates' ('minor' in the sense of inferior authority rather than necessarily of size). These tractates, first published together in this form in the BT edition Wilna 1886, fall into two categories: viz., seven independent writings and seven thematic collections of halakhot, most of which also appear elsewhere. Frequently only this second group is actually called 'minor tractates'.

English translation of all these tractates: A. Cohen (ed.), *The Minor Tractates of the Talmud*, 2 vols., London 1965, 2nd edn. 1971. (Cf. also the Hebrew-English Edition of the Soncino Talmud: *Minor Tractates*. London 1984.) Comprehensive treatment: M. B. Lerner, 'The External Tractates', in Safrai, *The Literature*, 1:367–403.

## *1) Abot de Rabbi Nathan (=ARN)*

***Bibliography***

**Finkelstein, L.** 'Introductory Study to Pirke Abot.' *JBL* 57 (1938) 13–50. **Finkelstein, L.** *Mabo le-Massekhtot Abot we-Abot de-Rabbi Natan.* New York 1950. **Goldin, J.** 'The Two Versions of Abot de Rabbi Nathan.' *HUCA* 19 (1945–46) 97–120. **Goldin, J.** *EJ* 3: 984–86. **Goldin, J.** 'The Third Chapter of Abot De-Rabbi Nathan.' *HTR* 58 (1965) 365–86. **Goldin, J.** 'Reflections on the Tractate Aboth de R'Nathan' (Hebr.). *PAAJR* 46–47 (1979–80) Hebr. section 59–65. **Kahana, T.** 'Le-habanat ha-Baraitah 'al Hilkhot Yerushalaim.' *Beth Mikra* 21 (1975–76) 182–92. [On ARN 35 and parallels.] **Kister, M.** *Avot de-Rabbi Nathan: Studies in Text, Redaction and Interpretation* (Hebr.). Diss. Jerusalem 1993. **Marmorstein, A.** *EJ* (Berlin 1928) 368–70. **Neusner, J.** *Judaism and Story: The Evidence of the Fathers According to Rabbi Nathan.* Chicago 1992. **Neusner, J.** *Form-Analytical Comparison in Rabbinic Judaism: Structure and Form in The Fathers and The Fathers According to Rabbi Nathan.* Atlanta 1992. **Saldarini, A. J.** *Scholastic Rabbinism: A Literary Study of the Fathers According to R. Nathan.* Chico 1982. **Zunz,** *GV*, 114–16.

***Text***

**Schechter, S.** *Aboth de Rabbi Nathan: Edited from Manuscripts with an Introduction, Notes and Appendices* (Hebr.). Vienna 1887; corrected repr. Hildesheim 1979. **Bregman, M.** 'An Early Fragment of Avot de Rabbi Natan from a Scroll' (Hebr.). *Tarbiz* 52 (1982–83) 201–22. [ARN A 38 and 36; the Genizah fragment is supposed to be no later than the 9th cent.]

***Translations* of Version A**

**Goldin, J.** *The Fathers According to Rabbi Nathan.* New Haven 1955; repr. New York 1974. **Neusner, J.** *The Fathers According to Rabbi Nathan: An Analytical Translation and Explanation.* Atlanta 1986. **Pollak, K.** *Rabbi Nathans System der Ethik und Moral.* Frankfurt am Main 1905.

**Version B**

**Saldarini, A. J.** *The Fathers According to Rabbi Nathan (Abot de Rabbi Nathan) Version B: A Translation and Commentary.* Leiden 1975. [Cf. J. Elbaum, *KS* 52 (1976–77) 806–15.]

ARN is preserved in two versions (A and B), comprising 41 and 48 chapters respectively. Version A was first printed in the Talmud edition of M. A. Justiniani at the end of Seder Neziqin (Venice 1550). S. Schechter reproduced it in the usual form, but corrected in accordance with MSS (Oxford Neubauer 408; MS Epstein of the year 1509) and medieval quotations. Version B was already published by S. Taussig, partly based on Cod. Hebr. Munich 222 (*Neweh Schalom* vol. 1, Munich 1872); S. Schechter took MS Rome Ass. 303 as his basis and also drew on MS Parma De Rossi 327 and MS Halberstam from the Bodleian, Oxford Neubauer 2635, along with medieval quotations. Meanwhile a number of Genizah fragments of ARN A and B, and of related material, have come to light (see the list in Bregman, 219–22; two fragments were used by Saldarini in his translation).

ARN is clearly dependent on the M tractate Abot, since it cites the latter and comments on it. Like Abot, ARN contains only haggadah. In further determining the relationship with Abot, Schechter distinguishes various parts: he sees ARN A 1–11 (B 1–23) and 12–18 (B 23–30) as a midrash on Abot, whose sayings Abot interprets one by one in detail and frequently with different explanations, often drawing on the Bible. ARN 20–30 (B 31–5) are more similar to M itself in that they merely present the rabbis' sayings without commentary. Like Abot 5, chapters 31–41 (B 36–48) consist primarily of numerical sayings; they quote Abot and supplement it after the manner of T (Schechter, xvi f.). Goldin and Saldarini follow Schechter, but consider the dominant genre to be midrash. The designation of ARN as Tosefta (e.g. D. Hoffmann, *The first Mishna and the Controversies of the Tannaim*, trans. P. Forchheimer (New York 1977), 47) or baraita on Abot (thus Zunz, *GV*, 114; Albeck, *Einführung*, 410) is based on the fact that ARN cites (almost) only Tannaites as authorities and is composed in Mishnaic Hebrew instead of the Aramaic of the Gemara.

The text of Abot differs in the two versions of ARN, and in both departs significantly from the present Mishnah Abot. Mishnah Abot contains much more material than what underlies ARN. In ARN some of the rabbis' sayings are in more appropriate chronological order than in M. There are, moreover, divergences in wording and in the names of tradents (frequently also between ARN A and B). L. Finkelstein (*Mabo*, 4f.; followed by Goldin and Saldarini) considers the form of Abot underlying both versions of ARN to be older than that of M.

According to S. Schechter (xx–xxiv), ARN A and B derive from a common, written original, while Goldin ('The Two Versions') regards them as independent formations of the oral tradition (with Finkelstein, *JBL* 57:16, 39). He considers the basic theme in A to be the study of Torah; and in B, good works ('The Two Versions', 98f.).

The name of R. Nathan is irrelevant for the historical origin of ARN. Is it not clear that the well-known Tannaite is intended, nor that he was seen as the author of ARN. J. Goldin (*EJ* 3:984) suspects that ARN is based on a recension of Abot by R. Nathan, and was therefore named after him.

Since ARN uses a version of Abot which diverges from M, the core of ARN might reasonably seem to have its origin in the third century – although Abot itself is later than M and cannot easily be dated. At the same time, it is impossible to say how long the active development of ARN continued. The widely accepted dating of the final version between the seventh and ninth centuries (Zunz, *GV*, 116: post-Talmudic) is essentially based on the fact that ARN is regarded as one with the minor tractates. Based on its language, contents and the cited rabbis, J. Goldin concludes, 'The composition of the contents of ARN cannot be much later than the third of following century, or at the utmost shortly thereafter' (*The Fathers*, xxi). However, each version must be assessed on its own. ARN B is very likely the older version; it is already quoted in the eighth century *Sheiltot*. Since it was was less widely known, it also suffered less from later alterations than version A (Schechter, xxiv) and therefore preserves the more primitive form. M. B. Lerner dates the final redaction of ARN B to the end of the third century; but for version A he concludes from the text published by Bregman that 'the basis for the extant arrangement. . . is a product of the latter half of the seventh or the early eighth century' (378), even if much of the material is close to the Tannaitic period. Kister 214–19, on the other hand, regards both versions as post-Talmudic, while allowing that A is further removed from the original than B. He dates their extant form no earlier than the end of the Amoraic era (after the fifth and before the ninth century, probably around the middle of this period).

## *2) Soferim*

### *Bibliography*

**Higger, M.** *Masseket Soferim.* New York 1937. **Higger, M.** *Seven Minor Treatises. . . and Treatise Soferim.* Vol. 2. New York 1930. [Incl. English translation.] **Müller, J.** *Masechet Soferim: Der thalmudische Tractat der Schreiber.* Leipzig 1878. [With detailed commentary in German.] **Ben Ifa, O.** *Massekheth Soferim ou le traité gaonique des 'Scribes'.* Dison 1977. [Müller's text with translation.]

**Kasher, M. M.** *Torah Shelemah.* Vol. 29: *The Script of the Torah and its Characters*

(Hebr.), 94–99. Jerusalem 1978. **Slotki, I. W.** Introduction to his Translation in A. Cohen (ed.), *The Minor Tractates of the Talmud*, vol. 1. London 1965. **Zunz**, *GV*, 100f. [*Derashot*, 275–77 adds notes by Albeck.]

German translation: H. Bardtke, *Wissenschaftliche Zeitschrift* (Leipzig 1952–53) 31–49.

The tractate Soferim survives in two versions, a Palestinian (in the Talmud editions) and a Babylonian one. The standard (Palestinian) version consists of several parts: chapters 1–5 give the rules for the production of biblical manuscripts using the minor tractate Sefer Torah; 6–9 continue this topic; 10–21 regulate the public reading of the Torah. Since BT is also frequently cited, this tractate (also cited as *Hilkhot Soferim* and *Baraita de-Soferim*) in its present form cannot be dated prior to the middle of the eighth century, even if earlier forms must be assumed. In some points Soferim contradicts the Talmudic halakhah and has prevailed.

Only the first two chapters survive of Version II (Babylonian). However, Higger (*Seven Minor Treatises*, Hebr. introduction, 12–15) shows by means of quotations in a Genizah document that the text must originally have been longer. (The fragment was published by E. N. Adler, *JQR* 9 (1897) 681–716 as a work of Yehudah ben Barzillai, but Higger attributes it to an eleventh cententury Babylonian Jew.) Hai Gaon repeatedly quotes this second version.

### *3) Ebel Rabbati*

#### *Bibliography*

**Brüll, N.** 'Die talmudischen Traktate über Trauer um Verstorbene.' *Jahrbücher* 1 (1874) 1–57. **Higger, M.** *Treatise Semachot.* New York 1931. [Critical edition.] **Horovitz, Ch. M.** *Uralte Toseftas*, Parts 2–3. Mainz 1890. [*Semachot Zutarti* and parts of *Ebel* tracts.] **Klotz, M.** *Der talmudische Traktat Ebel Rabbati.* Berlin 1890. [Critical edition of Chapters 1–4 with annotated German translation.] **Zlotnick, D.** *The Tractate 'Mourning'.* New Haven 1966. [Introduction, English translation, critical text.] **Zlotnick, D.** *EJ* 14: 1138f. **Zunz**, *GV*, 94.

The 14 chapters of Ebel Rabbati, the 'great (tractate) about mourning', euphemistically called Semaḥot by Rashi and others, describe halakhot and customs which must be observed with regard to the dying, suicides and the executed, mourning and burial customs. These subjects are broken up by means of numerous narrative illustrations (*ma'aseh*). Quotations from a work entitled Ebel Rabbati are given in MQ 24a; 26b; Ket 28a; but there must have been textual recensions of varying size and content (In *Torat ha-Adam*, Naḥmanides quotes a variant as *mekhilta aḥariti de ebel*; several medieval quotations are not in our text). Thus it remains possible that BT may indeed quote an early form or recension of our text. The Gaon Natronai (9th cent.) writes on the BT passages, 'Ebel is a M tractate containing funeral customs.

In it are found many of the halakhot which are taught in MQ 3; and there are two, a great one and a small one' (*Otzar ha-Gaonim*, vol. 8 (Jerusalem 1938), 95).

This text is missing in MS Munich of BT, but was printed already in the 1523 first printed edition of BT and is preserved in several MSS. It is usually dated to the eighth century (e.g. Brüll). However, the numerous parallels with BT and especially PT cannot simply be explained as taken from the Talmuds. Based on the cited rabbis, the structure and content as well as the language, a much earlier date is equally possible (Zlotnick: end of the 3rd cent.); this also finds support in archaeological facts, e.g. pertaining to burial customs (E. M. Meyers, 'The Use of Archaeology in Understanding Rabbinic Materials', in M. A. Fishbane & P. R. Flohr (eds.), *Texts and Responses: Studies Presented to Nahum N. Glatzer on the Occasion of his Seventieth Birthday by his Students* (Leiden 1975), 28–42, 93f.; idem, *Jewish Ossuaries: Reburial and Rebirth*, Rome 1971). On *Semaḥot de R. Ḥiyya* (i.e. *Semaḥot Zutarti*) see M. B. Lerner, 390f.

### *4) Kallah*

***Bibliography***

**Albeck**, *Mabo*, 601–14. **Aptowitzer, V.** 'Le traité de "Kalla".' *REJ* 57 (1909) 239–48. **De Vries, B.** 'The date of compilation of the tractate "Kalla rabbati"' (Hebr.). *4th WCJS* (Jerusalem 1967) 131–32. [Repr. in idem, *Meḥqarim*, 259–62.]

***Text***

**Coronel, N. N.** *Chamischa Quntarsim: Commentarios quinque doctrinam Talmudicam illustrantes*. Vienna 1864. [First edition of Kalla Rabbati.] **Higger, M.** *Massekhtot Kallah*. New York 1936. **Friedmann, M.** *Pseudo-Seder Eliahu zuta*, 13–19. Vienna 1904. [Repr., together with SER and SEZ, Jerusalem 1960.]

The tractate Kallah ('bride') represented in BT and Maḥzor Vitry comprises a chapter discussing engagement, marriage and conjugal relations. Shab 114a, Taan 10b and Qid 49b cite as a requirement for a rabbinic scholar knowledge of the *massekhet kallah*. Rashi et al. relate this to the tractate Kallah, while Ḥananel et al. see in it the institution of Kallah and the tractate prepared for this. The latter reading is to be preferred; in this regard the mention of the Kallah tractate in BT is already a gloss on the Palestinian tradition (Albeck; Goodblatt, *Instruction*, 157–59). Usually, however, Kallah is considered to be a work of Yehudai Gaon (8th cent.), or at any rate of Geonic origin (M. B. Lerner, 395: 'definitely. . . a post-talmudic compilation of the early Gaonic period').

*Kallah Rabbati*, published by Coronel from ME Halberstam-Epstein and also preserved in BT, consists of ten chapters, each with baraita and Gemara.

The Gemara of 1–2 comments on the tractate Kallah; 8, on the additional chapter 6 of Abot (*Qinyan Torah*); the other chapters constitute a Gemara on the tractate Derekh Ereṣ. Friedmann (p. 15) links this work with the school of Raba (i.e. 'BA4'); in this he is followed by de Vries, who bases himself primarily on linguistic proximity to the extraordinary tractates of BT. Most scholars, however, would attribute it to a student of Yehudai Gaon (Aptowitzer), or at any rate to this period.

### *5) Derekh Ereṣ Rabbah (DER)*

#### *Bibliography*

**Epstein, A.** *Qadmoniot*, 104–106. **Krauss, S.** 'Le traité talmudique "Déréch Éreç".' *REJ* 36 (1898) 27–64, 205–21; 37 (1899) 45–64. [Cf. W. Bacher, *REJ* 37 (1899) 299–303.] **Zunz**, *GV*, 116–18.

#### *Text*

**Higger, M.** *The Treatises Derek Erez, Pirke ben Azzai, Tosefta Derek Erez, Edited from MSS with an Introduction, Notes, Variants and Translation.* New York 1935; repr. Jerusalem 1970.

#### *Translation*

**Van Loopik, M.** *The Ways of the Sages and the Way of the World; The Minor Tractates of the Babylonian Talmud: Derekh 'Eretz Rabbah, Derekh 'Eretz Zuta, Pereq ha-Shalom. Translated on the basis of manuscripts and provided with a commentary.* Tübingen 1991.

*Derekh Ereṣ* (lit. 'way of the earth', hence 'rules of life') designates two entirely different tractates, which were later distinguished by being called Rabbah and Zutta, respectively. DER is a collection of baraitot supplemented by sayings of early Amoraim. Chapters 1–2 are absent in certain MSS that begin with chapter 3 (Ch. 1: illicit marriages – Elijah Gaon therefore prefers to take this piece with Kallah; 2: different classes of people, etc.). Chapter 3 is also called *Pereq ben Azzai* (Rashi in Ber 22a) and has frequently given its name to the entire tractate. Chapters 3–11 present rules of life, table manners, rules for behaviour in the bath, etc., and have a lot of material in common with ARN. In Ber 22a R. Yehudah's students ask him to teach them a chapter of Derekh Ereṣ; p.Shab 6.2, 8a cites a sentence from DER as contained *be-derekh ereṣ*. The basic core could already have developed in Tannaitic times; however, later on the text was not only revised but experienced considerable growth, resulting in a highly variant textual tradition.

### *6) Derekh Ereṣ Zutta (DEZ)*

***Bibliography*** (see also §5)

**Friedmann, M.** *Pseudo-Seder Eliahu zuta.* Vienna 1904; repr. Jerusalem 1960. **Sperber, D.** *Masechet Derech Eretz Zutta.* 2nd edn. Jerusalem 1982. **Sperber, D.** *A Commentary on Derech Erez Zuta Chapter Five to Eight.* Ramat-Gan 1990.

***Translations***

**Van Loopik, M.** [See §5.] German: **Tawrogi, A.** *Der thalmudische Tractat Derech Ereṣ Sutta.* Königsberg 1885.

DEZ, addressed primarily to scholars, is a collection of mostly anonymous maxims urging self-examination and modesty. The last chapter (10) is eschatological. The work is composite: 1–4 is also cited as 'fear of sin' (*yir'at ḥeṭ'*); the *Halakhot Gedolot* only designate 5–8 (taken from Maḥzor Vitry in the BT editions) as DEZ. Chapter 10 is no doubt also from different source. Van Loopik (p. 9) suspects that DEZ 1–3 (4) 'as a literary unit is a Tannaitic collection from the circles of the early Hasidim', but that the final redaction of DEZ probably only took place in the Geonic period (for a Geonic date see also D. Sperber, *Masechet*, 11, 179).

### *7) Pereq ha-Shalom*

***Text*** in **Higger** (cf. §5); also **Higger, M.** *Massekhtot Zeirot.* New York 1929. [Both versions.]

***Translations***

**Van Loopik, M.** [See §5.] German: **Wünsche,** *Lehrhallen,* 4:56–61.

This chapter, often reproduced as DEZ 11 (thus in BT Wilna), is a short composition with sayings about peace. It survives in two versions (cf. S. Schechter, *ARN*, 112f. n.19 on B). LevR 9.9 (M. 187–95) should be regarded as the likely source.

### *8) The other 'Minor Tractates'*

***Text***

**Higger, M.** *Seven Minor Treatises... and Treatise Soferim.* Vol. 2. New York 1930. [Introduction, text, translation.]

First edited by R. Kirchheim, *Septem libri Talmudici parvi Hierosolymitani* (Frankfurt 1851; repr. Jerusalem 1970) according to a MS of E. Carmoly; since then it appears in almost all editions of BT, after the texts discussed in §§1–7.

The seven tractates are thematic collections of baraitot which are first referred to as a whole in Nachmanides, *Torat ha-Adam* (*Kitbe Ramban*, ed. B. Ḥavel (Jerusalem 1964), 2:100) 'the tractate Ṣiṣit of the seven minor tractates'. Usually said to be post-Talmudic, these texts are regarded by M. Higger to be the first thematic compendia of the period after M; produced in Palestine, they were later revised in Babylonia. R. Neḥemyah says in LevR 22.1 (M. 496) that even the laws about Ṣiṣit, Tefillin and Mezuzah were already contained in the legislation at Sinai. This statement is adopted in EcclR 5.7, where however a later editor, assuming a reference to the minor tractates, added Gerim, Abadim, etc. (cf. Epstein, *ITM*, 50). These passages, therefore, are (for the Geonic period) only of indirect use as evidence for the minor tractates.

1. *Sefer Torah*: regulations about writing Torah scrolls; the basic form probably dates from the third century, albeit subsequently revised.

2. *Mezuzah*, 'door post'. A piece of parchment with Deut 6.4–9; 11.13–21 in a container affixed to the right door post.

3. *Tefillin*, 'phylacteries', derived from Exod 13.9, 16; Deut 6.6; 11.18.

4. *Ṣiṣit*, 'fringes' (Num 15.37ff.; Deut 22.12) on the four ends of the upper garment, later on the small and on the large Talit (prayer shawl).

5. *Abadim*, 'slaves'. German translation with notes: *Angelos* 1.3–4 (Leipzig 1925) 87–95.

6. *Gerim*, 'proselytes'.

7. *Kutim*, 'Samaritans'. The friendly attitude to the Samaritans in much of Kutim suggests that the basic core of this tractate must likely predate the final break at the end of the third century.

The last three tractates were already previously published (H. J. D. Azulai, *Mar'it ha-Ayn*, Livorno 1805; another version of Gerim already in *Simḥat ha-regel*, Livorno 1782); Jakob Naumburg already gave a commentary on Gerim in *Naḥalat Jakob*, Fürth 1793.

# PART THREE: MIDRASHIM

# I

# INTRODUCTION

***Bibliography***

**Bloch, R.** 'Midrash.' In W. S. Green (ed.), *Approaches*, 1:29–50. **Bloch, R.** 'Écriture et tradition dans le judaïsme – aperçus à l'origine du midrash.' *Cahiers Sioniens* 8 (1954) 9–34. **Boyarin, D.** *Intertextuality and the Reading of Midrash.* Bloomington 1990. [Cf. A. Samely, 'Justifying Midrash: On an "Intertextual" Interpretation of Rabbinic Interpretation', *JSS* 39 (1994) 19–32.] **Del Agua Pérez, D.** *El método midrásico y la exégesis del Nuevo Testamento.* Valencia 1985. **Elbaum, J.** 'On the Character of the Late Midrashic Literature' (Hebr.). *9th WCJS* (Jerusalem 1986) 57–62. **Finkelstein, L.** 'The Oldest Midrash: Pre-Rabbinic Ideals and Teachings in the Passover Haggadah.' *Harvard Theological Review* 31 (1938) 291–317. **Fishbane, M.** *Biblical Interpretation in Ancient Israel.* Oxford 1985. [On inner-biblical exegesis; cf. Y. Zakovitch, *Tarbiz* 56 (1986–87) 136–43.] **Fraenkel, J.** *Darkhê ha-Aggadah we-ha-Midrash.* 2 vols. Giv'ataim 1991. [Cf. M. Hirshman, *Jewish Studies* 32 (1992) 83–90). **Goldberg, Abr.** 'The Early and the Late Midrash' (Hebr.). *Tarbiz* 50 (1980–81) 94–106. **Goldberg, A.** 'Die funktionale Form Midrasch.' *FJB* 10 (1982) 1–45. **Goldberg, A.** 'Stereotype Diskurse in den frühen Auslegungsmidraschim.' *FJB* 16 (1988) 23–51. **Goldberg, A.** 'Midraschsatz: Vorschläge für die descriptive Terminologie der Formanalyse rabbinischer Texte.' *FJB* 17 (1989) 45–56. **Goldberg, A.** 'Paraphrasierende Midraschsätze.' *FJB* 18 (1990) 1–22. **Gottlieb, I. B.** 'Midrash as Biblical Philology.' *JQR* N.S. 75 (1984–85) 134–61. **Halivni, D. W.** *Midrash, Mishnah, and Gemara.* Cambrige, MA 1986. **Hallewy, E. E.** 'Biblical Midrash and Homeric Exegesis' (Hebr.). *Tarbiz* 31 (1961–62) 157–68. **Hartman, G. H.** & **Budick, S.**, eds. *Midrash and Literature.* New Haven 1986. **Heinemann, I.** *Darkhê ha-Aggada.* 3rd edn. Jerusalem 1970. [Cf. E. E. Urbach, *KS* 26 (1949–50) 223–28.] **Heinemann, J.** *Aggadah.* **Henschke, D.** 'The Midrash of the Passover Haggada' (Hebr.). *Sidra* 4 (1988) 33–52. **Herr, M. D.** *EJ* 11: 1507–14. **Hruby, K.** 'Exégèse rabbinique et exégèse patristique.' *Revue des Sciences Religieuses* 47 (1973) 341–72. **Jurgrau, M.** 'Targumic and Midrashic Methods of Interpretation' (Hebr.). *Bar-Ilan* 12 (1974) 179–99. **Kadushin, M.** *The Rabbinic Mind.* 2nd edn. New York 1965. **Le Déaut, R.** 'A propos d'une définition du midrash.' *Bib* 50 (1969) 395–413. **Maass, F.** 'Von den Ursprüngen der rabbinischen Schriftauslegung.' *ZTK* 52 (1955) 129–61. **Melammed, E. Z.** *Bible Commentators* (Hebr.), 1:5–128. Jerusalem 1975. **Muñoz Leon, D.** *Derás. Los caminos y sentidos de la palabra divina en la Escritura I: Derás targumico y derás neotestamentario.* Madrid 1987. **Neusner, J.** *Midrash in Context: Exegesis in Formative Judaism.* Philadelphia 1983. **Neusner, J.** *What is Midrash?* Philadelphia 1987. **Neusner, J.** *Midrash as Literature: The Primacy of Documentary Discourse.* Lanham, MD 1987. **Neusner, J.** *Invitation to Midrash.* San Francisco 1988. **Porton, G.** 'Defining Midrash.' In J. Neusner (ed.), *The Study of Ancient Judaism*, 1:55–92. New York 1981. [Revised from *ANRW* II 19/2 (Berlin/New York 1979) 103–38.] **Porton, G.** *Understanding Rabbinic Midrash: Texts and Commentary.* Hoboken, NJ 1985. **Samely, A.** 'Between Scripture and its Rewording: Towards a Classification of Rabbinic Exegesis.' *JJS* 42 (1991) 39–67. **Samely, A.** 'Scripture's Implicature: The Midrashic Assumptions of Relevance and Consistency.' *JSS* 37 (1992) 167–205. **Sarason, R. S.** 'Toward a New Agendum for the Study of Rabbinic Midrashic Literature.' In E. Fleischer & J.J. Petuchowski (eds.), *Studies in Aggadah, Targum and Jewish Liturgy, in Memory of Joseph Heinemann*, 55–73. Jerusalem 1981. **Seeligmann, I. L.** 'Voraussetzungen der Midraschexegese.' *VTSup* 1 (Leiden 1953) 150–81. **Shinan, A.** &

**Zakovitch, Y.** 'Midrash on Scripture and Midrash Within Scripture.' *SH* 31 (1986) 257–77. **Stemberger, G.** *Midrasch: Vom Umgang der Rabbinen mit der Bibel.* Munich 1989. **Vermes, G.** *Scripture and Tradition in Judaism: Haggadic Studies.* 2nd edn. Leiden 1973 (repr. 1983). **Vermes, G.** 'Bible and Midrash: Early Old Testament Exegesis.' In idem, *Studies*, 59–91. **Weingreen, J.** *From Bible to Mishnah.* Manchester 1976. **Wright, A. G.** *The Literary Genre Midrash.* Staten Island, NY 1967. [Cf. on this Le Déaut in the essay cited above.]

## *1) The Term*

***Bibliography***

**Bacher**, *ET*, 1:25–28, 103–105; 2:41–43, 107. **Frankel, I.** *Peshat in Talmudic and Midrashic Literature.* Toronto 1956. **Gertner, M.** 'Terms of Scriptural Interpretation: A Study in Hebrew Semantics.' *BSOAS* 25 (1962) 1–27. **Heinemann, I.** 'Le-hitpaḥut ha-munaḥim ha-miqṣo'iim le-ferush ha-Miqra.' *Leshonenu* 14 (1946) 182–89. **Loewe, R.** 'The "Plain" Meaning of Scripture in Early Jewish Exegesis.' *Papers of the Institute of Jewish Studies* 1 (London 1964) 140–85. **Meir, O.** 'The Problem of the Term "Midrash" in the Studies of Midrashim' (Hebr.). *11th WCJS* (Jerusalem 1994) C 1:103–10. **Wagner, S.** *TDOT* 3 (1978) 293–307.

*Midrash* derives from the verb *darash* 'to seek, ask'. Already in Scripture the verb is used with primarily theological connotations, with God or the Torah, etc. as object (e.g. Ezra 7.10 'studying God's law'; Isa 34.16 'searching in God's book'). The noun 'midrash' appears in two late passages: according to 2 Chr 13.22, the history of Abijah is recorded 'in the midrash of the prophet Iddo'; 24.27 speaks of the 'midrash on the Book of Kings'. The precise meaning of midrash in both passages is not certain: whether 'book, work' (LXX translates *biblion* or *graphé*, the Vulgate *liber*) or already in the later sense of an 'interpretative writing'. Sir 51.23 is the first instance of *beth midrash*, 'house of teaching, schoolhouse'. In the sense of 'teaching, instruction', the term is now documented at Qumran, too: *midrash le-maskil* occurs in 4QSb and 4QSd; the Scrolls also frequently use *darash* as 'to search out, interpret' (the laws or commandments: 1QS 5.11; 6.6; 4QFlor 1.11) and speak of the *midrash ha-torah* (1QS 8.15; CD 20.6).

This is already equivalent to rabbinic usage, where midrash means especially 'research, study' and is distinguished, as 'theory', from the more essential 'practice' (*ma'aseh*): Abot 1.17. In this regard it is synonymous with *talmud*, which is contrasted with practice e.g. in p.Pes 3.7, 30b. In the narrower sense of 'interpretation', Ket 4.6 says *zeh midrash darash*, 'he presented this interpretation' (the object of interpretation here is the Ketubbah). Midrash is more particularly applied to the occupation with the Bible: thus e.g. p.Yoma 3.5, 40c, according to which every interpretation of Scripture (*midrash*) must address the content. The *beth ha-midrash*, therefore, is the house of study, especially of the Bible (e.g. Shab 16.1; Pes 4.4). Midrash also comes to designate more specifically the result of interpretation or writings containing biblical interpretation. The *darshan* (Aram. *darosha*) is the Bible interpreter or preacher.

The term does not as such imply a particular method of biblical interpretation as distinct from *peshat*, the rendition of the literal meaning. Such a distinction was later asserted in medieval exegesis (even though a *derash/peshat* distinction existed already in Amoraic times: Heinemann, 188; cf. Arak 8b; Erub 23b; Sanh 100b, etc.). In the Talmudic period, even the *peshat* is not the simple literal meaning, but often merely an opinion sanctified by long tradition or teaching authority.

Midrash cannot be precisely defined, but only described, as Le Déaut stresses (p. 401). G. Porton describes 'midrash as a type of literature, oral or written, which stands in direct relationship to a fixed, canonical text, considered to be the authoritative and the revealed word of God by the midrashist and his audience, and in which the canonical text is explicitly cited or clearly alluded to' (*The Study*, 62).

The canonical (or perhaps more generally: religiously authoritative) text is certainly an essential prerequisite of midrash (even if Ket 4.6 identifies the Ketubbah as an object of interpretation). Midrash, however, is not merely 'a literature about a literature' (Wright, 74), as R. Le Déaut (p. 406) rightly cautions; it may allude not just to a biblical text, but just as easily to a biblical event. However, the hearers' or readers' attitude to the expounded canonical text (or biblical event) does *not* properly belong to the definition of midrash (*pace* Porton), since that would almost always remain unverifiable.

### *2) Origins of Midrashic Exegesis*

The beginnings of a midrashic exegesis of earlier Scripture texts were already contained *within the Bible* (cf. the comprehensive discussion by Fishbane): 'The oldest midrashic exegesis developed organically out of the distinctive character of the Biblical literature' (Seeligmann, 151). Thus, for example, the books of Chronicles have been understood as a kind of midrash on the books of Samuel and Kings, and Chroniclers' additions in earlier books have been seen in similar terms (e.g. the gloss in Gen 22.14 which identifies the mountain of the sacrifice of Isaac with the Temple Mount). The historical Psalms and the Psalm titles in particular must also be mentioned here.

Within *post-biblical literature* we may cite the Praise of the Fathers in Sir 44–50, the description of the work of Wisdom in the history of Israel in Wisd 10–19, as well as the midrashic element in the LXX and in the work of Philo or Josephus. The specific literary genre of the book of Jubilees and the Genesis Apocryphon is disputed. On *Jubilees* as 'Rewritten Bible', see J. C.

Endres, *Biblical Interpretation in the Book of Jubilees.* Washington 1987. The Genesis Apocryphon 'contains elements similar to a *targum* and to a *midrash*' (J. A. Fitzmyer, *The Genesis Apocryphon of Qumran Cave I* (2nd edn. Rome 1971), 10); according to M. R. Lehmann it is probably 'the oldest prototype of both available to us' (*RQ* 1 (1958–59) 251).

The *relationship between Targum and Midrash* is impossible to define precisely. Neh 8.8 is frequently cited as the point of departure, or even as the first instance, of both genres. There it says of the reading of the Torah under Ezra, 'And they read from the book, from the Torah of God, in paragraphs and with explanations, so that they understood the reading.' The Targum in any case is not merely a translation, but also an explanation and often expansion of the Bible by means of haggadah. With Le Déaut, 411, it must be assumed that many elements of Targum entered the midrash, and vice versa, so that there was no independent development of the two literary genres (see especially A. Sperber, *The Bible in Aramaic*, vol. 4 B: *The Targum and the Hebrew Bible*, Leiden 1973; and the texts in vol. 4 A: *The Hagiographa: Transition from Translation to Midrash*, Leiden 1968; on vol. B see A. Díez Macho, *JSJ* 6 (1975) 217–36; for parallels between Pentateuchal Targums and rabbinic literature see E. B. Levine in the appendix to A. Díez Macho, *Neophyti I. Targum Palestinense MS de la Biblioteca Vaticana*, vols. 2–5, Madrid 1970–78). The kinship between the two genres is clear also from their common *Sitz im Leben*, which in both cases must be seen in the school and the synagogue liturgy (cf. A. D. York, 'The Targum in the Synagogue and in the School', *JSJ* 10 (1979) 74–86); *meturgeman* and *darshan*, translator and preacher, will often have been identical. However, this does not say anything about the actual beginnings of the midrash, as Porton (*The Study*, 67) rightly emphasizes: 'Those who argue that the regular readings of the Torah within the synagogal service gave rise to midrash find little evidence upon which to base their theory'.

Since its discovery at Qumran (e.g. 1QpHab), the *pesher* has become well known as a distinct genre of biblical interpretation. Each respective verse of Scripture is followed by an interpretation of the prophetic text for the present experience of the congregation at Qumran. This reflects the congregation's conviction that over and above their straightforward sense the prophetic texts have a meaning for the end of days, which is being fulfilled in the interpreter's present. In this respect these commentaries are comparable to the fulfilment quotations in the New Testament. The Pesher should be regarded as a sub-genre of midrash (cf. W. H. Brownlee, *The Midrash Pesher of Habakkuk*, Missoula 1979; H. Gabrion, 'L'interprétation de l'Écriture dans la littérature de Qumrân', *ANRW II* 19/1 (Berlin/New York 1979) 779–848;

M. P. Horgan, *Pesharim: Qumran Interpretations of Biblical Books*, Washington 1979).

Midrash-like texts have also been identified in the *New Testament*; the term 'midrash' has been used especially for the infancy gospels and for the story of Jesus's temptation. To be sure, the classification of a text as midrash has become rather fashionable, especially in New Testament scholarship; in this context the particular character of rabbinic midrash has not always been properly recognized as a point of departure. Wright's work on the literary genre proceeds from this uncertainty in New Testament scholarship.

We should also mention the *Liber Antiquitatum Biblicarum*, which probably dates from the end of the first century; Porton (*The Study*, 72) calls it 'one of the oldest midrashic works' (contrast M. D. Herr, 1508: *LAB* is not a midrash). L. Finkelstein, on the other hand, regards the Passover-haggadah as the oldest actual midrash (cf. D. Henschke). An extended prehistory of the midrash before the rabbinic period is in any case undeniable.

### *3) The Character of Rabbinic Midrash*

As in the case of its predecessors, so for rabbinic midrash the *religious interest* of the treatment and exposition of Scripture is significant. Midrash is not 'objective' professional exegesis – even if at times it acquires such methods, knows the philological problems as well as the principle of interpretation in context (i.e. the explanation of Scripture from Scripture), and also manifests text-critical interests (although the *al-tiqrî* interpretation in rabbinic literature by no means always serves textual criticism: cf. Seeligmann, 160; I. Heinemann, *Darkhê*, 127–29). Similarly, midrash takes for granted the principle of exegesis in context, explaining the Bible from the Bible. The context, however, is the entire Bible; any of its verses can be related to any other, while the specific intention of an individual book is rarely of interest. One encounters the Bible as an integral whole, which accordingly carries a uniform divine message.

Midrash is primarily a religious activity: this is clear also from the recitation of the thirteen rules of Ishmael in the morning prayer (introduced relatively late). Midrash arises out of Israel's consciousness of an inalienable solidarity with its Bible; midrash therefore is always also *realization*, and must discover ever afresh the present significance of the text or of biblical history. To be sure, the present relevance of midrashic exegesis is not always obvious; but even where *prima facie* it merely appears to serve pious curiosity, the ultimate concern is always to let the Bible be the intellectual and religious milieu in which the Jew lives.

The *methods* of biblical interpretation in midrash are not restricted to the hermeneutical rules. G. Vermes distinguishes between 'pure exegesis' which deals with linguistic problems, real and apparent lacunae and contradictions in the text, and 'applied exegesis', 'providing a non-scriptural problem with a scriptural solution' ('Bible and Midrash', 62). One must also distinguish between halakhah and haggadah, as we stressed earlier. *Halakhic exegesis* not only has to supply details which are missing in the Bible but which provide instructions for the application of a biblical rule; it must also resolve contradictions (e.g. between Deut 15.12 and Exod 21.7, regarding the release of a female slave: Vermes, 'Bible and Midrash', 69), reconcile the biblical text with current practice (e.g. in the prohibition of images), find biblical support for regulations not yet envisioned in Scripture (a Scripture passage as *asmakhta*, 'support', or *zekher*, 'remembrance, reference'), etc. *Haggadic exegesis* is freer and more characterized by a playful element; yet in its own way it is strongly bound by tradition and at the same time open to contemporary influences (such as apologetic and polemical needs). The differences between halakhic and haggadic exegesis, at any rate, are due less to matters of principle than to differing intentions.

I. Heinemann (*Darkhê*) speaks of two main directions in the haggadah: '*creative historiography*' fills out biblical narratives by supplying details, identifying persons, drawing an anachronistic picture of the living conditions of biblical characters, attributing to the latter a knowledge of the entire Bible and of the future, resolving contradictions, linking the details of narratives by analogy, etc. '*Creative philology*' uses an argument from silence to interpret not only repetitions of words and sentences, expressions which are unnecessary for the meaning of a sentence, but also the absence of expected details. It takes into account stylistic divergences between parallel statements and narratives, different possibilities of vocalizing an unpointed word, and linguistically antiquated forms of Scripture. Convinced of the independence of the individual parts of speech, it often performs its own division of words and sentences (NB the MSS originally contained no spaces between individual words), divides a word into constituent parts or reads it as *notarikon*, counts the frequency of a certain letter in a paragraph in order to deduce something, inverts the sequence of words in a sentence, gives highly idiosyncratic explanations of proper names, etc.

What appears to be an arbitrary treatment of the biblical text arises in reality from the view that everything is contained in the Torah (Ben Bag Bag says in Aboth 5.22, 'Turn and turn it (the Torah), for everything is in it'). The rabbis are also convinced of the ambiguity of Scripture: 'A Scripture passage has several meanings' (Sanh 34a). Yet the rabbis remain aware that in their interpretation they occasionally do violence to the Bible; thus Ishmael reproaches Eliezer ben Hyrcanus, 'Behold, you say to Scripture: be still while I interpret you' (Sifra, *Tazria Negaim* 13.2, W. 68b). All the while, however, there is an indispensable awareness that Scripture remains relevant as God's Word to humanity today.

At the same time, a serviceable description of rabbinic midrash must be capable of distinguishing the latter from the midrashic literature on the Bible before and after the rabbinic period, and of identifying precursors and successors of rabbinic biblical interpretation. D. Halivni (*Midrash*, 118ff.) attempts to distinguish between 'simple' and 'complex' midrash. In comparing the Temple Scroll of Qumran (11QTorah) with early rabbinic texts, Abr. Goldberg similarly emphasizes that the Temple Scroll, as an 'early midrash', does not derive the halakhah from Scripture by means of exegetical rules, but places it indistinguishably alongside the biblical text and frames it with verses from Scripture. It is, however, impossible to substantiate the view that the Pharisaic halakhah was also presented in this form, and that traces of the further development towards 'late midrash' can be discerned in texts like Sot 8. Nevertheless, it is right to distinguish rabbinic midrash from earlier forms on the basis that the rabbinic texts often use the biblical text as proof, clearly separate it from the exposition, and frequently even indicate the rules by which its interpretation is derived. An additional characteristic is the identification of rabbis as authors or tradents of interpretations: in late midrashim the names of rabbis become less and less frequent, and finally disappear almost entirely.

### *4) Classification of the Midrashim*

The extant rabbinic midrashim can be classified as follows:

#### *a) Halakhic and Haggadic Midrashim*

The distinction is not precise, inasmuch as halakhic midrashim also contain haggadic material and vice versa, but it does signify the dominant interest of a given midrash. The designation of a group of midrashim as 'haggadic midrashim' occasionally encounters the objection that this expression is tautologous. The original meaning of haggadah, it is argued, is biblical interpretation, as is suggested by the introductory formula *maggid ha-katub* (Bacher, *ET*, 1:30; cf. Porton, *The Study*, 77). However, this objection applies at best to the origin of the term 'haggadah', since subsequent times clearly saw a restriction of the term. Bacher himself emphasizes (*ET*, 1:33) that 'early in its scholastic usage, the noun acquired the meaning of non-halakhic scriptural interpretation. In the oldest traditions, the word exclusively carries this meaning.' The received topical classification, therefore, should be retained. The designation of the halakhic midrashim as '*Tannaitic* Midrashim', however, is a consistent principle of classification only as long as one also speaks of Amoraic or Geonic midrashim, i.e. if the criterion is the time of origin. But for this the dating of many midrashim (and especially the halakhic midrashim) is far too problematic.

***b) Exegetical and Homiletical Midrashim***

A formal distinction is made between exegetical and homiletic midrashim (also known as expository and sermonic midrashim). Here, too, it is impossible to effect an easy distinction, since characteristic traits of one genre are sometimes also found in the other. It is nevertheless a basic difference whether a midrash expounds the biblical text verse by verse and often word by word, or whether it merely gives a devotional commentary on individual verses or on the main theme of the weekly reading from the Torah or the prophets. And the homiletic midrashim probably do not on the whole contain actual synagogue sermons but literary abridgements which in part were developed directly in the schools.

The mixing of the various genres in the midrash was undoubtedly also furthered by the fact that midrash, even more than other rabbinic material, is largely a literature of compilation and quotation. Especially in exegetical midrash there is a tendency to string together a chain of expositions according to the arrangement of the biblical text, usually identifying the authors or tradents of the individual expositions. The combination of interpretations with the repeated introduction *dabar aḥer*, 'another interpretation', suggests catena-like collections. Frequently, however, such juxtaposed interpretations are not alternatives but parts of a consciously composed overall presentation (see E. Ungar, 'When "Another Matter" is the Same Matter: The Case of Davar-Aher in Pesiqta DeRab Kahana', in J. Neusner (ed.), *Approaches to Ancient Judaism*, New Series 2:1–43 (Atlanta 1990); J. Neusner, *Symbol and Theology in Early Judaism*, Minneapolis 1991).

***c) Country of Origin***

Aside from the late compendia, almost all midrashim originated in Palestine. Scholars in Babylonia did work in the area of midrash, although apparently not to the same extent as in Palestine. While Babylonian midrashic texts partly incorporate Palestinian material, they frequently adapt this to their own interests and handle it independently. Such midrashim do not survive as separate writings but were incorporated into BT (see p. 199 above).

## *5) The Synagogal Reading Cycle*

***Bibliography***

**Bregman, M.** 'The Triennial Haftarot and the Perorations of the Midrashic Homilies.' *JJS* 32 (1981) 74–84. **Büchler, A.** 'The Reading of the Law and the Prophets in a Triennial Cycle.' *JQR* 5 (1892–93) 420–68; 6 (1893–94) 1–73. [Repr. in J. J. Petuchowski (ed.), *Contributions to the Scientific Study of Jewish Liturgy*, New York 1970.] **Elbogen, I.** *Jewish Liturgy: A Comprehensive History*, 129–63. Translated by R. P. Scheindlin. Philadelphia/New York 1993. **Fleischer, E.** 'A List of Yearly Holidays in a Piyyut by Qiliri' (Hebr.). *Tarbiz* 52 (1982–83) 223–72. **Fleischer, E.** 'Inquiries Concerning the Triennial Reading of the Torah in Ancient Eretz-Israel' (Hebr.). *HUCA* 62 (1991) 43–61. **Fleischer, E.** 'Annual and Triennial Reading of the Bible in the Old Synagogue' (Hebr.). *Tarbiz* 61 (1991–92) 25–43. **Heinemann, J.** 'The Triennial Lectionary Cycle.' *JJS* 19 (1968) 41–8. **Klein, M. L.** 'Four Notes on the Triennial Lectionary Cycle.' *JJS* 32 (1981) 65–73. **Mann, J.** *The Bible as Read and Preached in the Old Synagogue.* 2 vols. Cincinnati 1968 (repr. New York 1971 with an important prolegomenon by B.Z. Wacholder), 1966 (completed by I. Sonne). **Moore, G. F.** *Judaism in the First Centuries of the Christan Era*, 1:296–302. Cambridge, MA 1958 (=1927). **Offer, J.** 'The Masoretic Divisions (Sedarim) in the Books of the Prophets and Hagiographa' (Hebr.). *Tarbiz* 58 (1988–89) 155–89. **Perrot, C.** *La lecture de la Bible dans la synagogue: Les anciennes lectures palestiniennes du Shabbat et des fêtes.* Hildesheim 1973. **Rosenthal, D.** 'The Torah Reading in the Annual Cycle in the Land of Israel' (Hebr.). *Tarbiz* 53 (1983–84) 144–48. **Tabory, J.** *Jewish Prayer and the Yearly Cycle: A List of Articles.* KS Supplement to vol. 64 (1992–93).

The homiletical midrashim contain sermons on the synagogue readings of Sabbaths and holy days. They follow a Palestinian order of reading, even though most of them were subsequently divided according to the Babylonian order (the same procedure was followed for the halakhic midrashim, which originally reflected a completely different structuring principle).

### *a) The Reading from the Torah*

M.Meg 3.6 provides for a continuous reading of the Torah, although it is not clearly stated whether the weekday readings are included in the schedule or not. Meg 29b indicates that a one-year reading cycle was in use in Bayblonia and a three-year cycle in Palestine (the text is not datable; it is also unclear whether 'three years' is meant in the strict sense). However, even in Geonic times there were still *no standard cycles* in Palestine (for the rabbinic period cf. LevR 3.6 M.69; for the Geonic period see *Ha-Ḥilluqim she-bên anshê mizraḥ u-benê Ereṣ Yisra'el*, ed. M. Margoliot (Jerusalem 1938), 88), but the cycles varied from place to place. This is also substantiated by the different lists of pericopes (the Pentateuchal pericope is called 'seder' in Palestine, 'parashah' in Babylonia): 141, 154, 155, and 167 sedarim are attested. What is more, the readings were not tied to a particular time of year, as is seen from Yannay's *Qerobot.* Instead of a cycle of exactly three years, then, we must assume one of approximately three-and-a–half to almost four years. The cycle is moreover interrupted e.g. for the special Sabbaths (for which, as for the festivals, the reading had already been determined very early on). Thus there cannot have been a definite correspondence of certain Torah readings with certain prophetic readings.

The Babylonian one-year cycle divides the Pentateuch into 54 weekly portions. Even this lectionary, however, is likely to derive originally from Palestine (Wacholder, xxiii; Perrot, 146f.; D. Rosenthal). E. Fleischer sees evidence for this in a *Piyyut* by Ha-Kallir which he published; this text presupposes the one-year cycle and the feast of Simḥat Torah as its conclusion. He suspects that before the year 70 the Torah reading was the only item on the agenda of Sabbath congregations. Since it was therefore likely to be longer, it would have been closer to the *parashiyot* of the one-year cycle; the continuous lectionary was then introduced after 70, and later adopted in Babylonia as well. In Palestine, meanwhile, the extension of the service through prescribed prayers and the like made it necessary to curtail the readings; this led to the three-year cycle. Most of the Palestinian synagogues returned to the one-year cycle only later, when sermons were dropped from the service.

### *b) The Reading from the Prophets*

The prophetic reading is known as *Haftarah* ('ending, dismissal'; cf. the Palestinian expression *ashlemata*, 'completion', i.e. probably of the Scripture reading and not of the service as such). This is attested as early as the New Testament (Luke 4.17), but it came to be cyclically ordered only at a much later date. Unlike the Torah reading, that of the prophets was not subject to the requirement of a continuous reading (M.Meg 4.4). The readings for the festivals and the special Sabbaths were determined very early (t.Meg 3.1–7, L. 353–5; cf. Lieberman, *TK* 5:1164ff.). In other respects, freedom of choice prevailed for a long time, as long as the Haftarah somehow agreed with the Seder (Meg 29b). The Haftarot were frequently written up together in special scrolls (Git 60a); as far as we can tell from the late Haftarot lists of the 'three-year' cycle, Isaiah and the twelve minor prophets were especially favoured in their selection. On the three Sabbaths of mourning and seven of consolation (Tammuz 17th until Sukkot), for which the Haftarot were also fixed at an early date, the synagogue sermon kept to the Haftarot; to what extent it did so at other times cannot be generally determined (cf. Wacholder, xii, *contra* Mann). It is true that the (NB literary) homilies of the midrashim frequently quote the opening verse of the haftarah in their comforting conclusion (*ḥatimah*). However, many other *ḥatimot* do not correspond to a known haftarah, or do not end with a prophetic verse at all. For this reason it will only rarely be possible from the *peroratio* of the homily to infer the prophetic text which was read together with a given passage of Torah (Bregman).

### *c) Hagiographa*

According to Shab 16.1, the hagiographa are not read in the Sabbath synagogue service; p.Shab 16.1, 15c restricts this to the time before the Minḥah prayer, for which Shab 116b explicitly attests the reading of the Ketubim at Nehardea. There is very early evidence for the reading of Esther at Purim; that of Ruth, Cant and Lam is attested in Soferim 14.3. Of course the Psalms were also recited in the service, although perhaps rarely according to a fixed order.

## *6) Synagogal Sermon, Petiḥah and Ḥatimah*

**_Bibliography_**

**Cohen, N. J.** 'Structure and Editing in the Homiletic Midrashim.' *AJSR* 6 (1981) 1–20. **Goldberg, A.** 'Die "Semikha": Eine Kompositionsform der rabbinischen Homilie.' *FJB* 14 (1986) 1–70. **Heinemann, J.** *Sermons in the Talmudic Period* (Hebr.). Jerusalem 1970. **Heinemann, J.** *EJ* 13: 994–98. **Heinemann, J.** 'On Life and Death: Anatomy of a Rabbinic Sermon.' *SH* 27 (1978) 52–65. [On b.Shab 30a-b.] **Hirshman, M.** 'The Preacher and His Public in Third-Century Palestine.' *JJS* 42 (1991) 108–14. **Maybaum, S.** 'Die ältesten Phasen in der Entwicklung der jüdischen Predigt.' *19. Bericht der Lehranstalt für die Wissenschaft des Judenthums in Berlin*, 1901. **Zunz,** *GV*, 342–72.

**_On the Petiḥah_**

**Bacher, W.** *Die Proömien der alten jüdischen Homilie.* Leipzig 1913; repr. Westmead 1970. **Bregman, M.** 'Circular Proems and Proems Beginning with the Formula *"Zo hi' shene'emra beruaḥ haq-qodesh"*' (Hebr.). In E. Fleischer & J.J. Petuchowski (eds.), *Studies in Aggadah, Targum and Jewish Liturgy, in Memory of Joseph Heinemann*, Hebr. section, 34–51. Jerusalem 1981. **Fox, H.** 'The Circular Proem: Composition, Terminology and Antecedents.' *PAAJR* 49 (1982) 1–31. **Goldberg, A.** 'Petiḥa und Ḥariza: Zur Korrektur eines Mißverständnisses.' *JSJ* 10 (1979) 213–18. **Goldberg, A.** 'Versuch über die hermeneutische Präsupposition und Struktur der Petiḥa.' *FJB* 8 (1980) 1–59. **Grözinger, K. E.** 'Prediger gottseliger Diesseitszuversicht.' *FJB* 5 (1977) 42–64. **Heinemann, J.** 'The Petiḥtot in Aggadic Midrashim, their Origin and Function' (Hebr.). *4th WCJS* (Jerusalem 1968) 2:43–47. **Heineman, J.** 'The Proem in the Aggadic Midrashim – A Form-Critical Study.' *SH* 22 (1971) 100–122. **Heinemann, J.** 'Tannaitic Proems and their Formal Characteristics' (Hebr.). *5th WCJS* (Jerusalem 1972) 3:121–34. **Jaffee, M. S.** 'The "Midrashic" Proem: Towards the Description of Rabbinic Exegesis.' In W. S. Green (ed.), *Approaches*, 4:95–112. **Kern, B.** 'Paraphrasendeutung im Midrasch: Die Paraphrase des Peti-ḥaverses.' *FJB* 9 (1981) 115–61. **Schäfer, P.** 'Die Peticha – ein Proömium?' *Kairos* 12 (1970) 216–19. **Segal, E. L.** 'The *Petihta* in Babylonia' (Hebr.). *Tarbiz* 54 (1984–85) 177–204. **Shinan, A.** 'Letorat happetiḥta.' *Jerusalem Studies in Hebrew Literature* 1 (1981) 135–42.

**_On the Ḥatimah_**

**Goldberg, A.** 'Die Peroratio (Ḥatima) als Kompositionsform der rabbinischen Homilie.' *FJB* 6 (1978) 1–22. **Stein, E.** 'Die homiletische Peroratio im Midrasch.' *HUCA* 8–9 (1931–32) 353–71.

A rabbinic sermon could serve a number of functions. It might be a popular sermon in the synagogue, intended either for a wider circle in the schoolhouse outside the service (and hence under fewer time constraints) or as a lecture in the rabbinic academy; or it could be an abbreviated account of a real or a literary sermon. In accordance with the circumstances, and depending on the time and region, it was characterized by specific formal conventions. Of these, *Petiḥah* and *Ḥatimah* have been specially studied, while the main part of the sermon has so far remained rather neglected and in fact is less subject to clearly evident laws. As N. J. Cohen has shown, in the early homiletical midrashim the main body of the sermon is usually characterized by the treatment of thematic questions, followed by exegetical observations on the opening verses of the pericope. In later midrashim this order is no longer preserved; even petiḥot are blended into the main body. Nevertheless, Cohen does not see this as a corruption of the form: 'the breakdown in the fixed structure of the rabbinic derashah was due to a conscious decision on the part of the editors to enhance the artful editing of their homilies' ('Structure', 20). However, even if particular instances of the later homily do show closer thematic connections, the formal degeneration cannot be ignored.

***a) The Petiḥah***

The Petiḥah is probably the most common form of midrashic literature. W. Bacher counted almost 1,400 instances in the texts he had available; there are in fact many more examples. The name derives from the usual formula, *Rabbi X pataḥ,* 'opened (the sermon)' or 'preached'. Hence Petiḥah is usually rendered as 'opening', 'proem', but it can also simply mean 'sermon'.

The basic structure is in three parts: a Petiḥah verse, usually not from the biblical book (or group of books) from which the reading is taken, but mostly from the 'Writings'; the preacher expounds this verse so as to lead up to the concluding verse of the reading (usually the first or second verse, generally of the Pentateuchal reading, hence also called the 'seder verse').

Aside from this 'simple Petiḥah' there is the composite one, in which the interpretative transition from the Petiḥah verse to the seder verse is achieved in several steps by various quoted rabbis. Sometimes the seder verse is cited even before the Petiḥah verse. Occasionally the Petiḥah also makes use of Scripture verses from all three parts of the Bible: Bacher saw in this the idea of the unity of Scripture as the basic motif of the Petiḥah. However, Goldberg (*JSJ* 10) rightly objects that this is not characteristic of the Petiḥah but an independent, special form of argument.

The Petiḥah is occasionally found in halakhic midrash (but always doubtful), and even in the Talmud and Midrash it is sometimes put into the mouth of Tannaites. Its classic form at any rate was reached in the early haggadic midrashim (like GenR, LevR), while mixed forms increasingly developed later on. Especially worth mentioning is the form which concludes by repeating the Petiḥah verse instead of or in addition to the Seder verse; the Petiḥah verse thus frames the entire Petiḥah (Bregman calls this a 'circular proem'). This structure is used primarily, although not exclusively, in a special form of the Petiḥah in which the opening Petiḥah verse is followed by the stereotyped phrase 'this is what was said through X by the Holy Spirit' (on this *ruaḥ haqodesh* Petiḥah see also A. Goldberg, *Ich komme und wohne in deiner Mitte* (Frankfurt 1977), 14f.). Bregman ('Circular Proems') shows that both forms are late developments of the literary homily which enjoyed particular popularity in the Tanḥuma-Yelamdenu literature.

The function of the Petiḥah is disputed: is it the introduction to a sermon or the sermon itself? The question arises why so many proems are extant, but no actual sermons – unless the amorphous series of individual expositions which follow the proems were to be seen as such. J. Heinemann therefore explained the Petiḥah as an introductory short sermon before the reading. This finds support both in the brevity of the Petiḥot as well as in their 'inverted' structure; however, later on the Petiḥot will undoubtedly have been used as introductions to longer sermons, too. P. Schäfer, on the other hand, considers it impossible that *petaḥ* could mean both 'to open' and 'to explain, preach' at the same time. What is more, there is no evidence that such introductory sermons were in fact customary. Thus he concludes that the Petiḥah is the sermon pure and simple, and that the introductory formula *R. X pataḥ* properly means that he interpreted the verse of the pericope by means of the quoted Bible verse. Grözinger is probably right to consider this a false alternative: it is necessary to assume diverse functions of the Petiḥah in the history of the rabbinic homily, so that the Petiḥah can be either an independent homiletical unit or a component of a two-part homily, whether as an actual or a literary sermon – the latter would perhaps have been shaped only by the redactor (*FJB*, 43–47; for the history of the development see especially Bregman, 'Circular Proems').

***b) The Ḥatimah***

The Ḥatimah ('conclusion' of the sermon) is not properly a *peroratio*, since the latter, somewhat unlike the Ḥatimah, summarizes the arguments of a speech by rhetorical means in order to persuade the listener. Instead, the rabbinic homily is concerned to end on a comforting note (Sifre Deut §342, F. 391f., hearkening back to the example of Moses; PRK 13.14, M. 238: all prophets began with words of admonition and ended with words of comfort, except Jeremiah). The insertion of words of comfort at the end of tractates of M and T bears witness to the same trend.

The messianic or generally eschatological perspective in the Ḥatimah is analogous to the Petiḥah, but less pronounced. The Ḥatimah begins with the text of the pericope and normally passes from its first or last verse (the *'inyan*, the real theme of the sermon) to the Ḥatimah verse, which is usually taken from the prophets. This latter verse is introduced by a fairly clearly defined Ḥatimah formula in which God often appears as the speaker and which usually contrasts this world with the world to come ('not as in this world is it in the world to come', or 'thus it is in this world – how much more in the world to come', etc.). Unlike the Petiḥah, the beginning of the Ḥatimah is very difficult to determine, since it is not formally identified. Often it can only be perceived from the end.

As Goldberg emphasizes (20–22), the homiletical function of this form of the Ḥatimah, found especially in the Pesiqta and Tanḥuma homily, must be seen from the perspective of the typological interpretation of Scripture in the rabbinic homily. Taking the verse of the pericope, which usually addresses something imperfect and incomplete, the preacher deliberately expounds it with a view to the prophetic verse – thus leading on from the imperfect to the perfect. The Ḥatimah, therefore, is the concluding eschatological kerygma of the sermon.

# II

# THE HALAKHIC MIDRASHIM

## *1) General Introduction*

***Bibliography***

**Albeck, Ch**. *Untersuchungen über die halakischen Midraschim.* Berlin 1927. **Albeck**, *Mabo* 79–143. **Chernick, M**. 'The Use of Ribbuyim and Mi'utim in the Halakic Midrash of R. Ishmael.' *JQR* N.S. 70 (1979–80) 96–116. [No clear separation between Ishmael and Aqiba.] **Epstein, J. N.**, *ITL*, 497–746. **Finkelstein, L**. 'The Sources of the Tannaitic Midrashim.' *JQR* N.S. 31 (1940–41) 211–43. [Reprinted in idem, *Sifra*, 5:191*–223*.] **Goldberg, Abr**. 'Leshonot "dabar aḥer" be-midreshê ha-halakhah.' In Y.D. Gilat et al. (eds.), *'Iyyunim be-Sifrut Ḥazal, ba-Miqra u-be-Toldot Yisra'el* (*Festschrift* E. Z. Melamed), 99–107. Ramat-Gan 1982. **Harris, J. M.** 'Modern Students of Midrash Halakhah: Between Tradition and Wissenschaft.' In J. Wertheimer (ed.), *The Uses of Tradition*, 261–77. New York 1992. **Heschel, A. J**. 'Studies in Midrashic Literature' (Hebr.). In *The Abraham Weiss Jubilee Volume*, 349–60. New York 1964. [Differences between the schools of Ishmael and Aqiba in the Haggadah.] **Herr, M. D**. *EJ* 11: 1521–3. [Summary of Albeck.] **Hoffmann, D.** *Zur Einleitung in die halachischen Midraschim.* Berlin 1887. **Lightstone, J. N.** 'Oral and Written Torah in the Eyes of the Midrashist: New Perspectives on the Method and Message of the Halakhic Midrashim.' *Studies in Religion* 10.2 (1981) 187–93. **Lightstone, J. N**. 'Form as Meaning in Halakhic Midrash: A Programmatic Statement.' *Semeia* 27 (1983) 24–35. **Melammed, E. Z.** *Introduction*, 161–317. **Melammed, E. Z.** *The Relationship between the Halakhic Midrashim and the Mishna and Tosefta: The Use of Mishna and Tosefta in the Halakhic Midrashim* (Hebr.). Jerusalem 1967. [Summarized in *Introduction*, 223–58.] **Mirsky, S. K**. 'The Schools of Hillel, R. Ishmael and R. Akiba in Pentateuchal Interpretation.' In H. J. Zimmels et al. (eds.), *Essays Presented to Chief Rabbi Israel Brodie*, 1:291–99. London 1966. **Neusner, J**. *The Canonical History of Ideas: The Place of the So-Called Tannaite Midrashim.* Atlanta 1990. **Porton, G. G**. *Ishmael*, vol. 2.

The halakhic midrashim are exegetical midrashim on Exodus through Deuteronomy. As the name indicates, they are primarily legal in orientation. They endeavour to establish Scripture as the source of the halakhah, and to emphasize this (not necessarily always polemical) antithesis to the Mishnah's derivation of the halakhah even by the formal structure of their individual sections (cf. Lightstone, *Form*). However, since as continuous commentaries they do not omit the narrative passages, they are at the same time also strongly haggadic.

D. Hoffmann divided these midrashim into two groups, which he assigned to the school of *Aqiba* and that of his contemporary *Ishmael.* His criteria are the names of the cited teachers as well as the fact that many anonymous sentences in midrashim of the school of Ishmael are in the Talmuds derived from the school of Ishmael. According to Hoffmann, the two schools differ in their technical terminology as well as in exegetical method. Aqiba's school likes to apply verbal analogy (*gezerah shawah*); that of Ishmael employs this only if the word would otherwise be superfluous and therefore appears specifically intended for this interpretation. Inclusion and exclusion (*ribbui* and *mi'ut*), too, are held to be characteristic of the school of Aqiba; similarly the exposition of all linguistic peculiarities, such as the doubling of certain terms or individual particles and letters. On the other hand, a predilection for the literal meaning is attributed to R. Ishmael and his school, since the Bible speaks in human language. In keeping with these criteria, Hoffmann assigned Mekhilta and SifreNum, the beginning and end of SifreDeut and also MidrTannaim on Deut to the school of Ishmael; the Mekhilta de R. Simeon ben Yoḥai on Exod, Sifra on Lev, Sifre Zutta on Num and Sifre on Deut belong to the school of Aqiba.

Ch. Albeck, however, has demonstrated that the classification of midrashim according to schools must be considerably modified. Absolute differences exist only in terminology, even though these differences have occasionally become blurred in the course of textual transmission (Albeck compiles the characteristic terms of the various midrashim in *Untersuchungen*, 78–81). These terminological differences, however, do not go back to the differing nomenclature of the schools of Ishmael and Aqiba but to the redactors of these midrashim. They forged a standard terminology for material from different sources, as can also be seen from the parallels in the Talmuds (*Untersuchungen*, 86). The assignment to the schools of Ishmael and Aqiba is unproven, 'because the dependence of the methods of these midrashim on the principles of these Tannaites is all too weakly substantiated' (*Untersuchungen*, 139). Yet Albeck, too, considers it proven that Mek and especially SifreNum made use of sources from the school of R. Ishmael.

L. Finkelstein has taken up the question of the sources of halakhic midrashim. He basically agrees with Albeck's thesis. The haggadic material must on principle be considered separately, since it is based on different sources which were common to all groups and were only slightly adapted. The real differences between the schools were in the legal sphere. Finkelstein holds that after excluding the numerous interpolations in the halakhic midrashim, which were also pointed out by J. N. Epstein, S. Lieberman et al., one actually comes back to a core which originated in the schools of Ishmael and Aqiba, even if the differences between the two schools were later blurred.

However, the problematic nature even of Finkelstein's result has been demonstrated by G. G. Porton. The mass of exegetical material attributed to Ishmael does indeed seem to lend support to his role in biblical interpretation; but this is not enough to permit the inference that there was an Ishmael school of interpretation. In the transmitted material, Ishmael never uses the majority of hermeneutical rules attributed to him, particularly not in the Tannaitic texts and the halakhic Midrashim (*Ishmael*, 4:191). He occasionally abandons the literal sense where Aqiba holds to it, and in general makes use of methods attributed to Aqiba (conversely, Aqiba also uses those of Ishmael). A clear demarcation between Ishmael and Aqiba is therefore impossible, as is the assumption of two clearly opposing schools at the time of Ishmael. 'It appears that the standard picture of Ishmael's exegetical practices is, at earliest, an Amoraic construction' (*Ishmael*, 2:7; cf. 3:2f.). Not until the Palestinian Talmud do we find a wide methodological separation between Ishmael and Aqiba (*Ishmael*, 4:191).

This corroborates Albeck's thesis that the real terminological differences between the two groups of midrashim are the work of the redactors (although it remains open whether the first or final redactors are in view): they accommodated the material adopted from other sources to the terminology of their main sources, in which the school terminology had already gradually developed (Albeck, *Untersuchungen*, 86). Although the two groups of midrashim clearly differ in their exegetical terminology, they are by no means strictly separate in substance: each group also presents a good deal of material from the other, albeit with linguistic adaptations (frequently introduced by *dabar aḥer*: see Abr. Goldberg). G. G. Porton observes a fairly even distribution of the opinions attributed to Ishmael in both groups of halakhic midrashim, as well as a notable prominence of Aqiba in the group of midrashim ascribed to the school of Ishmael (*Ishmael*, 4:55f., 65f.). 'I would conclude, therefore, that our standard division of the Tannaitic texts into 'Aqiban and Ishmaelean is at least over-simplified, and it may be incorrect' (*Ishmael*, 4:67).

Thus we may record as a *preliminary result*: 1) Exegetical differences between Ishmael and Aqiba cannot be verified; nor can their foundation of schools of interpretation. 2) The halakhic midrashim fall into two categories which respectively favour traditions of R. Ishmael and of R. Aqiba or their students, although they frequently transmit them conjunction with those of the other side. 3) Haggadah and halakhah in these midrashim derive from different sources; the haggadic material is common to all groups. 4) In the halakhah there is a developing school terminology, which the redactors of the midrashim also applied to extraneous material. 5) With Albeck (*Untersuchungen*, 154), the halakhic midrashim should be classified as follows: a) Mek and SifreNum; b) Sifra and Sifre Zutta; c) SifreDeut and MRS. The midrashim of b) and c) frequently betray the same sources and thus somehow belong together, while MidrTannaim and fragments on Lev must be included in a group with a). 6) Anyone wanting to speak of midrashim of the schools of Ishmael or Aqiba (support for this can be found in Maimonides's preface to *Mishneh Torah*) would need to be aware of the purely pragmatic (not historical) nature of this nomenclature; with Herr (*EJ*), the more neutral classification in Group I ('Ishmael') and II ('Aqiba') is to be preferred.

The halakhic midrashim are also often designated as *Tannaitic midrashim*; this is due to the language of these midrashim (Mishnaic Hebrew) and to the teachers named in them (Tannaites and first-generation Amoraim). This designation, too, was criticized by Albeck on the grounds that the halakhic midrashim are never cited in the two Talmuds (*Untersuchungen*, 91ff.). Albeck does acknowledge the numerous parallels between halakhic midrashim and the Talmudic baraitot, but prefers to derive these from collections known to both. He bases this above all on the very inconsistent manner of citation of such sayings in the Talmuds: 'If the Talmud were to adduce e.g. our Mekhilta, it could not do so now with *tania*, now with *teni R. Ishmael*, now with *teni R. Shim'on*, etc. The Talmudic references, therefore, must be to other, clearly identified collections of baraitot, and not to our halakhic midrashim which contain baraitot from all these collections' (*Untersuchungen*, 110).

This line of argument is not entirely sound: it presses the Talmuds into an excessively rigid system of citation and fails to consider the diverse origin of the Talmudic material. Nevertheless, it is true that quotations from the halakhic midrashim in the Talmuds cannot be confirmed with absolute certainty. The argument from silence, viz., that the Talmud surely would have relied on the halakhic midrashim in certain discussions if they were known, is of no help to our question. Albeck (*Untersuchungen*, 119) moreover admits that the Talmuds' ignorance of the halakhic midrashim does not prove with certainty 'that they did not exist in Talmudic times'. But he considers it likely that they were written 'in late Talmudic times at the earliest'. M. D. Herr pegs the date of origin more precisely to the latter half of the fourth or the beginning of the fifth century (*EJ* 11: 1523). However, both maintain the Tannaitic origin of the material of these midrashim: they are baraitot.

By and large, the halakhic midrashim undoubtedly had their final redaction after the actual Tannaitic period, i.e. after the redaction of M. This is clear, for example, from the numerous quotations from M and T which Melammed has collected in the halakhic midrashim, even if in a particular cases a quotation can rarely be shown to derive from the final version of M or (especially!) T. It is nevertheless conspicuous that Melammed was unable to confirm a quotation in Sifre Zutta. This alone suffices to show that a general statement on the date of the halakhic midrashim cannot be made, but that each case must be judged on its merits. In any case, the late dating of the halakhic midrashim by Albeck and his school is not guaranteed simply by the fact that quotations from them in the Talmuds cannot be positively identified. Parallels between the halakhic midrashim and the Talmuds often find their more primitive expression in the former; indeed, even the relative priority of a midrashic tradition over against a parallel in M or T can frequently be demonstrated. This suggests that the final redaction of the halakhic midrashim should not be removed too far from that of M and T. The late third century as the date of redaction probably accounts for the majority of halakhic midrashim, even if this needs to be more accurately established for each individual midrash.

## *2) The Mekhilta de Rabbi Ishmael (=Mek)*

***Bibliography***

**Abramson, S.** 'Arba'ah Inyanot be-Midreshê Halakhah.' *Sinai* 74 (1974) 1–9. [On his proposed new reading from a MS Antonin see S. Lieberman, 'Pisqah Ḥadashah mi-Mekhilta u-Firushah.' *Sinai* 75 (1974) 1–3; repr. in *Studies*, 25–27.] **Albeck**, *Mabo*, 79–113, esp. 106–13. **Boyarin, D.** *Intertextuality*. **Cohen, N. J.** 'Analysis of an Exegetical Tradition in the Mekhilta de-Rabbi Ishmael: The Meaning of the 'Amana in the Second and Third Centuries.' *AJSR* 9 (1984) 1–25. [On the conclusion of Beshallaḥ 7.] **Davies, W. D.** 'Reflections on the Spirit in the Mekilta: A Suggestion.' *Journal of the Ancient Near Eastern Society of Columbia University* 5 (1973) 95–105 (*Festschrift* T. H. Gaster). [Repr. in idem, *Jewish and Pauline Studies* (London 1984), 72–83. Also *6th WCJS* (Jerusalem 1977) 3:159–73.] **Eckart, K. G.** *Untersuchungen zur Traditionsgeschichte der Mechilta*. Diss. Berlin: Kirchliche Hochschule, 1959. **Epstein, J. N.**, *ITL*, 545–87. **Ginzberg, L.** 'The Relation between the Mishnah and the Mekiltah' (Hebr.). In idem et al. (eds.), *Studies in Memory of Moses Schorr, 1874–1941*, 57–95. New York 1944. [Repr. in idem, *Al halakhah we-aggadah* (Tel Aviv 1960), 66–103, 284–90.] **Herr, M. D.** *EJ* 11: 1267–69. **Kadushin, M.** 'Aspects of the Rabbinic Concept of Israel: A Study in the Mekilta.' *HUCA* 19 (1945–46) 57–96. **Kadushin, M.** *A Conceptual Approach to the Mekilta*. New York 1969. **Klein, H.** 'Mekilta on the Pentateuch.' *JQR* N.S. 35 (1944–45) 421–34. **Kugel, J.** 'Song and Poetry in the Mechilta d'R. Yishmael' (Hebr.). *8th WCJS* (Jerusalem 1982) C:141–44. **Kvarme, O. C.** 'Skrift og tradisjon: En innføring i den rabbinske midrasjlitteratur med særlig henblikk på Mekilta de Rabbi Jismael.' *Tidsskrift for Teologi og Kirke* 49 (1978) 173–96. **Lauterbach, J. Z.** 'The Name of the Mekilta.' *JQR* N.S. 11 (1920–21) 169–95. **Lauterbach, J. Z.** 'The Arrangement and the Divisions of the Mekilta.' *HUCA* 1 (1924) 427–66. **Lauterbach, J. Z.** 'The Two Mekiltas.' *PAAJR* 4 (1933) 113–29. [On Mekilta quotations missing from both versions.] **Levine, H. I.** *Studies in Mishnah Pesachim, Baba Kama and the Mechilta* (Hebr.). Tel Aviv 1971. **Melammed E. Z.** *Introduction*, 181–88, 249–53. **Neusner, J.** *Mekhilta According to Rabbi Ishmael: An Introduction to Judaism's First Scriptural Encyclopaedia*. Atlanta 1988. **Neusner, J.** *Bab*, 1:179–83. **Neusner, J.** *Introduction*, 249–70. **Niditch, S.** 'Merits, Martyrs, and "Your Life as Booty": An Exegesis of Mekilta, Pisḥa 1.' *JSJ* 13 (1982) 160–71. **Stemberger, G.** 'Die Datierung der Mekhilta.' *Kairos* 21 (1979) 81–118. **Towner, W. S.** *Enumeration*. **Wacholder, B. Z.** 'The Date of the Mekilta de-Rabbi Ishmael.' *HUCA* 39 (1968) 117–44.

***a) The Name***

*Mekhilta* (root *kul*) is the Aramaic equivalent of Hebrew *middah* or *kelal*, 'rule, norm'. More specifically it means the derivation of the halakhah from Scripture according to certain rules; secondly also the halakhic exegesis itself and its result. It is thus often roughly equivalent to Mishnah or baraita (cf. Hai Gaon's Responsum in L. Ginzberg, *Geonica*, vol. 2 (New York 1909), 39). Finally, *mekhilta* can also mean a tractate containing such exegesis (i.e. a similar development as for Greek *kanôn*). The identification with *megilta* in the *Arukh* of Nathan of Rome is untenable. In the Talmud, Mekhilta does not designate our commentary on Exod but is contrasted as *baraita* with *matnita*: thus Pes 48a; Tem 33a; cf. Git 44a, 'Go and look up your *mekhilta*', i. e. written notes on the halakhah. Similarly p.AZ 4.8 44b: *appeq R. Yoshiyya mekhilta* (G. Wewers ad loc. somewhat misleadingly translates, R. Y. *edited* ('gab. . . heraus') the Mekhilta; but in the corresponding note he explains that this refers to a collection of halakhic questions on idolatry).

In Geonic times, Mek (perhaps originally plural: *mekhilata*, approximately equivalent to *massekhtot*) designates the halakhic commentary on Exod through Deut. This applies perhaps already in the *Halakhot Gedolot*, although the textual transmission here does not permit a confident assessment (cf. Epstein, *ITL*, 546), and later in Hai Gaon (A. Harkavy, *Responsen der Geonim* (Berlin 1887), No. 262) as well as Maimonides in the introduction to *Mishneh Torah.* In other texts, *Sifre (debê Rab)* is used just as comprehensively, sometimes without Sifra on Lev: thus also in Sanh 86a; Ḥag 3a, etc., even if there *Sifra* and *Sifre* do not yet denote our extant midrashim. The designation *Mekhilta* for our midrash is certainly later than Sifre.

Althouth a text attributed to Saadya quotes our Mek as *mekhilta de-we-elleh-shmôt*, this is perhaps still a description rather than a proper name (Lauterbach, 'Name', 174); similarly the term *mekhilta de-Ereṣ Yisra'el* (e.g. Harkavy, *Responsen der Geonim*, No. 229). The first definite references to our text as Mekhilta de R. Ishmael date from the eleventh century: Nissim of Kairouan (on Shab 106b in BT Wilna) and Samuel ha-Nagid in his introduction to the Talmud.

The work was named after R. Ishmael not because he was considered its author (but NB see Maimonides), but – in keeping with the medieval mode of citation – because the midrash as such begins in Pisḥa 2 (L. 15; Pisḥa 1 must be seen as an introduction) with the mention of Ishmael.

***b) Content and Structure***

Mek is a commentary on Exod 12.1–23.19; 31.12–17; 35.1–3. Thus it contains only c. 12 of the 40 chapters of Exod. It concentrates on the legal sections, but also does not omit the narrative portions. It is striking, however, that even some vital legal sections are not treated. The commentary on the directions for the construction of the covenantal tabernacle (Exod 25.1ff.) was apparently given in a separate work, which will have corresponded approximately to the *Baraita de-melekhet ha-mishkan* (whose basic core, in the opinion of Epstein, *ITL*, 549, may go back to the school of R. Ishmael). This document is composed in Mishnaic Hebrew and cites only Tannaites; it describes the construction of the covenantal tabernacle in 14 chapters. Text in *BhM* 3:144–54. Critical editions: M. Friedmann, Vienna 1908 (repr. together with Sifra, Jerusalem 1967); R. S. Kirschner, *Baraita DeMelekhet ha-Mishkan: A Critical Edition with Introduction and Translation*, Cincinnati 1992. A Genizah fragment of the *Baraita* has been published by Hopkins, *Miscellany*, 78ff. See also Ginzberg, *Ginzê Schechter*, 1:374–83. The commentary on Exod 29 was also an independent work, included in Sifra (on Lev 8) as *Mekhilta de-Milluim*, even though terminologically it belongs to Group I ('school of Ishmael').

In the original arrangement, Mek consists of nine tractates (*massekhtot*) which in turn are subdivided into a total of 82 paragraphs (*parashiyot*; MSS offer halakhot as a further subdivision): 1. Pisḥa (Exod 12.1ff.); 2. Beshallaḥ (13.17ff.); Shirata (15.1ff.); 4. Wayassa (15.22ff.); 5. 'Amaleq (17.8ff.); 6. Baḥodesh (19.1ff.); 7. Neziqin (21.1ff.); 8. Kaspa (22.24ff.); 9. Shabbeta (31.12–17; 35.1–3).

This arrangement is exclusively based on content, and does not follow the synagogal order of reading. Only the printed editions introduced the arrangement according to the Babylonian order of reading. This led to the designation of the first part of 'Amaleq as *Beshallaḥ*, the second part together with Baḥodesh as *Yitro*; the tractates Neziqin and Kaspa were combined as *Mishpatim*, while Shabbeta was divided into *Ki-tissa* and *Wa-yaqhel*. However, the original arrangement is to be preferred (thus ed. Lauterbach; ed. Horovitz-Rabin has unfortunately adopted the secondary arrangement, but adds the original one in small print).

### *c) Character, Origin, Date*

The assignment of Mek to Group I ('school of Ishmael') is due (e.g. Epstein, *ITL*, 550ff.) to the numerous passages in Mek which in other writings are cited either verbatim or by content as teachings of R. Ishmael, and which in BT are introduced by *tanna debê R. Yishmael* or, in BT and in the midrashim, by *teni R. Yishmael*. But we must note that many of the quotations thus introduced are absent from Mek or even contradict it; hence this cannot furnish proof. As for the method of interpretation, its classification in the halakhic portions is unproblematic (e.g. no evaluation of purely stylistic repetitions); the haggadic portion derives from sources in common with the other Group. The demarcation is straightforward in regard to the exegetical terminology (e.g. *maggid* instead of *melammed*, etc.).

Lauterbach (in the introduction to his textual edition) has proposed a number of theses on the genesis of Mek. 'one of the older tannaitic works' (xix). He considers that a number of factors make Mek 'one of the older tannaitic works (p. xix), 'one of the oldest midrashim': these factors include its early halakhah (which often contradicts the later one), many old legends not preserved elsewhere, and a still unsophisticated interpretation of Scripture which largely agrees with the ancient versions. In the Talmud it is not known by the name Mek, since in Amoraic times it was only a part of the larger collection Sifre (on Exod, Num, Deut). The midrash on Exod which was known to the Amoraim is also not identical with ours; it is only the latter's core, which in various redactions was subjected to considerable alterations in form and content before attaining its final shape (xxiii). Lauterbach regards the core as going back most probably to the school of R. Ishmael or at least to the teachings of his students; but the first redactor already added material from the school of R. Aqiba. Mek went through 'more than one revision and several subsequent redactions', one of which probably took place in the school of Yoḥanan bar Nappaḥa, in whose name rabbinic literature elsewhere cites many of the statements appearing anonymously in Mek. But Lauterbach also allows for even later redactions of Mek (xxvi).

A number of factors favour this picture of a series of subsequent redactions beginning in the Amoraic period with a core going back to the school of Ishmael, even if it does not fully agree with Lauterbach's designation of Mek as one of the oldest Tannaitic works. The date of the final redaction (apart from later interpolations, textual corruptions, etc.) is hereby left entirely in limbo. Given these manifold revisions, what actually remains of the Tannaitic core? It is probably no longer possible to speak consistently of a Tannaitic midrash.

An account of the origin of Mek can only proceed from the individual sources of Mek, allowing also for the relationship with MRS. A separate investigation of the halakhic and haggadic material (as enjoined by L. Finkelstein) is required as much as a discriminating form critical treatment of the individual pieces (as attempted by Eckart for the case of the tractate Pisḥa). In this regard we are still rather at the beginning of the task. This is true also for the investigation of the individual *massekhtot* of Mek as independent units. J. N. Epstein has pointed out the common interests as well as contradictions and differences between the individual tractates (*ITL*, 581–

87): 'Their correlation consists merely in their place in *one* collection and in *one* book', viz., in their connection with a midrash on Exodus (*ITL*, 581). This agrees with what E. Z. Melammed (*Introduction*, 249) concludes on the use of M and T in Mek (no quotation in Shirata and Shabbeta, only two in Beshallaḥ; but 45 in Piṣha, 36 in Neziqin, etc. The identification of genuine quotations remains problematic, but that does not alter these characteristic differences between the individual tractates). J. Neusner has demonstrated the close connection between Pisḥa and Neziqin, noting especially the disproportionate prevalence of Yoshiyya, Jonathan and Nathan, but also of Ishmael). Since the first three of these rabbis were all in Babylonia after the Bar Kokhba revolt, Neusner concludes 'that the Mekhilta sections in question were *originally* compiled on the basis of discussions between 135 and 150 CE, probably at Ḥuẓal' (*Bab* 1:179). Nowadays Neusner himself would no longer support this conclusion, and no longer comments on the date (*Mekhilta*, 24f.). His earlier observations, however, remain to be accounted for, along with his more recent statements about the distinctive style of argumentation in Neziqin.

It is easier to date the final redaction of Mek. B. Z. Wacholder indeed has proposed the genesis of the work in eighth-century Egypt or elsewhere in North Africa. He argues that Mek uses BT and post-Talmudic writings, invents Tannaites and is ignorant of conditions in the Talmudic period; Kaspa 5 even employs a Geonic tradition. However, a specific investigation of the individual passages shows that these arguments are not sound. On the contrary, in the case of parallel traditions Mek usually has the older version compared with works like BT, Sifre and MRS. The mention of the sons of Ishmael need not imply Islamic rule. The form of the individual traditions, the cited rabbis and the historical allusions suggest a date of final redaction in the second half of the third century (against Wacholder's theory see also M. Kahana, *Tarbiz* 55 (1985–86) 515–20).

***d) The Text***

***1. Manuscripts***

MSS of the complete Mek are MS Oxford 151, dating from 1291 according to Neubauer's catalogue (vol. 1 (1886), 24), and MS Munich, Cod. Hebr. 117, written c. 1435. Facsimile: *The Munich Mekilta – Bavarian State Library, Cod. Hebr. 117*, ed. J. Goldin, Copenhagen/Baltimore 1980. Parts of the text of Mek are also in Casanata MS H. 2736 (end of Beshallaḥ and all of Shirata) as well as fragments from Oxford. (No. 2756: parts of Wayassa; No. 2669: parts of Neziqin).

*Genizah fragments* have been published by E. Y. Kutscher ('Geniza

Fragments of the Meḳilta of Rabbi Yišma'el' (Hebr.), *Leshonenu* 32 (1968) 103–16: fragment Oxford 62d with a piece of Wayassa) and Z. M. Rabinovitz (*Ginzé Midrash*, 1–14: pieces of Beshallaḥ and Shirata from the British Museum, of the same kind as those published by Kutscher; according to Rabinovitz (p. 2), they belong to the oldest fragments of the whole Genizah; cf. also Kutscher on the great text-critical value of the fragments). Additional Genizah fragments from the libraries of Dropsie College in Philadelphia and of Columbia University were already used by Lauterbach in his edition.

### *2. Printed Editions*

First printed in 1515 at Constantinople; the edition Venice 1545 (facsimile Jerusalem 1981) uses Const. and corrects this text (only rarely, on the basis of one MS, viz., the same one used by Const.: E. Z. Melammed, 'The Constantinople Edition of the Mechilta and the Venice Edition' (Hebr.), *Tarbiz* 6 (1934–35) 498–509). Of the later editions, the one with commentary by J. H. Weiss, Vienna 1865, and the one with commentary by M. Friedmann, Vienna 1870, are especially often cited. They have now been replaced by two *critical editions*:

H. S. Horovitz & I. A. Rabin, *Mechilta d'Rabbi Ismael cum variis lectionibus et adnotationibus*, Frankfurt 1931, 2nd edn. Jerusalem 1960 (generally uses Venice 1545 as base text; cf. E. Z. Melamed, *Tarbiz* 6.1 (1934) 112–23). The Hebrew introduction announced by Rabin was not published.

J. Z. Lauterbach, *Mekilta de Rabbi Ishmael: A Critical Edition on the Basis of the MSS and Early Editions with an English Translation, Introduction and Notes*, 3 vols., Philadelphia 1933–35 (broader textual basis than in Horovitz/Rabin, but no complete critical apparatus; eclectic text; cf. Lieberman, *KS* 12 (1935–36) 54–65 = idem, *Studies*, 540–51). See also L. Finkelstein, 'The Mekilta and its Text', *PAAJR* 4 (1933–34), 3–54 (= idem, *Sifra*, 5:1*–52*).

A new critical edition is advocated by M. Kahana, 'The Critical Edition of Mekilta De-Rabbi Ishmael in the Light of the Genizah Fragments' (Hebr.), *Tarbiz* 55 (1985–86) 489–524; D. Boyarin is currently preparing such a new edition (see idem, 'From the Hidden Light of the *Geniza*: Towards the Original Text of the *Mekhilta d'Rabbi Ishmael*' (Hebr.), *Sidra* 2 (1986) 5–13).

### *3. Concordance*

B. Kosovsky, *Otsar Leschon ha-Tannaim: Concordantiae verborum quae in Mechilta d'Rabbi Ismael reperiuntur*, 4 vols., Jerusalem 1965–69.

### *4. Translation*

English translation in Lauterbach; see also J. Neusner, *Mekhilta Attributed to R. Ishmael: An Analytical Translation*, 2 vols., Atlanta 1988. German translation in J. Winter & A. Wünsche, *Mechiltha, ein tannaitischer Midrasch zu Exodus*, Leipzig 1909 (repr. Hildesheim 1990).

## *3) The Mekhilta de Rabbi Simeon ben Yoḥai (= MRS)*

***Bibliography***

**Abramson, S.** 'Arba'ah 'inyanot be-midreshê halakhah.' *Sinai* 74 (1973–74) 1–13. [On MRS 1–8.] **Albeck, Ch.** *Untersuchungen*, 151–56; *Mabo*, 82f. **De Vries, B.** *Meḥqarim*, 142–147. **Epstein, J. N.** *ITL*, 725–40. **Ginzberg, L.** 'Der Anteil R. Simons an der ihm zugeschriebenen Mechilta.' M. Brann & J. Elbogen (eds.), *Festschrift zu I. Lewy's siebzigstem Geburtstag*, 403–36. Breslau 1911. **Herr, M. D.** *EJ* 11: 1269f. **Kasher, M.** *Meqorot ha-Rambam we-ha-Mekhilta de Rashbi*. New York 1943; 2nd edn. Jerusalem 1980 under the title *Sefer ha-Rambam*. . . . [Cf. S. Zeitlin, *JQR* N.S. 34 (1943–44) 487–89, who believes that MRS repeatedly used *Mishneh Torah*, not vice versa.] **Levine, H. I.** *Studies in Talmudic Literature and Halakhic Midrashim* (Hebr.), 127–91. Ramat Gan 1987. **Lewy, I.** 'Ein Wort über die "Mechilta des R. Simon".' *Jahrbuch des jüdisch-theologischen Seminars*. Breslau 1889. **Melammed,** *Introduction*, 208–13.

The Exodus midrash MRS is frequently quoted in the Middle Ages (until the sixteenth century); however, it was not printed, and from the seventeenth century on was considered lost until its rediscovery in the nineteenth and twentieth centuries.

### *a) Name*

Medieval quotations from MRS are usually adduced as *Mekhilta de R. Simeon (b. Yoḥai)*: e.g. repeatedly in Naḥmanides' commentary on the Pentateuch, see on Exod 22.12; Ritba (Yom Tob ben Abraham of Sevilla) quotes the text as *Mekhiltin de R. Aqiba*; the name *mekhilta de saniyah* is also used ('Mekhilta of the thornbush', since it begins with Exod 3; thus Hadassi in *Eshkol ha-Kofer* 36a). A quotation also used in Naḥmanides is found in the Geonic Responses (Harkavy No. 229) as *Sifrê debê Rab* in contrast to the *Mekhilta de-Ereṣ Yisra'el* (due to the brevity of the quotation – two words and a Bible verse – it is uncertain that the Geonic text really quotes this passage, rather than just a parallel).

### *b) Text*

Already M. Friedmann collected the MRS quotations known to him in his edition of Mek; I. Lewy then showed that the majority of them are transmitted in MHG. D. Hoffmann subsequently reconstructed the text on the basis of MHG and three Genizah fragments of MRS (two at Oxford; another at

Cambridge can no longer be located): *Mechilta de-Rabbi Simon ben Jochai. . .*, Frankfurt 1905. However, in the wake of additional textual discoveries this edition, along with all the early literature on MRS, is of value almost exclusively for the history of research.

*MSS known at present* (gathered by J. N. Epstein): the most important is *MS Firkovitch* II 268, Leningrad, which preserves 20 unconnected pieces, about half of MRS, on 51 leaves in Rashi script. Other leaves held by various libraries are also part of this same Genizah manuscript. Additional fragments are at Cambridge (Ginzberg, *Ginze Schechter*, 1:339–73) and Oxford; MS Antonin 236 at Leningrad has a piece of MRS in an independent textual recension, which Melamed therefore prints separately in the appendix to the textual edition.

On the basis of these fragments, J. N. Epstein prepared an edition which has been completed by E. Z. Melammed. Approximately two-thirds of the text in this edition are covered by Genizah fragments; the rest (in small print) derives from quotations in MHG: J. N. Epstein and E. Z. Melamed, *Mekhilta d'Rabbi Sim'on b. Jochai: Fragmenta in Geniza Cairensi reperta digessit apparatu critico, notis, praefatione instruxit. . .*, Jerusalem 1955, repr. Jerusalem 1979. (In the introduction, 13–25, Epstein presents a history of research and classification of MRS; on pp. 33–45 Melammed describes the extant Genizah fragments).

Genizah fragments not yet considered in the textual edition: S. Abramson, 'A New Fragment of the Mekhilta de-Rabbi Shim'on bar Yoḥai' (Hebrew), *Tarbiz* 41 (1971–72) 361–72 (corresponds to Epstein/Melamed 9–10); A. Glick, 'Another Fragment of the Meḳilta de-RaSHBi' (Hebr.), *Leshonenu* 48–9 (1984–85) 210–15 (Cambridge, two unconnected leaves on Exod 14.10–15 and 14.16 = Epstein/Melamed 54–57 and 59, as well as on Exod 15.1 = Epstein/Melamed 74f.); G. Ṣarfatti, 'Qeta' mitokh Mekhilta de-Rashbi', *Leshonenu* 27/28 (1962–64) 176 (=Epstein/Melamed 157, l. 5–11; cf. Z. Ben-Ḥayyim, ibid. 177f.). The latter fragment is in the Jewish Theological Seminary, New York; another fragment in that library, on Exod 3.1, is mentioned in Ch. Albeck, *Mabo*, 83 n. 9. See further M. Kahana, 'Another Page from the Mekhilta of R. Simeon b. Yoḥai' (Hebr.), *Alei Sefer* 15 (1988–89) 5–20 (Cambridge, T-S AS 77.27 = Epstein/Melamed 85, l. 25–87, l. 18); idem, 'Ginzê Midrash be-Sifriot Leningrad u-Moskvah', *Asufot* 6 (1992) 41–70 (p. 50 for additional fragments).

***c) Content and Structure***

MRS is an exegetical midrash on Exod 3.2, 7–8; 6.2; 12.1–24.10; 30.20–31.15; 34.12, 14, 18–26; 35.2. The fragmentary transmission of course does not permit a definitive judgement as to whether the original body of text was greater. However, the beginning at Exod 3 is confirmed by the medieval citation as 'Mekhilta of the thornbush'. The original structure, too, (probably like Mek arranged in *massekhtot, parashiyot* and *halakhot*) cannot be precisely ascertained; the arrangement according to *parashiyot* in the edition Epstein/Melamed is a purely pragmatic expedient.

### *d) Character, Origin and Date*

Terminology and names of rabbis classify MRS with Group II of the halakhic midrashim ('school of Aqiba'). The frequent mention of the students of Aqiba with patronym, however, is noticeable, as is the recurrent preference for the literal meaning in interpretation. The haggadah concurs with Mek.

L. Ginzberg agrees with I. Lewy that R. Ḥizkiyyah (A1) was a redactor of MRS (many anonymous sentences of MRS are in the Talmuds attributed to R. Ḥizkiyyah), but unlike Lewy, according to whom MRS has no relation to R. Simeon or his school, Ginzberg continues to hold to the authorship of R. Simeon because of the many anonymous sentences in MRS which represent Simeon's teaching. However, J. N. Epstein (introduction, 18–22 of the edition) has shown that MRS frequently omits even sentences attributed to R. Ḥizkiyyah or – more seriously – contradicts him. He infers from this that the *tanna debê Ḥizkiyyah,* who is quoted in the Talmuds, in turn used Sifre *debê Rab* on Exod (i.e. MRS). R. Simeon's teaching is also used in MRS, but according to Epstein he cannot be regarded either as the author or as the main authority of the work. MRS has only been named after him because he is the first rabbi it cites.

Epstein stresses that MRS frequently used Sifra, Sifre and T, and thus originated later than the other halakhic midrashim. De Vries, moreover, has made it likely that (at least the final redaction of) MRS knew and used Mek as a finished book. Added to this is Levine's observation that MRS treats M in Amoraic fashion and formulates it in keeping with its own halakhic views. M. D. Herr holds the same to be true for the later stage of Mishnaic Hebrew in MRS; but it is questionable whether on this basis one should follow him (p. 1270) in dating MRS no earlier than the beginning of the fifth century. Any date in the fourth century seems equally possible – but we are still in need of pertinent detailed studies which would secure a precise date.

## *4) Sifra*

#### *Bibliography*

**Albeck, Ch.** *Mabo*, 113–23, 608–10. **Brown, R.** 'A Literary Analysis of Selected Sections of Sifra' (Hebr.). *10th WCJS* (Jerusalem 1990) C 1:39–46. **Epstein, J. N.** *ITL*, 645–702.

**Finkelstein, L.** *Sifra on Leviticus.* Vol. 1: *Introduction.* New York 1989. **Finkelstein, L.** 'The Core of the Sifra: A Temple Textbook for Priests.' *JQR* N.S. 80 (1989–90) 15–34. **Herr, M. D.** *EJ* 14: 1517–19. **Melammed, E. Z.** *Introduction,* 189–194, 233–43. **Neusner, J.** *Purities,* esp. vol. 7: *Negaim: Sifra* (Leiden 1975). **Neusner, J.** *Sifra in Perspective: The Documentary Comparison of the Midrashim of Ancient Judaism.* Atlanta 1988. **Neusner, J.** *Uniting the Dual Torah: Sifra and the Problem of the Mishnah.* Cambridge 1990. **Neusner, J.** *Introduction,* 271–304. **Porton, G. G.** *Ishmael,* 2:63–81.

### *a) The Name*

*Sifra*, Aramaic 'book', designates the book of Leviticus, because in the old Jewish school system this was the first book, with which instruction began: R. Issi justifies this in LevR 7.3 (M.156) by saying that children and sacrifices are pure, and the pure should occupy themselves with pure things. This explanation is surely secondary; nor is it possible to substantiate the assumption of an ancient priestly tradition that learning began with Leviticus (thus e.g. Finkelstein, *Sifra*, 1:5). On the beginning of instruction with Lev see also ARN A6 (Sch. 29) on Aqiba. It is worth noting that both references use the customary Palestinian term *Torat Kohanim*, 'law of priests'.

Both *Sifra* and *Torat Kohanim* also designate a halakhic midrash on Lev (NB not necessarily our Sifra): e.g. Ber 47b, according to which the subjects taught are Sifra, Sifre and halakhah; according to Meg 28b and Qid 49b, etc., halakhah, Sifra, Sifre and Tosefta. *Torat Kohanim* occurs e.g. in Qid 33a, Yeb 72b and regularly as a title in the MSS. Ber 11b and 18b use the name *Sifrê debê Rab*, the commentary on Lev taught in [Rab's] schoolhouse (Goodblatt, *Instruction*, 116f. thinks that *sifra debê rab* means simply a 'schoolbook', and that there is no connection with Rab. This in itself is possible, especially with regard to Rab. However, it appears that what is intended here is not just any text book, but a quite particular book which, in keeping with later tradition, is best understood as a commentary on Lev). All these names are also common in Geonic and medieval literature, where they now definitely refer to our Sifra.

### *b) Content and Structure*

Sifra is a halakhic midrash on Lev, which in its present state of transmission comments on all of Lev verse by verse, often even word by word. Its content, in keeping with the character of Lev, is almost exclusively halakhah. As in the case of Mek, the original structure was topical (nine tractates or *dibburim*, subdivided into *parashiyot*, and each of these in turn into two or three chapters, *peraqim*). However, in the textual transmission this was adapted to the *parashiyot* of the Babylonian reading order and adulterated in other ways.

| ***Original Structure*** | ***Structure Now in Use*** |
|---|---|
| 1) 1.1–3.17 Nedabah or Wayyiqra | 1) 1.1–3.17 Nedabah or Wayyiqra |
| 2) 4.1–5.26 Ḥobah (Nefesh) | 2) 4.1–5.26 (Wayyiqra) Ḥobah |
| 3) 6.1–7.38 Ṣaw | 3) 6.1–7.38 Ṣaw |
| | 4) 8.1–36 Mekhilta de-Milluim |
| 4) 10.8–12.8 Sheraṣim | 5) 9.1–11.47 Shemini |
| 5) 12.9–13.59 Negaim | 6) 12.1–8 Tazria |
| | 7) 13.1–59 Tazria Negaim |
| 6) 14.1–15.33 Meṣorah | 8) 14.1–57 Meṣorah |
| | 9) 15.1–33 Meṣorah Zabim |
| 7) 16.1–20.27 Aḥarê (Mot) or Qedoshim | 10) 16.1–18.30 Aḥarê (Mot) |
| | 11) 19.1–20.27 Qedoshim |
| 8) 21.1–24.23 Emor | 12) 21.1–24.23 Emor |
| 9) 25.1–27.34 Sinai | 13) 25.1–55 Behar |
| | 14) 26.1–27.34 Beḥuqqotai |

### *c) Character, Origin and Date*

The version of Sifra given in the printed editions is not homogeneous. With its terminology, its exegetical method and the most important rabbis, the basic core of Sifra belongs to Group II of the halakhic midrashim ('school of Aqiba'). However, there are a number of additions in Sifra. Among these is already the introduction with the 13 rules for the interpretation of the Torah (Epstein, *ITL*, 641f.; Porton, *Ishmael*, 4:167: 'the exegetical *sugyot* in Sifra. . . do not picture Ishmael's conforming to the opening section of the text'; Finkelstein, *Sifra* 1:186f.: this section was linked with *Sifra* no later than in the Geonic period). The *Mekhilta de-Milluim* (W. 40d–46b) on Lev 8.1–10.7 (i.e. including also the first part of the present tractate Shemini; cf. Albeck, *Untersuchungen*, 81–4 and Epstein, *ITL*, 681) is certainly from Group I as well. In Shemini 17–28 this piece itself has in turn been supplemented (W. 44c–45b; the latter is missing e.g. in Cod. Ass. 66, ed. Finkelstein, 192, and in the Genizah text of Rabinovitz, *Ginzé Midrash*, 42–50). Aḥarê 13.3–15 (W. 85d–86b) and Qedoshim 9.1–7; 9.11–11.14 (W. 91c–93b) on Lev 18.6–23 and 20.9–21 were added even later: this so-called *Mekhilta de–'Arayot* was only inserted from the *Yalqut* by Aaron Ibn Ḥayyim in his *Qorban Aharon*. It is still absent from the first printed edition; in Codex Assemani 66 (Finkelstein, 370–87) it was added from another source. This text was originally not expounded in public ('before three': M.Ḥag 2.1; t.Ḥag 2.1, L. 380, which in p.Ḥag 2.1, 7a is represented as the opinion of Aqiba); it too belongs in kind to Group I of the halakhic midrashim (Epstein, *ITL*, 640f.). Finally, even the tractate Beḥuqqotai does not entirely fit the rest of Sifra; it probably belongs to another branch of the exegetical orientation represented by Sifra. Apart from this, a number of smaller pieces also entered Sifra only at a later date (see Epstein, *ITL*, 682ff.).

In Sanh 86a R. Yoḥanan names R. Yehudah (bar Ilai) as the teacher of the anonymous sentences in Sifra (cf. Shab 137a, Erub 86b, etc.). The Amoraic tradition, therefore, ascribes to Yehudah a halakhic commentary on Lev. Certain anonymous sentences of Sifra are indeed cited as Yehudah's teaching in the Talmud. It may be that Yehudah's commentary on Lev (or the commentary ascribed to him in the Talmud) served as a basic core or source for our Sifra; alternatively, these sentences may be from the general school tradition. Finkelstein, on the other hand, goes far beyond the evidence with his thesis (*Sifra*, 1:12, 21ff.; 'The Core') that Sifra derives from a Maccabean or even earlier teaching manual for priests, which was revised by Eliezer ben Hyrcanus and then by Aqiba, before being edited by R. Yehudah and further augmented at a later time.

The name *Sifrê debê Rab* led Maimonides to state, 'Rab composed Sifra and Sifre in order to explain and make known the foundations (*'iqqarê*) of the Mishnah' (introduction to *Mishneh Torah*, edn. Jerusalem 1957, *Sefer ha-Maddah*, 9; based on Ber 18b). Weiss, too, supports this theory (introduction to his edition, iv), over against the other explanation (e.g. in *ITL*, 652) that the name merely designates the commentary on Lev which was usually taught in the school of Rab. Objections to the authorship of Rab include the fact that he sometimes appears to be unaware of, or even contradicts, the solution of a problem in Sifra.

Others regard R. Ḥiyya as the author of Sifra (e.g. D. Hoffmann, 22f.; on this see Albeck, *Untersuchungen*, 119f.). He was indeed frequently occupied with Lev, and some of his teachings are also in Sifra. Epstein supposes that Ḥiyya composed a commentary on Lev which perhaps was used by the final redactor of Sifra (*ITL*, 655). Strack's theory, that the basic core of Sifra derives from Yehudah and the final redactor is R. Ḥiyya, oversimplifies matters on the basis of tradition. Sifra in fact combines the teachings of very different rabbis and from very different sources.

As Melammed (*Introduction*, 233ff.) has shown, Sifra quotes M and T with particular frequency (more than 400 passages, esp. from Negaim). Based on his study of Negaim and Meṣorah (*Pur*, vol. 7), J. Neusner initially regarded Sifra as a massive polemic against the Mishnah. Sifra on this view frequently quotes M verbatim, in order to criticize its derivation of the law from reason rather than from Scripture. Following his study of the entire text, Neusner significantly modified this thesis: 'the authorship of Sifra is careful not to criticize the Mishnah' (*Uniting*, 176); even for Sifra, M serves as 'a valid source of law on its own' (p. 99). Sifra's main concern now is not the Mishnah's lack of biblical arguments, but a 'sustained critique of applied reason' (p. 180f.). Even a direct use of the finished M and T no longer seems assured: instead, Neusner believes the redactors of Sifra filled in an early layer of simple expositions on Leviticus with a larger layer of dialectical units, using 'abundant materials from completed, free floating pericopae also utilized in the redaction of Mishnah and Tosefta' (*Sifra in Perspective*, 24).

This theory of two layers in Sifra, therefore, involves a correspondingly earlier assessment of the work, although Neusner refuses to commit himself on the question of dating (*Uniting*, 3). It remains to be determined whether this (plausible) historical model of Sifra can be verified, and indeed whether Neusner is right to speak of the 'uniform and formally coherent character of the document' (*Sifra in Perspective*, 36) – a perspective that would appear to take insufficient account of the diverse origins of various parts of Sifra (e.g. the *Mekhilta de-Milluim*). What is certain is that Sifra fills its commentary on Leviticus largely, though not everywhere equally, with material known to us from M and T; it then goes on to derive from this material the questions it asks of the biblical text. We may assume that this close interweaving of Sifra with M and T brought in its wake further additions and accommodations. Sifra and its programme, must in any case be understood less as an alternative to M than as an important complement.

There is dispute about the extent to which the Talmuds quote Sifra or merely sources in common with it. However, this seems an insufficient reason for dating Sifra (with Herr) around 400 or later. A date in the second half of the third century seems justified for the basic core of Sifra, although this text in particular had an extensive afterlife of which a satisfactory account has yet to be given.

### *d) The Text*

#### *1. Manuscripts*

Aside from the Genizah fragments, *Codex Assemani 66* of the Vatican Library is the oldest extant rabbinic manuscript. It was probably written in the tenth century (thus M. Lutzki in the *Mabo* to the facsimile, 70ff.; L. Finkelstein, ibid., 1 assumes the ninth century, while H. Cassuto, *Codices Vaticani Hebraici: Codices 1–115* (Vatican 1956), 95 thinks that a hand as early as the eighth century corrected and vocalized the text). Babylonian vocalization. Facsimile: *Sifra or Torat Kohanim According to Codex Assemani LXVI*, with a Hebrew Introduction by L. Finkelstein, New York 1956.

A very different textual tradition is offered by Vatican MS *Vat. Ebr. 31*, dated to 1073. This MS is likely to be from Egypt (Finkelstein, *l.c.*, 1); its readings are close to some Genizah fragments and to MHG. Facsimile: *Torath Cohanim (Sifra), Seder Eliyahu Rabba and Zutta Codex Vatican 31*, Jerusalem 1972. Additional MSS: Parma de Rossi 139, Oxford Neubauer 151 and London, Margulies 2:341.

G. Haneman, 'On the Linguistic Tradition of the Written Text in the Sifra MS. (Rome, Codex Assemani 66)' (Hebr.), in E. Y. Kutscher et al. (eds.), *Henoch Yalon Memorial Volume* (Jerusalem 1974), 84–98, shows the disparate origin of the various parts of Sifra in Cod. Ass. 66 by means of linguistic and external criteria.

*Genizah fragments*: N. Alloni, *Genizah Fragments*, 67–70; Rabinovitz, *Ginzé Midrash*, 15–50 (these contain Weiss 2c–3b; 3c; 4a–b; 4b–c; 20a–c; 22d–23b; 35c–d; 43d–45c: a new text of the *Mekhilta de Milluim*). Another Genizah fragment at Dropsie University in Philadelphia is described in *JQR* N.S. 13 (1922–23) 12. There are photographs of numerous fragments in Finkelstein, *Sifra*, vol. 1.

***2. Printed Editions***

*First printed edition*: Constantinople, 1523 (only a small part of the text); followed by Venice, 1545. Today one normally cites according to the edition of I. H. Weiss, Vienna 1862, repr. New York 1947. M. Friedmann, *Sifra, der älteste Midrasch zu Levitikus*, Breslau [Wroclaw] 1915, repr. Jerusalem 1967, uses various MSS but includes only Nedaba 1–19 (up to Lev 3.9). L. Finkelstein, *Sifra on Leviticus according to Vatican Manuscript Assemani 66 with variants from the other manuscripts, Genizah fragments, early editions and quotations by medieval authorities and with references to parallel passages and commentaries* (Hebr.), 5 vols., New York 1983–91 (vol. 1: *Introduction*; vol. 2: the text of chapters Nedabah and Ḥobah according to Vatican MS Assemani 66; vol. 3: variants from other MSS, printed editions and early quotations; vol. 4: commentary; vol. 5: *Indices, Selected Studies in Midrash Halakha*); A. Shoshana (ed.), *Sifra on Leviticus: According to Vatican Manuscript Assemani 66 with Variants*, vol. 1: *Baraita de-R. Ishmael. . . with the Medieval Commentaries*, Jerusalem/Cleveland 1991.

***3. Concordance***

B. Kosovsky, *Oṣar Leshon ha-Tanna'im: Sifra.* 4 vols. New York/Jerusalem 1967–69.

***4. Translations***

J. Neusner, *Sifra: An Analytical Translation,* Atlanta 1988 (translates

Finkelstein as far as he was available, then follows the edition of S. Koleditzky, Jerusalem 1961). German: J. Winter, *Sifra: Halachischer Midrasch zu Leviticus*, Breslau 1938.

### *e) Commentaries*

Hillel ben Elyaqim (Greece, 12th cent.) wrote a commentary on Sifra which has been edited by S. Koleditzky according to MS Vienna 59 and a MS of the Bodleian: *Sifra or Torat Kohanim and Commentary by R. Hillel ben R. Eliakim*, 2 parts, Jerusalem 1961. Abraham ben David (Rabad) of Posquières (1120–98): his commentary, in part already published in the first printed edition of Sifre, was also used in the commentary attributed to Samson of Sens (early 12th cent.): cf. I. Twersky, *Rabad of Posquières* (2nd edn. Philadelphia 1980), 98f.). The latter is published e.g. in the edition *Sifra* Jerusalem 1959 (this edition contains numerous commentaries). Aaron Ibn Ḥayyim (born in Fez; died in Jerusalem, 1632) is the author of the detailed commentary *Qorban Aharon*, Venice 1609–11, repr. Jerusalem 1970, which also includes all pertinent Talmudic references. The annotations to Sifra by the Gaon of Wilna were first printed in *Sifra*, Jerusalem 1959; that edition also contains many other commentaries on the baraita of the 13 rules of Ishmael.

## *5) A 'Mekhilta' on Leviticus?*

***Bibliography***

**Epstein, J. N.** *ITL*, 634–43. **Klein, H.** 'Mekilta on the Pentateuch.' *JQR* N.S. 35 (1944–45) 421–34. **Melammed, E. Z.** *Introduction*, 213f. **Rabinovitz, Z. M.** *Ginzé Midrah*, 51–59.

The very fact of additions to Sifra from the alternative school of interpretation (*Mekhilta de-Milluim* and *Mekhilta de-'Arayot*) suggests that there may originally have been two commentaries on Lev as well. In support of this assumption, J. N. Epstein cites the interpretations of Lev which in the Talmuds are cited as *teni R. Yishmael* or *tanna debê R. Yishmael* (this material fully treated in Porton, *Ishmael*, vol. 3). Such quotations of course cannot prove, but may at best intimate, the existence of a continuous commentary on Lev from the 'school of Ishmael'. Further relevant material appears in T: Epstein identifies t.Shebu 3 (Z. 449f.) as a commentary of the school of Ishmael on Lev 5.1; and t.Shebu 1.5–7 (Z. 446f.), as the same on Lev 5.2. He also points out the insertion in Sifra Shemini 5.4 in MS Rome 31, as well as numerous pieces in MSS and editions of Sifre (cf. also L. Finkelstein, 'Prolegomena to the Sifre', *PAAJR* 3 (1932) 26ff.; repr. in idem, *Sifra*, 5:76*ff.).

Z. M. Rabinovitz has published a page of a Yemenite manuscript (c.

14th cent.) with a commentary on Lev 9.16–10.5, apparently a continuation of the text in L. Ginzberg, *Ginze Schechter*, 1:67–83. The text combines various midrashim, but most of them appear to belong to the so-called 'school of Ishmael'.

### *6) Sifre Numbers*

***Bibliography***

**Albeck**, *Mabo*, 123–27. **Epstein, J. N.** *ITL*, 588–624. **Herr, M. D.** *EJ* 14: 1519f. **Horovitz, S.** Introduction to his edition of the text. **Karl, Z.** *Meḥqarim be-Sifrê*. Tel Aviv 1954. **Melammed, E. Z.**, *Introduction*, 195–202. **Neusner, J.** *Bab*, 183–87. **Neusner, J.** Introduction to his translation. **Neusner, J.** *Introduction*, 305–27. **Pérez Fernández, M.** *Parabolas Rabinicas*. Murcia 1988. [Cf. also M. Pérez Fernández, *Sefarad* 46 (1986) 391–96; 47 (1987) 363–81, on biblical interpretation in SifreNum.]

#### *a) The Name*

*Sifrê*, 'books' (e.g. in the constellation 'Halakhah, Sifra, Sifre and Tosefta' in Ber 47b, Ḥag 3a, etc.), designates a halakhic commentary on Exod, Num and Deut. The Exod commentary was still included as late as the Geonic period; but in North Africa and Europe, the name Sifre was in the Middle Ages applied only to the extant halakhic commentaries on Num and Deut. The expression *she'ar sifrê debê rab* (Yoma 74a, BB 124b) in BT appears to designate simply 'the other schoolbooks', without reference to the person of Rab; their precise content cannot be determined (Yoma quotes an explanation of Lev, BB one on Deut). Ḥananel (on Shebu 37a) cites SifreNum §28 as *Sifrê debê Rab*, i.e. he relates the expression to our midrashim on Num and Deut and takes Rab as a proper name; he thus regards the two midrashim as composed by Rab (so also Rambam) or at least as having been taught in his school. One occasionally encounters the designation *Midrash Wishalḥu* for SifreNum (e.g. in the *Arukh*), since the commentary begins with Num 5.

#### *b) Content and Structure*

SifreNum is an exegetical midrash on Num. It begins with 5.1, the first legal portion of Num. Longer narrative units like Num 13–14 or 16–17 are completely omitted; but in the treated portions the narrative parts are included, so that some haggadah is also offered. The original structure was purely substantive and independent of the synagogal order of reading: parashiyot divided into baraitot. This arrangement was subsequently blurred in MSS and printed editions. The arrangement used today divides the text into paragraphs (*pisqa'ot*) which largely correspond to the verse structure of the Bible. In addition it is conventional to cite the name of the paragraph of the respective reading: §§1–58 = Parashah *Naso* (on Num 5–7); §§59–106 =

P. *Beha'alotekha* (on Num 8–12); §§107–15 = P. *Shelaḥ* (on Num 15); §§116–22 = P. *Koraḥ* (on Num 18); §§123–30 = P. *Ḥuqqat* (on Num 19); §131 = P. *Balaq* (on Num 25.1–13); §§132–52 = P. *Pinḥas* (on Num 26.52–30.1); §§153–58 = P. *Mattot* (on Num 30.2–31.24); §§159–61 = P. *Mas'ê* (on Num 35.9–34).

### c) Character, Origin, Date

SifreNum belongs to Group I of the halakhic midrashim ('school of Ishmael'). SifreNum prefers the same rabbis (especially Ishmael, Yoshiyyah, Jonathan, Nathan), the same terminology and the same exegetical method as Mek. Here, too, there are numerous texts which in other rabbinic writings are attributed to R. Ishmael, although along with differences and contradictions.

Sifre Num is not a homogeneous text. A long haggadic piece in *Beha'alotekha* (§§78–106) is conspicuous for its different terminology and different names of Tannaites. This evidently reflects an attempt to balance the two midrashic schools, which entailed tensions and inner contradictions. §131 (*Balaq*) belongs to Group II, and the Haggadah in §§134–41 also derives from a source different from the rest of SifreNum.

Yoḥanan's statement in Sanh 86a that the anonymous sentences in Sifre correspond to R. Simeon (b. Yoḥai) does not apply to our Sifre on Num and Deut, since the latter is a compilation of various midrashim. Only certain pieces in SifreNum appear to derive from the circles around Simeon b. Yoḥai (Epstein, *ITL*, 601 includes §§42, 119, 128). As in the case of the other halakhic midrashim, there is no certainty about whether the Talmuds knew and quoted SifreNum or whether they only quote common sources. The most likely date for the formation of Sifre Num is some time after the middle of the third century.

### d) Text

#### 1. Manuscripts and Printed Editions

H. S. Horovitz's critical edition *Siphre D'be Rab: Fasciculus primus: Siphre ad Numeros adjecto Siphre zutta*, Leipzig 1917, 2nd edn. Jerusalem 1966 (to be supplemented with the collation of MS Berlin in Kuhn's translation) is based on the following manuscripts: British Museum MS Add. 16006, which has numerous omissions due to homoioteleuton; MS Vatican 32 (10th or early 11th cent.; facsimile Jerusalem 1972; cf. M. Bar-Asher, 'A Preliminary Study of Mishnaic Hebrew as Reflected in Codex Vatican 32 of Sifre-Bemidbar' (Hebr.) *Te'udah* 3 (Tel Aviv 1983) 139–65); and a *Midrash Ḥakhamim* which contains *inter alia* excerpts of a large part of Sifre (formerly in A. Epstein's possession, now at the Jewish Theological Seminary, New York).

In addition there is MS State Library of Berlin (MS Orient. Quart. 1594), probably written in the fourteenth century in Northern Italy; K. G. Kuhn considers it to be the most important textual witness of SifreNum (see his translation of SifreNum, 708; on pp. 703–85 he presents a description and collation of the MS). M. Kahana (*Prolegomena*, 12–23), by contrast, assesses it much more cautiously. See also L. Finkelstein, *PAAJR* 3 (1931–32) 3ff. (repr. in *Sifra* 5:53*ff.).

*First printed edition*: Venice 1545, together with Sifre Deut (repr. Jerusalem 1970–71). Comprehensive list of textual witnesses: M. Kahana, *Prolegomena to a New Edition of the Sifre on Numbers* (Hebr.), Jerusalem 1986; idem, *Asufot* 6 (1992) 44–48: MS Firkovitch II A 269 (= ed. H. 7–37) in Leningrad.

***2. Translations***

J. Neusner, *Sifré to Numbers: An American Translation and Explanation*, 2 vols. (§§ 1–115), Atlanta 1986 (the concluding volume 3 is due to be produced in 1995 by W. S. Green). German: K. G. Kuhn, *Der tannaitische Midrasch Sifre zu Numeri übersetzt und erklärt*, Stuttgart 1959. Spanish: M. Pérez Fernández, *Midrás Sifre Números: Versión critica, introducción y notas*. Valencia 1989.

***3. Concordance***

B. Kosovsky, *Thesaurus 'Sifrei': Concordantiae verborum quae in 'Sifrei' Numeri et Deuteronomium reperiuntur*, 5 vols., Jerusalem 1971–74.

List of biblical passages and rabbinic parellels: D. Börner-Klein, *Midrasch Sifre Numeri: Voruntersuchungen zur Redaktionsgeschichte*, Frankfurt 1993.

***e) Commentaries***

The commentary of Hillel ben Elyakim (12th cent.) is important for textual criticism; he also quotes various earlier commentaries such as that of Hai Gaon. It is included in the Sifre edition of S. Koleditzky, 2 vols., Jerusalem 1983, which also contains the annotations of the Gaon of Wilna (cf. M. Kahana, 'The Commentary of R. Hillel on Sifre' (Hebr.), *KS* 63 (1990–91) 271–80). David Pardo's commentary (18th cent.) was published in 1799 at Thessaloniki, that of M. Friedmann in his edition of Sifre, Vienna 1864.

***7) Sifre Zutta (=SZ)***

***Bibliography***

**Albeck, Ch.** *Untersuchungen*, 148–51. **Albeck, Ch.** *MGWJ* 75 (1931) 404–10. [Critique of

Epstein.] **Epstein, J. N.** *ITL*, 741–46. **Epstein, J. N.** *Tarbiz* 3 (1931–32) 232–36. [Reply to Albeck, *MGWJ*; reprinted in *Studies*, 2:174–78.] **Herr, M. D.** *EJ* 14: 1522f. **Horovitz, H. S.** Introduction to his edition of the text, xv–xxi. **Lieberman, S.** *Siphre Zutta (The Midrash of Lydda)* (Hebr.). New York 1968. **Melammed, E. Z.** *Introduction*, 215–19, 249.

*Sifre Zutta*, 'the small Sifre' in distinction from SifreNum, is in medieval quotations also adduced simply as Sifre or Zutta, or as *Sifrê shel panim aḥerim*. Maimonides repeatedly cites the work as *Mekhilta (de. R. Yishmael)* in *Sefer ha-Miṣwot*. The *text* of SZ is only fragmentarily preserved in medieval quotations, in the Yalqut and MHG as well as in quotations in NumR. In addition there are two fragments from the Genizah, one of which was already published by S. Schechter (*JQR* 6 (1894) 656–63) and included by H. S. Horovitz in the appendix to SifreNum (330–34) in his textual edition (see above). J.N. Epstein, 'Sifre Zutta Parashat Parah', *Tarbiz* 1 (1929–30) 46–78 (=*Studies*, 2:141–73), published MS Firkovitch II A 313[43], a fragment comprising five leaves (corresponds to Horovitz, 300–15). Horovitz already remarked on his edition of SZ that 'much may have been included in the text which is not from *Sifre Zutta*; but with equal certainty one can claim that much is missing which was originally contained in *Sifre Zutta*' (xx). S. Lieberman sees this confirmed by comparison with the fragment published by Epstein, although the text compiled by Horovitz is probably almost complete (*Siphre Zutta*, 6). Lieberman (*Siphre Zutta*, 6–10) supplements the text of SZ with a number of other quotations.

Like SifreNum, SZ also probably began with 5.1 and gave a continuous halakhic commentary on Num, which was divided not according to the reading cycle but topically according to parashiyot.

SZ is closely connected with Group II of the halakhic midrashim ('school of Aqiba'); this is shown particularly in comparison with Sifra, with which SZ has numerous substantive and verbal parallels, but from which it also departs in many points. Especially in its exegetical terminology SZ has many forms not attested elsewhere, and several Tannaim quoted in SZ are not transmitted elsewhere. SZ quite frequently differs from M in matters of halakhah. It is also noticeable that the names of Rabbi and Nathan are never mentioned, but their teachings are instead rendered anonymously. S. Lieberman (91) regards this as a polemical concealment both of the Patriarch Rabbi and of Nathan who was related to the Exilarch.

Countering D. Hoffmann's suggestion of Simeon b. Yoḥai as the author of SZ (he applied Sanh 86a *stam sifrê R. Shim'on* to SZ), Horovitz (xvii) names R. Eliezer ben Jacob (T3), who is often named in SZ and is also repeatedly cited in rabbinic texts as the author of anonymous sentences in SZ. Epstein supposes Sepphoris as the place of final redaction (because Erub 83b mentions Sepphoris, where the parallel SZ 283, line 19 simply reads 'from us') and Bar Qappara (T5) as the editor (*ITL*, 745), while Melammed (*Introduction*, 216f.) prefers to think of the latter's contemporary, R. Ḥiyya. Like Epstein, Lieberman, 92ff. regards Bar Qappara as the final redactor, but considers Sepphoris to be impossible (it is the seat of the Patriarch, whereas SZ is so critical of the patriarchate); he therefore infers Lydda, which in late Tannaitic times was the only significant centre of Torah besides Sepphoris. In his opinion SZ is older than all other halakhic midrashim (early third century).

### *8) Sifre Deuteronomy*

***Bibliography***

**Abramson, S.** 'Arbaʿah 'Inyanot be-midreshê Halakhah.' *Sinai* 74 (1974) 9–13. **Albeck, Ch.** *Mabo*, 127–29. **Basser, H. W.** *Midrashic Interpretations of the Song of Moses*, New York 1984. [Translation and commentary on SifreDeut §§306–41.] **Basser, H. W.** *In the Margins of Midrash: Sifre Ha'azinu Texts, Commentaries, and Reflections.* Atlanta 1990. **Epstein, J. N.** *ITL*, 625–30, 703–24. **Finkelstein, L.** 'Hashpaʿat Bêt Shammai al Sifrê Debarim.' In M.D. Cassuto et al. (eds.), *Sefer Assaf* (*Festschrift* S. Assaf), 415–26. Jerusalem 1953. [Reprinted in idem, *Sifra*, 5:49–60.] **Finkelstein, L.** 'Concerning an Obscure Beraytha in the Sifre' (Hebr.). In E. Fleischer (ed.), *Studies in Literature* (*Festschrift* Simon Halkin), 181–82. Jerusalem 1973. **Fraade, S. D.** *From Tradition to Commentary: Torah and Its Interpretation in the Midrash Sifre to Deuteronomy.* Albany, NY 1991. **Fraade, S. D.** 'Sifre Deuteronomy 26 (ad Deut. 3:23): How Conscious the Composition?' *HUCA* 54 (1983) 245–301. [Also generally on problems of SifreDeut and its date.] **Goldberg, Abr.** 'The School of Rabbi Akiba and the School of Rabbi Ishmael in Sifre Deuteronomy, Pericope 1–54' (Hebr.). In M.–A. Friedman, A. Tal and G. Brin (eds.), *Studies in Talmudic Literature*, 7–16. Tel Aviv 1983. [Only §§31–54 belong to the 'school of Ishmael'.] **Gottlieb, I. B.** *Language Understanding in Sifre Deuteronomy: A Study of Language Consciousness in Rabbinic Exegesis.* Diss. New York University 1972. **Hammer, R.** 'Section 38 of Sifre Deuteronomy: An Example of the Use of Independent Sources to Create a Literary Unit.' *HUCA* 50 (1979) 165–78. **Hammer, R.** 'A Rabbinic Response to the Post Bar Kochba Era: The Sifre to Ha-Azinu.' *PAAJR* 52 (1985) 37–53. [On §§306ff.] **Herr, M. D.** *EJ* 14: 1520f. **Karl, Z.** *Meḥqarim be-Sifre.* Tel Aviv 1954. **Martínez Saiz, T.** 'La Muerte de Moisés en Sifré Deuteronomio.' In D. Muñoz León (ed.), *Salvación en la Palabra: Targum – Derash – Berith: En memoria del profesor Alejandro Díez Macho*, 205–14. Madrid 1986. **Melammed, E. Z.** *Introduction*, 202–7, 243–45. **Neusner, J.** *Sifre to Deuteronomy: An Introduction to the Rhetorical, Logical, and Topical Program.* Atlanta 1987. **Neusner, J.** *Introduction*, 328–51.

For the name see p. 266 above.

#### *a) Content and Structure*

SifreDeut is an exegetical midrash on Deut 1.1–30; 3.23–29; 6.4–9; 11.10–26.15; 31.14–32.34. Thus in addition to the legal core of Deut 12–26 there are also narrative portions (the historical prologue, the prayer of Moses, the Shema, the transfer of office to Joshua, Moses's song and blessing, as well as his death). The original structure was according to paragraphs (*Pisqa'ot*), each probably corresponding to one verse, and according to the open and closed *parashiyot* of the biblical text (not those of the Babylonian order of reading, those this was later taken into account): see Rabinovitz, *Ginzé Midrash*, 61.

***b) Text***

***1. Manuscripts and Printed Editions***

SifreDeut was first printed at Venice in 1545, together with SifreNum (repr. Jerusalem 1970–71).

Critical edition: L. Finkelstein, *Siphre ad Deuteronomium H. S. Horovitzii schedis usis cum variis lectionibus et adnotationibus*, Berlin 1939, repr. New York 1969. He follows an eclectic text. Important reviews of the first fascicles of the edition are J. N. Epstein, *Tarbiz* 8 (1936–37) 375–92 (=*Studies*, 2:889–906); S. Lieberman, *KS* 14 (1937–38) 323–36 (=*Studies*, 566–78). The edition is based above all on the following MSS (cf. L. Finkelstein, 'Prolegomena to an Edition of the Sifre on Deuteronomy', *PAAJR* 3 (1931–32) 3–42; repr. in idem, *Sifra* 5:53*–92*): *MS Rome* Assemani 32 (10th or 11th cent.) comprises the entire text of SifreNum and Deut (except on Deut 32–34); facsimile Jerusalem 1972; *Berlin* MS Orient. Quart. 1594 (see p. 268 above); *British Museum* MS Add. 16406; *MS Oxford*, Neubauer 151. The six Genizah fragments already evaluated by Finkelstein must be supplemented by another: Z. M. Rabinovitz, *Ginzé Midrash*, 60–65 (contains §§289–92, Oriental script, c. 14th cent.). T.S.c2 181 (on Deut 1.14–16; 1.30; 3.23), on the other hand, in M. Kahana's opinion does not belong here but with MidrTann; similarly a piece on 32.43ff. which is quoted in a Yalqut preserved in fragmentary form in the Genizah (see below, p. 274f.). *Quotations* in MHG, Yalqut and a Yemenite midrash (from the end of the fourteenth century, a compilation similar in kind to MHG: Leningrad Cod. II Firkovitch 225, part 4): L. Finkelstein, 'Fragment of an Unknown Midrash on Deuteronomy', *HUCA* 12–13 (1937–38) 523–57 (NB only part of the MS).

***2. Concordance***

B. Kosovsky (p. 268 above).

***3. Translations***

R. Hammer, *Sifre: A Tannaitic Commentary on the Book of Deuteronomy*, New Haven 1986; J. Neusner, *Sifré to Deuteronomy: An Analytical Translation*, 2 vols., Atlanta 1987. German: H. Bietenhard, *Der tannaitische Midrasch 'Sifre Deuteronomium'*, with a contribution by H. Ljungman, Berne 1984.

### *c) Character, Origin, Date*

SifreDeut is not a homogeneous work. §§1–54 and 304–57, i. e. the haggadic sections, do not belong together with the central legal section §§ 55–303 (Deut 11.29–26.15). By the usual criteria (rabbis, exegetical method and technical terminology), the halakhic section must be assigned to Group II of the halakhic midrashim ('school of Aqiba'); this is also demonstrated by the numerous and often verbal parallels with Sifra. Individual pieces are indeed quoted as R. Ishmael's teaching in other rabbinic texts, but these can be shown to be later additions: they generally appear late in the MSS tradition or can otherwise be identified as subsequent glosses. In the Finkelstein edition these doubtful texts are indicated in small print (cf. *ITL*, 706f., 711–24).

J. Neusner attempts to establish SifreDeut as an integral work characterized by rhetorical, logical and topical homogeneity, to which any later additions were also accommodated (*Sifre to Deuteronomy: An Introduction*). This approach, however, appears to employ criteria that are too crude, as can also be seen from the fact that on this basis it is difficult to delimit SifreDeut from Sifra and SifreNum. At least the halakhic midrashim can hardly be differentiated by means of Neusner's catalogue of criteria; another problem is that it does not enable us to isolate the blocks of material which are generally attributed to the 'school of Ishmael' on the basis of terminology and other considerations.

Sanh 86a states that the anonymous part of Sifre goes back to R. Simeon; Epstein (*ITL*, 705f.) considers that this applies best to the halakhic part of SifreDeut, since many of the passages here offered anonymously are in other rabbinic texts presented in the name of R. Simeon b. Yoḥai. The same is of course true for Rabbi and R. Ḥizkiyyah, but Epstein prefers to account for these rabbis by the use of SifreDeut in their schools (*ITL*, 709); he accounts similarly for Yoḥanan bar Nappaḥa, whom D. Hoffmann, 70f., regarded as the redactor of SifreDeut.

L. Finkelstein (in *Sefer Assaf* (S. Assaf Memorial Volume)) has proposed a detailed theory of the origin of SifreDeut in the halakhic section. Proceeding from passages in which SifreDeut advocates the halakhah of Shammai against that of Hillel, he traces these back to the Shammaite Eliezer ben Hyrcanus, whose students are assumed to have begun the redaction of SifreDeut as early as the time of Yoḥanan ben Zakkai (F. refers especially to passages which speak of the court at Yabneh). Aqiba later supposedly taught SifreDeut in his school, supplementing, correcting, and adapting it to the opinion of Hillel, but without obscuring all traces of the earlier redaction (423f.).

Finkelstein's theory goes far beyond the evidence. Eliezer cannot be considered a Shammaite, but agrees only sometimes with the opinion of this school (Neusner, *Eliezer*, 2:309). It is true that SifreDeut together with Sifra is more closely related to traditions of Eliezer than Mek (ibid., 226–33) for example, but no particular exegetical interest or even a special exegetical method can be demonstrated in it (387–98). For their reconstructions, both Finkelstein and Epstein interpreted their observations on individual traditions and possible sources of SifreDeut to imply the historical development of the writing as a whole. However, such judgements are still unfounded. Even for the halakhic part of SifreDeut we cannot affirm more than a date of the final redaction. The latter must be assumed, contrary to the school of Albeck, not around 400 but in the late third century.

The same is true for the *haggadic sections* §§1–54 and 304–57, which their terminology, names of rabbis, etc. show to be from the 'school of Ishmael' or related to it. J. N. Epstein (*ITL*, 627ff.) demonstrates the inconsistency even of the haggadic pieces. Only §§31–54 (Deut 6.4–9; 11.10–28) consistently manifest the typical characteristics of Group I (incl. also parallels to Mek); §§1–25, 26–30 and 304–57, on the other hand, are compiled from different sources, as can be seen from the names of rabbis and especially in the mixed terminology. At the same time, the haggadic material of the halakhic midrashim is to a much greater extent common property than is the halakhah. The early historical impact of SifreDeut (or at least of its material) is apparent in the Targums on Deut (I. Drazin, *Targum Onkelos to Deuteronomy* (New York 1982), 8–10, 43–47, demonstrates the dependence of Onkelos on Sifre; cf. also P. Grelot in *RB* 88 (1981) 421–25).

#### *d) Commentaries*

These are the same as for SifreNum, since the two works were transmitted as a unit (see p. 268 above). H. W. Basser has edited the Deut part of a 14th-century (?) commentary on SifreNum and Sifre Deut: *Pseudo-Rabad: Commentary to Sifre Deuteronomy Edited and Annotated According to Manuscripts and Citations*, Atlanta 1994 (the chapter Ha'azinu already appeared in idem, *In the Margins*, 182ff.).

### *9) Midrash Tannaim*

#### *Bibliography*

**Albeck, Ch.** *Untersuchungen*, 156f. **Epstein, J. N.** *ITL*, 631–33. **Herr, M. D.** *EJ* 22: 1518f. **Melammed, E. Z.** *Introduction*, 219–22.

MidrTann is the designation given by D. Hoffmann to his reconstruction of a halakhic midrash on Deut. Others prefer the designation *Mekhilta on*

*Deuteronomy*, in order thereby to stress the connection with Mekhilta, or in keeping with Maimonides's statement (in the preface to *Mishneh Torah*) that Ishmael wrote a Mekhilta on Exod through Deut.

***a) The Text***

As early as 1890, D. Hoffmann gathered quotations from MHG which were intended to prove the existence of a halakhic midrash on Deut (also on 12–26, not just on the peripheral chapters): 'Ueber eine Mechilta zu Deuteronomium', in *Shai la-Moreh* (*Festschrift* I. Hildesheimer, Berlin 1890), 83–98 and Hebrew section, 3–32. S. Schechter subsequently published two Genizah fragments: 'Genizah Fragments', *JQR* 16 (1904) 446–52; 'The Mechilta to Deuteronomy', *JQR* 16 (1904) 695–701. Together with quotations from MHG, these then became the basis for D. Hoffmann's textual edition: *Midrasch Tannaim zum Deuteronomium*, 2 parts, Berlin 1908/09; repr. Jerusalem 1984. Another Genizah fragment: S. Schechter, 'Mekhilta le-Debarim Parashat Re'eh', in M. Brann and J. Elbogen (eds.), *Festschrift zu I. Lewy's siebzigstem Geburtstag* (Breslau [Wroclaw] 1911), Hebr. section, 187–92. Since the fragment published by him in *JQR* 16:695ff. was incorrectly reproduced, J. N. Epstein re-edited it: 'Mekhilta le-parashat Re'eh', in *Abhandlungen zur Erinnerung an H. P. Chajes* (Vienna 1933), Hebr. section, 60–75 (=*Studies*, 2:125–40). Hoffmann had conjecturally 'corrected' it in his edition without reference to the MS. Additional textual sources from the Genizah, two of which were already known to L. Finkelstein but assigned by him to SifreDeut: M. Kahana, 'New Fragments of the Mekilta on Deuteronomy' (Hebr.), *Tarbiz* 54 (1984–85) 485–551; idem, 'Citations of the Deuteronomy Mekilta Ekev and Ha'azinu' (Hebr.), *Tarbiz* 56 (1986–87) 19–59; idem, 'Pages of the Deuteronomy Mekhilta on Ha'azinu and Wezot ha-Berakha' (Hebr.), *Tarbiz* 57 (1987–88) 165–201 (two leaves of 14th–15th cent. Yemenite MSS with the midrash on Deut 32.36–39 and 33.3–4). For reactions to the latter article see H. Fox, *Tarbiz* 59 (1989–90) 229–31 and H. W. Basser, ibid., 233f. (also idem, *In the Margins*, 63–66); M. Kahana's reply appears ibid., 235–41. See also H. Fox, 'The Relationship between the Midrashim Sifrei and Mechilta to Deuteronomy: on the Nature of the Yemenite Midrashic Compilations' (Hebr.), *Alei Sefer* 17 (1992–93) 97–107 (on SifreDeut 47 and Mek Deut).

Epstein (*ITL*, 632f.) infers from the comparison of the Genizah fragments with MHG that the author of the latter did not have access to a complete manuscript of the Mekhilta on Deut. That author combined texts with parallels in BT or SifreDeut, and furthermore did not simply fill the gaps in Sifre from the Mekhilta on Deut. Only about half of the MHG quotations in Hoffmann are in fact likely to derive from Mek on Deut. Such a judgement is possible on the basis of internal criteria (system of interpretation, names of rabbis, terminology). Further analysis of the textual fragments published by Kahana is bound to advance the discussion of MidrTann.

***b) Character and Origin***

MidrTann was a halakhic midrash which apparently comprised all of Deut. Fortunately the Genizah fragments happen to document precisely the transition from Deut 11 to 12, i.e. from the haggadic to the halakhic part. They generally justify Hoffmann's decision to incorporate SifreDeut §§1–54, supplemented by MHG, for the haggadic part; similarly §§304ff. The Genizah fragments show that the original arrangement was in parashiyot and halakhot.

The names of rabbis, exegetical method and terminology assign MidrTann to Group I ('school of Ishmael') of the halakhic midrashim. In view of the fragmentary and partly suspect textual condition, we cannot be specific about the origin and date. Our assessment of the other halakhic midrashim can by and large be adopted here as a preliminary working hypothesis.

At this point it is worth mentioning another halakhic midrash on Deuteronomy, which is related to Sifre Zutta and frequently quoted in the 11th-century Karaite Yeshua ben Yehudah. See M. Kahana, 'Citations from a New Tannaitic Midrash on Deuteronomy and Their Relationship to Sifre Zuta' (Hebr.), *11th WCJS* (Jerusalem 1994) C 1:23–30.

# III

# THE OLDEST EXEGETICAL MIDRASHIM

## *1) Genesis Rabbah (GenR)*


***Bibliography***

**Albeck, Ch.** 'Einleitung zum Bereshit Rabba' (Hebr.). In the appendix of the edition of Theodor/Albeck, vol. 3. 2nd edn. Jerusalem 1965. **Alexander, P. S.** 'Pre-Emptive Exegesis: Genesis Rabba's Reading of the Story of Creation.' *JJS* 43 (1992) 230–45. **Brown, R. N.** *The Enjoyment of Midrash: The Use of the Pun in Genesis Rabba.* Diss. Cincinnati: HUC-JIR, 1980 (University Microfilms, Ann Arbor 1980). **Brown, R. N.** 'A Note on Genesis-Rabba 48:17' (Hebr.). *Tarbiz* 51 (1981–82) 502. **Brown, R. N.** 'The Term 'Etmaha in Genesis Rabba.' *HUCA* 56 (1985) 167–74. **Epstein, J. N.** *IAL*, 287–90. [The relationship with PT.] **Guttmann, M.** & **Heller, B.** *EJ* 7 (1931) 241–47. **Heinemann, J.** 'The Structure and Division of Genesis Rabba' (Hebr.). *Bar-Ilan* 9 (1971) 279–89. [=Memorial Volume H. M. Shapiro, vol. 1, Ramat Gan 1972.] **Herr, M. D.** *EJ* 7: 399–401. **Lerner, M.** *Anlage des Bereschith Rabba und seine Quellen.* Berlin 1882. **Marmorstein, A.** 'The Introduction of R. Hoshaya to the First Chapter of Genesis Rabba.' In *Louis Ginzberg: Jubilee Volume*, 247–52. New York 1945. **Meir, O.** *The Darshanic Story in Genesis Rabba* (Hebr.). Tel Aviv 1987. **Meir, O.** 'Chapter Division in Midrash Genesis Rabbah' (Hebr.). *10th WCJS* (Jerusalem 1990) C 1:101–8. **Meir, O.** 'A Garden in Eden – On the Redaction of Genesis Rabba' (Hebr.). *Dappim* 5–6 (1989) 309–20. [On the chapter divisions.] **Meir, O.** 'Questions and Answers: On the Development of the Rhetoric of the Mahaloket (Conflict of Opinions) in the Palestinian Rabbinic Literature' (Hebr.). *Dappim* 9 (1993–94) 155–74. **Mirsky, A.** 'Midrash ha-Tannaim le-Bereshit.' *Sinai* 108 (1990–91) 97–128; 109 (1991–92) 212–35. [On the Tannaitic substrate of GenR.] **Neusner, J.** *Comparative Midrash: The Plan and Program of Genesis Rabbah and Leviticus.* Atlanta 1986. **Neusner, J.** *Judaism and Christianity in the Age of Constantine.* Chicago 1987. **Neusner, J.** *Introduction*, 355–81. **Odeberg, H.** *The Aramaic Portions of Bereshit Rabba: With Grammar of Galilean Aramaic.* Lund/Leipzig 1939. **Rabinowitz, L. I.** 'The Study of a Midrash.' *JQR* N.S. 58 (1967–68) 143–61. **Thoma, C.** & **Lauer, S.** *Die Gleichnisse der Rabbinen.* Part 2: *Von der Erschaffung der Welt bis zum Tod Abrahams: Bereschit Rabba 1–63.* Berne 1991. **Thorion, T.** 'MASHAL-Series in Genesis Rabba.' *TZ* 41 (1985) 160–67. **Zunz**, *GV*, 184–89.


### *a) The Name*

GenR (also known as Bereshit Rabbah in accordance with the Hebrew title of Genesis) already appears under this name in the *Halakhot Gedolot*, in the *Arukh* and elsewhere. Other early attestations include the designations *Bereshit de Rabbi Oshayah, Bereshit Rabbah de Rabbi Oshayah* and *Baraita de Bereshit Rabbah.* It is unclear why the commentary is called *Rabbah.* Zunz (*GV*, 187) supposed the original name to be *Bereshit de R. Oshayah Rabbah.* In his view the name of R. Oshaya (the midrash was named after him because it begins with *R. Oshayah pataḥ*) was later dropped, leaving *Bereshit Rabbah.* It can be objected that the best textual witnesses in fact read only *R. Oshayah*, not *R. Oshayah Rabbah.* It is unsuitable to regard Bereshit Rabbah as 'the great Genesis' in distinction from the biblical text itself, since in that case every biblical commentary would have to receive the epithet *Rabbah*. Thus we are left with the possibility that *Rabbah* distinguishes our commentary on Gen from another, smaller one. It may be intended either to contrast the more elaborate part of GenR (i.e. parashiyot 1–29) with the much more concisely worded remainder (thus J. Theodor, *MGWJ* 38 (1894) 518, who regards GenR as composed of two midrashim), or else to distinguish GenR from another, smaller midrash on Gen. The transmission of GenR together with other midrashim on the Pentateuch will have transferred the designation *Rabbah* onto them as well, and later also to the Megillot.

***b) Content and Structure***

GenR is an exegetical midrash on Gen. It offers partly simple explanations of words and sentences, partly short or elaborate haggadic interpretations and expositions, often only loosely tied to the text, which are frequently interlaced with maxims and parables. After parashah 92, the verse-by-verse exposition is abandoned. However, MS Vatican 30 transmits 95–97 in a different textual version, which must be considered original.

Printed editions usually have 100 *parashiyot*, MSS between 97 and 101, the latter number being contained in MS Vat. 30. The numbering here diverges beginning with par. 97 (=98 in Vat. 30). But in *parashiyot* 40–43, too, MSS and printed editions do not agree in their numbering. Part of the textual tradition divides 40 into 40 and 41, but combines its 43 with the 43 of the other tradition, so that agreement is restored.

By contrast to the halakhic midrashim, this work is particularly characterized by the *proems* (some of them admittedly late). All but seven *parashiyot* (13, 15, 17, 18, 25, 35, 37) contain one or more *petiḥot*. Albeck (12) counts a total of 246 *petiḥot* in GenR proper (parashiyot 1–94 as well as 95–97 according to MS Vat. 30); most of these begin with verses from the Ketubim and the majority (170) are anonymous. The number of *petiḥot* at the beginning of the *parashiyot* varies between one (in 38 cases) and nine (in parashah 53).

By what principle were the *parashiyot* divided? Albeck (97) follows Theodor in thinking that the *parashiyot* were divided largely according to the 'closed' and 'open' sections in the Bible (*setumot* and *petuḥot*; cf. J. M. Oesch, *Petucha und Setuma*, Freiburg/Göttingen 1979), and in isolated cases according to the three-year reading cycle of Palestine. However, this explanation still does not account for a large part of the *parashiyot*. For this reason J. Heinemann attempts an explanation on the basis of the *petiḥot*. These are normally to be expected before the *sedarim* which were preached on. The Palestinian cycle has a little over 40 *sedarim* for Gen. Wherever a parashah in GenR corresponds to the beginning of a *seder*, there are usually two or three proems; where this is not the case there is either no *petiḥah* (seven times) or a brief, rudimentary or even inauthentic *petiḥah*. This permits one to conclude that GenR was originally arranged according to the *sedarim* of the Palestinian reading cycle. Heinemann thinks that an excess of material led to the creation of a further 50–60 sections; proems were affixed where possible in order to achieve a homogeneous structure of the midrash, but substitute solutions were also employed. On the other hand, the considerable variations in the length of the *parashiyot* lead O. Meir to postulate a different dividing principle: she believes that the redactors were motivated by their desire to identify meaningful thematic units and to counteract the atomistic tendencies of exegetical midrashim.

***c) Sources of Genesis Rabbah***

The redactor of the Midrash draws on a wealth of rabbinic traditions. Nevertheless, in particular cases it is difficult to determine whether he has written texts before him and quotes freely, or whether he has recourse to earlier versions of the extant texts or indeed merely to a common oral tradition. The latter assumption might apply particularly to the parallels of GenR with Philo, Josephus and the intertestamental literature; on the other hand it cannot be excluded that such traditions, which of course were not cultivated in rabbinic Judaism (at least not openly), became known through contacts and discussions with Christians. Such mutual interactions in Palestine have not yet been adequately investigated.

On three occasions (ed. Theodor/Albeck 198, 461, 1152) GenR expressly appeals to Aquila's translation into Greek. There are numerous parallels with the Targums, often with explicit reference to the Targum. Differences in wording are only natural, since of course the Targums underwent an extended period of growth. But even in the numerous quotations from M and baraita (with or without reference), the redactor does not follow the precise wording as transmitted to us. Thus Albeck can deny direct borrowing from T even for verbal parallels, partly because many of these parallels also occur in PT, but above all because they tend to consist of haggadah, whose origin is difficult to substantiate. The situation is similar for the halakhic midrashim: Albeck denies their use in GenR, when it cannot be ruled out on other grounds, simply with the argument that PT itself also did not employ the halakhic midrashim (64).

As so often in the history of rabbinic literature, an unequivocal judgement regarding the direct use of certain writings cannot be achieved. It is certain, however, that the redactor of GenR will have been familiar with the content of M, T, the halakhic midrashim and the Targums.

Of particular significance for the date of GenR is the question whether the redactor used our PT or not. Frankel, *Mabo*, 51b–53a along with Zunz, *GV*, 185, took the view that GenR used and explained PT. Albeck on the other hand showed by means of a comprehensive comparison of the c. 220 parallels that GenR used a PT which resembled our PT but was different from it. That GenR used this other version of PT, rather than vice versa, is clear above all from the halakhic sayings in GenR. Almost all of them 'were initially taught to explain or supplement the Mishnah, and not on a text of Torah. That is to say, the redactor of GenR copied them from the Talmud which he had for the Mishnah' (67). From here one can also draw conclusions regarding the haggadah wherever in GenR it is parallel to PT, even if a variety of sources must be assumed for it.

***d) Redaction and Date of Genesis Rabbah***

Maimonides writes in the preface to *Mishneh Torah* that 'R. Oshayah, the pupil of our holy Rabbi, composed a commentary on the book of Genesis'. He apparently means GenR. This attribution clearly takes its point of departure in the beginning of GenR, where R. Oshayah is the first to speak. The name Genesis *Rabbah* seems to have occasioned the attribution of the work to Rabba bar Naḥmani (Babylonian, A3), for instance in a group of MSS of Abraham Ibn Daud's *Sefer ha-Qabbalah* (Cohen (123) designates this reading as a gloss, and relegates it into the apparatus).

However, a date in the third century (Oshaya) or around 300 (Rabba bar Naḥmani) is not tenable, since GenR quotes Babylonian Rabbis from c. 300, Palestinian Rabbis up to c. 400. Diocletian is also mentioned (GenR 63.8, Theodor/Albeck 688). Zunz (*GV*, 186) moreover considers that the reference in GenR 64.10 (Theodor/Albeck 710–12) to a subsequently retracted official Roman permission to rebuild the Temple cannot be seen to indicate the time of Hadrian; instead he deems this to be a misunderstood report of the attempt to build the Temple under Julian. In his opinion, the historical confusion shows that the redactor lived a long time after the events. However, such an interpretation of this text is by no means necessary. There is therefore no reason to date GenR in the sixth century. Based on the rabbis and events mentioned in GenR, only a date after 400 is required. Since GenR does not yet quote PT in its present form, but nevertheless knows even the latest layers of its content, the final redaction of this midrash will have been approximately contemporary with PT, i.e. in the fifth century, and probably in its first half.

We have no certain knowledge about the prehistory of GenR. It is impossible to verify the assumption that GenR is the expanded version of a midrash begun already by R. Oshayah; nevertheless, duplicate interpretations for certain passages might indeed be due to different preliminary stages of GenR (cf. R. N. Brown, 'Etmaha'). It is certain, however, that the redaction of GenR took place in Palestine. This is indicated not merely by the prevalence of Palestinian rabbis in GenR, but above all by its language: Hebrew predominates, with many Greek loan words; but some parts are in Galilean Aramaic. This is corroborated by tradition (Rashi on Gen 47.2 calls GenR *Aggadat Ereṣ Yisra'el*).

In the course of transmission, the text of GenR became subject to various *expansions* (but also omissions). This can be clearly seen by comparing Cod. Vat. 30 with the other textual witnesses. Such additions in parashiyot 75 (Theodor/Albeck 884–92, 894–96), 91 (Theodor/Albeck 1118–26) and 93 (Theodor/Albeck 1161–71) were already pointed out by Zunz; most of these derive from Tanḥuma. Other expansions were added only in the printed editions.

As for chapters 96–100, Zunz (*GV*, 265–67) has drawn attention to their different character as compared with the rest of GenR; he emphasized that much of the content agrees with Tanḥuma. What is more, most MSS contain the exposition of Jacob's blessing (Gen 49) in a later recension, partly adopted from homilies of Tanḥuma, which is also quoted in the *Arukh* and in the *Yalqut*. This version is called *shittah ḥadashah*. Albeck 103f. concedes that chapters 95 and 96 are homilies from Tanḥuma; but these should be replaced by the genuine GenR-parashiyot 95–97 preserved in Vat. 30. However, the four last parashiyot, 98–101 (or 97–100 in the usual printed editions), are a genuine part of GenR, with the exception of the paragraphs marked *lishana aḥarina* in the last two parashiyot. The parallels with Tanḥuma do not mean that Tanḥuma was the source of GenR. By means of new textual material, L. M. Barth (*An Analysis of Vatican 30* (Cincinnati 1973), 89ff.) has demonstrated the authenticity of certain passages in Vat. 30 which Albeck (104, 108) had suspected as additions.

***e) The Text***

***1. Manuscripts*** (Description in Albeck, 104–17)

*MS Vat. Ebr. 60* of the Vatican Library is the oldest extant manuscript of GenR; yet it was not used in the Theodor/Albeck edition. H. Cassuto, *Codices Vaticani Hebraici 1–115* (Vatican 1956), 87, dates the MS to c. the tenth century. Facsimile: *Midrash Bereshit Rabba: Codex Vatican 60 (Ms. Vat. Ebr. 60): A Previously Unknown Manuscript, Recently Established as the Earliest and most Important Version of Bereshit Rabba*, Jerusalem 1972; another facsimile: Copenhagen 1981 (with an English introduction by M. Sokoloff). M. Sokoloff, *The Genizah Fragments of Genesis Rabba and Ms. Vat. Ebr. 60 of Genesis Rabba* (Hebr.), Diss. Jerusalem 1971.

*MS Vat. Ebr. 30*, written in Egypt in the tenth or eleventh century by several scribes, is considered the best textual version of GenR (thus Albeck, Kutscher, et al.). It is superior to the older MS Vat. Ebr. 60, although the beginning and end as well as parts of the main body are missing. Facsimile: M. Sokoloff, *Midrash Bereshit Rabba (Ms. Vat. Ebr. 30) with an Introduction and Index*, Jerusalem 1971. L. M. Barth, *An Analysis of Vatican 30*, Cincinnati 1973; E. Y. Kutscher, *Studies in Galilean Aramaic* (Ramat Gan 1976), 11–41; M. Sokoloff, 'The Hebrew of Berešit Rabba according to Ms. Vat. Ebr. 30' (Hebr.), *Leshonenu* 33 (1968–69) 25–42, 135–49, 270–79.

*MS British Museum*, Add. 27169, containing GenR and LevR, was chosen by Theodor as the base text for his edition. Albeck, 105 maintains that this MS was written prior to the year 1000 (according to a gloss the Messiah is expected in that year), while Herr, 401 dates it to the middle of the twelfth century. Description: J. Theodor, 'Der Midrasch Bereschit Rabba', *MGWJ* 37 (1893), 38 (1894) and 39 (1895) in 12 instalments.

Additional MSS are in Paris (Bibl. Nat. No. 149: GenR, LevR and part of NumR, written at Arles in 1291), Leningrad (Firkovitch I 241, 43 leaves, 13th or 14th cent.), Oxford, Stuttgart and Munich.

### *2. Genizah Fragments*

The Theodor/Albeck edition already incorporated into the apparatus certain pages from the Genizah in the Bodleian Library at Oxford (parts of GenR 33, 34, 70, 74). In the index section, 146–50, Albeck reproduces three leaves from Cambridge (first published by E. Levine, *JQR* 20 (1907–08) 777–83) and one from Oxford (parts of GenR 1.4 and 5). The texts in A. S. Lewis/M. D. Gibson, *Palestinian Syriac Texts* (London 1900), Plates II and III (texts transcribed in L. M. Barth, *An Analysis of Vatican 30*, 329–35; parts of GenR 1, 2, 56, 57) are not evaluated. N. Alloni, *Genizah Fragments*, 51–62 described additional fragments (also reproduced in facsimile): however, the palimpsest texts which he regards as fragments of a single manuscript belong in fact to two different palimpsests, one over a Christian-Aramaic text and the other over a Greek uncial text from the New Testament. All the Genizah fragments known up to now, 12 manuscripts in total, have been linguistically analysed and transcribed (in addition to facsimile examples from every MS) by M. Sokoloff in the order of GenR: *The Geniza Fragments of Bereshit Rabba: Edited on the Basis of Twelve Manuscripts and Palimpsests with an*

*Introduction and Notes* (Hebr.), Jerusalem 1982. Generally on the palimpsests from the Genizah, with lists of the texts hitherto identified, see M. Sokoloff and J. Yahalom, 'Christian Palimpsests from the Cairo Geniza', *Revue d'Histoire des Textes* 8 (1978) 109–32. Yahalom 115f. on the whole assumes a date between 500 and 600 for the lower script; hence the upper script could have originated c. 600 at the earliest, although it could also be as late as the tenth century or later.

***3. Printed Editions*** (cf. Albeck, 117–38)
GenR was first printed at Constantinople in 1512 together with the other writings of the Midrash Rabbah on the Pentateuch, probably based on several MSS, one of which must have been of the nature of Vat. Ebr. 30. However, one also encounters here many additions not found in any MS; these are taken from PT, other midrashim, and from the commentary on GenR attributed to Rashi (Albeck, 127f.). GenR was printed a second time in 1545 in Venice, now including also the midrashim on the Megillot, which were first published in 1519 (in Pesaro?). In addition to the first printed edition, a manuscript was used; but many independent changes were also made in the text (Albeck, 131). The 1545 edition then became the basis for the numerous further editions of the Midrash Rabbah; the most important one is that of Romm, Wilna 1887, which also contains a good many traditional commentaries. The latter is the basis for M. A. Mirkin's *Midrash Rabbah*, 11 vols. (GenR in vols. 1–4), Tel Aviv 1956–67, although this edition also takes into account Theodor/Albeck. We should further mention E. E. Hallewy's edition, *Midrash Rabbah*, 8 vols., Tel Aviv, 1956–63. Both editions provide a vocalized text of the *Rabbot* on the Pentateuch.

The critical edition of J. Theodor & Ch. Albeck, *Midrash Bereshit Rabba: Critical Edition with Notes and Commentary*, 3 vols., Jerusalem 1965 (repr. of Berlin 1912–36, with corrections) is based on the British Museum MS, but incorporates in the apparatus almost all the MSS material which was known at the time. The edition is exemplary, even though Albeck himself already realized that MS Vat. 30 rather than MS London should have been the basis (this is also the judgement of L. M. Barth, *Analysis*, 120). However, a new edition seems desirable on account of both the Genizah material discovered in the meantime and also of MS Vat. 60, which was overlooked by Theodor and Albeck despite its correct identification in the catalogue of the Assemani brothers.

***4. Translations***
H. Freedman & M. Simon (eds.), *Midrash Rabbah: Translated into English*,

10 vols., London 1939, 3rd edn. 1961 (GenR in vols. 1–2, trans. H. Freedman); J. Neusner, *Genesis Rabbah: The Judaic Commentary on Genesis: A New American Translation*, 3 vols., Atlanta 1985. German: A. Wünsche, *Bibl. Rabb.*, Leipzig 1881, repr. Hildesheim 1967. Italian: A. Ravenna, Turin 1978. French: B. Maruani & A. Cohen-Arazi, Paris 1987.

### *f) Commentaries*

The 1567–68 Venice edition of GenR has in the inner margin the commentary wrongly attributed to Rashi (cf. J. Theodor in M. Brann & J. Elbogen (eds.), *Festschrift zu I. Lewy's siebzigstem Geburtstag,* Breslau 1911; R. N. Brown, 'An Antedate to Rashi's Commentary to Genesis Rabba' (Hebr.), *Tarbiz* 53 (1983–84) 478: at least some parts must be older than 1291), and in the outer margin that of Abraham ben Asher, a student of Joseph Karo at Safed, later a rabbi in Aleppo. The Venice edition entitles both commentaries together as *Or ha-Sekhel.* A MS at Mantua contains an anonymous 12th-century commentary (Y. Ta-Shma, 'An Unpublished Early Franco-German Commentary on Bereshit and Vayikra Rabba, Mekilta and Sifre' (Hebr.), *Tarbiz* 55 (1985–86) 61–75). In the mid–13th century, R. Isaac ben Yedayah commented on the entire Midrash Rabbah (MS 5028 of the Jewish Theological Seminary, New York); cf. M. Saperstein, 'The Earliest Commentary on the Midrash Rabba', in I. Twersky (ed.), *Studies in Medieval Jewish History and Literature* (Cambridge, MA 1979), 283–306; idem in *REJ* 138 (1979) 17–45. R. Issachar Baer ben Naftali ha-Kohen's very popular commentary *Mattenot Kehunnah* was completed in 1584 (on the entire Midrash Rabbah); the section on GenR was first published in the Cracow 1587–88 edition of the Midrash Rabbah. The author was very interested in textual criticism and attempted to correct mistakes in the printed editions by means of MSS. Further commentaries are given in M. Benayahu, 'R. Samuel Yaffe Ashkenazi and Other Commentators of Midrash Rabba' (Hebr.), *Tarbiz* 42 (1972–73) 419–60. A modern commentary is included in the Theodor/Albeck edition under the title *Minḥat Yehudah.* However, this has a primarily text-critical orientation. A simple substantive commentary in Hebrew is in the edition of Mirkin as well as in that of Hallewy.

## *2) Lamentations Rabbah (LamR)*

#### *Bibliography*

**Abrahams, J.** *The Sources of the Midrash Echah Rabbah.* Dessau 1881. **Baarda, T.** 'A Graecism in Midrash Echa Rabba I, 5.' *JSJ* 18 (1987) 69–80. **Cohen, S. J. D.** 'The Destruction: From Scripture to Midrash.' *Prooftexts* 2 (1982) 18–39. **Hazan-Rokem, G.** '"Echa?. . . Ayekah?" – On Riddles in the Stories of Midrash Echah Rabbah' (Hebr.). *JSHL* 10–11 (1987–88, Jerusalem 1988), 2:531–47. **Hazan-Rokem, G.** 'Perspectives of Comparative Research of Folk Narratives in

Aggadic Midrashim – Enigmatic Tales in Lamentations Rabba, I' (Hebr.). *Tarbiz* 59 (1989–90) 109–31. **Heller, B.** *EJ* 10 (1934) 48–50. **Herr, M. D.** *EJ* 10: 1376–78. **Neusner, J.** *The Midrash Compilations of the Sixth and Seventh Centuries: An Introduction to the Rhetorical, Logical and Topical Program.* Vol. 1: *Lamentations Rabbah.* Atlanta 1989. **Neusner, J.** *Introduction*, 510–32. **Stern, D.** *Parables in Midrash.* Cambridge, MA 1991. **Zulay, M.** 'An Ancient Poem and Petichoth of Echa Rabbati' (Hebr.). *Tarbiz* 16 (1944–45) 190–95. **Zunz**, *GV*, 189–91.

***Text***

**Buber, S.** *Midrasch Echa Rabbati: Sammlung aggadischer Auslegungen der Klagelieder.* Wilna 1899, repr. Hildesheim 1967. **Krupp, M.** 'The Yemenite Version of Midrash Lamentations Rabbah' (Hebr.). *10th WCJS* (Jerusalem 1990) C 1:109–16. **Rabinovitz, Z. M.** *Ginzé Midrash*, 118–54. **Rabinovitz, Z. M.** 'Genizah Fragments of Midrash Ekha Rabba' (Hebr.). *6th WCJS* (Jerusalem 1977) 3:437–39.

### *a) The Name*

LamR is also called *Midrash Threni* or *Ekhah Rabbati*, after its Hebrew opening. The latter name is already used by Rashi on Isa 22.1 and Jer 40.1. Originally this title probably applied only to chapter 1 (in Lam 1.1 Jerusalem is called *rabbati 'am*) and was subsequently extended to the other chapters (thus Zunz, *GV*, 189 n.(e); Buber, on the other hand (*Mabo*, 3 n. (a)), explains *Rabbati* as denoting the contrast with a small midrash on Lam, *Ekhah Zutta*). Other designations are *Aggadat Ekhah* (*Rabbati*) (thus Ḥananel); *Megillat Ekhah* (Arukh); *Midrash Qinot* (Rashi on Exod 12.3); *Midrash Ekhah* (Rashi on Isa 43.24).

### *b) The Text*

LamR, an exegetical midrash on Lam to which a number of *petiḥot* have been prefixed, is transmitted in two textual recensions. One is represented by the first printed edition, Pesaro 1519 (repr. Berlin 1926, together with the other Megillot), the other by the Buber edition, which uses as its textual basis MS J. I.4 of the Biblioteca Casanata in Rome. This textual version is attested by quotations in the Arukh and in medieval authors. However, Buber's MS (which records on the last page a purchase receipt dated 1378) *inter alia* lacks the *petiḥot*, which he therefore adopted from Cod. 27089 of the British Museum (dated 1504); yet even the latter manuscript, a compilation containing 19 different writings, lacks *petiḥot* 1–4, for which it simply refers to PRK as a source. Five additional MSS are preserved in Parma, of which MS De Rossi 1240 was written in the year 1270. Two MSS are in the Vatican Library, one at Oxford, another (dated 1295) at Munich; the text of the latter resembles the first printed edition and may have served as its basis. A description of the MSS is in Buber, *Mabo*, 73–77.

Rabinovitz has published several Genizah fragments: a fragment of three leaves in Cambridge contains the text of several *petiḥot*; one leaf in

Leningrad, the midrash on 1.17 and 16; another, in Cambridge, the midrash on 3.64–4.2. The fragments, all in oriental script and dated to the eleventh or twelfth century by Rabinovitz, significantly differ from the two familiar versions in textual arrangement, content and language, but are generally closer to the first printed edition than to the Buber edition. The fragments illustrate how in the course of transmission Greek words were adulterated, rare expressions altered, linguistic peculiarities assimilated to the style of BT or of medieval Hebrew, and how the arrangement of the text was also subject to multiple alterations. Thus, despite their small extent the Genizah fragments are valuable witnesses of a very early stage of development of the midrash. A critical edition is being prepared in Jerusalem by P. Mandel.

*Translations*: A. Cohen, *Lamentations*, in: *Midrash Rabbah: Translated into English*, ed. H. Freedman/M. Simon, London 1939, repr. 1961. J. Neusner, *Lamentations Rabbah: An Analytical Translation.* Atlanta 1989. German: A. Wünsche, *Bibl. Rabb.*, Leipzig 1881, repr. Hildesheim 1967.

***c) Content and Redaction***

LamR is introduced by numerous *petiḥot*, which will be further discussed below. The actual commentary is divided into five parashiyot in keeping with the five chapters of Lam. These provide a continuous, verse-by-verse exposition, including on the one hand simple lexical and substantive explanations, but also sundry parables and stories. On the 9th of Ab, Lam was read and expounded in the synagogues to commemorate the destruction of the Temple in the year 70. For this reason many stories about the destruction of Jerusalem in 70 have been incorporated but also about other times of crisis under Trajan and Hadrian as well as in the Bar Kokhba revolt. Similarly, themes of the earlier martyrdom tradition were also adopted, such as the well-known story from 2 and 4 Macc about the mother with her seven sons who die as martyrs. Interspersed in the text are other stories intended to show the superiority of the inhabitants of Jerusalem over those of Athens. The parallels with Flavius Josephus need not be explained by a direct use of his work.

In addition to Tannaites, LamR cites primarily Palestinian Amoraim, none of whom is later than the fourth century. This speaks for an early origin in Palestine; the same is also true for the language, in which Hebrew stands alongside Galilean Aramaic and numerous Greek (e.g. *nikétés barbarôn* in Petiḥah 23) as well as Latin phrases are found (e.g. Yoḥanan ben Zakkai's address to Vespasian in 1.5, *vive domine imperator*).

LamR uses M and T as well as Mek, Sifra and Sifre. The midrash has numerous parallels with PT (cf. e.g. 1.2 with p.Taan 4, 59d–60c). However, the major differences in the text would appear to speak in favour of the use of a common source rather than for a direct dependence. It is doubtful whether PRK has been used: what is said on Psa 77.7f. in 1.2 might be borrowed from PRK 17 (M. 281), but the reverse is more plausible.

LamR itself appears to have been used in LevR, RuthR, and in a number of other midrashim. However, despite the long collection of parallel material in Git 55b–58a, its use in BT cannot be assumed. The question of an influence of BT on LamR, on the other hand, belongs not to the redactional history of the midrash but to the history of its textual transmission; this is also illustrated particularly by the Genizah fragments.

Based on its supposed allusions to Arab rule, Zunz (*GV*, 190f.) dated LamR to the seventh century. However, the Buber edition 77 on 1.15 reads not (Edom and) Ishmael but Seir. Buber (*Mabo*, 9) on the other hand dates the text too early, viz., in the fourth century (because he dates PT 200 years after the destruction of the Temple!). Most likely is a date of origin in the fifth century, probably in its first half. However, the popularity of the midrash meant that the text was treated very liberally: even later on, pieces from other writings were incorporated or the text was adapted to parallel traditions, and conversely some genuine material was very likely deleted. Individual later traits, therefore, cannot be taken into account for the redaction of the midrash as such; on the other hand, the date here proposed covers only the basic form of the midrash, which is perhaps most nearly represented by the Genizah fragments.

***d) The Petiḥot***

The petiḥot at the beginning of the midrash constitute more than a quarter of the work. There are now 34, although Nos. 2 and 31 are each composed of two proems, so that there are a total of 36; perhaps this is intentional, since 36 is the numerical value of the word *êkhah*. The petiḥot correspond to the classical type; 20 are based on prophetic texts, 13 from the 'Writings' (NB two of them from Lam itself), three from the Pentateuch.

It is not possible to determine *by what principle the petiḥot were arranged*. Herr (1377) surmises that they are grouped according to the number of petiḥot in the names of the various rabbis, beginning with the rabbis who provide four petiḥot and descending to those of whom only one petiḥah is included. However, this proposal matches neither the arrangement of the Buber edition nor that of the other printed editions (which agree with Buber in this regard): first there are three petiḥot of Abba bar Kahana, then four each of Abbahu, Isaac and Ḥanina b. Pappa, two each of Abbahu, Abin, etc.; after three single petiḥot there are again two in the name of Zabdi, and in three cases (2b, 31b, 34) the name and introduction are missing. Above all, however, the Genizah fragment has a completely different sequence of petiḥot: 23, 16, 19, 18, 17, 24, 25; and in petiḥah 16 it cites Abun instead of Abbahu.

The Genizah text also shows a standard ending for all petiḥot: 'When they were exiled, Jeremiah began to mourn for them and to say, "How lonely she sits" [Lam 1.1].' In MSS and printed editions this stereotypical conclusion of the petiḥot has in part been deleted. On the other hand the Genizah text lacks *inter alia* a long piece on God's lament, etc., in petiḥah 24, which for various reasons has long been suspected as a late addition (e.g. A. Goldberg, *Untersuchungen über die Vorstellung von der Schekhinah* (Berlin 1969), 135).

S. Buber (*Mabo* 4) surmised that it was not the redactor of LamR who included the petiḥot in the text, but a later compiler who already used LamR, among other things. M. Zulay by contrast observes that the petiḥot are already presupposed in the ancient *Piyyut* and therefore must have been familiar in Byzantine times ('An Ancient Poem', 190). However, this argument is valid only for the individual pieces used in the *Piyyut* (at any rate 21 of 36, according to Zulay), and not for the totality of the petiḥot, some of which (e.g. the first four) appear to have been taken from PRK (or they have material in common; or vice versa?). The (late) Yemenite MSS lack the initial petiḥot of the printed editions (Krupp, 113). The textual history of LamR at any rate illustrates the susceptibility of this introduction to later supplementation and revision, even if a basic core of the petiḥot does in fact go back to the redactor of the midrash. Whether the petiḥot (or at least some of them) derive from actual synagogue sermons is of no consequence in the present context.

# IV

# HOMILETICAL MIDRASHIM

## *1) Leviticus Rabbah (LevR)*

***Bibliography***

**Albeck, Ch.** 'Midrash Wayyiqra Rabbah.' In *Louis Ginzberg: Jubilee Volume*, Hebr. vol., 25–43. New York 1945. **Cohen, N. J.** 'Leviticus Rabbah, Parashah 3: An Example of a Classic Rabbinic Homily.' *JQR* N.S. 72 (1981–82) 18–31. **Goldberg, Abr.** 'The Term *gufa* in Midrash Leviticus Rabba' (Hebr.). *Leshonenu* 38 (1973–74) 163–69. **Goldberg, Abr.** 'On the Authenticity of the Chapters "Vayehi baḥazi hallayla" (Ex. XII,29) and "Shor o Kesev" (Lev. XXII,27) in the Pesiqta' (Hebr.). *Tarbiz* 38 (1968–69) 184–85. [*Contra* Heinemann, *Tarbiz*.] **Heinemann, J.** 'Chapters of Doubtful Authenticity in Leviticus Rabba' (Hebr.). *Tarbiz* 37 (1967–68) 339–54. **Heinemann, J.** 'The Art of Composition in Leviticus Rabbá' (Hebr.). *Hasifrut* 2 (1969–71) 809–34. **Heinemann, J.** 'Profile of a Midrash: The Art of Composition in Leviticus Rabba.' *JAAR* 31 (1971) 141–50. [Summary of the previous article.] **Heinemann, J.** *EJ* 11: 147–50. **Kadushin, M.** *A Conceptual Commentary on Midrash Leviticus Rabbah.* Atlanta 1987. **Künstlinger, D.** *Die Petichot des Midrasch rabba zu Leviticus.* Krakau 1913. **Margulies, M.** Vol. 5 of his textual edition: *Introduction, Supplements and Indices* (Hebr.). Jerusalem 1960. **Neusner, J.** *Judaism and Scripture: The Evidence of Leviticus Rabbah.* Chicago 1985. **Neusner, J.** *The Integrity of Leviticus Rabbah: The Problem of the Autonomy of a Rabbinic Document.* Chico, CA 1985. [Summary in *PAAJR* 53 (1986) 111–45; cf. S. Fraade, *Prooftexts* 7 (1987) 179–94.] **Neusner, J.** 'Appropriation and Imitation: The Priority of Leviticus Rabbah over Pesiqta deRab Kahana.' *PAAJR* 54 (1987) 1–28. **Neusner, J.** *Introduction*, 382–410. **Rabbinowitz, Z. M.** 'Two Supplements to the Collection of Liturgical Poems by Yannai' (Hebr.). *4th WCJS* (Jerusalem 1968) 2:49f. [Use of LevR.] **Sarason, R. S.** 'The Petiḥtot in Leviticus Rabba: "Oral Homilies" or Redactional Constructions?' *JJS* 33 (1982 = *Festschrift* Y. Yadin) 557–67. **Visotzky, B.** 'Anti-Christian Polemic in Leviticus Rabbah.' *PAAJR* 56 (1990) 83–100. **Zunz,** *GV*, 191–95.

### *a) The Name*

In keeping with the Hebrew opening of Lev, the MSS usually cite this midrash as *Wayyiqra Rabbah* ('Rabbah' probably having been adopted from GenR), or occasionally as *Haggadat Wayyiqra*, *Haggadah de-Wayyiqra* and the like.

### *b) Text*

Margulies used as the basis of his edition *British Museum* Add. MS 27169 (Catalogue No. 340), which contains GenR and LevR and was also the foundation for Theodor and Albeck's edition of GenR (description of the MS by Albeck, ibid., *Mabo*, 105ff.). *Vatican Cod. Hebr.* 32 (facsimile Jerusalem 1972) contains LevR as well as SifreNum and Deut and probably dates from the tenth or eleventh century. For LevR the MS goes back to a common *Vorlage* with the MS of the British Museum, as can be seen from the common omissions and abridgments. MS 149 of National Library at Paris belongs to the same text family; it also contains GenR and the beginning of NumR, and is dated to 1291. Margulies used *MS Munich 117* (from the year 1433) only in part. Additional MSS are in the Bodleian at Oxford and in Jerusalem (all are late).

Margulies 5:3–86 describes and reproduces most of the *Genizah fragments* of LevR; all in all there are 40 leaves taken from 17 MSS. The oldest (Margulies 5:3: 9th cent.) and most important fragment, MS Heb. C. 18 F. 17–22 of the Bodleian, is partly vocalized. Description in N. Alloni, *Geniza-Fragments*, 63f., facsimile 155–66. In LevR, too, the text type represented by the Genizah fragments turns out to be the oldest and least corrupted.

*First printed edition*: Constantinople 1512, then Venice 1545. The printed editions are based above all on a MS of the type of MS Paris, but they also use other sources. LevR is contained in all traditional printed editions of Midrash Rabbah, in Mirkin, *Midrash Rabbah*, vols. 7–8, and in Hallewy, *Midrash Rabbah*, vol. 5. Critical edition: M. Margulies, *Midrash Wayyikra Rabbah: A Critical Edition Based on Manuscripts and Genizah Fragments with Variants and Notes*, 5 vols., Jerusalem 1953–60.

*Translations*: J. Israelstam & J. J. Slotki, vol. 4 of the Soncino edition of the *Midrash Rabbah*, London 1939, 3rd edn. 1961. J. Neusner, *Judaism and Scripture: The Evidence of Leviticus Rabbah*, Chicago 1986. [Translation.] German: A. Wünsche, *Bibl. Rabb.*, vol. 5, Leipzig 1883–84; repr. Hildesheim 1967.

***c) Content and Structure***

LevR consists of 37 homilies on Lev. Each homily begins with petiḥot (only 2, 5, 22 have just one petiḥah); these are followed by the sermon proper (in the Genizah fragments regularly introduced by *gufa*), which has an eschatological ending in the *Ḥatimah*. About two-thirds of the petiḥot are anonymous (88 of 126 according to Albeck; in Sarason's numbering 35 of 122 are attributed to a rabbi, although the mostly secondary nature of such attributions is clear from the citation of the same rabbi even within the petiḥah). Most of these are literary creations, as is shown by the stereotypical transitions to the seder verse as well as by the parallels in other rabbinic literature, where the same material appears outside the framework of a petiḥah (cf. Sarason).

The arrangement according to 37 homilies appears to follow the Palestinian reading cycle. However, the latter only knows of 20–25 sedarim for Lev. J. Heinemann believes the solution lies in a later addition of some sermons (although they would have been added shortly afterwards, since they are contained in all MSS): of the five chapters which are also contained in PRK, he regards LevR 20, 29, 30 (=PRK 26, 23, 27) as original components of the PRK, and possibly likewise for 27 (=PRK 9) (thus *EJ*, after Goldberg's criticism). Only 28 is almost certainly original in LevR and was later adopted in PRK.

Heinemann also considers LevR 2 as probably inauthentic; for like LevR 1, this chapter is a homily on Lev 1.1: the other two cases of two homilies for only one seder are LevR 4 and 5 as well as 20 and 21 – but 20 belongs properly to PRK and 4 should belong to a seder properly beginning with Lev 4.13 and not 4.1f. As for the remaining surplus of homilies in relation to the reading cycle, Heinemann attempts to explain this with the assumption that the cycle underlying LevR greatly diverged from the usual one, and that LevR was therefore supplemented with homilies on the standard pericopes.

The opposite standpoint is taken by J. Neusner (*The Integrity*), who wants to conclude from the rhetorical plan of the homilies that all of the five chapters in common with PRK belonged originally to LevR, with whose literary design they are entirely compatible. However, he does not respond to Heinemann's argument; nor does he address the problem of LevR 2. The adequacy of Neusner's criteria remains to be established.

The form of the sermons in LevR is that of literary homilies. Evidence of antecedent stages in real sermons can no longer be demonstrated; Neusner in fact doubts that the chapters can be formally regarded as sermons.

***d) Redaction and Date of LevR***

This question must be assessed above all from the connection with other rabbinic texts. LevR shares its language, as well as a great deal of material, with GenR. Margulies, (5:xii) thinks that both writings use common haggadic sources and derive from the same school. Albeck, on the other hand, believes that LevR used GenR. Abr. Goldberg wants to date LevR after GenR (*KS* 43 (1967–68) 73) on the basis of external form as well: it is a homiletic midrash instead of the exegetical midrash of GenR, which is still close to the halakhic midrashim; and the petiḥot have greater significance in LevR.

There is an even closer relation with PRK. In addition to the five common chapters, which – as we said – are due to later revision, there are numerous parallels. S. Buber and others inferred from this the use of PRK by the redactor of LevR. Conversely Albeck, 36ff., followed by Abr. Goldberg, regards PRK as dependent on LevR; Margulies (5:xiii) finally derives both works from the same author.

As for the parallels with PT, Albeck 30f. concludes that LevR used PT (indeed our PT and not another version of it, unlike GenR), but that in the haggadic parallels it also had access to another source. However, Margulies, (5: xix), advances plausible arguments to suggest that the parallels (at least most of them) are due not to the use of PT in LevR but to common haggadic sources, indeed that PT was able to employ an early stage of LevR: 'The haggadic book on Lev which lay before the redactor of PT closely resembled our LevR.' L. Moscovitz, too, considers that there was no direct borrowing from LevR on the redactional level of PT (unlike the later textual tradition): 'The Relationship between the Yerushalmi and Leviticus Rabbah: A Re-Examination' (Hebr.), *11th WCJS* (Jerusalem 1994) C 1:31–38.

The numerous parallels between LevR and Tanḥuma derive in part from LevR, where Tanḥuma found them and adopted them in abbreviated form (e.g. the parallels in Tanḥuma are usually anonymous, while in LevR they appear with tradents' names). Allusions to Tanḥuma in LevR, especially of a linguistic nature, entered this work only later; this is clear from the comparison with earlier MSS and with the Genizah fragments.

Since LevR quotes M, T, and the halakhic midrashim, and is in turn used already in the Midrash Rabbah on the Megillot (esp. CantR and EcclR) and by the early Payyetanim (esp. Yannai), the time of the redaction of LevR is restricted to between c. 400 and 500. The same follows from the rabbis named in LevR, who are mostly Palestinian scholars of the third and fourth century. A more precise assignment would result from the relationship to GenR, PRK and PT: but this cannot be unequivocally explained (Margulies, xxxii, dates LevR to the beginning of the fifth century, Albeck, 42, to the end of the fifth or early sixth century). That the midrash originated in Palestine is clear from its language (Galilean Aramaic, a lot of Greek), its preference for Palestinian rabbis, many Palestinian geographic references, and also from its halakhah, whose agricultural laws were valid only in Palestine.

### *2) Pesiqta de Rab Kahana (PRK)*

#### *Bibliography*

**Albeck, Ch.** *Derashot*, 105–107, 360f. **Baeck, L.** 'Haggadah and Christian Doctrine.' *HUCA* 23.1 (1950–51) 549–60. **Barth, L. M.** 'Literary Imagination and the Rabbinic Sermon.' *7th WCJS* (Jerusalem 1981): *Studies in the Talmud, Halacha and Midrash,* 29–35. [On PRK 15.] **Barth, L. M.** 'The "Three of Rebuke and Seven of Consolation" Sermons in the Pesikta de Rav Kahana.' *JJS* 33 (1982) 503–15. **Goldberg, Abr.** 'On the Authenticity of the Chapters "Vayehi baḥazi hallayla" (Ex. XII,29) and "Shor o Kesev" (Lev. XXII,27) in the Pesiqta' (Hebr.). *Tarbiz* 38 (1968–69) 184–85. **Mandelbaum, B.** 'Prolegomenon to the Pesikta.' *PAAJR* 23 (1954) 41–58. [Description of the MSS; structure of PRK.] **Mandelbaum, B.** *EJ* 13: 333f. **Neusner, J.** *From Tradition to Imitation: The Plan and Program of Pesiqta Rabbati and Pesiqta deRab Kahana.* Atlanta 1987. **Neusner, J.** 'Appropriation and Imitation: The Priority of Leviticus Rabbah over Pesiqta deRab Kahana.' *PAAJR* 54 (1987) 1–28. [On the priority of LevR in the chapters in common with LevR.] **Neusner, J.**

*Introduction*, 411–33. **Silberman, L. H.** 'A Theological Treatise on Forgiveness: Chapter Twenty-Three of Pesiqta Derab Kahana.' In E. Fleischer and J.J. Petuchowski (eds.), *Studies in Aggadah, Targum and Jewish Liturgy, in Memory of Joseph Heinemann*, 95–107. Jerusalem 1981. **Silberman, L. H.** 'Toward a Rhetoric of Midrash: A Preliminary Account.' In R. Polzin & E. Rothman (eds.), *The Biblical Mosaic: Changing Perspectives*, 15–26. Chico 1982. **Silberman, L. H.** 'Challenge and Response: Pesiqta DeRab Kahana, Chapter 26, as an Oblique Reply to Christian Claims.' *HTR* 79 (1986) 247–53. **Sperber, D.** 'Varia Midrashica IV.' *REJ* 137 (1978) 149–57. **Svedlund, G.** *The Aramaic Portions of the Pesiqta de Rab Kahana . . . with English Translation, Commentary and Introduction.* Uppsala 1974. **Thoma, C.** & **Lauer, S.** *Die Gleichnisse der Rabbinen.* Part One: *Pesiqtâ de-Rav Kahanâ (PesK).* Berne 1986. **Ungar, E.** 'When "Another Matter" is the Same Matter: The Case of Davar-Aher in Pesiqta DeRab Kahana.' In J. Neusner (ed.), *Approaches to Ancient Judaism*, New Series 2:1–43. Atlanta 1990. **Zinger, Z.** 'The Bible Quotations in the Pesikta de Rav Kahana.' *Textus* 5 (1966) 114–24. **Zunz**, *GV*, 195–237.

***Text***

**Mandelbaum, B.** *Pesikta de Rav Kahana: According to an Oxford Manuscript with Variants. . . With Commentary and Introduction.* 2 vols. New York 1962. [Cf. Abr. Goldberg, *KS* 43 (1967–68) 68–79.]

***Translations***

**Braude, W. G.** & **Kapstein, I. J.** *Pesikta de-Rab Kahana.* Philadelphia 1975. **Neusner, J.** *Pesiqta deRab Kahana: An Analytical Translation.* 2 vols. Atlanta 1987. [Vol. 2 also contains a substantial introduction to PRK, largely identical with *From Tradition to Imitation.*] German: Wünsche, A. *Bibl. Rabb.* Vol. 5. Leipzig 1884–85; repr. Hildesheim 1967.

### *a) The Name*

Pesiqta (perhaps originally in the plural *pesiqata*; cognate with *pasuq*, 'verse') corresponds to *pisqa*, 'section, chapter'. Zunz (*GV*, 203) supposes that Pesiqta originally designated only the individual sections of the collection together with each respective title, and that it became the title of the entire work only at a later stage. The name was chosen because this midrash does not offer a running commentary, but comments on lectionary pericopes from the synagogal liturgy.

The naming of the work (at first probably just Pesiqta) after Rab Kahana is attested from the eleventh century (R. Meshullam ben Moshe et al.: Zunz, *GV*, 204 n. f.). In the opinion of Zunz and S. Buber, this designation arose because the work's longest unit of text (the 12 chapters commencing with the Sabbath before the 17th of Tammuz) begins, *R. Abba bar Kahana pataḥ*. However, even if PRK should at one time have opened with this text, why then was the logically expected title *Pesiqta de R. Abba bar Kahana* abbreviated in this way? B. Mandelbaum (*PRK*, vol. 2, English introduction, xviii) therefore prefers to attribute the title to the mention of R. Kahana at the beginning of the chapter for the New Year (in two MSS), which he considers to be the original beginning of the text; this name was intended to distinguish PRK from other works entitled Pesiqta.

***b) Text***

For a long time PRK was known only from quotations, especially in the Arukh and the Yalqut. Zunz reconstructed the content and structure of the work from these quotations (*GV*, 1st ed. 1832). His relative success in this endeavour is attested by S. Buber's edition (Lyck [Elk] 1868) based on four manuscripts which had subsequently become known or useable. This edition in turn has now been replaced by the Mandelbaum's text; but because of its commentary and the quotations of medieval authorities, Buber's edition continues to be useful.

Buber used as his basis MS Safed, written at Cairo in 1565 (=MS 47 of the Alliance Israélite Universelle, Paris), supplemented (unsystematically) by three further MSS: Oxford MS Marshall Or. 24, dated to 1291 by the colophon; MS Carmoly, Cambridge Add. 1497, late fifteenth or early sixteenth century; Parma De Rossi Cod. 261:2 from the thirteenth or fourteenth century (11 chapters only). M. Friedmann (*Beth Talmud* 5 (1886–89), 46–53, 78–90, 108–14, 168–72, 197–206) described two further MSS: MS Casanata 3324 in Rome (early seventeenth century, incomplete) and a second MS from the Bodleian, Oxford (fifteenth century, text partly abridged).

B. Mandelbaum uses his base text the Oxford MS Marshall Or. 24; to the cited MSS he adds MS Oxford, Bodleian (Neubauer 2324/11). He also draws on seven *Genizah fragments* (Jewish Theological Seminary, New York; Cambridge; Oxford; Leningrad), of which those at Cambridge are of particular interest. However, in this regard Mandelbaum's description and reproduction of the variants must be corrected: see N. Alloni, *Geniza Fragments*, 71–75; N. Alloni & A. Díez-Macho, 'Pesiqta de Rab Kahana be-Niqqud Ereṣ–israeli', *Leshonenu* 23 (1958–59) 57–71. Two of the three units of text are palimpsests on Greek (Mandelbaum, 1: 13 inadvertently writes 'Latin', even though his photographic reproduction clearly shows the Greek uncials) and Syriac texts which can be dated to the eighth to tenth centuries (Abr. Goldberg, *KS* 43:71 n.1 has collated Mandelbaum's deviations from the text in *Leshonenu*).

***c) Content and Structure***

PRK is a homiletic midrash for the readings of the festivals and the special Sabbaths, which of course had fixed readings from early on. Zunz had originally inferred 29 pisqa'ot, beginning with the New Year, since the Arukh twice refers to *Rosh ha-Shanah* as *resh pisqot*. In keeping with the MSS it uses, the Buber edition on the other hand begins with Ḥanukkah and numbers

32 pisqa'ot (however, he has left out 31; 22 and 30 are doubles; 24 is not original). Mandelbaum also begins his edition with Ḥanukkah, but he acknowledges the soundness of Zunz's theory, based on MS Oxford 2324/11 as well as on a book list from the Genizah which cites the beginning of the *Pisqa Rosh ha-Shanah.* To retain the original order, therefore, one should begin with vol. 2 of Mandelbaum's edition. Goldberg, *KS* 72, doubts the conclusiveness of these arguments, especially since the book list of the Genizah elsewhere cites *parts* of books as well. See also Braude and Kapstein, xlviif.

Mandelbaum (2: xiv–xvii) numbers 28 pisqa'ot and nine appendices. Along with the festal sermons there are homilies for the four Sabbaths after Ḥanukkah, the three penal Sabbaths before the 9th of Ab and the seven Sabbaths of comfort after this date, as well as for the two Sabbaths after New Year (NB for these last twelve Sabbaths the sermon text is the *haftarah*). The appendices concern *Simḥat Torah*, which in Palestine would have made little sense (PRK clearly is a collection of annual sermons: the celebration at the conclusion of the cycle would only have been held once in about three-and-a-half years; but see now the piyyut of Ha-Kallir, edited by E. Fleischer, which presupposes *Simḥat Torah* (cf. p. 263); the second day of Sukkot, which originally was also celebrated only in Babylonia; and a number of additions which are alien to PRK (Goldberg, *KS* 72, considers Mandelbaum's appendix 4, i.e. the second sermon on Deut 14.12ff., to be genuine: the reading was given both on the Sabbath in the week of Easter and on that in the week of Sukkot; see E. Fleischer, 'The Reading of the Portion "Asser Te'asser" (Deut. XIV,22)' (Hebr.), *Tarbiz* 36 (1966–67) 116–55).

For the five chapters in common with LevR see p. 290 above. Albeck regarded all of them as original in LevR (cf. also Neusner); Heinemann, on the other hand, supposes only LevR 28 to be original in relation to PRK 8, but he considers PRK 9, 23, 26 and 27 to be original in the Pesiqta. But even the borrowing of LevR 28 does not convince him that the redactor of PRK knew LevR; instead, this borrowing took place at the stage of textual transmission. PRK 7 will have been adopted from PesR (thus Goldberg) or from material used by PesR, while PRK 12.12–25 is likely to derive from *Tanḥuma Yitro*. In both cases the *structure of the pisqa* (in addition to the MS transmission and the style) is an important argument, as Goldberg (*KS*) has shown: for in the genuine pisqa'ot the petiḥot (between 1 and 10 per pisqa) are always the longest part (on the petiḥot see Braude and Kapstein, xxx–xxxvi); they are sometimes followed by thematic treatises which can almost be regarded as a variation of the form of the petiḥah, before the pisqa concludes with expositions of a few verses.

***d) Redaction and Date***

With its inconsistent structure, order and extent, the MS tradition of PRK shows that the text of PRK, like that of PesR, remained indeterminate for a long time (H. Hahn, *Wallfahrt und Auferstehung zur messianischen Zeit* (Frankfurt 1979), 2: 'Both Pesiqtot were not fixed as complete literary works until they were first printed'). Discussions of the date, therefore, concern only the basic core or the substance of the work; but they must of course allow for a subsequent fluidity of this document, which, as a collection of sermons, arose out of practical usage in the synagogue.

Zunz, *GV*, 206f. supposed that PRK used PT, GenR, LevR and LamR, and that it was composed around 700. He was led to this late date also by the halakhic introduction to the haggadah, and by the feast of *Simḥat Torah*. As noted above, however, the homily for this feast is probably a later addition; the chapters in common with LevR were also discussed earlier. When Zunz (*GV*, 207) suggests that Eleazar ha-Kallir (who today is generally dated to the Byzantine period) already knew PRK, this is in fact an argument against the late date. Based on its content, structure, literary connections and language (on the latter see Svedlund, 9f.), the work must be dated to the fifth century, approximately contemporary with LevR. It is, however, impossible to prove Margulies's assumption (*Mabo* to LevR, xiii) that LevR and PRK derive from the same redactor. L. M. Barth (*JJS* 33) has attempted to narrow down the date of origin at least for PRK 13–22. These chapters are based on the prophetic readings for the three Sabbaths before and the seven Sabbaths after the 9th of Ab. The Haftarot in question are first attested here: although still unknown in PT, they are already presupposed by Yannai. According to Barth, these chapters were composed between 451 and 527, i. e. in the relatively quiet period for Judaism between the Council of Chalcedon (elevation of Jerusalem to the patriarchate) and the inauguration of Justinian. He sees the well-designed structure of these chapters as reflecting 'an elaborate homiletic acceptance of the status quo' (513), and within the stated period he considers the second half of the fifth century to be the most likely. However, the cited arguments do not suffice for a delimitation of this kind.

The date and Palestinian origin (the latter can be inferred from the language and the cited rabbis) appear to speak against a connection of the work with any of the six rabbis known to us by the name of Rab Kahana (all six were Babylonians, although three of them spent some time in Palestine). Buber had considered PRK to be the oldest homiletic midrash, composed in Palestine by Rab Kahana, the student of Rab. Svedlund, 4 also allows for the possibility that this Rab Kahana edited the Pesiqta in the third century.

Braude and Kapstein explain the name of PRK by saying that 'he was presumably the one who gathered, compiled and edited the pisqas that comprise the work' (p. x); however, they date PRK to the fifth century (xxviii f.), and hence seem to presuppose a later Kahana. None of these solutions is satisfactory; the naming of PRK after Rab Kahana still remains unexplained.

PRK is still frequently quoted in the Arukh and in Rashi; it is later displaced by PesR, and since the fifteenth century has been known only through the Yalqut.

### *3) Pesiqta Rabbati (PesR)*

#### *Bibliography*

**Aptowitzer, V.** 'Untersuchungen zur gaonäischen Literatur.' *HUCA* 8–9 (1931–32) 383–410. **Bamberger, B. J.** 'A Messianic Document of the Seventh Century.' *HUCA* 15 (1940) 425–31. **Ben-David, I.** 'Yiḥudê lashon mitokh Pesiqta Rabbati.' *Leshonenu* 44 (1979–80) 316–18. **Bogaert, P.** *Apocalypse de Baruch: Introduction, Traduction du Syriaque et Commentaire*, 1:222–41. Paris 1969. **Braude, W. G.** 'Overlooked Meanings of Certain Editorial Terms in the Pesikta Rabbati.' *JQR* N.S. 52 (1961–62) 264–72. **Goldberg, A.** *Erlösung durch Leiden: Drei rabbinische Homilien über die Trauernden Zions und den leidenden Messias Efraim (PesR 34.36.37)*. Frankfurt 1978. **Goldberg, A.** *Ich komme und wohne in deiner Mitte: Eine rabbinische Homilie zu Sacharja 2,14 (PesR 35)*. Frankfurt 1977. **Goldberg, A.** 'Pesiqta Rabbati 26, ein singulärer Text in der frühen rabbinischen Literatur.' *FJB* 17 (1989) 1–44. **Grözinger, K. E.** *Ich bin der Herr, dein Gott! Eine rabbinische Homilie zum Ersten Gebot (PesR 20)*. Berne/Frankfurt 1976. **Gry, L.** 'La ruine du Temple par Titus: Quelques traditions juives plus anciennes et primitives à la base de Pesikta Rabbati XXVI.' *RB* 55 (1948) 215–26. **Hahn, H.** *Wallfahrt und Auferstehung zur messianischen Zeit: Eine rabbinische Homilie zum Neumond-Shabbat (PesR 1)*. Frankfurt 1979. **Heinemann, J.** 'A Homily on Jeremiah and the Fall of Jerusalem (Pesiqta Rabbati, Pisqa 26).' In R. Polzin & E. Rothman (eds.), *The Biblical Mosaic: Changing Perspectives*, 27–41. Chico 1982. **Kern, B.** *Tröstet, tröstet mein Volk! Zwei rabbinische Homilien zu Jesaja 40,1 (PesR 30 und PesR 29/30)*. Frankfurt 1986. **Kern, B.** 'Pesikta Rabbati: Redaction and Canonization' (Hebr.). *11th WCJS* (Jerusalem 1994) C 1:111–18. **Lenhard, D.** *Vom Ende der Erde rufe ich zu Dir: Eine rabbinische Psalmenhomilie (PesR 9)*. Frankfurt 1990. **Lévi, I.** 'Bari dans la Pesikta Rabbati.' *REJ* 32 (1896) 278–82. **Lévi, I.** 'La Pesikta Rabbati et le 4$^{e}$ Ezra.' *REJ* 24 (1892) 281–85. **Marmorstein, A.** 'Eine messianische Bewegung im 3. Jahrhundert.' *Jeschurun* 13 (1926) 16–28, 171–86, 369–83. **Meijer, B. J.** *Midrasch Pesiqta Rabbati 42 – Und der Herr besuchte Sara*. Diss. Frankfurt 1986. **Neusner, J.** *From Tradition to Imitation: The Plan and Program of Pesiqta Rabbati and Pesiqta deRab Kahana*. Atlanta 1987. **Neusner, J.** *Introcution*, 434–63. **Prijs, L.** *Die Jeremia-Homilie Pesikta Rabbati Kapitel 26: Kritische Edition nebst Übersetzung und Kommentar*. Stuttgart 1966. **Sperber, D.** *EJ* 13: 335f. **Zunz**, *GV*, 250–62. [Supplemented in Albeck, *Derashot*, 119–21, 388f.]

#### *Text*

**Friedmann, M.** *Pesikta Rabbati: Midrasch für den Fest-Cyclus und die ausgezeichneten Sabbathe*. Vienna 1880; repr. Tel Aviv 1963. **Braude, W. G.** 'The Piska Concerning the Sheep which Rebelled.' *PAAJR* 30 (1962) 1–35. [Pisqa 2b edited on the basis of MS Parma 1240.] **Cohen, N. J.** *The Manuscripts and Editions of the Midrash Pesikta Rabbati: A Prolegomenon to a Scientific Edition*. Diss. New York: HUC, 1977. [Critique in H. Hahn, *Wallfahrt*, 24f.] **Cohen, N. J.** 'The London Manuscript of Midrash Pesiqta Rabbati: A Key Text-Witness Comes to Light.' *JQR* N.S. 73 (1982–83) 209–37. **Grözinger, K. E. & Hahn, H.** 'Die Textzeugen der Pesikta Rabbati.'

*FJB* 1 (1973) 68–104. **Hahn, H.** 'Wiener Pesiqta-Rabbati-Fragmente (einschl. neuer Funde).' *FJB* 7 (1979) 105–14. **Kern, B.** 'Die Pesiqta Rabbati 29/30 Naḥamu und die Pesiqta de Rav Kahana Naḥamu – Eine Gegenüberstellung zweier Textzeugen aus Parma.' *FJB* 11 (1983) 91–112. [PesR uses PRK or a common homiletical stock.] **Sanders, M.** 'The First Print of Pesiqta Rabbathi' (Hebr.). *Areshet* 3 (1960–61) 99–101. **Scheiber, A.** 'An Old MS of the Pesiqta on the Ten Commandments' (Hebr.). *Tarbiz* 25 (1955–56) 464–67. [Geniza fragment from the Kaufmann Collection, Budapest: an early form of PesR or a version of the Midrash on the 10 Commandments.]

***Translations***

**Braude, W. G.** *Pesikta Rabbati: Discourses for Feasts, Fasts, and Special Sabbaths.* 2 vols. New Haven 1968. **Neusner, J.** *From Tradition* contains the translation of PesR 1–5 and 15. Italian: M. Gallo, *Sete del Dio vivente: Omelie rabbiniche su Isaia* (Rome 1981) has 8 chapters from PesR on Isa 40–66. All the Frankfurt monographs cited also contain a German translation and a critical edition of the text.

### *a) The Name*

For 'Pesiqta' see p. 292 above. The designation *rabbati* is applied to distinguish this text from other sermon collections such as PRK. The name is first attested in Rashi on Isa 51.12; like Maḥzor Vitry, Rashi also uses the name *Pesiqta gedolah* (on Exod 6.14). In the thirteenth century Zedekiah ben Benjamin uses *Pesiqta rabbeta*; likewise the Prague edition. Occasionally PesR is also simply called *Pesiqta.*

### *b) Content and Text*

PesR is a collection of sermons for the feasts and special Sabbaths. Its extent was only finally determined by the printed editions. The first printed edition, Prague 1653 (thus Sanders) or 1656, comprises 47 *pisqa'ot*; the same is true for subsequent printings, which are all dependent on the first. M. Friedmann reproduces the edition Sklow 1806, corrected by the first edition and his own conjectures. As a first supplement to the 47 homilies he appends four sermons (from MS Parma? Grözinger & Hahn, 104 assume a separate source), and as a second supplement he has a piece of Bereshit Rabbati. Braude's translation counts these additions as chapters 48, 49, 50, 52 and 53. Braude's 51 is a homily on Sukkot from MS Parma, which was not included in the printed editions but which is necessary to complete the annual cycle.

The number of sermons is greater than the number of chapters. Friedmann therefore already divided chapters 23, 27 and 29 (23; 23/24; 27; 27/28; 29; 29/30–30). See, however, B. Kern (*Tröstet*, 24–27) on the textual problems of the last two chapters: Friedmann's 29/30 is missing in MS Parma and has been adopted by him from early printed editions, supplemented by pieces of LamR. On the other hand, MS Parma contains the beginning of the homily which is missing in Friedmann's 29/30–30, and which Kern counts as 29/30.

In the present structure, PesR traces the following annual cycle (Braude's numbering): New Moon Sabbath (1), Ḥanukkah (2–9), distinguished Sabbaths (10–16), Pesaḥ (17–19 and 48–49), Feast of Weeks (20–25), three Sabbaths of mourning and admonition before the 9th of Ab (26–29/30), seven Sabbaths of comfort after the 9th of Ab (29/30–30 to 37), New Year through Yom ha-Kippurim (38–47, 50), Feast of Booths and Shemini Aṣeret (51–52), Shabbat Bereshit (53).

Thus, PesR has only attained its greatest textual extent in Friedmann and Braude. The MSS, by contrast, do not recognize this form of PesR. The most important textual witnesses are *MS Parma* 3122 (formerly 1240; not yet used in Friedmann), *MS Casanata* 3324 in Rome, and *MS London* (now in Philadelphia, Dropsie MS 26). MS Parma (in De Rossi's Catalogue still incorrectly identified as *Leqaḥ Tob*), dated by Zunz to 1270, is a compiled MSS with a great many hasty errors; it divides PesR into four blocks, apparently not considering it as a whole (contrast Hahn, *Wallfahrt*, 15: the MS provides the fullest possible collection of homilies on the Sabbaths and feasts, including the midrashim on the festal scrolls). The MS contains in this order (see the table in Grözinger & Hahn, 88f.): Tanḥuma Buber; PesR 1–18; CantR; PesR 48, 49, 25, 19–24; empty pages; 29/30–43, 50, 44–47, 51–53; other midrashim; 26–28; LamR.

According to Grözinger & Hahn 87, *MS Casanata* has the best claim to being a Pesiqta MS, since it apparently aims to present a festive cycle from Ḥanukkah to Sukkot. Carefully written no later than in the early seventeenth century, this MS is incompletely preserved; the missing part can, however, be deduced from the table of contents and from the related MS in London. Over and above the *pisqa'ot* which are in common with PRK in MS Parma and the editions, this manuscript replaces a number of additional homilies with others from PRK, and thus mixes the *pesiqtot* even more than the tradition does elsewhere. However, the structure is somewhat similar to that of MS Parma: both have 25 before 19, 50 between 43 and 44, and both lack 46.

*MS London* was already described by M. Friedmann in *Beth Talmud* 5 (1892) 1–6, but was long forgotten and only recently rediscovered in the library of Dropsie College. Written in Italy in 1531, it has much in common with MS Casanata; it also supplies the text of the *pisqa'ot* which in the latter are missing but mentioned in the table of contents. It must on the whole be preferred to MS Parma.

There are significant fragments of a Pesiqta MS in Vienna, which probably dates to the thirteenth century and is important for textual criticism; 18 pages have so far been discovered (all or part of parashiyot 1, 5, 7, 8, 21, 22, 27, 27/28, 31 and 32).

Another textual witness is the copy of the *editio princeps* in the Jewish Theological Seminary; this contains not only numerous marginal glosses but also additional hand-written parashiyot, two of them from the Yalqut and another nine from a source related to MS Parma (cf. Grözinger & Hahn, 98–104). The PesR quotations in the Yalqut should also be taken into account, although for textual criticism they must be used with caution. Additional material is in L. Ginzberg, *Ginze Schechter*, 1:171–81, and S. A. Wertheimer, *Batei Midrashot*, 1:260–64.

***c) Redaction and Compilation***

The textual tradition already shows a blanket assessment of PesR to be impossible. This is a composite work. The first printed edition, MS Casanata/MS London, and MS Parma are three redactions of this Pesiqta; 'they draw on a common store of homilies, from which they have taken blocks of varying size and combined them according to their views or needs to form independent works' (Grözinger, *Ich bin der Herr*, 7; cf. Goldberg, *Ich komme*, 7). With Grözinger (*Ich bin der Herr*, 8f.) one must distinguish at least five or six sources:

1. A *Yelamdenu-Source* (MS Parma prefaces PesR 1–18, 'In the name of the Lord our God let us begin. *Yelamdenu*'. This may be intended as a title: Grözinger & Hahn, 90). Each of these sermons begins with a *Yelamdenu* paragraph, followed by a *petiḥah* in the name of R. Tanḥuma bar Abba. To this category belong PesR 1–14, 19, 25, 29, 31, 38–45, 47–49.

2. *Homilies which derive from PRK* or are known from it: PesR 15–18 (=PRK 5–8) and 32 (=PRK 18); partly 14 (=PRK 4); PesR 51, 52 (=PRK 27, 28). The manuscripts have included additional material from PRK.

3. *Formally related to 2.* are PesR 27, 27/28, 29/30, 29/30–30.

4. *Ruaḥ-ha-qodesh Homilies* begin by saying, 'This is what X said in the Holy Spirit'. They always have only one *petiḥah*, which has an independent structure: PesR 20 (this may not originally have belonged to PesR, and appears not to have been contained in the PesR used by the Yalqut: Grözinger, *Ich bin der Herr*, 19f.), 28, 30, 34–37. A mixed form appears in 50.

5. *Midrash of the 10 Commandments* (cited by Ha-Meiri as *Midrash Mattan Torah*): PesR 21–24. It differs in language and structure from the rest (large parts in Aramaic, numerous *Ma'asim)*. Only this part of PesR has thus far been attested in the Genizah.

6. *PesR 26* (but see Prijs, 21f., who sees no reason to attribute this homily to another author: he argues that 26 does not indeed begin with a Scripture verse, but nonetheless with a sentence composed of Scripture verses; the

fluent narrative style which characterizes 26 is in his view due to the subject matter). A. Goldberg, on the other hand, shows that formally the chapter is in fact neither a homily nor an exegetical midrash, but stands out as a unique text within midrashic literature, which can hardly have been fabricated by the compiler of PesR.

PesR 46 is missing in all three MSS. Friedmann, 186b n.1 already declared this homily to be secondary. As noted above, PesR 53 derives from Bereshit Rabbati.

Zunz (*GV*, 255) dates PesR to the second half of the ninth century; apart from the writings he believes to be quoted in PesR, his view is based esp. on PesR 1 (F. 1b): 777 years have passed since the destruction of the Temple (gloss: 'now it is already 1151'), i.e. the author wrote after 845 (since Jewish chronology regards 68 as the year of the Temple's destruction). This date has been widely accepted: e.g. J. Mann, *The Jews in Egypt and in Palestine under the Fâtimid Caliphs*, vol. 1 (London 1920; repr. New York 1970), 48 n.2; L. Prijs, 77, even if he considers the material to be older (11 n.3); D. Sperber, *EJ* 13: 335 (but only for the Yelamdenu part, while elsewhere he gives a date in the sixth or seventh century).

Friedmann ad loc. also bases himself on this figure, but relates it to the destruction of the First Temple: i.e., according to the chronology of SOR, to the year 355 (the Persian period is only counted as 52 years); the gloss should then be dated to 719. Friedmann is aware that this is not true for the whole work (24: some parts are undoubtedly from Geonic times), but for various reasons he wants to place the latter not much later.

H. Hahn also advocates a reference to the year 355 in this passage; for this reason he regards the attribution of the *petiḥah* to R. Tanḥuma as reliable (*Wallfahrt*, 110–13), although of course he draws no conclusions from this for the work as a whole. At any rate, the redactional history of PesR seems to him to suggest a fifth-century date (388ff.) and a Palestinian origin (397ff.) for this chapter. Regarding the *Yelamdenu* part of PesR, Hahn, 380 sees no reason against F. Böhl's general conclusion 'that the Yelamdenu materially existed around 400 at the latest' (*Aufbau und literarische Formen des aggadischen Teils im Jelamdenu-Midrasch* (Wiesbaden 1977), 90). Such an experimental result applies of course only to the substance of this extensive part of PesR and not to the collection of these homilies, although the latter may not need to be placed much later.

The *Ruaḥ-ha-qodesh Homilies* are another block of PesR, much of which has already been explored in detail. Friedmann, 24 had already attributed PesR 34–37 to a different author from that of the main part, and called them the earliest chapters of the book. B. J. Bamberger dates these homilies about the mourners of Zion and the suffering Messiah to the years 632–7, based on 36.2 (F. 162a): 'In the year when the Messiah reveals himself. . ., the King of Persia will wage war against a King of Arabia, and this King of Arabia will go to Edom in order to consult with the Edomites. Then the King of Persia will devastate the whole world.' However, this text might equally well apply to Odenathus; such a view is favoured both by the name of R. Isaac and by the contemporary expectations that the coming of the Messiah is preceded by a war between Persia and Rome.

The *mourners of Zion* are another point of reference: J. Mann, *The Jews in Egypt and Palestine under the Fâtimid Caliphs*, vol. 1 (London 1920; repr. New York 1970), 47–49 sees them as a movement of repentance in Islamic times, and he regards PesR 1 and 34–37 as the latest part of the work, composed by an Italian haggadist who in the first half of the ninth century joined the mourners for Zion in Jerusalem. Others arrive at a similar date by identifying the mourners for Zion with the occasionally mentioned Karaite group of this name: thus e.g. H. Graetz, *Geschichte*, vol. 5 (4th edn. Leipzig 1909), 269, 507f., and M. Zucker, 'Tegubot li-tenuat Abelê Ṣion ha-Qarayyim ba-sifrut ha-rabbanit', in *Sefer Yovel le-Rabbi Ḥanokh Albeck* (Jerusalem 1963), 378–401. For criticism, cf. A. Goldberg, *Erlösung durch Leiden*, 131–34.

Goldberg demonstrates that PesR 35 did not originally belong together with 34, 36–37, but he also stresses the problem of any dating of these texts. Nothing prevents a date of PesR 35 in the third or early fourth century (*Ich komme*, 20); likewise one must assume the origin of PesR 34 some time after the middle of the third century (*Erlösung*, 142). However, redaction in both cases may have taken place much later. The question is particularly complicated by the fact that clearly usable parallels with known and dated writings are only rarely available. Thus the question of the use of the *She'iltot* of R. Aḥa (seventh and eighth cent.) in PesR or vice versa remains unsolved: Zunz and Aptowitzer assumed such a use in PesR as assured, while S. Buber and Braude arrive at the opposite result. What is more, the decision would of course always hold only for the particular passages. Equally unclear is the relationship of PesR to ha-Kallir (according to Zunz, *GV*, 256, the latter knew PesR; contrast Aptowitzer, 403ff.).

As for the place of origin of PesR, Zunz had suggested Greece (*GV*, 256), while I. Lévi assumed Southern Italy because of the supposed mention of Bari (PesR 28, F. 135b). The choice of these localities of course is linked with the late dating of PesR. Numerous arguments favour an origin in Palestine: thus above all the names of the cited rabbis (third and fourth-century Palestinian Amoraim), as well as the absence of a pisqa for *Simḥat*

*Torah*, and perhaps also the language. Nevertheless, none of these arguments is absolutely conclusive, and it is appropriate to warn against hasty generalizations.

The genesis of PesR, therefore, is still largely uncertain. The idea of an individual final redactor is at any rate untenable. Instead, a lengthy process of development must be assumed. In the course of this, individual homilies which in turn used pre-edited material (e.g. apocalypses in PesR 36–37 or hekhalot material in PesR 20) were collected in groups of common form and spirit. Often these were made serviceable in the festal liturgy only at a later stage, and then connected with other texts (in this way, 34–37 will have been combined with other homilies to form the sermons of comfort, 29–37). This resulted in relatively fixed units of text, which in time merged into a cycle of sermons for the entire year. Some parts, however, still remained interchangeable, in keeping with the nature of a sermon collection as a functional manual. The indiscriminately late dating by Zunz et al. is in any case unwarranted. Nowadays scholars more frequently opt for a date in the sixth or seventh century (Braude; Sperber in *EJ* 13: 335); but even this can only be regarded as an appropriate time frame, which remains to be secured in detail.

## *4) Tanḥuma – Yelamdenu*

### *Bibliography*

**Albeck, Ch.** *Derashot*, 112–16, 373–75. **Aptowitzer, V**. 'Scheeltoth und Jelamdenu.' *MGWJ* 76 (1932) 558–75. **Böhl, F.** *Aufbau und literarische Formen des aggadischen Teils im Jelamdenu-Midrasch.* Wiesbaden 1977. **Bregman, M**. 'Stratigraphic Analysis of a Selected Pericope from the Tanhuma-Yelammedenu Midrashim' (Hebr.). *10th WCJS* (Jerusalem 1990) 117–24. **Bregman, M.** 'Early Sources and Traditions in the Tanḥuma-Yelammedenu Midrashim' (Hebr.). *Tarbiz* 60 (1990–91) 269–74. **Ginzberg, L.** 'Ma'amar al ha-Yelamdenu.' In *Ginzê Schechter*, 1:449–513. **Herr, M. D**. *EJ* 15: 794–96. **Marmorstein, A.** 'Zur Erforschung des Jelamdenu-Problems.' *MGWJ* 74 (1930) 266–84. **Marmorstein, A**. 'Die Gottesbezeichnung Elohim im Jelamdenu.' *MGWJ* 75 (1931) 377–79. **Milikowski, C**. 'The Punishment of Jacob – A Study in the Redactorial Process of Midrash Tanḥuma' (Hebr.). *Bar-Ilan* 18–19 (1981) 144–49. **Schlüter, M**. 'Ein Auslegungsmidrash im Midrash Tanḥuma.' *FJB* 14 (1986) 71–98. **Stein, M.** 'Le-ḥeqer Midreshê Yelamdenu.' In *Sefer ha-Yovel le-kabod Moshe Schorr* (*Festschrift* M. Schorr), Hebr. section, 85–112. Warsaw 1935. **Zunz**, *GV*, 237–50.

### *Text*

*Midrasch Tanḥuma.* Jerusalem 1960. **Buber, S**. *Midrasch Tanḥuma.* 2 vols. Wilna 1885; repr. Jerusalem 1964. **Adler, J**. 'Midrash Tanḥuma Ketab Yad Vatikan 44.' *Kobez al Yad* 8 [18] (Jerusalem 1975) 15–75. [14th-cent. MS, hybrid between regular text and TanB.] **Bregman, M.** 'Toward a Textcritical Approach of the Tanhuma-Yelamdenu Midrashim' (Hebr.). *Tarbiz* 54 (1984–85) 289–92. **Bregman, M.** Textual 'Witness of the Tanḥma-Yelamdenu Midrashim' (Hebr.). *9th WCJS* (Jerusalem 1986) C:49–56. **Bregman, M.** *The Tanhuma-Yelammedenu Literature: Studies in the Evolution of the Versions* (Hebr.). Diss. Jerusalem 1992. **Ginzberg, L.** *Ginzê Schechter,* 1:18–66, 96–102, 107–35. [13 Genizah fragments; cf. J. Mann, 'Genizah Studies',

*American Journal of Semitic Languages and Literatures* 46 (1929–30) 265–267, who rejects this identification in part.] **Mann, J**. *The Bible as Read and Preached in the Old Synagogue*. 2 vols. New York 1971 (=repr. of 1940, with prolegomenon by B.Z. Wacholder), Cincinnati 1966 (completed by I. Sonne). **Wertheimer**, *Batei Midrashot*, 1:139–75. Urbach, E. E. 'Seridê Tanḥuma-Yelamdenu.' *Kobez al Yad* 6 [16] part 1 (Jerusalem 1966) 1–54. **Wilhelm, J. D**. 'Qeta'im mi-midrash Tanḥuma le-Sefer Shemot u-mi-midrash Yelamdenu le-Sefer Debarim.' *Kobez al Yad* 6 [16] part 1 (Jerusalem 1966) 55–75. **Wilhelm, K**. 'Ein Jelamdenu-Fragment.' *MGWJ* 75 (1931) 135–43.

***Translations***

**Townsend, J. T**. *Midrash Tanḥuma: Translated into English with Introduction, Indices, and Brief Notes (S. Buber Recension)*. Vol. 1: *Genesis*. Hoboken, NJ 1989. German: **Bietenhard, H**. *Midrasch Tanḥuma B: R. Tanḥuma über die Tora, genannt Midrasch Jelammedenu*. 2 vols. Bern/Frankfurt 1980–82. [The Buber version; his text is based on Codex Vat. Ebr. 34, which frequently departs from Buber's text.]

## *a) The Name*

Tanḥuma or Yelamdenu designates a homiletic midrash on the whole Pentateuch which is known in several collections. The name *Yelamdenu* is taken from the halakhic introduction *Yelamdenu Rabbenu*, 'let our master teach us'. The name *Tanḥuma* is explained either by the fact that several addresses begin with 'R. Tanḥuma bar Abba introduced thus'; or else by the assumption that this Amora himself created the basis for these homilies in the second half of the fourth century (thus Bacher, *PAm* 3:502f.). And indeed there are more proems transmitted in the name of Tanḥuma than in that of any other rabbi. The title *Tanḥuma* is attested in Rashi and in the *Yalqut*; *Yelamdenu* especially in the *Arukh* and the *Yalqut*.

## *b) The Text*

Tanḥuma exists in two editions, representing two different textual recensions: *1. The Standard Edition.* First printed at Constantinople 1520/22 (facsimile Jerusalem 1971), then Venice 1545, Mantua 1563 (facsimile Jerusalem 1971; on additions in this printing which were also adopted in the later editions, see Buber, *Einleitung*, 163–80), Verona 1595, etc. Together with the *Etz Yosef* and *Anaf Yosef* commentaries, it appeared at Wilna/Grodno in 1831 (several reprints). *2. The Buber Edition* according to MS Oxford Neubauer 154 (of uncertain age) as the base text, along with four other MSS from Oxford, Cod. Vat. Ebr. 34 (which Theodor would have preferred as the basis for the edition), Munich Cod. Hebr. 224 (several chapters, partly also in *BhM*, 6:91–185) and MS Parma De Rossi 1240. For Gen and Exod, the text published by Buber (=TanB) strongly diverges from the ordinary edition; for Lev, Num and Deut, the two editions essentially agree. TanB is most likely a European recension (cf. I. Ta-Shma, *KS* 60 (1984–85) 302 envisions an Ashkenazic revision, while M. Bregman, 'Textual Witness', 51 suggests a final redaction in Italy; the relevant Genizah fragments are also of European origin).

Buber already knew a number of additional MSS. Only a part of them has been published in the meantime, e.g. MS Cambridge 1212 (early fourteenth century), edited by Urbach. Numerous fragments from the Cairo Genizah have been published, above all by L. Ginzberg and J. Mann. Further textual witnesses (esp. Genizah fragments) are discussed in M. Bregman, 'Textual Witness'.

*How are Tan and Yelamdenu related?* On the one hand the two names appear to be interchangeable: in the Middle Ages the same quotations are cited now as Tanḥuma, now as Yelamdenu; a large number of homilies in Tan connects the halakhic introduction, *Yelamdenu Rabbenu*, with a petiḥah in the name of Tanḥuma. On the other hand the compiler of the *Yalqut* seems to regard Tan and Yelamdenu as two different works which he cites side by side and which coincide only in part. Moreover, many Yelamdenu quotations of medieval literature cannot be found in either version of the midrash (the quotations, esp. on Num, are gathered in L. Grünhut, *Sefer ha-Likkutim*, 4–6). Must a lost Yelamdenu midrash therefore be assumed?

For a long time the discussion was determined by the question of an *Ur*-Tanḥuma or *Ur*-Yelamdenu, and focused on their relation to the two printed Tanḥumas and the other Yelamdenu quotations. Buber, for example, regarded his text as the *Ur*-Tanḥuma; Ginzberg saw the fragments he published as *Ur*-Yelamdenu. All the reconstructions had to take into account several unknown variables and were, moreover, highly subjective on the problem of dating: some took the presence of Aramaic in a text as an indication of a late, others of an early date; similarly in regard to divine names.

The MSS which have been published or become known since then show that the questions are much more complex than had been assumed. The Tanḥ-Yelamdenu midrashim are a group of homiletic midrashim on the Pentateuch which are transmitted in many versions, and to which belong not only the two editions of Tan and various handwritten recensions, but which also comprises ExodR II, NumR II, DeutR, parts of PesR and of other midrashim. E. E. Urbach, 3 thus rightly considers the search for an *Ur*-Tanḥuma to be hopeless, at least as far its preservation in a particular manuscript is concerned. This genre of midrash was so successful that it quickly took on regional differences. As functional literature, these midrashim continued for the longest time to be subject to changes, growth and loss of text.

Regarding the form of the Tan homilies, the stereotypical *Yelamdenu*

*Rabbenu* usually introduces the halakhic unit which is followed by a closely connected haggadic unit. Several proems precede the exposition of the first verse of the seder text and a Messianic conclusion. An analysis of the forms of the haggadic component has been presented by F. Böhl. Some of the sermons will have been actually delivered, while others will be literary products; there has undoubtedly been some reciprocal interaction, so that a clear assessment is not possible.

***c) Origin and Redaction***

Zunz (*GV*, 247) dates Tanḥ-Yelamdenu to the first half of the ninth century. For this he appeals above all to similarities with the *She'iltot* and Geonic writings, polemics against the Karaites, and a text (Tan Noaḥ 3) according to which the two academies in Babylonia are still in existence. Even today this dating is still very common (e.g. Herr, *EJ*, 795).

A dating by means of individual passages is most problematic, particularly in the case of a collection of sermons. The text about the two *yeshibot* of Babylonia (cf. Goodblatt, *Instruction*, 13–15; V. Aptowitzer, *HUCA* 8–9 (1931–32) 415–17) is also found, with variants, in a letter of Pirqoi ben Baboi (c. 800). To assume this letter as a source of Tan is hardly possible; and interpolations in Tan must be assumed at all times. This is true also for the other contacts with Geonic texts, especially with the *She'iltot* (cf. Aptowitzer, *MGWJ* 76), which are of interest more for the history of transmission of Tan. The proximity of Tan to the *She'iltot* is, moreover, primarily formal in nature.

F. Böhl notes that t.Ber 4.16 (L. 22–24) already attests a form that is comparable with the Yelamdenu, and sees this as 'evidence against the frequent assertions that Yelamdenu is dependent on R. Aḥai's *She'iltot*. This is more obviously the case because Tannaitic texts frequently employed the sequence of a) the students' request for instruction, and b) the Rabbi's answer' (*Aufbau*, 91). In BT, too, the Yelamdenu formula is repeatedly found in the context of halakhic instruction; formal similarities also appear in the sermon of Tanḥum of Newai in Shab 30a–b. Böhl observes a line of development of the Yelamdenu form, from the instruction of pupils via the halakhic responses of the BT to the halakhic-haggadic instruction of the literary Yelamdenu form, which in the midrash is used as the introduction to a longer unit of text. On the basis of the tradents named in Yelamdenu, he concludes that the latter 'existed in substance around 400 at the latest' (*Aufbau*, 90).

This assessment can probably be accepted, as long as it is not understood to posit an all-inclusive date without any further development. It is true that the customary late dating of homiletic works in particular has been based too much on individual observations that cannot be unequivocally confirmed. Form critical investigations may well prove helpful here, even if the dating of individual Tan homilies is likely to remain largely unattainable.

If there was a congregational need for a sermon collection on the festival cycle, the need for similar sermons on the Pentateuchal readings would not have been far behind (as Theodor showed, Tan originally followed the approximately triennial Palestinian order of reading). This is another argument for the early date of such collections, even if the multiplicity of MS versions and medieval quotations indicates that they never attained an absolutely final form.

The reading cycle, the cited rabbis and the material of Tan combine to make Palestine the most plausible place of origin for this genre, even if other countries later contributed to the further development of the textual recensions.

### *5) Deuteronomy Rabbah (DeutR)*

#### *Bibliography*

**Herr, M. D.** *EJ* 5: 1584–86. **Zunz,** *GV*, 263–65. [Cf. Albeck, *Derashot*, 122f., 391.]

#### *Text*

Editions of Midrash Rabbah, e.g. **Mirkin, A.** Vol. 11. **Liebermann, S.** *Midrash Debarim Rabbah*. 3rd edn. Jerusalem 1974. **Ginzberg, L.** *Ginzê Schechter*, 1:107–68. **Mann, J.** & **Sonne, I.** *The Bible as Read and Preached in the Old Synagogue*, vol. 2 (Cincinnati 1966), Hebrew section, 220–39. **Rabinovitz, Z. M.** *Ginzé Midrash*, 72–82. See also the bibliography on Tanḥuma.

#### *Translations*

**Rabbinowitz, J.** In the Soncino edition of *Midrash Rabbah*. London 1939; repr. 1961. **Wünsche, A.** *Bibl. Rabb.* Vol. 3. Leipzig 1882; repr. Hildesheim 1967. [Both give the standard version.]

### *a) Name*

In the Middle Ages, DeutR is cited as (*Haggadat*) *Elleh ha-Debarim Rabbah*, *Debarim Rabbati* and the like, but also as *Yelamdenu* or *Tanḥuma*, since the midrash in fact belongs to the Tan group.

### *b) Text*

All MSS diverge to some extent from the printed version of DeutR (first printed at Constantinople 1512; then Venice 1545). S. Buber, *Liqqutim mi-Midrash Elleh ha-Debarim Zutta* (Vienna 1885), 10–32, published the pericope Debarim (Deut 1.1–3.22) and the additions in Niṣabim from Cod. Hebr. 229 (dated 1295) of the State Library at Munich. Parashiyot 2 and 9–

11 are missing in this MS; the other chapters are the same as the printed edition. A MS in the possession of A. Epstein (described by him in *Qadmoniot*, 80–82) resembles MS Munich, but contains parashiyot 2 and 9 (*Wa-etḥannan* and *Wa-yelekh*) which diverge from the usual printed text, additions to 8 (*Niṣabim*) and augmentations of the last two parashiyot from Tanḥuma.

Oxford MS 147, edited by S. Lieberman, belongs to the same kind of manuscript as that described by Epstein (Oxford MS 2335 is also similar). It contains Midrash Rabbah on the whole Torah. In DeutR it includes additional homilies from Tanḥuma on parashah 2 (*Wa-etḥannan*), over and above the material from MS Epstein. The Lieberman edition renders in small print all those passages that are identical with Tanḥuma (*Wa-etḥannan*, pp. 34–54; *Ha'azinu* and *We-zo't ha-Berakhah*, pp. 125–31) or which correspond to the standard edition (*'Eqeb* through *Niṣabim*, pp. 83–116); these passages add up to more than half the text.

The fragment edited by Rabinovitz, a page from the Antonin collection in Leningrad, diverges in parashah *Re'eh* from both versions of Tan and DeutR, and might represent an early form. The fragment dates from about the eleventh century.

### *c) Structure*

In the printed editions, the ordinary version of DeutR is divided according to the Sabbath pericopes of the one-year cycle (the editions of Constantinople 1512 and Venice 1545 have only ten, since *Niṣabim* and *Wa-yelekh* are linked together). In reality, DeutR consists of 27 self-contained homilies which relate to texts of the roughly *triennial* cycle.

The homilies begin with a halakhic introduction: the question formula *Halakhah – adam me-Yisra'el* precedes the answer introduced by *kakh shanu ḥakhamim*. This is followed by one or several proems, which here are already fairly independent homiletical creations. The haggadah usually commences with the words *zeh she-amar ha-katub*, 'this is what the Scripture says'. After the exposition of the Scripture passage, the sermon usually ends in a promising or comforting eschatological conclusion.

In the Lieberman edition, DeutR does not always introduce the sermons with a halakhic question; and the question in each case begins without an introductory formula. The answer, however, always begins with *kakh shanu rabbotenu*, the haggadah with *zehu she-amar ha-katub*.

### *d) Origin and Date*

The textual transmission indicates a complex origin. When MSS Munich and

Epstein became known, the existence of a second, complete DeutR was inferred. Medieval quotations missing from both textual versions led A. Epstein to assume a third recension. However, the material peculiar to MS is not sufficiently extensive to require a second complete version of DeutR (different recensions exist only for the first two parashiyot and the beginning of the third).

Medieval quotations imply that the standard version was common in France and Germany, while that edited by Lieberman prevailed in Spain, where Naḥmanides was the first to quote it.

Both versions of the text use PT (often abridged), GenR and LevR; the ordinary version also employs LamR. Influence from BT, on the other hand, cannot be established (individual Babylonian expressions in DeutR are due to the textual transmission). Since the language (Hebrew, Galilean Aramaic, many Greek loan words) along with the places and rabbis' names indicate a Palestinian origin of DeutR, it must have ben composed prior to the circulation of BT in Palestine. Parallels with the later midrash *Petirat Mosheh* must probably be regarded as later additions. Thus, as Lieberman xxii stresses, Zunz's late dating (*GV*, 264f.) is entirely unfounded. The work certainly has an early origin; but due to its turbulent textual history (especially the constant mutual influence of the various Tan recensions), a more precise dating between c. 450 and 800 is extremely difficult.

### *6) Exodus Rabbah (ExodR)*

***Bibliography***

**Herr, M. D.** *EJ* 6: 1067–69. **Liebermann, S.** *Midrash Debarim Rabbah*, xxii, 2nd edn. Jerusalem 1964. **Shinan, A.** 'The Opening Section of Midrash Exodus Rabbah.' In E. Fleischer & J.J. Petuchowski (eds.), *Studies in Aggadah, Targum and Jewish Liturgy, in Memory of Joseph Heinemann*, Hebr. section, 175–83. Jerusalem 1981. **Zunz**, *GV*, 268–70. [Cf. Albeck, *Derashot*, 125, 396f.]

*Text:* in the standard editions of Midrash Rabbah, e.g. **Mirkin, A.** *Midrash Rabbah*, vols. 5–6. Critical edition of the first part: **Shinan, A.** *Midrash Shemot Rabbah, Chapters I–XIV: A Critical Edition Based on a Jerusalem Manuscript, with Variants, Commentary and Introduction* (Hebr.). Tel Aviv 1984.

***Translations***

**Lehrmann, S. M.** In the Soncino Edition of *Midrash Rabbah*, vol. 3. London 1939; repr. 1961. German: **Wünsche, A.** *Bibl. Rabb.* Vol. 3. Leipzig 1882; repr. Hildesheim 1967. Spanish: **Girón Blanc, L. F.** *Midrás Exodo Rabbah.* Vol. 1. Valencia 1989. [Translation of Shinan's edition.]

ExodR (or *Shemot Rabbah*) is preserved in MS Oxford Bodl. 147 and 2335, both of which contain the entire Midrash Rabbah on the Torah; similarly in

MS Jerusalem 24°5977 (Spain, 15th cent.); for additional textual witnesses see Shinan 24–28. The manuscripts have not yet been sufficiently analysed; a scholarly edition of ExodR exists only for the first part of the work. It was first printed at Constantinople in 1512, then at Venice in 1545.

The work is composed of two different parts. *The first part* (ExodR I) comprises parashiyot 1–14 and is an exegetical midrash on Exod 1–10 (11 is not treated in ExodR). *The second part* (ExodR II) with parashiyot 15–52 is a homiletical midrash on Exod 12–40 which belongs to the genre of the Tanḥuma-Yelamdenu midrash (this is clear e.g. from the repeated introduction, *kakh pataḥ R. Tanḥuma bar Abba*). The sermons follow the sedarim of the Palestinian reading cycle; the exposition usually only treats the first few verses. This part contains frequent sermon conclusions pertaining to the future.

Zunz, who does not yet divide the work, dates it as a whole to the eleventh or twelfth century, although he allows for many pieces from older works on the grounds that the work uses the entire older haggadah. Such a comprehensively late dating, however, is extremely doubtful (Lieberman). Herr considers the second part to be older than the first, which in his opinion used the lost beginning of the homiletic midrash on Exod as a source. For the dating of ExodR I he bases himself above all on linguistic arguments (partly Babylonian Aramaic) and on the use of BT, whose Aramaic in his view was at times rather unhappily rendered into Galilean Aramaic. He judges this part to be no earlier than the tenth century. Shinan, 19ff. considers it possible that the BT was not yet available to the redactor as a completed work, but only in partial excerpts. He assumes the origin of ExodR I in the tenth century; the place of origin cannot be determined.

Herr holds that ExodR II, whose language is essentially Mishnaic Hebrew with Galilean Aramaic and numerous Greek and Latin loan words, uses Tannaitic literature and PT as well as the early Amoraic midrashim and Tanḥuma, but not BT. The first explicit quotations of ExodR occur in Azriel of Gerona (first half of the 13th cent.) and in Naḥmanides' commentary on the Pentateuch (c. 1260); but the combination of the two parts of this midrash might of course be dated considerably earlier. A more precise dating must await further study.

### *7) Numbers Rabbah (NumR)*

***Bibliography***

**Albeck, Ch.** *Midraš Berešit Rabbati.* Jerusalem 1940; repr. 1967. **Albeck, Ch.** *Mabo*, 9–20; *Derashot*, 126f. **Epstein, A.** *Qadmoniot*, 64–69. **Herr, M. D.** *EJ* 12: 1261–63. **Mack, H.** 'Anti-Christian Sections in Midrash Numbers Rabbah' (Hebr.). *10th WCJS* (Jerusalem 1990) C 1:133–40.

[NumR as evidence for controversies in Southern France after the first Crusade.] **Zunz**, *GV*, 270–74.

***Text***

See the standard editions of Midrash Rabbah, e.g. **Mirkin, A.** *Midrash Rabbah.* Vols. 9–10. Cf. also **Ginzberg, L.** *Ginzê Schechter*, 1:91–102. [On Genizah material differing in part from our editions of Tan and NumR.] **Mack, H.** *Prolegomena and Example of an Edition of a Midrash of Bemidbar Rabba Part 1* (Hebr.). Diss. Jerusalem 1991. **Mack, H.** 'The Reworking of a Midrash by Printers in Istanbul in 1512' (Hebr.). *Pe'amim* 52 (1992) 37–46. [On the first printed edition.] **Rabinovitz, Z. M.** *Ginzé Midrash*, 66–71.

***Translations***

**Slotki, J. J.** In the Soncino Edition of *Midrash Rabbah.* London 1939; repr. 1961. **Wünsche, A.** *Bibl. Rabb.* Vol. 4. Leipzig 1883–85; repr. Hildesheim 1967.

The earliest complete MSS of NumR (in Hebrew *Bemidbar Rabbah*; in the first printed edition of Constantinople 1512 *Bemidbar Sinai Rabbah*) are from the fifteenth century (Oxford Bodl. 147 and 2335); MS Hebr. Paris 149 from the year 1291 contains NumR 1–5; MS Munich 97.2 of 1418 presents NumR 1–14.

The midrash consists of two very different parts. NumR I comprises sections 1–14, approximately three-quarters of the total work, and is a haggadic treatment of Num 1–7. NumR II (sections 15–23) is a homiletic midrash which discusses Num 8–36 much more briefly.

As for the origin of the midrash, I. H. Weiss (*Dor*, 3:236) is followed by Mirkin in regarding NumR as the homogeneous work of Mosheh ha-Darshan (11th century, Narbonne), while most would agree with Zunz in seeing NumR as a composite work.

*NumR I* on the two first sedarim of the one-year cycle (*Bemidbar, Naso*), albeit arranged in parashiyot according to the Palestinian, roughly triennial cycle, has as its textual basis a Tanḥuma midrash (anonymous proems, partly still with halakhah). This, however, was later greatly enlarged: 'instead of the short explanations or allegories of the elders, instead of their constant appeal to authorities, we read here compilations from halakhic and haggadic works, intermingled with artificial and often playful applications of Scripture; and for many pages at a time we find no named source' (Zunz, *GV*, 272f.). The expansions vis-à-vis Tan include numerous passages from various rabbinic writings (halakhic midrashim, PRK, PesR, MidrPss, etc.). With Ch. Albeck it must be assumed that these texts were inserted all at once, from a work of the school of Mosheh ha-Darshan, whom Rashi (e.g. on Num 32.41f.) already knows as an author of interpretations which are known to us only from NumR. *Bereshit Rabbati* and the *Midrash Aggadah* published by S. Buber, which stem from Mosheh ha-Darshan or his school, have much in common with NumR, and they too employ Mosheh ha-Darshan's method of assembling interpretations from very different works into a new midrash like a mosaic. His use of pseudepigraphs and quotation of rabbinic works by their (supposed) authors is characteristic. Thus e.g. *Midrash Tadshe* is in NumR repeatedly cited as Pinḥas ben Yair, *Seder Eliyahu* as Elijah (e.g. NumR 5.9, 'Elijah says'); 14.10 presents a quotation from Tan Shemot 3: 'R. Tanḥuma says'. With Zunz the development of the expanded version cannot be assumed prior to the twelfth century.

*NumR II* (Chapters 15–23) will originally have been divided according to the approximately triennial reading cycle; in the editions it is arranged according to the Sabbath parashiyot of the one-year cycle: only the parashah *Shelaḥ-lekha* (Num 13–15) contains has two sections. As was already recognized by M. Benveniste (preface to *Ot Emet*, Thessaloniki 1565), this part is essentially the Midrash Tanḥuma. At the beginning of the halakhic introduction the printed editions of NumR have 'halakhah', while the Paris MS Hebr. 150 reads the older form *Yelamdenu Rabbenu*. The excess text over against the printed Tan is generally covered by MSS of Tan. The two longer additions for which this is not the case are from Mosheh ha-Darshan: 18.15–18; 20.5–6; also 18.29, although this has also been included in the printed Tanḥuma.

Herr assumes a date of origin in the ninth century for this part of NumR, as for Tanḥuma; but an earlier date is more likely (see p. 305 above). Prior to editing, NumR I must have looked like NumR II; or perhaps one must suppose that an originally homogeneous Tan midrash on Num was truncated only in the course of revision in the school of Mosheh ha-Darshan, and subsequently reassembled. The coupling of the two parts probably took place at the beginning of the thirteenth century, since the Yalqut does not yet appear to know NumR as a complete work, while Naḥmanides already quotes it as such.

### *8) Smaller Homiletical Midrashim*

#### *a) Aggadat Bereshit*

Aggadat Bereshit is a collection of 28 homilies on Gen according to the c. triennial reading cycle. Each homily has three sections, resulting in a total of 84 (83 in the earlier printings; for only MS Oxford 2340, which incidentally calls the work *Seder Eliyahu Rabbah*, also contains section 42). The first section always relates to Gen, the second to a text from the prophets which must be regarded as haftarah for this seder; the third is about a passage from the Psalms (perhaps read on the same Sabbath). The beginning (Gen 1.1–6.4) and the final treatment of a Psalm verse are missing. The content is for the most part taken from TanB. The work is often attributed to Rab (thus Abraham ben Elijah of Wilna in his textual edition, Wilna 1802); M. D. Herr dates it in the tenth century.

***Bibliography***

***Text***

First printed by Menaḥem di Lonzano in Venice, 1618, at the end of *Shtê Yadot*. **Buber, S.** *Aggadat Bereshit*. Cracow 1903; repr. 1973. [Uses the first edition together with MS Oxford.] **Jellinek, A.** *BHM*, 4:1–116. See M. D. Herr, *EJ* 2: 366; Zunz, *GV*, 268.

### *b) Midrash Hashkem or Midrash We-hiẓhir*

J. M. Freimann edited a MS of the Munich State Library (Cod. Hebr. 205) which contains a midrash on Exod 8.16 to Num 5.11ff., structured according to the parashiyot of the one-year cycle. As early as the middle ages, this work is named after its opening word *hashkem* ('rise early!'). Freimann preferred the name *We-hizhir*, which is also attested in the middle ages and takes its origin from the many paragraphs beginning with *we-hizhir ha-qadosh barukh hu'* ('and God admonished' Israel). Quotations from early authors are published in L. Grünhut, *Sefer ha-Likkutim*, 1:2a–20a and in Enelow. Freimann thought that the two names designate different midrashim, since the parallels are often inexact. Others, including S. Assaf, hold that such alterations are common in medieval quotations, and that both names relate to the same work. In terms of both form and content, the text is dependent on R. Aḥa's *Sheiltot* (8th cent.); in both documents, halakhic questions follow the Torah reading and are augmented by haggadic passages. The work adopts additional halakhic material from the *Halakhot Gedolot* and takes further haggadic material from the Tanḥuma tradition; it also includes 12 of the 14 chapters of the *Baraita de-Melekhet ha-Mishkan* (cf. R. S. Kirschner, *Baraita de-Melekhet ha-Mishkan* (Cincinnati 1992), 57, 68f., 109f.). Now that Genizah fragments have considerably enhanced our knowledge of the *Sheiltot*, a new study of their influence on this midrash is urgently required. S. Assaf is probably right to suggest that this document was composed in Palestine in the tenth century.

***Text***

**Freimann, J. M.** *Sefer We-hiẓhir*. Vol. 1: Exod (Leipzig 1873); vol. 2: Lev, Num (Warsaw 1880). **Eisenstein, J. D.** *Ozar Midrashim*, 1:138–46. **Enelow, H. G.** 'Midrash Hashkem Quotations in Alnaqua's Menorat ha-Maor.' *HUCA* 4 (1927) 311–43. **Roth, A. N. Z.** 'A Fragment from Midrash ve-Hizhir' (Hebr.). *Talpioth* 7 (1958) 89–98. See S. Abramson, *Inyanot be-Sifrut ha-Geonim* (Jerusalem 1974), 382f.; Zunz, *GV*, 294; idem, *Schriften*, vol. 3 (Berlin 1876), 251–59.

### *c) Pesiqta Ḥadatta*

The 'new Pesiqta' is a brief homiletical midrash for the feast days (published in A. Jellinek, *BhM* 1:137–41; 6:36–70). It contains homilies for Ḥanukkah, Pesaḥ, Shabuot, Sukkot, Purim, Rosh Ha-Shanah and Yom Kippur. Early sources attest the name *Mah Rabbu*; this shows that the midrash originally began with New Year, whose homily begins with these words (S. Lieberman, *Midrash Debarim Rabbah*, 3rd edn. Jerusalem 1974, xiv f.). Sources include GenR, PRE and Sefer Yeṣirah. German Translation: A. Wünsche, *Lehrhallen*, vol. 5.

### *d) Midrash Wa-yekhullu*

This text is named after Gen 2.1. We know the work only from quotations (collected by L. Grünhut, *Sefer ha-Likkutim*, 2:16a–20a) in authors after the middle of the twelfth century. These quotations relate to Gen, Lev, Num and Deut; thus the midrash appears to have comprised the entire Pentateuch. An important source for it was Tanḥuma. Cf. Zunz, *GV*, 293f.

### *e) Midrash Abkir*

This work is known from more than 50 excerpts in the Yalqut and in other writings (the quotations in Tobiah ben Eliezer's *Leqaḥ Tob* are uncertain). It probably covered only Gen and Exod. Its name derives from the expression *Amen; be-yamênu ken yehi raṣôn.* Eleazar of Worms affirms that all of its homilies ended with this expression ('Amen; in our days, thus be it [God's] will'). The language and content suggest a late date. The whole work was still known to Azariah dei Rossi (d. 1578) and to Abraham Ibn Aqra.

***Text***

**Buber, S.** 'Liqqutim mi-Midrash Abkir.' *Ha-Shaḥar* 11 (Vienna 1883) 338–45, 409–18, 453–61. [Extracts in the Yalqut; a separate edition of these pages appeared in Tel Aviv, 1982.] **Abraham ben Elijah of Wilna**. *Rab Pealim*, 133–47. Edited by S. M. Ḥones. Warsaw 1894; repr. Tel Aviv 1967. Further quotations are given by **Epstein, A.** *Ha-Eshkol* 6 (1909) 204–7. See also **Marmorstein, A.** *Debir* 1 (1923) 113–44. [His quotations are not certainly from this Midrash.]

***Bibliography***

**Haag, H. J.** '"Dies ist die Entstehungsgeschichte des Himmels und der Erde" – Midrash Avkir zu Gen 2,4.' *Judaica* 34 (1978) 104–19, 173–79. **Herr, M. D.** *EJ* 16: 1516f. [He dates the work to the beginning of the 11th century]. **Spiegel, J. S.** 'The Latest Evidence to Midrash Abkir' (Hebr.). *KS* 45 (1969–70) 611–15. **Zunz**, *GV*, 293f.

### *f) Midrash Esfah*

This midrash on Num is named after Num 11.16, 'Gather for me 70 men from the elders of Israel'. Since it is almost exclusively known from a few excerpts in the Yalqut, its genre cannot be securely determined. The quotations are collected in S. Buber, *Knesset Yisra'el*, vol. 1 (Warsaw 1887), 309–20; and Abraham ben Elijah Gaon, *Rab Pealim*, ed. S. M. Ḥones (Warsaw 1894; repr. Tel Aviv 1967), 147–53; Wertheimer, 1:208–14. Cf. Zunz, *GV*, 292.

# V

## MIDRASHIM ON THE FIVE MEGILLOT

***1) The So-Called Rabbot***
***a) Lamentations Rabbah***: see pp. 283–87.

***b) Midrash Shir ha-Shirim or Song of Songs Rabbah (CantR)***
Because of the opening quotation of Prov 22.29 *ḥazitah ish mahir*, this midrash is also called *Aggadat Ḥazitah.* The 1519 *editio princeps* of Pesaro uses the designations *Shir ha-Shirim Rabbati* and *Midrash Shir ha-Shirim.* The oldest manuscript is MS Parma De Rossi 1240, where CantR is inserted after PesR 18 for the Pesaḥ festival, on which of course Cant is read. Z. M. Rabinovitz, *Ginzé Midrash*, 83–117, has published several Genizah fragments from Cambridge and Leningrad, a total of ten pages, all from about the eleventh century (on Cant 1.2, 5f., 8f., 12; 3.1). Especially in regard to language, their character is much more genuinely Palestinian; in contrast with the printed editions, these texts show no signs of borrowing from BT.

CantR is an exegetical midrash. In the first edition it was divided into two parashiyot (Cant 1.1–2.7; 2.8ff.); the later editions have eight parashiyot in keeping with the number of chapters in Cant. CantR offers an allegorical (or, more precisely, typological) exegesis of the Song of Songs, whose holiness was already discussed in the Mishnah (m.Yad 3.5). This midrash is marked by multiple repetitions and diverse material; Theodor attempted to explain this as a result of its catena-like character (cf. Lachs, *JQR* N.S. 55:243f.). However, CantR is not merely a catena but expresses a coherent design (see J. Neusner). The Genizah texts demonstrate that some of the repetitions were omitted from the printed editions. The main sources of CantR are PT, GenR, LevR and PRK; M passages and Baraitot are also adduced. The opening proems all end on the same sentence from Seder Olam. CantR (in another version) served as a source of PesR. The work must, with Herr, be dated to the middle of the sixth century (Lachs, *JQR* N.S. 55:249, follows Zunz in endorsing a later date: original composition between 650 and 750, final version in the second half of the eighth century); but it contains much older material. Urbach finds in this text valuable information on the Christian-Jewish controversy of the first few centuries; but cf. J. Maier, *Jüdische Auseinandersetzung mit dem Christentum in der Antike* (Darmstadt 1982), 193: despite the unmistakably apologetic and polemical character of the text, detailed analysis reveals very little concrete knowledge of Christian arguments.

*Text:* in the standard Midrash Rabbah editions. **Dunsky, S.** *Midrash Rabbah: Shir ha-Shirim.* Jerusalem/Tel Aviv 1980. [Presents merely the text of the Wilna edition, 'corrected' on the basis of parallels from rabbinic literature and conjectures of earlier commentators, but without using any MSS.] **Girón Blanc, L. F.** 'Cantar de los Cantares Rabbâ 4,7–8: Edición crítica.' *Sefarad* 52 (1992) 103–12. [The base text is MS 27 of the Kaufmann Collection, Budapest.] **Goldstein, N.** 'Midrash Shir-ha-Shirim Rabbah bi-ketab yad Parma 1240.' *Kobez al Yad* 9 [19] (Jerusalem 1979) 1–24. [Includes only a quarter of the text, with important variants.] **Rabinovitz, Z. M.** *Ginzé Midrash,* 83–117. **Rabinovitz, Z. M.** 'On the Ancient Form of Midrash Shir ha-Shirim Rabba' (Hebr.). In M. A. Friedman, A. Tal & G. Brin (eds.), *Studies in Talmudic Literature,* 83–90. Tel Aviv 1983. [On the Genizah fragment edited by Scheiber.] **Scheiber, A.** 'Ein Fragment aus dem Midrasch Schir Haschirim Rabba: Aus der Kaufmann Geniza'. *AcOr* 32 (1978) 231–43; repr. in idem, *Genizah Studies* (Hildesheim 1981), 500–12. [One leaf: CantR on 4:7–8.] **Steller, H. E.** 'Shir haShirim Rabbah 5.2–8: Towards a Reconstruction of a Midrashic Block.' In A. Kuyt et al. (eds.), *Variety of Forms: Dutch Studies in Midrash,* 94–132. Amsterdam 1990. **Steller, H. E.** 'Preliminary Remarks to a New Edition of Shir Hashirim Rabbah.' In G. Sed-Rajna, *RASHI 1040–1990,* 301–11. Paris 1993. [An edition prepared by M. C. & H. E. Steller; L. F. Girón Blanc is also working on a critical edition.] **Wertheimer, S. A.**, *Batei Midrashot,* 1:347–53. A critical edition is being prepared in Amsterdam by M. C. & H. E. Steller.

***Translations***

**Neusner, J.** *Song of Songs Rabbah: An Analytical Translation.* 2 vols. Atlanta 1989. **Simon, M.** In the Soncino Edition of the Midrash Rabbah, vol. 9. London 1939; repr. 1971. **Wünsche, A.** *Bibl. Rabb.* Vol. 2. Leipzig 1880; repr. Hildesheim 1967. [German.]

***Bibliography***

**Boyarin, D.** 'Two Introductions to the Midrash on the Song of Songs' (Hebr.). *Tarbiz* 56 (1986–87) 479–500. [On the Tannaitic exposition of the Song of Songs as typological, not allegorical or esoteric.] **Girón Blanc, L. F.** 'Exégesis y homilética en Cantar de los Cantares Rabba.' *MEAH* 40.2 (1991) 33–54. [On 2 proems.] **Herr, M. D.** *EJ* 15: 152–54. **Lachs, S. T.** 'An Egyptian Festival in Canticles Rabba'. *JQR* N.S. 51 (1960–61) 47–54. **Lachs, S. T.** 'Prolegomena to Canticles Rabba'. *JQR* N.S. 55 (1964–65) 235–55. **Lachs, S. T.** 'The Proems of Canticles Rabba'. *JQR* N.S. 56 (1965–66) 225–39. **Lerner, M. B.** 'Concerning the Source of a Quotation in the Epistle of R. Solomon b. Judah and Studies in Midrash Shir Hashirim' (Hebr.). *Tarbiz* 52 (1982–83) 581–90. [On an interpolation in the interest of the Palestinian Gaonate.] **Neusner, J.** *The Midrash Compilations of the Sixth and Seventh Centuries: An Introduction to the Rhetorical, Logical, and Topical Program.* Vol. 4: *Song of Songs Rabbah.* Atanta 1989. **Neusner, J.** *Introduction,* 467–86. **Theodor, J.** 'Zur Komposition der agadischen Homilien'. *MGWJ* 28 (1879) 271–75, 337–50, 408–18, 455–62; 29 (1880) 19–23. **Urbach, E. E.** 'Rabbinic Exegesis and Origenes' Commentaries on the Song of Songs and Jewish-Christian Polemics' (Hebr.). *Tarbiz* 30 (1960–61) 148–70. [English translation in *Scripta Hierosolymitana* 22 (1971) 247–75.] **Zunz,** *GV,* 274f.

### *c) Midrash Ruth*

This midrash contains a complete commentary on Ruth, traditionally read at Shabuot, in eight sections (probably originally four). The work as a whole is introduced by six proems; additional proems appear before sections 3, 4, 6 and 8. Extensive expositions of 1 Chr 4.21–23 and 11.13 (from p.Sanh 2.5, 20b–c) are included at the beginning of chapters 2 and 5, in an attempt to integrate Ruth into biblical history. The story of Elisha ben Abuyah, which is also included in Midrash Qohelet, serves in this text (6.4) as a contrast to

Boaz; here as elsewhere, material shared with other writings is clearly made to serve the purposes of Midrash Ruth. The main sources are Tannaitic literature, PT, GenR and PRK. The text mentions no rabbis after the fourth century; together with its language and its literary dependences, this locates it in Palestine around the year 500. It was called Midrash Ruth in the first edition, Pesaro 1519, and has been known as Ruth Rabbah since the Venice edition of 1545.

***Text:*** in the standard Midrash Rabbah editions. Critical edition with introduction: **Lerner, M. B.** *The Book of Ruth in Aggadic Literature and Midrash Ruth Rabba* (Hebr.). Vol. 2. Diss. Jerusalem 1971. [Basic text is MS Oxford 164; collation of Genizah fragments, etc.] **Alloni, N.** *Geniza Fragments*, 65f.

***Translations***

**Neusner, J.** *Ruth Rabbah: An Analytical Translation.* Atlanta 1989. **Rabinowitz, L.** In the Soncino Edition of *Midrash Rabbah*, vol. 8. London 1939; repr. 1971. German: **Wünsche, A.** *Bibl. Rabb.* Vol. 3. Leipzig 1883; repr. Hildesheim 1967.

***Bibliography***

**Hartmann, P. D.** *Das Buch Ruth in der Midrasch-Literatur.* Frankfurt 1901. **Herr, M. D.** *EJ* 14: 524. **Kronholm, T.** 'The portrayal of characters in Midrash Ruth Rabbah'. *Annual of the Swedish Theological Institute* 12 (1983) 13–54. **Lerner, M. B.** [See above.] **Lieberman, S.** 'Qeṣat he'erot le-teḥilat Rut Rabbah.' In S. Lieberman (ed.), *Henoch Yalon: Jubilee Volume* (Hebr.), 174–81.. Jerusalem 1963. [Reprinted in *Studies*, 45–52.] **Neusner, J.** *The Midrash Compilations of the Sixth and Seventh Centuries: An Introduction to the Rhetorical, Logical, and Topical Program.* Vol. 3: *Ruth Rabbah.* Atanta 1989. **Neusner, J.** *Introduction*, 487–509. **Niehoff, M.** 'The Characterization of Ruth in the Midrash' (Hebr.). *JSJT* 11 (1993) 49–78. **Zunz**, *GV*, 276f. [Supplemented by Albeck, *Derashot*, 130.]

### *d) Midrash Qohelet* (Ecclesiastes Rabbah)

This midrash, which in manuscripts and in the first printed edition (Pesaro 1519) is called *Midrash Qohelet* (quoted as *Haggadat Qohelet* in the Arukh; known as Qohelet Rabbah only since the edition Venice 1545), follows the biblical text verse by verse, leaving only a few verses (in the Pesaro edition 15 out of 222) without explanation. The first printed edition has three parashiyot (1.1ff.; 7.1ff.; 9.7ff.). Today the text is usually divided into 12 sections, in accordance with the biblical number of chapters. The work has numerous parallels in the older midrashim, especially in proems relating to Qohelet. PT is most extensively used, along with GenR, LamR, LevR and PRK; the parallels with BT, however, are probably later additions. The tractate Abot and several of the minor tractates (Gerim, Slaves, Fringes, Phylacteries and Mezuzah) are mentioned. Repetitions are not uncommon. Hirshman (*HUCA*) stresses the encyclopaedic character of this work, which uses the biblical text to discuss very diverse topics; in this form it might well have served as a school textbook (cf. already J. Heinemann), implicitly disputing the need for cultural borrowing from the environment. There is as yet no critical edition of this text (aside from chapters 1–4 in Hirshman's dissertation). It may have originated in Palestine in the eighth century; Hirshman wants to date it in the sixth or seventh century. The oldest manuscripts are Leningrad Firkovitch II A 272 (c. 14th cent.: cf. M. Kahana, *Asufot* 6 (1992) 60) and MS Vat. Hebr. 291.11b (14th or 15th cent.; the date of 1417, which is mentioned in the earlier part of this composite MS, need not apply to Midrash Qohelet); additional MSS are in Oxford and Jerusalem. The Genizah fragments are described in Wachten, 28–31; additional material can be found in Hirshman, Diss., 118–21.

***Bibliography***

**Ben-David, I.** 'Some Notes on the Text of Midraš Ecclesiastes Rabba' (Hebr.). *Leshonenu* 53 (1988–89) 135–40. **Grünhut, L.** *Kritische Untersuchung des Midrasch Kohelet Rabba, Quellen und Redaktionszeit.* Frankfurt 1892. **Herr, M. D.** *EJ* 6: 355. **Hirshman, M.** *Midrash Qohelet Rabbah Chapter 1–4: Commentary (Ch.1) and Introduction* (Hebr.). Diss. New York: Jewish Theological Seminary, 1983. **Hirshman, M.** 'The Prophecy of King Solomon and Ruaḥ Hakodesh in Midrash Qohelet Rabbah' (Hebr.). *Jerusalem Studies in Jewish Thought* 3 (1982) 7–14. **Hirshman, M.** 'The Priest's Gate and Elijah ben Menahem's Pilgrimage: Medieval Interpolations in Midrash Manuscripts' (Hebr.). *Tarbiz* 55 (1985–86) 217–27. **Hirshman, M.** 'The Greek Fathers and the Aggada on Ecclesiastes: Formats of Exegesis in Late Antiquity.' *HUCA* 59 (1988) 137–65. **Lieberman, S.** 'Notes on Chapter I of Midrash Koheleth Rabbah' (Hebr.). In E. E. Urbach et al. (eds.), *Studies in Mysticism and Religion* (*Festschrift* G. Scholem), Hebr. section, 163–79. Jerusalem 1967. [Reprinted in *Studies*, 53–69; esp. on Greek vocabulary.] **Lieberman, S.** 'Shesh Millim mi-Qohelet rabbah'. *Memorial Volume G. Alon*, 227–35. Jerusalem 1970. [Reprinted in *Studies*, 498–506.] **Wachten, J.** *Midrasch-Analyse: Strukturen im Midrasch Qohelet Rabba.* Hildesheim 1978. Zunz, *GV*, 277.

***Translations***

**Cohen, A.** In the Soncino Edition of *Midrash Rabbah*, vol. 8. London 1939; repr. 1971. German: **Wünsche, A.** *Bibl. Rabb.*, vol. 1. Leipzig 1880; repr. Hildesheim 1967.

### *e) Midrash Esther*

Midrash Esther, also less frequently called *Haggadat Megillah* or *Midrash Ahasweros*, is an exposition of the Esther scroll, which is read at the feast of Purim. The earliest MSS are from the early fifteenth century, the first printed edition is Pesaro 1519. The latter divides the midrash into 6 sections (1.1, 4, 9, 13; 2.1, 5) marked by petiḥot. The later editions have ten sections. The uneven treatment of the text (in Esth 1–2 every verse is discussed; for 3.1–8.15 there are many omissions) suggests a distinction between two different midrashim:

*EsthR I* (section 1–6) is characterized by classical proems which are rarely anonymous; according to its language it originated in Palestine. This text quotes PT, GenR and LevR, and is in turn quoted in EcclR, MidrPss, etc.; hence it must be dated after around 500.

*EsthR II* (sections 7–10) has only a few, non-classical petiḥot and mixes older with more recent material (sections 8f. contain a long interpolation of Septuagintal material on Esth from Josippon: dream and prayer of Mordecai, Esther's prayer and her appearance before the king). Herr (*EJ* 6: 915) surmises that this document originated in the eleventh century, as a replacement for the original continuation of EsthR I which was attested by quotations in EcclR, MidrPss and medieval authors. Z. M. Rabinovitz, *Ginzé Midrash*, 155–60, presents a Genizah text from Cambridge (c. 11th cent.) on Esth 6.11–7.8, which appears to be a continuation of EsthR I. The combination of EsthR I and II probably took place in the twelfth or thirteenth century.

***Bibliography***

**Neusner, J.** *The Midrash Compilations of the Sixth and Seventh Centuries: An Introduction to the Rhetorical, Logical, and Topical Program.* Vol. 2: Esther *Rabbah I.* Atanta 1989. **Neusner, J.** *Introduction*, 533–46.

***Text***

See the standard Midrash Rabbah editions. **Tabory, J.** 'Some Problems in Preparing a Scientific Edition of *Esther Rabbah*' (Hebr.). *Sidra* 1 (1985) 145–52.

***Translations***

**Neusner, J.** *Esther Rabbah I: An Analytical Translation.* Atlanta 1989. **Simon, M.** In the Soncino edition of Midrash Rabbah. Vol. 9. London 1939; repr. 1971. German: **Wünsche, A.** *Bibl. Rabb.* Vol. 2. Leipzig 1881, repr. Hildesheim 1967.

## *2) Other Midrashim on the Megillot*

### *a) Song of Songs* (Cant Zutta)

S. Buber, *Midrasch suta: Hagadische Abhandlungen über Schir ha-Schirim, Ruth, Echah und Koheleth, nebst Jalkut zum Buche Echah*, Berlin 1894; repr. Tel Aviv n.d. The edition reproduces MS Parma De Rossi 541 (now 2342.3); S. Schechter edited the highly defective MS Parma (written c. 1400) at the same time as Buber, and provided many annotations: *Aggadath Shir Hashirim*, Cambridge 1896 (from *JQR* 6–8 (1894–96); in *JQR* 8 (1896) 179–84 he criticizes Buber's very flawed reproduction of the MS). Schechter points out the significant aspects in common with Yelamdenu and dates the work to the tenth century, even though it contains a lot of old material. The sections on the war against Rome have aroused a great deal of interest (see Lieberman, *Greek*, 179–82; G. Alon, *Studies*, 43; Y. Baer, *Zion* 36 (1971)

131f.). Z. M. Rabinovitz, *Ginzé Midrash*, 250–95, has edited a Genizah fragment from Leningrad which on six pages contains about one-third of the text, and which is far superior to the version known up to now. Rabinovitz denies the connection of the text with Yelamdenu (different terminology; every verse is explained); the dating, too, requires renewed examination.

L. Grünhut has edited a third midrash on Cant: *Midrasch Schir Ha-Schirim*, Jerusalem 1897. New revision of this edition: E. H. Grünhut and J. C. Wertheimer, *Midrash Shir Hashirim*, Jerusalem 1971. See on this the sharp criticism of M. B. Lerner, *KS* 48 (1972–73) 543–49: for the text the old edition is to be preferred; introduction and commentary amateur are dilettantish. A Genizah MS dating from 1147 was edited by Grünhut, but is no longer to be found. Herr (*EJ* 16: 1515) dates the work to the eleventh century; but this still requires more detailed examination.

J. Mann published a fragment of another midrash on Cant from the Genizah: *HUCA* 14 (1939) 333–37; on the other hand, a fragment he published in *Texts and Studies*, vol. 1 (New York 1930; repr. 1972), 322 n.47 in his opinion derives from another midrash. See also M. B. Lerner, 'Perush Midrashi le-Shir ha-Shirim mîmê ha-Geonim', *Kobez al Yad* 8 (1976) 141–64; Ch. Albeck, *Derashot*, 129, 404f.

***b) Qohelet*** (Eccl Zutta)

Ecclesiastes Zutta is shorter than EcclR, although it is still unclear whether Eccl Zutta is older than EcclR or merely an abridged version of the latter, with some additions (thus Albeck, *Derashot*, 130f.). Rashi apparently knows only Eccl Zutta, while the author of Leqaḥ Tob in Greece knows only EcclR (Hirshman, *Midrash Qohelet Rabbah*, 44). Edition by S. Buber (see above on a); description of MSS: M. G. Hirshman, 117f.; J. Wachten, *Midrasch-Analyse* (Hildesheim 1978), 32–36; S. Greenberg, 'Midrash Koheleth Zuṭa', in S. Lieberman (ed.), *Alexander Marx Jubilee Volume* (New York 1950), Hebr. section, 103–14. See also L. Ginzberg, *Ginze Schechter*, 1:169–71 (a fragment of another midrash on Eccl).

***c) Esther***

S. Buber, *Sammlung agadischer Commentare zum Buche Esther*, Wilna 1886, comprises the Midrash Abba Gurion, the Midrash Panim Aḥerim A and B, as well as Leqaḥ Tob. The *Midrash Abba Gurion*, already quoted by Rashi, is also printed in A. Jellinek, *BhM*, vol. 1. German Translation: A. Wünsche, *Lehrhallen*, vol. 2. After the publication of a second version from the Genizah (fragments from the tenth century) by Rabinovitz, *Ginzé Midrash*, 161–70, the conventional late dating to the eleventh or twelfth century is subject to revision. The relationship with the *Targum Sheni* on Esther (Zunz, *GV*, 291) must also be examined. The *Midrash Panim Aḥerim* A dates perhaps from the eleventh century; version B (2.5–14 already in *BhM*, 1:19–24; German translation in A. Wünsche, *Lehrhallen*, vol. 2), which Buber edited on the basis of an Oxford MS of 1470, is already used in the Yalqut. Rabinovitz, *Ginzé Midrash*, 171–78, has published a Genizah fragment (Cambridge; c. 11th cent.) which provides a more complete text than the MSS.

S. Buber, *Aggadat Esther: Agadische Abhandlungen zum Buche Esther*, Cracow 1897, repr. Tel Aviv 1982, edited on the basis of two Yemenite MSS, must be attributed to the author of MHG (Ch. Albeck, 'Das verkannte Buch "Agadath Esther"', *MGWJ* 72 (1928) 155–58.

Other midrashim on Esther are *Midrash Yerushalmi 'al Megillat Ester*, in S. A. Wertheimer, *Batei Midrashot*, 1:318, 340–43; and two different versions of Mordecai's dream and Esther's prayer: *BhM* 5:1–8 (German translation A. Wünsche, *Lehrhallen*, vol. 2); S. A. Wertheimer, *Batei Midrashot*, 1:316f., 331–39. Another version is contained in M. Gaster, 'The Oldest Version of the Midrash Megilla', in G. A. Kohut (ed.), *Semitic Studies in Memory of Rev. Dr. A. Kohut* (Berlin 1897), 167–78 (repr. in idem, *Studies and Texts* (London 1925–28), 1:258–63, 3:44–49; text also in Eisenstein, 1:59–61).

***d) Ruth*** (Ruth Zutta)

Based on MS Parma (De Rossi 541), S. Buber edited a small midrash on Ruth (see above on Cant). Almost the entire text has meanwhile been attested in Genizah fragments, and a new edition is required: see A. Shinan, 'The Stories in Ruth Zuta' (Hebr.), *11th WCJS* (Jerusalem 1994) C 1:129–36.

# VI

## OTHER EXEGETICAL MIDRASHIM
(in order of the biblical books)

Bereshit Rabbati, Bereshit Zutta, Leqaḥ Tob, Sekhel Tob and Midrash Samuel: see Chapter VIII.

### *1) Midrash Jonah*

In the standard editions, Midrash Jonah consists of two parts. Most of the first part also appears in the Yalqut on Jonah (Yalqut II, §§ 550f.: both appear to have drawn on the same source). Chapter 10 of PRE is almost entirely re-used here; some material also comes from PT and BT. The second part, beginning with 2.11 ('then God spoke to the fish'), has been translated into Hebrew from the Zohar; it is not in MS De Rossi, which was used by H. M. Horowitz, *Sammlung kleiner Midrashim*, 1:11–23. Horowitz has three recensions. First printed edition: Prague 1595, then Altona (no date; around 1770), both following the account of Petaḥyah of Regensburg's travels. The text is also in A. Jellinek, *BhM*, 1:97–105 and Eisenstein, 1:218–22; German translation in Wünsche, *Lehrhallen*, vol. 2.

### *2) Midrash on Psalms (MidrPss)*

MidrPss or Midrash Tehillim is also called *Shoḥer Tob*, after the opening words from Prov 11.27. As Zunz, *GV*, 278–80 already recognized, it consists of two parts: the first comprises Psalms 1–118 (only these are in the manuscripts and in the first printed edition), and perhaps part of 119 (thus two MSS). This first part is not the work of a single redactor; for the manuscripts differ considerably, and there are not a few repetitions. Certainly there will have been haggadic collections on the Psalms from early on: GenR 32.3 (Theodor/Albeck 307) speaks of an *Aggadah de-Tehillim* of R. Ḥiyya; elsewhere, too, rabbinic literature mentions haggadic books with Psalms. The Psalms were also the preferred source for the petiḥah verse, so that numerous pertinent expositions were available. *Aggadat Bereshit* might appear to suggest that the Psalms were used as the third reading in the Palestinian synagogue service; but this is not certain. Remnants from these older collections will at any rate still have been available when the later haggadists compiled more numerous midrashim on biblical books. Homilies and expositions on individual verses were apparently being gathered from very diverse sources (cf. D. Lenhard). For this reason a definite date of composition cannot be given. Zunz envisioned the closing centuries of the

Geonic epoch; Buber proposed an early dating of MidrPss 1–118 and believed that only later additions create the impression of a more recent date. Albeck again holds to the late date. One must undoubtedly assume an extended period of development; this renders more accurate statements impossible. Most of the material certainly dates back to the Talmudic period (Braude, xi; on p. xxxi he maintains that MidrPss grew from the third to the thirteenth century). The expression and nature of the Haggadic expositions speak in favour of Palestine as the place of origin: the cited Amoraim are all Palestinians; or at least, in a few instances, they appear also in PT. The interpretation often takes into account *Qere'* and *Ketib*, *plene* and defective spelling. On several occasions the numerical value of the letters of a word is used. There are also dissections of words (*gematria* and *notarikon*).

The second part of MidrPss, containing Pss 119–50, was first printed separately at Thessaloniki in 1515. It is found in no manuscript and is in large part (Pss 122, 124–30, 132–37) borrowed verbatim from the Yalqut. For Pss 123 and 131, Buber compiled a replacement midrash from PesR, Sifre, NumR and BT. J. Mann published a Genizah fragment (Pss 13–16, 24–27) which resembles this second part (Pss 119–21, 138–50) in its stylistic traits. He inferred from this that originally there were at least two complete midrashim on the Pss: the second part does not use the expression *zehu she-amar ha-katub* but simply [Solomon, etc.] *amar*, presents the expositions anonymously, and is much shorter. Mann therefore assumes an earlier textual basis for the second part as well, though this is usually dated to the thirteenth century.

***Text***

Printed together with Midrash Samuel and Midrash Proverbs: Venice 1546, Prague 1613; by itself as *Midrash Shoḥer Tob*: Lemberg (L'vov) 1851, Warsaw 1873. **Buber S.** *Midrasch Tehillim.* Wilna 1891; repr. Jerusalem 1966. [Following MS Parma De Rossi 1332, with a comparison of 7 additional MSS.] See also: **Arzt, M.** 'Chapters from a Ms. of Midrash Tehillim.' In S. Lieberman (ed.), *Alexander Marx Jubilee Volume* Hebr. section, 49–74. New York 1950. **Jellinek, A.** *BhM* 5. **Mann, J.** 'Some Midrashic Geniza Fragments.' *HUCA* 14 (1939) 303–58.

***Translation***

**Braude, W. G.** *The Midrash on Psalms.* 2 vols. New Haven 1959 (=3rd edn. 1976). [Also valuable for textual criticism.] German: **Wünsche, A.** *Midrasch Tehillim.* Trier 1892; repr. Hildesheim 1967.

***Bibliography***

**Elbaum, J.** *EJ* 11: 1519f. **Grözinger, K.-E.** 'Prediger gottseliger Diesseitszuversicht: Jüdische "Optimisten".' *FJB* 5 (1977) 42–64. [On Psalm 34.] **Lenhard, D.** *Vom Ende der Erde rufe ich zu Dir: Eine rabbinische Psalmenhomilie (PesR 9)*, 98–116. Frankfurt 1990. **Rabinowitz, L.** 'Does Midrash Tillim Reflect the Triennial Cycle of Psalms?' *JQR* N.S. 26 (1935–36) 349–68. [His answer: probably yes.] **Zunz,** *GV*, 278–80. [And cf. **Albeck, Ch.**, *Derashot*, 132, 411f.]

### *3) Midrash Mishle*

This midrash on Proverbs (MidrProv) is quoted in the eleventh century, and perhaps already by the Geonim (thus Buber, but uncertain). For the most part, it is more commentary than midrash (but note 1.1, the four riddles which the Queen of Sheba poses for Solomon; 9.2, the death of Aqiba). A good deal of material remains without interpretation, including all of chapters 3 and 18, and almost all of 7 and 29. Quotations in the Yalqut show that a great deal must have been lost. BT and older midrashim served as sources, although in each case it remains to be determined whether a given quotation derives from BT, a parallel in PT, or from the midrashim. Buber and others claim that PT is never used, but this is by no means clear (Visotzky, *The Midrash*, 8). Rabinovitz argued for a Palestinian origin, based on the typically Palestinian style and terminology of the Genizah fragments he had published; but this is strictly valid only for the manuscripts, and not for the midrash itself. Buber had thought of Babylonia and Zunz of Southern Italy as the geographic origin of the work; but this issue cannot be clearly resolved (Visotzky, *The Midrash*, 10–12). The date remains similarly uncertain: while the Genizah fragments often have a more extensive text, they do not yet employ the later, biblical division into 31 chapters. Buber had in mind a date just after BT, while Zunz proposed the end of the Geonic period. In contemporary scholarship, Rabinovitz advocates a date around the seventh or eighth century, while Visotzky argues for the ninth century *inter alia* on the basis of the work's anti-Karaite polemic (*The Midrash*, 10).

#### *Text*

Constantinople 1512/17; Venice 1546. **Buber, S.** *Midrasch Mischle*. Wilna 1893. [Repr. Jerusalem 1965, together with MidrSam (according to MS Paris 152, compared with MSS from Parma and Rome, but not with the oldest MS, Parma 3122, from the year 1270).] **Visotzky, B. L.** *Midrash Mishle: A Critical Edition Based on Vatican MS. Ebr. 44*; with variant readings. . . . New York 1990. For the text see also **Ginzberg, L.** *Ginze Schechter*, 1:163–68. [New version of 31:22–25.] **Rabinovitz, Z. M.** *Ginzé Midrash*, 218–49. [Fragments in Cambridge: 2 leaves of a 10th-cent. palimpsest, though Visotzky prefers to date them in the 11th or 12th cent. (Edition, *Mabo* 9); 6 leaves from the 11th cent.: chapters 7–10, 14–15] **Rabinovitz, Z. M.** 'A Genizah Fragment of Midrash Mishle' (Hebr.). In *Michtam le-David: Rabbi David Ochs Memorial Volume (1905–1975)*, 106–19. Ramat Gan 1978. [Oxford, 2 leaves, c. 11th cent.: chapters 11–12, 17, 19.] Another version of Chapter 31 appears in **Wertheimer, S. A.** *Batei Midrashot*, 2:146–50.

#### *Translations*

**Visotzky, B. L.** *The Midrash on Proverbs*. New Haven, CT 1992. German: **Wünsche, A.** *Bibl. Rabb.* Vol. 4. Leipzig 1885; repr. Hildesheim 1967.

Cf. further **Elbaum, J.** *EJ* 11: 1517. **Higger, M.** 'Beraitoth in Midrash Samuel and Midrash Mishlei.' *Talpioth* 5 (1951–52) 669–82. [Considers these to be evidence of a Babylonian origin.] **Stein, D.** 'The Queen of Sheba and Solomon – Riddles and Interpretations in Midrash to Proverbs Chap. 1' (Hebr.). *Jerusalem Studies in Jewish Folklore* 15 (1993) 7–35.

***4) Midrash Job***

Its existence is attested e.g. in *Yalqut ha-Makhiri*. The extant excerpts and quotations are collected in S. A. Wertheimer, *Batei Midrashot*, 2:151–86. He attributes the work to R. Hoshayah Rabba (3rd cent.), since many anonymous statements in this midrash are elsewhere given in Hoshayah's name. Cf. Zunz, *GV*, 282. The question of the date, which is problematic already because of the fragmentary transmission, still requires detailed investigation (e.g. a comparison with the Targum Job from Qumran).

# VII

# OTHER HAGGADIC WORKS

## *1) From Midrash to Narrative Literature*

### *a) Seder Olam (SOR)*

Since the twelfth century (first in Abraham ben Yarḥi), Seder Olam has been called *Seder Olam Rabbah* (SOR), in order to distinguish it from the work introduced below. SOR is especially (but not exclusively) interested in the chronology of the time from Adam to the end of the Persian period; the latter is compressed into 52 years, or 34 years after the construction of the Second Temple. The second part of the concluding chapter 30 offers the essential dates from Alexander the Great to Bar Kokhba, perhaps abridging an originally more extensive version. Tradition attributes it to the Tannaite Yose ben Ḥalafta (c. 160): thus R. Yoḥanan in Yeb 82b and Nid 46b: 'Who taught Seder Olam? It is R. Yose.' Milikowsky (*PAAJR* 52: 124) regards R. Yose not as the author or redactor, but as the tradent of an earlier work which he revised; based on a comparison of several passages of SOR with t.Sot 12, Milikowsky concludes that 'Seder Olam already existed as a redacted book before the final redaction of T' (*Tarbiz* 49: 263). However, the work was probably redacted in early Amoraic times and later supplemented or revised. B. Z. Wacholder (*Eupolemus* (Cincinnati 1974), 109 n. 53) calls the surviving text 'a post-talmudic publication'; in view of this work's highly disconnected history of transmission (cf. Ratner), this suggestion merits further examination. SOR is frequently credited with the introduction of a chronology 'since the creation of the world'. However, this is here used only in relation to the Flood, and it only achieved widespread ascendancy in Judaism in the eleventh century. SOR also dates the destruction of Jerusalem to the year 68 (though this calculation needs to be pieced together from the various dates it provides).

#### *Text*

First printed at Mantua, 1513. **Ratner, B.** *Seder Olam Rabbah: Die grosse Weltchronik.* Wilna 1897. [Cf. the critique of A. Marx, *Zeitschrift für hebräische Bibliographie* 3 (1899) 68–70.] **Ratner, B.** *Einleitung zum Seder Olam* (Hebr.). Wilna 1894. [Repr. New York 1966=Jerusalem 1988, together with an introduction by S. K. Mirsky.] **Marx. A.** *Seder Olam (Kap. 1–10) herausgegeben, übersetzt und erklärt.* Berlin 1903. **Milikowsky, C. J**. *Seder Olam: A Rabbinic Chronography.* Diss. New Haven, CT: Yale, 1981. [Critical edition based especially on the Genizah text Antonin 891, 9th-cent. Leningrad; where this is impossible, the textual basis is the *editio princeps*, Mantua 1513.] **Milikowsky, C. J.** 'On the Printed Editions of Seder Olam – Introduction to a Critical Edition of Seder Olam: I' (Hebr.). *Alei Sefer* 12 (1986) 38–49. **Weinstock, M. J.** *Seder Olam Rabbah ha-shalem.* 3 vols. Jerusalem 1956–62. **Hopkins, S.** *Miscellany*, 78, 92–94. [Photographs of Genizah fragments.]

***Bibliography***

**Gandz, S.** 'The Calendar of the Seder Olam.' *JQR* N.S. 43 (1952–53) 177–92, 249–70. **Gaster, M.** 'Demetrius und Seder Olam: Ein Problem der hellenistischen Literatur.' In J. Fischer et al. (eds.), *Festskrift i Anledning af D. Simonsens 70–aarige Fødelsedag*, 243–52. Copenhagen 1923. **Milikowsky, C. J.** 'Seder 'Olam and the Tosefta' (Hebr.). *Tarbiz* 49 (1979–80) 246–63. **Milikowsky, C. J.** 'Kima and the Flood in Seder 'Olam and B.T. Rosh ha-Shana: Stellar Time-Reckoning and Uranography in Rabbinic Literature.' *PAAJR* 50 (1983) 105–32. **Milikowsky, C. J.** 'Seder 'Olam and Jewish Chronography in the Hellenistic and Roman Periods.' *PAAJR* 52 (1985) 115–39. **Milikowsky, C. J.** 'Gehenna and "Sinners of Israel" in the Light of Seder 'Olam' (Hebr.). *Tarbiz* 55 (1985–86) 311–43. **Milikowsky, C. J.** 'The Symmetry of History in Rabbinic Literature: The Special Numbers of Seder Olam, Chapter Two' (Hebr.). *JSJT* 11 (1993) 37–47. **Rosenthal, J. M.** *EJ* 14: 1091–93. Zunz, *GV*, 89.

### *b) Seder Olam Zutta (SOZ)*

SOZ draws up a list of 89 generations from Abraham to the exile and then to the end of the Talmudic period. Its main interest concerns the office of the exilarch, which according to tradition dates back to the time of the Babylonian exile and is hereditary in the family of David. This line ends with the emigration of Mar Zutra III to Palestine. The later exilarchs are not of Davidic descent and therefore not legitimate, as the book polemically implies. The work dates from the eighth century at the earliest.

***Text***

**Schechter, S.** 'Seder Olam Suta.' *MGWJ* 39 (1895) 23–28. [Text according to MS De Rossi 541 (first half of fourteenth century).] **Grosberg, M.** *Seder Olam zuta and Complete Seder Tannaim v'Amoraim.* London 1910; repr. Jerusalem/Tel Aviv 1970. **Weinstock, M. J.** *Seder Olam Zutta ha-Shalem.* Jerusalem 1957.

***Bibliography***

**Beer, M.** *Exilarchate*, 11–15. **Goode, A. D.** 'The Exilarchate in the Eastern Caliphate, 637–1258.' *JQR* N.S. 31 (1940–41) 149–69. **Rosenthal, J. M.** *EJ* 14: 1093. **Zunz**, *GV*, 142–47.

### *c) Sefer Zerubbabel*

This apocalypse, placed into the mouth of Zerubbabel after the Nebuchadnezzar's destruction of Jerusalem, was written at the beginning of the seventh century in the style of biblical visions (Dan, Ezek). It describes the eschatological struggle between Armilos, the leader of Rome and of Christianity, and the Messiah ben Joseph, who falls in battle but prepares the way for the Davidic Messiah. Armilos perhaps is shaped after the person of the Emperor Heraclius. The work draws only partly on rabbinic sources. Its great influence has led to many textual changes, which make a reconstruction of the original text all but impossible. An addition to Sefer Zerubbabel, published in Wertheimer 1:118–34 as *Pirqê Hekhalot Rabbati* and also reproduced in Eben-Shmuel 357–70, is a Sabbatian supplement to the work from the school of Nathan of Gaza (Eben-Shmuel 352–56).

***Text***

**Jellinek, A.** *BHM*, 2:54–57. [Translated in A. Wünsche, *Lehrhallen*, vol. 2.] **Wertheimer, S. A.** *Batei Midrashot*, 2:495–505. **Eben-Shmuel, J.** *Midreshê Ge'ullah*, 71–88. [Introduction: pp. 55ff.; this is a problematic mixed text with rearrangements and conjectures, but Eben-Shmuel 379–89 also offers other textual versions.] Genizah Fragments: **Hopkins, S.** *Miscellany*, 10, 15, 64f., 72f.

***Bibliography***

**Dan, J.** *The Hebrew Story*, 35–46. **Dan, J**. *EJ* 16: 1002. **Fleischer, E.** 'Haduta-Hadutahu-Chedweta: Solving an Old Riddle' (Hebr.). *Tarbiz* 53 (1983–84) 71–96, especially 92ff. [On a *piyyut* influenced by Sefer Zerubbabel or by one of its early layers.] **Lévi I.** 'L'apocalypse de Zorobabel et le roi de Perse Siroès.' *REJ* 68 (1914) 129–60; 69 (1919) 108–21; 71 (1920) 57–65. [Also contains text and translation.] **Martola, N.** 'Serubbabels Bok.' *Nordisk Judaistik/Scandinavian Jewish Studies* 3 (1979) 1–20. **Marx, A**. 'Studies in Gaonic History.' *JQR* N.S. 1 (1910–11) 75–78. **Stemberger, G**. *Die römische Herrschaft im Urteil der Juden*, 138–43. Darmstadt 1983. Additional Messianic writings appear in **Townsend, J. T**. 'Minor Midrashim.' In *Bibliographical Essays in Medieval Jewish Studies*, 360f. New York 1976.

### *d) Pirqe de Rabbi Eliezer (PRE)*

PRE, also called *Baraita de Rabbi Eliezer* (Arukh, Rashi), *Mishnah de R. E.* or *Haggadah de R. E.*, has 54 chapters in the extant version; but it is evidently incomplete. There is no trace of other chapters, even though medieval quotations of PRE often do not agree with our text; SEZ 19–25 also belongs in some way to the R. Eliezer tradition, but it is not a sequel of PRE. The author may not have completed the work.

Contents: 1–2 on the life of R. Eliezer; 3–11 creation; 12–23 Adam to Noah (announcement of God's ten descents to earth; the three pillars on which the world rests: Torah, worship, acts of love); 24–25 sinful humanity and the confusion of languages; 26–39 Abraham to Jacob; 40–48 Moses to God's revelation after the sin of the golden calf; 49–50 Amalek's descendants (Haman, Titus), remarks on the Esther scroll; 51 the future redemption; 52 seven miracles; 53–54 the punishment of Miriam for her criticism of Moses (Num 12). Here the narrative breaks off.

The work was evidently meant to be continued, since only eight of God's ten descents are presented. Chapters 27ff. are, moreover, connected with the Eighteen Benedictions, but the work only extends as far as the Eighth Benediction, the prayer for health. It must be assumed that the work was planned up to the death of Moses, i.e. that it was intended to cover the entire Pentateuch. M. Pérez Fernández (*Los Capítulos*, 22–26) attempts a different explanation of these problems, suggesting that PRE may have used only parts of a work about the ten descents of God. He further proposes that the Eighteen Benedictions serve only as a redactional bracket (No. 13 is cited at the end of chapter 10), and need not have been included in their entirety. Pérez Fernández's analysis of sources merits detailed consideration; but the abrupt conclusion of PRE remains to be explained even on his account.

The document is not a midrash in the real sense, but should rather be classified as 'rewritten Bible', i.e. a coherent biblical story, in some ways similar to Arabic biblical narratives, even if some midrashic traits are still present (individual traditions are cited in the names of speakers, although they often appear to be pseudepigraphical; contradictions between individual traditions are not harmonized). It is uncertain whether the author himself intended the pseudepigraphical attribution to Eliezer ben Hyrcanus. The book may simply have been named after Eliezer because it begins with him. However, since some manuscripts do not contain chapters 1–2, it is also possible that they were only subsequently connected with this work. This connection, however, would need to have been made at an early date, since Genizah fragments already attest the present chapter numbering (thus the text of PRE 26–29, 11th cent.; similarly the fragment containing chapter 46, published by Aloni). The title's connection with R. Eliezer also has early attestation, e.g. in R. Nathan's *Arukh*.

The work appears to have originated in the eighth or ninth century (it seems that Pirqoi ben Baboi in the early ninth century already quotes it: *Ginze Schechter*, 2:544). It alludes repeatedly to Arab rule, especially in the stories about Ishmael, as whose wives Aisha and Fatima are named (chapter 30). In the same chapter the Dome of the Rock on the Temple site is also known, and the joint rule of two brothers is mentioned; the latter is usually taken to refer to the two sons of Harun al-Rashid (809–13), while A. H. Silver (*A History of Messianic Speculation in Israel* (Boston 1959=1927), 41) thinks of the half-brothers Mu'awiya (caliph from 661) and Ziyad (ruler of the Eastern provinces from 665). Similarly uncertain is the interpretation of a text in PRE 28 in which the rule of the four kingdoms lasts for one day of God, i.e. 1,000 years. Starting from different presuppositions, the expectation of the messianic was thus calculated by Zunz (*GV*, 289) for the year 729, Friedlander (200) for 832, and A. H. Silver for 648; these differences suffice to illustrates the problems of a direct historical use of such data.

Interpolations must also be expected in PRE. It uses a wealth of older tradition and shows itself aware of the pseudepigrapha; it may also have adopted entire chapters from other sources, almost without alteration (e.g. the three astronomical chapters 6–8: cf. M. Steinschneider, *Mathematik bei den Juden* (Berlin/Leipzig 1893; repr. Hildesheim 1964), 44–48). Nevertheless, by and large the work must be regarded not as a compilation like other midrashim, but as the creative achievement of a personal author. Palestine is the most likely place of origin (almost all the cited rabbis are from there).

### *Text*

First printed at Constantinople, 1514 (with lacunae due to self-imposed censorship); Venice, 1544; Warsaw, 1852, repr. Jerusalem 1963 (incl. commentary by D. Luria; here, too, there are many lacunae due to censorship). **Higger, M.** 'Pirqê Rabbi Eliezer.' *Horeb* 8 (1944) 82–119; 9 (1946–47) 94–166; 10 (1948) 185–294. [Collation of three MSS of the Biblioteca Casanata, Rome; following C. M. Horowitz.] **Horowitz, C. M.** *Pirke de Rabbi Eliezer: A Complete Critical Edition as Prepared by C. M. Horowitz, but Never Published: Facsimile Edition of Editor's Original MS.* Jerusalem 1972. [Unfortunately the facsimile is missing several leaves; pp. 183ff. are out of order.] **Friedmann, M.** *Pseudo-Seder Eliahu Zuta*, 50–56. Vienna 1904. [Chapters 39–41 from MS Parma 1240 (where these chapters are inserted in PesR together with Seder Eliyahu Zutta 19–25, which also belongs to the Eliezer tradition).] **Wertheimer, S. A.** *Batei Midrashot*, 1:238–43. [Variant version of the final chapter, similar to MS Epstein.]

### *Geniza Fragments*

**Alloni, N.** *Geniza Fragments*, 76. [A palimpsest leaf of PRE 45f. at Cambridge.] **Rabinovitz, Z. M.** 'Genizah Fragments of the Pirke R. Eliezer' (Hebr.). *Bar-Ilan* 16–17 (1979) 100–111. [PRE 26–29 (begining), 11th cent.]

### *Translations*

**Friedlander, G.** *Pirke de Rabbi Eliezer.* London 1916; repr. New York 1981. [English translation of MS A. Epstein, Vienna, with introduction; cf. B. Halper, *JQR* N.S. 8 (1917–18) 477–95.] French: **Ouaknin, M.-A., Smilévitch, E. & Salfati, P.-H.** *Pirqé de Rabbi 'Eliezer (Traduction annotée).* Paris 1984. Spanish: **Pérez Fernàndez, M.** *Los Capítulos de Rabbí Eliezer.* Valencia 1984. [Based on the Luria edition, using the Venice 1545 edition and the three MSS published by Higger; includes an extensive introduction, which also comments on the relationship of PRE to the Targum.]

### *Bibliography*

**Blumenthal, D.** 'The Rationalistic Commentary of R. Ḥoṭer Ben Shelomo to Pirqe de Rabbi Eliezer' (Hebr.). *Tarbiz* 48 (1978–79) 99–106. **Hayward, R.** 'Pirqe de Rabbi Eliezer and Targum Pseudo-Jonathan.' *JJS* 42 (1991) 215–46. **Heinemann, J.** *Aggadah*, 181–99, 242–47. [Especially on the relationship to Islam.] **Heinemann, J.** ''Ibbudê aggadot qedumot be-ruaḥ ha-zeman be-Pirqê Rabbi Eliezer.' In B. Shakhevitch and M. Peri (eds.), *Simon Halkin Jubilee Volume*, 321–43. Jerusalem 1975. **Heller, B.** 'Muhammedanisches und Antimuhammedanisches in den Pirke R. Eliezer.' *MGWJ* 69 (1925) 47–54. **Herr, M. D.** *EJ* 13: 558–60. **Horowitz, C. M.** 'Iggeret Petuḥah.' *Bet Talmud* 1 (1881; repr. Jerusalem 1969). **Ohana, M.** 'La polémique judéo-islamique et l'image d'Ishmael dans Targum Pseudo-Jonathan et dans Pirke de Rabbi Eliezer.' *Augustinianum* 15 (1975) 367–87. **Pérez Fernández, M.** 'Targum y Midrás sobre Gn 1,25–27; 2,7; 3.7.21: La creación de Adán en el Targum de Pseudojonatán y en Pirqé de Rabbí Eliezer.' In D. Muñoz León (ed.), *Salvación en la palabra: Targum – Derash – Berith: En memoria del profesor Alejandro Díez Macho*, 471–87. Madrid 1986. **Pérez Fernández, M.** 'Sobre los textos mesiánicos del Targum Pseudo-Jonatán y del Midrás Pirqé de Rabbí Eliezer.' *Estudios Biblicos* 45 (1987) 39–55. **Schussman, A.** 'Abraham's Visits to Ishmael – The Jewish Origin and Orientation' (Hebr.). *Tarbiz* 49 (1979–80) 325–45. **Shinan, A.** *The Embroidered Targum* (Hebr.), 176–85. Jerusalem 1992. **Zunz,** *GV*, 283–90. [Cf. **Albeck, Ch.** *Derashot*, 136–40, 421–23; also idem, 'Agadot im Lichte der Pseudepigraphen.' *MGWJ* 83 (1939) 162–69, regarding parallels especially with the Book of Jubilees.]

### e) *Megillat Antiochos*

This work, also known as *Sefer Bêt Ḥashmonai*, 'the book of the Hasmoneans', or *Megillat Benê Ḥashmonai*, 'the scroll of the Hasmoneans', is a legendary portrayal of the Maccabean period up to the introduction of the feast of lights (Ḥanukkah). It is composed in Western Aramaic, though it was probably revised in Babylonia. Kadari proposes to date the work for linguistic reasons between thesecond and fifth centuries, but most would assume the eighth or ninth century and regard the language as a literary imitation of Targum Onqelos. (Similarly A. Kasher: along with earlier authors, he considers the text to be a festive scroll for Ḥanukkah; redacted in polemical reaction against the Karaites who rejected this feast, this work could not have been composed before the second half of the eighth century. The material might have originated in Antioch, from where there is early evidence for the veneration of the Maccabees.

The *Halakhot Gedolot* attribute a *Megillat Bêt Ḥashmonai* to the elders of the schools of Shammai and Hillel; but this text cannot serve as reliable evidence of the knowledge of our document, especially since MS Rome reads *Megillat Ta'anit.* Thus there is no unequivocal attestation of the work before Saadya, who translated it into Arabic and also wrote an Arabic introduction to it. The work is attested by several MSS and extensive Genizah fragments. It enjoyed great popularity in the Middle Ages, and was sometimes also used in the synagogue for Ḥanukkah.

#### *Text*

First printed edition Aramaic/Hebrew, c. 1481/82 in Guadalajara: see **Joel, I.** 'The Editio Princeps of the Antiochus Scroll.' *KS* 37 (1961–62) 132–36. [Reproduces Aramaic variants in relation to A. Jellinek's text in *BhM*; also the entire Hebrew text, which widely differs from the standard version.] **Filipowski, H.** *Mibchar Ha-Peninim.* London 1851. [Aramaic text given at the end.] **Jellinek, A.** *BhM*, 6:1–8. **Gaster, M.** *Studies and Texts*, 3:33–43. London [1925–]1928; repr. New York 1971. [Introduction and English translation in 1:165–83.] **Wertheimer, S. A.** *Batei Midrashot*, 1:319–30. **Kadari, M. Z.** 'The Aramaic Megillat Antiochus' (Hebr.). *Bar-Ilan* 1 (1963) 81–105; 2 (1964) 178–214. [This text is translated into Spanish by L. Diez Merino, 'Fuente histórica desconocida para el período macabaico: Megillat Antiochus', *Ciencia Tomista* 106 (1979) 463–501; he also adopts Kadari's earliest suggested date (2nd century), as does A. Vivian.] **Nemoy, L.** *The Scroll of Antiochus.* New Haven 1952. [Contains the facsimile of a European version.] **Vivian, A.** 'Un Manoscritto aramaico inedito della Megillat Antiochus.' In S. F. Bondi et al. (eds.), *Studi in onore di Edda Bresciani*, 567–92. Pisa 1985. **Vivian, A.** 'La Megillat Antiochus: Una reinterpretazione dell' epopea maccabaica.' *Atti del congresso tenuta a San Miniato, 7–10 novembre 1983*, 163–95. Rome 1987. [Introduction, translation and text of a MS at Turin.]

#### *Genizah Fragments*

**Hopkins, S.** *Miscellany*, 18f., 20–26 (almost a complete text), 29–39, 44f., 50–53, 55f., 102f., 110 (including two passages of Saadya's Arabic introduction).

***Early translations into Hebrew***

**Hopkins, S.** *Geniza Fragments*, 102f. [Slightly differs from A. Jellinek, *BhM* 1:142–46 (German translation in Wünsche, *Lehrhallen*, 2:186–92).] **Fried, N.** 'Nusaḥ 'Ibri Ḥadash shel Megillat Antiokhos.' *Sinai* 64 (1969) 97–140. [MS British Museum, containing an original translation from the Aramaic.]

***Saadya's Arabic introduction***

See also **Atlas, S.** and **Perlman, M.** 'Saadia on the Scroll of the Hasmoneans.' *PAAJR* 14 (1944) 1–23.

***Additional Bibliography***

**Abrahams, I.** 'An Aramaic Text of the Scroll of Antiochus.' *JQR* 11 (1898–99) 291–99. **Fried, N.** ''Inyanot Megillat Antiokhos.' *Leshonenu* 23 (1958–59) 129–45. **Kasher, A.** 'The Historical Background of Megillath Antiochus.' *PAAJR* 48 (1981) 207–30. **Rosenthal, F.** 'Saadyah's Introduction to the Scroll of the Hasmoneans.' *JQR* N.S. 36 (1945–46) 297–302. **Rosenthal, F.** 'Scroll of Antiochus.' *EJ* 14: 1045–47. [Rev. from the German *EJ* 2 (1928) 944–47.]

### *f) Midrash 'Eser Galuyyot*

The 'Midrash of the Ten Exiles' was transmitted in several recensions, the earliest of which may date from the ninth century. The idea of the 10 exiles as such, however, is earlier and can be found e.g. in Qilliri (*Tarbiz* 56 (1986–87) 510).

***Text***

**Jellinek, A.** *BhM,* 4:133–36. [German translation in A. Wünsche, *Lehrhallen*, vol. 2.]. A later recension is in **Jellinek, A.** *BhM,* 5:113–16. See also **Grünhut, L.** *Likkutim*, 3:1–22. **Ish-Shalom, M.** 'Midrash "Eser Galuyyot".' *Sinai* 43 (1958–59) 195–211.

### *g) Book of the Danite Eldad ben Maḥli*

Eldad ha-Dani (second half of 9th cent.) claimed to come from an independent Jewish state in East Africa, which was inhabited by members of the tribes of Dan (hence his epithet), Asher, Gad and Naphtali. He visited Babylonia, Kairouan and Spain. He created a considerable stir with his stories about the Israelites of the lost ten tribes beyond the river Sambation, as well as with his very unconventional rules of ritual slaughter which he had supposedly brought with him from his homeland. Eldad seems to have been a kind of itinerant bard, whose 'autobiographical' narratives constitute merely the framework for the stories which are drawn from very different traditions. His book had a powerful impact and was transmitted in numerous manuscripts; it was at the same time frequently revised and altered, so that today at least 17 different recensions are known.

***Text***

First Printed in 1480 at Mantua. Three recensions are given in **Jellinek, A.** *BhM*. Vols. 2, 3, 5.

**Epstein, A.** *Eldad ha-Dani, seine Berichte über die 10 Stämme und deren Ritus, mit Einleitung und Anmerkungen* (Hebr.). Pressburg (Prague)/Vienna 1891. [Repr. in *Kitbê A. Epstein*, vol. 1.] **Müller, D. H.** *Die Recensionen und Versionen des Eldad had-Dânî.* Vienna 1892. [Synoptic edition.] **Schloessinger, M.** *The Ritual of Eldad ha-Dani, Reconstructed and Edited from Mss. and a Genizah Fragment.* London 1908.

***Translation***

**Adler, J. N.** *Jewish Travellers*, 4–21. 2nd edn. New York 1966.

***Additional Bibliography***

**Dan, J.** *The Hebrew Story*, 47–61. **Rabinowitz, L.** 'Eldad ha-Dani and China.' *JQR* N.S. 36 (1945–46) 231–38. **Shochat, A.** *EJ* 6: 576–78.

### *h) Midrash 'Aseret ha-Dibrot*

The 'midrash of the Ten Commandments' is not properly a midrash, but a collection of Jewish and other stories, often only loosely connected with the Ten Commandments. The Genizah fragments document early versions of this text which sugest that it was originally closer to the genre of midrash (e.g. it had *petiḥot*), but in the course of later transmission it developed an increasing focus on the narrative element (cf. M. B. Lerner, *'Al ha-Midrashim*). A. Alba Cecilia proposes to date this collection no later than the 10th century. As early as the middle ages, however, the number and selection of stories aried considerably (the standard version has 17 narratives, some MSS up to 50). This is probably the oldest Hebrew collection of stories, apart perhaps from the *Alphabet of Ben Sira*.

***Text***

***Jellinek, A.*** *BhM*, 1:62–90. [German translation in A. Wünsche, *Lehrhallen*, vol. 4.] Other versions: **Gaster, M.** *The Exempla of the Rabbis*, 7–8, 142–48. New York 1968: repr. of 1924, with a prolegomenon of W. G. Braude. **Hershler, M**, ed. *Genuzot* 2 (Jerusalem 1985) 109ff. [From MS Vat. 285; cf. M. B. Lerner, 'Collected Exempla: Studies in Aggadic Texts Published in the Genuzot Series' (Hebr.), *KS* 61 (1986–87) 867–91.]

***Translation***

Spanish: **Alba Cecilia, A.** *Midrás de los Diez Mandamientos y Libro Precioso de Salvación.* Valencia 1990. [Includes an introduction on the medieval narrative tradition.]

***Bibliography***

**Dan, J.** *The Hebrew Story*, 79–85. **Dan, J.** *EJ* 11: 1515f. **Elizur, B.** 'On the Process of Copying Midrash 'Aseret Haddiberot' (Hebr.). *Leshonenu* 48–49 (1984–85) 207–9. **Lerner, M. B.** ''Al ha-Midrashim le–'Aseret ha-Dibrot.' In *Talmudic Studies*, 1:217–36. **Noy, D.** 'General and Jewish Folktale Types in the Decalogue Midrash' (Hebr.). *4th WCJS* (Jerusalem 1968) 2:353–55. **Zunz, L.** *GV*, 150–52.

### *i) Alphabet of Ben Sira*

This is a pungent satire on the Bible and rabbinic religiosity composed of biblical and haggadic elements. The first part recounts the life of Ben Sira from conception to his first birthday (he is regarded as the son of Jeremiah, since this name has the same numerical value as *Sîra'*). In the second part the one-year-old Ben Sira tells his teacher proverbs beginning with each of the letters he is supposed to learn; the teacher replies in each case by relating something of his life. In the third part Ben Sira is at Nebuchadnezzar's court and answers the latter's questions about the peculiarities of animals, etc. (here the structure is not entirely clear, and some material appears to have been added later). In the last part, Ben Sira's son and grandson, Uzziel and Joseph ben Uzziel, comment on his proverbs, again 22 in alphabetical order. The MSS do not attest the name *Alphabet* of Ben Sira for the work as a whole; this title in fact fits only part of the text, but has been customary since Steinschneider's edition.

E. Yassif grouped the numerous manuscripts into two recensions, both of which are attested in Europe since the eleventh century. One (A) was common in France and later throughout Europe; the other (B) was represented in Italy and in the Orient. Recension B is probably closer to the original text, while A has been significantly reworked and is transmitted in an inherently inconsistent form. However, Yassif's attempt to establish the various parts as originally independent writings of different authors is just as unconvincing as his endeavour to deny the element of satire and criticism of religion in this work (see J. Dan's critique). Despite or perhaps because of its ironic criticism of religion, the work was widely circulated, but also frequently censored and played down, so that it could later influence even the *Ḥasidê Ashkenaz*. It probably dates from the ninth or tenth century (Yassif gives detailed reasons for each of its parts), and its country of origin will have been Babylonia.

#### *Text*

First printed in Constantinople, 1519; Venice 1544. Scholarly editions: **Yassif, E.** *The Tales of Ben Sira in the Middle-Ages: A Critical Text and Literary Studies* (Hebr.). Jerusalem 1984. [Cf. J. Dan, *KS* 60 (1984–85) 294–97.] **Steinschneider, M.** *Alphabetum Syracidis*. Berlin 1858. **Friedman, D. & Löwinger, D. S.** 'Alfa Beta de-Ben Sira.' *Haṣofeh* 10 (Budapest 1926; repr. Jerusalem 1972) 250–81. [A different text.] **Habermann, A. M.** 'Alphabet of Ben Sira, Third Version' (Hebr.). *Tarbiz* 27 (1957–58) 190–202. **Eisenstein**, 1:35–43, 43–50. [Another version.] **Hopkins, S.** *Miscellany*, 57–60, 66, 78–85. [Genizah fragments.]

#### *Bibliography*

**Dan, J.** *The Hebrew Story*, 68–78. **Dan, J.** 'Ḥidat Alfa Beta de-ben Sira.' *Molad* 23 (1965–66) 490–96. **Dan, J.** *EJ* 4: 548–50. **Epstein, A.** *Qadmoniot*, 110–15. **Lieberman, S.** *Shkiin*, 32–42. Jerusalem 1939. **Marmorstein, A.** 'A Note on the "Alphabet of Ben Sira".' *JQR* N.S. 41 (1950–

51) 303–6. **Reifman, J.** 'Tekhunat Sefer Alfa Beta de-Ben Sira.' *Ha-Karmel* 2 (1873) 124–38. **Yassif, E.** 'Medieval Hebrew Tales on the Mutual Hatred of Animals and Their Methodological Implications' (Hebr.). *Folklore Research Center Studies* 7 (Jerusalem 1983) Hebr. section, 227–46. **Yassif, E.** '"The History of Ben Sira": Ideational Elements in Literary Work' (Hebr.). *Eshel Beer-Sheva* 2 (1980) 97–117. **Zlotnick J. L.** 'Aggadot minni qedem: Benê adam she-nishtalu she-lo ke-derekh ha-nishtalim.' *Sinai* 18 (1945–46) 49–58. **Zunz,** *GV*, 111.

### *k) Josippon*

Josippon is a history of the Jews from the fall of Babylon to the destruction of the Temple in Jerusalem. The work was written in 953 (?) by an anonymous author in Southern Italy; his sources included Josephus in particular, supplemented by Hegesippus, the apocrypha in the Vulgate version, and various early medieval Latin texts. Already in the eleventh century the author was identified with Flavius Josephus and his work thus became a pseudepigraphon, although in the original text the author clearly indicates his dependence on Josephus. Over time the work was greatly expanded, *inter alia* by a Hebrew version of the Alexander romance.

***Text***

First printed at Mantua in 1480, then in a longer version, Constantinople 1514, on which the standard editions are based. **Flusser, D.** *The Josippon (Josephus Gorionides): Edited with an Introduction, Commentary and Notes.* Vols. 1 (text and commentary), 2 (introduction, textual variants, indexes). Jerusalem 1978–80. **Flusser, D.** *Josippon: The Original Version MS Jerusalem $8^{0}$41280 and Supplements.* Jerusalem 1978. [Facsimile; on this and generally on MSS and editions see A. M. Habermann, *K'vusei Yahad: Essays and Notes on Jewish Culture and Literature* (Hebr.), (Jerusalem 1980), 27–47.] Flusser, D. *EJ* 10: 296–98.

***Latin translation:*** J. F. Breithaupt, Gotha 1707.

***Additional Bibliography***

See **Flusser, D.** *EJ* 10: 296–98. **Bowman, S.** 'Sefer Yosippon: History and Midrash.' In M. Fishbane (ed.), *The Midrashic Imagination*, 280–94. Albany, NY 1993. Sela, S. *The Book of Josippon and Its Parallel Version in Arabic and Judaeo-Arabic* (Hebr.). Diss. Tel Aviv 1991.

### *l) Midrash Petirat Aharon*

The 'midrash of the passing of Aaron' takes as its starting point Num 20. Text: Constantinople 1515; Venice 1544; A. Jellinek, *BhM* 1:91–95. Translations: B. M. Mehlman, 'Midrash Petirat Aharon; Introduction and Translation', *Journal of Reform Judaism* 27 (1980) 49–58. German: A. Wünsche, *Lehrhallen*, vol. 1. Cf. also Zunz, *GV*, 153.

### *m) Midrash Petirat Moshe*

The 'midrash of the passing of Moses' survives in several recensions dating from between the seventh and the tenth or eleventh centuries. The first version was printed at Constantinople 1516; Venice 1544; A. Jellinek, *BhM* 1:115–29. German translation in A. Wünsche, *Lehrhallen*, vol. 1. A long piece has been included in the Yalqut (Deut §940) as well as in DeutR.

The second version picks up on Prov 31.29 and is printed in Jellinek, *BhM* 6:71–78. A German translation of the first part appears in A. Wünsche, *Lehrhallen*, 1:122–25. For the second part there is a variant textual version from Bereshit Rabbati (Albeck, 136f.), which is printed in Jellinek, *BhM* 6:xxii–xxiii. See also Wertheimer, 1:273–75, 286f. Another recension is given by Eisenstein, 2:368–71; M. Krupp, 'New Versions of Midrash Petirat Moshe' (Hebr.), *11th WCJS* (Jerusalem 1994) C 1:119–23. The reconstruction of an early version is attempted by L. J. Weinberger, 'A Lost Midrash' (Hebr.), *Tarbiz* 38 (1968–69) 285–93. Cf. Zunz, *GV*, 154.

### *n) Dibrê ha-yamim shel Moshe*

The 'life of Moses' is written in a pseudo-biblical Hebrew. It belongs to the genre of 'rewritten Bible' and frequently just strings together biblical verses, always without an introductory formula. Some parallels can be found in Josephus. The rabbinic tradition is always used without the names of rabbis, and the selection from the sources is above all intended to exaggerate the miraculous traits in the life of Moses. The work employs ExodR and Josippon; it is mentioned in the *Arukh* and probably dates from the eleventh century.

#### *Text*

Constantinople 1516; Venice 1544; Jellinek, *BhM*, 2:1–11. **Habermann, A.**, ed. *Ḥelqat Meḥoqeq: Dibre midrash we-aggadah 'al Moshe Rabbenu u-petirato*, 7–24. Tel Aviv 1947. **Shinan, A.** 'Dibre ha-yamim shel Moshe Rabbenu.' *Hasifrut* 24 (1977) 100–16. [Introduction and text according to MS Oxford Bodl. 2797 of 1325; especially in the second half, this and the other MSS diverge significantly from the printed versions.]

#### *Translations*

**Wünsche, A.** *Lehrhallen*, vol. 1. **Gaster, M.** *The Chronicles of Jeraḥmeel*, Chapters 42–48. London 1899; repr. New York 1971. [Translates a similar text.] **Girón Blanc, L. F.** *Sefarad* 48 (1988) 390–425.

#### *Bibliography*

**Dan, J.** *EJ* 12: 413. **Dan, J.** *The Hebrew Story*, 140f. **Flusser, D.** *Josippon*, 2:151. [Use of Josippon.] **Zunz**, *GV*, 153.

### *o) Midrash Wa-yissau*

This work describes the conflicts of the sons of Jacob with the Amorites and Esau, based on Gen 35.5; 36.6. There are also parallels to *Jubilees* 34.37f. and *Testament of Judah* 2ff.; these may serve as a model for this medieval compilation, which was probably stimulated by heroic legends. G. Schmitt, *Ein indirektes Zeugnis der Makkabäerkämpfe* (Wiesbaden 1983), 48 assumes an early source of the midrash, 'probably no later than the Bar Kokhba war'; the present text is in his opinion the 'free renarration of a Hebrew original, or else a translation of an Aramaic original'.

***Text***

The text preserved in Yalqut Gen §133 is also printed in Jellinek, *BhM*, vol. 3. See also **Charles, R. H.** *The Greek Versions of the Testaments of the Twelve Patriarchs*, 237f. Oxford 1908. [Part One.] **Charles, R. H.** *The Ethiopic Version of the Hebrew Book of Jubilees*, 180–82. Oxford 1895. Critical edition: **Lauterbach, J. Z.** 'Midrash Wayissa'u o Sefer Milḥamot Benê Ya'aqov.' In *Abhandlungen zur Erinnerung an H. P. Chajes*, Hebr. section, 205–22. Vienna 1933. **Alexander, T. & Dan, J.** 'The Complete "Midrash Vayisa'u"' (Hebr.). *Folklore Research Center Studies* 3 (Jerusalem 1972) Hebrew section, 67–76.

***Translations***

**Gaster, M.** *The Chronicles of Jeraḥmeel*, 80–87. London 1899. [English translation of a somewhat different version.] **Rönsch, H.** *Das Buch der Jubiläen*, 390–98. Leipzig 1874. [German.]

***Additional Bibliography***

**Dan, J.** *The Hebrew Story*, 138–40. **Flusser, D.** *EJ* 11: 1520f. **Hultgård, A.** *L'eschatologie des Testaments des Douze Patriarches*, 2:123–27. Uppsala 1982. **Safrai, Z.** 'Midrash Wajisau – The War of the Sons of Jacob in Southern Samaria' (Hebr.). *Sinai* 100 (1987) 612–27. [Synopsis with *Test. Judah* and *Jubilees*; list of MSS.] **Schmitt, G.** *Ein indirektes Zeugnis der Makkabäerkämpfe*. Wiesbaden 1983. **Zunz**, *GV*, 153.

## *p) Midrash Wa-yosha*

An interpretation of Exod 14.30–15.18, the 'song at the Reed Sea'; in the style of the later haggadah. Much of its material derives verbatim from Tanḥuma; the *Dibrê ha-yamim shel Moshe* have also been used. 15.18 mentions Armilos who will slay the Messiah from the tribe of Joseph, but who will be killed by the Messiah ben David (cf. the book of Zerubbabel). Already known in the Yalqut, the work was probably composed at the end of the eleventh century.

***Text***

Constantinople 1519. **Jellinek, A.** *BhM*, 1:35–57. **Niedermaier, H.** 'Der altjiddische Midrasch Wojoscha.' *Judaica* 21 (1965) 25–55. German translation: **Wünsche, A.** *Lehrhallen*, vol. 1.

Cf. **Herr, M. D.** *EJ* 16: 1517; **Zunz**, *GV*, 294f.

### *q) Midrash Elleh Ezkerah*

The name derives from Psalm 42.5, 'These I will remember'. The work describes the execution of ten famous Tannaites: Rabban Simeon ben Gamaliel II, the high priest Ishmael, Aqiba, Ḥananyah ben Teradion, Yehudah ben Baba, Yehudah ben Dama, Ḥuṣpit, Ḥananyah ben Ḥakhinai, Yeshebab and Eleazar ben Shammua (the list differs in various recensions). The work does not report historical facts but is primarily literary in nature (the ten men are known not to have died in the same period). Initially the number 10 was not yet fixed; it was subsequently connected with Joseph's ten brothers who became guilty by selling him into Egypt, and for whom the martyrs now make atonement. Yet at the same time their martyrdom means the guarantee of the coming redemption and the approaching demise of Rome.

Together with the *Aqedat Isaac,* this work formed the basis of medieval Jewish martyrology. It is therefore preserved in numerous MSS and versions. The motif of the ten martyrs, along with lists of names, occurs in various midrashim (LamR 2.1, B. 100; MidrPs 9.13, B. 88f.; MidrProv 1.13, B. 45); this is the starting point of the story of the Ten Martyrs, an early version of which is contained in Midrash Cant, ed. E.H. Grünhut & J. C. Wertheimer (Jerusalem 1971), 9–24. J. Dan and others have considered the parallels with the hekhalot literature, of which a great many are present especially in Recension III of Reeg's edition (cf. also A. Goldberg, *FJB* 1 (1973) 16–19; I. Gruenewald, *Apocalyptic and Merkavah Mysticism* (Leiden/Cologne 1980), 157–59), to be the basis of the narrative as a whole. However, Reeg's comprehensive analysis of all textual recensions shows that this material was only incorporated in the course of transmission. Rabbinic parallels have also been included, above all in Recension III. The content of the story of the Ten Martyrs is presupposed by the Seliḥah (liturgical poem) *Elleh Ezkerah,* which in turn appears to be the basis of the midrash *Elleh Ezkerah* (= the first of the ten recensions in Reeg). Chronologically, therefore, the midrash represents a very late stage of this narrative tradition.

#### *Text*

**Reeg, G.** *Die Geschichte von den Zehn Märtyrern: Synoptische Edition mit Übersetzung und Einleitung.* Tübingen 1985. [Comprehensive edition with detailed discussion of the MSS and recensions.] Earlier editions of individual recensions: **Jellinek, A.** *BhM,* 2:64–72 and 6:19–35. **Herschler, M.** 'Midrash 'Asarah Harugê Malkhut.' *Sinai* 71 (1972) 218–28. **Oron, M.** 'Merkavah Texts and the Legend of the Ten Martyrs' (Hebr.). *Eshel Beer-Sheva* 2 (1980) 81–95. **Schäfer, P.,** ed. *Synopse zur Hekhalot-Literatur,* §§107–21. Tübingen 1981. [Presents 7 MSS for the version of the narrative in Hekhalot Rabbati.]

***Bibliography***

**Abrams, J. A.** 'Incorporating Christian Symbols into Judaism: The Case of Midrash Eleh Ezkerah.' *CCAR Journal* 15 (1993) 11–20. **Auerbach, M.** ''Aserah Harugê Malkhut.' *Jeshurun* 10 (1923) 60–66, 81–88. **Bloch, P.** 'Rom und die Mystiker der Merkabah.' In *Festschrift zum siebzigsten Geburtstage J. Guttmanns*, 113–24. Leipzig 1915. **Dan, J.** *The Hebrew Story*, 62–68. **Dan, J.** 'The Story of the Ten Martyrs: Its Origin and Developments' (Hebr.). In E. Fleischer (ed.), *Studies in Literature* (*Festschrift* S. Halkin), 15–22. Jerusalem 1973. **Dan, J.** 'Hekhalot Rabbati and the Legend of the Ten Martyrs' (Hebr.). *Eshel Beer-Sheva* 2 (1980) 63–80. [On the 'Italian' Recension (=Reeg's Recension III).] **Finkelstein, L.** 'The Ten Martyrs.' In I. Davidson (ed.), *Essays and Studies in Memory of L. R. Miller*, 29–55. New York 1938. **Herr, M. D.** *EJ* 15: 1006–08. **Krauss, S.** ''Asarah Harugê Malkhut.' *Hashiloah* 44 (1925) 10–22, 106–17, 221–33. **Toder, S.** '"Aseret Harugê Malkhut": Ha-sippur we reqa'o.' *Ha-Ummah* 9 (1972) 199–206. **Wahrmann, N.** 'Zur Frage der "zehn Märtyrer".' *MGWJ* 78 (1934) 575–80. **Zeitlin, S.** 'The Legend of the Ten Martyrs and its Apocalyptic Origins.' *JQR* N.S. 36 (1945–46) 1–16, 209f. [Repr. in idem, *Studies in the Early History of Judaism*, vol. 2 (New York 1974), 165–80.]

### *r) Midrash 'Al-yithallel*

This is named after Jer 9.22 ('let not [a person] boast. . .'). It contains stories from the life of Solomon the wise, David the mighty, and Koraḥ the wealthy. Text: A. Jellinek, *BhM* 6:106–108; L. Grünhut, *Sefer ha-Likkutim*, 1:21ff.

### *s) Sefer ha-yashar*

The 'book of the upright' (cf. Josh 10.13), also called *Toldot Adam* presents a review of history from Adam to the exodus from Egypt. It poses as an ancient work saved by an old man when Titus captured Jerusalem. The narrative is based on Scripture, the Talmud and midrash, but also on non-Jewish traditions. J. Dan (*The Hebrew Story*, 137f.) suspects that this work, which is usually dated to the eleventh or twelfth century and whose sources include e.g. *Midrash Wa-yissau* and the *Dibrê ha-yamim shel Moshe* as well as Josippon, was composed only at the beginning of the sixteenth century in Naples (NB there is no MS). In support of this date, J. Genot cites the description of Joseph as a Jewish astronomer at a Gentile court, the use of the astrolabe, and contemporary influences on biblical narratives.

***Text***

Venice 1625 (repr. Paris 1986, together with an introductory volume, ed. J. Genot-Bismuth). The Venice edition appeals to an earlier one printed in 1552 at Naples; but this apparently never existed (see J. Dan, *KS* 49 (1973–74) 242–44). Other editions: Berlin 1923 (ed. L. Goldschmidt); Jerusalem 1986 (ed. J. Dan). For two Yiddish adaptations of the work see **Turniansky, Ch.** 'The First Yiddish Translations of Sefer Hayashar' (Hebr.). *Tarbiz* 54 (1984–85) 567–620.

***Translations***

**Noach, M.** *The Book of Jaschar*. New York 1840; repr. 1972. French: **Drach, P. L. B.** In Migne, *Dictionnaire des Apocryphes*, 2:1070–1310. Paris 1858.

***Bibliography***

**Dan, J.** 'Matai nitḥaber "Sefer ha-Yashar"?' In S. Werses et al. (eds.), *Sefer Dov Sadan*, 105–10. Tel Aviv 1977. **Dan, J.** *The Hebrew Story*, 137f. **Dan, J.** [Introduction to his edition.] **Flusser, D.** *Josippon*, 2:17–24. **Genot, J.** 'Joseph as an Astronomer in Sefer ha-Yashar' (Hebr.). *Tarbiz* 51 (1981–82) 670–72. **Genot, J.** 'Censure idéologique et discours chiffré: Le Sefer hayašar oeuvre d'un exilé espagnol refugié à Naples.' *REJ* 140 (1981) 433–51. **Herr, M. D.** *EJ* 16: 1517. **Schmitt, G.** *Ein indirektes Zeugnis der Makkabäerkämpfe: Testament Juda 3–7 und Parallelen.* Wiesbaden 1983. **Zunz,** *GV*, 162–65.

### *t) Ma'aseh-Books*

For the numerous Hebrew and Yiddish *Ma'aseh-Books,* see M. Steinschneider, *Catalogus librorum Hebraeorum in bibliotheca Bodleiana* (Berlin 1860; repr. Hildesheim 1964), 3869–3942; J. Dan, *The Hebrew Story* (bibliography). Further bibliography in E. Yassif, 'Sepher ha-Ma'asim: Character, Origins and Influence of Folktales from the Time of the Tosaphists' (Hebr.). *Tarbiz* 53 (1983–84) 409–29.

## *2) Ethical Midrashim*

### *a) Derekh Ereṣ Rabbah and Derekh Ereṣ Zuttah*: see pp. 230f.

### *b) Tanna de-bê Eliyahu*

The structure and much of the content of this work, which is also known as *Seder Eliyahu* (SE), is indebted to the narrative of Ket 106a: the prophet Elijah taught Rab Anan, a student of Rab, *Seder Eliyahu Rabbah* (SER) and *Seder Eliyahu Zuttah* (SEZ). Of the various Talmudic passages linked with the expression *Tanna debê Eliyahu*, some are contained in the book at hand. Its intention, expressed at the outset by an explanation of Gen 3.24, is to urge right moral conduct (*Derekh Ereṣ*) and to glorify the study of the law. It contains on the one hand interpretations of legal provisions, enlivened by parables, sentences, prayers and admonitions, and on the other hand stories about the author's travels (he claims to be from Yabneh and to have moved to Babylonia) and adventures. Elijah appears repeatedly; but he is probably not intended as the narrator throughout, even where he is not explicitly named.

The language of SE is a pure but flowery, 'classicistic' Hebrew (Urbach), embellished with peculiar expressions and numerous new idioms. The date and place of composition are disputed. According to some, SE is essentially identical with the work cited in the Talmud as *Tanna de-bê Eliyahu*. For these scholars, its basic core goes back to third-century Babylonia (Friedmann, Margulies, Braude), or was at any rate composed in the second half of the fifth century, prior to the final redaction of the BT, since it presupposes the persecution under Peroz and the power of the Magi

(Mann; Epstein, who regards Anan as the initial redactor but assumes several editions in the Babylonian academies). Others (e.g. Zunz) date the work to the tenth century, based on the data in chapters 2 (F. 6f.), 7 (F. 37) and 29 (F. 163). The parallels in BT and GenR in this case would not derive from SE, but would instead have given rise to it. However, a comparison of the first historical reference in SER (more than 700 years of the intended Messianic period have already passed in servitude because of our sins: this would point to a redaction after 940) with the quotation of this passage in Yalqut Makhiri on Zech 14.7 (here 664 is given, i.e. the year 904) shows that copyists continually updated these references. It is moreover clear that Natronai Gaon (ninth century) already quotes the work. Hence a date of composition before the ninth century, and probably after BT, is likely (thus e.g. Albeck). Further clarification may result from discoveries of additional texts, such as the Genizah fragment of a Palestinian character (halakhah, style) which has been published by Rabinovitz. This has also made the Babylonian origin of the text highly questionable.

According to the *Arukh*, which does not itself contain any quotations, the first part (SER) has 30 chapters, the second (SEZ) 12; in the 1598 Venice edition according to a MS from the year 1186, the first part has 31, the second 25 chapters. Zunz already recognized that chapters 15–25 of the latter are additions. On the basis of a Vatican manuscript of 1073, Friedmann divided the first part more suitably into 29 chapters. He ends the second part with chapter 15 of the Venice edition, but the last chapter is not authentic. In the edition of Ch. M. Horowitz, SEZ has only 12 chapters. With respect to SEZ, the manuscripts, printed editions and excerpts in the Yalqut are so divergent that one is inclined to assume different recensions. The edition of S. Haida, Prague 1677, is not an edition of the actual text of SE. Instead, the author himself discloses that in view of the corrupt transmission of the text he persuaded Elijah after prayer and fasting to reveal the work to him anew. . .!

***Text***

**Friedmann, M.** *Seder Eliahu Rabba und Seder Eliahu zuta (Tanna d'be Eliahu).* Vienna 1902. **Friedmann, M.** *Pseudo-Seder Eliahu zuta.* Vienna 1904. [Repr. with the above, Jerusalem 1960. Cf. J. Theodor, *MGWJ* 44 (1900) 383–84, 550–61; 47 (1903) 77–79.] **Ginzberg, L.** *Ginzê Schechter*, 1:235–45. [SEZ.] **Horowitz, Ch. M.** *Bibliotheca Haggadica*, 2:3–19. Frankfurt 1881; repr. Jerusalem 1967. **Rabinovitz, Z. M.** *Ginzé Midrash*, 296–301. Facsimile: *Torat Cohanim (Sifra): Seder Eliyahu Rabba and Zutta: Codex Vatican 31.* Jerusalem 1971.

***Translation***

**Braude, W. G. & Kapstein, I. J.** *Tanna debe Eliyyahu: The Lore of the School of Elijah.* Philadelphia 1981. [Cf. J. Elbaum (Hebr.), *JSHL* 7 (1985) 103–19.]

***Bibliography***

**Aptowitzer, V.** 'Seder Elia.' In S. W. Baron and A. Marx (eds.), *Jewish Studies in Memory of G. A. Kohut*, 5–39. New York 1935. **Brand, J.** 'Seder Tanna de-be-Eliyahu Rabbah we-zutta (zemano u-meḥabero).' In B. Z. Luria (ed.), *Zer li'gevurot: The Zalman Shazar Jubilee Volume*, 597–617. Jerusalem 1973. **Braude, W. G.** '"Conjecture" and Interpolation in Translating Rabbinic Texts: Illustrated by a Chapter from Tanna debe Eliyyahu.' In J. Neusner (ed.), *Christianity, Judaism and other Greco-Roman Cults: Studies for Morton Smith at Sixty*, 4:77–92. Leiden 1975. **Braude, W. G.** 'Novellae in Eliyahu Rabbah's Exegesis.' In E. Fleischer and J. J. Petuchowski (eds.), *Studies in Aggadah, Targum and Jewish Liturgy, in Memory of Joseph Heinemann*, 11–22. Jerusalem 1981. **Elbaum, J.** *EJ* 15: 803f. **Elbaum, J.** 'The Midrash Tana Devei Eliyahu and Ancient Esoteric Literature.' *JSJT* 6 (1987) Hebr. section, 139–50. **Epstein, J. N.** *ITM*, 762–67, 1302f. **Goldberg, A.** *Erlösung durch Leiden*, 28–31. Frankfurt 1978. [SEZ 19–25 and PesR 34–37 not directly related; 'however, one cannot exclude the possibility that PesR 36–7 has indirectly influenced SEZ 21' (p. 31).] **Kadushin, M.** *The Theology of Seder Eliahu.* New York 1932. **Mann, J.** 'Date and Place of Redaction of Seder Eliyahu Rabba and Zuṭṭa.' *HUCA* 4 (1927) 302–10. **Margulies, M.** 'Le-ba'ayat qadmuto shel Seder Eliyahu Rabbah.' In M.D. Cassuto et al. (eds.), *Sefer Assaf* (*Festschrift* S. Assaf), 370–90. Jerusalem 1953. **Urbach, E. E.** 'Le-she'elat leshono u-meworotaw shel sefer "Seder Eliyahu".' *Leshonenu* 21 (1956–57) 183–97. **Werblowsky, R. J. Z.** 'A Note on the Text of Seder Eliyahu.' *JJS* 6 (1955) 201–11. **Zucker, M.** *Rav Saadya Gaon's Translation of the Torah* (Hebr.), 116–27, 205–19. New York 1959. [Anti-Karaite polemic in SE, which he dates c. 850–60.] **Zunz**, *GV*, 92f., 119–25. [Cf. Albeck, *Derashot*, 55–57, 292–96.]

### *c) Midrash Ma'aseh Torah*

A compilation of teachings and rules in accordance with the numbers from 3 to 10, hence also called *Midrash Shloshah we-Arba'ah.* Another name is *Pirqê Rabbenu ha-Qadosh.* There are several, only some of which have so far been published. The midrash probably originated in the ninth century, but used older sources.

***Text***

Constantinople 1519; Venice 1544. **Jellinek, A.** *BhM*, 2:92–101. [German translation in A. Wünsche, *Lehrhallen*, vol. 4.] Another recension: **Schönblum, S.** *Shloshah Sefarim Niftaḥim.* Lemberg (L'vov) 1877. [*Pirqa de rabbenu ha-qadosh.*] Also in **Grünhut**, *Sefer ha-Likkutim*, 3:35–89; and **Wertheimer**, *Batei Midrashot*, 2:45–73. **Higger, M.** 'Pirqê Rabbenu ha-Qadosh.' *Horeb* 6 (1941) 115–59. [A Yemenite MS of the JTS, which served as the *Vorlage* of the MS edited by Grünhut.] Cf. also the *Ḥuppat Eliyahu* in **Horowitz, Ch. M.** *Kebod Ḥuppah.* Frankfurt 1888. – See further **Herr, M. D.** *EJ* 16: 1516. **Zunz**, *GV*, 297f.

### *d) Midrash Temurah*

This small ethical-haggadic work is designed to illustrate the necessity of reverses and contrasts in the world. In the first two of five chapters, Ishmael and Aqiba appear as teachers (deliberate pseudepigraphy?); this is followed by an interpretation of Psalm 136 in relation to Eccl 3.1–8. The language along with the earliest quotations of this work suggest a date in the second half of the 12th century.

***Text***

First printed as an appendix to **Azulai, H. J. D.** *Shem ha-gedolim.* Livorno 1786. **Jellinek, A.** *BhM,* 1:106–14. Critical edition: **Wertheimer**, 2:187–201. **Perani, M.** *Il midrash temurah: La dialettica degli opposti in un' interpretazione ebraica tardo-medievale; Introduzione, versione e commento.* Bologna 1986. Cf. **Herr, M. D.** *EJ* 16: 1518; **Zunz**, *GV*, 124.

### *e) Midrash Ḥaserot wi-Yterot*

This midrash deals with the words of the Bible that are written with or without *mater lectionis.* It was probably composed in Palestine under the influence of the Masoretes (ninth century or earlier; it was already quoted by Hai Gaon). The work does not follow the biblical order, which was introduced only by a later redactor. Several versions of the work are preserved.

***Text***

**Wertheimer**, 2:203–332. **Berliner, A.** *Pletath Soferim* (Breslau [Wroclaw] 1872), 34–41; Hebr. section 36–45. **Marmorstein, A.** *Midrash Ḥaserot wi-Yterot*, London 1917. **Mainz, E. M.** 'Midrash Male' we-Ḥaser.' *Kobez al Yad* 6 [16] (Jerusalem 1966) 77–119. [MS Vat. 44, partly in Arabic, probably from Yemen.] **Ginzberg, L.** *Ginze Schechter*, 1:206–9. A related text (on the mutually contradictory verses of Scripture): J. Mann, *HUCA* 14 (1939) 338–52.

## *3) Esoteric and Mystical Writings*

***General Bibliography***

**Chernus, I.** *Mysticism in Rabbinic Judaism: Studies in the History of Midrash.* Berlin/New York 1982. **Gruenwald, I.** *Apocalyptic and Merkavah Mysticism.* Leiden/Cologne 1980. [Cf. J. Dan, *Tarbiz* 51 (1981–82) 685–91; G. Vajda, *REJ* 140 (1981) 217–24.] **Halperin, D. J.** *The Merkabah in Rabbinic Literature.* New Haven 1980. **Halperin, D. J.** *The Faces of the Chariot: Early Jewish Responses to Ezekiel's Vision.* Tübingen 1988. **Schäfer, P.** *Hekhalot-Studien.* Tübingen 1988. **Schäfer, P.** *Der verborgene und offenbare Gott: Hauptthemen der frühen jüdischen Mystik.* Tübingen 1991. [ET *The Hidden and Manifest God: Some Major Themes in Early Jewish Mysticism.* Albany, NY 1992.] **Scholem, G.** *Major Trends in Jewish Mysticism.* 3rd, revised edn., New York 1954. [Frequently reprinted.] **Scholem, G.** *Origins of the Kabbalah.* Edited by R. J. Z. Werblowsky and translated by A. Arkush. Philadelphia/Princeton 1987. **Scholem, G.** *Jewish Gnosticism, Merkabah Mysticism, and Talmudic Tradition.* 2nd edn. New York 1965. **Scholem, G.** *EJ* 10: 489–653. [Also published in book form, together with other *EJ* articles by Scholem: *Kabbalah*, Jerusalem 1974; repr. New York 1987.] **Séd, N.** *La mystique cosmologique juive.* Paris 1981.

### *a) Sefer Yeṣirah*

In concise language, the 'Book of Creation' portrays the origin and constitution of the world. In the '32 Paths of Wisdom', it appears to combine two originally independent parts: one is about the *ten Sefirot*, the basic numbers, which are at the same time the basic principles of the world, viz., the four basic elements (divine spirit, ether, water and fire) and the six dimensions of space (North, South, East and West, as well as height and depth). The second part discusses the *22 letters* of the Hebrew alphabet. The relationship between the letters and the *Sefirot* is not indicated. The letters uphold creation; they are divided into three groups: the three 'mothers', *Alef*, *Mem*, and *Shin*; the seven 'double' (twice pronounced) letters (*b*, *g*, *d*, *k*, *p*, *t* and *r*); the twelve remaining letters. Each group of letters is interpreted both cosmologically and in relation to man. All things exist by the combination of these letters.

This work used to be commonly dated to the Geonic period; Scholem now dates it to the time between the third and the sixth century, and locates it in Palestine. Because of the work's links with Valentinian Gnosticism, the Pseudo-Clementines and similar writings, P. Hayman suspects a Syrian origin in the late second or early third century; but detailed evidence is yet to be provided. With Gruenwald we must at any rate distinguish between the origin of each of the two parts and their amalgamation in the final redaction (probably in the early Islamic period); more specific conclusions, however, are not yet possible. The work first appears in the tenth century, and then immediately in three recensions: a short recension was the subject of a commentary by Dunash b. Tamim around 956; a long one underlies the commentary of S. Donnolo (10th cent.); a version related to the latter is contained in Saadya's commentary of 931. Subsequently, the short version came to be preferred, and commentaries on it were produced by Jacob ben Nissim, Yehudah ben Barzillai, Moses ben Naḥman and others.

***Text***

First printed at Mantua, 1562. [A short form with several commentaries; the appendix contains the longer recension without commentary.] **Goldschmidt, L.** *Das Buch der Schöpfung: Text nebst Übersetzung... und Einleitung*. Frankfurt 1894; repr. Darmstadt 1969. [Critique: A. Epstein, *MGWJ* 39 (1895) 46–48, 134–36.] **Gruenwald, I.** 'A Preliminary Critical Edition of Séfer Yeẓîra.' *Israel Oriental Studies* 1 (Tel Aviv 1971) 132–77. [Textual basis MS Vat. 299(8), probably tenth century.] **Weinstock, I.** 'Le-birur ha-nusaḥ shel Sefer Yeṣirah.' *Temirin* 1 (Jerusalem 1972) 9–61. [Rather arbitrary reconstruction of the text: cf. Gruenwald, *REJ* 132 (1973) 435 n.1.] – **Allony, N.** '"Sefer Yeṣira" nusaḥ RaSa"G be–ṣurat megillah mi-genizat Qahir.' *Temirin* 2 (1982) 9–29. [Reprinted in idem, *Collected Papers*, vol. 1 (Jerusalem 1986), 335–55.] **Castelli, D.** *Il commento di Sabbathai Donnolo sul libro della creazione*. Florence 1880. **Habermann, A. M.** 'Abanim le-ḥeqer "Sefer Yeṣirah".' *Sinai* 10 (1945) 241–65. [Genizah fragment of Saadya's commentary, tenth century.] **Lambert, M.** *Commentaire sur le Séfer Yesira ou le livre de la Création par le Gaon Saadya de Fayyoum*. Paris 1891; repr. 1986. **Vajda, G.** 'Le Commentaire de Saadia sur le Séfer Yeçîra.' *REJ* 106 (1941) 64–86. **Vajda, G.** 'Le commentaire kairouanais sur le "Livre de la Création".' *REJ* 107 (1946–47) 99–156; 110 (1949–50) 67–92; 112 (1953) 5–33. **Vajda, G.** 'Deux nouveaux fragments arabes du commentaire de Dunash b. tamim sur le "Livre de la Création".' *REJ* 113 (1954) 37–66. **Vajda, G.** 'Deux nouveaux fragments arabes....' *REJ* 122 (1963) 149–62.

***Additional Bibliography***

**Allony, N.** 'Ha-shittah ha-anagrammatit shel ha-milonut ha–'ibrit ba-Sefer Yeṣirah.' *Temirin* 1 (Jerusalem 1972) 63–100. [Reprinted in idem, *Collected Papers*, vol. 6 (Jerusalem 1992) 23–59. Based on the second part of the book, he argues for an Islamic date.] **Dan, J.** 'The Religious Meaning of *Sefer Yeẓira*' (Hebr.). *JSJT* 11 (1993) 7–35. **Dan, J.** 'The Language of Creation and Its Grammar.' In C. Elsas et al. (eds.), *Tradition und Translation: Zum Problem der interkulturellen Übersetzbarkeit religiöser Phänomene* (*Festschrift* C. Colpe), 42–63. Berlin/New York 1994. **Dan, J.** 'Three Phases in the History of the Sefer Yezira.' *FJB* 21 (1994) 7–29. **Gruenwald, I.** 'Some Critical Notes on the First Part of Séfer Yeẓîrâ.' *REJ* 132 (1973) 475–512. **Hayman, P.** 'Some Observations on Sefer Yeṣira: (1) Its Use of Scripture.' *JJS* 35 (1984) 168–84. '(2) The Temple at the Centre of the Universe.' *JJS* 37 (1986) 176–82. **Séd, N.** 'Le Séfer Yeṣîrâ, L'édition critique, le texte primitif, la grammaire et la métaphysique.' *REJ* 132 (1973) 513–28. **Scholem, G.** *EJ* 16: 782–88. **Toaff, G.** 'Gnosticismo e Sepher Yezirah.' *Annuario di Studi Ebraici* 9 (1977–79) 19–26. Rome 1980. **Toaff, G.** *Sefer Yezira (Il libro della creazione)*. Rome 1979. **Zunz**, *GV*, 175.

### *b) Midrash Tadshê*

The work is named after Gen 1.11, the verse addressed at the beginning; it is also called *Baraita de Rabbi Pinḥas ben Yair* (P. is mentioned twice in the text and once, as the author, at the end). It comments on various passages of the Torah and of Lamentations. It is closely linked with rabbinic esotericism and shows a clear knowledge of the Book of Jubilees. G. Scholem (*Origins of the Kabbalah*, 17) locates the origin of the work in Southern France or in adjacent centres. It is quoted by Mosheh ha-Darshan (see Albeck, *Bereshit Rabbati*, 16f.), whom A. Epstein actually considers to be the author of the work.

***Text***

**Jellinek, A.** *BHM*, 3:164–93. **Epstein, A.** *Qadmoniot*, 144–71. German translation: **Wünsche, A.** *Lehrhallen*, vol. 5 b.

***Bibliography***

**Belkin, S.** 'Midrash Tadshê o Midrash de-Rabbi Pinḥas ben Yair: Midrash Hellenisti Qadmon.' *Horeb* 11 (1951) 1–52. [Sees a common source with Philo for the allegorical exegesis.] **Epstein, A.** *Qadmoniot*, 130–43. **Epstein, A.** 'Le livre de Jubilés, Philon et le Midrasch Tadsché.' *REJ* 21 (1890) 80–97; 22 (1891) 1–25. **Zunz**, *GV*, 292f.

### *c) Midrash Konen and Other Texts on the Work of Creation*

A midrash on the creation of the world, first printed in Venice, 1601; *BhM* 2:23–39 (German translation in Wünsche, *Lehrhallen*, vol. 3). Together with a number of other texts, the work belongs to the *Ma'aseh Bereshit*, the second branch of Jewish mysticism alongside the *Ma'aseh Merkabah*: *BhM* 5:63–69; Wertheimer, 1:1–48 (*Seder Rabbah de-Bereshit*); L. Ginzberg, 'Nusaḥ ḥadash shel Seder Ma'aseh Bereshit', *Ginze Schechter*, 1:182–87. N. Séd, 'Une cosmologie juive du haut moyen age: La Berayta de Ma'aseh Bereshit', *REJ*

123 (1964) 259–305; 124 (1965) 23–123 (introduction and text). See also the texts in *Synopse zur Hekhalot-Literatur*, §§ 428–67.

***d) The Greater and the Lesser Hekhalot***

The writings about the 'throne halls' or heavenly 'palaces' are the most important texts of the merkabah literature, which prepares or simply describes the mystical ascent to God's throne chariot (*merkabah*). The way through the seven heavens and the seven throne halls is full of dangers which can only be overcome if one knows the right formulas (many expressions in these magical texts are in Greek). Most of the texts are devoted to the heavenly liturgy. They quote hymns sung by the angels or by the four beings that carry the divine throne. These songs usually end with the threefold 'Holy' of Isa 6.3. The solemn and monotonous uniformity of the hymns is doubtless also meant to encourage ecstasy. A. Goldberg sees in the Hekhalot Rabbati three major parts which were later redactionally interwoven: the Qedushah songs; the initiation of the adept regarding the ascent to the seven hekhalot; the mystery of the Torah.

G. Scholem dated Hekhalot Rabbati and Zutrati in the Talmudic period. P. Schäfer, on the other hand, emphasizes the inconsistent manuscript tradition particularly of Hekhalot Zutrati, the irregular internal structure of the work, as well as the fact that the manuscripts neither make use of the title nor indicate the beginning or end, but seamlessly append additional material. Schäfer regards this as the 'classic example of a textual fiction whose redactional unity probably never existed' (*Hekhalot-Studien*, 62). In *JSJ* 14:180 (cf. *Hekhalot-Studien*, 15), he speaks similarly about hekhalot literature as a whole. For this reason, the question of the dating of these works is not a meaningful one; one can only 'assume as relatively certain that macro-forms of *Hekhalot Rabbati* and *Zuṭarti* were in circulation no later than the tenth century' (*Übersetzung*, 2:xx–xxi). There are many later (even Sabbatian) additions and alterations of the textual tradition.

***Text***

**Schäfer, P.**, ed. (with M. Schlüter and H.G. von Mutius). *Synopse zur Hekhalot-Literatur.* Tübingen 1981. [The most comprehensive publication of hekhalot material thus far, a synopsis of 7 MSS; see J. Dan, *Tarbiz* 53 (1983–84) 313–17.] **Schäfer, P.**, ed. *Übersetzung der Hekhalot-Literatur.* Vols. 2–4. Tübingen 1987–91. [Vol. 1 will contain §§1–80 of the Synopsis, i.e. 3 Enoch.] **Schäfer, P.**, ed. *Geniza-Fragmente zur Hekhalot-Literatur.* Tübingen 1984. **Schäfer, P.**, ed. *Konkordanz zur Hekhalot-Literatur.* 2 vols. Tübingen 1986–88. **Schäfer, P.** *Hekhalot-Studien*, 96–117 [new fragments of hekhalot texts], 154–233 [description of MSS]. **Davila, J. R.** 'Prolegomena to a Critical Edition of the Hekhalot Rabbati.' *JJS* 45 (1994) 208–26. **Elior, R.** *Hekhalot Zutarti.* Jerusalem 1982. [Cf. P. Schäfer, *Tarbiz* 54 (1984–85) 153–57.

Older (partial) editions are given in **Musajoff, S.** *Sefer Merkabah Shlemah.* Jerusalem 1921; repr. Jerusalem 1972. **Wertheimer**, 1:65–136. **Jellinek, A.** *BhM*, 3:83–108.

***Bibliography***

In addition to Scholem's writings cited earlier, see **Scholem, G.** *EJ* 11: 1386–89. Also: **Alexander, P. S.** 'Comparing Merkavah Mysticism and Gnosticism: An Essay in Method.' *JJS* 35 (1984) 1–18. **Chernus, I.** 'Individual and Community in the Redaction of the Hekhalot Literature, *HUCA* 52 (1981) 253–74. **Chernus, I.** 'Visions of God in Merkabah Mysticism.' *JSJ* 13 (1982) 123–46. **Goldberg, A.** 'Einige Bemerkungen zu den Quellen und den redaktionellen Einheiten der großen Hekhalot.' *FJB* 1 (1973) 1–49. **Gruenwald, I.** *Apocalyptic*, 98–123, 142–73. **Gruenwald, I.** 'The Song of the Angels, the Qedushah and the Composition of the Hekhalot Literature' (Hebr.). In A. Oppenheimer et al. (eds.), *Jerusalem in the Second Temple Period* (Memorial Volume for A. Schalit), 459–81. Jerusalem 1980. **Halperin, D. J.** *The Faces of the Chariot*. Tübingen 1988. **Maier, J.** *Vom Kultus zur Gnosis*, 128–46. Salzburg 1964. **Maier, J.** 'Serienbildung und "numinoser" Eindruckseffekt in den poetischen Stücken der Hekhalot-Literatur.' *Semitics* 34 (1973) 36–66. **Schäfer, P.** *Hekhalot-Studien*. [In English see also idem, 'Tradition and Redaction in Hekhalot Literature', *JSJ* 14 (1983) 172–81; 'New Testament and Hekhalot Literature: The Journey into Heaven in Paul and in Merkavah Mysticism', *JJS* 35 (1984) 19–35.] **Schiffmann, L. H.** 'The Recall of Rabbi Neḥuniah Ben Ha-Qaneh from Ecstasy in the Hekhalot Rabbati.' *AJSR* 1 (1976) 269–81. **Schlüter, M.** 'Die Erzählung von der Rückholung des R. Neḥunya ben Haqana aus der Merkava-Schau in ihrem redaktionellen Rahmen.' *FJB* 10 (1982) 65–109. **Wewers, G.** 'Die Überlegenheit des Mystikers. Zur Aussage der Gedulla-Hymnen in Hekhalot Rabbati 1,2–2,3.' *JSJ* 17 (1986) 3–22.

## *e) Other Merkabah or Hekhalot Texts*

The *Sefer Hekhalot* was edited by Odeberg as 3 Enoch. It describes R. Ishmael's heavenly journey under the guidance of Enoch, who has been transformed into Metatron in heaven. Although Odeberg dated it in the late third century, it must probably be moved to the end of the Talmudic period: see P. S. Alexander, who argues for a post-Talmudic final redaction.

***Text***

Partly published in **Jellinek, A.** *BhM*, 5:170–90. **Odeberg, O.** *3 Enoch or The Hebrew Book of Enoch*. Cambridge 1928; repr. New York 1973 (with a prolegomenon by J. C. Greenfield). **Schäfer, P.** (ed.). *Synopse zur Hekhalot-Literatur*, §§1–80. Tübingen 1981. [A new edition with translation is being prepared by P. Schäfer.] English translation with commentary and detailed introduction: **Alexander P. S.** In J. H. Charlesworth (ed.), *The Old Testament Pseudepigrapha*, vol. 1 (London 1983), 223–315. German translation: **Hofmann, H.** *Das sogenannte hebräische Henochbuch*. Königstein (Taunus)/Bonn 1984.

***Additional Bibliography***

Cf. **Alexander, P. S.** 'The Historical Setting of the Hebrew Book of Enoch.' *JJS* 28 (1977) 156–80. **Alexander, P. S.** '3 Enoch and the Talmud.' *JSJ* 18 (1987) 40–68. **Gruenwald, I.** *Apocalyptic*, 191–208. **Morray-Jones, C. R. A.** 'Hekhalot Literature and Talmudic Tradition: Alexander's Three Test Cases.' *JSJ* 22 (1991) 1–39.

The *Visions of Ezekiel (Re'uyyot Yeḥezkel)*, a kind of commentary on Ezek 1, originated even earlier, probably in the fourth or early fifth century.

***Text***

**Mann, J.** 'Pereq Re'iyyot Yeḥezqel.' *Haṣofeh* 5 (Budapest 1921; repr. Jerusalem 1972) 256–64. [Genizah text.] **Wertheimer, S. A.** *Batei Midrashot*, 2:127–34. [Text of Mann plus conjectures.] **Marmorstein, A.** 'A Fragment of the Visions of Ezekiel.' *JQR* N.S. (1917–18) 367–78. [Genizah fragment.] Critical edition and Commentary: **Gruenwald, I.** *Temirin* 1 (Jerusalem 1972) 101–39. Cf. **Gruenwald, I.** *Apocalyptic*, 134–41. **Halperin, D. J.** *The Faces of the Chariot*, 263–89, 495–504. Tübingen 1988. [Translation on pp. 264–68.]

*Merkabah Rabbah* is a composite work whose main topic is the 'great mystery' (of the Torah) which R. Ishmael acquires. Rich in magical passages, it is connected with a piece of Shi'ur Qomah and other texts such as the 'Conjuration of the Sar ha-Panim'.

***Text***

**Musajoff, S.** *Merkabah Shlemah*, 1a–6a. Jerusalem 1921; repr. Jerusalem 1972. **Schäfer, P.**, ed. *Synopse zur Hekhalot-Literatur*, §§623–712. Tübingen 1981. **Schäfer, P.** *Hekhalot-Studien*, 17–49 [Merkabah Rabbah], 118–53 [Sar ha-Panim]. German translation in **Schäfer, P.** *Übersetzung der Hekahlot Literatur*, vol. 5. See also **Gruenwald, I.** *Apocalyptic*, 174–80.

*Ma'aseh Merkabah* was first edited by G. Scholem, *Gnosticism*, 101–17; a more broadly based text appears in *Synopse zur Hekhalot-Literatur*, §§544–97. A German translation and an extensive introduction are given in P. Schäfer, *Übersetzung der Hekhalot Literatur*, vol. 3. See further I. Gruenwald, *Apocalyptic*, 181–87; N. Janowitz, *The Poetics of Ascent: Theories of Language in a Rabbinic Ascent Text*, Albany, NY 1989; M. D. Swartz, *Mystical Prayer in Ancient Judaism: An Analysis of Ma'aseh Merkavah*, Tübingen 1992.

This document should be distinguished another work known as *Massekhet Hekhalot* (cf. A. Jellinek, *BhM*, 2:40–47), which Wertheimer (pp. 51–62) also called *Ma'aseh Merkabah*: see K. Herrmann, *Massekhet Hekhalot, Traktat von den himmlischen Palästen: Edition, Übersetzung und Kommentar*, Tübingen 1994. According to Gruenwald, *Apocalyptic*, 209–12, *Ma'aseh Merkabah* probably originated in German Hasidic circles in the 12th or 13th century.

For the *Shi'ur Qomah*, see M. S. Cohen, *The Shi'ur Qomah: Texts and Recensions*, Tübingen 1985; German translation in P. Schäfer, *Übersetzung der Hekhalot-Literatur*, vol. 4. In light of the extremely fluid text material, Schäfer doubts that a finished redaction of Shi'ur-Qomah documents ever existed.

***Bibliography***

**Cohen, M. S.** *The Shi'ur Qomah: Liturgy and Theurgy in Pre-Kabbalistic Jewish Mysticism.* New York/London 1983. **Dan, J.** 'The Concept of Knowledge in the Shi'ur Qomah.' In S. Stein & R. Loewe (eds.), *Studies in Jewish Religious and Intellectual History: Presented to Alexander Altmann on the Occasion of His Seventieth Birthday*, 67–73. University, AL 1979. **Herrmann, K.** 'Text und Fiktion: Zur Textüberlieferung des Shi'ur Qoma.' *FJB* 16 (1988) 89–142. **Schäfer, P.** *Hekhalot-Studien*, 75–83. **Scholem, G.** *Gnosticism*, 36–42.

### *f) Alphabet (Otiyyot) of R. Aqiba*

This work of merkabah mysticism is preserved in several recensions; among other things it also contains elements of Shi'ur Qomah speculation. Graetz once attempted to prove that this work is the main source of the hekhalot literature. In actual fact the relationship between these writings must be viewed in reverse. The work is quoted from the tenth century on, so that a date between the seventh and ninth century is likely. However, a new study of this document is needed.

***Text***

**Jellinek, A.** *BhM*, 3:12–64. [Two recensions. German translation in A. Wünsche, *Lehrhallen*, vol. 4.] **Wertheimer, S. A.** *Batei Midrashot*, 2:333–477. [The same two recensions as well as similar writings. Cf. D. F. Sawyer, *JJS* 42 (1991) 115–21; idem, *Midrash Aleph Beth*, Atlanta 1993.] See also Jellinek, *BhM* 5:31–33.

***Bibliography***

**Graetz, H.** 'Die mystische Literatur in der gaonäischen Epoche.' *MGWJ* 8 (1859) 67–78, 103–18, 140–53. [The two latter instalments deal mostly with Shi'ur Qoma.] **Herr, M. D.** *EJ* 16: 1516. **Scholem, G.** 'Über eine Formel in den koptisch-gnostischen Schriften und ihren jüdischen Ursprung.' *ZNW* 30 (1931) 17–176. **Zunz,** *GV*, 178.

### *g) Sefer Raziel and Sefer ha-Razim*

*Sefer Raziel*, first printed in Amsterdam in 1701, is probably not much older in its present form. However, it compiles a number of older writings from the hekhalot literature and similar writings, as well as a long version of *Shi'ur Qomah*. The name probably derives from the angel Raziel, the revealer of the mysteries, who already plays a part in the old *Sefer ha-Razim*. This work, which has been reconstructed from a Genizah text and various MSS, may have been written in Palestine as early as the third or fourth century (Gruenwald, *Apocalyptic*, 226: 6th or 7th cent.). It is related to the hekhalot texts in that it describes the seven heavens. However, what is characteristic of the work is the predominance of magic, which often transgresses the boundaries of 'orthodox' Judaism and has its closest parallel in the Greek magical papyri of Alexandria. The work even contains a Greek hymn to Helios.

***Text***

**Margalioth, M.** *Sepher ha-Razim: A Newly Recovered Book of Magic from the Talmudic Period* (Hebr.). Jerusalem 1966. [His detailed introduction is relevant as well for the Book of Raziel (on which cf. also J. Dan, *EJ* 13: 1592f.). On this edition see further J. Dan, '"Sepher Harazim" edited by M. Margalioth' (Hebr.). *Tarbiz* 37 (1967–68) 208–14.

***Translation***

**Morgan, M. A.** *Sepher Ha-Razim: The Book of Mysteries.* Chico 1983.

***Further Bibliography***

**Gruenwald, I.** *Apocalyptic*, 225–34. **Niggemeyer, J.–H.** *Beschwörungsformeln aus dem 'Buch der Geheimnisse'*. Cologne 1974. [Critique of Margalioth's edition.] **Séd, N.** 'Le Séfer ha-Razim et la méthode de "combinaison des lettres".' *REJ* 130 (1971) 295–304.

# VIII

## COMPILATIONS; COMMENTARIES KNOWN AS 'MIDRASH'

### *1) Yalqut Shim'oni*

Usually simply known as Yalqut, this is a midrashic thesaurus on the whole Old Testament, compiled from more than 50 works, some of which are lost to us (Sifre Zutta, Yelamdenu, the midrashim Abkir, Tadshe and Esfah, etc. are in part attested only in Yalqut). The Yalqut is also valuable for the textual criticism of extant works. However, this should be qualified inasmuch as the author of Yalqut of course also uses defective MSS as his *Vorlage*, partly corrects them by conjectures, and also combines and abbreviates his sources. Moreover, the Yalqut itself suffered in transmission; one must take into account both the first printed edition of Thessaloniki and the only virtually complete manuscript (MS Oxford 2637), which also underlies the critical edition. The sources of the work are always marked at the beginning of the quotation (thus the first printed edition) or in the margin (in the later editions); this probably may well go back to the original compiler.

The Yalqut has two parts, the Pentateuch with 963 paragraphs (*remazim*) and the other books of the Bible with 1085. The order of the Biblical books is as given in BB 14b, except that Esth precedes Dan: i.e. Isa after Ezek; hagiographa: Ruth, Pss (NB only 147 instead of 150; this is perhaps due to MidrPsa 22.4, where the number of Pss is said to correspond to Jacob's 147 years of life), Job, Prov, Eccl, Esth, Dan, Ezra, Neh, Chr. Later editions kept to the usual order of the biblical books and thus confused the system of *remazim*. The individual paragraphs are of very unequal length, ranging from a few lines to several pages. It is likely that they were never intended as textual divisions but as an internal reference system: this follows from the fact that in MS Oxford, as in the first edition, the numbers appear not at the beginning of the paragraphs but next to a text which is also used elsewhere in the work (thus Hyman). Only the first edition of the Yalqut adds an appendix to the text (*Qunderes aḥaron*), which in 256 *remazim* presents haggadot of the PT, and in 55 *remazim* quotations from Yelamdenu.

The author of the Yalqut is Shim'on ha-Darshan. Beginning with the Venice edition (whose editor M. Prinz probably relies on traditions), the title pages of the editions suggest that the author is from Frankfurt (on Main). S. I. Rapaport (*Kerem Ḥemed* 7 (1843) 4ff.) and others make this Shim'on ha-Darshan a brother of Menaḥem ben Ḥelbo, the father of Joseph Qara; in this case he would have lived as early as the second half of the eleventh century. This identification was soon rightly criticized by A. Geiger, and especially by

A. Epstein; the latter also refuted M. Gaster's conjecture (p. 38f.) that the author lived in Spain not before the 14th century. The date must instead be assumed to be the 12th or 13th century. This follows, firstly, from the evident (though not explicit) use of this work in *Capistrum Judaeorum* by Raymond Martini (1220–85), which was written c. 1267 (cf. U. Ragacs, *Das Capistrum Iudaeorum des Raimund Martini*, Diss. Vienna 1995); and from the oldest manuscript (MS Oxford 2637 dates from 1307). On the other hand, such a date is also implied by the writings that are quoted in the Yalkut, including *inter alia* Bereshit Rabbati and Midrash Abkir. First cited by Isaac Abrabanel, the Yalqut has continued to increase in popularity since the end of the 15th century – thereby contributing to the fact that several of the midrash texts excerpted in it ceased to be independently transmitted.

***Text***

Thessaloniki 1526–27 (part 1), 1521 (part 2) [Repr. Jerusalem 1968 (part 1), 1973 (part 2)]; Venice 1566 (many changes), the basis of subsequent editions. On the printed editions see A. Epstein, *Kitbê*, 2:278–308.

***Critical edition***

**Hyman, D., Lerrer, D. N. & Shiloni, I.**, eds. *Yalqut Shim'oni al ha-Torah le Rabbenu Shim'on ha-Darshan.* 9 vols. Jerusalem 1973–91. [There is a brief introduction at the end of vol. 9.]

***Bibliography***

**Abramson, S.** *Sinai* 52 (1963) 145–47. **Elbaum J.** *EJ* 16: 707–709. **Epstein, A.** *Qadmoniot (Kitbê*, vol. 2), 278–327, 351–54. **Hyman A. B.** *The Sources of Yalkut Shimeoni* (Hebr.). 2 vols. Jerusalem 1965–74. **Hyman, D.** [=A. B.]. 'Rimzê Yalqut Shim'oni.' *Hadorom* 12 (1960) 144–47. **Finkel, C. Z.** '"Yalqut Shim'oni" u-feshar "Remazaw".' *Moria* 7.8–10 (1977–78) 62–92. **Gaster, M.** *The Exempla of the Rabbis*, Engl. section, 21–39. New York 1968 [repr. of 1924]. **Greenbaum, A.** *Sinai* 76 (1975) 120–33. [Review of Hyman.] **Zunz,** *GV*, 308–15.

### *2) Yalqut ha-Makhiri*

Makhir ben Abba Mari (ben Makhir ben Todros) is commonly thought to have lived in Southern France, although this can be deduced only from the name. A medieval note to the effect that he wrote 'before the persecutions in Spain' would agree with the initial circulation of his writings in Spain as well as with his use of DeutR edn. *Lieberman*, which was particularly common in Spain (thus already A. Marx, *OLZ* 5 (1902) 295f.). If the aforesaid note is correct, the *terminus ante quem* would be 1391; otherwise 1415, when MS Leiden was sold. Thus the late thirteenth or fourteenth century should probably be assumed as the time of composition. M. Gaster wanted to relocate the work to twelfth-century Spain and to see it as a source of Yalqut II, but A. Epstein refuted this. The two Yalqutim probably originated independently of one another.

Yalqut ha-Makhiri comprises the prophetic writings proper and the three great hagiographa; i.e. it deliberately excluded the writings already covered in the Midrash Rabbah. The work employs as sources most of the midrashim known to us, including such late ones as Midrash Job, MidrProv and SER, but also writings that are not otherwise preserved. The author sometimes quotes Midrash Yelamdenu alongside Tanḥuma, which implies that these were two different works for him and not simply different names of the same work. The text of his quotations, moreover, does not agree with the two printed editions of Tan. Evidently, numerous MSS were available to the author, and for some writings more than one. Since on the whole he quotes accurately, his variants for the text of otherwise familiar sources are of great significance.

***Text***

**Spira, J.** *The Yalkut on Isaiah of Machir ben Abba Mari.* Berlin 1894. [According to Codex Leiden, from which 20:4–40:20 and 63:2–end are absent.] **Buber, S.** *Jalkut Machiri... zu den 150 Psalmen.* Berdyczew 1899; repr. Jerusalem 1964. [Additional source references: M. Margulies, *MHG Gen* (Jerusalem 1947=1967), 6f.] **Grünhut, L.** *Sefer ha-Yalqut ha-Makhiri al Mishlê.* Frankfurt 1902. [On Prov 18–31; repr., with J. Spira on Isaiah, Jerusalem 1964. Supplements in *Sefer ha-Likkutim* 6 (Prov 2, 3, 13, 14); further supplements (on Prov 2, 3, 14) published by I. Berdehav, Jerusalem 1927.] **Spiegel, Y. S.** 'A New Section of Yalqut ha-Makhiri on Proverbs' (Hebr.). *Sidra* 1 (1985) 91–130. **Greenup, A. W.** *The Yalkut of R. Machir bar Abba Mari.* 2 vols. London 1910–13; repr. Jerusalem 1967. [Based on Codex Harley 5704 (minor prophets), incomplete at beginning and end.] **Greenup, A. W.** 'A Fragment of the Yalkut of R. Machir bar Abba Mari on Hosea (I.9–XIV.1).' *JQR* N.S. 15 (1924–25) 141–212. [From MS Vat. 291; repr., together with Berdehav, Jerusalem 1968.] **Lauterbach, J. Z.** 'Unpublished Parts of the Yalkut ha-Makiri on Hosea and Micah.' In B. Schindler (ed.), *Occident and Orient* (*Festschrift* M. Gaster), 365–73. London 1936.

***Bibliography***

**Elbaum, J.** *EJ* 16: 706f. **Epstein, A.** 'Le Yalkout Schimeoni et le Yalkout Ha-Makhiri.' *REJ* 26 (1893) 75–83. [*Contra* Gaster.] **Gaster, M.** 'La source de Yalkout II.' *REJ* 25 (1892) 44–52. [In support of his thesis he adduces (53–64) the preface of Yalqut ha-Makhiri and excerpts on Isa 10f. and Obad.]

### *3) Yalqut Reubeni*

This work on the Torah, also called *Yalqut Reubeni gadôl* to distinguish it from the same author's *Yalqut Reubeni* which was first printed at Prague in 1660, was written by Rabbi Reuben Höschke Kohen (Höschke is a Polish diminutive for Yehoshua), who died in 1673. This Yalqut (Wilmersdorf 1681, then Amsterdam 1700; Warsaw n. d., 2 vols.) is a collection of kabbalistic interpretations of the Pentateuch, and hence is of importance for the history of the Kabbalah, but not for midrash research. Cf. G. Scholem, *Major Trends*, 31f.

***4) Midrash ha-Gadol (MHG)***

MHG on the Pentateuch is the largest of all midrash collections. David ben Amram of Aden is today almost universally regarded as the author of MHG, even if its rhyming technique leads A. Steinsaltz to doubt the Yemenite origin of MHG and to favour Egypt. David ben Amram is usually dated in the thirteenth century; however, a Yemenite manuscript dates his halakhic queries for a descendant of Maimonides to 1346 or 1352 (Y. Raẓhabi, *Tarbiz* 54:556). The attribution to Abraham the son of Maimonides is only extremely weakly attested.

The author has divided the Pentateuch according to the annual reading cycle. Each parashah begins with a rhyming proem of two stanzas leading up to the paragraph to be discussed, and it ends with a preview of the coming redemption and the return home to Israel. In between, he compiles for each verse the interpretations of the entire midrashic tradition, of the two Talmuds, many Geonic writings, Alfasi and especially those of Maimonides. Nevertheless, the author does not specify his sources. What is more, a comparison of MHG with some of its sources shows that the latter are handled quite freely. The author divides them into the smallest units, frequently corrects the halakhah of the halakhic midrashim in accordance with the wording of M, adds from the Talmud and other writings, and inserts his own explanatory glosses. Thus there results a mosaic-like composition, an entirely new work with its own style, whose sources can often no longer be reconstructed. This reduces the value of MHG for the restoration of lost midrashic texts such as the MRS, Sifre Zutta and MidrTann. This is shown *inter alia* by a comparison of the two editions of MRS by D. Hoffmann and by Epstein/Melamed (cf. in the latter the introduction by Melamed, 45–58); but even Horowitz in his reconstruction of Sifre Zutta did not always succeed in separating genuine quotations of Sifre Zutta from those of Maimonides. It was once commonly believed that MHG had no access to Mek or Sifre and therefore made use of the other midrashim, MRS, Sifre Zutta and MidrTann. Since then, however, it has been recognized that the author does indeed know and quote both Mek and Sifre, but that for certain reasons he has neglected them, sometimes combining them with the other midrashim to make the halakhic differences disappear. MHG attained great popularity in Yemen and largely displaced other midrashim. With Ch. Albeck, *Midrash Aggadat Esther* (cf. p. 348) must also be attributed to the author of MHG. In Europe MHG only became known in the nineteenth century: the first manuscript was brought to Berlin by M. W. Schapira. Numerous other MSS have since become known.

***Text***

The following were early, partial editions: **Schechter, S.** *Midrash ha-Gadol Forming a Collection of Ancient Rabbinic Homilies to the Pentateuch... Genesis.* Cambridge 1902. **Hoffmann, D.** *Midrasch ha-Gadol zum Buche Exodus.* Berlin 1913–21.

***Critical editions***

Gen: Margulies, M. 2nd edn. Jerusalem 1967.
Exod: Margulies, M. 2nd edn. Jerusalem 1967.
Lev: Rabinowitz, E. N. New York 1932.
Steinsaltz, A. Jerusalem 1975.
Num: Fisch, S. London 1940. [only part 1; detailed introduction in English, 1–136.]
Fisch, S. 2 vols. Jerusalem 1957–63.
Rabinovitz, Z. M. 2nd edn. Jerusalem 1973.
Deut: Fisch, S. Jerusalem 1972.

***Bibliography***

**Belkin, S.** 'Ha-Midrash ha-Gadol u-Midreshê Philon.' In S. B. Hoenig and L. D. Stiltskin (eds.), *Joshua Finkel Festschrift*, Hebr. section, 7–58. New York 1974. **Fisch, S.** *EJ* 11: 1515f. [Cf. also his introductions to MHG Num and Deut.] **Kasher, M. M.** *Sefer ha-Rambam we-ha-Mekhilta de Rashbi*, 29–47. 2nd edn. Jerusalem 1980. **Morag, S.** 'The Rhyming Techniques in the Proems of Midrash Haggadol and the Authorship of this Midrash' (Hebr.). *Tarbiz* 34 (1964–65) 257–62. **Nahum, Y. L.** *Mi-Tsefunot Yehudê Teiman*, 181–205. Tel Aviv 1962. **Ratzabi, Y.** 'The Authorship of Midrash Haggadol' (Hebr.). *Tarbiz* 34 (1964–65) 263–71. **Ratzabi, Y.** 'Linguistic Study in "Midrash Haggadol"' (Hebr.). *Bar-Ilan* 13 (1976) 282–320. **Ratzabi, Y.** 'She'elot Hanagid – A Work by R. Yehoshua Hanagid' (Hebr.). *Tarbiz* 54 (1984–85) 553–66. **Ratzabi, Y.** 'Leqet leshonot mi-Midrash ha-Gadol.' In Y. D. Gilat et al. (eds.), *'Iyunim Be-sifrut Ḥazal, Ba-Miqra u-be-Toldot Yisra'el* (*Festschrift* E. Z. Melammed), 376–97. Ramat Gan 1982. **Sperber, D.** 'Al kammah millim ba-Midrash ha-Gadol.' *Sinai* 77 (1974–75) 13–16. **Steinsaltz, A.** 'Rhyming Techniques in the Proems of Midrash Haggadol' (Hebr.). *Tarbiz* 34 (1964–65) 94–97. **Tobi, Y.** *Ha-Midrash ha-Gadol: Meqorotaw u-Mibnehu.* 2 vols. Diss. Jerusalem 1993. **Zucker, M.** 'Pentateuchal Exegeses of Saadia Gaon and Samuel ben Chofni Incorporated into the Midrash ha-Gadol' (Hebr.). In *The Abraham Weiss Jubilee Volume*, 461–81. New York 1964.

### *5) Bereshit Rabbati*

Mosheh ha-Darshan of Narbonne (first half of the 11th cent.), frequently quoted by Rashi and his grandson Jacob Tam, wrote commentaries on biblical books and compiled midrashim, the extent of which is still unknown (the entire Torah? other biblical writings?). In his *Pugio Fidei*, written c. 1280, Raymond Martini (1220–85) frequently quotes a *Midrasch Bereschit Rabba major* of Mosheh ha-Darshan. The authenticity of these quotations was often denied, until a MS of Bereshit Rabbati was discovered. However, since a number of quotations in *Pugio Fidei* and in Rashi are missing here as well, A. Epstein (followed by Albeck) regards Bereshit Rabbati as an abridged version of the work of Mosheh ha-Darshan, whose school also produced the *Midrash Aggadah* published by S. Buber (Vienna 1894) and the revision of NumR I.

The work is a typical midrashic compilation which uses the entire rabbinic literature, but also frequently quotes Midrash Tadshe (so that the latter was occasionally attributed to Mosheh ha-Darshan himself) and makes extensive use of the pseudepigraphical literature, above all Enoch, Jubilees and Test XII. The work is hardly of value for textual criticism of earlier midrashim, since the author freely revises, combines and abridges his sources.

***Text***

**Albeck, Ch**. *Midraš Berešit Rabbati ex libro R. Mosis Haddaršan collectus e codice Pragensi cum adnotationibus et introductione*. Jerusalem 1940; repr. 1967.

***Bibliography***

**Epstein, A**. *Moses had-Darschan aus Narbonne, Fragmente seiner litterarischen Erzeugnisse... mit Einleitung und Anmerkungen*. Vienna 1891. **Elbaum, J**. *EJ* 7: 401f. **Himmelfarb, M**. 'R. Moses the Preacher and the Testaments of the Twelve Patriarchs.' *AJSR* 9 (1984) 55–78. **Lieberman, S**. *Texts and Studies*, 285–300. **Ta-Shma, I**. *EJ* 12: 429. **Zunz**, *GV*, 300–306. [Cf. **Albeck**, *Derashot*, 149f., 447.]

### *6) Leqaḥ Tob*

This work is named after Prov 4.2 (a 'good teaching') and alludes at the same time to the author's name, Tobiah ben Eliezer. In Zunz's opinion the latter was from Mainz and later lived in the Orient; but with S. Buber (18, 20–26), Kastoria in Bulgaria must be assumed as his place of residence. He probably wrote his book in the year 1097, and personally edited it in 1107 and 1108 with additions and corrections. It contains allusions to contemporary events such as the persecution of Jews in 1096. Leqaḥ Tob covers the Pentateuch and the Megillot and is 'part commentary, part haggadah, primarily from older works' (Zunz, *GV*, 306f.). It makes particular use of BT and many midrashim as well as of mystical literature, mostly without mentioning the source and not quoting verbatim, but casting the whole in a homogeneous Hebrew and blending it with many of its own interpretations. The author also shows a particular interest in grammar and matters of halakhah. The work was later erroneously cited as *Pesiqta* or as *Pesiqta zutrata*.

***Text***

Venice 1546 (Lev, Num, Deut); Wilna 1884 (incl. commentary by A. M. [Katzenellenbogen of] Padua). **Buber, S**. *Lekach tob (Pesikta sutarta), ein agadischer Commentar zum ersten und zweiten Buche Mosis von R. Tobia ben Elieser*. Wilna 1884; both vols. repr. in Israel, n. d. **Nacht, J**. *Tobia ben Elieser's Commentar zu Threni, mit einer Einleitung und Anmerkungen*. Berlin 1895. **Greenup, A. W**. *The Commentary of R. Tobia b. Elieser on Echah*. 2nd edn. London 1908. **Feinberg, G**. *Tobia ben Elieser's Commentar zu Koheleth (Lekach tob) samt Einleitung und Commentar*. Berlin 1904. [Repr., together with Greenup, Jerusalem 1967.] **Bamberger, S**. *Lekach Tob (Pesikta Sutrata): Ein agadischer Kommentar zu Megillat Ruth*. Aschaffenburg 1887.

**Greenup, A. W.** *The Commentary of Rabbi Tobia ben Elieser on Canticles.* London 1909. [Repr., together with Bamberger, n.p., n.d. (Jerusalem 1968?).] Leqaḥ Tob to Esther: **Buber, S.** *Sifre de-Aggadeta*, 85–112. Wilna 1886.

***Bibliography***

**Elbaum, J.** *EJ* 11: 1516f. **Ginzberg, L.** *Ginzê Schechter*, 1:246–97. **Zunz,** *GV*, 306–8.

## *7) Sekhel Tob*

This is a midrashic anthology on the Pentateuch by Menaḥem ben Solomon. It was written in 1139, perhaps in Italy (loan words in the text are Italian). In addition to the rabbinic literature, the author quotes Geonic writings like the *She'iltot* and the *Halakhot Gedolot*, but also Alfasi and the *Midrash Leqaḥ Tob*. It was still known in its entirety by medieval authors, but is extant only for Gen and Exod.

***Bibliography***

**Buber, S.** *Sechel Tob: Commentar zum ersten und zweiten Buch Mosis von Rabbi Menachem ben Salomo verfasst i.J. 1139... herausgegeben... commentiert und mit... Einleitung.* Berlin 1900/1901; repr. Tel Aviv n.d. [Cf. I. Ta-Shma, *EJ* 11: 1307f. ] **Lockshin, M. I.** 'The Connection between R. Samuel ben Meir's Tora Commentary and Midrash Sekhel Tov' (Hebr.). *11th WCJS* (Jerusalem 1994) 135–42.

## *8) Midrash Samuel*

Zunz (*GV*, 281f.) dated this compilation of individual interpretations on Sam not before the eleventh century. However, the work undoubtedly originated much earlier, even though it was later revised (late petiḥot). This is confirmed by quotations in Samuel ben Ḥofni (10th cent.) under the title of *Aggadat Shmuel*, as well as in Rab Nissim Gaon's *Megillat Setarim* (S. Abramson, *'Inyanut be-Sifrut ha-Geonim* (Jerusalem 1974), 154; idem, *Rab Nissim Gaon* (Jerusalem 1965), 311). The *Qiṣur Aggadot ha-Yerushalmi* from the Genizah quotes 'Samuel Rabbah' (*Ginze Schechter*, 1:392); book lists of the Genizah refer to an *Aggadat Shmuel* (J. Mann, *Texts and Studies*, vol. 1 (New York 1972 = repr. of 1931), 644). The work employs not only rabbinic midrash literature, but also makes use of material not otherwise attested, some of which is very old. It comprises 32 chapters (24 on 1 Sam, 8 on 2 Sam), and probably originated in Palestine: the cited Amoraim and the quoted sources are all Palestinian. MS Parma 563 is the only MS, but very defective; Rabinovitz has published eight leaves from the Genizah which feature a very divergent text (without the later additions, but instead with other material which apparently was later omitted).

***Text***

Constantinople 1517; Venice 1546. **Buber, S.** *Midrasch Samuel... kritisch bearbeitet, commentiert und mit einer Einleitung*. Cracow 1893. [Repr., together with *Midrash Mishlê*, Jerusalem 1965. Cf. A. Ehrlich, *MGWJ* 39 (1895): 331–36, 368–70: numerous typographical errors, omissions, etc.] **Rabinovitz, Z. M.** *Ginzé Midrash*, 179–217. [C. 13th cent.] A further fragment in **Alloni, N**. *Geniza Fragments*, 77. German translation: **Wünsche, A**. *Lehrhallen*, vol. 5.

***Bibliography***

**Elbaum, J**. *EJ* 11: 1517f. **Higger, M.** 'Beraitoth in Midrash Samuel and Midrash Mishlei' (Hebr.). *Talpioth* 5.3–4 (1952) 669–82. **Zunz,** *GV*, 281f.

## *9) Bereshit Zutta*

This is the title S. Buber assigned to the Gen commentary of Samuel b. R. Nissim Masnut, who taught in Aleppo in the thirteenth century but probably came from Toledo. His identification with Samuel b. R. Nissim, whom Alḥarizi visited c. 1218 in Aleppo, is uncertain (the latter does not mention the name Masnut; and the author of the midrash wrote a commentary on Dan as late as 1276). The sole surviving manuscript calls the work simply Midrash of R. Samuel Masnut. The work is a compilation from the entire rabbinic literature (not cited by name), composed like a mosaic from very small units. It clearly favours the literal meaning. There is no commentary on Gen 1.23–8.16; a single leaf on 3.6–8, apparently taken from the same work, suggests that this paragraph will have been lost. The same author produced a *Midrash Sefer Iyyob Ma'ayan Gannim* as well as midrashim on Dan, Ezra (with Neh) and Chr. Part of a commentary on Num is also preserved (Jewish Theological Seminary), so that one can probably assume that the author commented on the entire Bible. Samuel Masnut also relies heavily on the Targums and the Peshitta; his commentary on Chronicles simply copies that of David Qimḥi (c. 1160–1235) and supplements it with rabbinic quotations. Perhaps he did the same for Ezra and Dan, on which no commentary of Qimḥi is extant (apart from an explanation of the Aramaic expressions).

***Text***

**Buber, S.** *Samuel b. R. Nissim Masnut, Ma'ayan Gannim... al Sefer Iyyob*. Berlin 1889; repr. Jerusalem 1970. **(Ha–)Cohen, M.** *Midrash Bereshit Zutta*. Jerusalem 1962. **Lange, I. S. & Schwartz, S.** *Midras Daniel et Midras Ezra auctore R. Samuel b. R. Nissim Masnuth (Saec. XIII)* Jerusalem 1968. **Richler, B.** 'Completion of a Lacuna in R. Samuel b. Nissim Masnut's Midrash on Genesis' (Hebr.). *KS* 63 (1990–91) 1323–26.

***Bibliography***

**Díez-Macho, A**. 'Las citas del targum palestinense en el midras Bereshit Zuṭa.' In A. Caquot et al.

(eds.), *Mélanges bibliques et orientaux en l'honneur de M. Mathias Delcor*, 117–26. Neukirchen 1985. **Ta-Shma, I.** *EJ* 11: 1097f.

### *10) Pitron Torah*

A collection of interpretations and sermons on Lev, Num and Deut, probably composed in the ninth century in Babylonia. The work is preserved in a MS of 1328; apart from rabbinic sources, it also quotes the *She'iltot* of R. Aḥai as well as interpretations of the Karaite Benjamin al-Nahawandi. It is significant for the history of the text and transmission of rabbinic literature.

#### *Text*

**Urbach, E. E.** *Pitron Torah: A Collection of Midrashim and Interpretations*, Jerusalem 1978. [An English summary of the introduction appears in *7th WCJS* (Jerusalem 1981) 3:21–27.] For the piyyutim at the beginning of the individual chapters see **Fleischer, E.** 'On the Payytanic Heritage of Rav Hai Gaon – The Introductory Poems in the Midrash Pitron Torah' (Hebr.). *JSHL* 10–11 (1987–88; Jerusalem 1988) 2:661–81.

### *11) Other Midrashim and Related Works*

A number of additional midrashim are contained in the collections of Eben-Shmuel, *Midreshê Ge'ullah*; J. D. Eisenstein, *Ozar Midrashim*; L. Grünhut, *Sefer ha-Likkutim*; Ch. M. Horovitz, *Sammlung kleiner Midraschim*, part 1 (Berlin 1881), parts 2 & 3 (Frankfurt 1881–82, repr. in 2 vols. (Jerusalem 1966–67); A. Jellinek, *BhM*; and S. A. Wertheimer. Yemenite midrashim include *Midrash ha-Ḥefeṣ* by R. Zechariah ben Shlomo ha-Rofeh, a kind of Yalkut in Arabic, which according to the colophon was completed in 1427: M. Ḥabaṣelet, *Bereshit-Shmot*, Jerusalem 1990 (with Hebrew translation); A. Y. Wertheimer (ed.), *Yalkut Midreshey Teiman... by an unknown medieval Yemenite scholar* (Hebr.), 2 vols., Jerusalem 1988 (vol. 1: Gen–Lev; vol. 2: Num–Deut; not before the 17th cent.). A compilation of the midrashic tradition is provided by M. M. Kasher, *Torah Shelemah*, Jerusalem/New York 1927ff. (42 vols. to 1991); abridged translation ed. H. Freedman, New York 1953ff. Very valuable for locating scattered biblical interpretations in the entire rabbinic literature: A. Hyman, *Torah Hakethubah Vehamessurah*, 2nd edn. rev. and enlarged by his son A. B. Hyman, 3 vols., Tel Aviv 1979; further additions: *Sepher Hahashlamoth*, Jerusalem n.d. (1985?).

For additional bibliography see J. T. Townsend in *The Study of Judaism*, vol. 1 (New York 1972), 35–80; vol. 2 (New York 1976), 333–92.

# APPENDIX

## EDITOR'S POSTSCRIPT:

## ELECTRONIC RESOURCES FOR THE STUDY OF THE TALMUD AND MIDRASH

Since the 1991 edition of this work, we have seen an explosive growth in the availability of computer-based scholarly resources for the study of rabbinic Judaism. It therefore seems appropriate to offer a very brief list of available materials to supplement the more traditional publications discussed in the text.[1] In view of this rapidly changing field, the information here provided is likely to be out of date within months; a brief beginner's list, therefore, seems more suitable for present purposes than any attempt at completeness. While numerous academic institutions around the world are sponsoring ongoing computer-based research projects in Jewish Studies, for reasons of space we must here confine ourselves to material published either on floppy disk or compact disk (CD-ROM), or else made available 'on line'.

For convenience, our discussion is here divided into (i) resources on CD-ROM, and (ii) bibliographies, electronic journals, and discussion forums accessible on the Internet.

### A. Resources on CD-ROM

At present, the standard equipment configuration is usually a Windows-based PC with a Pentium processor, SVGA graphics, 16 megabytes of RAM, and a quad-speed or faster CD-ROM drive. Some of the resources listed are also available in Macintosh format, and require equivalent equipment configurations.

#### 1. Davka Software

This company has released a series of affordable disks offering standard traditional texts of most of the rabbinic literature, together with efficient searching software. Initially based on the MS-DOS operating system, the most recent revised versions now operate in the standard Microsoft Windows interface; most are also available in Macintosh format. The address in the UK is 56 Benwell Road, London N7 7BA (Tel. 0171–607–6661, Fax 0171–700–4520). In the USA: 7074 N. Western Ave., Chicago, IL 60645 (Tel. (312) 465–4070).

---

[1]The Editor gratefully acknowledges advice on this Postscript received from Robert Kraft, Douglas de Lacey, Chaim Milikowsky, David Reimer, and Günter Stemberger.

While limited (cheaper) editions exist, the most complete disks include:

**a) The Judaic Classics Library, Deluxe Extra Edition CD**

Tanakh (pointed) with Rashi and other commentaries
Tosefta
Palestinian Talmud
Babylonian Talmud with Rashi's Commentaries and Tosafot
Halakhic Midrashim: Mek, Sifra, Sifre Num & Sifre Deut
Misc. Aggadic Midrashim
Shulḥan Arukh
Zohar

**b) The Soncino edition of the Babylonian Talmud** (bilingual: Hebrew/Aramaic and English), including a bilingual keyword and English subject index.

**c) The Soncino Midrash Rabbah** (bilingual) with English subject index.

**d) Geoffrey Wigoder (ed.), *The Encyclopedia of Judaism*** (New York/London: Macmillan, 1989); **and idem (ed.), *Dictionary of Jewish Biography*** (New York: Simon & Schuster, 1991).

Other editions include the following:

**2. The Global Jewish Database (The Responsa Project) of Bar-Ilan University**

The most recent CD-ROM from Bar-Ilan ('Taklit-Shu"t' No. 3) includes *inter alia*

Tanakh (with Rashi, Ramban, Onkelos et al.)
Mishnah
Babylonian Talmud (with Rashi)
Palestinian Talmud
halakhic and haggadic midrashim
Maimonides' Mishneh Torah
Shulḥan Arukh
253 books of Geonic Responsa.

The software requires MS Windows, but no special Hebrew ROM is needed; complex morphological searches are possible. Contact: The Responsa Project, Bar Ilan University, P.O. Box 90000, Ramat Gan 52900, Israel. Tel.: +972–3–531–8411; fax: +972–3–534–1850; E-mail: R70018@mvsa.biu.ac.il. In the USA: Torah Educational Software, 750 Chestnut Ridge Road, Spring Valley, NY 10977; tel. (800) 925–6853 or (914) 356–1190; fax: (914) 356–1343.

**3. The Saul Lieberman Institute of Talmudic Research**

This Institute, based at the Jewish Theological Seminary in New York, publishes *inter alia* the *Sol & Evelyn Henkind Talmud Text Databank*, which is slated to contain all manuscript and early printed versions of the BT, and in its present form includes over half of the major manuscript texts of the BT. (The Lieberman Institute has also produced a line collation program which can produce synopses for the comparison of manuscripts.) Subscribers to this ongoing and expanding project receive periodic updates of the database, which is distributed not on CD-ROM but for installation on a hard disk. The software works on a minimal PC compatible system: it needs 30 MB on a hard disk, 512 KB of memory and any version of DOS. For further information, contact Dr Bruce Nielsen (Co-ordinator of the Talmud Project, E-mail: brnielsen@theo.jtsa.edu) or Dr Mayer Rabinowitz (Director of the Lieberman Institute and Librarian of the Jewish Theological Seminary, E-mail: marabinowitz@theo.jtsa.edu). The postal address is The Saul Lieberman Institute, The Jewish Theological Seminary, 3080 Broadway, New York, NY 10027–4649, USA.

**4. Pertinent Greek and Latin Texts**

a) *Thesaurus Linguae Graecae*

The TLG Institute publishes a CD-ROM containing virtually all of ancient Greek literature up to the year 600 (including Jewish and relevant early Christian texts), in a format allowing fast and complex searches. Contact Thesaurus Linguae Graecae, University of California at Irvine, Irvine, CA 92717–5550, USA (Tel. (714) 824–7031, Fax (714) 824–8434, E-mail: tlg@uci.edu). A convenient Windows-based software package for this CD-ROM is TLGWorkplace by Silver Mountain Software, 1029 Tanglewood, Cedar Hill, TX 755104–3019, USA (E-mail John Baima: jbaima@ onramp.net).

b) *Patrologia Latina*

Many of the equivalent Latin Patristic texts in the more than 220 volumes of J. P. Migne (ed.), *Patrologia Latina* are accessible through the ongoing (and rather expensive) CD-ROM database project of this name published by Chadwyck-Healey. The software is based on DOS and Windows. Contact Chadwyck-Healey, The Quorum, Barnwell Road, Cambridge CB5 8SW, England (Tel. (01223) 215512, Fax (01223) 215515; E-mail: mail@ chadwyck.co.uk); in the USA: Chadwyck-Healey Inc., 1101 King Street, Alexandria, VA 22314 (Tel: (800) 752–0515 or (703) 683–4890; Fax (703) 683–7589).

*c) CETEDOC Library of Christian Latin Texts* on CD-ROM

Another, less complete collection of Christian texts is published by CETEDOC, University of Louvain, Belgium. The software is DOS-based and the texts follow the *Corpus Christianorum Series Latina* edition. Contact Brepols Publishers, Baron Frans du Fourstraat 8, B-2300 Turnhout, Belgium (Tel. +32–14–41–54–63, Fax +32–14–42–89–57).

*d) Packard Humanities Institute*

PHI have published a Latin CD-ROM with all classical texts up to the year 200 (No. 5.3), as well as a Greek Documentary CD-ROM with a large number of inscriptions and papyri including the texts from Nag Hammadi and the Coptic New Testament (No. 6). For further information contact PHI, 300 Second Street, Los Altos, CA 94022, USA (Tel. (415) 948–0150; Fax (415) 948–5793; E-mail: 74754.2713@compuserve.com).

**B. Resources on the Internet**

The growth of scholarly activity based on the worldwide electronic Internet has, if anything, been even more explosive; and there is as yet no convenient way of indexing the available resources.

Access to internet resources has become much easier with the *World Wide Web* (WWW) system, which allows free browsing of a wide range of resources on the Internet. The 'home pages' of a growing number of institutions now provide convenient entry points for resources in Jewish and biblical studies. Useful international examples include the following:

- CCAT at the University of Pennsylvania (http://ccat.sas.upenn.edu)
- University of Toronto Centre for Computing and the Humanities, resources in religious studies and theology (http://www.cch.epas.utoronto.ca/cch/disciplines/religious_studies)
- Religious Studies home page at the University of Oxford (http://info.ox.ac.uk/departments/humanities/rel.html)
- Religious Studies Home Page at the Free Faculty of Theology in Oslo (http://www.hivolda.no/asf/kkf/rel-stud.html)
- The Hebrew University, Jerusalem (http://www.aleph.huji.ac.il)

Major university home pages (e.g. http://www.utoronto.ca) usually offer comprehensive indexed information about Internet resources. Another convenient way to search the Internet resources is via indexing and searching facilities like GNN (http://gnn.com/gnn.html) or Edge Internet Resources (http://www.edge.net/edge/spider.html).

Many materials are freely accessible, while others require paid subscription. The most important resources for the study of rabbinic Judaism fall into four categories: 1. bibliographies, 2. texts, 3. electronic journals, 4. electronic discussion forums.

**1. Bibliographies**

Many of the world's major research libraries are now freely accessible on the Internet. Examples include Harvard (hollis.harvard.edu) and Cambridge (ul.cam.ac.uk) University Libraries, and the valuable resources of the Center for the Computer Aided Study of Texts (CCAT) and the Hebrew University in Jerusalem. The latter are useful for both library facilities and the Global Jewish Information Network; anyone can use the English interface, but full access to titles published in Hebrew requires the use of Hebrew keyboard mapping. The best access to these resources is either direct (issue the command 'telnet [address]') or via the home pages of various institutions like those listed above.

**2. Electronic Texts**

A large and growing number of classic religious texts is now available 'online'. Many biblical (Tanakh, LXX, New Testament, etc.), apocryphal, patristic and other ancient texts are freely accessible from the various 'home pages' listed above. An index to early Christian texts is also available through http://www. iclnet.org/pub/resources/christian-history.html. Further afield, it is also worth noting the various indexes of 'Online Books' (e.g. http://www.cs.cmu.edu/ web/bookauthors.html).

**3. E-journals**

A number of electronic journals for the study of Judaism have begun to appear. Here, it may suffice to note three publications.

*a) IOUDAIOS-REVIEW*

A periodic service of scholarly reviews of books on Ancient Judaism is available by sending the following message to listserv@lehigh.edu: "sub ioudaios-review [your name]" (alternatively, the World Wide Web address is http://www.lehigh. edu/lists/ioudaios-review).

*b) JUDAICA E-journal*

A. J. Hyman at the Ontario Institute for the Study of Education (E-mail: ajhyman@oise.on.ca) publishes a monthly journal containing a variety of articles, information and announcements of interest to scholars of Judaism. To subscribe, send the message "sub h-judaic [your name]" to listserv@uicvm.earn (Europe) or listserv@uicvm.bitnet (North America).

*c) Bryn Mawr Classical Review*

A more general source of scholarly reviews of books on the Graeco-Roman world is the *Bryn Mawr Classical Review*, freely available by sending the message "sub bmcr-l [your name]" to listserv@cc.brynmawr.edu.

*d) ABZU Journal Index*

This index is accessible through the World Wide Web home page of the Oriental Institute, University of Chicago (http://www-oi.uchicago.edu). It includes journals and periodicals relevant for the study and interpretation of the Ancient Near East which are at least partly available on the Internet. The scope of this index is fairly broad, ranging over the whole breadth of Ancient Near Eastern Studies and including items from Archaeology and Classics. The stated intention is 'to provide an easy point of entry to a wide variety of formally published periodicals'. The index also allows access to resources like the home page of Scholars Press in Atlanta (http://scholar.cc.emory.edu), which includes, *inter alia*, publishers' catalogues and experimental access to reviews from the *Journal of Biblical Literature*.

**4. Electronic Discussion Forums**

There are now a large number of specialized discussion forums for the study of religion and of ancient texts. Most of these are too general for present purposes; but perhaps the most useful and prominent for this context is IOUDAIOS-L, a lively discussion network of Ancient Judaism involving about 600 scholars worldwide. To join, send the following message to listserv@lehigh.edu: 'sub ioudaios-l [your name]'. Another important list is JEWISHNT (listserv@bguvm.bgu.ac.il). Others include HUMANIST, RELIGION, and ELENCHUS.

## C. For Further Reference

For up-to-date information about currently available resources, it is always worth consulting the discussion lists like IOUDAIOS-L and JEWISHNT, as well as the resources described above.

The following bibliographical resources may also be helpful, if in part somewhat dated:

Greenstein, Daniel I. *A Historian's Guide to Computing*. Oxford Guides to Computing for the Humanities. Oxford/New York 1994.

Hughes, John J. *Bits, Bytes & Biblical Studies*. Grand Rapids, MI 1987.

Krol, Ed. *The Whole Internet: User's Guide and Catalog*. 2nd edn. Sebastopol, CA 1994.

Strangelove, Michael. *The Electric Mystic's Guide to the Internet: A Complete Directory of Networked Electronic Documents, Online Conferences, Serials, Software and Archives*

*Relevant to Religious Studies*. 2 vols. 2nd edn. Ottawa: Research Centre for the Study of Religion, 1993. Includes indexes. The author can be contacted on E-mail: 441495@acadvm1.uottawa.ca.

Since 1988, Oxford University Press has published the annual *Humanities Computing Yearbook*, edited by Ian Lancashire.

## LIST OF WEEKLY READINGS (SEDARIM) FROM THE TORAH ACCORDING TO THE ONE-YEAR CYCLE

**Genesis**

| | |
|---|---|
| 1.1–6.8 | Bereshit |
| 6.9–11.32 | Noaḥ |
| 12.1–17.27 | Lekh lekha |
| 18.1–22.24 | Wa-yera |
| 23.1–25.18 | Ḥayyê Sarah |
| 25.19–28.9 | Toldot |
| 28.10–32.3 | Wa-yeṣe |
| 32.4–36.43 | Wa-yishlaḥ |
| 37.1–40.23 | Wa-yesheb |
| 41.1–44.17 | Miqqeṣ |
| 44.18–47.27 | Wa-yiggash |
| 47.28–50.26 | Wa-yeḥi |

**Exodus**

| | |
|---|---|
| 1.1–6.1 | Shemot |
| 6.2–9.35 | Wa-era |
| 10.1–13.16 | Bo |
| 13.17–17.16 | Beshallaḥ |
| 18.1–20.26 | Yitro |
| 21.1–24.18 | Mishpaṭim |
| 25.1–27.19 | Terumah |
| 27.20–30.10 | Teṣawweh |
| 30.11–34.35 | Tissa |
| 35.1–38.20 | Wa-yaqhel |
| 38.21–40.38 | Pequdê |

**Leviticus**

| | |
|---|---|
| 1.1–5.26 | Wa-yiqra |
| 6.1–8.36 | Ṣaw |
| 9.1–11.47 | Shemini |
| 12.1–13.59 | Tazri'a |
| 14.1–15.33 | Meṣora' |
| 16.1–18.30 | Aḥarê |
| 19.1–20.27 | Qedoshim |
| 21.1–24.23 | Emor |
| 25.1–26.2 | Behar |
| 26.3–27.34 | Beḥuqqotai |

**Numbers**

| | |
|---|---|
| 1.1–4.20 | Bemidbar |
| 4.21–7.89 | Naso |
| 8.1–12.16 | Beha'alotkha |
| 13.1–15.41 | Shelaḥ |
| 16.1–18.32 | Koraḥ |
| 19.1–22.1 | Ḥuqqat |
| 22.2–25.9 | Balak |
| 25.10–30.1 | Pinḥas |
| 30.2–32.42 | Mattot |
| 33.1–36.13 | Mas'ê |

**Deuteronomy**

| | |
|---|---|
| 1.1–3.22 | Debarim |
| 3.23–7.11 | Wa-etḥannan |
| 7.12–11.25 | 'Eqeb |
| 11.26–16.17 | Re'eh |
| 16.18–21.9 | Shofṭim |
| 21.10–25.19 | Ki Teṣe |
| 26.1–29.8 | (Ki) Tabo |
| 29.9–30.20 | Niṣabim |
| 31.1–30 | Wa-yelekh |
| 32.1–52 | Ha'azinu |
| 33.1–34.12 | We-zot ha-Berakhah |

## LITERATURE CITED IN ABBREVIATED FORM

This list only contains works that appear throughout the book, not those given in the bibliographies of specific chapters.


Albeck, Ch. *Einführung in die Mischna.* Berlin/New York 1971. [*Einführung*].

Albeck, Ch. *Introduction to the Talmud, Babli and Yerushalmi* (Hebr.). Tel Aviv 1969. [Mabo].

Albeck, Ch. *Untersuchungen über die halakischen Midraschim.* Berlin 1927. [*Untersuchungen*].

Albeck, Ch. *Derashot*: see under Zunz, L.

Alloni, N. *Geniza Fragments of Rabbinic Literature, Mishna, Talmud and Midrash, with Palestinian Vocalization* (Hebr.). Jerusalem 1973. [*Geniza Fragments*].

Alon, G. *The Jews in their Land in the Talmudic Age.* 2 vols. Jerusalem 1980–84. [*The Jews*; revised translation of *Toldot ha-Yehudim*, 3rd edn. Tel Aviv 1958.]

Alon, G. *Jews, Judaism and the Classical World: Studies in Jewish History in the Times of the Second Temple and Talmud.* Jerusalem 1977. [Selection of the most important essays from the Hebrew edn. (2 vols., Tel Aviv 1958).]

Assaf, S. *Tequfat ha-Geonim we-Sifrutah.* Jerusalem 1955. [*Geonim*].

Bacher, W. *Die Agada der Tannaiten.* Vol. 1, 2nd edn. Strasbourg 1903; vol. 2, 1890; repr. Berlin 1965–66. [*Tann*].

Bacher, W. *Die Agada der palästinensischen Amoräer.* 3 vols. Strasbourg 1892–1905; repr. Hildesheim 1965. [*PAm*].

Bacher, W. *Die Agada der babylonischen Amoräer.* 2nd edn. Frankfurt am Main 1913; repr. Hildesheim 1965. [*BAm*].

Bacher, W. *Die exegetische Terminologie der jüdischen Traditionsliteratur.* Leipzig 1899–1905; repr. Hildesheim 1965. [*ET*].

Bacher, W. *Tradition und Tradenten in den Schulen Palästinas und Babyloniens.* Leipzig 1914; repr. Berlin 1966. [*TT*].

Baron, S. W. *A Social and Religious History of the Jews.* 2nd edn. New York 1952–83. [*History*].

Beer, M. *The Babylonian Exilarchate in the Arsacid and Sassanian Periods* (Hebr.). Tel Aviv 1970. [*Exilarchate*].

Beer, M. 'Exilarchs of the Talmudic Epoch Mentioned in R. Sherira's Responsum.' *PAAJR* 35 (1967) 43–74. ['Exilarchs'].

Beit-Arié, M. *Hebrew Codicology.* Paris 1976; supplemented reprint, Jerusalem 1981. [*Codicology*].

Dan, J. *The Hebrew Story in the Middle Ages* (Hebr.). Jerusalem 1974. [*The Hebrew Story*].

Daube, D. 'Alexandrian Methods of Interpretation and the Rabbis.' In *Festschrift Hans Lewald*, 25–44. Basle 1953: repr. in H. A. Fischel (ed.), *Essays*, 164–82. ['Alex. Methods'].

Daube, D. 'Rabbinic Methods of Interpretation and Hellenistic Rhetoric.' *HUCA* 22 (1949) 239–64. ['Rabb. Methods'].

Dor, Z. M. *The Teachings of Eretz Israel in Babylon* (Hebr.). Tel Aviv 1971. [*Teachings*].

Eisenstein, J. D. *Ozar Midrashim: Bibliotheca Midraschica*. 2 vols. New York 1915: repr. Jerusalem 1969.

Eben-Shmuel, J. *Midreshê Ge'ullah*. Jerusalem 1954, 3rd edn. 1968.

Ephrathi (Efrati), J. E. *The Sevoraic Period and its Literature in Babylonia and in Eretz Israel (500–689)* (Hebr.). Petaḥ Tiqwah 1973. [*The Sevoraic Period*].

Epstein, A. *Me-Qadmoniot ha-Yehudim: Beiträge zur jüdischen Alterthumskunde*. Wilna 1887; repr. in A. M. Haberman, ed., *Kitbê Rabbi A. Epstein*, 2 vols., Jerusalem 1950–57 (vol. 2). [*Qadmoniot*].

Epstein, J. N. *Introduction to the Text of the Mishna* (Hebr.). Jerusalem 1948. [*ITM*].

Epstein, J. N. *Introduction to Tannaitic Literature: Mishna, Tosephta and Halakhic Midrashim* (Hebr.). Edited by E. Z. Melamed. Jerusalem 1957. [*ITL*].

Epstein, J. N. *Introduction to Amoraitic Literature: Babylonian Talmud and Yerushalmi* (Hebr.). Edited by E. Z. Melamed. Tel Aviv 1962. [*IAL*].

Epstein, J. N. *Studies in Talmudic Literature and Semitic Languages*. Edited by E. Z. Melamed. 3 vols. Jerusalem 1983–91. [*Studies*].

Fischel, H. A., ed. *Essays in Greco-Roman and Related Talmudic Literature*. New York 1977. [*Essays*].

Fischel, H. A. *Rabbinic Literature and Greco-Roman Philosophy*. Leiden 1973.

Frankel, Z. *Mabo ha-Yerushalmi: Einleitung in den jerusalemischen Talmud*. Breslau 1870; repr. Jerusalem 1967. [*Mabo*].

Frankel, Z. *Darkhê ha-Mishnah: Hodegetica in Mischnam librosque cum ea coniunctos*. (*Introductio in Mischnam*; *Additamenta et Index*.) Leipzig 1859–76; repr. Tel Aviv n. d. [*Darkhê*].

Gafni, I. M. *The Jews of Babylonia in the Talmudic Era: A Social and Cultural History* (Hebr.). Jerusalem 1990.

Gerhardsson, B. *Memory and Manuscript: Oral Tradition and Written*

*Transmission in Rabbinic Judaism and Early Christianity.* Uppsala 1961.

Ginzberg, L. *A Commentary on the Palestinian Talmud.* Vol. 1. New York 1941; repr. 1971. Hebrew Introduction. [*Mabo*].

Ginzberg, L. *Genizah Studies in Memory of Doctor Solomon Schechter.* Vol. 1: *Midrash and Haggadah*; vol. 2: *Geonic and Early Karaitic Halakah* (Hebr.). New York 1928–29; repr. 1969. [*Ginze Schechter*].

Goodblatt, D. *Rabbinic Instruction in Sasanian Babylonia.* Leiden 1975. [*Instruction*].

Graetz, H. *Geschichte der Juden von den ältesten Zeiten bis zur Gegenwart.* Vols. 4–5. 4th edn. Leipzig 1908–09. (Earlier English Translation: *History of the Jews from the Earliest Times to the Present Day.* Edited & translated by B. Löwy. 4 vols. London 1891–92.) [*Geschichte*].

Green, W. S., ed. *Approaches to Ancient Judaism: Theory and Practice.* Vol. 1: Missoula, MT 1978; vol. 2: Chico, CA 1980; vol. 3: Chico, CA 1981; vol. 4: Chico, CA 1983; vol. 5: Atlanta, GA 1985. [*Approaches* 1–5].

Green, W. S., ed. *Persons and Institutions in Early Rabbinic Judaism.* Missoula, MT 1977. [*Persons*].

Grünhut, L. *Sefer ha-Likkutim: Sammlung älterer Midraschim und wissenschaftlicher Abhandlungen.* 6 Fascicles. Jerusalem 1898–1903; repr. Jerusalem 1967. [*Sefer ha-Likkutim*].

Halevy, I. *Dorot Harischonim: Die Geschichte und Literatur Israels.* Vols. lc, le, 2, 3. Frankfurt am Main 1897–1918; repr. Jerusalem 1967. [*Dorot*].

Halivni, D. W. *Sources and Traditions* (Hebr.). 2 vols. Vol. 1: Tel Aviv 1968; vol. 2: Jerusalem 1975. [*Sources*].

Heinemann, I. *Darkhê ha-Aggadah.* 3rd edn. Jerusalem 1970.

Heinemann, J. *Aggadah and its Development* (Hebr.). Jerusalem 1974. [*Aggadah*].

Hopkins, S. *A Miscellany of Literary Pieces from the Cambridge Genizah Collections.* Cambridge 1978. [*Miscellany*].

Juster, J. *Les Juifs dans l'Empire Romain.* 2 vols. Paris 1914; repr. New York 1968.

Lauterbach, J. Z. *Rabbinic Essays.* Cincinnati 1951; repr. New York 1973.

Levine, L. *Caesarea under Roman Rule.* Leiden 1975.

Lieberman, S. *Greek in Jewish Palestine.* 2nd edn. New York 1965. [*Greek*].

Lieberman, S. *Hellenism in Jewish Palestine.* 2nd edn. New York 1962. [*Hell.*].

Lieberman, S. *Texts and Studies*. New York 1974.

Lieberman, S. *Tosefta Ki-Fshutah: A Comprehensive Commentary on the Tosefta* (Hebr.). 10 vols. and supplement to *Moed*. New York 1955–88. [*TK*].

Lieberman, S. *Studies in Palestinian Talmudic Literature* (Hebr.). Edited by D. Rosenthal. Jerusalem 1991. [*Studies*].

Maier, J. *Jesus von Nazareth in der talmudischen Überlieferung*. Darmstadt 1978.

Mantel, H. *Studies in the History of the Sanhedrin*. Cambridge, MA 1961.

Melammed, E. Z. *An Introduction to Talmudic Literature* (Hebr.). Jerusalem 1973. [*Introduction*].

Neusner, J. *A Life of Rabban Yohanan ben Zakkai*. 2nd edn. Leiden 1970. [*Life*].

Neusner, J. *Development of A Legend: Studies on the Traditions Concerning Yoḥanan ben Zakkai*. Leiden 1970. [*Development*].

Neusner. J. *A History of the Jews in Babylonia*. 5 vols. Leiden 1965–70. [*Bab*].

Neusner, J. *The Rabbinic Traditions about the Pharisees before 70*. 3 vols. Leiden 1971. [*Phar*].

Neusner, J. *Eliezer ben Hyrcanus: The Tradition and the Man*. 2 vols. Leiden 1973. [*Eliezer*].

Neusner, J. *A History of the Mishnaic Law of Purities*. 22 vols. Leiden 1974–77. [*Pur*].

Neusner, J. *Introduction to Rabbinic Literature*. New York 1994. [*Introduction*].

Neusner, J. *Rabbinic Judaism: The Documentary History of its Formative Age, 70–600*. Bethesda, MD 1994. [*Judaism*].

Neusner, J., ed. *The Modern Study of the Mishnah*. Leiden 1970. [*The Modern Study*].

Neusner, J., ed. *The Formation of the Babylonian Talmud*. Leiden 1970. [*Formation*].

Neusner, J., ed. *The Study of Ancient Judaism*. 2 vols. New York 1981; 2nd edn. Atlanta 1992.

Porton, G. G. *The Traditions of Rabbi Ishmael*. 4 vols. Leiden 1976–82. [*Ishmael*].

Rabinovitz, Z. M. *Ginzé Midrash: The Oldest Forms of Rabbinic Midrashim according to Geniza Manuscripts* (Hebr.). Tel Aviv 1976.

Safrai, S., ed. *The Literature of the Sages*. Part 1: *Oral Tora, Halakha, Mishna, Tosefta, Talmud, External Tractates*. Assen 1987. [*The Literature*]

Safrai, S. and Stern, M., eds. *The Jewish People in the First Century*. 2 vols. Assen/Amsterdam 1974–76. [*Safrai/Stern*].

Schäfer, P. *Studien zur Geschichte und Theologie des rabbinischen Judentums*. Leiden 1978. [*Studien*].

Schürer, E. *The History of the Jewish People in the Age of Jesus Christ: A New English Version*. Rev. and ed. by G. Vermes, F. Millar, & M. Black. 3 vols. Edinburgh 1973–87. [Schürer/Vermes].

*Talmudic Studies*: *Mehqerei Talmud: Talmudic Studies*. Vol. 1, edited by Y. Sussmann & D. Rosenthal. Jerusalem 1990. Vol. 2, edited by M. Bar-Asher & D. Rosenthal. Jerusalem 1993.

Towner, W. S. *The 'Enumeration of Scriptural Examples'*. Leiden 1973.

Urbach. E. E. *The Tosafists: Their History, Writings and Methods* (Hebr.). 2nd edn. Jerusalem 1955.

Vermes, G. *Post-Biblical Jewish Studies*. Leiden 1975. [*Studies*].

Vries, B. de. *Mehqarim be-Sifrut ha-Talmud*. Jerusalem 1968. [*Meḥqarim*].

Weiss, A. *Studies in the Literature of the Amoraim* (Hebr.). New York 1962. [*SLA*].

Weiss, A. *Meḥqarim ba-Talmud*. Jerusalem 1975.

Weiss, I. H. *Dor Dor we-Dorshaw: Zur Geschichte der jüdischen Tradition* (Hebr.). 5 vols. Wilna 1871–83; repr. Wilna 1904, etc. [*Dor*].

Wertheimer, S. A. *Batei Midrashot*. 2 vols. 2nd edn. Jerusalem 1968.

Wünsche, A. *Bibliotheca Rabbinica: Eine Sammlung alter Midraschim: Zum ersten Male ins Deutsche übertragen*. 5 vols. Leipzig 1880–85; repr. Hildesheim 1967. [Bibl. Rabb.]

Wünsche, A. *Aus Israels Lehrhallen*. 5 vols. Leipzig 1907–10; repr. in 2 vols., Hildesheim 1967. [*Lehrhallen*].

Zunz, L. *Die gottesdienstlichen Vorträge der Juden historisch entwickelt*. 2nd edn. Frankfurt am Main 1892; repr. Hildesheim 1966. [*GV*; Hebr. trans. *Ha-Derashot be-Yisrael*, Jerusalem 1954, supplemented by Ch. Albeck, *Derashot*; quoted only in case of important additions by Albeck].

# ABBREVIATIONS

## I) Journals and Collections

*AcOr* — *Acta Orientalia* (Budapest)
*AJSR* — *Association for Jewish Studies Review*
*ANRW* — *Aufstieg und Niedergang der Römischen Welt*, vol. II 19/2, ed. H. Temporini & W. Haase.
*Archive* — *Archive of the New Dictionary of Rabbinica! Literature*, 2 vols. (Ramat Gan 1972–74).
*BhM* — *Bet ha-Midrash: Sammlung kleiner Midraschim*, ed. A. Jellinek, Parts 1–4 (Leipzig 1853–57), 5–6 (Vienna 1873–77); repr. 2 vols. (Jerusalem 1967).
*Bib* — *Biblica*
*BSOAS* — *Bulletin of the School of Oriental and African Studies*
*CCSL* — *Corpus Christianorum: Series Latina*
*CSEL* — *Corpus Scriptorum Ecclesiasticorum Latinorum*
*DBS* — *Dictionnaire de la Bible*, Supplément
*EJ* — *Encyclopaedia Judaica*, Jerusalem 1971 [references to the German *EJ* (Berlin 1928–34) indicate the year of publication].
*FJB* — *Frankfurter Judaistische Beiträge*
*GCS* — *Die griechischen christlichen Schriftsteller*
*HR* — *History of Religions*
*HTR* — *Harvard Theological Review*
*HUCA* — *Hebrew Union College Annual*
*IEJ* — *Israel Exploration Journal*
*JAAR* — *Journal of the American Academy of Religion*
*JBL* — *Journal of Biblical Literature*
*JE* — *Jewish Encyclopedia*
*JJS* — *Journal for Jewish Studies*
*JQR* — *Jewish Quarterly Review*
*JSJ* — *Journal for the Study of Judaism*
*JSHL* — *Jerusalem Studies in Hebrew Literature*
*JSJT* — *Jerusalem Studies in Jewish Thought*
*JSS* — *Journal of Semitic Studies*
*KS* — *Kiriath Sepher*
*MGWJ* — *Monatsschrift für Geschichte und Wissenschaft des Judentums*
*OLZ* — *Orientalistische Literaturzeitung*
*PAAJR* — *Proceedings of the American Academy for Jewish Research*
*REJ* — *Revue des Études Juives*
*RHR* — *Revue de l'Histoire des Religions*

| | |
|---|---|
| *RQ* | *Revue de Qumran* |
| *RSR* | *Recherches de science religieuse* |
| *SH* | *Scripta Hierosolymitana* |
| *TDOT* | *Theological Dictionary of the Old Testament* |
| *VTSup* | Supplements to *Vetus Testamentum* |
| *WCJS* | *World Congress of Jewish Studies* |
| *ZDMG* | *Zeitschrift der deutschen morgenländischen Gesellschaft* |
| *ZTK* | *Zeitschrift für Theologie und Kirche* |

**2) Other Abbreviations**

| | |
|---|---|
| ed. | editor, edited by |
| edn. | edition |
| Hebr. | Hebrew |
| MS(S) | Manuscript(s) |
| Rabb. | Rabbinic |
| repr. | reprint |
| vol(s). | volume(s) |

**3) Rabbinic Texts**

a) Mishnah, Tosefta, Talmuds

| | |
|---|---|
| BT | Babylonian Talmud |
| M | Mishnah |
| PT | Palestinian Talmud |
| T | Tosefta |

The tractates of these works are abbreviated consistently, but quotations are distinguished as follows: M is quoted according to chapter and halakhah (e.g. AZ 1.1), BT according to folio, side a or b (e.g. AZ 2b). Quotations from PT are preceded by 'p.' (e.g. p.AZ 1.1, 39a: the first two digits represent the chapter and halakhah as in M, the third gives the folio and column), those from T by 't.' (e.g. t.AZ 1.1, followed by the first letter of the relevant critical edition: L. = S. Lieberman, R. = K. H. Rengstorf, Z. = M. Zuckermandel).

| | |
|---|---|
| Abot | |
| Arak | 'Arakhin |
| AZ | 'Abodah Zarah |
| BB | Baba Batra |
| Bek | Bekhorot |
| Ber | Berakhot |
| Beṣah | |
| Bik | Bikkurim |
| BM | Baba Meṣia |
| BQ | Baba Qamma |
| Demai | |
| Eduy | 'Eduyot |
| Erub | 'Erubin |
| Git | Gittin |

| | |
|---|---|
| Ḥag | Ḥagigah |
| Ḥal | Ḥallah |
| Ḥul | Ḥullin |
| Hor | Horayot |
| Kel | Kelim |
| Ker | Keritot |
| Ket | Ketubbot |
| Kil | Kilayim |
| Maas | Ma‘aserot |
| Mak | Makkot |
| Makh | Makhshirin |
| MSh | Ma‘aser Sheni |
| Meg | Megillah |
| Me‘ilah | |
| Men | Menahot |
| Mid | Middot |
| Miqw | Miqwa’ot |
| MQ | Mo‘ed Qatan |
| Naz | Nazir |
| Ned | Nedarim |
| Nid | Niddah |
| Neg | Nega‘im |
| Ohal | Ohalot |
| Orlah | |
| Parah | |
| Peah | |
| Pes | Pesaḥim |
| Qid | Qiddushin |
| Qin | Qinnim |
| RH | Rosh ha-Shanah |
| Sanh | Sanhedrin |
| Shab | Shabbat |
| Shebi | Shebi‘it |
| Shebu | Shebu‘ot |
| Sheq | Sheqalim |
| Sot | Sotah |
| Suk | Sukkah |
| Taan | Ta‘anit |
| Tam | Tamid |
| Tebul Yom | |
| Tem | Temurot |
| Ter | Terumot |
| Uqṣin | |
| Yad | Yadayim |
| Yeb | Yebamot |
| Yoma | |
| Zab | Zabim |
| Zeb | Zebahim |

b) Other Texts

| | |
|---|---|
| A. Ibn Daud | G. D. Cohen, *A Critical Edition with an Introduction and Notes of the Book of Tradition (Sefer ha-Qabbalah) by Abraham Ibn Daud*, Philadelphia 1967. |
| ARN | *Abot de Rabbi Nathan.* Text A or B; Sch. = edn. S. Schechter, Vienna 1887; repr. Hildesheim 1979. |
| DeutR | Deuteronomy Rabbah; L. = S. Lieberman, *Midrash Debarim Rabbah*, 3rd edn. Jerusalem 1974. |
| ExodR | Exodus Rabbah |
| GenR | Genesis Rabbah; Theodor/Albeck = J. Theodor & Ch. Albeck, *Midrash Bereshit Rabba: Critical Editions with Notes and Commentary*, 2nd edn. Jerusalem 1965. |
| CantR | Song of Songs Rabbah |
| EcclR | Ecclesiastes Rabbah |

| | |
|---|---|
| ISG | *Iggeret Rab Sherira Gaon*; page references according to edn. B. M. Lewin, Frankfurt 1920; repr. Jerusalem 1972. |
| LamR | Lamentations Rabbah; B = S. Buber, *Midrasch Echa Rabbati*, Wilna 1899; repr. Hildesheim 1967. |
| LevR | Leviticus Rabbah; M. = M. Margulies, *Midrash Wayyikra Rabbah*, 5 vols., Jerusalem 1953–60. |
| Mek | Mekhilta de R. Ishmael; L. = J. Z. Lauterbach, *Mekilta de Rabbi Ishmael*, 3 vols., Philadelphia 1933–35. |
| MHG | Midrash ha-Gadol |
| MidrPss | Midrash on Psalms; B. = S. Buber, *Midrasch Tehillim*, Wilna 1892; repr. Jerusalem 1966. |
| MidrProv | Midrash on Proverbs; B. = 5. Buber, *Midrasch Mischle*, Wilna 1893; repr. Jerusalem 1965. |
| Midr Tann | Midrash Tannaim; H. = D. Hoffmann, *Midrasch Tannaim zum Deuteronomium*, Berlin 1908–09. |
| MRS | Mekhilta de R. Simeon b. Yoḥai; E.–M. = Edition J. N. Epstein & E. Z. Melamed, Jerusalem 1965. |
| NumR | Numbers Rabbah |
| PesR | Pesiqta Rabbati; F. = M. Friedmann, *Pesikta Rabbati*, Vienna 1880. |
| PRE | Pirqe de Rabbi Eliezer; L. = Edition D. Luria, Warsaw 1852; repr. Jerusalem 1963. |
| PRK | Pesiqta de Rab Kahana; M. = ed. B. Mandelbaum, 2 vols., New York 1962. |
| SER | Seder Eliahu Rabbah; F. = ed. M. Friedmann, Vienna 1902; repr. Jerusalem 1960. |
| SOR | Seder Olam Rabbah |
| SOZ | Seder Olam Zuttah |
| STA | Seder Tannaim we-Amoraim |
| SZ | Sifre Zuttah; H. = ed. H. S. Horovitz, 2nd edn. Jerusalem 1966. |
| Tan | Tanḥuma |
| TanB | Tanḥuma Buber |

# INDEX OF SUBJECTS

# INDEX OF PASSAGES

# INDEX OF ANCIENT AND MEDIEVAL NAMES

# INDEX OF MODERN AUTHORS